QUITE A LIFE!

From Defeat to Defeat ... and *Back*

by CAROL SCHWARTZ

Quite a Life!: From Defeat to Defeat ... and *Back*/ Carol Schwartz –
1st edition
ISBN 978-1-54391-570-9

™© 2017 Carol Schwartz unique author display:
Carol
Schwartz

DEDICATION

This book is dedicated generally to family, friends, colleagues and animals, here and gone, who have enriched my life—and they know who they are. It is dedicated specifically to my intellectually disabled and only sibling, Johnny, who defined me, and put me on the path I followed of trying to be a caretaker, both personally and professionally; to the role models of my youth, Grandma Carrie, Aunt Doe, Aunt Betty and Uncle Seymour—all of whom loved me unconditionally; to wonderful Aleida whose help for 31 years has made it easier for me to lead the life I do; to my dear children, Stephanie, Doug and Jen, and especially Hilary, who for the last several years helped enable me to finally write my story (in fact, no one but the two of us worked on this book); and to my precious grandchildren, Sylvie and Wally, whose existence gives me much happiness—and hope for the future. To each and every one of them, I say a heartfelt thank you.

My Pictorial Journey
From Youth to Not ...

(If you want bad or normal pictures of me, you'll have to look elsewhere as I only picked good ones for my book.)

Birth is a beginning
And death is a destination
And life is a journey
From childhood to maturity and youth to age
From innocence to awareness and ignorance to knowing
From weakness to strength or strength to weakness
And often, back again
From fear to faith
From defeat to defeat to defeat
Until, looking backward or ahead
We see that victory lies
Not in some high place along the way
But in having made the journey stage by stage
A sacred pilgrimage"

- Rabbi Alvin I. Fine*

The above poem has always been one of my favorites since I first read it decades ago. It is featured in the Union Prayer Book, which is used in Reform Jewish congregations across the country.

*Alvin Fine was Rabbi of Temple Emanu-El in San Francisco from 1948 to 1964. (Rabbi Fine was known as a civil rights activist and invited Martin Luther King and Maya Angelou to speak to his congregation in the early days of the movement. Impressive person. Impressive words.)

PREAMBLE

This book is coming from my memory of a packed 73-year life. It is also brought to you after going through 105 equally packed scrapbooks filled with news articles and letters and then leafing through some of my archived Council documents. If you're looking for a tightly written polished memoir which only touches the surface, you will not find it here. I hope much of it you will find compelling. What I have attempted to do is allow you to get to know me. I have even had second thoughts about my outright honesty while writing this book—both about myself and others—but I'm going to keep it that way. I have also tried to bring you into my thought process, which can be somewhat hyper. Whenever I think I have an idea of merit, which is often, I don't just let it go. I try to act on it, whether personally or professionally. Or at least speak about it—as I do in this book.

You may get far more detail here about certain subjects, which I found important and which you may not. (Let's face it, every aspect of one's life is not entirely fascinating.) I have included some of my speeches and op-ed pieces, as well as a few letters because they are part of my story that you are welcome to read—or skip. What you can't skip are the old, fuzzy pictures, and there are many. As has been said, "What is the use of a book without pictures?" (Hope you can still see them as I realize I blinded you with the book cover—made up of my political colors for four decades.)

This is a catch-all book. I wanted to cover my life. I also wanted to talk about the political history of D.C., especially post-Home Rule, as well as legislation and what it took to make it into law—or not. I am also using this book as therapy, thus I include my feelings on practically every subject. I also wanted to speak about my family and friends who have touched my life—for better or worse.

I know I am not an author. Still, I'm going to paraphrase something that was attributed to novelist Herman Melville, which came to mind when I thought about this book: I fear if I do not write it now, I never will; and I fear if I do write it, it will not be as good as it should be. I hope it is at least good enough.

Since it's probably the only book I'll ever write as it took me 73 years to do this one, with two and a half years of research and writing to get it out, it's long. As you keep reading, you may think, "Why didn't she edit it?" I did. It could have been 1,500 pages.

This is not a tweet. This is my life.

INTRODUCTION

In the fall of 2013, I started working on my autobiography, something I had thought about doing—and actually had been encouraged to do by others—for many years. But once I finally started just shy of age 70, I really got into it. Of course I began with my childhood, the family, their background, college, marriage, children. It was going along smoothly. But in the spring of 2014, when I got into my career which was mainly spent in elected office, that's when I started hitting a roadblock. The deeper I got into the laws I helped pass and the changes I helped bring about, I could no longer just sit and write. The reality became very vivid to me: Why am I taking the time to write about my life when all I want to do is continue to live it?

So I put the book aside in May of 2014 to get ready to run for Mayor of Washington, D.C.—for the fifth time. It was a short and tough five months from announcement to defeat—getting by far my worst percentage ever, costing me personally the most money, but ultimately feeling more good than bad about the effort.

But losing wasn't new to me. In 1944, I started out a loser in life (or so I thought, and some people might agree), and then completed my 40-year span of mostly elected public life (which began in 1974 and ended in 2014) as a loser (and this time, all would agree). But in between, there were plenty of times I won—literally and figuratively. And my race for Mayor in 1994 against Marion Barry remains the closest Mayoral general election ever in Washington, D.C. I lost, but did get 42% of the vote as a Republican despite the registration in D.C. being 77% Democrat to 7% Republican (an 11 to 1 ratio). I tackled those same odds when I ran for Mayor again and again. So you may ask, "Why even try?"

What makes me run ... and run ... and run? Even when I know deep down that it's probably a lost cause, I think the reason is a strong desire to overcome the odds, the undying optimism in my soul, an overwhelming drive to effectuate change, and a survival mechanism which allows me to surmount fear, risk failing and falling, and still get up, dust myself off and carry on.

Honestly, I think my life made me used to battling fear. My first memory when I was about four or five years old was of my father throwing a pot of hot soup across our small living room at my mother. It was so scary.

But little did I know at four, that it was just the beginning of many such experiences which made me frightened all my life. Most people wouldn't be aware of that about me except a few really close friends and family. You who may know me less, if at all, might think how did I get the nerve to do such things as run for Mayor of D.C. against Marion Barry twice?

A better question might be, how did a Jewish child who had to face being from the poor side of the tracks in a nouveau riche town with only a few Jews and lots of prejudice against them, who had an abusive father, who had an only sibling with intellectual disabilities, who was made to work starting at the age of eight, who was scared and anxious all of the time, overcome those things enough to tackle later on even greater challenges—some unavoidable but many of them willingly?

Here is the story of my life—the good, the bad, and everything in between. I've had wins. You'll hear me speak proudly of these wins when they happen. But the wins have been more than balanced out by the losses—losses of elections and personal losses.

For years, I didn't want to write my life story as I didn't want to have to relive it. And even in the rare times I thought about it, the title was always: *An Interesting Life, but Don't Ask Me to Live It Again.* Yet now that I did finally write it and did relive it, I decided that title doesn't work. I feel more blessed than it implies. And I wanted the poem I love to be part of my story—and it is. So I have now gone with *Quite a Life!: From Defeat to Defeat ... and Back.*

I have found this experience of writing about my life to be a learning one—and even liberating. I have also found writing a book about yourself makes you terribly self-absorbed. It's all about you—what you did, who hurt you, your honors, your loves, your kids, your friends, your thoughts, etc. But then, isn't that the purpose of writing an autobiography?

Now that I'm finished, I'm relieved I can get back to my normal life with less self-reflection and more time with friends on a personal level and with strangers on an activist level, though I have tried to keep up with at least some with both during this period.

Thank you for taking the time (and due to the length, a lot of it) to go through the journey of my life with me.

CHAPTER 1

My Background

I was born toward the end of World War II on January 20, 1944, at King's Daughters Hospital in Greenville, Mississippi. My brother Johnny was born in the same hospital 18 months earlier. Our mother had returned to her family's hometown to give birth, as was then the Southern custom.

Mom told me I was a very quiet child, which must come as a shock to anyone who has made my acquaintance. (I was even shocked myself when I heard this.) Because of my mother always working, my father's temperament, and my brother needing so much attention due to his disability, I guess I instinctively knew to keep quiet and stay out of the way—at least in the early years.

My mother was born Hilda Janet Simmons, her parents' first born, at the same hospital in Greenville on September 30, 1917. Her father, Seymour Simmons, of German ancestry, worked for the Illinois Central Railroad for 50 years and had been born on January 7, 1885 in Leland, Mississippi, an even smaller town near Greenville. He was perhaps the sweetest man I ever met. Mom's mother, my beloved grandmother, Caroline Sternberger Simmons (later called Carrie), of German and Polish descent, was born on January 26, 1892 in Brownsville, Tennessee, 30 miles from Memphis. She was a working woman long before it was fashionable, as well as a fun-loving person, a good cook, and a great card player.

I never found it unusual that both of these grandparents were born in the United States, and that two of my great grandparents on the maternal side were born in this country as well. However, I learned later that this background of having ancestors here as early as the 1850s is highly unusual for Jewish families.

(Speaking of "greats" ... my great great grandfather Joe Davis, a handsome 1850s immigrant ended up at the Brownsville, Tennessee train station, smoking on the platform when the train took off with his possessions. He went into town where he later married and became a widower three times, siring 9 or 10 children until he died at age 96 in 1930 after being hit by a car—supposedly chasing after his fourth wife.)

My mother, who had two younger brothers, was a talented student and writer. She wrote the Bass Junior High School official song, which was still being used in Greenville, Mississippi a few years ago. She received a full scholarship to Sophie Newcomb College (the women's college at Tulane). Mom wanted instead to go up North to a co-ed school and went away to the University of

Wisconsin, where her pretty face and Southern accent made her an instant hit. But she found the frigid weather there made her too sick to capitalize on that popularity. She returned down South for her sophomore year at Louisiana State University (LSU), where she graduated first in her journalism class in 1939.

My father, Stanley Levitt, was larger than life—and not necessarily in a good way. His middle name was originally Manuel, but I found it interesting that he legally changed it to Nickoll, his mother's maiden name, when he was an adult. He was born, the third of four children, on December 24, 1914, in Portland, Oregon. He was raised there before the family moved to New York City during his teen years, where he attended George Washington High School in Washington Heights.

His father, Samuel John Levitt, known as either S.J. or John, was born February 11, 1885 of ancestors originally from Bulgaria, but whose family lived in Russia. As a young boy of seven, Grandpa's family left their small village for America and settled in Milwaukee, Wisconsin.

(Speaking of Bulgaria, here's a story that took place in the 1990s. A friend was involved with an organization which helped arrange elections in emerging democracies around the world. One day after her return from Bulgaria, we had dinner. Since I knew my grandfather's ancestors were from there and he and his children were very good-looking blue-eyed brunettes, I said, "I bet they are very attractive people, those Bulgarians." And she said, "Are you kidding? Those are the ugliest people I ever saw. Why do you ask?" And I said, "Oh, I was just curious," not wanting to make her feel badly by telling her those were my relatives.)

Now back to the 1800s: Dad's mother, Bertha Nickoll, known as Bonnie, was born in Russia on January 22, 1888 and her family immigrated to Milwaukee when she was three. Many years later, in Wisconsin, she met and married Samuel John Levitt. They then started a business in Nebraska before moving on to Portland, Oregon where they raised their children and opened a shoe store.

I had always thought that these paternal grandparents had been born in the United States as well because they led us to believe that. It was only during my daughter Hilary's search for ancestral information to satisfy her own curiosity that I learned that they came here as small children. I guess they just wanted to be American bred—*and* born.

A little bit more on Grandpa's family: Grandpa John's older brother Adolph moved from Milwaukee when he was 37 years old, and started selling donuts from a pushcart in New York City. He soon decided to make the donuts himself to avoid the middleman, and is credited with inventing the donut machine. Adolph approached his brothers to go into business with him, but Grandpa, who already had a wife and four kids to support, was afraid to take the risk. Big mistake. The business went on to become the Donut Company of America, which was hugely successful; and after opening the Mayflower Coffee Shops, he and his family became zillionaires. Years later, my Grandpa approached Adolph about becoming a partner but it was too late. He did, though, become Vice President for Human Resources and thus moved the family to New York when my dad was 13. Grandpa John made a good living, and they lived well, but mostly above their means. Yet he kicked himself for the rest of his life for not becoming a partner when he had the chance. (I do know my dad and his siblings were surrounded by first cousins who were extremely rich, and they were very envious. I always thought that surprising because from my perch as a child I found my dad and his siblings' childhood with help in the house, no requirement to work, and their choice of colleges enviable. I guess it's all relative.)

My father Stanley was quite intelligent and extremely handsome with an olive complexion, bright blue eyes and a great cleft in his chin. He graduated with a degree in civil engineering from the Massachusetts Institute of Technology (MIT) in 1936 after having spent his freshman year at the University of North Carolina at Chapel Hill. His first job after graduation was working on building the Bronx-Whitestone Bridge in New York City. Then Dad headed to Washington, D.C. where he continued his work as a civil engineer in what is now the Commerce Building. Interestingly, a half century later, I ended up in an office right across the street from where he worked in D.C. in the late 1930s. (Note that this is just the first of many not-so-interesting "interestinglys.")

My parents met after Dad graduated from MIT and was living in Manhattan. My mom was visiting her Aunt Hilda (an opera singer originally from Brownsville, Tennessee) in the city that summer on a free train pass, a perk of her dad's job. There, Mom had a date with a male friend from the University of Wisconsin. That friend saw Dad during intermission of the Broadway play, *Idiot's Delight*, and he introduced the two of them. My father was immediately struck by this fair complected brunette beauty with the wide-set, pretty brown eyes and the lilting Southern accent.

(I'm aware many say that their parents are good looking. So I am including pictures of my family in their early years in this book so you can judge for yourself. And by the way, I'm happy with the way I look. I'd guess I'd give myself a solid 7, and on a few good days maybe even an 8, for most of my 73 years. But my parents in their youth were definitely 9s or 10s.)

Dad, at 22, fell in love at first sight and he was determined to have her. So the next day he called up his friend and asked about the nature of their relationship. The guy said, "Unfortunately we're just friends," and when Dad asked for her number, he got it. Mom had only enough time for one date before she was traveling back home and at 18, starting her sophomore year at LSU. But that one date was memorable. Dad took her out drinking at some great New York bar, dinner at an expensive restaurant, and finally dancing at the Rainbow Room. It was also memorable because at the end of the date, as Dad dropped her at her Aunt Hilda's place, he had to ask her for a quarter to take the trolley home.

To be closer to her, my dad took a job surveying the Vicksburg Battlefield in Mississippi. He then went to Baton Rouge during Mom's last year of school, and enrolled in graduate courses at LSU. *Unusually* for the 1930s, my mother insisted upon finishing college before she would get married.

She did and then Mom and Dad were married on October 17, 1939, 18 days after she turned 22. My dad's parents flew in from London—where for two years Grandpa John had been working for the donut company—to Greenville for their lovely wedding at Hebrew Union Congregation.

The Early Years

After marrying, my parents moved to Youngstown, Ohio for another engineering job. In the early 1940s, they headed to Oak Ridge, Tennessee where my father worked as a draftsman for seven years on the Manhattan Project which developed the atomic bomb. (My dad left and lost many different jobs, not for lack of competence but because he was so difficult to work with. He never liked having a boss—he just wanted to be the boss.)

In Oak Ridge, Mom owned and ran the book and cosmetics sections of a department store in one of the first shopping centers in America. (In those days, department stores usually leased out their separate sections.) Seeing how well my mother did in retail during the town's boom war years, and continuing to find it hard to work for other people, my father decided to join her.

But just as he quit his job to work with Mom in her successful business, the department store lost its lease to one of Senator Estes Kefauver's buddies and they were both out of work. My father was so infuriated by the political shenanigans that he drove up overnight to Washington, D.C. and parked himself in Senator Kefauver's office until he was able to have a word with him. Needless to say, it made no difference. But Dad was proud that he had tried. I guess some of that tenacity passed on to me.

My only other memories of Oak Ridge were two in number, both traumatic. One was Dad throwing that pot of soup. The other was a memory that involved my brother Johnny (who was intellectually disabled and who attended a special education program in a public school—quite rare in those days—in Oak Ridge in the late 1940s.) Johnny had the top part of his index finger cut off while helping to fold up a rollaway bed, which was scary. I had the sisterly task of holding the finger as we rushed to the hospital where thank goodness they were able to re-attach it.

Because my parents lived very frugally in a small track house, they saved much of the money they had both made during their nearly eight years in Oak Ridge. Frugality came naturally to both of them, but they were also conscientious about planning for Johnny's future financial needs.

Thus in 1950, after becoming jobless, they were able to pick up and go to Oklahoma City. They had heard about a department store downtown which needed a lessee for their men's department—an opportunity Dad grabbed. As soon as we moved there, Mom found a bookstore nearby to lease and run. We lived in a tiny one-bedroom apartment where Johnny and I shared a rollaway bed in the living room.

A good thing about Oklahoma City is that my parents were able to find Naomi Ruppe, who ran a private school for the intellectually disabled. (Unlike Oak Ridge, Oklahoma City did not have special education public school programs at that time.) Johnny's IQ was 47, which would have categorized him as "trainable" but not "educable" (both terms of that day). However, Mrs. Ruppe was able to teach Johnny how to read, which seemed very unlikely given his IQ. That ability proved to be a saving grace as he got such enjoyment from perusing the newspapers, which helped him be somewhat conversant about the news of the day as he grew older. The Ruppe School had both a day program and a boarding school. Johnny went to the day program and was able to live at home.

In Oklahoma City, I was what is now called a latch-key kid starting at the age of six. My parents would pick up Johnny from school and they would not arrive home until dark. Because coming back to the small apartment with no one there was very lonely, I often stayed at the playground where I was also usually alone. I would sit or stand on the swing set, swing back and forth, and escape into my own little world where I was a trapeze artist. The interesting part when thinking back on this is that I grew up to be petrified of heights—so I'm sure glad *that* dream didn't come true.

As a child, I also fantasized as I swung back and forth—and even when I wasn't swinging—about saving people. I'd jump in the water to rescue drowning swimmers. I'd rush people to the hospital in the nick of time. I guess that was just the beginning of a lifetime need to be needed.

And speaking of need, since I was so needy for attention having rarely gotten any, I began to seek it out at school. When I was in the second grade in the fall of '51, I often finished my work quickly and proceeded to act out in mostly playful and silly ways. At midterm, the Principal, at the teacher's request, gave me a battery of tests in his office and they ended up putting me into the third grade for the second semester. I'm not sure if I was that smart—although I did well enough on the tests—but I am sure that the 2nd grade teacher just wanted to get rid of me—and she succeeded.

In Oklahoma City, I also vividly remember sitting in Mom's bookstore on the weekends while she worked and always watching out for Johnny either there or at home.

Unfortunately, both the men's department and the bookstore were located in dying downtown locations, and my parents proceeded to lose in the two years we were there all of the money they had saved in Oak Ridge. We were lucky if we sold a book a day at the store. Also, my father and his two brothers became partners in a clothing store in Okmulgee, Oklahoma, which did not do well either. So once again, Mom and Dad had to re-group.

Texas

Dad had heard about the Sprayberry Boom, which was a big oil discovery in West Texas. Being close to destitute, Dad hopped on a train in late 1951, leaving Mom, Johnny and I back in Oklahoma, and headed to Midland, Texas (which got its name due to being midway between Fort Worth and El Paso). Although my parents made little money in the Oklahoma businesses, they had once again lived very frugally and made sure that they always paid all their bills on time. So when Dad arrived in Midland with only a few dollars in his pocket, he was able to walk into a bank, not knowing a soul, and say he needed to borrow money to open a store—and get it. The bank had run Mom and Dad's Dunn & Bradstreet credit report and found out that they had an A credit rating. Thank goodness for Mom being a good bookkeeper and their steadfast rule of paying on time. My parents owned nothing—but they also owed nothing. I admired that trait in them and have always tried to replicate it.

Dad scouted locations. He found a small, white brick place for rent at 300 East Florida St. that was on the two-lane highway coming into town. He thought the best way to make a living for his family was to open a store that catered to the people who worked in the oil fields. So he opened the "General Clothing Store."

He immediately started pounding nails into the wood and built the fixtures for the store himself. He ordered merchandise, which consisted of work clothes: steel-toe boots, steel helmets, khakis, overalls, as well as underwear for people who worked on the rigs and drove the oil trucks. He and Mom eventually added western wear (jeans, cowboy shirts, hats and boots) to supply weekend outfits for this same type of customer as they headed to the honkytonks (which were located in Odessa—a town 20 miles away—as Midland was a dry county). The store was stacked with all these goods from floor to ceiling. He was ready for business within a few weeks.

While we stayed back in Oklahoma, Dad worked alone day and night seven days a week for six months. This was my Dad who grew up so differently. He had gone to one of the most expensive private universities in the country while owning a car. His parents were not that wealthy but lived like they were. They had both a housekeeper and a cook come in to help with the household chores. But here he was in Midland at 37 years old living in the back of the store on a rollaway bed, where there was only one window fan in very hot West Texas. There was a tiny bathroom with only a sink and toilet. Once a week Dad went to a fleabag (probably literally) motel for a bath and a good night's sleep.

From the combination of the loan and the store making money, Dad was able to buy a small house with a small yard five blocks from the store, on the corner of Midland's two main highways where all the oil trucks came in. (Speaking of good nights' sleep, after we moved into the house, we hardly got any. There was a traffic light right outside so the sounds of 18-wheelers screeching to a stop, loudly shifting gears, and roaring up again could be heard all night long.)

After the house and store were set up and the school year was complete, Dad sent us train tickets in the summer of 1952 to travel from Oklahoma City to Midland, Texas. They decided to keep Johnny at the Ruppe School, where he seemed happy, and they could now afford the boarding program. Mom and I got on an overnight train to Midland. We just brought ourselves and our few clothes. My parents had no other possessions to lug along as they had always only rented furnished homes and rarely bought anything for themselves or us.

I did have one extra piece of cargo—my pet snapping turtle. It was the only pet I was allowed to have and I named him Snappy. (Wasn't that original?) During the trip, I kept Snappy in a valise with the top partly open for air. In the middle of the night I heard a woman screaming. Snappy, a pretty large turtle, had gotten out of the case. But I was able to retrieve him then. Unfortunately, in Midland one day when I let him out in the small fenced-in side yard, I lost him for good. I have never been able to even try turtle soup in my whole life because of dear Snappy.

Midland, then a town of about 30,000, was in big sky country. The land was so flat that you could see an endless horizon. That was the most beautiful thing about it, and maybe the only beautiful thing. It was a desert with no mountains, hills, or even an oasis. There was very little vegetation, unless you count the tumbleweeds. Dust was everywhere. It was hot as hell, oftentimes 110 degrees during the day but would cool off at night to about 60. When it was 110, all the Midlanders would say "at least it's a dry heat." At 110, you really don't care—it's hot. The crackle of cicadas could be heard all summer long, especially at night. The barren landscape was dotted with oil rigs. They would churn away during the boom years and at other times, stand silent. (This is the most vivid and poetic description you'll get in the whole book, so I hope you enjoyed it.)

There were the proverbial train tracks separating the town, with most of it by far being north of the tracks. We lived on the south side, which was considered to be the "wrong" side. My side of town—whatever you want to call it—consisted of working-class people, when people were working. After I enrolled in elementary school for the 4th grade, I had to fill out forms with information such as my parents' educational background. When I completed the form, a school official read it and said, "Your parents graduated from high school?" "Yes." "Both of them?" "Yes." They graduated from college?" "Yes." "Are you sure?" "Yes." "Both of them?" "Yes." Then the official said, "There's not one student in this elementary school whose parents graduated from high school much less college." She wanted to "car" me, as there was no busing then, to the north side of town. I was not interested in doing so, and thank goodness, neither were my parents. South Elementary School (and that was its name) was two blocks from the house and four blocks from the store so convenience won the day.

General Clothing Store

I had to work at the store starting at age eight, including operating the cash register. (Being tall for my age helped.) The store did a decent business but not a thriving one. During the oil booms my parents did well. But in their over 30 years in business, most of them were not boom years. Many days we would sit or stand on a concrete floor for hours (as there was only one chair at a desk upfront and one stool in the back for trying on boots) waiting for someone to come in. The store was open seven days a week, 10 a.m. to 10 p.m., Monday through Saturday, and Sunday from 12 p.m. to 6 p.m.—until the Blue Laws came in and then we had to close on Sunday. I had to be at the store after school until about 8 p.m. Mom and I would then go home and Dad would close the store at 10. I also had to be there on weekends unless Johnny was in town and then I would take care of him instead.

One of the few times I was not in the store, fate played a very cruel trick on me. A young Elvis Presley, who was performing in Odessa, came into the store when only Mom was there and bought practically every belt we had. In those days instead of throwing sweaty scarves to the audience, which became his trademark, he gave out belts to his fans. (I sure hope he didn't throw them.) Unfortunately, I missed my idol that time. However, when I was 13 and Elvis had just gotten out of the Army, he did a train tour to say hello to fans around the country and came through Midland. I made sure that I was at the train station to wave. Not quite the close-up Mom had years before, but at least some face time.

Though Dad bought the merchandise, my mother worked in the store longer hours. This is because when people would walk in after no one had been in for hours, Dad would yell at them. Needless to say, most then left. It was really insane. Instead of welcoming customers, he took out his anger on the few who came in.

So Mom would say, "Stan, it's time to leave. Either go take a nap, go play tennis, or go to the stock market. Just please go."

He often did go to the stock broker's office, where he would watch the stock prices scroll by and purchase sometimes. Good thing he did as they started making some real money that way—even though I never knew it. They sure didn't live like they had any money. They certainly didn't look like they had any money.

Dad was usually disheveled. He wore only loose-fitting slacks. Given that he belted those slacks under his barrel chest and not having a big rear, it looked like he was always about to lose them. (Little did I know then that it would become the "in" style 50 years later.) He wore a plaid shirt every day, oftentimes the same one. Mom couldn't have cared less about clothes either at that point and never wore jewelry or makeup. They were attractive because they were born that way but they certainly did little to enhance themselves except for some dress-up days. Mom always carried a few extra pounds. Dad was trim in his youth and ate like there was no tomorrow. But as he reached his tomorrows in his 40s, he put on weight. I think that added to his foul moods.

We were glued to the store other than the week from Christmas to New Year's when we closed every year. We drove to visit my grandparents in Greenville, Mississippi during that time. The only family trip we ever took that didn't involve visiting family was when we drove to Mexico City when I was 13. On the drive down, we spent a night at a nice hotel in Monterrey, Mexico and I developed a crush on the 20-something-year-old son of the owner. (Me and my crushes, ever-present from age eight to about age 60, a 50-plus-year run.) Other than going to the Pyramids in Mexico City, where I only went up ten steps (my fear of heights had already kicked in), all we did on that trip, or so it seemed, was look at cathedrals, one after the other. Finally, and memorably, Johnny sat down on a bench in a plaza across the street from one, crossed his arms and declared, "I'm not going into another church." He could not be moved. (I'm sure it wasn't just cathedrals or churches—any religious structures would have applied.)

Johnny

My dear brother Johnny, who early in my life consumed much of my time and later defined me, was born on June 29, 1942. At first they didn't realize that anything was wrong with him. He was kind of thin and wasn't as alert as a lot of other babies, but there was nothing very obvious then. About the time he should have been crawling, though, he didn't, and he was behind in other ways developmentally as well. Then when he was 9 or 10 months old the doctor said, "I believe there may be some mental deficiency here." In those days, they thought that mental retardation (the term of the day) was genetic.

I learned later on when I was studying special education at the University of Texas in the early '60s that 98% of "mental retardation" was caused by injury before, during, or after birth. Only 2% then was caused by chromosomal incompatibility or other genetic issues. In Johnny's case they thought the cause may have been one of two things or neither: Mom had taken medication for varicose veins during pregnancy and Johnny was a high forceps delivery. But in 1942 before a lot of studies had been done on it, couples mainly blamed each other—or themselves.

Johnny was very loved by my parents. But they would not have planned to have another child after finding out about his problems. They would have feared that each of their offspring would have similar issues. However, just about the time they found out about Johnny, Mom discovered she was pregnant with me. If I hadn't been conceived right then and there, I probably wouldn't be here (and you would not have to be reading this book). Mom confirmed to me later that they would have quit having kids. But my timing was impeccable, at least that time.

It was a scary period for them. They didn't know if I was going to be mentally disabled as well and had to wait until I developed to find out. Fortunately, I was pretty bright-eyed and bushy-tailed and started to do things like crawl and talk pretty early. That was very consoling for them. And thank goodness they had me because I think I gave them some pleasure as well as helped take some of the burden of Johnny off of them.

Because Johnny had stayed behind in Oklahoma City at the Ruppe School, for the first time in our lives we were separated. Even though I was just a little girl of eight, I worried about his well-being. And this time, it turned out to be a good premonition.

During the summer when I was nine, I went to visit him for about 10 days, and stayed at the boarding school with him. I found that some of the young people who worked there, who I believe were related to Mrs. Ruppe, were abusing the kids. They would help the students make wood carving boards that were shaped like pigs or apples and some were fairly large. Then they would use those boards to spank them. When I protested, they did the same to me. I wanted to tell my parents over the phone about what was going on, but as the school officials always listened in on phone calls, I couldn't. As soon as I got home, though, I told my parents and they immediately brought Johnny home.

We were all angry about the behavior that was allowed to go on there. But we were also always grateful to Mrs. Ruppe herself for the love and attention she gave to Johnny as well as her gift of teaching him to read. Therefore, nothing was said at first about the circumstances of his leaving other than we wanted him back because "we missed him."

Even though I was only nine years old, I insisted that my parents tell Mrs. Ruppe about the abuse. Instead, they wanted to cut and run because of their fondness for her. But I felt that she should know the truth in order to be able to clean up the situation and make it better for the remaining and future students. "If you don't tell, they'll keep doing it!" I cried. For the first time in my life with my parents, I got my way. They did call.

When it came to Johnny, my parents often deferred to me because I was a natural caretaker and they were so distracted by work. It was the only subject on which I could speak my mind and have it matter. Feeling such responsibility for my brother at such a young age made me grow up fast. Others used to say I was a wise old lady even as a child. (As an adult in my own home, I started reversing that and now as an older lady, I have become often childlike. And it's not dementia yet. I'm letting myself be the child I never got a chance to be. And it's fun.)

When Johnny left the Ruppe School, he moved back for a while until my parents found him a new place: the Brown School in San Marcos, Texas, which was known to be one of the finest—and most expensive—in the country. Even though Johnny lived away, he came home often—not just for the holidays, but about every six to eight weeks for a week or so.

I normally worked at the store on Saturdays, but when Johnny was in town, I'd look after him. We'd walk eight blocks up Main Street to go to the movies at the Ritz Theater. I'd eat sour pickles and Johnny ate popcorn and then we'd have candy, all of which we enjoyed as much as the movie. (Starting as a young adult, I had little interest in pickles, and popcorn became my favorite food.) It was usually a western or comic book action movie. The common thread was that the films always only had male heroes. (The only exception was Dale Evans—who played Roy Roger's dutiful wife.)

While we were at the movie theater, sadly Johnny was too often the subject of cruel taunts by other young people, many of them far bigger than we were. They would call him terrible names and make fun of the way he looked and acted. I remember one guy saying, "I bet you can't read, you idiot." "He can read," I yelled back proudly. It was scary, though. It would have been easier to ignore the bullies and wither away. But something inside of me made me fight back. I'd go up into their faces and say, "You should be ashamed of yourself for making him feel bad when he can't help it." And they would sometimes wither away themselves.

Other times they would just keep coming back at me, but at least not at Johnny. That's when I became a fighter. And I have used those same tactics throughout my life to fight for causes I've cared about. I never, though, have used the Judo I learned at the local YMCA as a kid in order to protect myself and Johnny. It's a good thing as I was never very good at it anyway.

And speaking of fights, I got into one doozy with Johnny. It was probably back in Oklahoma City, when I was about seven years old and Johnny was about eight and a half. There were big piles of magazines in the house. Johnny would take them and strewn them across the floor. Because he would never pick them up and put them back into a pile, I would have to do it. This occurred at least once a day. Finally, it came to me that if he was smart enough to take them out and toss them, why couldn't he put them back?

So I did something very reminiscent of a movie I later saw about Anne Sullivan and Helen Keller called *The Miracle Worker*. I told Johnny we were going to have to put the magazines back and this time we were going to do it together. I showed him, "I'll put one on. You'll put one on." He said, "No, I'm not going to do it." He could be very stubborn. And I said, "Yes, you are. We are going to do this." This conversation went on for a very long time. Finally, I just took his hand and put it on the magazine and took the magazine and put it on the pile until after some struggle, he at last began to do it himself. It finally worked. It helped that Johnny loved and respected me, and didn't want me to be mad at him. Every day after that, when he had spread the magazines on the floor, we would put them back together. Not exactly a miracle worker, but it got that job done. It was a great learning experience. Johnny was getting very spoiled because everybody was trying to compensate for his disabilities. He just wanted to do what he wanted to do and usually got away with it. It was also a good learning experience for me too. Situations like that helped me realize I wanted to be a teacher and also helped give me the tools that I would use both in teaching—and in parenting.

More on My Parents

My father's dominance and mercurial temperament ruled my childhood and the house we lived in. His rage brought me tremendous anxiety every day. When he came home around 10 p.m., I never knew what mood he would be in. I would hear the front door open and clench in fear. I was always so frightened. If it was a bad day at the store, he would come into my room and just start beating me with a belt. And it was often a bad day. I hadn't done anything wrong. I was just in my room, not bothering anybody. In fact, I was a really good kid. I wish my mom were here to attest.

After my father beat me, ten minutes later he'd come into my room and hug me. But he would never say he was sorry.

Unfortunately, my mother never intervened. She never walked in and stopped it. Never even tried. And their room was right next door in our tiny little house. Even when the beatings ended, she never even came in to pat my arm or anything.

I loved my mother dearly, but in retrospect I'm mad at her for never protecting or consoling me. After some especially bad instances, I would beg her to leave him. She'd say, "Where would I go, especially with Johnny?" I wanted to yell out sometimes, "How about home to your sweet parents and my loving grandparents in Mississippi?" But I never argued with my parents. I just understood that my mother had a tough life herself. With working all the time, worrying over Johnny, and bearing my father's unbearable temperament, I felt she did the best she could. But it still hurt that she did not protect me. And it still hurts today just thinking about it.

As an adult I have always been a forgiving person, probably too forgiving. I guess that came from the immediate need to forgive, or at least move on when I was a child in order to survive.

We did, though, occasionally have some good times. Every year or so, Mom, Dad and I (and Johnny when he was in town) would go over to Odessa to a honkytonk with great country music. Mom and Dad were a joy to watch on the dance floor. They were both excellent dancers and had a unique move where they would walk arm and arm to the beat and then go back into a couple's stance—like real professionals. I became a good dancer— and an able follower (only at dancing)—due to Dad, and that served me well over the years. Johnny could also dance and really got the beat—in fact we all did. My dad also had a nice singing voice and would sometimes break into song when he was driving. Mom was a good whistler. I was a good listener since I was not good at either of the above.

Sometimes Dad would decide to close the store at 9:30 if he was in an up mood. He'd call to say he'd pick us up in five minutes and we'd be off to the Yucca Theater for a 10 p.m. movie, always on a school night. Or we'd go to Borden's for a hot fudge sundae or the Ranch House for chocolate pie—rushing in at closing time. When I was sick, Dad would sometimes bring me chocolate ice cream and movie magazines. My good memories revolved around chocolate and movies then—and by the way, they still do.

But even those fun trips to the movies caused stress. The films were very chaste in those days, but not enough for my father's standards. If the couple on screen kissed, more than just a peck on the lips, Dad would get up in a fury and leave. I would spend the remainder of the movie constantly turning around in my seat, wondering whether he would return and sit back down, or come back in and announce that we were leaving. I spent each trip to the movies practically praying the couple would not kiss so we didn't have to go through all that.

My folks did try to give me some advantages along the way. I don't actually remember taking a ballet class in Oak Ridge, but I've seen a picture of me in a tutu when I was four or five. They also offered me an art class early Saturday mornings, but I just went a couple of times because Saturday was the only day I could sleep in a little, so I chose sleep. I still have the one still-life oil painting I did. Mary Cassat I was not, but I wasn't bad. I did make it through several piano lessons, but I hated to practice so that did not last long either. My favorite was a modern dance class I took for a while. I do appreciate that they gave me those opportunities, some of which I had asked for—probably to just get a break from working at the store.

Yet I never could have friends over to the house because Dad wouldn't allow it. I wasn't allowed to talk on the phone either because the telephone line always had to be open in case he wanted to get through. Dad would call from the store and if he heard a busy signal, he'd close the store, rush home, and pull the phone out of the wall in anger. In those days, we had the type of phone where the phone company had to come to take the whole mechanism out of the wall, fix it, and put it back in—a little more troublesome than the clip-in wires we have today. This routine cost plenty of money, and it probably happened every two weeks until I stopped using the phone entirely.

I was scared to death of my father and his violent temper. I was constantly anxious, which later developed into heartburn which later developed into a hiatal hernia which later developed into acid reflux.

My father also demanded to be the center of our world. I think that's why he didn't allow me to talk on the phone or have friends over. I think he was jealous of anything else in my life. The same rules applied to my mother. She never went out or spent time with friends because she wasn't allowed any. Once in a while she'd go to the library and get books. But mostly she went to work and came home, and that's it. The only time we had any freedom was when Dad went to New York to visit his parents, which was once or twice a year.

My father tried his best to keep us isolated and all to himself. No one ever came to our home. Let me correct that. One person, a salesman, once came to our house before we went to dinner with him. He stood at the doorway as we got ready to go. He never sat down nor was invited to.

I wasn't allowed to have pets either besides Snappy. He was just low maintenance enough to get approval from my father. However, one time when Dad was away visiting his family, I found a stray, malnourished kitten. She was the cutest thing. She was black and white with all white feet. In another burst of pet name creativity, I named her Boots. I brought her home and was able to nurse her to better health. Mom, who was fond of Boots too, said, "You have to get her out of here by the time Dad gets back." But I didn't. He came home and said, "You have to get rid of that damn thing." I said, "I have a lot of homework now but I will do it to-morrow." But next thing I knew—and I was sure that it was going to happen—he started petting her and fell in love. So now I had a fluffy four-legged pet. We had her until she died many years later.

In Midland, we lived in a small stucco Spanish-style house. The living room was dismal with dark black-out curtains that were never opened. I mean, never. We also never sat in the living room, not once to visit together. It was just the pass-through room. My parents sat in their twin beds in their small bedroom. That's where we congregated when we congregated, which was only late at night or on Sundays after the Blue Laws.

We never had a television set, as my father wouldn't allow it. We would just sit on their beds usually playing gin rummy and listening to operettas (Mario Lanza was my favorite), show tunes, and big band dance music on a record player console. I became very smart about every song and who the band leaders were. I knew every show tune and I could tell you the show it came from. I could have won *Name That Tune* at that time but I didn't know about that show until years later as remember, we didn't have a TV. When I went to college, I'd listen to classical music at bedtime. My exposure to all kinds of music from bluegrass to symphonies and everything in between enlarged my life and I've loved all types of music ever since, with my favorites being old country, bluegrass, and the sounds of the '50s and '60s with others sprinkled in between. It probably also helped that my dad seemed to be in a better mood when he was listening to music.

My parents barely owned anything other than bare essentials. The only knick-knack in our house was a Holiday Inn ash tray, which Mom constantly used. When I was about 10, I bought Mom a pretty, flowery tin canister set for Mother's Day at Woolworths. The very next day, Dad in a fit of anger put his fist through the bread basket. It had to be thrown away, but at least the sugar, flour, and coffee/tea canisters remained.

There were no pictures in our home except 2x4-inch black and white family photos that my father taped on a small area of their bedroom wall. When I was 13, I got an opportunity to breathe some life into my own bedroom. I got twin beds instead of a roll-away bed, like the one I had slept on since I was a small child in Oak Ridge. I arranged the beds in an L-shape. And off I went to Woolworths again and bought some pictures, $2 apiece, and I put them on the wall. It was nice to finally have a pretty room. Decorating has remained a distraction and a joy throughout my life.

(I guess as an act of adult rebellion over the lack of televisions and pictures at home growing up, I now have a TV in almost every room, including a bathroom, and pictures on every inch of wall space. Maybe I would have done it anyway, but who knows ...)

Food played a central role in my family but we rarely ate at home. Mom in all the years I knew her only made two dishes. One was boiled tongue with rice and the other was chopped chicken liver, which we spread on white bread. I know these dishes sound awful, but they were actually kind of good. My father occasionally fried up a steak or made a pot of chicken soup with lots of noodles and vegetables, which was also good. That was it and those meals were served a total of four times a year—maximum.

Most of the time I ate at Jo Pal's, the little truck stop next to the store. I'd have the blue plate special for 69¢ and then it went up to 99¢. It was Southern cooking at its worst health-wise but taste-wise, delicious: heavy on meat and potatoes with lots of gravy on everything. The vegetable (when it wasn't lima beans, black-eyed peas or corn) was fried okra or green beans with ham hock. I looked forward to those meals and I loved every bite.

Sometimes we ate at the one Chinese restaurant in town, the Blue Star Inn, which was just awful. Mom and Dad would have chicken chow mein, which tasted like it came out of a can. It probably did. Johnny and I couldn't stand it. For years after that, I thought I hated Chinese food. Much later, when my husband would want to go out for Chinese, his favorite food, I'd protest and say, "I don't like Chinese food," but I went anyway. I soon found that I love Chinese food. I just hated the Blue Star Inn.

I did like Furr's Cafeteria. The million-dollar pie, with pineapples and pecans in a cream-cheese-type filling, was my favorite item. (Now that I'm describing it, I'm not sure why I liked it but in those days I just grasped at any and every straw I could.) I loved seeing the food before choosing it. That remains true today with buffets being a preference, where all the food is visible and plentiful. Even now, when I go to a restaurant, I often walk around and look at every table and see what they're eating before I order. I then point and say to the server, "I'll have what's she's having."

I know I'm mentioning food a lot. But the only time my father was reliably in a good mood was when we were eating (or listening to music). And Dad's moods ruled everything. I guess that joy associated with food has stuck with me. Plus, I like to eat.

My parents were amazingly smart. My father was maybe the smartest person I ever knew. He bought a set of the *Encyclopedia Britannica* supposedly for me but he always had his head in one of the volumes. He constantly lectured too, which was annoying in and of itself, but made much worse because most of his views were so intolerant and prejudiced.

My mother was a sweet, even-tempered woman. She was likely as smart as my father but more quiet about it. She devoured books and could do a *New York Times* crossword puzzle in just minutes.

I didn't want to be anything like my folks who were brilliant but hermits. I equated being an intellectual with being isolated. Though born with a decent brain, I did not want their anti-social life. So I developed a personality, craved being around people, and made intellectual pursuits secondary if not thirdary then. (I'm intellectual enough to know "thirdary" is not a word, but I don't like "tertiary" so I'm going with this, hoping it will maybe catch on.)

CHAPTER 2

My Religion or Lack Thereof

If you asked my parents their religion, they would say they were Jewish but they certainly didn't bring up the subject much less practice it at all. I vaguely knew about Passover only because my grandparents in New York would send us Passover petit fours. I had no knowledge of what Passover meant, but I sure looked forward to those chocolate treats.

I did have a Jewish confirmation in a sense. I carpooled twice over to a temple in neighboring Odessa at the request of my paternal grandparents. After those two classes, they handed me a confirmation certificate. It was a bit of a joke, but I did get some checks from relatives and thus my new bedroom furniture I mentioned earlier. As a result of the lack of Jewish education in my childhood, I had to read all the prayers during my kids' Bar and Bat Mitzvahs with the Hebrew words spelled out phonetically, and yet I still managed to mispronounce them, much to their embarrassment. They sometimes ask me to say certain words so they can get a good laugh. But my Spanish pronunciation is not much better. I guess I have no ear when it comes to pronunciations—or singing. But back to the Jewish issue ...

My father didn't even particularly like Jews, or any other group for that matter. But at least he would say he was Jewish if asked. His siblings preferred not to be. Period. As an example, his sister, Marguerite Levitt, who I only saw a couple of times, married a man named Monroe Levin, an orthodontist, in the 1940s. They both decided decades later to take away the Jewishness of their name and legally changed it to "Levis." Although I think they intended the second syllable to be pronounced like the verb "is," most people, including the family, pronounced their name like Levis jeans. It seemed obvious to us that they did not accomplish the goal they had in mind. Why not just "Lewis"?

Although I didn't know much about my religion growing up, it didn't stop me from being a target of my classmates. I heard more than my share of anti-Semitic comments and the expression "Jew you down" while working in the store. At South Elementary School, I had a crush on a boy named Jimmy Murphy who I thought was my friend. One day he screamed out to me in front of the whole class, "Dirty Jew!" "What are you talking about?" I asked. He said, "When I told my Dad about being friends with Carol Levitt, he said, 'You mean that dirty Jew?'" Jimmy used that phrase all around school and everyone started repeating it. I knew

I was Jewish but I didn't know I was a "dirty Jew." I ran to the store crying and my mom just turned me around and pushed me saying, "Go back to school." I did. But that whole experience, especially for a child, was so hurtful, actually scary. Interestingly, many years later I heard that Jimmy became Pastor Murphy.

In high school, several guys who asked me out ended up breaking the date. I later learned that when they asked for the family car, their parents said, "Who do you have a date with?" They said, "Carol Levitt." The parents responded, "You're not going out with that Jew from the wrong side of the tracks." I never knew which bothered them more, nor did I ask. It just seemed like double jeopardy. All of these things were very painful.

I remember when I was 12 years old, I wanted to throw a birthday party for myself. My mom and dad would take me out to dinner for my birthday but I never had an actual party. I called up the *Midland Reporter-Telegram* because we got our town's newspaper at home and I knew they reported such events. I was excited to bring them the scoop of my own party. When I told the person at the paper about the fete, she said "fine" and then asked for my address. I said, "311 West Florida." Immediately she said, "Oh, we don't have any space." It was not even subtle—another rejection. That incident rained on my parade enough that I did not have the party after all. It did sting at the time but now I consider it totally ridiculous. When a paper has so few standards that they consider a kids' party newsworthy, who were they to reject me?

There were other instances. One time my friend Robin Redfern had a slumber party and I was not invited. That was weird because we were really good friends in school. Our mutual friend, Liz Hitt, confided to me that Robin had wanted to invite me but her parents said no because I was Jewish. I guess they thought Jewish was some dreaded disease they could catch.

Another time, on the day of the only snowfall I ever witnessed in Midland, school let out early. We all walked over to the Redfern house for hot chocolate. Everyone was allowed in except for me. I just waited outside the house in the snow. Because that snow incident was so traumatic, I had actually suppressed the memory. But at our 40th high school reunion several friends, including Liz, reminded me of it. And of course, I then remembered.

(About eight or nine years after high school, when I was married and pregnant with my first child, I was back in Midland visiting the family, which I did at least every year. Several years earlier, Mom had gotten involved with the American Auxiliary of

University Women (AAUW). There she met the Society Editor for the *Midland Reporter-Telegram* and next thing we know, my every visit is mentioned in the social column as if it were big news. AAUW had some social functions and during that visit, Mom asked me if I wanted to go to a luncheon at one of the women's homes. Many had said, "Bring your daughter. We read about her all the time in the society section of the paper." So I went to that event, which was held in one of the quintessential, huge ranch-style houses in Midland.

Several women immediately surrounded me, "We're so happy to meet you. I bet it's exciting in Washington." They were acting like there was a celebrity in town. That's when I spotted Mrs. Redfern, who was like the grande dame of Midland, at the far end of the next room. She saw me and came running with her arms outstretched like she was seeing her long-lost daughter. She burst into the circle around me, and said, "Carol! I'm so glad to see you." I replied, "Excuse me. [pause] Do I know you?" Of course I knew exactly who she was. I would never have forgotten the woman who banned me from her home. She said, "Yes. Don't you remember? You were good friends with my daughter Robin in high school." I said, "Oh yea." I've always been more of a forgiving person than a get-even one. But I must admit that day, I feigned a loss of memory to snub her—and enjoyed every minute of it.)

Even though I've tried to add some levity here, those experiences in my youth wounded me considerably at the time—and the scars remain. However, I do want to emphasize that those childhood occurrences did contribute to the life I ended up living. In a way I hate to even say that, because the individuals who brought me so much pain should not feel a sense of credit. I actually prefer that they feel guilty. But credit them I must to some degree.

I always wanted to be recognized as something special by those people who looked down on me. Their disdain was a huge motivator for me to prove that I was just as good as they were—no, probably better. Those incidents also made me aware that I would never wish the type of prejudice I received—or Johnny and others, especially individuals of darker skin, received—on anyone, and taught me to hate prejudice and hurtfulness of any kind.

Being ridiculed for being Jewish and from what they considered to be the "wrong" side of the tracks, and having a brother who* they considered not "normal," helped me choose to become different from them—and I am grateful for whatever got me here. I feel similarly about the pain my father put me through. It all helped me become not only a survivor, but a fighter, as well as a nicer, more forgiving person, albeit somewhat scarred—and those qualities have served me well over the years.

*I will be using "who" instead of "whom" most of the time because it's mainly the way I speak. In fact, I don't know many who use "whom." Or should I say, I don't know whomever "whom" is used by.

Too Early Bloomer

To add to those experiences, I became a woman at eight years of age, far too young. I developed breasts and had to wear a bra then. I basically went from practically being a toddler to adulthood, with not much childhood in between.

My mother rarely went out of town but one spring she had a family wedding in Denver. I had just turned nine years old and was in the latter part of the fourth grade. I left class to go to the bathroom. I saw that I was bleeding profusely and started thinking that I was bleeding to death with no idea why. It was so scary. I just started crying and stayed in the bathroom waiting for somebody to come in. When someone did, I told her to get my friend Carolyn Price, who came in and said, "Oh yea, that just happened to my sister Evelyn. It's mens-something. I can't remember the name." She went to the teacher and explained, and then we went over to Carolyn's house. Her mother gave me a pad to put on and told me what was going on. My mother never had because I'm sure she didn't expect me to start menstruating so early. I told my own daughters when they were six or seven to try to avoid the same experience and that was a good thing as my older daughter started at eight and my younger, ten.

I had always been pretty good at track and participated in school competitions. When I became fully developed in the fourth grade, I gained weight, which I was afraid would affect my running ability. However, in the sixth grade, I represented South Elementary School in the 50-yard dash in the citywide competition.

Developing early made me look twice my age. It also made me a target of ridicule. But there were some benefits.

I found being advanced for my age opened a way for me to get some of the attention that I was starved for. One time when I was working in the store, a cute guy of about 16 or 17 came in, and I helped him pick out a shirt. The next day he called the store and asked me out. I told him I was not allowed to date. He asked, "Why not?" And I responded, "I'm only nine years old."

I began dressing somewhat sexily to continue the attention. Before that I just wore jeans and men's western or white shirts. By sixth grade, at 11, I got a tight pink skirt paired with an equally tight black sweater, which were *the* colors of the '50s.

I was boy crazy starting at the age of eight. Of course there was my crush on Jimmy Murphy in elementary school, and as you know, that one didn't work out so well. One of the Barker brothers in sixth grade used to write me love notes. But my first real boyfriend was Ronnie Morelock at Cowden Junior High School. He was sort of short (but taller than I), very handsome, and we used to dance to "My Special Angel" by Bobby Helms. I spent my share of time necking at the movies during that time, but never more.

Though boy crazy and fond of wearing tight sweaters, I was in fact, very cautious. A lot of the kids in Midland were really fast and it made me slow down. When I was in the 7th grade, I went to a slumber party and the boys came over and we danced for a while. Then they left and we girls went to our mats on the floor to sleep. Next thing I remember is being awakened in the middle of the night by a boy who was coming on to me. I pushed him away. It appeared he was not the only boy who had returned. There was a couple next to me having sex. I could barely see them but I sure could hear them. And these kids were just kids. I went home the next day and I didn't hang around with that crowd again.

The south side was the rough area of town, which required you to grow up quickly. Many people I knew had brothers and fathers in prison, if they had fathers they knew at all. It was rough to deal with such things as the smartest student at my elementary school getting shot while playing Russian roulette with a friend. He remained physically and mentally disabled for the rest of his life.

When I was 11, I went to camp—another advantage Mom pushed for. Compared to the other campers, I looked like an adult. The camp directors, being aware of my not fitting in, brought me back as an unpaid counselor the next year, even though I was three years under the 15-year-old threshold to be one. Since I never could nap—once up, I'm up—I was the one chosen to walk up the huge hill each day to ring the bell to awaken the campers. That was just another example of being deprived of my childhood by such early development. I would much rather have been one of the regular campers than have the responsibility for them.

A Risky Ride

One night I did try to take advantage of looking older since I was stuck with it anyway. But let me set the stage:

When I was 12 years old, Dad taught me to drive. You couldn't get a license until you were 16, but maybe since I looked like I was older than that, Dad thought I was ready. He took me out on the highway and then pulled over and let me drive. About a block from the house coming home, I took a wide turn and hit a car. We had to go to court. Because Dad had let a 12-year-old drive, he got a reprimand and a fine from the judge as well as being forced to pay to fix the other driver's car. A fun time with Dad until it wasn't. (By the way, since age 12, I have had a really good driving record—knock on wood.)

A few months after that, my dad went to New York to visit his parents. As I said, I always loved when he was away—about twice a year—because I was free from him and free to do things I liked.

My two best friends in junior high were Danelle Reese and Pam Walling. Neither had a father in their lives then. Danelle's mother had been married four or five times. Pam's mom had been married five times. (And I swear, I'm not exaggerating.) It was later that I realized those two mothers were in their early 30s then. Now I wonder how many more times they married.

Anyway, that time when my father was away, my friend Danelle spent the night. She was a pretty blue-eyed blonde. Like me, she was fully developed. We were quite a pair.

That night Danelle and I made a plan. My mother was a really heavy sleeper. After taking her car keys, we snuck out my window, got in the car and drove to the neighboring town, 20 miles away. We arrived in Odessa around midnight. We went to a drive-in and ordered sodas. There was a group of four guys there who were 20 or 30-something, looking at us in an aggressive way. I said, "We should get out of here." We started driving back and those guys followed us. I was scared to death that they would attack us and started speeding to get away from them.

Suddenly, I heard a police siren. The other vehicle had slowed down when they saw the police car stopping me. The officer walked to my window and said, "Let me see your driver's license." I just said, "Sir, I don't have a driver's license. I'm Carol Levitt and I'm 12 years old. My father is out of town. He's really strict. He just taught me how to drive. I was driving so fast is because a car full of guys was following us." The officer said he saw them. I continued, "I did a really stupid thing. I promise if you don't tell my parents, I will never do anything like this again." The police officer said, "I don't know. This is unbelievable. You're 12 years old. It's nearly 1 a.m. You were really speeding." I kept pleading with him.

The officer finally said, "Alright. I'm going to get you to the Midland line. Follow me. Then I want you to go directly home, and never repeat this kind of thing." I said, "I swear." (And I did not: 1) because I swore I wouldn't, and 2) because the experience scared the sh... out of me.) The officer did as he promised. He led us to the line and waved goodbye. I went home, put the key back, and was thankful to have gotten home safely. The officer never told my parents, nor did I. Bless him. I surely would have gotten a beating, and this time, a deserved one.

I actually did get a legal license to drive when I was only 14 in the fall of my sophomore year of high school. There was a program at the school where several students could be selected to take a driver's ed course. I was fortunate to get chosen and afterwards received my driver's license.

(In addition to being a decent driver, I'm good at directions. Once I've been somewhere, especially if it is something I like, such as a friend's home, a restaurant or shop, I become like a homing pigeon—and can always find it again. But I must admit I'm a bit of a nervous passenger these days when others are driving, with very few exceptions. By the way, my mother would have qualified as an exception as she was the best driver I've ever known.)

Mississippi

The best times of my childhood happened in my birthplace—Greenville, Mississippi. Mom, Johnny and I would go there every summer for the month of August, and it was my favorite thing to do. Mom was always so happy to be away from work and Dad, and to be back with her loving and fun parents and her childhood friends. I felt the same way. I valued Greenville as an escape from Midland and a place to relax and have a really good time. Oh, how I wished for August to last forever, as my life in Midland was so different, with much brutality and lots of loneliness.

I loved Greenville mainly because of my family and friends there, but also because it was such a pretty town with much greenery. Its main street, Washington Ave., was canopied by tall, gorgeous trees on the sides of the streets and in the median.

My grandparents were industrious people. After retiring from working for the Illinois Central Railroad for 50 years, Grandpa Seymour got at a job at Weatherby's Hardware Store. I always appreciated the slogan that was on the side of its building in downtown Greenville. It said, "If We Don't Have It, You Don't Need It." Grandpa had a heart attack when he was in his late 50s, but he recovered nicely. He would come home for lunch (called "dinner" there) for their main meal of the day and then take a nap before going back to work. (Their evening meal was called "supper" and consisted of things we have for lunch.)

Grandpa and his younger brother, Uncle Benny, introduced me as a child to baseball, which became a sentimental favorite of mine. Greenville had a farm team of the then Milwaukee Braves and we spent many a night at their games—just me and the guys. I read the programs and knew all the players' names, had pictures of them with autographs, and kept the box scores. I loved every minute of watching those cute players play ball—and didn't even mind the many mosquito bites as a result.

(In fact, Midland got a farm team when my kids were quite young, enlarging my beloved memories centering around baseball. Those teams probably contributed to my liking so many baseball-themed movies, like *The Rookie*, *A League of their Own*, *42* (about Jackie Robinson), *Bull Durhum* and *The Natural*. My favorite is *The Rookie*—see it if you haven't.)

Another special memory with my Grandpa when I was a child was spending time with him when he came home for lunch and before his short nap. I would give him a hug and we would sit and visit a little. He would make me laugh by doing duck quacking noises. Even as I grew older, we kept up that tradition.

Grandpa had to quit working at age 83 when the hardware store closed. Weatherby's was being torn down to enlarge the Stein's discount store next door, which went on to be Stein Mart, the national chain. Sadly, we lost dear Grandpa about six months later on July 11, 1968. I always had the feeling he would still be with us if he could have continued working at Weatherby's.

My grandfather was such a dear that when he passed away, the *Delta Democrat-Times*, whose publisher was Hodding Carter Sr., wrote an editorial about him. It said, among other things, "He was a not only a gentleman, he was gentle man. He was a faithful and good friend and we mourn his passing. Would that Greenville had ten others to take the place he has vacated."

Grandpa, one of seven children, was a green-eyed blond (who grayed early), handsome, so sweet and mellow—actually pretty passive. But I guess anyone would have seemed passive next to my dynamo Grandma Carrie, his beloved wife.

Grandma Carrie, a simple but nice looking brown-haired woman with warm brown eyes, always worked. She owned a downtown grocery store called Simmons Cash and Carry, along with her brother-in-law Ben and sister-in-law Pearl, neither of whom ever married. In addition to walk-in customers, the store did bicycle deliveries as well as took food in the middle of the night to the boats that came in on the Mississippi River. The latter was a pretty good business. But because they let too many customers "carry" (run up bills on credit) without paying the "cash," they eventually had to close.

(Aunt Pearl and Uncle Benny lived together in the old family home downtown. Once Aunt Pearl died, though, my grandma took her brother-in-law in. As Uncle Benny was a grouchy and messy old bachelor, we all thought that was a very generous thing to do. Yet after Grandpa died and Grandma started becoming senile, having Uncle Benny there turned out to be actually a blessing.)

Once the store was closed, Grandma sold notions—promotional merchandise—to banks and auto dealerships. These were things like notepads, fingernail files, calendars and pencils with the company name on them. She kept the notions stuffed under her bed and in the trunk of her old Dodge, which she drove like an automatic when it was actually a stick shift. It was a wonder that she and her notions survived on the road as she drove around fulfilling orders well into her 80s.

Grandma was also an amazing cook. I would dream all year of her yummy fudge and coffee cakes, shrimp gumbo and fried catfish—not exactly a kosher home. Even her Jewish dishes had a heavy dose of the South: She sometimes flavored her matzo balls with bacon grease.

My grandparents had a fig tree in their backyard and boy, did I enjoy discovering them. Grandma would make fig preserves—just sugar, some figs and more sugar. I often had that on white bread for breakfast or fresh figs with cream. (I still love figs but now only eat them plain—as a small concession to fight obesity.)

When Grandma finished all of her delicious preparations in the kitchen it was like a whirlwind had been in there. With the food she produced, though, we all didn't mind cleaning up after her. In fact, that was Grandpa's regular job when we weren't around. He liked doing it. Interestingly enough, my Uncle Seymour, their oldest son, inherited that same trait. Even though he was President and CEO of a major company in Denver, at 7 p.m. you could find him doing the dishes with a smile on his face. It was sweet to see men who were helpful in the kitchen. They were ahead of their time, or at least their wives were.

Although her cooking wasn't kosher, Grandma Carrie was a proud Jewish woman, albeit a Southern one. In fact, she had taught at a Jewish Sunday school in Brownsville, Tennessee, where she was born and raised. And it was at a Sunday school convention in Jackson, Mississippi where she met my grandpa at the railroad station he was assigned to for a brief time. In the typical Southern tradition, she always had a Christmas tree—a tradition my parents followed and I as well. My grandparents did go to temple every Friday night, which appeared to be more social than religious. There was a Rabbi, but we knew that if he dared to speak one word of Hebrew during the brief service, he would be ushered onto the next train heading North. (The temple now has a woman Rabbi.)

My Mississippi relatives were highly assimilated. The names tell the story. Traditional Jewish families do not name their children after a living relative and thus don't typically have Sr.'s and Jr.'s and certainly not thirds. Our immediate family has had a Seymour Simmons first, second and third; a Jack Simmons first, second and third; and a father-son Joseph Simmons. My mother Hilda was named for her living Aunt Hilda. And Johnny was named after our paternal grandfather. You get the picture.

In Greenville, we occasionally went out to Doe's Eat Place, which remains my favorite restaurant anywhere. (I've heard it was also Bill Clinton's favorite once it opened its second place in Little Rock.) Doe's was originally the owners' home and customers would enter through the kitchen, where the delicious smells would greet you before you'd sit in the bare-bones dining areas with tables draped with plastic, red-and-white-checkered table cloths. With lemony salad, spaghetti and meatballs, hot tamales (which I like with ketchup) and shrimp gumbo, it was an enormous treat even if we were forbidden by Grandma from ever ordering the more expensive steak—its real trademark. She used to say it was not very good. Years later, after she passed, when I finally ordered it, I realized the steak was phenomenal. She was just frugal. If Doe's was ever missing any sugar packets, all they had to do was find Grandma's purse.

Grandma Carrie was a down-home woman, who unbelievable to me, had been a debutante in her youth in Memphis (and I have the program from 1910 to prove it). She always had spots on her dresses—the same ones. And I watched as she'd say, "Oh, that must have just happened." Yea, Grandma, 20 years ago. (I inherited some of that—not the spots necessarily, but I would put on pantyhose and see a run, and being too lazy to start all over again, off we'd go. If anyone pointed it out, I would say, "Oh, that must have just happened.")

Grandma was the most fun person I ever knew. In addition to her energy working and cooking, she played bridge and canasta and played them well. I inherited a love of cards from her and some of her skill. I played gin rummy a lot with Grandpa and my great uncle Benny. I also played gin at home with my father but when I would beat him, even at eight or nine years of age, he'd get furious, throw down the cards and quit playing. My mother actually said to me, "Carol, why don't you just let your father win so he won't get mad?" I always found that to be a little weird because I knew that in most families, they would actually let the children win. Oh well, we were never normal. I was also told to let Uncle Benny win because he would get mad as well if he lost. But I refused. I always played to win, except with Johnny and my kids (and only when my kids were young).

Grandma had a huge cadre of friends and they were always stopping by the house or we were running to see them. Life at that house was just one big fudge cake in every way. Grandma loved to laugh. Even in her 70s and 80s she would giggle like a teenager—and that was before her senility. Although thrifty, she was so generous of spirit. She would make coffee cakes and fudge cakes and bring them when she visited friends and even dropped them off to strangers who were in the hospital (even though now I'm thinking that maybe all that sugar and butter were not the best medicine for their recovery—or maybe they were). Grandma was indefatigable—which I can spell but don't ask me to pronounce it. But she was that. She was never too tired to be there whether it be for fun and games—or for a person in need.

Grandma was also bossy and a control freak and I'm sure my mother, when growing up, found a lot of those traits to be maddening. (It skipped a generation, but landed on me so I'm sure my children find me maddening as well.) But as her granddaughter, I just loved and adored her.

I had a bunch of friends in Greenville. Our main activities included going to Beulah's Drive-In on the highway, the Fountain Terrace downtown, and just cruising. My friends and I would drive in groups in our cars with the radio blaring, listening to such songs as Elvis's "Don't Be Cruel" and Fats Domino's "Blueberry Hill." There was a strip, a couple of miles long, where we all would drive back and forth and then back and forth again. We would pass each other about 12 times in a single afternoon, but we'd honk and wave like it was the first time. It was great fun at the cost of a soda and some gas, which was fortunately pretty cheap in those days.

The family cars we drove meant a lot to us. We'd name them shortened versions of our boyfriends' combined names. Grandma's car became "An-Jer-Jim-Bil." (Weren't we creative?— and this time, I wasn't solely responsible for the name.) I bet you can break the code of the guys' names if you really try. It was all so meaningful then, so ridiculous now.

Speaking of the Fountain Terrace, my friend Beth Stovall and I would rent horses and ride them downtown to have a soda there— certainly harking back to a time that no longer exists.

At this point, I have a confession. I became very friendly with Kitty Solomon, who was Miss Greenville High School and its head cheerleader. I had another friend named Sister Etheridge who was equally slim and beautiful and the head majorette of the school band. I couldn't come close to their beauty, athletic prowess or popularity. At home, I was only an *alternate* cheerleader and that was back in junior high. I didn't make the main squad. I was plump and couldn't jump very high, though I tried to make up for it with a lot of enthusiasm and a big booming voice. There were a few times when a main cheerleader could not fulfill her duties, and I got to substitute. But when I was with my friends in Greenville, the alternate and junior high parts conveniently got lost. I was simply a cheerleader. I just couldn't admit to my summer pals that I had only had a brief moment as a second stringer years earlier. It's actually a relief now to finally get this off my chest. And if any of my Greenville friends read this, I hope they will forgive me. (They probably always knew the truth anyway.)

For three summers, I went out with one of the few Jewish boys I dated growing up. Charles was 17 when we met in 1956 and was set to attend Vanderbilt University in the fall. I was 12, but remember, big for my age as well as mature, and thus Mom let me go out with him—unbeknownst to Dad. (In Midland, Dad did not let me date until I was 16.) Like all my early romances, it was very innocent. By the second summer, I had a bigger crush on his friend Julian, a handsome boy with striking dark eyes, who had lost a leg earlier in a car accident. He used to come over after Charles and I went out and we'd talk and smooch a little. We never told Charles to avoid hurting his feelings. (My second Greenville confession.) Sorry, Charlie! But that's what you get for dating a 12-year-old.

(Charles wound up becoming a surgeon, not in Greenville. Julian became a dentist, standing a lot, which I found extraordinary given his circumstances. Unfortunately we lost him many years ago. Charles called me about 10 years ago to catch up and we had such a good visit, talking about our professions and our families.)

While in town, Kitty, Sister, a fourth person, and I would play canasta. Kitty and I would always be partners. And we were also partners in "crime." We both liked to win so we devised a way to cheat: Step 1) We would let each other know what cards we needed. If it was a four, she would say, "*Do* any of you want something to drink?" Or if it was a six, "*For* goodness sake, I can't ever win." Do you get it? Step 2) Since it was summertime in the South, we of course would have our shoes off. If I had a four or a six or whatever she needed, I'd slip her the card between my toes and vice versa. We did often win. (You will not find this in my confessions of "bad" episodes later on, though, because it was all in good fun with no money involved. I'm sure our opponents were doing something similar. And besides, I'm a reformed card cheater anyway. In fact, I'm so reformed that I feel too guilty to even cheat with the solitaire cards I deal out these days.)

The only non-fun thing about Greenville for me were the mosquitos, which were ever-present in spite of the twice-a-week fog trucks that sprayed disinfectants. And when I got a mosquito bite, it would swell up and itch for weeks. (By the way, mosquitos still love me, and I've often said that I wish I was as popular with men.)

Despite these pests, my friends and I had a lot of good times on the narrow portion of the Mississippi River which ran by the town levee. We'd waterski on the river and sun on the barges. Waterskiing was not my specialty. I was worse at that than cheerleading, not even a second-stringer. But I did actually stay up a few times—for a minute. Regardless, I loved being down by the river and in the town nestled by it.

Note: Sadly, I learned later that Greenville had been a hotbed during the Civil Rights era. That made me upset and even embarrassed about not being aware. My world in Greenville was fortunately different. But I do feel terribly for those whose lives in that town were so tragically otherwise.

CHAPTER 3

Aunt Doe and Linda

Aside from Greenville and Grandma, there was finally another ray of sunshine that entered my life. When I was nine years old, a wonderful family named Garmon moved in next door and became my family as well. (Just noted all G's—and all good.)

Right before they moved in, Calvin, who worked at the filling station across the street, told me, "This family is moving in. They have a daughter your age named Linda, and she's seen you around. She said she doesn't like you and she's going to beat you up." Meanwhile he had said the same thing to Linda about me. He had us both so revved up. When they moved in, Linda and I would stare over the little fence between our houses, sizing each other up. Finally, we spoke and she said, "Calvin said you want to beat me up." I said, "He told me exactly the same thing about you." That broke the ice, and Linda, who we often called Linda Gayle and who was only three months older, became the sister I never had.

Linda had suffered with polio as a child, and one leg was three or four inches shorter than the other. When I met her at nine years of age, she walked with a terrible limp when she wasn't using crutches. I tried to help her overcome that. The shorter leg seemed so weak. There was that shin-high fence between our houses so I said to Linda, "Let's try to jump over it. Maybe if we make that leg stronger, it will get better." I really didn't know what I was talking about. I just thought it was worth a try. So we started jumping over the fence with me holding her hand so she wouldn't fall. Then we started dancing as another way to build the muscles of that leg. I had learned the jitterbug and taught it to Linda, who became so much better at it, as she was at everything.

In a year, her leg was just an inch shorter, barely noticeable. She got rid of the crutches and was able to walk pretty normally. She later even became a majorette. She used to give me the credit. She'd say, "I used to be crippled and Carol helped me not be." That made me a little hero around the elementary school. But I loved her and I loved to dance too so it was no great sacrifice.

Linda was my sister and her mother, Dora Faye, who I called Aunt Doe, was my salvation. (A Southern tradition was to call close unrelated elders "aunts" and "uncles.") Aunt Doe was warm, loving, and the world's greatest listener. I so needed all of the above. Her background was very different from my own family. Aunt Doe had only gone to school up until the fourth grade and could hardly spell. But she still wrote me beautiful, loving notes then and for the rest of her life, which I still have. She had an adorable sense of humor, like Grandma Carrie, and brought needed laughter to my Midland life.

She was a heavy-set woman and pretty, though faded. Ten years older than my mother, Aunt Doe had her first two children when she was very young—a daughter and son. Then fifteen years later she had two daughters around my age. By the time they moved in, her son Buddy was away in the Army and her daughter Kitty was married and living on the West Coast.

Aunt Doe always looked out for my best interests. During my pink skirt, tight black sweater stage, I added to the ensemble a white cap with a Navy logo. In hindsight, it may have had a too flirtatious tone. I wore it a lot until Aunt Doe stole it. She revealed that she had taken it later—and only after I got over its loss. She didn't want me wearing something so inappropriate. Thank goodness she really protected me from myself.

As I said, Aunt Doe was a good listener and boy, had I become a talker. It was sure good to have a listener because Mom and Dad certainly were not. Mom was so distant and Dad never stopped talking himself. With Mom, you really felt like you had to knock on her door, even when the door was open. She was always in the right-side twin bed, reading, doing crossword puzzles, or just sleeping. I think she wanted to get away from the world. I don't blame her. Her life was hard. Happily, though, when I was an adult and living far away, my mother became a great confidante.

Aunt Doe's door was always so open, literally and figuratively. Of course, there was a difference. Unlike my mother she was home all the time and didn't work outside the house, nor could she drive. So she was always available. If you had something to talk about, whatever she was doing—cooking, cleaning, sewing— she'd stop and just listen to you. She would pat and comfort you. I felt an angel had arrived in my life and I used to thank God for her. (In fact, as I and they got older, I used to pray to God to keep Grandma and Aunt Doe alive—and later my dear Aunt Betty and Uncle Seymour—as these four were my lifelong caretakers.)

Aunt Doe was a terrific cook. She made feasts of fried chicken, biscuits and cream gravy, black-eyed peas with ham hock, hash browns, and so much more. I watched and learned. Years later, it became my husband's favorite home-cooked meal. The only thing green Aunt Doe ever cooked was fried okra. I loved it all, except for her husband's meal of choice—a glass of buttermilk with cornbread in it, which he ate with a spoon.

I got to spend a lot of time with Aunt Doe, drinking her sweet tea, but I had to sneak around and conspire to do so. Thus, even my moments of escape were stressful as I was always worried about being caught. Dad was very jealous of my relationship with anybody, especially her. Mom became a co-conspirator because she thought my lack of freedom was terrible and she knew Aunt Doe was good for me.

The Garmons moved away from the house next door to a house a block away from the store when I was about 11, so Mom had to work harder to help sneak me out. When Mom was working at the store and I was supposedly there helping her, Dad would call from home and ask, "Where's Carol?" She'd fib, "She just went across the street to Modern Grocery to get a soda." When he would then go to the store and not find me there, he'd arrive at Aunt Doe's and bark, "It's time to get back to work." I think deep down my dad really liked Aunt Doe. You couldn't help but like her. But he had to be in control at all times.

Aunt Doe had a tough marriage. Her husband, Floyd—who most called Dutch and I called Uncle Dutch—worked in the oil fields and was a gallivanter. The mother of my junior high school boyfriend, Ronnie Morelock, used to run around with Dutch. It was Aunt Doe who told me about it as well as other things that worried her, and I felt badly. I often felt badly about the sad things around me, and hated the fact that I could do nothing about them.

Aunt Doe's son Buddy once told me, "My mother relies on you." I thought Aunt Doe was my salvation. It turned out she looked at me similarly. I was very mature and I kept confidences. Being so mature, I always gravitated toward older people. I loved my friends, but often found that I enjoyed hanging out with their mothers just as much—if not more.

Aunt Doe was a born-again Christian. She did not force it on anyone, including me. Once in a while, I would go with them on Sundays to the nearby Calvary Baptist Church. There they preached things like, "If you don't do this or that, you will burn in hell." The minister took a liking to me. In fact, he contacted my parents and said, "We really love your daughter. We can't stand the thought of her going to hell and we want to have her baptized." My parents said no. I didn't go that much after that. I did believe in God but the God I believed in was too benevolent to sentence someone to an eternity of hell for practically anything, much less not going to church every week.

Aunt Doe's daughter Linda was very smart and had a beautiful singing voice. She was really special, and we had a special and wonderful relationship—all of our lives. Linda used to talk about wanting to be a country music singer, but she ended up getting married at 17 to a sergeant in the Army named Kirby Reed. Then they took off to Italy and Germany. (In fact, my husband and I visited them in Regensburg.) She had four children early on, one right after the other. I'll never forget, soon after she got married and before she went away to Europe, she came to spend the night with me when Dad was out of town, and she described going "all the way." I remember it so vividly and my eager responses, "Then what? Then what?"

I was close to the whole Garmon clan. Dad really liked Linda's sister, Charlotte, who was two years younger. We girls used to play silly games when we were adolescents. In school there was a girl named Georgene Harden, who was gorgeous, so a game became, "Who's the prettiest? Georgene, Linda Gayle or Carol?" My father piped in the one time he overheard this discussion when he came to pick me up to go to the store: "I think Charlotte is the prettiest." It was so unlike him to 1) like someone and 2) join in. I found it refreshing. (By the way, I had crushes on Georgene's two brothers, and even went out a couple of times with Kenneth, the oldest one, a few years later. Who I didn't have crushes on then would make for a shorter list.)

But the one I was really smitten with was Linda's brother, Buddy Garmon, who was 15 years older than I was. When I was nine and first living next door to them, I saw his picture. He was so handsome with such beautiful blue eyes. He looked and was built like a lighter-haired Tommy Lee Jones in his prime, except better. When he came home from the Army and I met him for the first time, I fell madly in love—as much as you can at 11 years old. More about that later.

Aunt Doe remained a major part of my life. Into my adulthood, we always kept in touch through letters, phone calls, and visits back and forth. Although she had some Social Security through her husband and had never asked me for anything, after I got married I started sending her $100 a month in 1968, and later more, and some additional help when she needed it until she died. Early in life, Aunt Doe had given so much to me that later, when I could, I just wanted to make her life a little easier.

Her husband, Uncle Dutch, died in a car accident coming out of the Modern Grocery Store—a short block away from their rented house. Aunt Doe was in the car and got injured but survived. She had such difficulties: a philandering husband who died in a car accident in which she nearly died. They never had any money. She suffered from diabetes and heart disease. Three of her children died during her lifetime. Charlotte passed away at age 42 of cancer. Kitty and Buddy both died in their early 50s, one of cancer, the other of a heart attack when Aunt Doe was in her late 60s.

And then she experienced another horrifying thing. Not long after Dutch died and Aunt Doe had recovered from her injuries, she was living in the house by herself and watching a religious program on her little black and white television when a man broke in and raped her. She was in her 70s. She had to crawl to a neighbor's house afterwards to get help. Why? Why should such a good soul have to endure so much?

Through it all, Aunt Doe was such an inspiration in how she went on. I know people who have one bad thing happen to them and they can't even get out of bed. But she just forged ahead. More than that, she brought love and light to every person and situation she touched. She was the most amazing person I ever met.

At that time, Linda lived in San Antonio in a trailer. She had been divorced from Kirby for many years and then met the love of her life, Frank Mungia, and they married. After Aunt Doe's awful experiences, Linda moved her mom there. With my help, they bought another trailer and put them together in an L-shape. That way they each had their own space but could also look after each other. So there were some good years then. Linda was a good artist and decorator, and those trailers were like works of art. I visited them at least once a year, usually with Johnny, and would fly Aunt Doe up to Washington to spend time with me and my family.

Aunt Doe stayed in pretty good shape and she helped Linda raise her granddaughter, Brandy Gayle. from the age of one. She was the product of Linda's drug-addicted son, Rocky Lee, and his drug-addicted girlfriend. It was a bad circumstance but Brandy did bring them lots of pleasure in her early years. Sadly, though, Frank took off when Brandy was still young, and Linda was heartbroken, but she did receive a lot of solace from her dear son Allen, who lived nearby. Allen was gay and tragically Linda and all of us lost him to AIDS in 2002. Linda's oldest child, Charles, is in the service and lives in Oklahoma. Her daughter, Kristy Kee, called "Sissy," the baby of the family, also lived nearby with her female partner of many years and they were close to Linda as well.

In her later years, Aunt Doe used to tell Linda, "When I die I want to be put in the coffin with my arms crossed over my chest." Never a vain woman, she would only wear a little pink lipstick. But Aunt Doe always took pride in her hair. It was short, and she put it in rollers every night without fail.

In the early morning of July 28, 1996 in San Antonio, Linda brought her mother coffee as she did every morning. Aunt Doe, then in her mid-80s, had not been particularly sick and certainly not more so than usual considering her health issues. When Linda entered the room, she found her mom, my Aunt Doe, in her bed lying on her back with her hands crossed over her chest. She had the most peaceful look on her face. Her hair did not have rollers in it for the first time in any of our recollections. And she had on a touch of pink lipstick. It was a natural death. She must have just thought, "I want tonight for God to take me." She must have just laid down on the bed and crossed her arms over her heart. Then she was gone. But she is still here in my heart and in the many pictures I have always had of her around my homes.

My First Aunt Betty and Uncle Seymour

My mom's two younger brothers both married women named Betty. Uncle Seymour married Betty Jane Block, who was petite and pretty with a smile second to none. He met her on a trip to Denver to visit relatives when he was 16 and she was 15. (My grandpa Seymour's two sisters, Rubie and Ruchiel, had moved to Denver as young women and married there.) Uncle Seymour went on to LSU, where he was a track star and held several records which lasted for many decades, and then entered the service.

Afterwards, he went back to Denver, married very popular Aunt Betty when they were 21 and 20, and had two children, Seymour III and Beverly. Uncle Seymour, though reserved, was a natural-born leader—a delightful combination of his parents. He became President of the Miller Western Wear Company, the Denver Rotary Club and Temple Emanuel, the largest congregation in Denver. He also sang and played the piano beautifully. Uncle Seymour and Aunt Betty lived in Denver for the rest of their lives, where they had many wonderful friends as well as relatives, and were known as the most loving couple and superb bridge players.

(My mother and her brothers graduated from LSU. When my daughter Stephanie asked Aunt Betty Jane years later why none had gone to Ole Miss as they lived in that state, she responded that LSU was regarded as being more accepting of Jewish students.)

Aunt Betty and Uncle Seymour in Denver were wonderful guardians in my life. I was born before their own children, and my aunt liked to refer to me as their first child. As I grew older, she was a great confidante.

I hardly got to see Aunt Betty and Uncle Seymour when I was very young. Then when I was 11 years old, my mom found out about a camp called Geneva Glen outside of Denver. I think she wanted me to have time away from work and Dad. Maybe she even wanted me to get to know my large extended family in Colorado. And what a gift Mom gave me. My real relationship with Aunt Betty and Uncle Seymour started in Denver around those camp days. I got to spend some time in their home before and after they drove me to camp—which was a long, mountainous drive, but they did it happily.

I loved them so much—and the normalcy of their lives. Every night Aunt Betty made dinner, and the family would sit at the table in their nice kitchen, talking and playing intellectual games like trivia. It was so different from my own home, where we rarely ate meals together and the only games that were played usually ended with my father throwing the cards.

At camp, I enjoyed—and was good at—archery and target shooting with BB guns. One of my best memories of camp during my two years there was the talent show toward the end of our stay. My musical talent was limited, but with all the girls in the cabin singing, my voice was thankfully pretty much drowned out. However, I danced okay. We did a rendition of "I'm Gonna Wash That Man Right Out of My Hair" from *South Pacific*. How little did I realize then that song would get plenty of use over the years.

One of my other favorite things about camp was going to Red Rocks, an outdoor amphitheater etched into the mountains. As we drove to and from there on the bus, we always sang "Climb every mountain, ford every stream, follow every rainbow, 'til you find your dream." It sort of, at that age of 11, became my anthem.

Whenever I went to Denver as a camper or later, alone or with my own family, Aunt Betty and Uncle Seymour always had a party. They'd invite friends, great aunts and uncles, and cousins so the family could be together. Aunt Betty kept a lovely home and was a great hostess. I was so touched by the time and attention they gave me then and over the years. They wrote to me often and sent presents to me as well as my family. Not a holiday season went by when my own children didn't receive a card and check from them, even into their adulthoods.

Among the most generous things Aunt Betty and Uncle Seymour ever did was come to Midland after my dad died to help me and the kids go through everything. They were always there in every way, shape and form, no matter how difficult.

As the years went on and they got older, I tried to see them a lot. I went to Denver alone and with my family, and they came to visit me at my homes. I tried to give them the love and attention they had always given me. I really felt like they took me under their wing at a young age and left me many decades later, far stronger than they found me.

I lost both of them over the last few years and continue to miss them terribly. But given their conditions at the end, I feel relief for them. And for me, I feel blessed to have had them in my life for nearly 70 years.

My Second Aunt Betty and Uncle Joe

Uncle Joe was my mother's youngest brother. At college at LSU, Uncle Joe, a tall, handsome guy with lots of personality, met Betty Jean Moyse, a very smart gal who had beautiful graying hair even in college and a lovely, slim figure. This Aunt Betty had been born and raised in Baton Rouge, as had her parents, so when they married, they settled there and had three children—Becky, Jean, and Joe. Uncle Joe had a car dealership and then went into the real estate business.

Aunt Betty Jean came from a very wealthy family, even though she is very down to earth. Every several years in August during our time in Mississippi, we would drive to Baton Rouge for a few-day visit. We stayed in one of their four nice houses on the family compound, which was a treat. Uncle Joe was a casual-type guy and a big fisherman. He and Aunt Betty made great meals—his pork roast and her potato salad are especially memorable.

Grandma Carrie and I had this special relationship where we could say whatever we wanted to each other and teased a lot. Then, I think Uncle Joe saw that as disrespectful, although I know my grandma loved and enjoyed the fun tone of our relationship. He never said anything, but I could feel his disapproval. However, I think he grew to appreciate that relationship as well as my caretaking of Johnny. Thus years later, we grew much closer, and they joined us for many special family occasions, joyous and sad.

Uncle Joe with his twinkly eyes, great wit, and fabulous deep, thick-as-molasses Southern accent, died in 2008 and is missed a lot. Aunt Betty and I treasure each other and share one of the dearest relationships in my life.

The Levitts

I went up to New York City to visit my Grandma Bonnie and Grandpa John once every two or three years on my own, starting when I was 10. That first trip, alone on a bumpy plane ride, was pretty scary but still fun to see New York. It began a lovely affair with that city that I still really enjoy. And now having two daughters, a rescue grand-dog, and a rescue grand-cat there makes it even more special.

I had lots of fun with Uncle Albert, my dad's older brother, who lived in New York for the rest of his life after arriving there with the family at age 15. We'd sit on the balcony of my grandparents' apartment, and he'd take the lead eating cherries and spitting the pits many floors down. I sure hope no one was hit by them. (I was 10 years old and stupid, but what was his excuse?) Uncle Albert married three times—and had one son with the first wife. His third wife, though, committed suicide. I remember answering the phone in our Midland store when he called to tell us that sad news. After that, he did not marry again.

But because Uncle Albert was handsome and fun, he always had about 10 different girlfriends. Often when we would go out to places like P.J. Clarke's, due to his youthfulness and my looking so much older than I was, people would think we were a couple. Even when I would call him "Uncle Albert," people would respond, "Oh, sure he is." He had a biting humor, though, which sometimes could be hurtful. But I loved him and have many fond memories. Uncle Albert, although having gone to law school because his parents insisted, made his living as a philatelist (stamp dealer) and also a real estate agent.

My dad's oldest sibling was Marguerite Levis--remember her? Aunt Marguerite was pretty, interesting, talkative and very opinionated—as all the Levitts were. (I certainly qualify, at least with the latter two.) She and my dad were not very close (they probably had different opinions on one subject one time), so contact with her and her family was limited. Uncle Albert thought it continued to be limited because my husband and I were Jews who admitted it. In fact, he told me that one of Marguerite's daughters moved to Washington 35 years or more ago, but has kept her distance because people might find out she's Jewish by association.

Sorry to possibly blow her cover, but I did leave out her unusual first name to "protect" her.

The sweetest one in this family was Uncle Earl, the youngest. He tended to never stop talking and to lecture like my dad—like most of that family. I myself have inherited some of those traits but I'm an amateur compared to them. He lived in Williamsburg, Virginia with his wife Maxine and had two children, Bruce and Brook. I would visit them sometimes there or they'd come to D.C. He and Maxine owned wonderful men's preppy clothing stores called Earl N. Levitt in both Williamsburg on the main downtown street near the College of William and Mary as well as in Lexington, Virginia near Washington and Lee University. As the years went on and Uncle Earl was widowed, we became very close and visited back and forth more often. He too did not claim to be Jewish, nor his wife who was half.

My grandparents were not as sweet. Grandpa was small of stature, dapper, had deep blue eyes, and was a bit gruff. But he did call me every year on my birthday and sang in his nice voice, "Let Me Call You Sweetheart." Grandma was petite and slim, with a very shapely figure and she dressed beautifully. Quite a class act. With a very delicate pretty face, lovely blue eyes, and a tiny nose, she looked like the dancer and actress Leslie Caron but with short white hair. Grandma Bonnie could be nice but was very demanding and a perfectionist. She insisted that you always dress appropriately, quite an extreme difference from my life in Midland. I even had to wear white gloves when I was in New York in the '50s and early '60s.

Those grandparents lived in a beautiful apartment on the east side overlooking the river on Sutton Place South near 55th St.—so luxurious in comparison to anything I knew and certainly to my life back in Midland. It was nice to be spoiled for those couple of weeks every couple of years with meals at nice restaurants and always one Broadway play with a good seat.

My grandparents were attentive to me when I was around but not to my brother Johnny. They did help some financially with his schooling for a time—as did my maternal grandparents—but I remember the few times they were with him, you could see how uncomfortable they were. I did love them and was respectful because they were my grandparents and I tried to be a good granddaughter. But, honestly I did not like them so much. I always gauged everybody by how they treated Johnny. Friends of mine who weren't nice to Johnny simply weren't my friends anymore. With grandparents, it was more complicated.

Grandma Bonnie lived until six weeks' shy of 90, and remained an attractive lady until her passing. Grandma lied about her age, but I always told her she should instead wear a sign announcing it to give others hope. She lived long enough to hear Paul Harvey on his radio show wish her and Grandpa a happy 70th anniversary on April 11, 1978. Grandpa John lived until two months' shy of 98. He remained feisty up until the end, even outrageously flirting with his nurses.

In most marriages I've seen in my many years here on earth, there's usually a boss and a non-boss. In this grandparents' case, they were both bossy, unbelievably bossy. I would often think about them and wonder how they had lasted for seven minutes— much less for 70 years. But they did, and really seemed to love and enjoy each other.

Grandma Bonnie's (far right) parents, Jennie and Ura Nickoll, and siblings Elizabeth, Benjamin and Jacob

Grandma Carrie's parents, Jennie (Davis) and Joseph Sternberger

Grandma Carrie

Grandma Carrie (far left) with siblings Saul, Herbert and Hilda

(Picture on right) Mom (left) with parents, brothers Joe and Seymour and his wife Betty Jane

Mom with her brothers Joe and Seymour on either end

Dad (top left) with parents, Bonnie and John, and siblings Earl, Albert and Marguerite (left to right)

Mom and her family

My great great grandfather, Joe Davis

Grandpa Seymour and Grandma Carrie

Pictures of My Parents in their Youth

Mom, Johnny and Me Early On
with Grandma Carrie, Grandpa Seymour and Great Grandma Nancy

Our neighborhood
in background

Our Oak Ridge house behind us

Me (top center) at five in Oak Ridge at the beginning of my dancing career

Jimmy Murphy   Carolyn Price   Linda and Charlotte Garmon

My partner-in-crime,
Danelle Reese

Three-month-older Linda at age nine with her crutches
(I told you I developed early.)

Me at 10 and same-aged
cousin in Saybrook, CT

Grandparents C and S by Midland house

My beloved
Aunt Doe

No wonder
I was pudgy

Ronnie Morelock,
my junior high boyfriend

Me at 11 showing my
dance moves to
gas station customers
across the street

Our first
non-family-
visiting
trip: a day
at Carlsbad
Caverns
three hours
away when
I was 11

Our only other non-family-
visiting trip was when I was 13:
a week in Mexico (below)

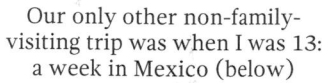

Me at 11 with family and our nice car

Poor donkey!

My best buddy and brother Johnny and me, looking much older than the 12 I was

Also at 12 by house

Grandma Bonnie's only visit to Midland when I was 12 (Dad wrote on the back of this picture: "Mom never smiling because of the way we lived.")

Summer friend and me by the Mississippi River

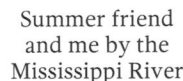

Junior high school graduation, age 14

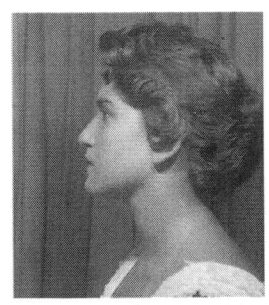

At this time, around 1956, people used to say I looked like Elvis. What do you think?

CHAPTER 4

Difficult Dad

I was really a good kid. I have mentioned a few instances, two relating to cars: 1) hitting one and 2) "stealing"—actually borrowing—one, plus a couple of indiscretions you'll hear about later (and which Dad never knew about), as well as sneaking out to see Aunt Doe. But that was it in the "bad" department. I did well in school, worked hard in the store, wrote letters to my grandparents, and took care of my brother. But in spite of all that, my father's beatings continued into my high school years. I often couldn't even suit up for gym class because of the belt welts on my back and legs. Our gym teacher, Mrs. Selbo, could verify.

When I was 16, my mom went on her second trip to Denver for another family occasion. One evening during that time, I was in the bathtub. Out of nowhere, my dad burst in and started beating me with a belt. Who knows why? That night, for the first time, I decided to get help. I called my friend Ann Gilbert, now Wylie, and she came and picked me up. I think he was so embarrassed by what he had done and now he knew someone else knew. I just said, "I'm going to stay at my friend Ann's house." I called my mother that night and she came home.

I had blocked out another incident from my senior year, but my friend Liz Hitt, now Burks, reminded me recently. My father had hit me so hard, he left a terrible bruise on my face. Liz covered it with lots of makeup so I could go to the high school dance.

I often wondered what made my father be so mean. I asked his older brother, Uncle Albert, about my dad's temper since I was close to him, although I never told him about the beatings. He said that my dad had been an amicable young man—very smart, athletic and popular. He believed that it was Johnny's birth in 1942 when Dad was 27 years old that made him mad at the world. By having his first-born son be so disabled, he felt that God was punishing him. I'm sure that played a role—and his own parents' reactions were certainly not helpful. As mentioned, they seemed uncomfortable and ashamed. My maternal grandparents, on the other hand, were the opposite—so loving. When we spent August with them as well as most Christmases, they paraded Johnny around town like he was a prince.

When it comes to my fathers' anger, in retrospect, I think there were even more contributors. My father, in spite of his brilliance, impressive degree, athleticism and great looks, never really found himself professionally. He had gone to MIT because his parents wanted an engineer in the family, just as Uncle Albert had gone to law school at their insistence but did not practice. And although Dad made a decent living most of the time, his business pursuits were never fulfilling or that successful. He did run for office once for Justice of the Peace in Oak Ridge, but didn't win. I think he felt a strong frustration with having so much promise unrealized.

This is not a definitive diagnosis, but I also think he suffered from some degree of depression, maybe even manic. Along with his frequent rage, he had such behavioral extremes. He would laugh it up with people in the store and the bank when he ran errands. Then he'd come home and live like a hermit. It was also strange that he grew up in a comfortable upper-middle-class family or better, and even had a car at MIT, then chose to live in such extreme austerity for most of his adult life. He would write me letters even when he was in his 70s with resources about how he had eaten at a restaurant for $1.57 like it was a badge of honor. (Of course in this area I often qualify for a badge too.)

Dad, to my recollection, was not at all a drinker which might have been at least some excuse for his abuse. I understand, though, that he did drink earlier on. In fact, I remember Mom talking about when she was in Greenville for those August visits, Dad would sometimes get into fights while drinking at honkytonks in Odessa. Later, it appeared that he gave it up to not get so roughed up.

As far back as I can remember, Dad would say regularly, "One day I'm going to blow my brains out," sometimes over something minor—or just out of the blue. The fact that he had at least three guns that I knew about—one in the glove compartment of the car, one in the trunk, and one in his nightstand—added to my fear that he might do it. Although he mistreated me so, he was my father and I loved him and the thought of his doing himself in was terrifying and sad. I would even say sometimes, "Dad, please don't think about doing that."

There was some mental illness in his family. It was known that some of his cousins had depression. His father even had shock treatments at Grandma's behest in the late 1960s, when he became depressed after retiring in his late 80s. My husband and I actually went down to visit Grandpa John at Duke University Hospital where he received the treatments.

My father's prejudice also contributed to the negative atmosphere of our home. I hated it and wanted to scream "Just stop it," but I was too scared of him. Maybe he knew that I felt that way and it added to his anger at me. Later, I certainly took him to task for such things. In fact, in the late 1980s, I was hanging out with my friend Barbara Blum by a pool when I read an article that the correct term was now "African American." I said to Barbara, "Oh no. I just got my father to start saying "black" instead of "negro."

Over the years, as my dad got to know and spend time with many of my close African American friends, it was obvious that his feelings started to change in that regard. The same was true after he got to know some of my gay friends. I was happy to see him grow to be a better person later on.

Most of his life, my dad was a paradoxical character. On one hand, he said such nasty things. Yet he hired S.W. Watson, a 19-year-old African American man who had just gotten out of the Army. S.W. started out cleaning up the store and house part-time and ended up running it when Mom and Dad semi-retired. He worked with my folks for 30 years. (When I was new to Midland and quite lonely, S.W. became my best friend. He was such a sweet man and I loved to talk to him. He usually did not say much—as if he could get a word in. He was like a Gary Cooper and tended more to "yep" and "nope," more than a real conversation.)

Dad paid S.W. well. He also got him into an IRA long before employers would do that for a full-time much less a part-time worker. He said, "We must protect you for your future." Dad also got him worker's comp. My parents had this tiny business in the '50s, '60s and '70s and probably by law didn't have to do that. But they were an example of what you should do with an employee.

When S.W. went from cleaning up to helping customers, people would actually call up and say, "I'm not coming in your store to be waited on by some [n-word]." And you know what my father would say to them? "Then shop elsewhere because he's working here." There were things about him that were such a dichotomy. How do you reconcile that with the bigot he seemingly was? He didn't like Jews either. He didn't like anybody. I think it was self-hatred. He didn't feel good enough about himself so he had to belittle other people. I have found that to be true of most bigots.

Although Dad had many problems and caused many others, he did have some good qualities. Customers would occasionally come into the store and give a hard-luck story. They weren't trying to get anything out of it. They were just talking. They may say, "I haven't worked in a long time." Maybe somebody was in an accident or sick. After they left, if they gave a check with an address, Dad would sometimes walk over to the grocery store and get bags of food. He would wait until dusk. Then he'd go to their house, ring the bell, and walk away before they opened the door. It was an anonymous gift. Now I'm charitable and I do a lot of volunteer work and financial giving, but I admit I enjoy getting credit for it. But Dad would do the few things he did completely anonymously. So there were some redeeming features about Stanley Levitt.

He certainly loved his parents and wrote them and his in-laws all the time. He used to write to me and Johnny often as well, and I still have every letter of his—and everybody else's except those you'll learn about later.

I used to think when I got beaten, "Thank God it's not Johnny." Even though my dad was so impatient and mad at the world, he rarely took it out on his son. He would yell at him sometimes, but nothing more. That's the main reason I forgave him for the physical and emotional abuse I received: At least he was good to my brother. If he had treated Johnny like he treated me, even though I was scared to death of him and not a violent person, I probably would have figured out a way to do him great harm.

My father defined me in so many ways. He was often a role model for what I did not want to be. He was a hermit. I became so not a hermit. He had no one over to the house. I always had a house full of people. He had no TV. I have a TV in practically every room. He was prejudiced. I became totally not prejudiced. I almost didn't become a Republican because he was such an obnoxious one. (I was drawn to the Party those many years ago in spite of him for reasons I'll talk about later.)

But for better or worse, my father made me who I am. And in my own crazy way, I am grateful. Yet don't ask me to go through those many years when he beat me and controlled—or tried to— my every move, my every thought. And even when he wasn't present, I was always anxious and scared about his calls, his pending arrival, his wrath. I get anxious even thinking about it today at 73 years of age, and he died over 23 years ago.

Intolerant of Intolerance

Hearing my dad's prejudice and people's reaction to S.W. in that provincial, somewhat bigoted town, really affected me starting as a small child. During the long hours at the store waiting for customers, I had lots of time to think. I remember these specific thoughts as a little girl: "I can understand not liking people because they're cruel. But why be nasty to someone like my brother who has special problems and can't help it, or S.W., because of the color of his skin? People *can* control their behavior. You can dislike them based on that. But how can you be mean to somebody based on what they cannot control? And even if they could, how dare you decide what is okay and what is not?" I remember thinking, "That is terrible. It's not right." I was just a child, but already knew right from wrong—and this time, not from my parents.

At that early stage, I became outraged by prejudice. And this was before the "dirty Jew" incident at school, so it was just based on the prejudice toward Johnny and S.W. Even then I was so intolerant of intolerance. That feeling has informed my whole life and I know has enlarged it as well. Not only is it morally wrong to be bigoted and so hurtful to those you aim your prejudiced bow at, but also how stupid it is to narrow your experiences.

I also became a feminist at a young age by observing the unfairness around me. I saw my mother being bossed around by my father night and day, both at home and at work. I thought as a girl, "He's smart, but she's smart. He graduated from college, but she did too. He works, but so does she, and actually harder. What gives him the right to tell her what to do?" Gender inequality confused me then, later made me mad, and now enrages me.

Early Activism

My background really made me want to help others. Starting at age 11, I'd stand on the street corner to raise money for the annual March of Dimes campaign. I did so for many years. Thinking back fairly recently, I realize that I probably started doing volunteer activities for people who were physically disabled or sick in some way because they, along with Johnny, made me feel fortunate.

I do believe I was getting depressed as a very young person because of the circumstances surrounding me. Helping others made me feel better and luckier. I would suggest this—and actually do—to all the people I know now who are feeling sorry for themselves. Volunteering is good for three reasons: 1) It helps the people or animals whose lives you are trying to improve; 2) seeing people worse off gives you a more realistic perspective of your own situation; and 3) just doing the act itself makes you feel more productive and worthwhile—and thus, feel better about yourself.

I also gravitated toward leadership positions, though obviously not of the highest order. In elementary school, I was Captain of the Safety Patrol. That one was such a natural as I've always liked directing people, especially where to go. In the sixth grade, I was elected President of my homeroom (you can find that one on my resume). When I was in junior high, I was on the Student Council and often put in charge of lots of important activities, such as decorations for the school parties.

Beginning at 15, I became very active at the Youth Center. I started student volunteer programs there such as implementing an idea I had to take physically disabled children to the Ice Capades in Odessa. I arranged all the logistics, including raising the money for the bus, getting discount tickets for the show, coordinating volunteers, and contacting the families. My senior year, the Center gave me its Youth Leadership Award for such work.

At school, I was a decent student. I preferred the liberal arts, and did pretty well in them as opposed to science. In fact, I had the opportunity to represent Midland High School at a regional poetry reciting competition in Abilene. I read, quite dramatically I must add, one of my favorite poems, "Renascence" by Edna St. Vincent Millay. Although I didn't win, I did place.

My algebra teacher was Mr. Selbo, whose wife was the gym teacher I mentioned who showed compassion for my situation. In algebra, I had no confidence and didn't think I would be good at it. I had friends who were and they let me copy their answers (one of those indiscretions). One day, Mr. Selbo caught me and I was so embarrassed. He took me to the hallway, and said, "Carol, you are a very smart girl and I am extremely disappointed in you." He said, "My wife really loves you and I'm not going to report this to the office. But you're going to have to catch up on your own."

So I took the algebra book home and studied. I ended up making an A in his class with no help. He appropriately made me feel badly about cheating (actually just getting caught did the trick) and I even became good in math thanks to him and that experience. And I never cheated again.

Other than the above and the episode of taking the car, I never did anything bad except for the two following incidents: One was taking a Big Hunk—a long taffy-like candy bar—from a grocery store near my elementary school, where we were allowed to eat in class. As soon as I started to open it, I felt so guilty that I not only didn't eat it, I walked into the store after school and told the man at the counter that I had stolen it earlier and gave it back to him. The other incident occurred around that same time when I was with some friends at Woolworths and we all took a lipstick. But then I could not bring myself to use it. So one day, I went there with the tube in my pocket and just dropped it back in the case. I decided then and there that thievery was not my strong suit.

I did come with a very strong guilt complex. I don't know where I got it from because my mother and father did not guilt-trip me. But the fact that they were honorable people in that regard probably set an example. Regardless, I often joke that I'm not really a nice person, I just do nice things so I won't feel guilty. And to this day, I don't know why I wasted one of two steals on taffy instead of much-preferred chocolate. That's probably why I took it back (just kidding).

Two High School Friends

Liz Hitt's father was Superintendent of the Midland Public Schools so she was fairly well-known, and Liz was well-liked because she was such a sweetheart. She also stood out because she was a magnificent artist. Liz took a bridge class and told me the basics of the game. So on those lonely nights in Midland, I would deal out four hands and play them—with just rudimentary knowledge of the game—and try to figure out how to make the hand I bid. I never took a class or read a book about bridge. I just taught myself, and I'm a pretty good player. And it has been a source of enjoyment since then. I've been trying to teach my kids for years, but they just fade out on me. It's really a great mind-challenging game, and it should not die off with my generation. (I did get the girls to try recently so I'm not giving up yet.)

Liz and I were really close since we met our sophomore year, and she was a very good friend to me during those tough teenage years. When we went off to college nearby one another, we would sometimes drive back to Midland together. One time when I dropped her off, I went inside to say hi to her folks and they were watching TV. They had not seen their daughter in four months, and all they did was say "shh." No hugs, not even a look. Just "shh." At that moment, I was glad Dad wouldn't allow a television.

Ann Gilbert, who was a year behind me in school, and I met later in high school while dating friends. She was pretty and smart, becoming salutatorian. We instantly became best friends then—and even after we stopped dating those guys, remained so—and to this day. Whenever I could get out of working we had some good times together, which mainly centered around going to her house (remember, no one could come to mine) and playing honeymoon bridge—a fun but silly two-person version of the card game. We would sometimes run over to the Shrimp Boat, which was a drive-in near her home, to order delicious fried shrimp and onion rings, which we'd eat in the car. In spite of that, Ann is slim even to this day—darn her.

Leaning on Lifelines

There again, I just related a good memory involving food and a friend. In writing this book I'm trying to dwell on the good memories as well as the others that were not. But make no mistake, my bad memories make up the vast majority. You know the bad parts—my dad's frequent beatings, taking care of Johnny, having to work, kept mostly isolated—but I also wanted to show you that I did grab on to every happy instant like a lifeline, and felt I should share them with you as well. I guess this is just indicative of trying to keep the glass half full. But I still know that I would *not* wish my childhood on my worst enemy—in fact, *any* enemy.

Boy Crazy

I've almost always been overweight, inferiority complexed, and never a flirt. So I found myself usually surprised when a male liked me. I see other women flirt and appreciate their skill, but just can't do it myself. I treat men just like I do my women friends. Fortunately, though, in spite of those three things, I did attract a decent number of men, especially when I was younger. But at this point, we're at the boy stage. So let's go.

I started having major crushes when I was about eight years old. (Remember, I did develop early.) In fact, I was boy crazy. I think those crushes helped me get through some tough circumstances then and later, like doing good works did.

When you go through this journey with me, you're going to hear about boys and men, sometimes ad nauseam. But just when you may be thinking, "Oh spare me," it may make you feel better to keep in mind that none of them really worked out. In the last ten years, since around age 60 or so, there has been nothing going on. I haven't been interested in anyone and not many have been interested in me either. These days I'm not so much male crazy as I am crazy about being alone. I was lucky, however, to have had some days in the sun when it came to boys or men. And I feel fortunate for that as I'm aware that many have not.

First, here are some distant crushes: several movie stars like Rock Hudson, Troy Donahue, Tab Hunter—and all of them turned out to be gay. And then there was James Dean, who I understand was probably bi-. Thank goodness there were non-gay (I think) backups: Gregory Peck, William Holden, Harry Belafonte and Paul Newman. (I did get to meet Gregory Peck when I was in college and snuck in with the help of the doorman to a reception at the Driskill Hotel in Austin. Wow. He was more tall and handsome in person than in the movies and his voice was to die for. And I also got to meet him again many years later, along with Paul Newman and Harry Belafonte, at the Kennedy Center.)

Buddy

When I was a young teenager, on afternoons, Linda, Charlotte and I used to go out driving in an old Studebaker. Buddy, the older brother who you may recall I had a pitter-patter for, would join us when he was in town. It was so much fun. We'd drive out to the wide-open spaces outside Midland, listening and singing along to country songs.

Buddy was a truck driver for many years, before and after his stint in the Army, as well as a talented amateur songwriter. He wrote a wonderful song about his travels called "Truck Driver's Road," which Linda and I used to sing it all the time. She had a great voice; I did not but it rarely stopped me.

One day, when I was 16, Buddy was home, divorced from his first wife, and we went driving by ourselves. He stopped the car and we started necking. Quite frankly, because I'd been so into him for seven years at that point, it might have been hard to stop him. But thank goodness he stopped himself.

He said, "Carol, you have a better life waiting for you than the rest of us. You're going to be something special and I'm not going to let you ruin that. Do not let anybody ruin that for you. You just keep on going." I never forgot what he said, and I was always grateful. Buddy's words reinforced what I wanted for myself—a bigger and better life away from Midland. (I do like Midland and would pick again as a place to be raised—but maybe with different circumstances. I would also pick again not to spend my life there.)

Buddy, a heavy drinker and smoker, went on to two or three more marriages with several children before dying of a heart attack at age 52. I still think about him and his ballad and am so happy that my son, who is a performer, sings it on stage: "Where is my destiny, where will it end? Around the next corner, around the next bend. Up in the mountains, the valley so low. I know I'll meet God on truck driver's road."

Andrew

Dad's brother Albert had one child, a son named Andrew from a previous marriage. I met Andrew for the first time on a trip to New York City when I was 15 and going into my sophomore year in high school, and he was 19 and going into his sophomore year at Syracuse University. Right away, I developed a crush on my first cousin. He really liked me as well. There was just immediate chemistry (maybe it was the common genetic material). I was a down-home Texas girl with a big accent in those days and I thought he was just so debonair and glamorous. The next thing I know he invited me up to New Rochelle, a ritzy suburb, to meet his mother. Although his mom was divorced from my uncle, and not amicably, she was fond of my mom and was curious to meet me. He took me out to dinner that night and we were smitten.

The whole family became very concerned. It was not like we were sleeping together or anything, but the family was going nuts. Only my great aunt Esther, Grandpa's younger sister, who was visiting from San Francisco, was supportive. She said to my parents and grandparents, "They're so young and it probably won't work out." She also reminded them that the most successful member of our family, Uncle Adolph of donut fame, married his first cousin and they had children who turned out fine.

When I returned to Midland, I would receive beautiful letters from Andrew. This went on for eight months. Then when I was 16, Andrew wrote to say he had another girlfriend. I was sad, but realized the first-cousin thing is not what I was looking for anyway. (Although marrying a cousin would at least rectify: "Whose family should we go to for Thanksgiving?")

I didn't see Andrew until several years after our few-months "romance." I was again in New York and he took me to lunch—I believe on our grandparents' dime. I realized then that though I had some sentimental feelings left, I certainly did not "love" him. What had seemed debonair before now seemed snobbish and even patronizing.

The night I got engaged for the first time, which was on my 21st birthday about three years later, Andrew called sounding a little drunk, saying, "I love you, always have, and want to be with you." I was flattered and appreciated the turnaround from his dismissiveness of me, but I had no other feelings. However, as we both married and had families, we talked or saw each other on occasion, and were sort of friends until he died on November 23,

2005 at only age 65, having been a very successful and well-known stamp collector and dealer.

A Varsity Jacket

I had gone to Cowden Junior High School, which was the school made up of the kids from the south side of town and other poorer sections of Midland. In 1958, I entered Midland High School, the one high school at the time (although the fall after I graduated in 1961, a new school was added—Lee High, where Laura Bush went). At Midland High, the kids from Cowden joined together with students from San Jacinto Junior High School, where the middle class and wealthier kids had gone. Bottom line: There was a whole new crop of boys to be seen.

My old partner in crime, Danelle Reese—remember her from the 12-year-old car escapade—and I were back to our conspiring ways. We were both boy crazy, so on the first day of school we decided to look for the cutest guy. We met up later and I said, "I found him." She said, "No, my guy is better." So we hooked up the next day to show off each other's picks. It turned out to be the same guy: Daniel Everett. [I'm changing the name to protect the innocent/guilty.] He was tall and lanky with blue eyes.

Everybody had a thing for Dan. But he was just not interested. He was a late bloomer. In my junior year of high school, I had a speech class with him. Our teacher was from the North and would correct our Southern accents. She would try to get us to say "get" instead of "git"—some of it stuck.

It was a small class, but unfortunately Dan, who I loved looking at, was assigned to a seat behind me. I was really upset that I couldn't see him. But being a person who makes the best out of every situation I find myself in, I bought a purse that had a mirror on the inside flap (pretty smart, eh?), which I just placed on the edge of my desk. I lifted the flap a lot.

Dan called me "Miss Levitt." "How are you doing, Miss Levitt?" He had this great deep voice as well as a great Texas accent.

I was overweight, always weighing about 150 lbs at less than 5'4". That was what I weighed since right after puberty when I went from skinny to plump—or so I liked to call myself. Diet pills started to be the big thing, and that spring, I began taking them and lost 25 pounds in three months. (I never took diet pills even once after that as they made me shaky and I knew they were bad.) I still had big thighs, but who cared as I wasn't wearing a bathing suit to school that often.

After the weight loss, I had a pretty good figure for the first time. So for a brief period, I became the "belle of the ball." I had gotten some attention from boys and a few other recognitions along the way. For instance, in junior and senior high school, when the school newspaper was putting together the ideal gal (again, not much news to report on in Midland), one year I got "hair," another year "eyes," and once "teeth" (I think I remember having those). But after the weight loss, I started getting major attention from some of the cuter guys and was even nominated for Yearbook Queen. I didn't win but it was fun to even be in the running. (Speaking of "creative names," Midland's only high school then called its yearbook "Catoico," which stood for cattle, oil and cotton. Clever, but not nearly as good as "An-Jer-Jim-Bil.")

I got asked out that summer by Luke Franklin [another name change]. He was athletic, attractive and a nice guy—and knew Dan well. I really didn't want to go out with him because of that, but at least he asked me out—and he was cute. I went to a couple of movies with him. After one, he gave me a brief kiss goodnight.

Then I went to Greenville for August before my senior year where I was equally popular during my brief moment at 125 lbs. There were days when I had three dates. (During that time of lots of dates with lots of people, I had a hard and fast "request": to not say the f- or s- word. Maybe I had heard them too much at home.)

While in Greenville, Luke wrote me and I wrote him back. About a week later, I got a long letter from Dan. It said, "Miss Levitt, I've been crazy about you since I first saw you." (Now remember that was 25 lbs. fatter.) "When my friend Luke started taking you out, I realized I could not allow this to happen. I asked Luke about you two, and he said that it had not advanced yet. I told him how I felt and he said he'd back away. But if you care about him, I'll try to move on." I wrote him back that I also had a thing for him since our sophomore year. When I returned to Midland in early September, we started going steady and he gave me his varsity lettered jacket—practically like being engaged in Midland in those days.

The first time that Dan came to pick me up at my house for a date, he got an unexpected greeting at the door. My dad yelled, "I don't like you dating my daughter," and threw a tennis shoe at his face. With welcomes like that, thank goodness no one was ever invited to the house.

At first, it was really great to get to know Dan. He was all he appeared to be: smart, funny, curious—easy to fall for. But Dan, the late bloomer, had blossomed. He put constant pressure on me to sleep with him, but I was more than reluctant. It wasn't uncommon to be pregnant at 16 in Midland. I had a few girlfriends who got pregnant even at 13, 14 and 15—some got married, others didn't. That was not going to be me.

I was crazy about Dan. But because of the pressure and the way he would get mad when I refused, I kept breaking up with him. Since we cared a lot for each other, he'd promise that he would do better. So we would get back together, but the pressure would only start again a minute later.

Recently, while writing this book, I saw *Splendor in the Grass* on television. It so reminded me of our relationship, which took place in 1960-61. And the movie came out in 1961—the exact same time. That story was about Bud pressuring Deanie (Natalie Wood) to sleep with him and was so reminiscent of us. In the movie Deanie went stark-raving mad, at least for a while. Thank goodness that wasn't my fate. Instead I just *got* mad.

Because the situation with Dan was so turbulent and emotionally stressful, and never got better in spite of the promises, I decided to really move on. I started dating Glen McKenzie, who was class president and All-State in baseball, and was a darling guy with blue eyes and a blonde crew cut. Dan was still in my heart, but I was trying to get over him and Glen cared a lot for me without the same pressure—until later, and then we ended too.

One night I was at a Youth Center dance with Glen. Dan was there too, and he was drinking and making a scene. He left with Debbie Brady [name change], a pretty blonde. They started dating, but occasionally Dan would come back to try to get me away from Glen. But at that point, I had given up on him. Not only did I not like his pressure and anger when I wouldn't respond, I also didn't like his drinking and the behavior it caused when he did.

It was really hard to let Dan go because I had fallen for him two years before we started dating. (I did learn then in that brief but important relationship with Dan that I was attracted to only strong, smart men with strong opinions. It certainly made for interesting couplings, but also not easy ones.)

I had also become good friends with Dan's sister and close to his parents. Although his parents were not happy initially when he asked me out because I was Jewish, they seemed to really care about me after they got to know me. I continued to have visits in Texas with members of his family. Unfortunately, both of the parents died several years ago. What a dear and attractive couple they were. Dan also stayed in touch with my brother. He had always been kind to Johnny when we were dating and he remained so for decades. And by the way, Dan and Debbie got married at age 19 and 18, and had a child soon thereafter.

In July of 1966, the night I got engaged to the man I married, we were in Midland and decided to go honkytonking with a group of friends, including Dan and his then wife Debbie. Dan asked me to dance and he said, "Please don't marry him. My marriage is falling apart. I want to marry you." I said, "Dan, I am marrying David. You are married. So stop it. You're just drunk." I walked away and went back to the table. (They did eventually divorce.)

For years, Dan would call me occasionally to say that he cared about me. "The biggest regret I've ever had is we never slept together," he'd say. One day decades later (I wish I thought of it earlier), I finally said, "Dan, you missed nothing. I'm not that good. I even have references to prove it"—though not necessarily true, I just wanted him to stop the melodrama and to stop drinking, which is what activated his calls. He said, "I only drink beer." I responded, "I know plenty of alcoholics who only drink wine, and the same is true of beer. Alcohol is alcohol. Don't kid yourself."

Dan did sober up and those calls stopped. However, we have stayed in touch on occasion. Dan and his second wife came to my brother's funeral. He was sober and like a different person. I was proud of him for making the difficult change—and proud that such a good guy remains a friend.

All in the Family

I had one last hurrah before I went to college. That summer when I was 17, I went up to New York and met Bob Rukeyser, who was a student at Cornell. Bob was a distant relative of my great uncle Norman (I thought just by marriage), and it turned out, an even more distant relative of his wife, my great aunt Hilda (Grandma Carrie's sister)—feel free to draw a graph if needed. So of course then Bob and I were very related, through both Aunt Hilda *and* Uncle Norman. We often kept it in the family. It was a fun and mellow several-week romance. We used to sit in his parent's magnificent house in Great Neck (that had 11 bathrooms to give you an idea of the size of it) and listen to Ella Fitzgerald, one of my favorites.

After I left and went to Greenville, we talked often and continued some when I first got back to Texas. But soon enough, the calls stopped and we both moved on. Another cousin bites the dust.

CHAPTER 5

University of Texas

I had worked at the store from age eight to 17 and my folks said they would put the money aside that I had earned so I could go to any college I wanted. But when the time came to apply, any college became a single one—the University of Texas (UT). The tuition there was $50 a semester for in-state students, which went up to $100 a semester my senior year. The money I earned that had been set aside remained set aside. Now Dad promised it would go for my wedding instead.

I had dreamed of going to Cornell or Syracuse in New York, but that wasn't to be. I had never really looked into the matter and there was no one to help me look into anything other than those two camp experiences at ages 11 and 12. So since I had two minor romances with two guys (who happened to be my cousins of some sort), who happened to have gone to those schools, they became my choices. Maybe I could have even gotten a family discount. In hindsight, considering how much I hated the cold, my dream schools could have turned into frigid nightmares, like Mom's did. Going to UT was one situation where my father's broken promise may have worked out for the best. And my childhood had been so difficult in Midland that just being away from my dad *wherever* was a dream come true.

One fun aspect of college, especially at UT, was football. I attended every in-town game and even a couple out of town. The Longhorns won two national championships during my four years there, but I really can't take credit for that. I've often said that UT won't let you graduate unless you pledge allegiance to football for the rest of your life. And I've been a good graduate. I was a big Dallas Cowboys fan and even remained one when I first moved to Washington. Several years in, I switched to becoming a big fan of the Washington football team.

I went off to school a week before it officially started because of sorority/fraternity pledge week. There were three Jewish sororities on campus, but they had no knowledge of me so I had not gotten any invitations to their first party—usually a given for everyone. I had gotten invited to one non-Jewish sorority party, but called to decline. I was determined to join a Jewish sorority because I really didn't know many Jews, had only dated a few (and two of the three were family), and had been barely exposed to Judaism in my upbringing. I wanted that exposure big time. Since the University of Texas, which had about 26,000 students in those days, only had around 400 Jewish students, it would be hard to meet them without that sorority connection.

Most of the Texas Jewish kids knew each other through national and state organizations like B'nai B'rith that had statewide conferences. They also came from the bigger cities like Dallas and Houston so they had a real network that I had not been part of. I did get in touch with the three Jewish sororities once I arrived in Austin, and then went to each of their first parties. Two invited me to the second party. I was most interested in AEPhi and let the second group know that. I was so glad when I got an invitation to AEPhi's third and last party, which meant I was close to getting in. It was considered to be the ritziest of the Jewish sororities and I was certainly not that, which would soon become more obvious.

Dad had taken me to buy a few dresses in preparation for college. Mom never participated in those things as she was usually working in the store and besides, she hated to shop. I really had no interest in it myself, for the most part, until my mid-30s. Anyway, back to the sorority party. I put on the only dressy dress I owned—a green scoop-necked number with small pink flowers all over it—and no jewelry as I had none.

When I got to the sorority house and we were on the lawn waiting for the doors to open, I looked around and saw that every single girl—without exception—had on a black dress with pearls. Of course there was *one* exception, me and the pink flowers. Like always, I stuck out—and not in a good way. I looked like Flo, the truck-stop waitress from the TV show *Alice* on an outing—and on a bad day. I was always so self-conscious about not fitting in and this one was a doozy. (Now, 55 years later, I realize I actually work hard at—and enjoy—not fitting in. But back then, I cared.)

I got into the sorority anyway. I think they liked my personality and down-homeness. I was so proud to be accepted by them, especially considering that I was usually rejected by the same non-Jewish types in Midland. In fact, my sophomore year and beyond, the sorority asked me to head up rush week as they thought I was good with people and helpful in selling the sorority to a lot of non-stuffy, outgoing girls like myself.

I guess because of my activism in causes and volunteer work, they also asked me to chair the Activities Committee. I organized a dance at the State Home for the Retarded (what it was called then) and got most of my sorority sisters to attend. My college boyfriend Ivan, who is still a dear friend, remembers me not giving anyone a choice in the matter. Some of the gals still talk about it. My sorority sisters elected me Parliamentarian not because I knew Robert's Rules of Order, but because they felt it would shut me up from disrupting the meetings. For the most part, it worked.

Soon after I joined, the sorority pushed me to run for Secretary of the Freshman Class (numbering nearly 10,000). I was a reluctant candidate then. Hard to believe, right? There was a large field of contenders, probably 20 or 30. One of the rivals was Kay Bailey, later known as Kay Bailey Hutchison. There was to be a run-off for the contenders who were in the top 50 percentile. I was one of the three who made it to the run-off and was thrilled to be in that number, even though I ultimately lost the election. Kay did not make the run-off, but in spite of that bitter defeat, she managed to pick herself up and eventually became a United States Senator.

I did have one win my freshman year. I was named Campus Chest. I did not remember this prestigious award, but in digging through my 100+ scrapbooks, my daughter Hilary found it, which then 'jug'ged—I mean— jogged my memory. I didn't really put myself in the race; I was drafted without consent. It is a dubious honor, but considering I was competing in a highly competitive field of buxom Texas women, it was quite an achievement. I think I still would have preferred being Secretary of the Freshman Class.

I did not get into a campus dormitory at UT. By the time I put in an application, it was too late. (These things were pretty overwhelming for a 17-year-old with lots of other responsibilities.) A woman from New York had taken a motel-looking building near campus and turned it into a dormitory called Rosie's with mostly Jewish girls living there. (It really was a dorm, though I know it sounds like a brothel.) And that's where I spent my freshman year.

They assigned me a roommate, the only non-Jewish resident that year, Gloria Garza, who had been Miss Weslaco, Texas. A girl named Sandy Mendlowitz lived down the hall. She had a nightmare of a roommate, a girl named SueSue who went on to Hollywood and had roles in a couple of sitcoms. (Now, I repeat, it really was a dormitory!) Anyway, SueSue would sit in her room amidst lighted candles and would not let Sandy put the lights on to study. Gloria and I felt so badly for Sandy that, with Rosie's permission, we moved another bed into our room—making for tight quarters—but the three of us lived happily together.

We all started smoking cigarettes toward the end of the first semester of our freshman year. It's surprising that I didn't smoke before then because my parents smoked as did many of my friends, including boyfriends. My father smoked cigars and my mother chain-smoked heavy-duty cigarettes. I must have been addicted to nicotine and craved it at college. As my friends Gloria, Sandy and I were studying for exams in December, we all started smoking to calm our nerves, or so we said. We coughed and coughed but fought through it and taught ourselves to inhale. Starting then, I smoked for 39 and a half years until I quit in 2001. Sadly, Sandy died of lung cancer several years ago.

(Speaking of dear Sandy, I roomed with her for several years and we were both very messy. One Friday afternoon during our sophomore year, we arrived to our small dorm room and could barely get in—dirty clothes strewn around the floor, brimming ashtrays everywhere. We looked at each other and said, "Enough." We spent the whole weekend washing clothes and cleaning up. In one full swoop, I went from being a total slob to the proverbial "neat freak"—from the sublime to the ridiculous [actually, from the ridiculous to the sublime]. And I have remained so.)

During my freshman year, I was slender for me. I was still weighing that 125 lbs. As a result, my social dance card was pretty full, though I kept with my abstinence program. However, I was enjoying myself and the newfound freedom too much. And as a result, I got put on academic probation after my first semester.

Actually it wasn't just my active social life that got me into trouble; it was a frog. My biology class had a lab element, but I had such a weak stomach that I would gag when I tried to dissect anything. Since I couldn't do that work, I knew I'd fail the lab. So I had to get a B on the written test, as the lab part was 25% of the grade, or I would fail the whole class. I hunkered down and really studied biology, ignoring my other classes. I did wind up getting that B on the test. But when grades were posted, I still got a big fat F. There was some small-print rule that if you failed lab, you failed the class entirely. I had no idea that was the rule—but no one cared.

And because I ignored my other classes to focus on the biology test, I got a D in geography. Although I was good at memorizing countries, capitals, rivers, etc., it was topography that did me in. Needless to say, I did not become a biologist or geographist or topographist, if there are any such things as the latter two. Though I never drank—and don't to this day—this humiliating academic probation "sobered" me up in a sense and I got really serious about my studies. There was no way I was going back to Midland—and Dad. The spring semester, I doubled my average and after that, I made Dean's List every semester from what I remember.

Speaking of drinking, I never started drinking for several reasons: 1) I always had a weight problem so I didn't need the calories and preferred using those calories instead for hot fudge sundaes (that was and is my favorite "high"). 2) I didn't need it to loosen up socially because I'm naturally outgoing, and finally, 3) I like being in control of myself at all times. I have watched so many of my friends over the years start out the evening attractive and together and then just dissipate right before my very eyes. It hasn't been a pretty picture—and I certainly didn't want that to be me. (I have also never done marijuana—never had one puff—nor any other addictive drug, prescribed or not. I do not want to alter the mind I was given; old age may do it but it will never be my choice.)

Here's the only drunk experience in my entire 73-year life: In August of 1962, my roommate Gloria was getting married in Weslaco and had asked me to be her maid of honor. Her family owned the big funeral home in town and turned out to be very wealthy people with a gorgeous two-story house. She also had a gorgeous, sophisticated older brother who was in medical school. Even though I am outgoing, I'm not very forward with men and as I've said, have never been much of a flirt. The brother, whose name I do not remember, was very reserved. So I made a conscious decision to drink, thinking maybe it would be helpful in making me flirtatious.

So here we were late the night before the wedding in their beautiful upstairs library, and I—the girl who had never had a drink—started chug-a-lugging the martinis the brother was making. Next thing I know I am running down the stairs and out the front door, falling on the lawn (where the wedding was to take place a few hours later), violently throwing up. My only interaction with that gorgeous brother I was trying to entice was his hosing me off on that lawn. Speaking of "not a pretty picture." In the space of 30 minutes of drinking, I hit rock bottom, and have been totally sober for 55 years now.

Back at school, there was no doubt that I would become a teacher. My brother's circumstances drew me to working with handicapped children, one of the terms of the day. Thus, I majored in special education. College special education degree programs were very rare in the early 1960s, but the University of Texas had one—and a good one. The Dean of the department was named Dr. John Peck and I admired him very much.

After that first semester debacle, I really tried to do well in my classes, both in education as well as general studies. There was one education professor who, no matter how hard I tried, would not give me above a B in her class. I was always aiming for an A and doing extra work to get it. Unfortunately, a year or so later, I had that teacher for a second class, and the same thing happened. Each semester I would have all A's except the two times I was in her class. It was so frustrating. I tried to talk to her about it, but she showed animosity toward me. Finally, as I was graduating, a year or so after my last class with her, Dr. Peck came over to me and said, "I've wanted to tell you this for a long time but I just couldn't. That instructor has one child, a daughter with special needs, and her husband left her several years ago and ran off with a woman who looks exactly like you. That was your one and only problem, and something you couldn't help. You did 'A' work."

Marbridge

I went to visit Johnny at the Brown School a lot when I was in college. My sophomore year I took the second family car to school to make it easier to visit him, and I could also transport both of us to and from Midland. It was a 1960 red and white, two-door Chevy Impala, with a three-gear stick-shift on the wheel—one of the best-looking cars in the world then or ever.

San Marcos, where the Brown School was located, was 30 miles from Austin. I'd pick Johnny up and usually spend all day Saturday with him at least once a month. Then I would drop by to see him sometimes in between. I started noticing that when I arrived, especially unannounced, I would find him just rocking in the chair on the porch. He was doing nothing really most of the day but feel sorry for himself because he couldn't date or do other things that were "normal" for people his age, which was then 19. I felt there was too much time on his hands and that if he were busier, he would be happier.

Johnny was always on my mind anyway, but I then started to really worry that his school in San Marcos did not offer enough for him. I learned about the Marbridge Ranch through one of my special education classes. Dr. Peck had some association with the school and he brought two young men who were residents there to speak to our class. They talked about their studies, their responsibilities on the ranch, and the many social activities they had. They seemed so engaged and content.

Marbridge was located in Manchaca, just outside of Austin. It was a fairly new facility for intellectually disabled men (a little while later women were added) that was started by a wealthy couple in Austin, Jim and Marge Bridges, who had a son with special needs. Their son had been to the best schools in the country, including the Brown School, and the parents felt that he needed more. So they started Marbridge and made sure that the program included a wide range of activities for the men that encompassed both fun and challenges to make for a fuller, more satisfying life. The program featured gardening, dairy production, chorus, sports, and forays off campus like attending UT football games and rodeos. I just knew it was the place for Johnny.

At the ripe old age of 18, I was determined to make the transfer to Marbridge happen. I did not tell my parents that I was unhappy with the Brown School and wanted to make a change because I didn't want to worry them, and why put them through that if Johnny couldn't get into the program. (And I knew that Marbridge only accepted a small percentage of applicants.) So I brought Johnny in for an interview without my parents' knowledge. He was excited but I swore him to secrecy. Not easy for him, but he did it. I told the school about the situation and why I was doing it the way I was, and I think they trusted me because of my relationship with Dr. Peck. And lo and behold, Marbridge accepted Johnny. He was pleased. And I was ecstatic.

Only after his acceptance did I drive to Midland to tell my parents in person of my concerns about Brown and about this extraordinary new place that would serve my brother better. Mom and Dad wanted the best for Johnny and had always deferred to me on issues concerning his care. So they enthusiastically concurred. Right away, I moved Johnny from Brown to Marbridge. My parents didn't see the school/ranch until years later. He continued to fly home with help by the airlines every couple of months for a week or so, or I drove both of us home on occasion.

Thank goodness Johnny was immediately very content at Marbridge and remained so for 42 years. He kept busy working in the laundry. Soon, because of his adorable personality, he became the person who gave tours of the school. When not working, he enjoyed those many outings to UT sports events, concerts, etc. It was a good move and I've always been proud of bringing it about in such a smooth and successful way.

Ivan

The beginning of my freshman year, I met Ivan Edelman. He was also a freshman and was from Baytown, Texas. He had this country boy aspect to him and a great Texas accent (which I, by the way, used to have). He was such a doll and attractive but I can't tell you I was attracted to him at first.

I think in me Ivan saw a comparable spirit—a small-town Texas girl not from a rich family, with the same down-home quality he had. We certainly weren't, though, comparable in our religious upbringing. He was raised an Orthodox Jew and I practically a Christian. (An FYI: Judaism has different sects. Reform Judaism, to which I belong, is the most liberal, least observant form. Orthodox is the most strict in customs and practice. Conservative is midway between the two. Another movement is Hasidic Judaism, which is very Orthodox, and most wear traditional garb.)

Ivan and I hit it off personality-wise and became great friends that first semester. He told me much later that he plotted to get me and decided that his best approach would be to act like he just wanted to be my friend.

Ivan was in a Jewish fraternity, Tau Delta Phi. One of his fraternity brothers at the time was the singer and comedian Kinky Friedman. Another member who came to campus a couple of years after we did was a guy from New York who we all found to be really arrogant. No one paid much attention to him, but considering his later success, maybe we should have. His name was David Geffen.

Ivan never acted like he was interested in me or flirted, which was fine because there was no pitter-patter here. So that whole first semester, he was just my buddy. He would call up after I'd come from dates with mostly upper-classmen and he'd ask, "How did it go? What did you do?" It was fun to have somebody who was so enjoyable just to talk to. He was one of the nicest people I've ever known and clearly many thought so too. He had tons of friends and was named Social Director of his fraternity.

Ivan kept kosher and was observant, which was so unusual in Texas even in a Jewish fraternity. It was also unusual for me as I had come from a family who was not only unobservant but Jewish in name only. Although Ivan did not wear a yarmulke (skull cap) all the time (actually only at temple), he would not carry money on Jewish holidays and the Sabbath (Friday evening to Saturday evening). He'd get movie tickets and buy the candy before sundown on Friday and then we'd go that night. Ivan did not drive on the Sabbath either, but walked everywhere instead. Although different from my upbringing, I admired him for his religious commitment—not in your face, but just did it easily and naturally.

Even though I went with a lot of different people as I was the "new girl in town" in that community, I never really clicked with any of the many guys I dated that first semester of my freshman year. Then I went home for the Christmas holidays and missed Ivan, but still was not thinking of him romantically at all. After I got back to school, he came over to my off-campus dorm and we sat outside on the grass to catch up. He said, "I sure missed you over the holidays," and he leaned over and gave me a kiss. He had never kissed me before. I just swooned. I liked him as a friend. He was the most fun person I knew. Then when he kissed me dreamily, I became enormously attracted to him. I immediately fell in love, which he later claimed to have done at our first meeting.

From then on, it was Ivan and I. We were a couple, and a pretty popular one. We were both funny but we were *really* funny together. We had a great time. Ivan loved to go and do. He loved to see every movie—the silly comedies and the dramatic foreign ones alike, as did I. We would go to all the dances and never sit down. He was a great dancer, just a ball of fun, and was mostly sober like me—only an occasional beer. We went to all the football games. Every October, we went up to Dallas for the Oklahoma-Texas game, and where I enjoyed visiting his extended family. We also hung out a lot with Johnny. First we'd go pick him up in San Marcos and then at Marbridge. Johnny really loved Ivan too.

I also liked to go to Baytown with him and I was crazy about his parents, Hannah and Abe, who I called Aunt Hannah and Uncle Abe. They lived in a small, modest house—but still much nicer than my own. His maternal grandparents, immigrants from Poland who didn't speak a word of English, lived with them. His father and grandfather wore yarmulkes all the time and as they walked through that small Texas town to temple. It was so foreign to me but interesting. I loved his mother, who was such a personality and she seemed to love me as the daughter she never had.

Ivan's parents owned a small shoe store in the tiny and dying downtown. (I had only a few clothes in those days—but thanks to their generosity, lots of shoes.) Ivan and I had that in common—parents owning and working in a small business. But there was a difference: Ivan never had to work in his family's store—not a day. I wish I could have said the same.

For all her great qualities, Hannah was not a particularly good cook. Her only meal was dry kosher chicken. The first night we had it warm, and the rest of the time, chilled. I didn't care and would eat it happily—of course I always ate happily. But she more than made up for it by the warmth and joy she brought into our lives. (Because of this experience, I always thought kosher meat meant dry, but certainly have learned that is not the case.)

Ivan spoiled me like he had been. He was an only child of older parents, and then when you add in adoring grandparents, he was really spoiled. And his parents and grandparents indulged me too. It felt wonderful to be spoiled by such wonderful people.

In January when Ivan and I started romantically dating, I still weighed that 125 pounds I had gotten to the end of my junior year of high school. By spring I weighed about 180, literally. Ivan loved to feed me. He enjoyed taking me out to meals and bringing me candy. This may have been part of another plot—this time to keep me. As if I was going anywhere—I could barely move. Ivan had gained some weight himself too, even though he still had a fabulous physique. Thank goodness we both lost weight when we were apart that summer.

Ivan and I had great chemistry and it didn't matter what my weight was. When I gained and looked like a balloon, he could have cared less. He couldn't keep his hands off me whether I weighed 130 or 180. I, however, did care that I weighed that much so I got myself down to my more normal 150 lbs. But the fact that Ivan loved me no matter my weight was such a good thing. It really was a very loving, validating relationship.

Speaking of it now reminds me of the popularity I enjoyed from the end of my junior year of high school through the first semester of my freshman year of college—the only period of my life when I was somewhat trim. Even though it was fun to attract new people who had never seemed to notice me before, it actually annoyed me at the time. I would think, "Where in the hell were they when I weighed 150 pounds? I'm the same person with the same personality with the same strengths and weaknesses. Yet 25 pounds was the difference between liking me or not liking me." How superficial is that? "Who needs you anyway" was my feeling.

Being with Ivan and his appreciation of me regardless made me realize that I wanted that and nothing less. And that has remained my feeling. Take me or leave me as I am. The men who would be interested in me or not for my weight—or age—I would not be interested in anyway. It was such a lesson to me that I've never forced myself to be unnaturally trim since. And I've never wanted to artificially alter my appearance, including getting rid of my wrinkles and gray hair. And I've never regretted those decisions.

Here's another decision I have not regretted: Some weekends, Ivan and I would rent either one motorcycle with me on the back, or two so I could drive my own. We would ride up into the lovely hills outside Austin. One day, when I was on my own bike and we were heading to return them, my choice was to hit a parked car or slide the bike onto the road with me on it. I chose the latter and got a real wicked scraped knee, not to mention ruining my favorite jeans. I also chose that day not to drive a motorcycle again.

Ivan and I continued to have a very special relationship. I really loved him, the University of Texas, and the many close friends I was making. It was such a good time of my life.

Unfortunately, though, at the end of our sophomore year, Ivan flunked out and he didn't come back to school until the next January. He remained in Baytown. I was really mad at him for having to leave school as we had already been talking about getting married. And I had tried to warn him that he could flunk out if he continued acting so irresponsibly about his classes, but he went about his merry way.

I felt his neglect of his studies indicated a lack of serious consideration of our future. Plus, his leaving for a semester meant we would be apart and we weren't going to graduate at the same time. We would then have to delay the wedding to the following year in January rather than the summer after we were both supposed to graduate. My anger grew when he didn't try to get a job in Austin so we could be together. Instead he went home to his parents.

I've never been a fair-weather person and I certainly don't like leaving someone when they're down—but this was somewhat of his own choosing. This whole episode made me start to question whether his maturity and dependability matched mine at this stage. They had two years earlier when we were 18. But nearing 20, I felt ready for the responsibilities of the future. I was not sure about him. As far as I was concerned, we were really on the outs.

A Memorable Day in November

In November of 1963, my junior year and the same semester Ivan was in Baytown, I was serving as an elected dormitory advisor at Kinsolving, which was the biggest dorm at UT at that time.

Lynda Bird Johnson, the daughter of Lyndon Johnson who was then Vice President, was on my wing and lived just down the hall from me. She was very reserved and I didn't get the chance to say more than hi to her usually. That day, November 22nd, though, I saw her in the mailroom downstairs and we finally chatted. I said, "You must be excited about your father coming to town this afternoon." President Kennedy and the Vice President had gone to Dallas that morning for a parade, and later were heading to Austin. She said she was looking forward to the festivities. We then went up the elevator together, and she went to the right into her room and I went to the left into mine.

I sat down on the bed and started reading my mail. (My parents and grandparents, as well as Aunt Betty and Aunt Doe, were good about writing to me.) A few minutes later, I heard noise in the hallway. I walked out of my room and saw the one-day-a-week housekeepers crying. Before I could ask them what was happening, I heard a radio coming from Lynda Bird's room and walked in there. She had her back to me and was looking out the window. The radio announcer said the President had been shot, as well as Texas Governor John Connally, but there was no word about the Vice President. Lynda fell to her knees and began to cry. I put my hand on her shoulder. A minute later the secret service men, who lived downstairs, came in and whisked her away. Other agents came back soon thereafter to pack up her things and we didn't see her again at the dorm. Later that day, her father would be sworn in as President of the United States after we learned President Kennedy had died. I've run into Lynda Bird every so often throughout my years in Washington and we've had pleasant visits but we've never talked about that sad day.

And what a sad day it was. We didn't have TVs in our rooms, so we gathered together in the dorm's common areas to watch the news. We were glued to it all day and night. We never even went to bed. We never bathed. I don't remember eating. I just remember the shock of it all—and crying.

A Man from Iran

The next day, after our sleepless night, grubby as all get-out, Sandy and I took a walk to the drug store nearby, probably to get cigarettes. Though the timing was strange, we met this good-looking Iranian man and a Turkish friend of his. I had seen the Iranian guy around campus, and he certainly was someone you noticed.

He was very dark-skinned with black hair, 6'4", slim, sophisticated, and drove around in a small red MG convertible.

When we met them at the cash register, we shared a few words about the tragic event and that was it. A week later, I ran into the Turkish man, who looked like Anthony Quinn, at the library. He asked me for my phone number and said it was for his Iranian friend, so I gave it. Next thing I know, the Iranian man I found attractive called and asked me out.

His name was Monsour Nikai Barami, but people called him "Duke." He was a 25-year-old graduate student in engineering and a teaching assistant. It turned out his father was one of the Shah's best friends. He was Muslim, and his father, who lived in Tehran, had at that time three wives.

Duke and I started dating and were together most of the time. He wrote me beautiful love letters. He asked me to marry him, but I was only 19 years old, still not over Ivan, and regardless, I did not want to be the first of three wives. In March, I started to really miss Ivan, who had come back to school in January. I was also getting a lot of pressure from Duke to sleep with him as he was older and used to that being part of his relationships.

I then broke up with Duke. He got very upset. I returned the star sapphire ring, encircled with small diamonds, he had given me for Christmas. (Only in Texas would a Muslim give a Jew such a lovely Christmas present.) He insisted I keep the ring, and when I kept handing it back to him, he ran into the bathroom and threw it in the toilet. I immediately went and fished it out, but he refused to take the ring back. I still have it.

Back to Ivan

I went back to Ivan. I did finally sleep with him when we got back together. I was in love with him and was probably going to marry him, and I didn't want to marry someone without having experienced really being together. It was wonderful. But I was worried about getting pregnant, so after a month we stopped and he, bless his heart, went along with it. He was such a good—and understanding—guy.

In my senior year, the day I turned 21, Ivan and I went out for dinner and he asked me to marry him. He gave me a beautiful marquise 1.5-karat diamond ring, which he and his family picked out and bought. It was so extravagant, especially for people of such modest means. When I got back to the sorority house around 11 p.m., that's when cousin Andrew called on the hallway phone to say that he missed and loved me, drunk of course. (Men sure like me when they're drunk.) I still can't believe the timing, even as I write this over 50 years later.

That spring, I went to Congregation Beth Israel in Austin where the few Jewish Marbridge students, including Johnny, attended services, which I had helped arrange. The temple had such a beautiful setting. I loved their openness and had already gotten my parents to contribute to the temple because of Johnny. That is where we were going to be married in January of 1966. I had already started making the arrangements myself, which as usual and unfortunately, I had to do on my own as again, Mom was working and never that interested in those things anyway.

I graduated from UT in May of 1965. Of course, my parents did not come to the ceremony. I was hoping they might at least make the wedding.

Visiting Washington

Before I started teaching that September in Austin, a friend Sherry from Houston and I decided to go to New York for two weeks. I had gone to New York over the years to visit my grandparents, but was pretty restricted and had a curfew. Sherry and I were planning to stay at an apartment-hotel. It was kind of my graduation present to myself.

When my friend Carol Ablon from Dallas, who had been one of my younger—and closest—sorority sisters, found out I was headed east with a friend, she urged us to stop and visit her in Washington, D.C. Carol had a summer internship there through Texas Senator Ralph Yarborough at the old Department of Health, Education and Welfare. (Carol was always involved with Democratic politics and still is.) In those days, you could do free airline stopovers and Sherry was game, so off we went.

A family friend of Sherry's picked us up at the airport the evening we arrived. He immediately took us to one of his favorite places for drinks and a bite. It was a German restaurant called Old Europe. Interestingly, eight years later the chef and subsequent owner of the restaurant, Karl Herald and his wife Isabel, became our next-door neighbors and are still dear friends to this day. There are lots of restaurants and neighbors in our town, and yet the first establishment I stepped foot into in D.C. was theirs. Life seems to always throw us some curious coincidences.

It did not take long for me to fall in love with Washington. It happened within minutes. I was just ga-ga. I was in D.C. for only

72 hours and I literally did not put my head on the pillow for even five seconds. I did not want to waste one minute of my time sleeping in the most beautiful place I'd ever seen with its plethora of trees, gorgeous architecture, not to mention the magnificent monuments. I loved the diversity. I heard people speaking different languages on the street. To me, it was so cosmopolitan and such a contrast from Midland. Austin was more diverse, worldly and pretty, but still nothing like Washington. In D.C. something just awakened in me. It was like a magnet drawing me to it.

The next day, our first real day in the District, Sherry and I went up to the Capitol. I led us straight to the Senate members' dining room. Sherry, a more reticent person, warned, "We can't go in there. It says, 'Members Only.'" But I was not going to miss this opportunity. I said, "Just walk in and act like we belong here. Leave it to me." The maître d' stopped us and asked whose guests we were. I just pulled out a Senator's name from the top of my head. I think I said, "Henry Jackson," better known as "Scoop," from the state of Washington, because I had just read something about him. The host let us sit down. I don't know if he bought it or was just amused at the gall of these girls with big Texas accents. So here we were fifteen hours after arriving in Washington, sitting in the Senate dining room with Senators and their friends and family. It was really fun. Never too concerned with couth, I even walked up to several Senators and secured autographs. I'm sure you can't get away with that today and even I wouldn't try now for fear of getting arrested. Or maybe I would.

We stayed at Carol's place in Georgetown called Hamilton Arms, which had a great history. It was a group of houses that had been divided into apartments located between 31st St. and Wisconsin Ave. and M and N Sts., N.W.

The last night of our three-day visit, Carol was out and Sherry was spending time with the friend who picked us up, so I was on my own. Carol was friendly with two older guys who lived above her. One of them, Don Landers, suggested that we walk up M St. to a fairly new restaurant. So we headed over to Clyde's. I was sitting at the bar, drinking my usual cola. (Now the usual is diet soda or seltzer water.) A friend of Don's walked in, whose name was Ben Noble. He was a bit short, a little pudgy and was legally classified as blind, though he had some peripheral vision. That fact was especially striking as I later took rides through D.C. with him on the back of his motorcycle. Thank goodness for the peripheral vision! (And thank goodness, my youthful stupidity wore off.)

That night, Ben and I got into a very good conversation. He was one of the most fascinating people, though a bit scandalous. He was married with nine children and his wife lived in the Midwest. And he had a mistress in Washington who also carried his name and with whom he had two children. Both women knew about each other, or so he said.

He was a lawyer in private practice and was not only interesting, but really smart. He had gone to Georgetown Law School with a reader. He was quite a bit older than I, probably 20 years or so. I was intrigued by him because he was so unique, but that was it.

Our bartender that night who participated in the conversation was Stuart Davidson, who was the co-owner of Clyde's and its successor restaurants. Stuart asked me out, but I told him I was engaged. Even though I declined the offer, he still came over to our friend Don's the next day for a short visit. Such a nice guy, and Clyde's became one of the major eating establishments in the D.C. area. (Years later, Stuart and his lovely wife Sally supported several of my Council campaigns before he passed away.)

Then the next day, Sherry and I went up to New York. I must admit I just wanted to be back in D.C. and Sherry was like a duck out of water or a fish out of water, or however it goes. (Like my fellow Midlander George W. Bush, I never get those idioms right. Maybe it was something in the West Texas water, or lack thereof.)

Also, during the week, I received a postcard from Ben via Don who had given it to Carol, who sent it to me. Anyway, after a week in the big city, Sherry and I were both ready to go elsewhere, she back to Houston and me back to D.C. to Carol's place for another week of exploration. I actually saw more of Washington during the 10 days I spent there as a tourist in the summer of 1965, including the Luray Caverns in Virginia, than I have ever seen since.

The combination of the beauty of the city, the diversity, and the kind of people I met in D.C. made it an irresistible draw. I could not fight the realization that I wanted a bigger, more diverse life than what was planned in Texas with Ivan—even though I still loved him dearly.

So that was it. I went back to Texas. Having flown all night, I arrived at 7 a.m. when my new job teaching started at 8 a.m. that same day. Ivan picked me up at the airport and dropped me right at school, keeping my suitcase in his trunk. That day, I gave the school notice that I would be leaving at mid-year (after one semester). I just knew I had to go back to Washington. Not long after, I broke my engagement to my best friend.

Last Days of Texas

In September of 1965 I started a job teaching special education at Porter Junior High School in Austin. My salary was $4,800 per year. The school district was mainstreaming where possible, which was a pretty advanced strategy in those days. That meant that my special education students were in my homeroom most of the day, where I worked with them on basic skills. Then for part of the day, I funneled some of them into classes with other students—called mainstreaming. I loved teaching. The students were great and the multiracial nature of the school appealed to me.

I took on a small battle against what I perceived as an injustice while at Porter. My kids, who were a mixture of mentally and emotionally challenged students, weren't technically in a grade as their ages ranged from approximately 12 to 15. I had one particular student, Nick Perez, who was a gifted basketball player. There was a rule that you had to be in a grade to be on the team. Thus, special education students couldn't even try out. This seemed particularly unfair to me in general and specifically deprived Nick of being able to participate and foster his talent.

I spoke to the coach and the principal regarding Nick: "He is 13 years old. Since that is the age of most 8th graders, just act like he is in the 8th grade and let him try out for the 8th grade team. If he qualifies, let him play." That made sense to me. Nothing happened.

I wrote a letter to the school system. I never heard back. Finally, I just showed up at a School Board meeting and spoke of how there was no process in place to allow special education students to even try out for, much less participate on sports teams. I explained that I wasn't asking for special treatment on his behalf, just a fair chance. He should be allowed to try out like any other student. I got a sympathetic ear there and the school was told to at least let him try out. He did get on the 8th grade team and played well. I was so proud of him—and myself.

On the personal front, that autumn was hard in that Ivan and I continued to go out as friends to football games and dinner occasionally, while he pushed me to change my mind. But I was intent on building my own life. I shared a two-bedroom apartment near campus with three other women. My roommate was Karen Glosserman from Sequin, Texas, who I did not know but liked a lot. She was legally defined as deaf, but was a gifted pianist. I found her ability, especially under the circumstances, quite extraordinary.

When I was living in that apartment complex, there was a group of guys who lived across the courtyard. One of them was just darling, so nice looking in an all-American way. He and I started hanging out a lot when we both got back from work. We would just sit on the grass on the complex and visit. One time we shared a kiss and he told me he wasn't sure if he wanted to be with girls. He was the first person who ever openly discussed that with me, the possibility that he might be gay. To all my gay friends, let this be proof of my frequent quip: "I've turned a lot of guys gay so you owe me big time."

I was also busy that fall with preparing to move to Washington. Carol, who was back in Dallas working at this point, felt the same as I did about returning to the District, and we had made plans to move up together.

I needed to find a job there. I called Ben Noble and asked him to send me names and addresses of school districts in and around D.C. I then sent them resumes. (It's so much easier these days with the Internet, but then far more difficult.) Since I had a special education degree, a rare commodity in those days, I got replies back from every jurisdiction except D.C.

I kept writing and calling the D.C. Public Schools to get an application as that is where I wanted to live and work. I never received one. I subsequently found out that they had no in-house special education programs but I might have been willing to teach elementary education, which my degree also qualified me for, if they had ever responded.

(Interestingly enough, while I was on the D.C. Board of Education starting in 1974 and on the Council starting in 1985, I used many opportunities to inform the school system of that story at public hearings and would always end by saying, "And to this day I have never received the application." Finally, in 2003, nearly 40 years later, then Superintendent Paul Vance heard my same old song and sent me one with a note attached, "Herein lies your requested teaching application." I loved it and it sure shut me up. Kudos to him! [Unfortunately, Paul died a couple of years ago, but I always think of him with humor.])

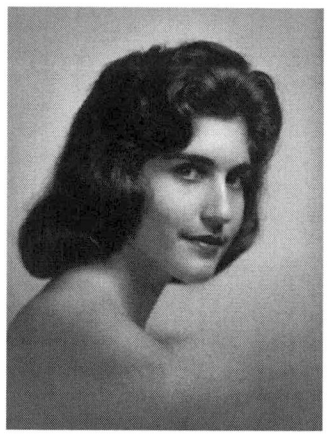

My official portrait in high school as a Catoico Queen nominee—the only brunette, I think (I did not win.)

High School graduation

Glen McKenzie: one of a few fun romances

The 1960 Impala

Dear friend Liz Hitt and Johnny

THE GENERAL CLOTHING STORE

With Uncle Albert in front of store

With S.W. Watson (left), Grandma C (middle) & Grandpa S (right)

I told you the store was stuffed to the rafters.

This picture was used in the
Washingtonian where I said,
"My hair should have been higher."

The picture to the left was not my
normal hair style. This one was.

Duke from Iran

A real love, Ivan Edelman,
and me in cowperson casual

In college I was one of the girls ... and one of the guys.

Grandparents (on ends) having one and only dinner together with Great Aunt Hilda and husband Great Uncle Norman (center) in New York

Grandpa S in the '30s

Grandparents B & J (above) and Grandparents C & S (left) as they age beautifully

Mom and Dad

Lovely pen and ink composite by cousin Seymour Simmons III

CHAPTER 6

Moving to Washington

On January 21, 1966, I set out for Washington, D.C. It was the exact month I was to be married to Ivan. He was still very hurt and I was very sad—about hurting him and about leaving a man I loved who was really and truly my best friend, and a little sad about leaving Texas, which had been my home for most of my life.

But I knew I had to go. There was that magnet drawing me to Washington. I am not a psychic nor really into any of those types of things but it was really like that. I had never had such a feeling before or since, just then.

The day I left Austin, I went over to Ivan's. I had already said goodbye to him but I just went over to say goodbye again. He was so generous. Though he said I was breaking his heart, he wished for me to be happy more than anything. He really was my friend.

On that January day in 1966, as I was leaving for D.C. to seek that happiness, I was ridden with anxiety. I'll never forget driving the Impala out of Austin off to my new life. I looked into the rear-view mirror, seeing the University of Texas tower getting smaller in the background, tears flowing down my face. I had just turned 22 the day before and here I was heading to Washington, not really knowing anybody except my friend Carol and the couple of people I met while visiting her. I was leaving the life I'd known— my family, friends and Johnny—and heading to a total unknown. I felt lonely, scared and yet, hopeful.

It was the middle of winter and I hated the thought of driving alone for 1,200 miles in bad weather. So I put an ad on the UT student center bulletin board to find someone to ride with me. A young man, a new student at UT, responded. Although, his final destination was New York, he did go with me to D.C. It now seems funny in hindsight that to ease my fear of being on the road alone, I drove with a perfect stranger. He was very nice, though, and listened to my blathering all the way about the wonderful ex-fiancé and the life I was leaving behind and the new life and whatever it was that I hoped to find. (I'm sure he wished he had just bought his own plane ticket—or even a two-day bus pass.)

We had to stop in Nashville as we were exhausted. We shared a room, me in the bed and him on the floor—in case you're wondering. The more suspicious me would not do that now, but I was so trusting then. Thank goodness it was fine. The next morning, he called his parents' friends who lived in a beautiful gated estate in Nashville and we had brunch with them—a relief from the road.

The rest of the trip was very icy and I was sure glad to have company. My car was a stick shift, the roads were slick, and no one in Texas had ever heard of snow tires. A couple of times we did go off the road—and some moments I felt myself careening off the mountain. But I just kept blathering away. I think at that point, my passenger even appreciated my chatter as a distraction from the scary icy conditions we were driving through.

I arrived in D.C. on January 22, 1966. Carol Ablon met me there and brought along a friend of hers from Dallas, a petite, young woman named Rita, to room with us as well. As we looked for an apartment, we stayed at a downtown apartment-hotel on M and 15th Sts., N.W. We found a two-bedroom apartment in Capital Park, which was in Southwest D.C. on 4th St. As Rita and Carol had grown up together, they shared one room while I took the second.

Carol worked for Robert Kennedy in his Senate office where he represented New York. I didn't have a job yet. I had several offers from suburban jurisdictions, but wanted to get the lay of the land before I signed on—and was still hoping for a response from the D.C. Public Schools. Fortunately, I had saved half the money from my teaching job in Austin as I had lived frugally, knowing I couldn't ask my parents for anything, or at least didn't feel comfortable doing so. Because of those savings, I was okay for a while.

After finding the apartment, the next step was to lease furniture. We went out to a place called Certified Leasing, where a guy named Mark worked. It was obvious he really liked Rita and seemed excited to meet these new Jewish girls with these Southern accents. He suggested that he get a couple of friends of his together to go out. We said yes as he appeared nice enough.

Carol and her date really clicked. He was David Pensky, and he and Carol immediately fell madly in love and were married four months later. So our furniture trip to Certified Leasing resulted in more than a couch—Carol and David for the long haul; Rita and Mark, for a time.

Not getting the D.C. application, I interviewed in several neighboring jurisdictions in February. It was one of the worst winters in history and I spent that cold month slipping and sliding through the icy, curvy roads of the D.C. suburbs while not knowing my way around places like Falls Church, Virginia and Prince Georges County, Maryland—I still don't. I survived and ended up taking a special education job with the Montgomery County Public Schools. I began teaching at Rock Terrace High School in Rockville, Maryland on March 1, 1966—five weeks after moving to D.C.

Meeting David

I had just gotten out of an engagement. After four and a half years with Ivan, I was looking to be footloose and fancy-free. I had a few dates, including going out with a doctor several times, but there were no real sparks. That was fine as I was liking my new hometown and was satisfied with that.

I did discover through family that there were distant cousins who lived in D.C., Arnold and Elaine Levitt and their young sons, John and Mark. They were very welcoming to me as a newcomer. Unfortunately, after they separated, Elaine called me when she couldn't reach Arnold, and asked me to go with her to his apartment where we found him deceased in his bed. It was my first time seeing anyone not alive. I thought it would be frightening, but he actually looked peaceful, which was consoling to her then—and to me for a lifetime.

I hung out with a guy named Harry Davies once in a while. He lived in that Hamilton Arms complex—and was a roommate of Don Landers—and I had met him on my first trip that past summer. He was a lawyer, real tall, about 38 years old, and was from a well-known Maryland family who looked like they arrived on the Mayflower. And they actually had. When I moved up to D.C., he began calling me to play bridge. One night, he put his arm around me, obviously wanting to advance our friendship. I said, "Harry, I enjoy your company but you're my friend. Let's keep it that way."

We still got together a week later to play bridge. He said that he understood that he couldn't get anywhere with me because he wasn't Jewish. (I immediately thought being Jewish had nothing to do with it, but why not let him continue to believe that.) Harry then went on to say that he knew a young man named David Schwartz who was Jewish, about 26 years old, a lawyer who had gone to Columbia Law School, and was from New York. Harry said, "He's very smart, has a great sense of humor, and sounds very nice." Harry had never actually met David, thus the "he sounds nice" comment. But they talked on phone all the time as David was a real estate lawyer and Harry was an attorney for one of the title insurance companies David's firm used. Harry announced that night that he was going to get the two of us together.

Meanwhile, I was having a decent time and enjoying my freedom so I didn't pick up on it. David Schwartz worked at the law firm of Arent, Fox, Kintner, Plotkin and Kahn, and was dating the boss's daughter, Margie Arent, who was away at graduate school.

It had been a fix-up by the boss/father, Al Arent. So David didn't encourage Harry either.

A couple of weeks later, the last day of February, Harry and I had just finished playing bridge with a couple at his apartment. As soon as they left at about 8 p.m. that Sunday night, Harry said, "Since I'm not getting anywhere with either of you, I'm calling David Schwartz right now." I said, "No, Harry," but he already had David on the phone. He then said to David, "I'm sick of trying to get you two together so here, talk to each other," as he handed the phone to me. It was basic small chit-chat for a minute.

Then David asked where I lived and I said 800 4th St, S.W. David exclaimed that was unbelievable as he lived in the other building in the same development at 301 G St., S.W. He then asked when I was coming home and I answered about 11 p.m. (I had actually planned on going home earlier, but I said 11 in order to discourage any attempt to meet that evening.) I also was starting my teaching job the next morning and said so. Undeterred David said, "I'll meet you at 11. What's your apartment number?"

I was so put off by that. I would have yelled, "Are you kidding, buster? You can't ask me out for a soda tomorrow night? You're just going to run to my apartment at 11 p.m. to give me a look over? How obnoxious of you. And I have no intentions of meeting you then or any other time." But I didn't say any of that. I agreed because Harry was standing right there. He was my friend and seemed so happy about this. I didn't want to disappoint him.

So at 11 p.m. on February 28, 1966, I arrived at my apartment and there was David H. Schwartz. I saw him down the long hallway. He was standing right outside my door in a casual disheveled-looking outfit. And I was not impressed. I guess he was okay looking. But he wasn't very tall—about 5'8". He wore glasses. He was not an Adonis. And me, I've got on this giant, thick, bright-pink flowing coat. I was not skinny and this fuchsia thing made me look even bigger. It probably made me look like I weighed 300 pounds instead of the 155 I did weigh. I also didn't wear makeup in those days. All in all, I didn't look so hot myself.

Politely, I invited him in. Everything about this scene was so not pleasant for me—not just his looks (or lack thereof), but the audacity of his inviting himself over to give me a once-over at practically midnight the night before a work day—and my first work day in D.C. But I tried to be civil. I asked if he wanted something to drink. He said, "Yea, what do you have?" I said we had iced tea, cola, lemonade. He remarked, "Don't you have wine, beer, liquor?" We didn't have any of that stuff. I think I ended up handing him a glass of water.

So we sat there at the rented dining room table in the little living room drinking our water. And he started lecturing. He just started talking *at* me. He was not asking me about myself. He just lectured about religion and politics—the things you're not supposed to talk about on a first date if you would even call this scene a date. He was smart and knew it. It was like Stanley Levitt, my father, who lectured on every subject all my life. Dad thought he was the end all and be all of all intelligence. And here was a replication—but shorter and not nearly as good looking. But unlike my father, David, especially in those days, was the classic New York liberal Jewish person. I really didn't agree with him on anything he was saying. He was just going on and on, not noticing my lack of enthusiasm for his speechifying. Meanwhile, there were no questions like, "Why did you move here? How long have you lived here?" NOTHING.

He went on and on and on. I know I'm going on and on now about his going on and on. But I just really want you to get the picture, and it's still so much less than what I received that night. I don't even know how he got on those subjects. I didn't really care. I was so not attracted to him. I sat there listening for what seemed like a very long while.

I finally said, during one of his long proclamations, one word: "Bullshit." That was it—the only word I could get in edgewise.

Now keep in mind this was 1966, a very different time. An overweight Jewish girl with no family money or connections, who went to a state school for college and who was still not married at the old age of 22, did not say such a thing to a "Prince." And what, you may ask, is a "Prince"? It is an eligible Jewish man who was either a doctor or a lawyer, especially one from a prestigious Ivy League school. You just didn't do it. You were supposed to hang on the guy's every word. I knew the rules. I just couldn't follow them—still can't.

But I actually did get this guy, whatever his name was, to finally stop speaking. It was like throwing cold water on him. He just looked at me, stunned.

David was an only child of older parents, who were both the youngest of large, nearby families. So he was surrounded by a huge extended family in which he was the only one to have gone to college, much less law school. So he was used to everyone—not just his dates and parents—but everyone hanging on his every word.

Now here I was some pudgy gal with no makeup, without much class, a little like Ma Kettle visits the big city, calling his lecturing "bullshit."

I remember silence. Then he said, "Nobody's ever said anything like that to me." I said, "Well, maybe they should have. You don't even ask me out for a soda. No, you had to come over here to look me over at 11:00 at night. Then you walk in and go on like a professor."

I didn't use the word "insufferable." I'm sure I would have if I had known the word then. But "bullshit"—a word I did know well—certainly got the point across. I think he just became enthralled by me. I had the nerve to say something like that to him and he couldn't believe it.

As David turned around to leave, he said, "I guess I got off to a bad start. How about letting me take you out for dinner on Saturday night?" Even though I sincerely wasn't interested in him, I thought at least I had to give it a shot for Harry. How bad could one real date be? At least I could tell my bridge pal, "Okay, I went out with him and there just wasn't anything there but thanks for trying." I already had my speech for Harry ready. I was not looking forward to the date and told my roommates so.

David: The Beginning

The night of the dinner David came to pick me up. Rita opened the door when he arrived. She came back to my bedroom and said, "What are you talking about? He's very nice looking." I said, "Maybe he sent a friend."

I went out to the living room, and she was absolutely right. He was standing there in a suit and tie. When I first met him, that bedraggled casual outfit that he had just thrown together did nothing for him. Also, the suit and tie even made him carry himself differently. I thought, "He *is* attractive."

And he couldn't have been more gentlemanly. We went out to dinner to one of the ritziest French restaurants in town, Sans Souci on 17th St., N.W. I got the feeling he really liked me because that night he had gotten all of his ducks in a row. He had friends join us for dinner: a lawyer colleague at the firm and another lawyer who was on the Board of the American Civil Liberties Union (ACLU), and their then wives.

I was so impressed by them, the food and the atmosphere. I did notice that David had a couple of drinks before dinner, several glasses of wine with the meal and an after-dinner liqueur, as did several of his friends, which was totally a first for me to witness as I had never seen so much drinking. I remember thinking that, "At least he seems to hold it well." I drank my usual soda.

After dinner, we went to the Holiday Inn on Rhode Island Ave. near 14th St., N.W., which had a great piano bar where the drinking continued. We watched Carmen McCrae perform. Wow! She was great. David had Ardith and David Myerson, his good friend from law school and his wife, meet us there and they brought along another couple. The Myersons were quite a glamorous duo. In fact, all of his friends were sophisticated and smart. I had my usual feelings of inadequacy, but it was mostly muted as we got to know one another and listened to the wonderful music.

David created an incredible impression that night. He had all these friends. Little did I know that they were basically the sum total of his friends, other than his few glee club pals from NYU. When I went home that night I thought, "Ooh, I like this man."

Ardith has said that she called David that very night as soon as he got home. The way she tells it, she stated, "I love that woman. Marry her. She's perfect for you." She said he said, "I think I will."

After our first real date, David called several times, and when I mentioned that I was trying to do my taxes—Dad had always done them before—he came over and did them for me—seeing up close and personal how little money I had. We went out another time after that but no advances—and only a few calls. He did say he went to New York occasionally and if I wanted a ride to call.

David wasn't forward at all. I think he really liked me, but it may have scared him. The positivity from his friends may have scared him even more. Plus, he wasn't that experienced in relationships. Other than Margie Arent, I think he had only briefly dated a couple of other women.

After I hadn't heard from him in a while, I called and asked if he was going up to New York anytime soon. I wanted to visit my grandparents over spring break from teaching. He said in fact he was going up to New York then and suggested we drive together.

That weekend he took me up to the Bronx to meet his mother. His mom and I seemed to hit it off pretty well until the fact that I was a Republican came up. How it came up, I don't remember but I could see that her attitude changed.

It was interesting to see the walk-up apartment where David grew up on Walton Ave. and 177th St. So I got to see that we were financial equals. (In fact, after we married and were surrounded by some very rich friends who had married richer friends, I would often privately joke, "In comparison to those guys, David and I were really a merger of poverty.")

While in New York, I stayed with my grandparents. They met David when he came to pick me up for dinner one night. My grandma Bonnie had the same reaction as Rita. She was effusive: "Oh, what a marvelous young man. He's perfect, everything I would want for you." This was in spite of the fact that he did not come from a wealthy family, which was her real preference for me. He actually came from a lower-income family.

Both of my grandmothers used to say that "it's just as easy to fall in love with a rich man as a poor one." I found over the years I tended to do just the opposite. I seemed to fall in love with more people who were not of means. I guess I wanted to be part of building any success rather than inheriting it—or marrying into it.

Grandma Bonnie just fell in love with his looks, his demeanor, and what he did for a living. Unlike Ivan who was too Jewish for her and the rest of my family's taste, David was just right. He carried himself like he had been manner-born. He knew about and liked good wines. He said as a kid he used to read *The New Yorker*, *Gentlemen's Quarterly* (*GQ*), and other such magazines in which he learned about the good life, and it was something he strived for. It certainly wasn't my thing, but I found his worldliness appealing. He was just born with class. I was born without it—I think I have developed some over the years, but the down-homeness is the still the prevalent characteristic, and that's fine with me.

After that weekend, David and I saw each other more frequently. But he tended to call at the last minute, assuming I would just be available. One time, a glee club friend who lived in California was coming to town. David called and said, "We're having dinner with Joel tomorrow night." I said, "I can't do that because I have a date." And he said, "Break it." I answered, "No." He could not believe I would do such a thing.

I found out later that he spent the whole evening with Joel fretting about my having a date, and not breaking it for him. I think Joel set him straight about his presumptuousness about me with no commitment from him. In fact, David came over late that night, quite drunk, to talk it over. That should have been a clue. Instead, after that, we became more involved.

When David and I got serious, he broke up with Margie Arent, who I understand was hurt. David did feel like it put a strain on his relationship with the big boss, who had arranged their dating.

Let's go back a few years. When David graduated from Columbia Law School in 1963 as a Harlan Fiske Stone Scholar, one of his professors he'd gotten to know well asked if he would be interested in moving to Washington, D.C. David, having spent his entire life in New York, including college and law school, was thrilled to move away. It turned out that this professor had a cousin who had recently started, along with others, a law firm in D.C. called Arent Fox, and he thought David would be a great fit. Turned out he was.

After David had been with the firm for a year or so, the lead partner, Al Arent, invited him to his house for a party. Once there he discovered all the guests were much older except for himself and the boss's daughter. Obviously a set-up was at work. David was a little slow in these matters and nothing came of it.

Then Al invited him over for Passover. It was just the immediate family, including the boss's daughter Margie—and David. Once again, he didn't get the hint. Margie then called him and said her folks had given her tickets to the symphony and would he join her. Finally, David caught on and they started dating until he and I were on solid ground.

I was always baffled that he picked me. He was a poor boy from the Bronx and her parents were very rich. He could have written his own ticket. So I remember thinking she must be chunky or unattractive or something. I did meet Margie once many years later. She was obviously smart, a Fulbright Scholar, and slim, pretty and nice. I guess her only flaw was not saying "bullshit."

As we were dating, I would have been willing to sleep with David. I had slept with Ivan that second semester of our junior year as I did not want to marry someone without having done that. David knew about Ivan and knew that if he wanted to sleep together, I was willing. But he didn't push it. In fact, he said we would likely get married soon so why not just wait. I went along—a characteristic that ended up being consistent in our marriage.

Terms of Engagement

I did go with Ivan as a friend to Carol Ablon and David Pensky's June wedding in Dallas six months after we had broken up. I let him know that night I would probably be getting engaged soon.

(I still remain intrigued with Carol and my similarities. She and I were both Carol J.'s [middle name] from Texas who had one sibling—a brother named John—who both were raised with limited means, who moved to D.C. together and who within months married David H.'s, each originally from the Bronx and also of limited means. David Pensky soon opened Britches men's stores, my David did well in law, while Carol and I went into politics—but in different parties. Only there the similarity ended.)

My parents' initial reaction to my being with David was, "What? David Schwartz?" Being so non-Jewish themselves, they were surprised I'd end up with someone Jewish again. After the wedding, I went to Midland. David was set to fly in two days later to meet my family. I had told him all about my background and our sort of shack-like house on the poor side of town.

My parents picked me up at the airport. But instead of heading to the house, they veered in another direction. I asked, "Where are we going?" They responded, "Some friends invited us over." That should have made me suspicious as they had so few friends.

We pulled up to Sutton Place Apartments. It was the nicest apartment development in town (and interestingly, the same name as my paternal grandparents' building and street). My parents claimed that their friends had left the door open and we should just come on up to the second floor. We walked up the stairs and into this beautifully decorated large one-bedroom apartment. Finally, they announced, "This is our new home."

What had happened was my grandmother in New York, who only came once to Midland because she couldn't stand the way my parents lived, called up my father after meeting David and liking him. She ordered, "You are not going to let this young man come into that horrible place you live in. You will leave that hovel and get a nice place to show him." That's exactly what they did.

It was amazing to me that my mom and dad after that conversation just left the house where they had lived for nearly 15 years. It was even more amazing to me that my dad, who was the boss of everyone and everything, could be so intimidated by his own powerful, 4'11" petite mother.

The new apartment was magnificently furnished and had pots, pans, paintings, and practically everything else. They really didn't need much for the move, which was good since they really didn't have much. So they packed one suitcase apiece and never went back to get the rest of their clothes. They were done. They left everything just as it was and the old house became a storage unit.

It was a good move for them, especially for Mom. She loved to swim, and she met a lot of nice people hanging out by the pool. So that move opened up her world some, thank goodness.

But at the time, I resented it. Here I had told David all about how I was this poor kid from the south side of town. Instead, he'd see my family suddenly in the nicest complex in Midland surrounded by lovely furnishings. How deceptive—like I had lived in such luxury all my life when I hadn't even for a minute! But I couldn't rain on their parade. I said how nice everything was, although inside I was just furious at their rewriting our history.

Johnny came into town the next day and was thrilled about the new place. The following day, the four of us picked David up at the airport. As we were driving home with Johnny, David and I in the back seat, no one was talking. It was all a bit awkward. Then Johnny spoke up: "David, I have one question. [pause] What are your intentions?" We all burst out laughing and the ice was broken. It was so precious. That was Johnny.

That night, after we got back from having dinner, David and I went out alone. I immediately took him to the old house. We sat on the outside step of the place where I had so many lonely and harsh memories—but it *was* my home. So it was fitting that it was there that David asked me to marry him. There was no ring, which I didn't care about anyway—just a request. I said yes. This was the right time, the right place, and the right person.

I was 22, and by Texas—especially Midland—standards, that was old to be getting married, particularly for the first time. At least it was my second engagement. But in their minds, that really didn't count. Friends actually told me that they had been having worried discussions about me: "She was always sort of a pretty girl. I wonder what's wrong with her." (Imagine how they felt about Laura Bush, another Midlander—but not one I knew—who didn't get married until age 31, speaking of a pretty girl.) I always found it interesting that in Midland getting married at 22 was considered old, whereas in D.C. I was thought of as practically a child bride. Oh well, just another example of how I never really fit in.

Sort-of Wedding

David and I got engaged at the beginning of July. We flew back to Washington and right away, I went up to New York where we decided to have the wedding. There was no temple in Midland and we did not belong to anything in D.C. yet. Furthermore, his mother and my grandparents lived in New York, and my grandparents belonged to Temple Emanu-El in midtown so we could use their membership to get married there. Since we planned the wedding for August 28th, the turnaround was quick—only seven and a half weeks. We rushed because we wanted to have the wedding while I was still on summer break from teaching, with time to devote several days to a honeymoon before school began after Labor Day. As before, I had to do all the arrangements myself.

The pressure about the wedding started immediately. My mom and dad were saying, "We don't want to spend much money." My soon-to-be mother-in-law, Blanche, who I called "Ma," wanted to invite everybody she had met on the subway. My grandparents, who were not contributing one cent to the wedding, were saying, "You only get married once. You should do things first-class." Pressure was coming from every direction.

I had always loved the Plaza Hotel, and I decided I'd rather have something simple there than something less simple elsewhere. I was determined to get my dream place on a reasonable budget. Not easy to do but worth a try. So off I went to the Plaza and met with the head of catering, who asked, "What do you want?" I responded, "Cheap." The head of catering was struck. "I've been working here for years and no one has ever said 'I need the cheapest thing.'" But he seemed to like my honesty. We worked together well and both decided that the best way to spend the least amount of money was to have an early afternoon wedding and then a wedding tea. We would serve finger sandwiches, cheese and crackers with some fruit, one hors d'oeuvres-type thing but I can't remember what, punch, and then champagne to have a toast with the wedding cake.

With that happily accomplished, I then went to Grand St. in the Lower East Side with Ma, who had told me they had discount wedding dress shops there. I got a sample size-12 wedding dress, which they cleaned, and even threw in the veil—all for $100. And by the way, I had seen a similar dress at Bergdorf Goodman for about $600, so I was really pleased. I found the florist and the photographer and told them we were on a tight budget.

I got back home to D.C. and we put the list together for about 100 people. But David and I knew that many of our out-of-town friends and family might not make it with so little advance notice. This was perfect because we'd get the credit for inviting them, they'd get an easy out, and my parents would not have to spend the additional money.

At the end of July, David and I traveled up to New York for the weekend to do our blood work as well as to address the invitations with David's mother. Those invitations ended up being a wedding gift from the printing company where Ma worked part-time as a bookkeeper. In the Bronx at her place on Sunday, we addressed and stuffed envelopes. Thank goodness we did not seal them. That was to be Monday's job. Meanwhile, Ma kept adding to her list. My folks kept complaining about the cost. My grandparents were urging me to make the reception more sumptuous. (Imagine thinking finger sandwiches and punch weren't sumptuous enough!)

(I cannot avoid as I'm writing this book 51 years later finding some humor in this experience. Truthfully, though, it was a very stressful and sad time when it should have been a happy one. I was really working hard by myself in a short period of time to put together a nice wedding. Instead, it was so unpleasant. I became very upset, especially with my parents. When I worked at the store, starting at age eight, they said they put the money I made aside for a college of my choice. But then they made me go to the University of Texas because it was just $50 a semester. At that point, they said they'd give me a nice wedding with the money that I had earned as a child. When my wedding arrived, I did all the preparations—on the cheap—and they still were giving me a hard time about the minimal cost. It seemed so unfair and uncalled for.)

That Sunday night, after we addressed the invitations, Mom and Dad called me at my grandparents' apartment and gave me more grief. I called David in the Bronx, crying. They were driving me crazy. The next morning David phoned and said, "The hell with all this. Let's just get married tomorrow." I said, "Let me think about it," which I did as he drove to pick me up for the planned blood work. When he arrived, I said, "That's a good idea."

We called my parents to tell them, "Since all the fun has been taken out of our wedding, we are just getting married tomorrow." They didn't try to talk us out of it. Mom went to the airport and sat there a while—there was an airline strike—until she could get on a flight. My dad didn't even bother to try to come.

The invitations never got sealed and mailed that day. Instead we ordered announcements and replaced the invitations with them using the same envelopes, which we sealed and mailed later.

The wedding took place on August 2, 1966 at 6 p.m. in Rabbi Julius Mark's chambers—we didn't need the chapel for nine people. Aside from the Rabbi, David and I, the guests included our mothers, my grandparents, the maid of honor Ann Gilbert (my Midland friend who was getting her Ph.D. in geology at Columbia), and the best man Peter Reill (David's glee club friend from NYU). Thank goodness they were available on 24-hour notice.

Rabbi Mark was the legendary head of Temple Emanu-El for 20 years from 1948 to 1968. The Temple itself, located on Fifth Ave. is the oldest Reform temple in New York City, and at that time had the largest Reform congregation membership in the United States. (Interestingly enough, I was serving on the Board of Washington Hebrew Congregation [WHC] in the mid-1990s, when it surpassed the Manhattan Temple Emanu-El in membership, giving WHC that distinction.)

For the short-notice wedding, I was able to re-arrange the florist and photographer. The head of catering at the Plaza was so nice. Not only did he give me back the entire deposit, but he threw in a beautiful wedding cake for the dinner we planned for seven people in the Edwardian Room of the Plaza Hotel (the Rabbi and Ann could not make the dinner). The whole affair cost less than $900, including dinner; the limo, which took us and then the whole wedding party the six blocks to the Plaza; dress and veil; some pictures; the bouquet and corsages; a centerpiece; and a contribution we made to the Temple. That did not include the $10 gold wedding band I had given David and the $5 one he gave me. (By the way, I did end up getting an engagement ring before the wedding because David's mother's oldest sister Helen passed away, leaving Ma her ring. So Ma then generously gave me her own ring, which we quickly got reset.)

Sort-of Honeymoon

We stayed at the Plaza that night and traveled right back to Washington. We had booked four days in S. Yarmouth, Cape Cod, Massachusetts for our honeymoon four weeks later. I had paid for that as David only had $300 in his bank account. He always bought nice work clothes and even took a cab to and from work. So with that plus student loans, he never saved. I, on the other hand, rarely bought anything (boy, have I changed!) and had $1,200 in my savings account. (This was actually quite impressive as I only made $4,800 a year before taxes teaching in Austin and just a little more in Montgomery County.) So the honeymoon was my treat, but David certainly made it up to me in spades over the years.

At the end of August on our way to the Cape, we stopped at the Roxy Delicatessen—David's favorite—in the Bronx and had lunch with now my mother-in-law. Being a Southern girl, I ordered my usual: corn beef on white bread with mayonnaise—exactly the way I like my baloney sandwiches growing up minus the onions. This turned out to be quite an unusual order at a New York Jewish deli, even this non-kosher one. The owner actually came out of the kitchen to meet the person who ordered "that" as it was a first.

I have one of my fondest memories from that stop-over in New York. We took a carriage ride and David sang to me. Our song was "Strangers in the Night" by Frank Sinatra. I think it exemplified our being conscious of our short-span relationship.

After our three-night honeymoon, we returned to our newly rented one-bedroom apartment at a place called Parkside off Wisconsin Ave. a little north of Bethesda, Maryland. Although we both preferred D.C., we were able to get so much more for our money further out and besides, I was working in nearby Rockville so it was in between our two jobs. We were living on a budget. I now made $5,300 as a teacher; David made $8,400 as an associate at Arent Fox. We decided to live on David's salary and save mine as we owned no furniture, not even our mattress—all were leased. In addition to saving for that, we wanted to travel before starting a family—because neither of us had ever really traveled.

Since we both worked, David did not seem to mind helping me with the domestic chores. (I just caught myself saying something I hate: "*helping me*" with the chores. Even with both people working, housework was thought of as the woman's job—and the man was generously helping her, which I went along with, but now believe was unfair.) Anyway, I did the cooking, bed making, cleaning and grocery shopping. David did the vacuuming and the laundry.

(When David and I were dating, he told me an inside story about how he hated to do chores around his mom's apartment as a kid. So when she asked him to put out the trash, he would make sure as he headed from the kitchen through the living room and the entranceway to the outside, to strewn a few things on the floor. It worked. She never asked him to throw out the trash again or assigned him any other duty. Thus, whenever David helped around our place, and screwed up the task, I would say, "Honey, I'm not your mother. It ain't gonna work here." He seemed to get a kick out of that. I still bet he was sorry he told me that story.)

But I was glad to have his help. And even though I was very neat and he not so much, he did try which I appreciated. What I did not appreciate was that every single night at dinner from day one, David would spend the entire meal complaining about work. It was usually about his feeling that everyone was out to get him. At that point, I just became his counselor—trying to reassure him that could not possibly be the case given a recent raise or positive comments he'd received. He also didn't like the work, which we discussed a lot too. Dinner was such a downer each night.

In attempts to brighten his mood, I had lots of little casual dinner parties with close friends. I may have done so anyway, since growing up in a closed home, I wanted ours to be open. I had never cooked other than being a helper for Grandma Carrie, but really did attempt to make good meals. I always wanted to be the best wife, the best teacher, the best cook, the best friend, the best decorator, the best counselor, the best everything—not easy to accomplish—and probably not easy for those watching me try.

More on David: His Upbringing

As mentioned, David didn't enjoy being a commercial real estate lawyer nor the low salaries that were being paid to entry-level lawyers in those days. But he did love the thought of the money he could eventually make in that field. David had grown up in the Bronx with parents who had very little financial resources. His father, Herman, worked in a bank and died at age 56 of heart disease when David was only 19. I obviously never met his dad, and when I tried to find out about him and the rest of the family from David and his mom, I could get little information. David was talkative about the things he cared about—Shakespeare, politics, music, his views on various subjects—but not his family or his upbringing.

David's mom, "Ma," was equally reserved about everything. I did know she was home full-time when he was growing up, taking care of the apartment and her son. Her social outlets were with family and a few friends, which included playing mahjong. She started working part-time as a bookkeeper after her son was grown. And interestingly, Ma's maiden name was also Schwartz. When she married Herman Schwartz, she became Blanche Schwartz Schwartz—or in foreign tongues, White Black Black.

Ma and Herman married when they were both in their 30s. Each of them was the youngest of large families and they wanted their own right away. Ma had several miscarriages before giving birth to David at age 37. I did meet the large extended family at several Sunday brunches in the Bronx over our early years. Those brunches had taken place every Sunday for decades. I watched as the entire family made over David—his brains, looks and talents, which I understand had gone on all of his life. (I must admit I did somewhat envy what appeared to be lifelong and constant reinforcement from that whole big clan.)

David was a smart student and was always in the advanced programs at school. He was expected to go to the Bronx High School of Science. But in spite of his mom getting the application and watching him fill it out, he never mailed it. He didn't tell her until it was too late to do anything about it. He told me that he just did not want to go there. He was sick of smart kids like himself and just wanted to be in a school for "normal" students.

David also grew up in a culture where you were expected to succeed. As a student in Howard Taft High School in the Bronx, he intended to become a doctor. But he hated the sight of blood. And where he grew up, what did you do if you were smart but couldn't stand the sight of blood? You became a lawyer. And that's what he did—and became a good one.

David went to New York University. At the time the school had a campus at University Heights in the Bronx so he could easily commute from Walton Avenue. He was accepted to go to Harvard and Yale for law school where they both offered him a full scholarship, but no housing. With no money to pay for room and board at those schools, he took instead the full scholarship offered by Columbia Law School where he could go and still live at home. Several summers while he was in college, he did take a job as a waiter at one of the hotels in the Catskills in order to earn the money he needed for books, commuting, and school expenses.

After I learned all this, I did resent the fact that his mom did not work when her brilliant son—her only child—was younger so she could better enable his advancement. Although Columbia is hardly chopped liver, why couldn't he at least have gotten the room and board money from his mom, instead of being denied Harvard and Yale as choices, and having to remain living at home? We never discussed it, but I think he felt the same.

By the way, David liked to tell this story about his time in the Catskills: The waiters got paid very little money as they were expected to get most of their salary from tips. At these hotels, a family would come for a week and would usually only tip the last day. Often though, it appears, some families would just try to drive away without tipping. So each Saturday the waiters would line up outside to thwart the getaway of the people who were trying to stiff them. Sometimes they'd even hoist their bodies onto the windshields so the culprits couldn't see to drive away. Quite a picture, but it seemed to work.

CHAPTER 7

Back to School

After Labor Day in September of 1966, I returned to my job at Rock Terrace High School, which I loved. It was an all-special education school for 13 to 21-year-olds, and had a cross-section of students who were physically challenged, emotionally and/or intellectually disabled, or had discipline issues. (The last category came from other schools, and at the time they were able to foist them on us instead of dealing themselves.) So there were kids with 40 IQs next to a kid with a high IQ who happened to be in a wheelchair. I had 15 students in my class with no assistant. It was an enormous challenge—probably would not even be allowed today.

In my first year of Rock Terrace, across the hall from me was another teacher named Jeff Stamos [name change]. He was a tall, huge, nice-looking Greek guy. He was married to a lovely German woman and we were friendly as couples for a long time.

The first day of school, all the kids were saying, "I want to be in her class," meaning me. Here I was—a short, non-intimidating-looking 22-year-old. And they looked at him, this great big guy and decided I was the way better choice. Then by the second week they were all begging to get in his class because I was such a strict disciplinarian. Meanwhile, Jeff's kids were out of control. They were roaming the halls and causing chaos in the class, while my students behaved, even the ones with supposed disciplinary problems. So once again, you can't tell a book by its cover.

(I found at an early age that when you're a young, short, friendly-looking female, you really have to work so much harder to be taken seriously and to get respect. Nothing has changed.)

While at Rock Terrace, I was elected as a union representative and I had the great honor of receiving tenure after only one year of teaching in that system, although the standard was two. I was also invited to be a member of the review and evaluation committee for instructional materials, which was unusual for a new teacher. I loved the principal, an older African American man named Dr. Louis Monk, and I admired the work he did—and valued his appreciation of me.

Back to D.C.

David and I really didn't like living in the suburbs as we missed D.C. There was really nothing wrong with it—we just liked being in the city. We had a year lease at the Bethesda apartment, but broke it after nine months. We really wanted to leave after six and gave the landlord three months' notice. We hoped they would rent the apartment early, which I presume they did because they never came after us for the rest of the year's rent.

Moving out of the city for that short period was a cure-all. We decided then and there that we would rather live in a smaller house in the city than get more space outside of it. Being in D.C. proper was just more valuable to us (even before my political life), and we never thought about living elsewhere again. We moved to a much smaller one-bedroom apartment on MacArthur Blvd., N.W., not far from Georgetown. Beginning then I started to say, "I'd rather live in a tent in the city than a mansion in the suburbs."

Box of Letters

I used to keep a box of special personal letters I received from my old boyfriends and close girlfriends. Apart from this, I also kept every letter I ever received from all my family members and other friends, but they were back in Texas. I was a hoarder of such things at a very early age. This special box, though, contained treasured material including letters and poems I received from boyfriends such as Dan Everett, Charles, and even my first junior high school boyfriend, Ronnie Morelock. There were letters from Ivan, Andrew, Duke and others. As soon as I got married, I thought that maybe it was not appropriate to keep such things, so I threw the box away. I have regretted it ever since. I would have loved to have kept those mementos and to look over them when I felt lonely during my marriage and after. Oh well ...

Out of regret for throwing away that box, I have rarely thrown anything out since. I keep tons of scrapbooks that contain all the letters I've ever gotten and even small items like phone messages and old covers of matchbooks from restaurants. I became a real environmentalist, even if not originally intended. All the scrapbooks are categorized by year. I must be the most organized hoarder in America, if not the world. I'm sure my kids will make a big bonfire out of all that stuff when I'm gone. (And I have—and do—apologize to them for not being able to get rid of it myself.)

Fun Times

Our first more formal evening of entertaining took place at our new apartment on MacArthur Blvd. We invited a business friend and his wife over for coffee and dessert after they took us to the theater. Although I had not made the dessert before, I knew I had this in the bag—or in this case, the box. Someone had given us a silver-plated pie dish as a wedding present, so I decided to make a banana cream pie, using the instant banana cream custard package you buy in the store with simple instructions, and then put some whipped cream and bananas on top. I could do that—and I did.

We got to the apartment where I had set the table earlier with nice plates and forks. I brought out my lovely pie from the refrigerator and announced that we were having banana cream pie to some "oohs" and "ahs." I excitedly cut into the first pie I ever made. As soon as I took the first piece out, the area where it came from filled in. I was horrified, but I didn't laugh, I didn't cry. I just picked up the plates and forks and replaced them with bowls and spoons, and said, "Did I say pie? I meant banana cream pudding!"

During our early marriage one of our favorite activities was to go to see the Washington Senators play baseball at RFK Stadium in the years before the team left for Texas. I always looked forward to D.C. getting a new team and was glad we finally did (and little did I know that I would end up being part of bringing it back after a tough fight for a fairer contract in 2005).

We went out every week or so to our favorite eateries—A.V. Italian restaurant at New York Ave. and 6th St., N.W. (a landmark until it closed several years ago) and the Astor, a Greek restaurant on M near 19th St., N.W., which has been gone for decades.

We hung out a lot with the Myersons, who lived in the Capitol Park development in Southwest D.C., where David and I coincidently both lived when we started dating. As they had a young daughter named Marni, we usually went over there on Sundays after having dinner at a fast food joint like Roy Rogers or Arby's, and played Monopoly into the evening. I would always go bankrupt very early (due to bad luck of the dice) and would have to sit there and watch the others play for hours, which was really no fun. One night, after a year of this Sunday activity with always the same result, I went bankrupt after just 15 minutes and started crying. I wasn't such a big crybaby in those days, but I guess I just had had it. Still nothing disrupted the weekly games—or my losing.

I really liked Ardith a lot but was intimidated by her overwhelming glamour—her New York sophistication, upscale clothes, and perfect makeup. I was dying to impress her. One night early in our marriage, we were meeting them for a movie downtown and while walking on 14th St. near G, I came upon a store: Simca of Fifth Avenue. Seeing that New York name, I thought, "Oh, that's a place where Ardith probably shops!" I bought a pair of shoes and strutted to meet the three of them, knowing I would finally score some points. When I arrived, I prominently and proudly showed off my shopping bag. They just started laughing. It turns out that Simca's was the Payless Shoes of its day, at best. I bombed out again, but did enjoy the hilarity of it as well—sort of.

Another night we went out to that same movie theater downtown with the Myersons to see *Goodbye, Columbus* with Richard Benjamin and Ali MacGraw (who factored in my life later on). About midway through the movie, where every seat was occupied, Richard Benjamin appeared with his shirt off, displaying his trim, not very macho body. David blurted out for all to hear, "Another great Jewish physique," to some laughter. After the movie, David and I left quickly because the garage was closing. Later, Ardith called and said they ended up walking out with Charlton Heston and his wife Lydia. Darn—I hate to miss anything!

One Sunday afternoon, David and I traveled up to Columbia, Maryland, which was a new planned town a little south of Baltimore—keeping up our free activities. While sitting toward the back of the bus on the tour of what the driver was describing as a "real city," David yelled out again, "But where are the poor people?" The guide took umbrage even at the question, saying, "We don't have any poor people." At which point David replied, "Then you are not a real city." (I always appreciated David calling it as he saw it—and usually humorously.)

Music Fans

David and I went to see live music at venues like Blues Alley, a well-known jazz club, as well as plays—not at first but as we could afford them. I was always star-struck and would wait outside the stage door to get autographs from the likes of Peter O'Toole, Eddie Fisher and Lana Turner. I was such an enthusiastic concert-goer and autograph seeker that I remember jumping over the fence at Carter Barron Amphitheater in D.C. to get an autograph from Andy Williams. One of our favorite performers was a dynamic local singer named Phil Flowers, who was kind of like an African American Tom Jones. We got acquainted with him through someone who worked in David's office and we became Phil Flowers devotees. We followed him around to his every show and I collected each flyer and program, and we got to be friends.

Soon we became more than fans with another singer. David was in a cab in D.C. when the female cab driver broke into song.

He came running home and said, "I have just heard the most fabulous voice. Her name is Beulah Barnes (isn't that a great name?) and we're going to make her a star." David was so happy about his new discovery that I invited her over for dinner the next day. She did have a good voice. She was probably 55 years old and quite a character. I shared David's enthusiasm. We spent many nights over the next few months running around to the clubs in the area, trying to get her a gig, as well as working with her on her performance skills and song choices. And her stage moves did need some honing. When she sang the song "Pennies from Heaven" and got to the lyrics "upside-down," she would lift her arms in the air and then push them down with great drama. We tried to have her do it a little more subtly but were never very successful.

Beulah was practically a full-time evening and weekend job, which we enjoyed because we were so fond of her. We did succeed in getting her a few bookings where she earned a little money (and we were certainly doing our part totally for free). But unfortunately it turned out she was a better cab singer than she was a club one, and I think she preferred that as well. We stayed in contact with Beulah for a long time afterwards, but unfortunately lost touch as so often can happen.

It's obvious that a lot of our fun times revolved around music. In the early 1970s, David and I went to Las Vegas, which he especially liked as he enjoyed gambling. I did not because I'm too cheap. I would only drop my usual $20 at a then $2-a-bet blackjack table. Afterwards, I would watch others or move on to the live musical performances, which I enjoyed more. Back then, those were pretty cheap too.

(Speaking of Las Vegas and gambling: Once after an education conference in California in the 1970s relating to a National Advisory Council I served on, I had planned to meet a friend in Las Vegas for the weekend on the way home as you could do a free stop-over then. Linda couldn't make it at the last minute, and David talked me into going alone. The first night I just went to my room to order in dinner and sleep. At 10 a.m. the next morning, I decided to take the $60 I was prepared to lose to a $2 blackjack table—and to only bet $2 a deal, no more. Twenty-two hours later, I got up from that same table. I never ate. I only drank orange juice, sodas, and Bloody Mary mix. Good thing I had situated myself near a bathroom. At 8 a.m. the next morning, I left with still $23 of the original $60, rushed to my room to pack and then on to the airport just in time to catch my 10 a.m. flight home.)

Now back to that trip David and I took in the early 1970s: My mom had a first cousin who lived in Denver. He and his wife went to Las Vegas all the time. David would make up these witty things about people when he thought there was something mysterious about them. Because this cousin was a gynecologist and always got front-row seats at the shows in the big hotels, David said he must be an abortionist for the Mafia. Everyone in David's imaginative mind was in the Mafia if they had extra money or connections.

That cousin could hook you up with those same good seats. I said to David, "I want to go to the Elvis show." David said, "You couldn't pay me to see Elvis." He had always liked show tunes and Frank Sinatra. And by that point, I had gotten him to listen to country music as well, which ultimately became his favorite; before that, David claimed he wouldn't listen to such noise. Yet, since our rule was whoever drives gets to pick the station, within months of our marriage he was addicted to country. But Elvis was beneath him; he wouldn't budge. Finally, I stated, "I love Elvis, and I'm going with or without you." David responded, "Okay, I'll go," but he was not a happy camper.

So we went to the concert, where we had seats next to the stage, thanks to the cousin. David sat there resentful and scowling, just trying to make sure it was no fun at all—to the point where I wished he had not agreed to go. Then the show began. The curtain remained closed. Orchestral music began to play that sounded like it came out of a biblical movie. It went on for about five minutes and really built up anticipation. It was like you were waiting for the curtain to part and for God to walk out. Finally, the curtain did part, Elvis appeared, and you weren't at all disappointed it wasn't God. Then he started performing.

This was Elvis in his chubbier stage. He had also begun to use karate moves in his act, done perfectly in time with the music. I had never seen him perform in person, but had watched his TV specials and even have to admit that I saw most of his movies.

As Elvis started singing a wide range of numbers, from "In the Ghetto," to "Don't Be Cruel," to "Are You Lonesome Tonight," I watched as David's whole expression changed. He became enthralled. David had very strong entrenched opinions and it was hard to lead him away from them. But he went from scowling to appreciation to admiration—all within the first 20 minutes. As much fun as it was watching Elvis, it was just as much fun watching David's transformation. He became a huge fan.

At intermission, I went to the ladies' room. As I was walking in, a gorgeous woman with beautiful green eyes was walking out. It was Priscilla Presley. They, though, divorced soon thereafter.

Elvis was the best performer we ever saw. He was on stage for over two hours and was mesmerizing. The most versatile performer we ever saw live was Sammy Davis Jr., who sang, danced, was humorous, and played several instruments well. Tina Turner was marvelous, who we saw from the second row at the Shady Grove Theater outside of D.C. Tony Bennett was good in the '70s, but he only did a 45-minute set at the Shoreham Hotel at a high cost with no encore. (But just several months ago, I saw Tony, now at age 90, for the second time live. He performed for over an hour, including a song without a microphone, after his quartet and daughter did their sets. And it was fabulous.) But Elvis is the King.

Worst Dressed List

One Saturday night in our early marriage, one of the partners at Arent Fox invited us to a charity costume ball—our first formal affair together. We were told that the attire was either costume or black tie. The black tie should have been a clue. When we walked in, everyone was decked out in either the most magnificent, elaborate costumes or in the most stunning gowns and tuxedos. When it came to us, it looked like we had just thrown on jeans, cowboy boots, and matching cowboy shirts—and we had, all from the General Clothing Store. We hadn't even splurged on a cowboy hat. We felt ridiculous and looked worse. I spent the whole first part of the evening sitting glued to my seat as I was so embarrassed about how under-dressed we were. We should have been on a hayride and not at the ballroom of the Washington Hilton. Even on the hayride, we would have gotten "worst dressed."

Then midway through the evening, the Master of Ceremonies stated there was going to be a costume competition. He invited those who wanted to compete up to the stage to be introduced and then to walk across the stage to be judged. It was not mandatory, only volunteer. The vast majority, even in their beautiful costumes, did not choose to participate. Only about 15 or 20 couples did out of the nearly two thousand people there. But David stood up and said, "Let's go." I was astonished: "Are you kidding?" David kept insisting. I then said, "Why would we want to draw more attention to ourselves? Haven't we humiliated our hosts enough?" But no. "Let's go. I've got this."

The next thing I know we were on the side of the stage and David was whispering something to the MC. I assumed he told him we were Roy Rogers and Dale Evans, which is what I had suggested as we were walking up. At least they did wear cowboy clothes. Instead when we walked across the stage, we were introduced as "Ferrante & Teicher" (a piano duo sort of popular in the '60s and '70s). What was he thinking? He just enjoyed making no sense at all. I barely made it across the stage from laughing. It was so absurd. There was some laughter from the audience, but I'm not sure if it was directed at the ridiculousness of the claim—or just at us. I still cringe when I think about this. (And our hosts never invited us anywhere again.)

And by the way, it was the first time I had seen Lynda Bird Johnson since that tragic day in college six years earlier. She was there with her handsome husband—and future Senator—in his tuxedo, while she looked lovely in a beautiful gown. I was so glad she didn't recognize me, or at least she pretended not to.

First Time Overseas

I was eager to start a family. David did want kids but his enthusiasm was less than mine. I guess most men are not as enthusiastic as women in this regard. But before we started that family, we yearned to see the world a little. Neither of us had ever been out of the country, other than my five-day family excursion to Mexico when I was 13. We took some of the money saved from my teacher's salary, and we went on a wonderful three-week tour of Europe (Paris, Brussels, Amsterdam and London) in mid-July of 1967. We also took a long weekend trip to Puerto Rico that fall.

Before we went on our European jaunt, we vowed that while there we would not buy anything for ourselves or anybody else as we still needed to return the rented furniture and buy our own. But in Paris, we went to Montmartre and on our way there we spotted a small, beautiful painting of a mother and a daughter in a store window. We traveled to look at the picture every single day, but kept our vow that we weren't going to buy anything. The last day in Paris we went to the store window to say goodbye to our painting—but it was gone.

We were so sad. The store owner saw us and came out. I said, "You sold our painting," with near tears in my eyes. He responded, "No, I have it. I just re-arranged the window as I do each week." At this point we realized we couldn't live without it. He sold it to us for only $80 with the frame and mentioned that he had seen this same artist in a shop on Bond St. in London selling for much more money. When we got to London, we did go by the shop and sure enough, there were several pictures by the same man, and they were several hundred dollars each.

(Not too long later, back in D.C., we went looking at model homes as we did most weekends because it was inexpensive entertainment. I saw a large print of what looked like the same French artist hung in a roped-off area of one of the homes. I told David, who scoffed at me, "Oh sure, they are making prints by the same painter of our original $80 oil painting." So I crawled under the rope and sure enough, it was the same artist. Then a few years later in an ad in the *Washingtonian Magazine* for an art investment firm, there was also a picture by that artist. David took ours there, got it appraised, and we were thrilled. So our little painting turned out to be a good investment, at least then, although we were totally ignorant of that at the time—and had just liked it. Later on, we did occasionally buy art with an investment value in mind and it didn't necessarily work out. *C'est la vie!*)

We celebrated our first anniversary in London and splurged by going to the very snooty restaurant at the Savoy Hotel. Our waiter, in the most upper-crust accent, said "May I tell you about our specialties?" I asked in my typical classiness, "What's good in the meat department?" Instead of being appalled, he let down his façade. His upper-crust British accent suddenly disappeared, and it turns out he was from Italy. And we became fast friends. He invited us out to dinner the next night, which was his day off. By then I had developed a terrible cold (how is that possible in sunny, warm London?) and was too sick to go, but insisted that David do so. I just asked that he bring me back something to eat when he returned. Little did I know that at 7 p.m., when he left his sick, generous wife—the one who encouraged him to go and the one who had no food nor did the hotel—he would arrive back at 2 a.m. with a cold McDonalds-type hamburger. Another *c'est la vie.*

Before my pneumonia-like sickness took over, David and I had a nice evening roaming the streets of London. At one point, I was outside while David went to the restroom. An elderly, distinguished-looking gentleman with a cane walked by me. Then he backed up several steps, looked me in the eye and said, "How much?" I replied immediately, "Too much" and he moved on. I high-fived myself for that quick comeback.

Because we lived up to our commitment about purchases in Europe, other than the painting, we still had the savings to be able to buy our first furniture sets out of the Sears Early American collection for our dining/living room, then a little more modern Sears set for the bedroom. Those items still reside in my current home.

A few years later, we took another European vacation. In Rome, David was buying cigarettes and I, while standing at the newsstand, spotted a man who looked familiar. I said, "You're that Frenchman from *The French Connection* (which was a very popular movie with Gene Hackman that had won the Academy Award earlier that year). Sure enough, it was he, who was actually a Spanish actor named Fernando Rey. We visited with him for a while and then he asked us to meet him the next night at the Via Veneto, which is like the Champs-Elysees of Rome. We did, and as we were sitting having a drink with him, I heard someone say, "Fernando?" I looked up and saw Jack Palance, a then well-known actor, with his beautiful daughter. They joined us. What a thrill—and certainly a far cry from reading movie magazines in Midland.

David Up Close

David and I exchanged many sweet notes when we were first married. "Stop working so hard, Pie," I'd write him. He wrote things like, "I love you, Pump. Love, Pump," short for "Pumpkin." After we had kids, he'd sign "Pumpkin Senior."

He was charming, funny and intelligent. We only knew each other five months—and had only dated seriously for two and a half months—before we got engaged in July and then married on August 2nd. That was hardly a long courtship, but we both seemed mature, felt we were in love, and at 26 and 22 years of age, marriage was the natural next step in those days.

Very soon thereafter, I discovered David had a good deal of sadness. I certainly had my own share of sadness from my childhood, but my innate positivity usually won out. I guess David had depression. The late '60s was a less enlightened time. (As time went on and more discussion on such things occurred, I became much smarter about it—as did we all.) David, through most of the years, was in denial about his mental state and the drinking problem that was adding to it. I used to urge him to go seek help and he would say, "You're my counselor." But my best counseling efforts weren't nearly enough and I told him so. And there were at least some anti-depressants available by the '70s. We actually knew several people who were on Lithium, which seemed to help them. Yet he refused to seek outside help either through therapy or medication, with the exception of two crisis periods later on.

Even though David had a great amount of confidence in his intelligence and capabilities, he had an even greater amount of paranoia, and it only seemed to revolve around his work. Most nights as we sat around the table having our dinner, starting even in those first few months of marriage, those demons dominated the conversation. I tried to remind him how appreciated he was at his office given his frequent raises and bonuses. I soon learned that reality and affirmation had nothing to do with it.

It was constant work to pick him up, and becoming harder with nobody there to pick me up. When he'd arrived at the house, I'd usually say, "Hi Honey. How was your day?" And then we would spend literally an hour or more talking about his bad day. But on the few times I would say my day wasn't good, he would immediately counter, "You think your day was bad? Wait until you hear about mine." And we never quite got back to my day.

I still kept trying to boost him. I usually wrote him notes that would say things like, "Good morning, Pump" or "I hope you have a good day, Honey." But as I was going through my scrapbooks recently in preparation for writing this book, I found one of my early notes to him, which read, "I love you. I just hope you stop your bad habit."

David would come home and immediately hit the liquor cabinet to get a Jack Daniels on the rocks and then more would follow. After dinner, when we had no plans, he would usually get into bed at 8 p.m. and be asleep soon thereafter. I guess he was using drinking as self-medication for depression. During our short dating period, we did not live together so I didn't see his habitual drinking. In retrospect, we should have lived together first. I certainly have advised my children and others to do just that.

I learned his drinking was a long-standing issue. It appeared to have started when David was 16 during the first semester of his freshman year in college. When he got together with his college glee club friends, all their stories involved drinking heavily.

At their concerts, they would have to take their belts off, link them together as one big belt, and then wrap that around all of them so one or more wouldn't fall off the risers. They would talk about participating in parades and how they would be out there peeing all over themselves because they were so drunk. The stories were pretty gross. Most of his glee club buddies ended up having drinking problems as well.

There were, though, good moments. David loved to sing. Sometimes in bed, I'd lay my head on his shoulder and I'd ask him to sing, but more often he would just break into song himself. I liked listening to his nice voice. And he did seem happier when he was singing. I think he would have loved to have been Neil Diamond—one of his favorites.

I attempted to keep the good and fun times front and center. I always looked at the glass as half-full, even the bourbon glass. After my father, everything was relative. I would think, "At least he doesn't beat me and I can talk on the phone." So I trucked along in my own inimitable way—probably my own form of denial. And I did love David. So soon we decided for me to go off my birth control pills, and try to start a family.

By the end of 1967, I was pregnant with our first child. When I called to tell my parents the news, the only thing my 53-year-old father said—speaking of inimitable ways—was not "That's great" or "I'm happy," but "I'm too young to be a grandfather."

Because of his strong, unending feelings in that regard, I had the kids call them "Texas Mom and Dad" instead of anything sounding grandparenty. Thank goodness, my mother-in-law was more normal and Grandma suited her just fine.

CHAPTER 8

First House

David and I got our first house in March of 1968. It was about the same time as many of our friends were getting theirs. All of us were looking for homes costing around $30,000. We soon discovered that our friends, for that money, were finding in Maryland three to four decent-sized bedrooms, two and a half baths, a family room, central air conditioning, an eat-in kitchen, and usually a garage. But we were not going to leave D.C. again and quickly found for that budget, of course we got far less for location and vitality.

We'd been looking and looking for months, starting in December when we learned I was pregnant. We finally found this darling house in American University Park on 47th St., N.W. It cost exactly $30,000. We needed $6,000 for the deposit. That's when I called my parents and said, "Please send me the money I made working in the store for those many years right now." I had no idea of the amount owed but it had to be at least $6,000, especially considering the interest it must have earned since then. That was the same money my folks never used for my college or my wedding, though promised. So I just finally demanded it—the one and only demand I ever made of my parents. And that's how we were able to buy our first house. (And even though the riots started three weeks after we moved into our new home in D.C., our feelings about laying our roots here in Washington never wavered.)

The house only had one bathroom (not even a powder room) and three tiny bedrooms, but it had a lot of charm—and at least an eat-in kitchen. Outdoor steps led up to a cute front porch. Upon walking in, you nearly tripped over the steps going up to the second floor. To the left was the living room, a dining room behind it, and straight ahead was a nice eat-in kitchen with fairly modern appliances. The bedrooms were actually smaller than tiny. The master bedroom only held a double bed and small nightstands. The room's one closet was four-feet wide and that was for both of us to share. Thankfully I didn't have many clothes in those days.

I did get creative in prettifying the home. I would buy felt material from nearby G.C. Murphy's which I would cut into flowers. Then I'd hand-sew them onto gauzy curtains, also bought there. I would cut pictures out of calendars and magazines and put them in cheap frames, ditto from G.C. Murphy's, and hang them on the wall, adding those to the few nicer paintings we had. (By the way, I still continue doing that, but I'm running out of room.)

I also took to entertaining, which was really a pleasure, especially after having a small one-bedroom apartment to now having a separate living room *and* dining room. I started taking *Gourmet Magazine* as the banana cream pudding episode made me realize I had to up my game. We had company all the time, whether invited or not. I did enjoy planning nice dinner parties where I loved to throw people together who may have never socialized otherwise, such as Gilbert Hahn, Republican Chair of the D.C. Council, and General Hassan, head of the Blackman's Development Center. I also started doing holiday parties where we would invite everyone we knew and some would actually show up. I'd spend days rolling hundreds of meatballs myself that I would pair with a sweet and sour sauce as well as a huge number of rum balls (which is the only way I like my liquor) myself as I wanted them to be perfect.

That house had sweet memories as our three children were all born when we lived there. One unsweet memory was getting rid of my 1960 Chevy Impala and going down to one car—David's much more conservative four-door sedan—as public transportation was nearby. We sold my beautiful car with only 50,000 miles on it in 1968 to a colleague at Rock Terrace for $150. Whenever I see that classic vehicle in a movie or photo, which is often, I have a tinge of regret for letting it go—especially so cheaply. Later, I was successful in making sure, when we finally got a second car, that it was not so conservative—always a convertible, usually red.

Stephanie's Birth

I taught up until I was six and a half months pregnant but had to leave at the end of May, two weeks before school let out, when the gnats in the playground and the non-air conditioned school became unbearable.

Near my due date, David and I went out to a shopping center to browse, and there in a pet store window was the most adorable little kitten. We just fell in love. We brought her home and named her Buttons as she was as cute as one. Right away, David showed allergic reactions. Even so, we weren't going to let her go. He decided he would just get medication. No more than two days later, though, she came down with distemper—not unusual for animals from pet stores we later found out. We took her to a vet, who said the disease was untreatable. All we could do was take her back home and make her as comfortable as possible, which we did.

On August 11th, 1968, I started going into labor just as Aunt Doe, Linda, her husband Kirby and their four children were arriving for an early dinner. Aunt Doe was visiting them in Aberdeen, Maryland where Kirby was stationed. Thank goodness I had prepared everything in advance. While serving the meal for the nine of us, I had to sit down every so often because of the labor pains. I called the doctor, who said the first child would be a long labor so there was no rush to get to the hospital.

David and I had planned to take our guests on a caravan tour of D.C. after we ate. Trying to be a good sport in spite of being in labor, I suggested they go without me. I didn't really mean it—but off they went. There I was alone in labor, doing the dishes, while they were on route to the monuments. That cured me of saying what I don't mean—well, most of the time.

The labor ended up lasting 21 and a half hours. That was not fun. But I had only gained 20 pounds during the pregnancy, and lost it immediately. That was fun.

I didn't sleep that whole night before I gave birth, not just because of labor pains but because I nursed Buttons, who by then was dying. I sat on the floor and kept her on my lap in a towel, trying to keep her warm all night long. She'd vomit on herself and I'd clean her. I would look over and be envious of David soundly sleeping. When the sun came up and it was finally time to go to the hospital, David and I put her in an open box on a little pillow.

After I gave birth to Stephanie on August 12, 1968, David returned home to find Buttons had passed away. He buried her and then came back to the hospital. A little later, I asked him for my wedding ring, which I had given to him to hold as I was being wheeled into the delivery room. He said, "Oh dear." It turned out that he had buried it with Buttons. He had wrapped it in a tissue and threw the tissue in the box with our poor little kitten. He ran home and dug up the dirt to retrieve it.

The month before I gave birth, I lost my beloved grandpa Seymour Simmons Sr. in Greenville. The "S" in Stephanie was to honor him and very secondarily, my father Stanley. We had already decided on names beforehand. If it had been boy, he was going to be "Jason Levitt Schwartz," the "J" for Johnny and "Levitt" being my maiden name. The name Stephanie came from an across-the-hall sorority sister. I had never heard the name before and fell in love with it at age 19. In actual fact, David really lost interest in the name game during my pregnancy. It was disappointing at first, but it did give me leeway to pick the names.

Her middle name came to me as David and Ben Noble (who you may remember I met that first trip to D.C. and who had become a friend of both of ours) were drunkenly singing the Irish ballad, "I'll Take You Home Again, Kathleen." I wanted a "C" name for Grandma Carrie so that "Kathleen" became our "Cathleen." The night I heard them sing, we were at a party in the apartment of Harry Davies, the guy who had introduced David and me. I found it fitting that those people who helped lead me to D.C. and to David also led me to the middle name of my first daughter.

As early as the 1960s, fathers were allowed to go into the delivery room, and even encouraged to do so. But when we went to the doctor a week before, we were told that the baby was going to be breech (which means legs first), so they might have to do an emergency Caesarian. So David could not come in. As it turned out, at the last minute, Stephanie turned herself before birth so no Caesarian was necessary. (She was always a helpful child.) And I think David was relieved he was not in the delivery room.

After the birth, David seemed very tired, even though he appeared to sleep well the night before. I thought maybe it was because of Buttons and running home to get the buried ring, but now I'm not sure. He only stayed a little while after returning to give me my ring and then he went back home to sleep—and did not come back. I was so happy to have a child, a beautiful little girl, but I felt so alone at the same time—and I was.

Since I never babysat, had rarely even been around children, I wasn't sure about being able to handle this alone. So I asked both my mom and my mother-in-law if they'd like to come and help when I got out of the hospital, thinking they would be thrilled to as Steph was the first grandchild for both—and there would be none but mine. They both declined. My mom said, "I want to come later when you're feeling better so we can go out." Ma had some other excuse. (I would have given my right arm to have a daughter or a daughter-in-law ask me for help at such a time.) Oh well ...

Thank goodness, I immediately got the hang of caring for a baby. Mom and Ma did come to visit separately for a couple of days several weeks later. And David was helpful. Then in March of 1969, I was pregnant again—and by choice. I had always wanted three or four children, and I wanted them to be close together in age. Since I had felt lonely as a child with only Johnny who was away at school much of the time, I wanted them to always have built-in companionship.

The Sound of Mom

I would have loved for my mother to be around more at that time, not only for help but because I found her soothing. One of my favorite things about her was her sweet Southern accent and her melodic speaking voice. I just loved her voice. Hearing it in person or on the phone relaxed me. I'd often call her just to listen to it. I feel the same thing today about my daughter Stephanie, who has a similar mellifluous voice without the Mississippi drawl.

About a month after Stephanie was born and Mom was visiting, I was in the bathtub when the phone rang. Mom answered, then came to the bathroom and said, "Mrs. Burka called." I thought, how formal is that for my 25-year-old friend to call herself. Later, when I called back, Janie said, "Since when do you have help?" I said, "Janie, I don't. That's my mother."

Mom could never quite pronounce my married name, Schwartz. She'd say, "Here's my daughter, Carol Swartz." I'd say, "Mom, it's Schwartz. Let's work on that. It's 'Sh' and then 'wartz.' Now put them together, Mom." "Okay, Honey. Swartz." She never quite got it right. And I'm so glad because I love this story.

Unlike me, my mother was not an advice giver. I give strangers in the airport advice, whether I know them or not or whether they want it or not. My mother was totally the opposite. But two times in my life she did so. Once was when I was 22 and getting married. She said two things: "Do not start out doing more than you're prepared to do for the rest of your life." Those were her exact words. I did not follow those words then. I started out doing everything—working, decorating, cooking, entertaining, writing thank you notes, making my own Christmas cards—and did most of them pretty well. But it all just became expected, not really appreciated—just expected. Exactly what Mom had warned me about.

Later in life, though, especially in personal relationships, I did follow her advice. If a man asked, "Are you a good cook?" I'd say, "No," even though I'm actually a decent cook. Sometimes I would eventually show that skill but I never wanted it to be a "selling point" or expected. I wanted it to be a surprise—and appreciated.

(Regarding cooking: My friend Marc Albert often talks about what a great cook I am. He once had my spaghetti and meatballs and bugs me all the time to make it. I keep telling him his memory is better than the real thing. I do make tuna fish salad now and then, and that's become my "cooking," except for a decent gazpacho in the summer—hardly cooking either.)

That piece of advice my mother gave me is the best I ever received. I pass on this bit of wisdom all the time as I do now to you: "Do not start out doing more than you're prepared to do for the rest of your life." She also advised me as I was getting married to always have some money put aside. She said, "That way if you want to leave him, you don't have to ask him for money to do so." The only other piece of advice Mom gave me I will talk about later.

Midland Reporter–Telegram Social Column

As mentioned, in addition to reporting on national and state news, the *Midland Reporter-Telegram* also printed the happenings in the community. After my mother became friendly at AAUW with the Society Editor, Mom was suddenly featured in the pages of the paper under headlines like "Mrs. Levitt Enjoys Apartment Living." It was fun to see that particular article with my working, totally non-domestic mother showing off her rented and pre-furnished abode at Sutton Place Apartments and her select never-made recipes, which were mine. But Mom had her own skills.

When David and pregnant me, with nearly one-year-old Stephanie, arrived in Midland for a visit in the summer of 1969, Mom and Dad had a welcome party for us, inviting some people from AAUW and their apartment complex. Her society reporter friend had told Mom she would like to do a piece about the party and our visit in her column, so asked that we write something and get it to her. Mom said of course and passed the assignment on to David.

The day after the party, David and I were leaving Stephanie with my folks as we were taking a trip to Los Angeles and then San Francisco—my first time in either—to visit my great aunt Esther who was nearly 100 years old, literally. (An aside: Aunt Esther drove us around San Francisco, speeding up and down those hills. True story. To this day, I still can't believe we survived.)

While in Midland, David and I had read that President Nixon was going to Los Angeles at the same time as we were and would be speaking at a dinner at the Century Plaza Hotel. We had decided we would go there to watch the President land in his helicopter so we could wave at him.

Right before we left for California, David, knowing the history of the *Midland Reporter-Telegram* and my birthday party experience, set about writing the piece to be given to the paper, which I never read nor did my parents before he dropped it off.

Several days later while we were in California, my father was stopped every two feet in downtown Midland. (Everyone knew my dad from the store and because he was such a character.) They all said things like "Stan, I just read about your daughter and her husband. Oh, how exciting! You should be so proud that they're going to the President's dinner." Dad had no idea what they were talking about. As soon as he got home, Dad asked Mom, "What in the hell was in the paper?"

Here's what David had written: "Mr. and Mrs. Stanley Levitt have been hosting their daughter Carol Schwartz, son-in-law and granddaughter, and they had a lovely party to welcome their visit. Now the Schwartzes are on their way to L.A. to arrive in time for the President's dinner."

And we did. There we were standing outside the hotel with a crowd in the rain watching the President land for his dinner. It *was* exciting. And Dad should have been proud of David's ingenuity and honesty, and the fact that we *did* arrive in time—to wave.

Hilary's Birth

On December 9, 1969, I gave birth to our second daughter. It was another challenging birth. She was in a posterior position, which means her head was down instead of up. So once again David could not go into the delivery room, even though he was in scrubs and ready to go. I believe, though, given his career switch from doctor to lawyer due to his queasy stomach, he was probably relieved again.

I was looking for a name that began with "H" to honor David's late father Herman as well as my mother Hilda. While I was pregnant, we went over to our friend Bob O'Regan's house for brunch. He had an adorable new springer spaniel. The minute I walked in the door, the dog jumped up on me and Bob yelled, "Down, Hilary." I thought, "That's the name." I don't know if my second daughter ever forgave me for getting her name from a dog, but at least we're both animal lovers.

When people called and asked what the new baby's name was, I said, "Hilary Beth Schwartz." Beth was for my mother-in-law Blanche in addition to Grandma Bonnie. I told them both the day of her birth and they were so pleased. But the more I said Hilary Beth Schwartz to friends, the more I realized it did not roll off the tongue, especially if you have a lisp (which Hilary did have for a while). Try it yourself. [pause] I made an adjustment to the easier-to-say Hilary Elizabeth Schwartz the day after when I filled out the birth certificate. I never told either Ma or Grandma Bonnie about the change. What would be gained?

When Hilary was born she was quite unattractive. She had red blotchy skin. Her black hair stood up like a porcupine. Her eyes bugged out and a large tongue hung from her mouth. I felt sorry for her right away because she was not very pretty, especially compared to her older sister. When friends and family called and said, "Congratulations on another beautiful Schwartz daughter," I said, basically, "Not so much." I wanted to forewarn them before they came to visit and saw her. I immediately became very protective of Hilary because I felt she might have a hard row to hoe. I've always had a bent toward people I perceived as vulnerable.

Soon, though, my concern was totally alleviated. She grew into the most beautiful little girl with wavy golden-brown hair, porcelain skin with rosy cheeks, and gorgeous blue eyes. My mother-in-law and I used to have silly fights over which one she resembled the most. We both wanted the credit. That competition certainly wasn't taking place at the beginning.

David was a helpful mate with the kids. He never minded changing their diapers. When they were infants on six feedings a day, he would always take the 6 a.m. feeding and sometimes the 8 p.m. In those days, most mothers were not breast-feeding. In fact, I could count my friends who breast-fed on one finger. It was kind of the thought of the day that not breast-feeding helped fathers participate and gave them an equal shot at bonding with their children. (I do regret, though, that I never had that experience, and I also understand now the benefits.)

One day, when Hilary was about seven months old and crawling, I asked her nearly 16-month older sister to please hand her a toy. Stephanie took the toy and threw it hard at Hilary. I immediately jumped up, grabbed Stephanie, gave a swipe of my hand to her rear, and said, "Don't you ever hurt your sister again." I then put her in her bed to think about it for a while. (Although I'm not sure how much thinking you really do at that age.) I did have some trepidation at the time because I wanted the girls to be close. I didn't want to create the opposite effect—Stephanie resenting my coming to Hilary's defense and thus, being angry at her as a result. But my initial instinct of immediately punishing the bad behavior turned out to be the right one. Stephanie never really harmed Hilary again. And they have been best friends ever since.

An Open Book

While growing up, I'm the first to admit that I never read except for movie magazines and occasionally *True Confessions*, which I would sneak into the house and read under the covers with a flashlight. The movies stars offered an escape from my life. Those glamorous people brought me to another place where I'd be happy. *True Confessions* was just scandalous and fun.

I was also trying to avoid my intellectual parents' way of life, which consisted of reading good books and the *Encyclopedia Britannica* incessantly. This to me equaled a hermit-like existence with no friends. And I sure did not want that to become my life.

David was such an intellectual, and he did use to say I was the smartest person he knew. And when we debated on different subjects, I often came out ahead, even though he was quite a good debater. (Actually, a lot of people over the years have commented on my debating skills and said I should go to law school. I kind of thought about it, but I ruled it out because I knew it might cause an issue in our marriage. David and I had no professional competitiveness—and I thought it was better to leave it that way.)

But early on, I did feel more than a little academically inferior to him, my own family, and his group of friends. Speaking of his friends, they were all politically liberal, but intolerantly so. One of the worst culprits was the guy who was on the National Board of the American Civil Liberties Union [ACLU]. Oftentimes he along with David's other friends would back me into a corner and harangue me just for having a differing viewpoint. My being a Republican, who did not apologize for it, drove them nuts. It was interesting to see people who claimed to believe in civil liberties not allow others the liberty to have another opinion. And I would tell them, "I have a civil liberty to express thoughts without your permission and y'all of all people should appreciate that." (I'm sure the "y'all" annoyed them too.) Some liberals!

Now that I was home raising children instead of working or in school, I decided it was time to do some catch-up. I asked David to go to the library and get me all the great ones in the "good books" area I should read. And he did. He got wonderful works of literature: *Of Human Bondage, War and Peace, The Brothers Karamazov, Sister Carrie.* (My favorite, though, was my own choice, *A Tale of Two Cities*, which I actually had read in high school and then read again and again over the years.) The list went on and on. I always had a book in my hand. Late at night after the kids had gone to sleep, I would read. In fact, David would get up at his regular 5 a.m. time and sometimes I would still be reading. So in those years of childbearing and raising my little ones, before I went back to work when my last child was two and a half, I expanded myself intellectually through that reading. It also kept me from being bored as well as making me feel better about myself.

Reconnecting with Ivan

I hadn't seen or spoken to Ivan, my ex-fiancé, for five years. In the summer of 1971, David and I were visiting Midland with the girls and I was pregnant with our third child. It was easy for Ivan and me to keep up with each other's happenings as we had so many mutual friends. I knew that he was in Dallas, married to a woman named Sandra, and that they had a daughter. I had talked to David about what a dear man Ivan was, and though my romantic feelings for him were gone, I did miss his friendship. David had also heard a lot about him from mutual friends like Sally and Stanley Bernstein, Patty and Larry Fallek, and Carol Pensky. I asked David if he'd mind if I called Ivan to say hi and he said he thought it was a great idea.

The name Ivan Edelman was easy to find in the Dallas phone book. When I did call, he could have chosen to blow me off. Instead he seemed thrilled. "I'm so happy you called!" He asked if we were coming to Dallas. I mentioned we were changing planes there. He insisted we change our flight to a later one to give us some time to come to his home for a visit and meet his family. That was easy to do in those days and they didn't charge the exorbitant change fees they do now.

Ivan picked us up at the airport and took us back to his and his wife's apartment for lunch. While driving, I asked about his daughter and what she looked like. Ivan said, "Well, she really looks like her," pointing to our daughter Hilary.

His wife Sandra was waiting for us as we pulled up. She was a pretty blonde with slim, long legs, which were quite visible in her short-shorts. I joked to the group that I could see how he had replicated me. And Ivan was sure right about his daughter Robin. She and Hilary did look so much alike—they could have been twins.

David and Ivan really hit it off, as did we girls. Sandra couldn't have been nicer. It was a great bonding experience. The next year, Ivan called me on my birthday and every year since then we have talked on our birthdays. We spoke those two times a year, and David and I would visit them every so often when we were in Texas. It was really nice to be reconnected.

Ivan and Sandra divorced after seven years and two children. He was footloose and fancy free for about seven more years, living mostly in San Antonio. He then met and fell in love with a woman named Bunny McLeod who he dated for 14 years before entering their now 21-year marriage, which I helped promote. Bunny was and is adorable in looks and personality. If you were casting the quintessential Texas blonde, she would get the part. And I mean that in the best way. We may not look alike, but we are like sisters.

Bunny loves to tell this story: After she and Ivan fell in love 35 years ago and at their most romantic stage, the first trip he took her on was to come and visit me (his ex-fiancé), David and our kids, bringing along his two kids as well. Wasn't that romantic?

Ivan even now jokes about our break-up. He's very knowledgeable and smart, but has never claimed to be academically inclined (which at this stage is not accurate). So now when he uses a really big word, he'll say, "And you didn't think I was smart enough for you!" He still has that wonderful sense of humor.

He also has a great relationship with his ex-wife Sandra, who married again after their divorce and had another child. I'm sure it wasn't easy after the divorce but for decades now, that too has been a special relationship. His wife loves and worships him. His ex-wife loves him. His ex-fiancé loves him. His daughter Robin even displays a picture of Sandra (her mother), Bunny and me smiling with our arms intertwined. I think that says it all. Ivan is really the best guy I've ever known.

Years later, Ivan and Bunny moved to D.C. for a bit for Bunny's work. (His job then allowed him to work anywhere.) Bunny stayed with me for a month until Ivan joined her and they got their own house nearby. I would take her around to parties, where she'd say, "See that woman over there: Carol Schwartz. That's the love of my husband's life and I'm so glad she dumped him because now I have him." Although I've tried for years, I can't stop her from telling that story that exact way—which I doubt is even true.

Bunny and Ivan are really my family and I know they feel the same way. In fact, I just spent several days with them in Dallas.

David at Law

In 1969, David remained unhappy practicing law at Arent Fox even though he was a big success there. He got regular bonuses and raises, and had been assured that he would become a partner. But he felt that breaking up with the boss's daughter when we got serious put a bit of a pall on the place. In retrospect, I think it was practicing law that put a pall in his mind everywhere he practiced. He just didn't like being a commercial real estate lawyer even though he was mighty good at it and became well remunerated.

Another real matter at the firm concerned David. They had told him that he would become a partner, along with a couple of others, in seven years which was the firm's rule. But one of the others, instead, was made a partner after six years. That on top of David's general unhappiness put him even more in the dumps.

He would come home every night complaining about work. I'd constantly ask him why he didn't he do something else. He had other interests. He seemed to care about city issues. What about doing something in urban affairs? Maybe something in the political sphere. There were lots of jobs out there other than with a law firm. But he liked making money, and given his deprived background, that was somewhat understandable. Plus, having children, maybe he wasn't sure he had much choice.

I tried to make him feel differently. I told him I was ready to go back to work. I also argued that there were plenty of families who had children and were having good lives with average incomes and even less. I would say, "You know, David, you didn't grow up with money. Money doesn't have to be the end all and be all. Why don't you do something that would make you feel better?" He continued saying no for months and months. I knew when the year passed and he did get that partnership he was due and promised, the additional money he would make would rope him in forever.

I finally got him to sit down for an interview with me so I could put his resume together. I then had him look at employment ads in the newspaper and I would mail his resume out in response to those he found appealing. One he really liked was an urban planning position in Lansing, Michigan. They were quite interested in him and asked him to come for an interview.

Immediately I thought, "Oh my God, be careful what you ask for. What have I done with my life? I hate cold weather and I had given up my life in Texas because I specifically wanted to be in Washington, D.C., and here I am having to go to Michigan." I never told him about these thoughts because I was so anxious for him to be happy and situated in a job he liked.

He went to Lansing for the interview and they offered him the job. I thought, "Oh well. I could get a master's degree in special education at Michigan State," as I had learned that they had a solid program. I put on a good show. But David had reservations himself. Then I said, "David, we don't have to live there forever. It will be a good experience. And we can always come back. It will build your resume." Finally, David announced his decision: "I don't want to move to Michigan." I responded with a relieved, "Okay."

CHAPTER 9

Council Secretary

Then I heard of another opportunity. The D.C. Council Chair, Gilbert Hahn, was looking to fill the position of Counsel to the Council of the District of Columbia—the number two job there. (As background, in the years before Home Rule in Washington—and this was one of them, 1970—the Mayor and Council were appointed by the President and confirmed by the Senate. The ability to elect these positions was passed in 1973 and enacted in 1974.)

I took the step of calling Chair Hahn, who happened to be a Republican although most of the Councilmembers were not. I didn't know him at all. I said, "My name is Carol Schwartz and I'm a Republican, but am married to a Democrat. He's a very smart lawyer at Arent Fox, who is in line to be a partner soon. I think he would be great doing something like this, and I think you'd be very impressed with him." Mr. Hahn said to send him in. So David agreed to meet and they liked each other. Right away, David left private practice to become the Counsel of the Council; and then six months later, when the Secretary (Chief of Staff) left, the Council asked David to take that top position.

So here David was running the entire staff of the Council of the District of Columbia—a very prestigious job. He loved it. He loved the political world. He loved advising all the people who were making decisions about running the city, albeit somewhat limited because of the tight and active control by Congress in those days. Among the appointed Councilmembers were Democrats Sterling Tucker, the Vice Chair, and Polly Shackleton, and Republican Reverend Jerry Moore, all of whom would later factor into my own elected political life.

(A fun aside which tells a lot about David: One night we were at a big outdoor party at friends Judy and David Irwin's house. I observed this attractive gal flittering around to each and every group with the same question, and then she approached me with it as well: "And what do you do?" I said, "I was a special education teacher, but now I have children and am home taking care of them." I saw she was bored with me already so I then said, "But my husband is the Chief of Staff of the D.C. Council." And she said, "Oh. And which one is he?" I pointed over to him and described the outfit he had on. And she said, "No. He works for Sears." I said, "No, he doesn't. He's Chief of Staff of the D.C. Council." I then got the whole story from David and his group. When this woman approached with the "And what do you do?" David had her number.

So he said, "I work for Sears." She immediately started to move away. But David grabbed her arm and said, "I just don't work at Sears. I'm the Manager of the appliance department." She still could not get away fast enough. But that was my adorable David.)

David was with the Council a total of two years and was never happier. He did get down once in a while and did drink some, but his mood was certainly better. It was at the District—now Wilson—Building where we met Dwight and Linda Cropp, who would later be my colleague on both the D.C. Board of Education and the D.C. Council. Dwight was a Yale fellow at the Council when David was there. We became good friends then and remain so today. In fact, the crib we used for our children went right to their house when we were through and they were just starting.

Others who became good friends were the Assistant Secretary to the Council Bob Moore and his wife Evelyn, who we hung out with a lot. The only thing annoying about it was that Evelyn and I used to have to sit there and listen as the guys raved on about how gorgeous Connie Chung, a young (just out of college) TV reporter, was with her mini-skirts. In the spring, David and I got invited to the Cherry Blossom Festival. I saw a really stunning Asian woman in a lovely kimono, elbowed David and said, "You think your Connie Chung is so beautiful. Look at *her*." David glanced up and said, "Oh, that is Connie Chung." I could have kicked myself.

Due to David's job, Chair Hahn awarded us the low license plate number 6. The Mayor, Walter Washington, had number 1, Gilbert Hahn had number 2, Sterling Tucker had number 3. Not bad, eh? It was fun to drive around in our then one-and-only car, a red Chevy convertible, with that low number. I was about 26 but people thought I looked younger then, especially since I wore no makeup and rarely shoes. I went around barefoot a lot, even to the grocery store (allowed in those days). I would drive up to shop in our neighborhood market, and someone would see the license plate and comment, "Your daddy must have an important job." I said, "My daddy owns a small clothing store in Texas but my husband is Chief of Staff to the D.C. Council"—with great pride.

Doug's Birth

In late December of 1971, when David was still at the Council, I was nine months pregnant with our third child. The morning of December 30th, a storm had dumped a foot of snow on Washington. Stephanie and Hilary were sleeping in their shared bedroom. At 8 a.m., I got out of bed and went into the bathroom where my water broke. I immediately went into hard labor. I called the doctor right away. In a blizzard this could have been a catastrophe except for one fateful thing: David was still at home. He had overslept. He was a very early riser and never, ever, ever overslept. But amazingly enough, he did that one day. It never happened before and it never happened after. But thank God it happened then.

I woke David up and he ran the girls to an older neighbors' home. Then he helped me get dressed, and we rushed to the hospital where they put me in a room alone. When I had the girls, they had used a stethoscope on my tummy to measure the baby's heartbeat. Now they hooked me up to a monitor as technology had progressed. The doctor was running late, and I presumed it was: 1) because of the snow storm and 2) because he thought there was no rush as my previous labors had been 21 and a half hours and 9 hours respectively. But this labor was only 2 hours and 13 minutes from water breaking to birth, but of course no one would have been able to predict that.

The interns kept coming in to check on me and would look at the monitor. I knew there was something wrong because they kept giving me sympathetic looks and patting my shoulder. So I started looking at the monitor as well. I could see the number sometimes drop down to zero. That was clearly not good and I really got scared. Actually, it was pretty terrifying. I started to cry.

Finally, the doctor arrived and they rushed me into the delivery room. I could see the worried looks all around. It turned out my baby was choking on the umbilical cord. I wasn't sure if the child would make it and if so, if there would be brain damage from the lack of oxygen. At last, after pushing hard, I heard the loudest infant scream. They didn't even have to slap the rear to stimulate that crying. Tears streamed down my face, this time with relief, when I saw this beautiful, pink vibrant newborn.

After two girls, I was hoping for a boy but by the time of the birth, I was just so grateful to see a healthy-looking baby that I didn't care. About when I was going to ask the doctor what gender, I looked over at the table where the baby was being cleaned and saw what looked like a stream of water spouting out above the child and landing right on the face. I knew then it was either a boy or an unusually built girl. We named him Douglas Levitt Schwartz. (By that point, I was tired of my previous choice of "Jason" as it had become too popular.) I also really wanted a "D" for David. My friend Beth from Greenville had a brother named Douglas, and I thought that was a great name including its shorter Doug. And of course, Levitt was my maiden name. (If a girl, the name would have been "Jessica Diane"—"J" for Johnny and "D" for David.)

Doug was the last baby our doctor Louis Goldstein delivered. In fact, he was going to retire before, along with his nurse who was his wife Janet, but he stayed on long enough to deliver Doug as he had Stephanie and Hilary. I've always been grateful.

Raising Children

Before David and I had children, several of our friends already had some. We would go out with them and their kids to a restaurant and the children would yell and run all over the place. The parents would say, "If you do that again, we're going home." The kids would do the same thing and the parents would repeat the threat: "We're leaving the restaurant *now*." But they would never follow through. On the way home, David and I would talk about it and both of us had just wanted to scream, "Just leave the $%?# restaurant! Don't say you're going to leave and never leave. You're losing any hope of ever having any credibility with those kids." We just found too many of these children to be out-of-control and the parents the same. We decided then and there, that was not going to be us and our kids.

Other times, we would go over to Aberdeen, Maryland where my "sister" Linda Garmon, now Reed, lived for a time. Linda and Kirby had small children who were like four little stair steps. Whenever she needed something, she'd ask them to go get it and they would happily do so. She was very loving to them, but she had taught them to behave—and be helpful. They also knew that when adults were talking not to interrupt—unlike today when most kids are programmed to interrupt. Never before or since have I seen kids like Linda's. They were such darling children. Linda became our role-model, and thankfully it worked for us too.

When we had children, we decided to continue leading our normal lives. So we would take Stephanie when she was a month old wherever we were going and kept up that practice as our family grew. They learned at an early age how to behave. We'd go into a restaurant and you could see the looks on people's faces when we came in with these three little ones. You knew they were thinking, "Oh no. Who's punishing me?" Then we'd sit down, have our meal, and the kids would act like little dolls. They were just so good. They'd talk but they didn't scream. Often people would come over and say, "I've never seen children who behave so well."

Because I had help only one day a week and with three small children and with lots of things to do, I would often be up until the wee hours of the morning. That was my norm even before I had children, always the night owl. That's when I would write letters to friends and family, pick out recipes for an upcoming dinner party, clean out drawers, do my reading, etc. Because of this and my desire to be in a good mood rather than a foul, foggy, sleepy mood, I got the children to be on my schedule when they were quite young.

I was able to do that by using these ways: After the children were out of the four-hour feeding schedule, instead of putting them to bed at 7:00 or 8:00 p.m. as many families do, I kept them up until 10:00 p.m. or so. Then they would wake up later in the morning and just entertain themselves for a while in their cribs or beds where there were soft toys available to them. The oldest two, who shared a room would even chat with each other, usually Steph doing most of the talking. They all seemed content—and never cried. When I came in at 10:00 a.m. singing "Good morning, good morning, it's time to say good morning, good morning to Miss (now Ms.) Stephanie," etc., saying "You're such good kids," we all would start our day in fine spirits.

Some friends, though, took great exception to the fact that my day did not start with the kids until 10:00 a.m., even though my day before didn't finish until 3:00 a.m. or later. When I had my first-born Stephanie on that schedule, they said she was just "an unusual child." Then 15 and a half months later, when I had Hilary on the same schedule pretty quickly, they said, "That's just girls." And finally, when I had Doug 24 months later soon on the exact same schedule, they shut up.

My children joined me at the weekly lunch/bridge game. My good pals Tay Hahn, Carol Schuman, Janie Burka, Judy Irwin initially, and I rotated homes and all brought their kids. Whoever was "dummy"—a bridge term for not playing the hand, which rotated—would be responsible for feeding the babies and changing the diapers. It takes a village—or in this case, a bridge group.

I really believe that if children fit into your lifestyle more than you adjusting your own style, you are a happier and more well-adjusted parent. And when a parent is happy usually the children are too, as long as the patterns are consistent. It also makes the children more adaptable people, which is helpful to them in life.

We had our kids being helpful themselves at an early age. They loaded the dishwasher with their dirty dishes starting at age four (no sharp items included of course). And we always said "thank you" and praised their good behavior.

And speaking of that, it reminds me of something I practiced not only in child rearing but when I taught school as well. Most of us are starved for attention, especially children. And I never understood why teachers and parents tended to give far more attention to the misbehaving child and usually literally none to the well-behaved one. To my mind, that was the opposite of the way it should be. So as a teacher, I tended to walk over to students who were quietly doing their work, put my hand on a shoulder and say, "I'm so proud of you for working so hard" and/or "Anything you want to ask me?" I did the same thing with my children, giving physical contact and saying things like, "I'm so proud of you for playing so nicely."

My philosophy was always reward good behavior and punish bad behavior, or better yet, ignore as much as possible bad behavior unless it was dangerous. Why does the kid who is screaming and not getting his or her way get picked up and get the hug, and the kid who is not acting out is left to fend for her or himself? That really made no sense to me. And still doesn't.

So I did it differently. For instance, if a student acted up in my special education class, I would make that individual stand in the hallway alone with no attention for a while, even though I would inconspicuously check on them. If my children took toys away from another, they would have to go to their room. I would explain that, "You do not take toys away from other children. That is not nice." And they would certainly not get affection or any type of positive attention until they apologized for their bad behavior. (Of course, before they talked, the apology wasn't mandatory.)

David and I also realized early on that it was important and effective to set strong, predictable rules—and certainly not "sometimes you mean it, sometimes you don't" rules. That is only confusing to children and even invites challenges from them, thinking maybe this time it will work. Below is an example:

One night as we were having dinner at a restaurant in Greenville with my parents, grandparents and Johnny when Stephanie was about a year and a half old, she started acting up in her high chair. We said, "Stop it." She continued. David said, "If you do that one more time, I'm taking you outside." Steph, as she persisted, must have thought, "Sure you're going to take me outside in the cold in front of the whole extended family." But David did take her out of the restaurant, away from her food and without her coat, to show her he meant business. They came right back in. And Stephanie's behavior improved significantly.

Leading our normal lifestyles with our children in hand, with our expectations for them set and clearly understood, made for peaceful, fun times, most of the time—at least until puberty hit when, as we all know, things get far more complicated and less peaceful and certainly less fun. Regardless, I think boundaries and expectations also help during those times as well.

Hotel Schwartz

David and I found we were particularly popular with out-of-town friends, relatives and even acquaintances when we had a home in Washington, D.C. Everyone would call, wanting to stay with us. Initially, I really enjoyed having the company and would welcome them especially when I was young, extremely helpful, wanting everyone to like me—and more energetic.

I don't even remember who, what, or why—they just came and went. In fact, not long ago I met a relative's friend from France I thought for the first time, but it turned out he had stayed at our house 40 years ago for a weekend. We would even welcome strangers on occasion, such as when about 30 students from Syracuse University came to protest on the Mall, and slept on our floor for several days. It was particularly interesting looking at the line to our one and only bathroom.

But sometimes more was not merrier. A relative on my father's side who occasionally came to stay with us happened to be in town, this time at a hotel on business. She gave us a call and said, "I have the flu and have been throwing up all day. I feel awful and would like to just come to your house to rest and recover." I said, "I hate to say no, but I would also hate for all three of my small children to get your flu, so I must." I never heard from her again. Sometimes it's good to separate the wheat from the chaff—especially when they do it themselves.

Early Volunteer Work

I stopped teaching while raising kids, but tried to be of service in other ways. I volunteered several days a week at the Blackman's Development Center. The Center was founded by Colonel Jeru-Ahmed Hassan, a Muslim black activist. I had heard him speak at a Council hearing and got interested in helping. The Center's main mission was drug recovery. I counseled and tutored drug addicts, and found it very rewarding. When I couldn't get a sitter, I often took the kids with me.

At the Blackman's Development Center, I first met Marion Barry. He had started, along with his then wife Mary Treadwell, a group called Pride Inc., which provided job training among other things. Wearing his trademark dashiki in those days, he was outgoing, cocky and charismatic.

I also got involved with the cooperative pre-school program at the Friendship Recreation Center which Stephanie started attending when she was four. As a cooperative, a parent was required to volunteer several days a week. Joanne New, the program director, found me friendly and efficient so out of the 20 or so mothers, she asked me to be our delegate to the citywide Parents Pre-School Council, which met several times a year. At the first meeting of the Pre-School Council, I was asked to run for Secretary and immediately got elected. I was the only white person on that Council at that time, so perhaps they were looking for some leadership diversity. So my first "election" was, "Hey, lady, will you please do this?" I wish my subsequent elections had been that easy.

Around that time, the D.C. public libraries announced they were getting rid of the separate children's reading rooms because they were trying to save money. I helped start a campaign to overturn this. I wrote letters to the Board telling them that this would be a mistake of "monumental proportions." That may have been a bit hyperbolic, but it got the point across.

I got the point across even better when the Library Board conducted an open meeting on the issue. I made sure that a large group of parents and their small children showed up to the meeting. On my cue, all the children made as much noise as possible. With kids, that's a lot of noise. I don't know how the other parents got their kids to respond, but I pinched mine. Then I said to the Board, "This is what the library will sound like when you close the children's rooms." The verdict: those rooms were *not* closed.

David's Firm

When David left the Council at the same time the Chair, Gilbert Hahn, departed, he decided to go to work in Hahn's law firm rather than join up with a former colleague from Arent Fox who had asked him to start a firm of their own. I had tried to get him to stay at the Council as he was a Democrat and the other members liked him a lot; but David felt he had his break—and was ready to make more money again.

Right away, he was miserable. He called me several times a day. He just hated it. I said, "If you're not happy, don't keep doing it. Dick Aronoff is an option as he wants to set up a commercial real estate firm with you—or you could always go back into public service" (which was my preference).

Dick used to come over to the house in the evenings to talk about establishing the firm, which he said would be named "Aronoff and Schwartz." I was really disturbed by that. David was the older one with more time practicing law, and now had high-level experience in the D.C. government. It also bothered David, but he told me instead of telling Dick.

One day when they were talking about "Aronoff and Schwartz," I jumped in and said it should be "Schwartz and Aronoff," or at least flip for it. Dick was a good lawyer as well as good at selling himself—something that David wasn't as he was not a self-promoter. So I knew Dick would probably bring in more clients. But I also knew that David was going to do most of the work.

Therefore, I stood my ground on the name as I knew David cared a lot. They did finally flip for it and it became "Schwartz and Aronoff." Later joining as a third partner in the firm of *Richard* Aronoff and *David* Schwartz was a guy aptly named Richard David. Thus, it became Schwartz, Aronoff and David.

Dick tended to be a big spender. Without concurrence, he just went out and bought the most expensive furniture although they all shared the cost. That was really annoying to the other guys—and to me. We were friendly with Dick—remember he and his wife were on our first date—but by this time, he was newly divorced. He dated a lot and would bring these dates over to our house practically every Sunday night for me to feed. His dates were always a lot younger than the three of us, but amazingly, did not have the energy to help cook or even help clear the table.

Melrod, Redman and Gartlan was another successful, bigger firm in town that did commercial real estate law. Leonard Melrod had approached the guys to merge firms when they first established Schwartz and Aronoff, but David and Dick were not interested and excited about doing their own thing. But when Melrod came calling again a couple of years later, David jumped at the opportunity and the other guys were willing to merge as well.

Turning Point

In 1972, after David left the D.C. Council and went into those private practices, he was aggravated most of the time and was not a happy camper. I was also tired from taking care of three small children, all under the age of four. I was lucky enough by then to have help come in once a week, and David was also helpful with them. But he worked hard all day, getting to work around 8 a.m. and coming home between 5:30 and 6:00 p.m., by then really tired. He continued the habit of pouring himself a couple of drinks and unloading about the day before going to sleep around 8 p.m. It was certainly not a good time for either of us.

I tried to perk him up. But by this point I had had six years of this; and I was getting weary from trying to keep him above water while never getting the attention, affection and appreciation I craved—and needed.

I could never tell my friends David was depressed and my marriage was unhappy. I didn't want to do anything to undercut him or his reputation. Plus, people loved us as couple. We could be the life of the party. We were funny. With his quick wit, David could be so entertaining in a crowd. We really could put on quite a show, even though we didn't think about it as a "show" at the time. But the minute we'd leave the party and close the car door (I was the designated driver before the term was used), he would never talk.

It was such a dramatic change. He was silent and if not, grouchy. Maybe he was drained from putting on that show. But the contrast between our outside selves as a couple and what happened once we closed the door was extreme. I used to think, "Why not save some of that fun spirit just for me as I try to do for you?" But I never said anything (and I know that's hard to believe for those who know me, especially now), but because he was so sad, I did not want to pile on.

Again, in the early '70s, I didn't have an understanding of clinical depression nor did most of us. It was not something understood as a disease or discussed at all then. Mental illness and just going to a psychiatrist were stigmatized, even as late as the 1980s, when Tom Eagleton had to drop out from being a Vice Presidential nominee for having been in psychiatric treatment. I never thought to label the problem depression or mental illness at that time. I just knew there was a constant sadness in David that was quite a burden to live with and was starting to make me awfully sad as well.

I would rationalize that it was okay. "He is a good father and provider. He works hard." I remember continuing that mantra and the following one countless times: "Carol, at least he does not beat you. He lets you talk on the phone and have friends, unlike your dad." That's what an effect my father had on me. I had no right to complain about the lack of affection and attention in my marriage because at least he didn't hit me and I had phone privileges. I guess the scars of my childhood ingrained in me that regardless of what is swirling around you, you just keep going. That tendency was certainly of great use later in my professional experiences as well.

I also knew I wanted to keep the family together—and I took marriage very seriously. And besides, I would constantly say to myself, "He needs me." And he did. I've always been first and foremost a loyal person, and reluctant to leave people, especially those who are vulnerable. That kept me there—along with knowing the kids needed their dad and he, them.

But most of the times I would need him, he wouldn't be there. I could give probably fifty examples, but I'm going to give just one: A dear friend from the University of Texas moved to D.C. with her very reserved, non-social husband. I immediately invited them over for dinner, but she explained that he was just terribly awkward around people so she always declined invitations. David knew the whole story. I did finally talk her into coming over with just the four of us for a relaxing, non-intimidating, casual dinner. An hour or so in, David excused himself to go to the restroom. After about 15 awkward minutes of waiting for him to return, I went upstairs, and he was asleep in bed—in his pajamas. And I could not wake him. I then went downstairs and explained that he was not feeling well. Needless to say, that was our last get-together with my college friend.

Through these times, what helped keep me there, in addition to the kids, was having a crush on Johnny Carson. Despite all of the loneliness at that time, I looked so forward every weekday to seeing him on *The Tonight Show* at 11:30 p.m.—just the beginning of my evening. His humor, manner, mannerisms and cuteness did help me through some tough times, as did other such crushes.

In December of 1972, as we usually did, David, the kids (then ages four, three and just turning one on the 30th), and I went to visit Grandma Carrie in Greenville, Mississippi for the holidays. Mom and Dad would close down the store for the week, and they and Johnny would drive there and join us.

That winter, the unhappiness was becoming unbearable. I remember David was particularly down then. And my ability to bring him up was lessened due to my own downward spiral. While in Greenville, I was able to get Mom away from Dad long enough to have a private talk—an accomplishment in and of itself.

When I was growing up, Mom would never want to talk to me much about anything. And if you started talking to her, she would say, "I'm tired." I understood that between working all the time, my impossible father, the issues with my brother, and no real break, how difficult her life was. So I tried not to bother her.

But then when I was an adult and needed someone to talk to about my marriage, Mom really was there for me. I didn't get to talk to her in depth often because we weren't with each other that much. And when I called home, Dad was always right there, front and center, so we couldn't have our own conversation. But sometimes when we were together we would steal away a few minutes by going to their apartment complex pool or out shopping (something neither of us liked to do at the time but it was an excuse to get away). During those times she became my confidante. I told her everything and she was very supportive and helpful.

So she wasn't surprised when that December evening in 1972, I said, "Mom, I need to talk to you. I am miserable in my marriage. I really can't do this anymore. I just want to cry all the time." She then said, "Carol, I understand. But what are your choices? Are you going to go out on the market with three little kids and no money? Are you going to come home with three babies to your father?" Mom said simply, "Go to work." She continued, "Just fill your life with other things." (That was my mother's third piece of advice—the only ones she ever gave me.)

I grabbed at that idea like a lifeline. I had already been trying: volunteering at the kids' pre-school and serving on the Parents' Pre-School Council, going to the Blackman's Development Center once or twice a week, as well as playing bridge once a week with the kids in tow. But now, I was determined to fill my life far more.

I never told David about my unhappiness with our marriage because as I've said before, I did not want to add to his depression. I did tell him that I had spoken to my mom about being with the kids most of the time and not being stimulated enough. I said, "I'm going to go do some additional volunteer work and maybe it will even lead to some regular work. I just need to get out of the house more." He agreed. And that's what I did. And it led me toward expanding my interest in politics.

My Husband, David H. Schwartz

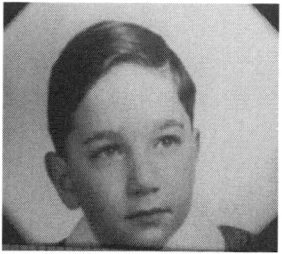

Young David, and with his father Herman and mother Blanche (right)

David (far left) with some NYU glee club buddies

Hilary insisted on below.

Stephanie arrives. (I took the same-type picture of each child.)

Mom with us four weeks after Steph was born

Steph was named for Grandpa S (right), who passed the month before she arrived. (above with his brother, Uncle Benny)

Welcome Hilary

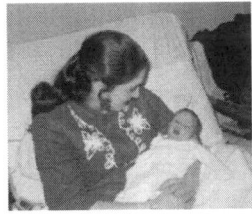

For not wanting to be a grandpa, Dad sure seemed into it.

Family in Midland with one more on the way

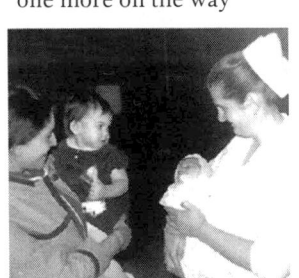

Stephanie meets Hilary.

See #6 license plate (if you have bionic eyes).

Great grandparents B & J

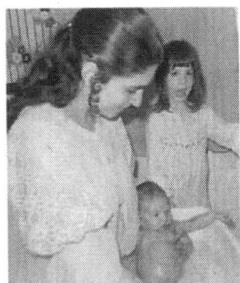

And then came Doug

Johnny loved being
an uncle.

Hilary's favorite cap

Great Grandma Carrie

Kids' first holiday card cover photo

I did the haircuts,
or lack thereof.

At airport to visit
great grandparents
in Miami Beach

With Grandma Carrie
and college friend
Sandy Mendlowitz
Handler

I loved dressing them
in cute outfits.

Johnny's
32nd birthday

Great Aunt Esther,
Grandpa John's sister

Grandma Blanche (r) with
friend Miriam in D.C.

CHAPTER 10

How I Became a Republican

I was pulled toward the Republican Party as a young person because of my belief in certain principles at its core, principles that I still believe in. Among these are a fiscally conservative viewpoint—not taking more taxes out of people's pockets than that which is absolutely needed, and then not wasting them; the promoting of business, especially small businesses—and jobs; showing toughness—but fairness—on crime; and having a strong military to keep us prepared and safe. I tried to put my beliefs into actions during my elected positions in D.C.—obviously not the military part. (Well, that's not true, because I did make sure that ROTC was brought back as an option for high school students in the late '70s when I was a member of the D.C. Board of Education.)

I never saw any reason why fiscal responsibility could not be coupled with compassion to care for our neediest. I've often called myself a "bleeding-heart conservative," even back in the '60s and '70s. And while I've always believed in a strong safety net, I feel it should be executed with financial and performance accountability—both often missing. And encouraging independence for those who are able should always be the goal.

I do believe in limiting taxes, which in spite of what you're thinking is not a disconnect to the safety net. The more money taxpayers can keep and spend themselves and the more they can shop and eat out, the more the economy is boosted—enabling jurisdictions to produce more jobs and obtain more taxes, which can go to the safety net, which also can produce more jobs that then produce more taxes. There really is a circular effect.

Reality has also shown that if you tax the wealthy too much (always considered a quick fix), the rich just establish their residency in another state—or another country—with less taxes to avoid yours. I've always said that, "In an effort to gouge every last nickel, we end up with no nickels. How stupid is that?" And when you force people to leave your town for six months and one day (the requirement of residency elsewhere), you not only lose their income taxes and probably get less property taxes—as they downsize in your town if they stay part-time at all—you also lose their sales and entertainment taxes for that period as well. I think it is much smarter to keep taxes competitive—and to keep those residents and businesses *and their taxes*—thus helping the safety net for those in need.

On a national level, I am a firm believer in a strong defense. This is not because I want to take over the world or like killing people, but because I want to discourage others from doing so. I so vividly remember a local TV commercial from decades ago where a little kid did some karate chops and said, "Nobody bothers me." As much as we'd like to believe otherwise, we do not live in a "Kumbaya" world. I do want peace, but I believe being prepared militarily encourages rather than obviates it.

I also think it's important to take a tough stance to deter crime, as long as it is administered equally on the rich and the poor and everyone in between, and regardless of ethnicity, skin color, sexual orientation, religion or gender identification.

For those who have been fairly tried—and DNA and the appellate process have certainly helped there—and do end up in prison, I've always believed in making it a rehabilitating experience—through drug treatment, counseling, educational opportunities, or all the above. (I was appalled when D.C. was funding a private rehab hospital for *returning* prisoners. My main question was why in the hell are prisoners coming out of prison drug addicted? Maybe the rehab part should take place before or during prison time—not *after*.) It's also important that the incarcerated are not sent to facilities way across the country, which isolates them from their families when keeping those connections is so important.

I do have a strong libertarian streak, and feel that government should be limited in saying what we can do with our bodies and who we can love. I have always been strongly pro-choice when it comes to reproductive freedom and active in the promotion of LGBTQ rights.

In my mind, those positions should fall neatly into the Republican philosophy of liberty and limited government. But unfortunately, it usually does not in the current Party. It wants government *out* of your business in certain areas it favors, but *in* it in others which they do not favor—like the above. I hope Republicans will see the hypocrisy here and will rethink it.

I was drawn to a Party that had a great history of expanding rights and of inclusiveness. A Party that had room for different points of view. A Party whose philosophy really was liberty. For some, this may now come as a surprise, but Republicans do have a history of being the Party of many meaningful firsts. And here are some of them:

It was a Republican Congress that passed the 13th Amendment outlawing slavery. A Republican Congress passed the 14th Amendment, recognizing African Americans as citizens. A Republican President, Theodore Roosevelt, appointed the first Jewish person (Oscar Straus) to a cabinet position. The Republican Party was the first to support women's suffrage. A Republican, Jeannette Rankin, was the first woman to serve in the House of Representatives. The Republican Party was the first to endorse an equal rights amendment for women in the 1940s. A Republican, Edward Brooke, was the first African American elected to the Senate. Republican President Dwight D. Eisenhower worked with Republican Senators Prescott Bush and Everett Dirksen to pass the 23rd Amendment granting D.C. residents votes in the electoral college for President and Vice President. (In fact, Eisenhower also pushed for voting representation for D.C. residents in the U.S. Congress until Democratic Chairmen in the House nullified those parts of the provision.[1]) Republican President Dwight D. Eisenhower and his wife Mamie refused to attend segregated theaters in Washington, D.C. and then Ike got his Attorney General to file a brief which resulted in legally ending segregation in restaurants, theaters, and other public places in D.C.[2] It was a Republican President, Richard Nixon, who signed and thus enacted the Home Rule Act of 1973, which allowed D.C. to elect its own Mayor and Councilmembers for the first time in more than century.[3] It was also Richard Nixon who gave back millions of acres to Native Americans in Alaska, then gave money and resources for economic development, and ensured a policy of self-determination for American Indians.[4] A Republican President, Ronald Reagan, appointed the first woman, Sandra Day O'Connor, to the Supreme Court. And it was Ronald Reagan who signed into law the first national holiday to honor an African American, Dr. Martin Luther King. It was a proud history.

I had been a Republican ever since I was a young girl, starting at age eight. I remember passing out "I Like Ike" buttons on election day at a nearby voting site, the Calvary Baptist Church to be exact. When I grew up in Texas, practically everyone was a Democrat. Texas itself had a de facto one-party system and it was worrisome. This one-party dominance always disturbed me as it left the process without needed checks and balances, and thus ripe for malfeasance of all kinds. And Texas seemed to have a lot of malfeasance in its political environment when I was growing up.

Seeing that kept me a Republican—and made me a believer in alternative voices in government.

This belief continued when I moved to D.C. in early 1966, where a one-party regime was even more pronounced. My terms in elected office, especially in the early decades, reinforced my view as I saw more up close and personal that the single-party system here was not serving the District well at all, just like in Texas. So I remained a Republican here where I was politically outnumbered 11 to 1 because I believed in the Party as well as alternatives to the status quo. And it was helpful to the city to have at least one elected Republican to fight its causes in Congress. I took on that task with great enthusiasm and became an effective advocate in helping push back against Congress's constant undermining of our limited Home Rule—which unfortunately continues to this day.

But in spite of that, I did get a lot of grief—and even sometimes abuse—about being a Republican, both personally and professionally, in D.C during those years. But I was a proud Republican then because of the Party's philosophy and because of its history. The history I mentioned earlier obviously remains. But the philosophies of most in the recent Party have certainly moved away from that history—and me.

Inauguration Volunteer

Let's get back to January of 1973. After my heart-to-heart with Mom about my marriage, and her encouraging me to do outside things, I came back to D.C. from the holidays in Greenville determined to do just that.

I was clearly interested in politics and although I had not gotten involved with Richard Nixon's campaigns for President, I knew his reelection inauguration was just three weeks away—actually on my 29th birthday—so I decided to volunteer for the Presidential Inaugural Committee. (I've always kidded about how nice it is to have that parade every four years on January 20th in honor of my birthday.) I found out that the Committee's office was at the Navy Yard in Southeast D.C. so I arranged for a babysitter and went. We had gotten home from the holiday trip on January 2nd and I was there on January 3rd.

When I arrived at the office, there was an African American woman behind the front desk. She asked me what I wanted to do. I admitted that although I could type, I wasn't a great typist but said I could do just about anything else. I spent the day on the very complicated task of alphabetizing 3x5 cards. (I sat there wishing I had said I was a good typist.) At the end of the day, the woman from the front desk came to where I was and asked, "Are you going to be here tomorrow?" I said I wasn't planning to be but could be there if I was needed. I had really only planned to go a couple of days a week. She went on to say that she had to go to a doctor's appointment the next day and thought I seemed friendly and competent, and asked if I would fill in for her at the front desk. I said, "Of course." She then gave me a brief tutorial on the various tasks that were involved.

I immediately scheduled a babysitter for the next day. There were several senior ladies who lived in our neighborhood who babysat. They were really grandmotherly, close by, and reasonably priced. It was a win-win-win. Oh, I forgot: and I could get out of the house. So it was actually a win-win-win-win!

The next morning, I sat outside the main office directing people where to go. The woman I filled in for ended up being out for a while so they needed me every day. I was thrilled to be occupied, if only until January 20th, and it was also good to have less time to think about other things. Because I was positioned so prominently, and was efficiently doing the job, the major operators of the Inaugural Committee started giving me other tasks to do. Next thing I know I was asked to be the Special Assistant to the Director of the Will Call operation at the Commerce Department (where everyone would go to pick up their tickets). So I moved over to 14th St. and Pennsylvania Ave., N.W. the following week.

The Director was oftentimes busy doing logistics for the Inauguration so I became the go-to person in the office. He really seemed to depend on me. In the space of less than a week, I had gone from changing diapers to having Congressmen and Senators calling me. The word had quickly spread that if you needed tickets or anything, call this Carol Schwartz. The phone constantly rang. Sometimes I would find the Director to ask about a problematic issue and he'd say: "Carol, just do what you think is the right thing to do. I trust you."

It was one of the most fun experiences I ever had and boy did I need it. It also gave David a big boost. Due to my role at the Committee, I got invited to every event, including the Governors' Brunch. So off David and I went. Although he was a Democrat, he seemed to love every minute. He appeared so happy and I was so proud to have contributed to that.

One of the well-publicized events we attended was the pre-Inaugural party at what was then the Jockey Club. It was there where

Frank Sinatra put a $2 bill in columnist Maxine Cheshire's glass, calling her a two-bit not-so-nice epithet, which made news around the world.

David and I had a natural tendency to be drawn to the most awkward people at a party and we'd take them under our wing. That night at the Jockey Club, we came across an older couple probably in their 70s (which now doesn't sound so old to me), who were sitting alone and clearly out of their element. We felt sorry for them and we could tell they needed some company. We spoke to them a good part of the evening—as much as you could carry on a conversation with all that noise.

Much later we found them in the middle of the street in the rain at about 2 a.m., trying to hail a non-existent cab. We were already giving a ride to a nearby hotel for an acquaintance and her date, the well-known former baseball player Bob Usher. We also offered this couple a ride even though their hotel was in Virginia. While all six of us were loaded into our two-door Chevy convertible, just to make conversation, I asked the couple if they liked baseball, planning to mention Bob. They said, "Oh yes. We own the Cleveland Indians."

I've often been struck by the happenstance of that whole situation. This "poor, pitiful couple" turned out to be the Stouffers who founded Stouffers Foods, and I guess all may have worked out for them even without our help ... but who would have thunk it? And the fact that I would have a famous baseball player in my car for the first and only time in my life and wanted to introduce him to a couple who turned out to own a baseball team. Who would have thunk that either?

Our adventures with the Stouffers continued because as we were dropping them off, they asked if they could go to the parade with us the next day and we made plans to meet them after the Governors' Brunch. At that brunch, we met a big-time Greek shipping magnate, who invited us to an exclusive party on his yacht out on the Potomac that afternoon. But since we had already made plans to chauffeur the Stouffers, disappointingly we felt we couldn't say yes. And he seemed disappointed as well.

After a not-so-fascinating afternoon with the Stouffers, we dropped them back at their hotel and gave them our card, maybe hoping for a thank you note for our two-day taxi service. We didn't get that—and not even one frozen dinner. With or without, I still regret not going on that yacht with the shipping magnate, who we often read about in the paper. What is *c'est la vie* in Greek?

During the brief time on the Inaugural Committee, I met a soon-to-become friend named Ed Morgan. He had a political appointment to a Governor's office in D.C. at the time, and also volunteered at the Committee. David and I both hit it off with him. Since Ed was newly divorced with two children living with their mother and was still adjusting to those circumstances in his small apartment, our home became like his second home. David and I basically adopted him—he became a wonderful friend to us and just as significantly, another "uncle" to our children.

After the Inauguration wrapped up at the end of January, I felt a little better about life but was still thinking about where to find my next work experience. Then the Watergate scandal erupted. I thought that it was going to bring down not only President Nixon but the entire Republican Party, and felt that now good Republicans had to rally. So in August of 1973, I went to volunteer at the Republican National Committee (RNC).

I was at the RNC for two or three days a week doing clearances for possible Presidential appointments. If the President wanted to appoint someone to a board or commission or other position, his office would send those names to the RNC, and I would call the State Chair where the person hailed from to clear him/her. It was a position of responsibility and I liked doing it.

I also became part of the after-hours RNC softball team, where I pitched sometimes and George H.W. Bush, who was the RNC Chair at the time, sometimes played first base. In fact, not long ago, I came across a book about him—and there in it was a picture of him with some members of the softball team, including me.

Thoughts on Nixon and LBJ

I had an experience of meeting President Nixon during his first term. It was when my David was the Secretary of the D.C. Council and was probably in 1971. President Nixon was the guest speaker at an event we attended in honor of Robert Brown, who was an African American aide to the President. With several hundred seated at tables in the ballroom waiting for him to speak, I spotted President Nixon standing in the vestibule. It was quite apparent he was very nervous. I walked over to him and said, "Oh Mr. President, I'm looking so forward to hearing you." I took his arm and really helped him walk out. He spoke and did fine. But this experience was enlightening as I could see his anxiety beforehand, and it was obvious to me then that he just didn't have a personality well-suited for his role, even though he undeniably had the brains.

I recognize today that Nixon is a controversial figure and always was to a degree. Of course, we all know about Watergate. However, philosophically, in many areas he was a moderate to liberal Republican, certainly by today's standards. He formed the Environmental Protection Agency, engaged China, and implemented the first federal affirmative action program. He appointed more women to administrative positions than President Johnson. It is also widely known, as Jackie Kennedy spoke of it, that President John F. Kennedy admired him and often sought his counsel.

And significantly, President Nixon, as I mentioned, signed the D.C. Home Rule Act into law, which gave Washington an elected Mayor and Council. In addition, he supported voting representation for D.C. in Congress, saying, in 1969, "It should offend the democratic sense of this nation that the citizens of its Capital ... have no voice in Congress."

It's easy after the Watergate scandal, and the hardline right stances some Republicans take today, to forget the moderation and even progressiveness of many of Nixon's policies. What he participated in with Watergate was unconscionable, but compared to some of the practices in Texas (my home state), was almost child's play. But still unconscionable. He paid the price and I'm glad he did. Crime should not pay—for anyone.

Speaking of Presidents who did not do everything right and went out with a cloud over them makes me think of Lyndon Johnson. He certainly was known to have more than his share of election dirty tricks under his belt and he also left with the stigma of lying about the bombing of Cambodia. But in my mind, I do give him enormous amounts of credit for the monumental things he made happen: the Civil Rights Law of 1964, the Voting Rights Act of 1965, and the War on Poverty.

Selling Our First House

By the end of the summer of 1973 we had been in our house in American University Park for nearly five and a half years. We moved there when I was pregnant with Stephanie and now we had three children. It had become a challenge to share our only bathroom with two kids toilet trained and one on the way to being. And at that time we could afford more so we started looking. (Aren't we spoiled these days? I lived in a house until I was 17 with often four adults there and with one bathroom—and there are so many who live with none.)

We had paid $30,000 for our house in 1968 and figured that after five and a half years, we would get nearly double for it, in spite of no remodeling. Generally, homes in D.C. in good locations turn out to be good investments—and that was the case for us.

The houses we were looking at that were bigger with more bathrooms were listed at around $110,000. Then we really lucked out. My dear friend Tay's in-laws, Maxine and Arthur Hahn, had good friends their age who were retiring elsewhere. So the Hahns hooked us up with Muriel and David Dreyfus, who had lived in their home in North Cleveland Park for decades. They had been told we were a nice couple, but not rich.

We saw the house and loved it. It had a finished basement and attic, a lovely family room in addition to a living and dining room and a small side porch, as well as three full bathrooms and two half-baths. The only thing missing was an eat-in kitchen. It was a real contrast to our present house. Muriel and David were quite wealthy and I don't think really cared about what they got out of their home. They offered us the house for $80,000, far less than what it was worth and what we expected to pay. We grabbed it fast at that great buy. And we felt very fortunate.

For our new home, I wanted to decorate the whole new living room around a Kirman rug, like Grandma Bonnie had. Around that time, I saw that Woodward and Lothrop was having a sale on carpets. I went there and found the large (practically wall to wall) gorgeous, pastel-colored Kirman rug of my dreams. It was $6,000 (and that was legit) but was on sale for half-price at $3,000. Regardless, it was still a whole lot of money. What to do? I then came up with a great idea.

I gave David the proposal: "Let me try to sell the house and if I do, I get to keep the 'realtor commission' and buy the rug." (The commission for the sale would be about $3,000.) I knew I was a decent salesperson, having had years of experience at the General Clothing Store, and David, being a commercial real estate lawyer, could easily do the legal work. So between the two of us, we had it covered. David told me I had a deal but only had two weeks. (He didn't want to have to get a bridge loan because we had already bought the other house; and with such a good price, we did not want to add a sales contingency.) I fought for three weekends— just two days more—and he relented. I immediately wrote an ad listing the house for $59,500 and put it in the paper.

The first weekend, I straightened up, turned on all the lights, and turned on as many window air conditioners as I could without the fuses blowing. David took the kids out while I showed the house. It was cutely decorated and seemed to show nicely. Unfortunately, though, many of the prospective buyers who came said, "Where's the garage?" Of course there wasn't one.

So the second week, I changed the ad headline to, "If you're looking for a garage, look elsewhere." I went on to say, "But if you're looking for an adorable house with a nice front porch ..." That solved that. But even with the change in the ad and a reduced price to $57,500, nothing happened. The third and last weekend came around and before he left, David reminded me, "This is it."

Late that Sunday—and final—afternoon, I was getting really discouraged. But then this darling couple walked in. They looked like they were 18 to my nearly 30-year-old eyes. At first they seemed interested, but then they just left. It was all over. "There goes my rug." I went out front to the porch to ruminate. I then looked over at the little hill down the street and saw that same couple sitting there. Encouraging? Maybe, but I wasn't sure.

It got to be 5:00 p.m., which was closing time. "Oh well ..." At that moment, just when David and the children walked into the house from their outing, the young couple knocked on the door. "We'll take it," they said. They offered $55,500—just $2,000 less—which we accepted. But I thought it would be contingent on their getting financing, which worried me. I said, "I know you're probably going to have to get financing. Aren't you going to have a difficult time in this market when the banks are being so tight about giving mortgages?" He said, "Oh no, we have no problem at all. My father owns the National Capital Bank." What luck was that! I was doing a jig in my mind I was so happy. And I was able to get my Kirman rug, which I still have, granted with my granddog's pee here and there. (Guess it is the rug of her dreams too.)

Home Again

In September of 1973, we moved into our new house at 3600 Cumberland St., N.W., which was my favorite home other than the apartment I live in now. I really loved that house and its location. It was one block away from the elementary school, four blocks from the junior high, and three blocks from the high school, and a lovely home for us and the children. We had wonderful next-door neighbors and friends, Isabel and Karl Herald, who owned the Old Europe restaurant, and whose kids, Alex and Oliver, played with ours. (They later had Sarah and Elizabeth.)

Our across-the-street neighbors were Senator John Stennis and his wife who he called Miss Coy—I followed suit. Because of my Mississippi roots, we became really good friends and I would often stop in during the day to visit with her. For the holidays one year, Miss Coy gave me a Menorah she had, which I still treasure.

Not long before we moved in, Senator Stennis had been shot by his house one night while being mugged by two teenagers. (We did not know this when we bought but maybe that was part of getting the good price.) He did thankfully recover and continued to serve in the Senate for a total of 40 years before he retired in 1981.

Each year, Miss Coy sponsored the Mississippi Nurses' Association's annual fundraising luncheon and card party in a big reception room in the Russell Senate Office Building. She asked me if I would get some friends together and attend. I said, "Of course," and invited my occasional bridge girlfriends, which included Linda Cropp. (By the way, Linda tells everyone that I'm the one who taught her how to play bridge, but she plays far more regularly and bypassed me years ago.)

Off the four of us went to Capitol Hill to this luncheon with several hundred people. Keep in mind this is 1975. Linda was the only African American guest, and I may have been the only Jewish person. If those two things didn't draw enough attention to us, these did: They had four raffle prizes and each of us bought a minimum amount of tickets as did many others. When they called out the winners, two of my three guests won two of the four raffle prizes. The last and only other giveaway, the door prize—a big beautiful lounge chair—was announced: And the winner is ... Carol Schwartz. It was sure embarrassing, but I loved the chair—and diversifying the crowd. Not sure if I was invited back the next year.

South Toward Home

Speaking of Mississippi, each December, David, the kids and I continued heading south to Greenville. David did enjoy those holiday visits with my grandmother, Uncle Benny, parents and Johnny. He would take the kids to feed the ducks on the Mississippi River. Then he would drive in circles on the tilted levy, while the kids whooped and hollered in the backseat like it was a rollercoaster ride. I'm scared of heights and rollercoasters so I was glad when I wasn't invited.

David asked if he could speak at one Friday night service at Hebrew Union Congregation in Greenville, which is the temple my family belonged to. He entitled the speech "South Toward

Home," and in it he spoke of being a Northerner finding the values of home, family and love in that Southern town with its front-porch culture. It was a beautiful and touching talk. I was glad to see he gained some peace through those visits with my family.

Turning 30

I was depressed about turning 30 years old. It reminded me of when I turned 20 in college. Becoming 20 in 1964 occurred at a wonderful time in my life. I was with Ivan and had lots of friends. I was doing well in school. I was 350 miles away from my tough dad and close to my sweet brother. All was good.

My parents called to wish me happy birthday at the stroke of midnight (they were night owls too). There I was crying in my dormitory room (we had an 11:00 pm curfew). They asked, "Why are you crying?" I said, "I'm not going to be a teenager anymore." It's funny how I thought I was getting so "old" then. It's also interesting now looking back that I didn't want to move on from my teenage years—especially considering how horrible my childhood and teenage years were at home with my father. But I think what got to me, as ridiculous as this sounds for age 20, was impending mortality. As tough as my life had been back in Midland, I still loved and valued life. And I guess I feared death. So much so that when I was a kid I would double my age in my head, just to reassure myself that I still had plenty of time to live. At 9, I'd double it and think, "I'll only be 18." At 13, doubling meant just being 26. Death was so far off. Perhaps my fear of death is why I'm such a night owl. I never want to pack it in.

There on the brink of 30, I had three lovely children, my husband was starting to do very well professionally, we had a lot of friends and what appeared to be a good life. And I wasn't as sad then about the marriage as I was focusing on exciting new outside experiences. Yet, I was sad about turning 30. I guess it's not unusual. Many people are. David himself was particularly despondent as he turned 30. Trying to analyze it, I said to him then, "Maybe it's because you'll no longer be the youngest this or the youngest that. At 30 and beyond, you're expected to achieve." He understood the point back then as I now did. But turning 30 still sucked.

For that semi-traumatic birthday, David had made reservations at a new expensive restaurant in town. We never went out to really nice establishments, except for special occasions. But the morning of my birthday, I woke up in a lousy mood and said, "I don't think we should go out and spend all that money. Why don't we just go to A.V.'s?"—and that's what we did. David called in Ed for reinforcement. The three of us went there and had the garlic white pizza we loved. At quarter to midnight, sitting at the table, I started to cry and it continued until at least 12:15 a.m.

I remember thinking that if I was so depressed at 20 and this depressed at 30, at 40 they may have to institutionalize me. But instead, I welcomed my 40th birthday, and my 50th, 60th and 70th. I was fine through them all, and hopefully will live long enough to welcome my 80th. But I must admit, I have stopped doubling my age as a stave-off-death strategy. At this point, my double age would be 146. And even with the new medicines and my mostly continuing positivity, I don't want to see it even if I could. (Well, maybe only to watch season 159 of *The Voice*—that is, if they continue with two seasons a year.)

Standing Up to Dad

One Christmas, when we met in Greenville for the holidays, we decided to rent a car so David, the children and I could follow my folks and Johnny back to Texas. There we planned to spend some time in San Antonio, Austin and then Midland, before getting rid of the car and heading back to D.C.

In San Antonio, my parents babysat one evening so David and I could have dinner with several of my college friends who lived there. We were only gone a couple of hours, but when we got back to the motel, my dad gave us a hard time about spending time with friends, the same old barrage I had always gone through.

But David would have none of it. He said to me, "We should leave." I was scared but agreed. David went into another room for a bit, came back and announced to my folks and Johnny: "We're leaving tomorrow morning." He had actually changed our reservations. David just put his foot down. I could never really stand up to my father as I was always so frightened of him. But David did—and I cheered him on in my mind, realizing of course, Dad would never have beaten David. Regardless, I had never been more proud of my husband.

First Home Rule Election

The first Home Rule election of 1974 in D.C. not only had an impact on my life as a Washingtonian in that we could finally vote for our own Mayor and Councilmembers, but it also had a deep impact on me personally.

A little background: Washington, D.C., the city I have called home for nearly 52 years now, has had a long struggle for any self-governance. Residents of the District were granted the right to electoral college votes in Presidential elections in 1961. When I moved here from Texas in January of 1966, the city was governed by three Commissioners appointed by the President and confirmed by the Senate. The next year, the three Commissioner form of government was replaced by a Mayor and nine Councilmembers, all still federally appointed and confirmed.

The first elected body the city was granted by Congress was the Board of Education in 1968, consisting of eight representatives from each of the eight Wards and one at-large member. Anita Allen was elected as the first President of the Board. She then lost her at-large seat to Marion Barry in 1971, who went on to be elected President by the Board as well.

In 1973, the Home Rule Act was passed by a Democratic Congress and signed by Republican President Nixon. Residents could at last elect their own Mayor and Councilmembers. (They had been able to elect their own Mayor in 1820 but that was done away with in 1871.)

The Council would now consist of 13 members. Eight of the members would represent each of the city's eight Wards. A Chair would be elected citywide along with four at-large (citywide) members, two of whom had to be not of the majority party.

But all these years later, we still don't have voting representation in the House or Senate, in spite of paying federal income taxes, making D.C. a sad but true illustration of taxation without representation.

And Congress still has a strong hold on the local affairs of the District to this day. Any law that is passed by the Council and the Mayor has to go through Congress. The budget also has to be approved by Congress, but there is an ongoing battle over this. (D.C. voters passed a referendum in 2013, calling for passive approval of the budget by Congress, which a judge upheld in early 2016.)

The Home Rule Act's implementation in 1974 did give us some degree of local self-determination, though, albeit unfairly limited. Still, it was precious to Washingtonians. And it did open the door for my entry into elected office.

Taking a Leap

It was the spring of 1974. The first Home Rule general election was scheduled for November 5, 1974 with the primary being in

September. By that point, David had been gone from his job as Secretary of the Council for about two years. As the election approached, I said to David that he should run for the Council. As you know, he had some challenges settling into a palatable private firm situation after leaving the D.C. government. He had loved working with the Councilmembers, and I knew he would love being one himself. I told him he'd be great at it, that I would help put together his campaign, and would also go to work full-time in a paid position to add to the family finances—which would have been quite affected if he did go into the public sector again.

David was a high-level partner at the merged firm at this point and was starting to earn really good money, which had always been his primary goal. I still believe he would have been much happier had he abandoned the pursuit of money, but I could not persuade him—even though he wasn't that materialistic while making that money. David liked nice clothes and an occasional fine meal, but he wasn't looking for the most expensive car or the grandest trip. I think he had just grown up with wanting to get out of that Bronx walkup apartment and into at least the option of a life of luxury. When he got there, he did not even choose luxurious items very often. But it was impossible to steer him away from that deeply embedded childhood dream of wealth.

David said, as I was bugging him, "You're the real politician in this family with your people skills. You're smart, have a big heart, and get things done. You should run for the Council." That pushback went on for a while.

Honestly, it was hard to imagine myself being a politician in my own right. Growing up in the '50s and early '60s, women didn't necessarily envision that for themselves. The furthest I could see was maybe marrying an aspiring politician and being helpful to him. In these past few decades we have seen a significant change, thank goodness, and I have felt some pride in helping that along. Many doors have swung open, though many still stick. I wish more women would run for office, especially nationally. I hope the future brings no limitations—in our own minds or anywhere else.

But at that time in 1974, I felt intimidated even at the thought of running for office. I had not grown up with much confidence and still had very little. Besides, I was not interested then in being on the Council, though later its issues did become part of my passion. At that time, though, education was my main concern and I had a good background for it. And interestingly enough, an opportunity, due to the new Home Rule Act, presented itself right away.

Now that elected Council seats were available, several members of the elected Board of Education were gearing up to run for them, leaving their positions open. For instance, Abe Rosenfield, who had been the Ward 3 School Board member for many years, was leaving to run for the Council. The procedure to fill a vacancy on the Board was that the remaining members would appoint somebody to fill that seat until the next election. Running for election was intimidating; an appointment was a whole different story.

Some people may be surprised at my great fear of running for office, considering I've now done it oh so many times. I was always outgoing and showed a lot of bravado, but people who truly know me understand that I'm someone who is a little afraid of everything. I later found out that most people lack confidence—even those you wouldn't guess that about. However, then, I thought I was the only person on earth who felt that way. Same happens with happiness too. As Charles de Montesquieu, an 18th century philosopher, said: "If we only wanted to be happy, it would be easy. But we want to be happier than other people, which is ... difficult, since we think them happier than they are."

Despite my insecurity, at least I was ready to take the small step of applying for the Ward 3 appointment. Our good friend Dwight Cropp was Secretary (Chief of Staff) of the Board of Education at that time. Although he could not recommend me per se, I knew he would probably say I was okay if asked. My public school credentials were immaculate having been a public school special education teacher and Secretary of the Parents Pre-School Council, had only attended public schools myself, kindergarten through college, and my oldest daughter was in our neighborhood public school with the second one headed there the next year. David had also gone to public schools through 12th grade, and we both had planned all along to send each of our three children only there, long before I ever thought about running for the School Board.

I wrote a letter submitting my application. I got people from the Pre-School Council and the Blackman's Development Center, as well as other D.C. friends, to write letters on my behalf. I worked really hard to get the appointment, but there were lots of other people going for it as well.

Then, all of a sudden, there were four vacancies on the Board of Education with three running for the Council and another leaving because of personal reasons. The five remaining Board members decided they did not want to appoint four of their colleagues. So they asked Congress to put the School Board's open positions on the first Home Rule election ballot. Congress agreed, so overnight, the appointment became an elected position. By that point, many people were invested in me, and I thought, "I've done all this work. I really want this job. I'm not stopping now."

So I jumped in. These many years later, I still am astounded—given the mush of inadequacies I felt inside—that I did it. But it was a huge lesson and the real beginning of training myself to by-pass certain fears. Don't think about it, just do it.

What I found then and over the years, is that I could not erase fears. But I could rise above them when it was for a cause I really cared about. Believe me, I still have a tremendous number of fears that I don't even bother to surmount. I am afraid of heights, so I don't jump out of planes. I fear bugs, so I don't go camping. Those things are just not that important to me.

But when I have wanted to accomplish something like trying to make a difference in people's lives, those fears—the fear of failing, the fear of losing friends, supporters and elections—become secondary to me. Even when some of those worst-case scenarios have come true, I know I would do the same thing all over again because the cause was worth it. Fears are ever-present in all of us—at least in all of us who are thoughtful and sober. They can either render us immobile or we can just forge ahead regardless. Remember, losing—or failing—is better than not even trying.

I guess what really motivates me the most is my biggest dread of all: winding up as that old lady on the nursing home porch in the rocking chair, going back and forth and saying to myself, "I could have, I should have, why didn't I?" That fear of regret pushed me into my first election.

CHAPTER 11

Running for the Board of Education

There had been at least 12 of us going for the appointment. When it became an election, all dropped out except two. My only opponent for the Ward 3 seat was a man named Bob McClure. I liked him and his wife a lot. Bob was in his 40s and had kids who went to Lafayette Elementary School. He had quite an impressive resume and served as Vice President of the National Education Association (NEA). The years that I had been taking care of babies, he was out giving speeches on education across the country.

Bob and I did a bunch of campaign forums. I was so nervous that my voice would shake. And my mouth would become so dry that my top lip would stick to my teeth. My personality would sometimes show through and I could occasionally be articulate, but not often. I knew I could be a good School Board member, but was not sure I was such a good candidate because of those nerves, the lip sticking to the tooth issue, and a general lack of confidence. (By the way, I did become a less intimidated and better speaker later on by using this practice: I would pick out several friendly faces in a crowd in different locations and would just *talk* to them. It made a big difference in calming my nervousness.)

Bob McClure, though, in contrast to me then, was a great public speaker and had confidence up the wazoo. He was also advantaged by being a Democrat. The School Board election was supposed to be a non-partisan race. But Councilmember Polly Shackleton, who had been appointed by the President and later would be elected as the Ward 3 representative, decided to insert herself into this race and make it partisan. She walked around with Bob the whole campaign telling voters, "You have to vote for the Democrat. Schwartz is a Republican. Vote for the Democrat." Educating our very needy students on a local level was not a partisan issue, but Polly sure made it one with Bob joining in. And it could be pretty effective in a Ward where Democrats outnumbered Republicans 7 to 1.

The combination of his poise and speaking ability as well as Polly's advertising him as the Democrat in the race really made me feel like I was burnt toast. But I was not going to let that stop me. I was into the race, and so was David.

We had a campaign "army," which consisted of me, David and Ed. I designed the posters. We picked a picture for it that made me look nice and friendly, with my hair pulled back and very little makeup (both of the latter were my usual), and a dress (not so usual) with a big 1970s winged collar.

Practically every night the "army" went out in David's and my convertible. I drove and the guys jumped out and put up the posters. Oftentimes they would get ripped down, so we'd have to go out the next night to replace any that had disappeared the night before. We were so good at keeping them out there that I'm sure most voters thought we truly had an army of volunteers. (In a Ward race, we could take care of the posters ourselves, but when I later ran for an at-large Council seat, I really needed an army of volunteers—and thank goodness, by then, had it.)

Recently, forty years later, I came across a poster from that first campaign we had found near a trash can in 1974. (As I said, I never throw anything away.) On it, black dots were drawn all over my face and the letters "sch" and "z" were blacked out of my last name, leaving just "wart." "Head" was added to make the poetic, "warthead." This is the kind of crap you face when you put yourself out there. (And besides, when I had warts they were on my hand, not head, so it should have been "warthand," stupid!)

One Saturday there was a candidates' forum at a Cleveland Park home, filled with an intimidating group of D.C. intellectuals. Some reporters were also there. (Because Polly Shackleton got so involved, the race was getting more attention.) Bob McClure and I were in the large living room answering questions. I was doing fairly well that day. I was holding my own for once.

Then my husband raised his hand and said, "I have a question." He proceeded to ask about something I had never heard of. It was some little-known term that only a few Ph.D.'s in education at that moment in time might have been familiar with. But there was my husband, who must have read the term in some article in *The New Yorker* or *The Atlantic*, asking the one question I could not answer. But of course Bob McClure, Mr. NEA Vice President, could.

Realizing how David had handed him the knock-out question (probably from the look on my face), Bob said, "Carol, why don't you answer that question first?" I was trapped. I probably should have said, "I'm going to need a moment to collect my thoughts on this." Instead the truth-teller that I am said, "I have no idea what he's talking about." Then Bob spoke very eloquently on the subject, whatever it was. When the question came back to me, I said, "I think Bob covered it." I'm laughing now, but then, the episode was humiliating. Walking to the car, I said to David, "What were you thinking?" It was probably the most ineloquent moment in my entire political history—and it came courtesy of my husband.

During the race I did a lot of door-to-door campaigning. I wrote and laid out my own brochure. I remember writing, crossing out and re-writing, and cutting and pasting the prototype together while sitting on our bed. (I have always used the bed as my desk.) The brochure included a lot of positive quotes from people I worked with in various volunteer ventures. I even made up a catchy handout for election day: a thick glossy paper ruler that read, "Rule for the day ... Vote for Carol Schwartz."

My kids got their first taste of campaigning during that race, particularly my daughters, though they were only five and four at the time. Hilary even remembers walking up to a voter with a flyer and saying, "Vote for my mom." They would say that phrase a lot in their lives. Poor babies.

But between Bob's experience, the debacle at the Cleveland Park forum, and my being a Republican, I thought I was a goner. When the results came in, I had won with 58% of the vote.[5] It was thrilling then—and is now thinking back on it. And it still gives me a special thrill that my name was on the first Home Rule election ballot on November 5, 1974. (And in 2008, my last full year on the Council, Marion Barry and I were the only two remaining elected officials in public office who could make that claim.)

After I won, people often asked, "How did you win? The odds were so against you." I never really knew why, but it reminds me of something that happened early in my political career. I was at a reception and was running around talking to all present. As I was leaving, a couple said, "We had such a good time watching you 'work the crowd.'" Though probably not intended, I actually took umbrage at that as it made it sound all feigned and false. It's not. It's just me. I really am a friendly, outgoing person who sincerely cares about people—and I guess that shows. Maybe that was the answer to those people's questions back in 1974.

But I still give the credit for the victory to that conversation with my mom back in December of 1972: "Carol, go to work. Fill your life with other things." That first School Board win did propel me into a whole new interesting—and challenging—life.

The Board of Education

My daughter Stephanie was in 1st grade, Hilary in kindergarten, and Doug was a year away from pre-school when I went on the Board of Education at the end of November of 1974. Because of the four vacancies on the Board, the four of us who won those seats were sworn into office as soon as the election was validated, when normally it would not have happened until January 2nd of the following year.

It was originally a non-paid position with reimbursement of expenses up to $2,400 annually, and then became a salaried position of $1,200 a year. In the late 1970s, near the time I was leaving, it went to $16,000. The Council probably did that increase to keep members of the School Board on the Board instead of running for their seats on the Council, as many had done.

It was ostensibly a part-time job. I ended up devoting 50+ hours a week to it. We had been using just occasional sitters like Mary Riston before. Mrs. Riston was with us until she was in her 90s— and long after we needed her. We kept her coming as we wanted her company—and to keep her busy in addition to her weekly bowling league. Sometimes I would actually have to beg one of the kids to stay home so she had someone to "babysit."

Marie Slater, who answered an ad, worked for us one or two days a week for several years when the kids were small, and I was very fond of her. But because she had a drinking problem, sometimes I would have to drive to N.E. where she lived and pick her up—and sober her up—before she could do any work; she was worth it. But now, I had to get a person who could live in as many of my work hours were at night. For various reasons, we had a series of people over the years. Some we liked a lot like Edith, who was older and then retired to move back to Jamaica, as well as Letitia and Gloria, who went on to different careers. Then there was Suzette who was okay, and there was another I had to fire. But we were generally lucky to find good people during those years, who enabled me to work, knowing my kids were in good hands when I wasn't home. I am grateful to all who helped and the several who are good friends to this day.

Our public schools, with well over 100,000 students then, were in crisis. Too many of our kids weren't graduating or hadn't mastered basic skills when they did. Sound familiar? There were so many stories of D.C. public school graduates not even being able to qualify for the military because of being ill-prepared. These stories were heart-wrenching as our kids deserved so much more.

Our school system also had a Superintendent, Barbara Sizemore, who was exacerbating the problems rather than solving them. From day one, I got entangled in the fight to remove her, which had started before I got there. The majority of the five veteran members were ready to fire her, but at first I tried to remain neutral and give her a chance. I felt that way especially because, from the sidelines, I had taken great pride as a woman when an African American woman was appointed to the post in the first place by then School Board President Marion Barry and the Board in 1973. Unfortunately, it did not take me long to arrive at the same conclusion that she needed to go. It was not an easy battle—truly baptism by fire.

But even before that battle heated up, the environment was a taxing one. Although I was glad to be there because I cared deeply about the issues, I still felt insecure and intimidated. So at the first meetings, talkative me did not speak at all. I just absorbed what was going on—and learned.

Barbara Lett Simmons sat next to me on the dais. (We sat in alphabetical order.) Barbara was a strong, overpowering person, who had been on the Board for a while and was at least 20 years older than I was. She spoke with such confidence and authority: "On February 2nd at a meeting, such and such happened ..." It was only later that I realized that February 2nd was a Sunday and we had no such meeting. A lot of that confidence was just b.s, but she, Ms. B.S.—figuratively and by initials literally—was forceful and quite good at it.

After about a month of observing, I finally worked up the nerve to take the microphone and speak. Barbara, from her seat next to mine, immediately started whispering in my ear the type of things my father used to say to me: "What do you have to say that anybody would ever want to listen to? Why are you talking? You don't know what you're talking about. Just shut up." It was so uncalled for and so brutal. I said back to her, "Barbara, be quiet." But she kept on doing it, not just at that first meeting when I spoke but during several subsequent ones as well. Meanwhile there was always an audience present and we were broadcast on television. The audience and TV viewers could not hear her nasty comments, but they sure could hear my non-sequiturs of "Barbara, stop. Leave me alone." I bet they wondered why I was constantly interrupting myself like a loony bird.

Those situations, cruel as they were, became good learning experiences. They taught me to use the same skill that I had used most of my life—just forge ahead regardless of the chaos around me. So I trained myself to just keep talking and block her out. On the other side of me sat Frank Shaffer-Corona. He was always ranting so I had to double-train myself to block both of them out. Boy, did that come in handy over the years, both at home and at work. In a strange way, I was always grateful to Barbara. She meant me harm then—but she ended up doing me a favor. Interestingly, she would, years later, do me many well-intended favors.

Reinstituting Standardized Tests

I represented Ward 3, west of Rock Creek Park, where most schools were performing comparatively well. We couldn't really measure it, though, because at that point in 1974/75, there were no standardized tests taking place in the D.C. Public Schools (DCPS) as Sizemore, with the Board's concurrence (including its President, Marion Barry) had done away with them. So we didn't even have a measuring stick to determine how badly we were doing—or how well in the few cases that was so.

Once I found my voice on the Board of Education, I began using it. And the first cause I took on was a return to standardized testing. But I encountered firm resistance. Superintendent Sizemore claimed that standardized tests were racist. I responded strongly: "That may certainly be true. But this is a racist world and we must give our students the tools to compete in that world. Imperfect or not, we needed some kind of comparative measuring device. Having none is doing our children no favors."[6]

My argument prevailed and standardized testing was reinstated by a majority vote of the Board. It was my first hard-won victory, which gave me a new feeling of confidence and strength.

The Battle Over Barbara Sizemore

I needed that strength as we headed into 1975 and the battle to remove a sitting Superintendent, who did not want to leave. There was a long list of failures for which to hold her accountable. One of the most egregious was hiring over 2,200 people in positions that had not been budgeted. So in the middle of the school year, an enormous number of students had to be shifted into other classes when their teachers had to be removed because there was no money to pay them.

Not just that, but numerous plans that were required by the courts to be submitted had not been. There was failure to deliver a plan to equalize distribution of resources in schools, failure to deliver required playground safety reports, failure to provide curriculum development, and failure to provide a legislative package that would allow more school control of construction and maintenance. No annual report was done to give recommendations for permanent tenure as was required for the '73-'74 school year, etc.

When school was set to start that fall in early September, students did not even have textbooks—and they didn't arrive until October. Obviously, so little was being done. And this was all on top of having a failing school system in general.

Sizemore took no responsibility for these failures and instead tossed blame. Amazingly, she made her failings somehow a racial issue. Just how did her not turning in reports that were due translate to racism? It didn't. She even accused some members of the Board of attacking not only her, but black children. This seemed particularly nonsensical as we were legitimately holding her accountable for failing to serve the students of DCPS, 95% of whom were African American. Shame on us for trying to give them a better education. How terribly racist! Those children were being attacked by her failures, not the other way around. Many of us on the Board, black and white, found it maddening, but this is what we had to contend with.

Superintendent Sizemore also lambasted Congress for being a racist power structure, which was not helpful in that Congress had so much control over District affairs. Whether there was legitimacy to her claim or not (and I feel there was some), the District still had to get its budget through Congress—and our gripe was not about funding then as we had the highest per capita expenditures in the nation. Thus, that rhetoric was counterproductive. (And we needed those funds to be at least at that level as we also had the highest percentage of disadvantaged students in the country.)

The racial divisiveness continued. At a workshop we held at *The Washington Post* in early 1975, before we made a move against her, Superintendent Sizemore said that we had to recognize that black children just learn differently than white children. I was so overcome by that statement, without even meaning to, I stood up and said that was one of the most racist things I had ever heard.

Black children learn differently from white children? That's something I would expect the Ku Klux Klan to say, certainly not her. I could understand saying some children who come from impoverished single-parent backgrounds, white or black, might need some extra attention, or that there should be educational materials that acknowledge various ethnic cultures. But to just say black children learn differently from white children made no sense to me and yes, I thought it was racist and said so. And by the way, it did end the conversation that day.

Removing the Superintendent wasn't easy. The Board had offered her a chance to resign by buying out her contract, which was worth about $46,000. (Now remember, this was 1974 and considered a good salary then.) But she rejected the buy-out, opting to fight to keep her job. Her faults and inadequacies were many and well-known, but we needed to build a formal legal case that would stand up in court if it should come to that—and we knew it probably would. We also wanted to diffuse the racial charges by articulately and understandably presenting the facts.

As we approached the firing of Sizemore that summer, the atmosphere was chaotic and emotional charged. She had supporters who heckled and disrupted the Board's every meeting. This caused many delays, which further elongated the process.

The six of us on the Board who wanted Superintendent Sizemore dismissed—Julius Hobson Jr., Reverend Ray Kemp, Bill Trainor, Hilda Mason, Betty Ann Kane and I—worked very hard, along with the Board's General Counsel David Splitt, on planning the strategy and putting together the charges and specifications to file against her. Hilda Mason and I had also recruited our husbands, Charlie Mason and David, both gifted lawyers, to help in this whole process. It really saved the taxpayers a huge amount of money to have their free and valuable expertise.

We were a mixed-race group, and as a group, we decided to beat Sizemore at her own racial game. We chose to use an arbitration format since we felt our case was solid. To hear the case, we selected Herbert O. Reid, who was a nationally, even internationally, prominent and well-respected African American civil rights lawyer. He had represented Adam Clayton Powell in the Bronx and was very involved in fighting racism. I'm sure even Barbara Sizemore was not unhappy to see him named by us.

The procedure went on for months. Toward the end, when Sizemore saw that our case was so strong, she came back to the Board and said she was ready to take the settlement—the $46,000 we had offered before. But at that point, because of the enormous amount of time, effort and money we had expended on the case (transcripts, court reporters, Reid's salary, etc.) we were not about to settle. And furthermore, we were not about to reward the chaos she had caused.

In May of 1975, the Committee of the Whole adopted charges of inefficiency against Superintendent Sizemore. The Board was subsequently due to adopt those charges in June and we were anxious to do so. As I told *The Washington Post* on June 17th, "[I] didn't want to go through another year of the shambles we have now."[7] But the meeting had to be adjourned when Sizemore supporters rushed the conference tables and a stink bomb was set off in the chambers. We did adopt the charges on August 20th with a vote of six to three. The three Board members against the dismissal of Sizemore and fighting it all the way were Barbara Lett Simmons, Frank Shaffer-Corona and Bettie Benjamin.[8]

We had presented 13 charges with 17 legal specifications to support her dismissal. After an ironclad process that lasted several months, Herbert Reid upheld all of them.[9] It was a huge victory for the Board members who stood up to her—and for our public school children. And I felt a tremendous amount of pride personally. We could now move on and find a Superintendent who could lift the D.C. Public Schools.

Picking Up a Pen

Even in the midst of our battle against Sizemore, we had to contend with a critical *Washington Post*. Their editorials were almost comical in their criticism. One day they said the process was going too slow, the next week they'd say it was too fast. In addition, the *Post* painted their criticism with such broad strokes. The Superintendent and some members of the Board certainly deserved criticism. But they wrote scathing editorials directed at us all—both the Superintendent and the Board in its entirety, urging voters to clean house. There was no discerning between ineffective and effective Board members or those who were taking on the legal battle. There wasn't even recognition that it was a legal battle that had to be played out in formal hearings. It was so unfair. And speaking of counter-productive!

Instead of just sitting on the anger I felt at their misguided blame, I got out a pen and paper and wrote a scathing letter myself to the editor of the *Post*. I even verbatim quoted their contradictory editorials, which was quite satisfying at the time, and was even more so when they published it. Then and there, I found my voice not only verbally but through writing. This new-found communication outlet served me well during my long political career. And it also proved to be quite therapeutic for me both professionally and personally over the years.

I also began writing a regular column, "Carol Schwartz Reports," (bet you didn't know I was a poet too) for the *Northwest Current* and the *Uptown Citizen*, at their request, and which kept constituents apprised of the happenings on the Board of Education. Soon I was also writing for *The Georgetowner*—and all for free for those free newspapers. Even though I represented Ward 3 where these papers were based, *The Washington Informer* Publisher and Editor Calvin W. Rolark (also President and Founder of the United Black Fund) called and asked me to write a regular column on education for his paper as well, although it was based in Anacostia/Ward 8. Of course I said yes and was very flattered to have been asked. (Calvin Sr. sadly passed away in 1994 at the age of 67. He is also fondly remembered for his phrase: "If it is to be, it is up to us." Calvin Rolark Jr. called from Indiana yesterday. We have been friends for decades and I am fond of his sister Denise Rolark Barnes, who still own and runs *The Washington Informer*.)

When I'm passionate about an issue or angered at a situation, I have proven to be a pretty good writer. But just writing on demand is much harder for me. Still, it was good to have these regular columns as a soapbox to promote my educational philosophy. Later the columns allowed me to speak up on other important city issues, which I continued to do in those papers as well as *Washington Jewish Week* at their request. I also wrote additional op-ed pieces and letters to the editor—that were *not* requested.

Dr. Vincent E. Reed

After the battle to fire Barbara Sizemore was over and won (and we had also won a less fraught battle against head lice which had broken out among students at several Northwest schools),[10] I was selected for the committee charged with finding a new Superintendent. We succeeded when we promoted from within Dr. Vincent E. Reed, a well-respected African American educator in his mid-40s. Vince had been, among other things, a Principal of Woodrow Wilson High School and was serving as Associate State Superintendent when he was appointed.

Dr. Reed lived up to our expectations as an outstanding Superintendent because he was a strong leader and had a real and demonstrated commitment to children. We worked very well together and were on the same page regarding eliminating social promotions, raising graduation standards, improving teacher qualifications and evaluations, implementing a back-to-basic curriculum, and enlarging the number of pre-school programs— all of which we did. (In fact, we were practically the only school system in the country that had pre-school programs in our elementary schools in the mid-1970s.) We also tried to bring D.C. its first model academic high school, but more on that later. I admired

Vince so and we became friends. In fact, I remain good friends with him and his dear wife Frances to this day, visiting recently.

A Presidential Appointment

Back in 1974 when I was running for the D.C. Board of Education, I was appointed by President Gerald Ford to the National Advisory Council on the Education of Disadvantaged Children (National Advisory Council). This was a 15-member advisory group which oversaw the federal Title I funds used to supplement education for children from low-income homes. The National Advisory Council reviewed the effectiveness of compensatory education programs using those funds, and made recommendations for improvement. It was a real honor to receive that appointment. Even when my term expired in 1977, President Jimmy Carter kept me on so I served until 1979 and was elected Vice Chair all five years. I made some really good friends there, including Dorothy Fleegler from Florida and Alan Woods, who became somewhat of a mentor here in D.C.—and both were helpful in opening up doors for me later on.

During my term, I wrote major papers on the state of education for disadvantaged students, including one published by Ohio State University. I was also invited to speak at several educational conferences around the country. One time, when I stopped by Midland for a couple of days on the way to California, where I was scheduled to be the keynote speaker at a statewide conference of 3,000 school administrators, my father was his usual supportive self. I was sitting there working on my speech and he asked me what I was doing. I told him. He said, "Why would anyone want to hear anything you have to say?" Although I was insecure about speaking in front of so many people, his nastiness helped spur me on. I ended up doing an unusually good job. Take that, Dad.

I also served from 1975 to 1978 as a member of both the D.C. Advisory Panel on the Education of Handicapped Children as well as the Mayor's Ad-Hoc Committee on Special Education.

Education Reform Before It Was Fashionable

Learning to speak and write more forcefully allowed me to air the passionate concerns I had, and still do, about education. The issues I brought up then are still being debated today. But in the mid-'70s, things like a longer school day and ending social promotions were not in vogue, and it really took a lot of courage to speak up on those topics. Yet I was so excited not only to be speaking up on those topics. Yet I was so excited not only to be speaking up, but to be on the Board of Education, where I could actually do something about them. And being on the National Advisory Council, which exposed me to successful programs at work throughout the country, put me in a better position to evaluate problems here and attempt to make needed changes. I was also active with the National School Boards Association and served on its Task Force on Improving the Quality of Teaching in the late '70s.

Superintendent Reed and I as Chair of the Education Programs Committee led a renewed focus on teacher competency through putting in place higher recertification requirements and improved personnel evaluations. Though not to disparage the great many teachers of quality, we needed to make certain all teachers met a high level. Vince and I also made sure that a competency-based curriculum for students was implemented. And even though student testing was controversial in the District at the time, I consistently beat the drum for it.

An op-ed I wrote that ran in *The Washington Post* on May 17, 1977 articulated my views on raising standards: "How can we expect our teachers to teach the basic skills if they themselves don't possess them? ... A common cry is that testing, both of teachers and students, is culturally and thus racially biased. I say 1/3 plus 1/4 equals 7/12 in any language, any culture. My main concern is the 95% black and 5% other students who are being cheated scholastically while we debate the relevancy of tests." Finally, in the same piece, I put the onus on everyone in the community: "Taxpayers and holders of the purse strings have the responsibility of providing us with the adequate resources (both authoritative and financial) to do our job. Even the media have a responsibility. They should encourage us by highlighting our successes as well as exposing our failures."[11] Our public education system is something we all need to be invested in. I felt that way then and still do today.

Early in 1974, the Duke Ellington School of the Arts was established by the Board of Education, led by Marion Barry, after it had been promoted by art activists Mike Malone and Peggy Cooper Cafritz. Right after entering office in November of 1974, I worked to support their efforts for Ellington which was to take over the old Western High School building on 36th St. and Reservoir Rd, N.W. As the then Chair of the Committee on Capital Improvements, I immediately made sure that dollars were found to enable the complete remodeling of the Duke Ellington School. I was anxious to see this valuable arts center readied and put to use right away for our talented students who qualified.

Duke Ellington School of the Arts has truly been an asset to our school system for over 40 years. Many esteemed artists have been part of the programs such as dancer/choreographer/actor Debbie Allen, who was a teacher there, as well as comedian Dave Chappelle and opera singer Denyce Graves, who are alumni. Ellington has also found a good ally for many years in the John F. Kennedy Center for the Performing Arts.

Precious Pets

Pets have always had a special place in my life. Early on, I had cats and still adore them. But since David was allergic, we sadly decided not to get another one. Thank goodness, though, my daughter Hilary has had two magnificent rescue cats, Poochie and V.V., who I've gotten to hang out with a lot. (Very sadly, Poochie just passed away at 13 from various illnesses, which we spent a fortune on over the years, but she was more than worth it. Imagine a beautiful, neat cat who would lick you like a dog. That was her.)

In 1975, when the kids were 7, 6 and 4, we adopted our first dog Candy from a rescue shelter. (Guess who named her? The same mind that had previously come up with Boots and Snappy.) She was a beautiful large shepherd mixed-breed, and we and the kids really loved her. We always adopted mixed-breed rescues and all my children in adult life have continued that practice.

Candy loved us too, and in fact, too much. She was so protective that it started to be a problem. She became aggressive. When the kids would have friends over, we were worried Candy was going to attack them. And she did attack a man who was just walking down our street. Although he was unharmed other than his suit, which we paid for, we realized it was too dangerous to keep her.

When we had to part with her, I was the hysterical one, even though it was David and the kids' idea to get her in the first place. For days I went around the house crying because I'd turn the corner and expect to see beautiful Candy there. I missed her so. Thankfully, not long after that, we learned that one of our babysitters had a friend who was keeping a dog outside, chained to a porch day and night, in hot and cold weather. When I found out about this dog being abused as well as missing Candy, I had to rescue this animal for her sake and mine. Midget filled the void for the whole family. (Please note that she came with the name. We certainly wouldn't have chosen it, but kept it because that's what she knew and answered to—if she decided to answer.)

Midget was an adorable fairly large multi-breed mix, who was about two years old when we got her. She was never that well-trained but she was so mild-mannered and precious. What a wonderful dog with the small exception that we couldn't ever leave the door open or out she'd go. That would always cause quite a production as the kids would run out to catch her, yelling "Midget!" throughout the neighborhood. The kids next door would inevitably get recruited into the chase. They'd develop creative ways to bring her back. Getting in the car was a favorite. They'd all climb in, pretending they were going on a trip, and Midget never wanted to be left behind. There would be cheers of joy when she climbed into the car and they got her, until she got smart enough not to fall for that trick.

We did manage to train Midget not to go into the living room because of fearing harm to the expensive Kirman rug (remember that story?) and furniture. It seemed like she was always so good about staying out of that room. But every time we'd drive up to the house when she was home alone, we'd see her through the large front window, relaxing on the living room couch. As soon as she'd hear the car, she'd run out of the room like no one was the wiser. The worn-out spot on the sofa where she sat was also a tell-tale sign. I still have that sofa (in fact I'm sitting on it right now) and when I look at it, I think of her. We finally gave up keeping her out of the room, 1) because we couldn't and 2) because she was so cute when she sat on that couch like a real person, her butt on the seat and front paws on the floor.

Midget was my company after the kids went off to college. We had her about 14 years until 1990. She was really old by then. She couldn't walk. I would lift her up—and she was a big dog—to take her outside to relieve herself and she would just collapse. It was so sad. I took her to the vet, who said it was cruel at this point to keep her around, and that it would be more merciful to let her go. I petted her, crying, saying goodbye while they put her to sleep. She was a sweet, loving and marvelous addition to the family and she helped me through some very trying times. I loved her so. And I still miss her to this day.

Elvis Has Left the Building

Back in 1977, August 16th to be exact, Elvis Presley died. He was only 42. Elvis had played a role in my life: skipping school to run to the train station as he rolled through after his army stint, dancing to "Don't Be Cruel" in junior high and beyond, having people tell me when my hair was short that we looked alike, seeing him perform in Las Vegas and watching David become enamored, his buying belts in our store, the fact that we were both born in Mississippi and then both moved to Tennessee. I learned the news of his death while we were in Rehoboth Beach, Delaware for a few weeks at a rented condo. I didn't get dressed all day. I just sat on the couch in my nightgown watching the news reports and sometimes crying. Too young, too talented—it really was a loss.

It was obvious that Elvis died from drugs (even though we don't exactly know which kind) and probably alcohol. But it was just another example of losing so many great talents in the same sort of self-abusive way: Judy Garland, Jimi Hendrix, Janis Joplin, John Belushi, Michael Jackson, Whitney Houston, Philip Seymour Hoffman, Prince, Kurt Cobain and countless more.

Ma

My mother-in-law Blanche, who, as mentioned, I called "Ma," had beautiful short white hair, which was always perfect, and striking blue eyes. She dressed well in spite of having modest means, and wore lots of bright colors. Ma loved to buy our daughters cute matching outfits. (I often did so as well with Steph in red and Hilary in blue.)

One interesting quirk about Ma is that she never would tell her age. I asked David when we were dating how old his mother was and he said he did not know. And I thought maybe that was because he never asked. So after we were married, I said, "Ma, how old are you?" And she said, "I do not tell my age." I said, "But Ma, we're your children. You can tell us. We won't tell anybody if you don't want anyone to know." She said, "I just don't tell." Obviously she didn't like the question so I never asked again.

Over fifteen years later, I got a call from Ma in the fall, and she said, "Carol, I know you've always wanted to know my age, so I'm going to let you know that my next birthday, I will be 80 years old." I was pleased that she told me and was especially pleased that she did so in time for me to help plan an 80th birthday party for her and her friends. (Ma did tell me later that one of the reasons she kept her age to herself was because she didn't want to discourage her younger friends from traveling with her for fear she would get ill.) She lived for nearly five more good years after that call.

Ma had her share of physical difficulties. Her neck was locked in place so she could not turn it at all. If she needed to look to one side, she had to rotate her whole body. This condition had occurred when she was in her 50s, long before I met her. While she was on a vacation in Arizona, her neck just froze. But I admired the fact that she never complained. I certainly would have. She also had a pacemaker since the mid-1970s.

When my husband David and I first got together, Ma seemed to just tolerate me. I could tell my being a Republican made her nauseous and caused her great embarrassment. And she would get in a jab here and there. Despite that, I was always nice to Ma. I am nice to strangers so I sure would be nice to my mother-in-law, and did try to include her. I also felt for her because she was alone. Her husband had died in 1958, and David was her only child.

Born and raised in the Bronx, Ma was of Hungarian descent. She did not like to cook much except for one dish, stuffed cabbage, a recipe from her Eastern European heritage. It was sublime. I always asked her to make it for me, and she was pleased to be asked.

Ma was reluctant to leave the Bronx, even when the neighborhood got more dangerous, first because she was born and raised there and then because she had a very large two-bedroom rent-controlled apartment which was hard to give up. But in her last couple of years in New York, she made the switch to Manhattan and a large subsidized efficiency apartment, which she and I enjoyed decorating together.

Several years later, around 1978, Ma mentioned wanting to move down to West Palm Beach, Florida. During the last seven or eight years of her life in New York, she spent a couple of months in Florida on her own during the winter where she would rent a small place. Ma started out in Miami Beach and then each year would head further north, including Deerfield and finally, West Palm Beach, which was her favorite. I always admired that this 65 to 70-something-year-old would just take off to a strange place knowing no one and explore, especially since she didn't even drive. Usually I would go visit her for a long weekend wherever she landed.

Ma wanted to move to West Palm Beach full-time and was pleased that her best friend Miriam, who was a little younger and just retiring, also wanted to relocate there. They had gone down and found a new development that was being built—a Century Village-type senior community, but smaller and a teensy bit more upscale. Ma said she might rent from an owner because if she bought she was worried she would not have enough money to live on and certainly not be able to travel. That's when I said, "Ma, we can do this for you. We can buy it and you can carry the maintenance." (It cost $23,000 in 1979 and not so much more than that today.) David was starting to do well so I felt comfortable saying what I said, and David certainly agreed.

I tried to talk Ma into getting the one-bedroom plus den option, but she refused and said that a one-bedroom was enough. Afterwards, for those ten years I slept in the twin bed next to her on visits, and now decades later (I still go there when I'm not working for a few months in the winter), I sure wished she had gone with the option. (Okay, I could have upgraded myself over the years, but I'm sentimentally attached to this place because of her.)

Ma was overwhelmed by the move and all the details, and the fact that she didn't drive made it even harder. So I decided to take a very active role in helping her through the process. I carved out time from a busy School Board schedule, not to mention the kids (9, 8 and 6), and flew down to meet her to pick out and order the furniture. As luck would have it, I had terrible plantar warts on one foot during the trip. (My nickname on posters could now be "warthand" *and* "wartfoot.") I was in pain and could barely move.

We stayed at a Holiday Inn and we ran around to all the stores. (Well, I should say I hobbled around with a cane.) We had decided which pieces she would bring from New York, but picked out new items, like bedroom furniture and a living/dining room set, which she bought. She loved a marble table and a mirror, but they were too expensive for her to buy. They became David's and my housewarming gifts to her.

About a month later, the apartment was ready and the furniture was set to be delivered. So I flew back down to meet her. By this point, I had plantar warts on the bottom of both feet (now make it "wart*feet*"). I felt miserable, in so much pain. I was no longer using a cane; I was now on crutches. We shopped for the remaining items, such as curtains and other odds and ends. After five or six days, we got her completely moved in. Every picture was on the wall. I hung the curtain rods and curtains. (I've always been cheap so had become handy.) I'm not sure how I did all that considering my condition. But the place was absolutely perfect in our eyes. And she was the happiest I'd ever seen her.

From that day on, Ma thought I walked on water. She was so grateful to have somebody just orchestrate that whole move, which was so intimidating for her. And she appreciated my decorative touches as she was not so strong in that area. It was an incredible transformation in how she felt about me. It was no longer, "My son used to buy me nice gifts before he was married." She began telling her friends how much she loved me and that she could never have done it without me. In fact, a couple of those friends told me that she felt closer to me than she did her own son. I then did feel like I became the daughter she never had. I had always tried to be kind to her. But once Ma started to be so loving and appreciative, I began to really love her more too and it became a wonderful relationship—a real friendship. Was it enough to make her forgive me for being a Republican? I'm really not sure, but at least she didn't talk about it anymore.

Ma's Son

Meanwhile I stayed busy with work and it helped distract me from my relationship with David. He was a nice man—a great father and provider. But he was not very affectionate and loving toward me in ways I needed. My mother sadly commented once 20 years into my marriage, "I knew David wasn't the right person for you. He's a cold fish like your mother." It was shocking to hear that from her. I had never thought about him that way—or even her. But with the exception of his children, he was not affectionate except when he was needy or ready.

Recently I saw a quote from Loretta Lynn about her husband of many years, who she called "Doo," which was in her second autobiography. I'm going to substitute the names: "[David] was a good man and a hard worker. But he was an alcoholic, and it affected our marriage all the way through."[12] That's exactly the way I felt then and feel now, nearly 30 years later.

With David, the drinking, which became more pronounced over the years, added to his isolation, self-absorption, and darkened mood—at least the David I got to see. What most people saw was a humorous, light-hearted life of the party. David would even take the microphone to sing at firm parties—after a few drinks. During a couple of these parties, he sang satirical songs he had written about people at the firm, and with his wit, got many laughs. He really was a showman.

At home, he continued to love to sing too and often would pick up a brush to use it as a "microphone." I must have seen it a thousand times but I giggled every time. He could be goofy. Sometimes at home while playing LPs he'd break out into a chicken dance.

At times I would ask him to do imitations, which perked both of us up as they were so amusing. He had a good ear like my son Doug does, who is also great at accents. David could skillfully mimic the singing of Dean Martin, Sammy Davis Jr., Tom Jones and Frank Sinatra—well the last one, not so skillfully.

I did appreciate when David would sometimes say to me, after I had made a special effort with an older, struggling or sick person in need: "Carol, you are such a sweet person." And when out at parties, I also always appreciated that David was one husband you did not have to drag onto the dance floor. He loved to dance, which I thought was really great.

That life-of-the-party David would dim some as the evening out wore on, though, as he continued drinking. If we played cards, which he loved doing, we who sat around the table often got the benefit of his hand as it was well-displayed. My usual refrain, "David, please breast your cards," was heeded until five seconds later when the card faces would come again.

David would also often get grouchy and snap at me. He had a somewhat cruel-type humor, which sometimes made me the target. I was glad at first for the attention—any attention; but as it went on, and got meaner, I really got my feelings hurt. He was usually sorry afterwards and wrote notes of apology. "I'm sorry, honey, to be so grouchy." I still have all his notes. And I always forgave him, or at least tried. But I was becoming very sad and bitter in the process.

It was especially hard to forgive him, though, for not being particularly nice to his mother. He was her only child, and even if she annoyed him, I thought he should have paid more attention. When we would call Ma, he'd talk to her for a minute or less—if you call this talk: "How are you?" she'd ask. "Fine." "How's work?" "Fine." And then he'd hand the phone back to me. When she came into town, he never invited her to his office or out to lunch. Not once. I certainly did that and always tried to keep her busy and/or with me even though I also worked. He basically outsourced the relationship to me. I admit I never liked that about him. It affected my respect and feelings for him. Remember the old adage—how a man treats his mother ...

CHAPTER 12

Reelection and More Challenges

In 1977, I was reelected to the School Board, garnering 77% of the vote in a three-way race.[13] I was then elected by my fellow members to be Vice President and was reelected as such for the next two years. I took pride in being the first Ward 3 member to be elected to a position of leadership on the Board, as well as being the only person at that time who had ever been elected to a leadership role three years in a row.

The Board of Education had a lot of in-fighting with many strong personalities. I had some continual issues with my old nemesis, Barbara Lett Simmons, who insisted upon creating tension instead of using her skills and energy for more positive things. In November of 1977, Barbara convened a separate meeting of only the African American members of the Board to discuss the future direction of the body. It was needlessly divisive, especially when we were a tiny group and racially evenly represented; plus, we were never racially split on any issue.

I had to confront it head on because 1) being me and 2) now in a leadership role, I felt a need to keep us moving forward together. I wrote her a letter that stated, "I can only imagine the furor if I, as a white member of the Board, had convened a white caucus for the purpose of discussing the same issue." I cc'd "Board members (without regard to race, creed, color or national origin)." Thank goodness, the "caucus" disappeared.

Over those years in the mid-to-late '70s, we also had to contend with constant cuts to the school system's budget. For the 1977 budget, Board members and Superintendent Reed had to battle Mayor Walter E. Washington to limit the cuts to $11 million rather than a proposed $15 million. In the meantime, Mayor Washington recommended an 18% pay increases for certain city employees—and none of them education-related.[14]

In 1977, we instituted another test: the Comprehensive Test of Basic Skills (CTBS) for 3rd, 6th and 9th graders. We wanted another tool to measure D.C. students against national benchmarks while getting a measurement of the school system itself.[15]

Around the same time, I also had to fight a battle to keep open Ward 3 schools, which were the ones thriving in the District, both in enrollment and test scores. Some mandatory closings were needed as enrollment overall had dropped—not only because of concerns about our schools, but also because both our city population in general was diminishing and the current generation was having fewer children. Calvin Lockridge, the Ward 8 member, wanted to do all the closings in Ward 3 and distribute those students elsewhere. Some on the Board wanted the closings to impact all Wards. But I fought hard for the Ward 3 schools. I fought not just because I represented them, but because they were succeeding academically as well as growing in population, boosted by their open-enrollment policy of taking kids from all around the city. My argument won the day: no Ward 3 schools were closed. And Calvin and I even became friends afterwards.

In an effort to keep all the schools in D.C. open and with full enrollments, I came up with the idea to do a bumper sticker that read, "A D.C. Public School—Try It, You'll Like It," and personally funded it. It did generate a lot of interest and many bumper stickers were distributed.

We also worked to increase pre-k programs even back in the mid-'70s for two reasons: 1) For disadvantaged children, it is particularly helpful to get them into school as soon as possible with socialization, nutritious meals and early learning. 2) The programs were helpful in attracting middle-class and above families to the public schools under the philosophy of "try it, you'll like it"—and maybe they would stay for the upper grades as well.

(In order to universalize pre-k thirty years later, the Council of the District of Columbia in May of 2008, led by Chair Vincent Gray and co-introduced by me and others, passed the "Pre-K Enhancement and Expansion Act of 2008." It expanded by law pre-k programs in elementary schools to all three and four-year-olds. It has been quite a success. By 2015, 86% of D.C.'s three and four-year-olds were attending a publicly funded pre-school program.[16] And it has particularly helped our disadvantaged children as well as helped increase our public schools' student population.)

Sumner School

Even amid tension on the Board, we did often successfully work together. One thing I'm most proud of in my career is that even when I disagreed with people on issues, I never made it personal. That enabled me to move from issue to issue with ease, making positive, collegial relationships—and often good friendships—along the way, even with the people I battled with most bitterly. That was certainly true of my relationship with Barbara Lett Simmons. In my whole career, there is only one exception—and I will address that later.

Barbara and I worked hand in hand on one of the most gratifying accomplishments I took part in, which was saving Sumner School. Dating back to 1872, Sumner was one of the first schools for African American students in D.C. and was the headquarters of the black school system. (Washington sadly had a segregated system.) Sumner is a beautiful landmark with a significant history.

The then unused building was being sold by the Barry Administration to the real estate and publishing magnate Mortimer Zuckerman from New York, who planned to tear it down to build an office building. Barbara Lett Simmons and I joined together to fight the demolition. The day they were to begin the destruction, Barbara and I got a group together and literally stood in front of the bulldozers. We would not be moved—and they stopped.

Once publicity began and consciousness was raised about Sumner's history, Zuckerman agreed to leave Sumner alone; well, actually something even better. In a deal worked out with the city, Zuckerman was able to buy the building next door for offices— half the original size—and renovated Sumner School for free. We saved the school and later helped it achieve National Landmark status. It became a museum, thanks to the efforts of the late and great Dick Hurlbut, the longtime government employee who came up with the idea, implemented it, and became its archivist. Sumner displays art exhibits, houses the archives of the D.C. Public Schools, as well as provides space for non-profit-type events. Today, it still stands proud and strong on 17th and M Sts., N.W. Go see it—Monday-Friday, 9-5! I remain pleased to have worked closely with Barbara on such a worthwhile—and winning—effort. And Mort Zuckerman deserves a lot of kudos as well.

Israel

In 1978, David and I made our first visit to Israel. Stuart Bernstein, who was a client of David's, and his wife Wilma organized a trip for the Weizmann Institute of Science there. David and I loved Israel. It was amazing to see such a small country with such distinctive cities just a few miles from each other. Haifa, sitting on a hill overlooking the Mediterranean Sea, is reminiscent of a small San Francisco, Tel Aviv is a modern metropolis not unlike a smaller and much warmer Chicago, Jerusalem is like you've walked back into biblical times, and the small desert city of Eliat is like Saudi Arabia.

Most of the people we went with, which numbered about 60, were cliquish as they had been friends since childhood. So David and I were basically on our own other than the group activities. Our tendency had always been to bring out-of-their-element people under our wing (even when we were out of our element). Thus, we struck up an acquaintance with a man, Harry Friedman, from the group who was traveling alone without his wife, Joy. She was a wealthy woman who had gone back to school in her 60s to become a family therapist. And since one of her families was in crisis, she wouldn't leave them—but insisted that her husband go.

Harry was the nicest guy, lots of fun, and looked like Kirk Douglas. I remember his patience as David and I both spent time shopping for leather coats for each of us. When we arrived back, Joy was at the airport to pick Harry up. Although they were over 20 years older, we became good friends. Unfortunately, not many years later, Joy got cancer, and I was grateful to be one of the few people she would see before she passed away. What a dear lady, and I'm so glad to have known her.

I found Israel to be a fascinating, marvelous country and the trip was an eye-opening, enriching experience. By eye-opening, I mean seeing up close and personal the reality of Israel being surrounded by enemies, most wishing to annihilate it, and who are poised just yards away to do so. It made me so much more appreciative of the courage and strength of the Israelis.

And as a Jew who has gone through some persecution for being part of a small religious minority, it is very gratifying to know that there is one tiny spot in this very big world where I could go without fear or worry of being targeted by a majority who could turn against us in a heartbeat—as history has often shown. I wish everybody would just take out a map of the world and label the countries by major religion (Christian, Muslim, Hindu, Jewish, Buddhist) and notice the fact that only Israel is majority Jewish. And then look at the size of Israel in comparison to all the countries on this earth and notice that Israel is just slightly larger than the state of New Jersey. Maybe then you would recognize that it's not too much to ask to have this one small place for Jewish people to call our own.

The fact Israel's extinction is always on the tongues of its enemies is abominable. And not just that, but in their constitutions, preambles, by-laws, etc. That kind of hatred should not be tolerated, and it should never be a basis for negotiation. Also watching the uneven coverage of Israel in the media is maddening as it is so blatantly biased. If Israel is responsible for anything not good, it gets big headlines and coverage. When it is victimized, the coverage is hard to find. Its leaders are also held up to the harshest possible light. And many of those who take Israel to task never mention the behavior of its multitude of enemies and *their* leaders. Such a different and unfair standard.

Strike

The Washington Teachers Union (WTU) contract expired on July 25, 1978, and the Board of Education reinstated it for 90 days to prepare a new contract.[17] It was not going to be easy. The present contract was extraordinarily favorable for teachers, who I believe should have a good contract. But the current contract made it so difficult to get the improvements the D.C. schools so desperately needed. Under its guidelines, principals couldn't enact policies in their own school without getting approval from their union members. And overly strict protections and required arbitration processes made it nearly impossible to remove incompetent teachers.

The school crisis was real. We had among the lowest test scores in the country and certainly the lowest in the metropolitan area. And even with having at least 75% of our students categorized as disadvantaged, it appeared D.C. had the shortest school day. In comparison to my teaching experience in Austin and Montgomery County nearby, it was short. I then got someone to help me and we started calling jurisdictions, digging into the data, and verified that D.C. *did* have the shortest instructional day in the country.

The other school systems in the region started school at 8:30 a.m. and ended at 3:30 or 4:00 p.m. Most had a one-half hour lunch break. And all of them met a minimum instructional time of six hours. On the other hand, D.C. had a school day from 9:00 a.m. to 3:00 p.m. with a one-hour lunch period, so only had five hours of instructional time. Then when you looked at the nation, the time that District children spent in school was about 180 hours per year *less* than the average. At the same time, D.C.'s starting teachers had the highest salary in the region. I felt strongly it was wrong to have the kids in the area who were most in need of teaching time getting the least amount. And I knew we had to try to do something about it.[18]

I initially proposed an increase in the instructional time to six and half hours a day so that our students could go from having the shortest instructional time to among the highest. It could be achieved by adding one hour to the day with a half-hour lunch, for example. I proposed that this extension be mandatory for any new contract. I was glad to have started the ball rolling in this direction and was pleased that most of my colleagues did a buy-in. Since all of us on the Board understood it was a negotiation, we compromised early in the process and asked for an increase to six hours of instructional time instead of the six and a half. This proposed increase was not outrageous at it would only put us in line with surrounding jurisdictions and the national average. And it should have been done decades ago.

In previous years, contract negotiations mainly centered around minutia such as how much room on the bulletin board should be devoted to union material and how many sodas should be available in the lounge vending machines. Not this time, as far as I was concerned. With so many critical issues at hand, it was time to get serious.

Some could have thought it unfair that we were asking for a longer day without being able to give additional money—even if our teachers worked a shorter day than surrounding school districts while being paid a higher starting salary—but all we were asking for was more parity.

Also, even if we had wanted to offer more money (which had already been done anyway), we couldn't. The Board of Education did not have the power to bargain over teachers' salaries and benefits. Those financial matters were under the jurisdiction of the Mayor and the Council, *not* the Board of Education.

But here's the most *crucial* point: As we were trying to accomplish what I thought was a novel idea, I learned that a few years before, in 1971, the Washington Teachers Union actually *agreed* to a longer school day in exchange for the Board supporting a pay increase. The Board kept its part of the bargain and advocated to get the pay increase, which the teachers then received. WTU, though, then reneged on its agreement to a longer day. In the seven years since, teachers went on receiving big increases annually. So it turned out we were only asking for what had previously been agreed to—and what we for seven years had been *paying for*.

At the end of 1978, as we continued negotiations with the Washington Teachers Union, the longer day was an important stipulation. The only other crucial specification we asked for was an improved grievance process to make it possible to remove incompetent teachers. Superintendent Vincent Reed was completely on board with these recommendations. We also had the public and media consistently complaining about the school system, and demanding improvements. A contract that at least insisted upon these important improvements—more time in school for our kids and better teachers to teach them—was an attempt to fulfill those demands as well as our own heartfelt convictions.

I asked for needed support from the public and media, as I knew the fight would get tough. As I wrote in my regular column in the Ward 3 newspapers and *The Washington Informer*: "I believe our cause is just and I will persevere—I only hope you will do the same if the need arises."[19]

The need did arise. WTU refused any lengthening of instructional time. It wanted a grievance process that was even more favorable to the teachers (as if that was humanly possible in those days). It stipulated additional requirements for transfer, such as in no case would a teacher who has received an involuntary transfer be subjected to an interview by a principal at the receiving school. It also demanded a union fee from all teachers, even those who didn't want to belong to the Union. We were at a stalemate.

Union President William Simons leveled the charge that the Board's conditions were tantamount to attempting to break the Union. We weren't trying break WTU; we were only trying to help children and work with the teachers to do so, with just a few conditions that were needed and reasonable.

Now it is commonplace to take on teachers' unions, almost too much, painting them as *only* thing blocking good education in America. In the late '70s in Washington, D.C., it was quite different. Making any demands of the Union, even minimal, was heretic. Today, totally blaming the unions is fashionable. Back then, it took a lot of bravery and stamina. And I found it to be maddening because the teachers and WTU knew as well as we did that incompetent teachers not *only* hurt students, but they also drag down the school system and its reputation—*and* hurt good teachers and their Union in the process.

At that time, *all* teachers upon condition of their employment had signed a contract *not* to strike, as it would be too detrimental to the students of the District. So it was actually illegal to strike. But starting on March 6, 1979, strike they did.[20]

Since I was a leader in bringing forth the contract conditions that led to the strike, it was a highly stressful period in my life. For the second time on the School Board, I received death threats (the first having taken place during the Sizemore dismissal hearings). Outside my home on Cumberland St., picket lines formed. Even one of my children's classmates marched outside our house. Always the affable hostess, I took lemonade and snacks out to them.

Considering how many in the public were demanding improvements in the school system, it was shocking when so many abandoned us when we took up that fight. The same held true for the media. *Washington Post* editorials put equal blame on the Board of Education for the strike after it had been begging us for years to do something about the state of the schools. Not only begging us to do something, but condemning us for not. However, when we did something and needed their support, they not only didn't offer it, they cut and ran—just like they did during the Sizemore firing. Like I said in the *Washington Star* on March 19, 1979, "It's the same people who cry out for quality education who want us to buckle."[21] It was crazily hypocritical and to this day, I don't understand it.

But I felt undaunted. As I wrote in my column in November of 1978, "I look upon my role as a Board of Education member as tantamount to being the chief negotiator for the approximately 117,000 students ... We represent children and their parents ... I do not intend to compromise the education of our young people."

During the strike, we tried to keep the schools open by recruiting volunteers, even ourselves. I volunteered at Sharpe Health School, a special education school, at 13th and Taylor Sts., N.W.

Again, the School Board was divided. Calvin Lockridge, Alaire Rieffel, Conrad P. Smith and I supported President Minnie Woodson and Superintendent Reed on the stipulations for the contract (our black woman President, two black men, two white women and our black male Superintendent), while Barbara Lett Simmons, Frank Shaffer-Corona, Bettie Benjamin and Victoria Street did not (three black women and one half-Latino man). Again, black and white members were equally divided on both sides of the issue.

Those of us who supported changing the contract filed contempt charges against the Union. A finding of contempt was found by Superior Court Judge Gladys Kessler, who ordered an initial fine of $7,750 and a $5,000 fine for each day the strike continued. And the collection of union dues was stopped.[22]

By March 16th, the Board agreed to reinstate the union dues and sadly rescinded its demand for a longer school day. The Union continued the strike. "We gave them a loaf and they gave us a crumb," I said on March 17th to *The Washington Star*.[23] The Union was so emboldened that by March 18th, Union President Simons made new demands for a 10% pay increase.[24]

Then Mayor Barry, who had received the support of the Washington Teachers Union during his campaign, intervened. He had his lawyer fight for the reinstatement of the old contract until an outside panel could review conditions for a new one.[25] Judge Kessler, after three weeks of the teachers' strike, folded. She restored the contract through July 15th of the next year until the Board and WTU could formulate a new contract with the aid of a fact-finding board.[26] The teachers returned to the classroom. So we were back to the same substandard conditions as when we started. It was so frustrating—and sad.

One night soon thereafter, while I was soaking in the tub, I just started writing in my mind. I jumped out, grabbed a pencil and paper, and wrote "Isn't It Wonderful?"—an op-ed piece for *The Washington Post*, which ran it. It read: "The striking teachers have returned to the classroom. Mediocrity rules the day once again with no hope for improvement." I added, "The media after wringing its hands about the break in children's education can start asking the question—'Why are our children not receiving the quality education they so justly deserve?'" Meanwhile, "The Mayor can continue his campaign and say education is the priority. ... The School Board did try to improve our children's education. We tried to negotiate a new contract and rid this system of the 12-year-old noose around its neck—the old contract. Now due to the Mayor's intervention and Judge Kessler's ruling, the noose is tighter than ever. ... Will test scores go up? Will incompetent teachers miraculously become competent? Will our children who receive the least amount of instructional time in the country receive any more? ... The answer is no. ... But the strike is over. Isn't it wonderful?"[27]

WTU, which broke the law, came out the victor. And those who had been crying for better education—the media, the Mayor, even the public—enabled the outcome. But I had no regrets in taking on the battle that needed to be fought. Even though it didn't end as I hoped, I was honored to work with our President Minnie Woodson, Superintendent Vincent Reed, and colleagues Calvin Lockridge, Alaire Rieffel and Conrad P. Smith in taking on the fight. (My friends Minnie, Calvin and Conrad are now sadly gone.)

Seven months later, on October 29, 1979, the Board and WTU signed a new contract. We did recapture some policy determinations for the Board while protecting the rights of teachers. I can't say we won much in that particular struggle, but my colleagues and I who tried were good soldiers for a good cause. I am proud to have been at the forefront of fighting the powers that be for better education, and I know we did help lay down the path for others to follow. And I am so pleased—although it's taken far too long—that progress on more instructional time did finally start and continues, e.g. DCPS announced in February of 2016 that 10 schools would add a month to their learning time starting in the 2016-2017 academic year.[28]

I am also glad to have continued to maintain cordial relationships with even my worst adversaries. Union President Bill Simons and I remained friendly. When I left the Board of Education a few years later, he sent me a beautiful note that said how much he admired my work on the Board and no matter how heated the debate got, he liked the fact that I never personalized it. He also stated that he respected my being a straight-shooter on where I stood as well as my passionate advocacy for my side. In the end, I respected him for the same.

35th Birthday

In the midst of the strike, I had a special birthday. A best girl-friend, Tay Hahn, invited me to their home for a dinner party for my 35th birthday. The gathering was set for 7:30 p.m. in Potomac, Maryland. Then David got an invitation from his law firm for an event it was having for Western Development (David's client), which started at 6 p.m. in D.C. I told David, "I know we need to make an appearance at the firm party, but we have to leave by 6:45 at the latest as I'm getting stressed about being in Potomac on time for the party Tay and Roger are so generously having for me."

We walked into the Holiday Inn in Georgetown for the law firm event exactly at 6:00, greeted by "Surprise!" David and Tay had orchestrated the whole thing, which was so precious of them. So many of my friends were there, and it was such a fun time.

Speaking of Tay, her father was a Wing Commander in Britain's Royal Air Force, so as a child she lived in many different countries and became quite worldly. However, in her 15 years in this country, Tay had never been to New York City other than its airports. So for Tay's 40th birthday, we took her and Roger on a weekend trip there. We told her about it in a fun way by leaving clues in her home, taking her from the refrigerator to the washing machine, until she opened up the last door to the sounds of "New York, New York." So off we went, leaving all the kids with Ed, including theirs, Phil and Missy, who were like cousins. When we came home from our fabulous time in NYC, the kids put on a soap opera-type play they had written and which left us all in stitches.

A Makeover

In the summer of 1979, I went to Baton Rouge, Louisiana for my cousin Becky's wedding. Mom came in from Midland. (The first thing Mom and I talked about was August, when she and Dad would be hosting Hilary and Doug [Steph was going to camp] in Midland for a few weeks, similar to the summer before when they hosted Steph and Hil for two weeks. The kids found those visits to be fun in that they swam a lot, went to minor league baseball games, and saw shows like *South Pacific* in Odessa. They enjoyed hanging out with Texas Dad at the bank, with Texas Mom at the library, and with both of them amid jeans and boots at the store.)

In Baton Rouge, Mom and I were looking forward to driving to New Orleans after the wedding for several days—just the two of us on a trip for the first time ever. Mom's cousin by marriage from Colorado was also in town for the wedding, and next thing we know, she invited herself on our trip to the Big Easy. Marianne was newly widowed so it was hard to say no. Her late husband, Mom's first cousin, had headed up a successful family-owned business in Denver. Marianne spoke proudly of having been heavy, but had recently lost 50 pounds by dieting and jumping rope. She now looked as glamorous as anyone I'd ever seen.

In New Orleans, we went to store after store where Marianne looked at jewelry. I had always loved looking at antiques, but found jewelry to be of no interest. Boy, did life change! As Marianne took us to an endless number of jewelry stores, in order just to occupy myself, I started glancing in the display cases and discovered that these antique pieces of jewelry were true works of art just like the antiques I adored, but smaller.

I even saw a ring with small sapphires and diamonds which cost $165. I called David to see if he minded if I bought it, and he was actually thrilled that I finally liked a piece of jewelry. That moment started my subsequent lifetime love of jewelry of all kinds, and I admit to having amassed quite a collection.

Marianne amassed more than jewelry in New Orleans, and I played a role. A college friend of Mom's at the wedding told me her younger brother, a newly divorced doctor, lived in New Orleans. I ended up calling him, introducing myself, and telling him about Marianne. He was open to meeting her. They wound up going out that night, and six months later they were married and had 36 lovely years together before he passed in 2015.

It was quite a fruitful trip in other regards too. Not only did I discover jewelry, but I guess due to Marianne's classy style, I began to realize that my non-stylish few items of clothing from basically the G.C. Murphy's of fashion were not befitting of an elected official in D.C. and the wife of a rising lawyer in a prestigious firm—or any 35-year-old for that matter. The old beat had gone on too long. In the early part of my marriage, I didn't even own a pair of earrings. I barely wore makeup. I dressed mostly for comfort. Even in my first years on the Board of Education, I looked like something the cat dragged in. It was time for a change.

After New Orleans, I did buy a few more appropriate clothes and did start wearing a little makeup. For years, I had worn my longer hair straight back with a barrette at the nape of my neck. But then I decided to cut my hair into a more chic style. I actually did start to look better. In fact, at work, many of the secretaries complimented me and several even said, "We always thought that you were pretty and hoped you would fix yourself up more." I always responded with, "I decided to get my act together while there was still an act to get together."

Finding Treasures

Once I started finally getting my act together, I found that the best and cheapest places, other than big sales at some stores, were next-to-new/thrift shops. I really love those. To me it's a threefer: 1) It's recycling, 2) it's inexpensive, and 3) it's often charitable since I normally pick those types of shops that are operated by a charity. I really am a fiscal conservative and I don't like spending more for something than I have to, unless it's really extraordinary.

I like nice shoes but I don't want to pay the hundreds of dollars a pair for them. So I go to charity shops—and sometimes consignment stores—and buy wealthy people's used shoes. Oftentimes rich people don't wear their shoes or purses until they're worn out. In fact, they get rid of them pretty quickly. And I'm waiting to buy them. Same is true of designer clothes. If I need a formal, I have always gone to these types of stores with a couple of exceptions in the last few years, like Sabella Mikesell in Palm Beach. I will buy new clothes now and then, especially when I'm trying to keep local and independently owned boutiques in business. By the way, any savings I get from the next-to-new shops is not hoarded away. It goes to a charitable contribution or to my one purchase passion: jewelry. (I know we all have our own purchasing habits as we should, but I just wanted to share some of mine with you.)

David had always enjoyed, as he was working his way up the economic ladder, buying me nice presents. I must admit, I didn't really appreciate them until the New Orleans trip. But then I was as enthusiastic as David. During this period of time (beginning in 1976), we as a family started spending several weeks in August in Rehoboth Beach, Delaware. In addition to spending time on the beach itself and eating pizza at Grotto's, we enjoyed going to the Stuart Kingston auctions at its gallery on the boardwalk—the last two were David's favorite things to do.

But the highlight of my time there was an annual antique show at the Convention Center. I so preferred browsing through display cases rather than yelling out prices at an auction for all to hear. At one of those display cases in 1977, we met Tom DePrince and Vernon Crawford, a couple of many years from New Jersey, who had wonderful antique jewelry. We soon became very good friends, and they gave us very good prices. Their friendship has remained quite a wonderful part of my life. And since they moved to Rehoboth year-round and I spend more time there now that I'm not working full time, I have more opportunity to see them, as well as Tom's sister Carolyn, and their four adopted children, who are now mostly grown.

Another treasure in Rehoboth was Lucile McCoy who was my across-the-street neighbor, 17 years older, originally from North Carolina and kept the accent. She was my best friend there and we hung out all the time. She was always game to do and go anywhere in spite of her type 1 diabetes. Lucile was a devout Catholic, attended church regularly, and worked with people in prison. She lost her beautiful daughter Louise in a car accident not long after we met. She often told me how our new friendship was comforting, especially during that time. We lost Lucile, who really was a gift to me, in June of 2008 at age 80. I have stayed close to her children, Mary and Tom, who live nearby in Bethel, Delaware.

My Parents' 40th Anniversary

October 17, 1979 was my parents' 40th anniversary. I wanted to do something special for them. They had never traveled except to visit their parents and siblings other than the one-day trip to Carlsbad Cavern in 1955 and that five-day trip to Mexico in 1957.

I decided I would send them to beautiful San Francisco for a week. Neither had ever been. The timing was right as they were winding down from working at the store and had S.W. managing it for them. A few weeks before their anniversary, I began planning the surprise. I purchased the plane tickets and made reservations at a nice hotel in a great part of town. Knowing Johnny's schedule for a trip to Midland, I decided to have the surprise revealed to them at the airport when they would be seeing Johnny off for his return flight to Austin. This was back in the days when you could call the airport and actually get the ticket counter. I did so and recruited the agents there to help me execute the plan.

I knew my parents would stand at the gate and watch to make sure Johnny's plane left. I called the counter, and when told the plane had taken off, I said, "Now." On the airport loud speaker, my parents heard, "Mr. and Mrs. Stanley Levitt, please return to the airline ticket counter." When they came up to the counter, they were handed an envelope with two tickets to San Francisco, a receipt for a paid hotel room for a week, and a $100 check for their first meal there. It was all wrapped in a letter from me, which read: "You have never taken a real trip on your own. Enjoy your 40th anniversary." I was so excited to hear their reaction.

So I waited. I heard nothing. I figured it would take time for them to get home, so I waited more. Nothing. I called the ticket counter again and was assured that they had been there and got the envelope. I thought, "They probably stopped for dinner before returning home. I'll wait some more." I got no call. Nothing. I couldn't believe it. It wasn't just the money I had spent on the trip and the long-distance calls, it was the thought and the planning.

Later that night, having never heard one word, I finally called them. Mom answered the phone and said, "This was very nice to do but I don't think we're going." I said, "That's ridiculous." She then gave Dad the phone and he said, "I won't go to San Francisco. It has too many fags." I yelled, "Then don't go," and I hung up. I had never hung up on my father before, but this was beyond the pale. It was so hurtful to be slapped in the face like that with such non-appreciation; and more importantly, I hated his use of that word, not to mention the feelings behind it.

The next day, they called and said, "We slept on it and decided to go. Thank you." They did go, and it was the best time they ever had in their whole marriage. My father had never bought my mother hardly anything, much less jewelry. All her jewelry came from her mother and Aunt Hilda. But in San Francisco, he bought her a fresh-water pearl necklace, which she wore every day, and a jade pin from Gump's which she adored. They went to many wonderful restaurants and sites, and especially loved eating down at the Wharf. If they were alive today and you asked them the best time they ever had, they would say, "San Francisco for our 40th anniversary." I am happy they enjoyed it, but their initial rejecting reaction and the reason for it still stings.

David's 40th

November 14th of 1979 brought a fun event (sort of)—David's 40th birthday. We took the kids and Ma, who was in from Florida, to dinner at the Palm restaurant. Friends had told me they would be sending a little birthday surprise that night. About 30 minutes in, a clown, balloons, animals, and horns started. The clown then gave out marzipan candies in the shape of a man with a large erection. I must admit I cringed for Ma and the kids. But I thought as it ended, "Oh, that has to be their surprise," and even said, "At least no one knows who we are." Then about 20 minutes later, along comes a very loud singing telegram, which said, "Happy birthday to David Schwartz, a lawyer at ..." and they named the firm ... "and his wife is Carol Schwartz and she is on the Board of ..." and they named the children, etc. It went on and on. It turns out the singing telegram was from the initial friends and the first ballyhoo was courtesy of others. Both were generous and somewhat fun; yet we were relieved when it was over—but I'm sure not as relieved as the other customers.

The Outlaw

As we approached 1980, we on the Board of Education were making some improvements to the school system and had the benefit of a very good Superintendent. But there were many challenges, including the fact that the Board itself was often splintered. This tension sometimes rose to the level of absurdity.

During a Board meeting that lasted past 3 a.m., one member, Calvin Lockridge, grabbed another, Frank Shaffer-Corona, by the throat and started choking him. We all just sat there for a minute or so. Finally, our Superintendent Vince Reed stopped it, and fortunately no one was hurt. Any display of violence is inexcusable—except maybe in this case. We all delayed in reacting for very good reason. The attack recipient was a singularly maddening character. In D.C., like elsewhere, we've had good officials and bad ones. Frank Shaffer-Corona was a legend in the latter category.

He was a perennial thorn in our side as he was always in opposition to any changes and went out of his way to belittle those who tried to make them. But that was nothing compared to his other actions. He used school funds to pay his way to Cuba to give a speech to a "Youth Against Imperialism" rally, as well as to Beirut, Lebanon to conduct a meeting with the Palestinian Liberation Organization (PLO). One of the last straws was when he charged the school system $1,900 on long-distance phone calls to Iran to supposedly negotiate the release of the American hostages—activities and expenses we did not know about until later. And by the way, the calls were not successful. But when he announced that he planned to travel to Tehran, again at the school system's expense, to continue "negotiations," I pounced. I led the Board in passing a resolution censoring him for the non-approved expenditures with declarations such as, "Why should our shrinking education dollars have to pay for his international activities?" We also cut off his ability to charge anything as well as sought reimbursement.

Thankfully, the democratic system worked. He badly lost his seat in November of 1981 after one term. With his own unique point-of-view which never quite dealt with reality, Shaffer-Corona claimed that enemies falsified the returns. He attributed his loss to the CIA and the State Department. I wish I had said to him, "No, Frank, it was not them—it was the intelligent voters."

After his defeat, Frank went back to Texas. He called me several times from there just to chat. That's one nemesis I'm not proud to have stayed on friendly terms with. The last I heard of Frank Shaffer-Corona is that in the late '80s, he escaped to Mexico with $31,000 that was "mistakenly placed in his bank account." He was returned to D.C. and in 1989, pled guilty to the theft of funds.[29]

Running for Board President

After serving since 1974 on the Board of Education and then elected as its Vice President for three years, I ran for President at the beginning of 1980. I had worked hand in hand with all three Presidents (a different one was elected each year) as Vice President and two of them even called me the de facto President.

Gene Kinlow, a newly elected member who was an African American male and part of a coalition supported by Mayor Barry to gain more control of the Board, ran for President as well. Some members, including me, resented the Mayor's interference in the strike and now on the Board through his emissaries. I had support from some because of this as well as my past effectiveness as a leader. Because President Minnie Woodson did not run for reelection, I as Vice President became the Acting President. Thus, as I was running for the Presidency, I was serving in that position.

When I asked other Board members for their vote, some, even a few friends and allies, did not want to support me because they said the School Board of the predominantly black school system was not ready for a white President. They explicitly said so.

At this time, Barbara Lett Simmons and I were on the same page about not wanting the Kinlow/Barry contingent to assume leadership. So late one evening, from home, I called Barbara to recruit her vote. We had a very long and memorable conversation.

Barbara said, "Carol, I cannot vote for you for President because you are white. I just can't do it and I'm not going to be coy about it. But I want to tell you that you are our real leader. You have grown more as a politician than anybody I've ever seen in my life. When you first got elected, you had good intentions but you were so shy and overwhelmed when it came to speaking. But now you're exceptional."

I said, "Barbara, you had a lot to do with that. I don't know if you remember all those years ago when I was first on the School Board, every time I'd open my mouth, you would just go on and on about how I should shut up. I realized I had to become a quick study to survive the constant negativity you directed at me. And so I want you to know the politician you see now, you deserve a lot of credit for." She actually loved that story, and so do I.

(And years later, we really did become friends. In fact, when I ran for the Council and during my 1998 and 2002 races for Mayor—even when she was the elected Democratic National Committeewoman for D.C.—she not only supported me, but put my campaign poster in her front yard. Besides remaining in touch, Barbara and I jointly worked to promote full voting rights for D.C. Sadly, we lost Barbara Lett Simmons about three years ago. Even through the sometimes bumpy road with her—or perhaps even because of it—I look back on her with fondness and appreciation.)

The Board of Education met at Eastern High School on Capitol Hill for the vote for President in early January of 1980. It was a contentious back and forth, which included several meetings, spanning two days. After 12 rounds of voting, neither candidate received the majority needed (even though I had the most votes), so we were really at a standstill.[30] It was quite a hullabaloo. We were the front-page story as well as the lead-in on TV and radio. I already had the job of President (albeit acting) and I could have kept it as long as the stalemate lasted, which probably would have been a very long time as nobody was even close to budging.

I really wanted this job badly and felt I deserved it far more as I had worked hard on the Board for nearly six years and been an elected leader for three. I also resented the fact that this newcomer, boosted by Barry, would waltz in if I gave in. But as I always cared more about D.C. than myself and realized that all this endless publicity was doing harm to the city and our children, I decided to withdraw. I then threw my support to an incumbent of several years, also an African American male, who won on the 13th ballot. I was sad about this withdrawal, but was glad to have made sure it was a loss for Kinlow—and Mayor Barry as well.[31]

Here's another instance of professional adversaries becoming friends: Gene and Nan Kinlow and I became friends decades ago. They've been to my home, and I was thrilled to be at their 50th anniversary several years ago—and to be one of very few political types invited. It would have been hard to have imagined that back in January of 1980, but I'm happy that the outcome has been water under a long-ago bridge.

CHAPTER 13

Stressful Time

Soon after the stressful vote on the Board of Education, I discovered I was pregnant. My children at that point were eleven, ten and eight years old. My marriage was not a good one. My husband's terrible depression had not improved, and I was afraid of bringing a new baby into the situation.

My three children were adolescents—in reality, if not in fact since the girls had developed early—and needed all the support they could get from two busy parents. I didn't feel like we should add to the burden of any of our family members at that time. Thus, early on David and I made a decision to end the pregnancy.

I wasn't sure if I even wanted to talk about this abortion here. I've told very few people. In fact, even most of my closest friends have not known until now. But it's a part of my life—a sad part. I was then and am still very much in favor of a woman's right to choose. And in this case, my husband was making the same choice. But having opted for it, I've been left with some sadness.

I look at my three children, and I feel sometimes that it would be nice to have another one like them. But I still think it was the best decision for me and our family at the time and would make the same decision now under those circumstances. I remain grateful to have had the choice and that others have that freedom today—and I will fight tooth and nail for the right to keep it.

After the drama of the Board presidency and the trauma in my personal life, I really needed to get away.

New Hampshire-Bound

I was contacted about a campaign trip to New Hampshire which Barbara Bush was putting together with a group to support her husband, George H.W. Bush. I was anxious for the respite and supported the senior Bush as a moderate as opposed to his chief rival in that campaign, Ronald Reagan, who I feared then was too conservative (or at least that was the media's take on him, but I think he proved otherwise). And besides, Bush was my old RNC softball teammate. I grabbed it as my getaway opportunity.

About 50 of us, including Barbara Bush, flew up together to Boston on one plane and then went by bus to Manchester, New Hampshire. That bus ride turned out to be a very special experience in that I became dear friends with several of the people on it—Joy Waters who later became Joy Safer, Tom Hill who worked on Capitol Hill, and an attractive woman I won't name who worked for a member of Congress.

The whole group spent several days canvassing for Bush. We froze during the day out on the streets and then congregated around the hotel's fireplace at night. It was a truly enjoyable time in every way, and just what the doctor ordered.

In August of 1980, I traveled to Detroit for the Republican National Convention as the elected Vice Chair of the D.C. delegation for Bush. But before the Convention, it had become obvious that Reagan was going to get the nomination. We D.C. delegates took along buttons we wore as well as passed out which promoted Bush for Vice President and felt like we played a small role when he was selected as the running mate. I even got to formally announce the vote for Bush for Vice President for our delegation—and my children said they got a kick out of seeing me on national television.

In Detroit, I was the designated driver of the van for our delegation, and the self-appointed navigator in the passenger seat was Oliver Carr. I had not met him before we both became delegates, but we had had a phone conversation where I had given him a hard time about tearing down Rhodes Tavern, a 150-year-old establishment at 15th and F Sts, N.W. and *not* even putting up a plaque.

(A group led by Joe Grano had wanted a plaque put up on Carr's new building to commemorate Rhodes Tavern, but Carr refused. Joe did finally succeed in getting that plaque on June 7, 1999—20 years later. But that whole episode did help lead to the establishment of the D.C. Historic Preservation Office. Yay, Joe! [Sadly, we lost him in 2013.])

It was my first political convention, and very exciting. It was also enjoyable because the well-connected unnamed woman I met on that bus trip took me under her wing and had me go as her guest to the glamorous parties that week. At one, a well-known—married—Congressman approached and basically propositioned me. I was quite taken aback and said, "How dare you? I am Vice President of the Board of Education in Washington, D.C. and I am a married woman" (probably in that order)—and walked away.

It turned out that my new friend was pretty well-known in that group for being a partier and I guess people presumed that her guest might be the same. But I must admit that because the Congressman was so attractive and famous, I did feel a teeny bit flattered in the midst of my appalled state.

More Fun Times with Friends and Family

We still spent time with the Myersons (who had moved back to New York after three years in D.C.), including many memorable Thanksgivings together in Washington. At one, during the Iranian hostage crisis, we basically forced our kids to stage a protest at the Iranian embassy. But they really got into it. They spent an entire evening writing protest signs, including "Honk If You're for America." We dropped them off at the embassy and our five kids constituted the entire protest. Cars honked as they drove by, including ours driving back and forth about 100 times.

Every Thanksgiving along with turkey, cornbread dressing, candied yams, etc., I made a green bean casserole. No one ate it but me. This happened year in and year out. So finally after about 15 years, I decided I did not want to eat green bean casserole for the next month as I usually did. So, instead, I made a spinach casserole after getting recipes from several friends, including Carol Pensky and Carol Schuman, and then combining all the best ingredients from each. I put it on the table and my kids and the Myersons all said mournfully, "Where is the green bean casserole?" I was stunned. I guess they were just upset that they had nothing to totally ignore. Well, the hell with them. Spinach casserole then became the green dish, with or without their permission.

We did have more fun times with the Myersons such as when we traveled to Atlantic City. The singer John Davidson, who was very popular in the early 1980s and who I thought was cute, was performing at one of the hotels. I was always game for getting close to celebrities, as you may recall.

We didn't have tickets for the John Davidson concert because the guys wouldn't go, but I persuaded Ardith to sneak in with me at least just to get a glimpse of him. She was usually too suave to do such a thing, but I guess I brought out the silliness in her. Before the performance began, we tried to talk our way through security. It didn't work. Finally, in mid-performance, we snuck in and literally crawled down the aisle. Suddenly, we were blocked by two legs belonging to the same security guard who had stopped us before. This time, thankfully, he just took mercy on us and seated us right next to the stage. During the performance, John, unbeknownst to me, always picked out a woman to kiss, and lo and behold, that night it was me. A little too wet, though, for my taste for a first kiss.

The next day I got my daughter Hilary and son Doug in on the celebrity stalking. We saw John Davidson walking through the lobby. I said, "There he is" and we all chased him through the hotel until he outraced us to the elevator. There went my second kiss—but it was okay due to the above.

That same weekend, Ardith and I had our palms read on the boardwalk, which I usually do not do either. Even though we were dressed up looking like we had never worked a day in our lives, the palm reader told me, "You have had a very tough life and have worked very hard. But one day, you are going to be famous." Maybe this book is my chance! Please tell your friends.

David and I had a really fun experience when one of his clients got us to buy into a fundraiser that took a plane-full of D.C. people dressed in black tie up to New York on a Friday night. We were met by a caravan of limousines that delivered us to the Pierre Hotel for a magnificent buffet dinner and then on to the Metropolitan Opera. David and I had grand seats in the second row, a little to the right. I had to leave to go to the restroom, but when I returned to the opera hall, even from the back row, I could hear David snoring. Everybody could hear David snoring. That tended to happen at movies and plays, especially if he had a couple of drinks. This evening qualified. The limousines were waiting as we left the Opera House to take us back to the plane, and we were in D.C. by 1 a.m. In spite of the embarrassment, which lots of people kidded David about, that night at the Opera was a beautiful and memorable time—and at least he snored in a rich baritone.

Back at home, we continued to enjoy entertaining friends. I still loved to do my dinner parties. Among our most notable was having over another of David's clients, John McLaughlin, who became most known not as David's client but as the host of *The McLaughlin Group*, and his then wife Ann who later became Secretary of the Department of Labor.

Although some days at home were stressful and sad, there were also pleasant ones where we all just sat around, listening to music, and singing along to John Denver, Roberta Flack, Kenny Rogers, the Eagles, Barry Manilow, Donny Hathaway, and musicals like *West Side Story* and *My Fair Lady*. David seemed happiest hanging around the house with the kids and the dog. He liked going outside to play catch and taking the kids on outings, such as going out some Sunday afternoons for bowling or pony riding. I joined in occasionally, but more often, it was their special time—and besides, I needed some time on my own.

And David could be creative and playful with the kids. He made up something called "baby school" as well as made up imaginary friends for our son. They weren't Doug's friends; they were imaginary friends his father created for him. When he was in a better mood, he was up for anything.

I also have very fond memories of many evenings at the back garden of the Roma Restaurant with David—sometimes with kids or friends, but usually just the two of us. David could be such a good conversationalist. I especially liked the conversations when he would say, "I've never had a boring day with you." And I would respond, "Is that a good thing?" He always said either "Yes" or "Absolutely."

Banneker Academic High School

When the 1980 summer recess ended, I was gearing up for another big battle on the Board of Education, and one I had helped to create again. It concerned starting a model academic high school in Washington. Other major cities had such secondary schools like the Bronx High School of Science and Stuyvesant in New York, and Boston Latin in that city. A similar model academic high school was something that both Superintendent Vince Reed and I very much wanted—to give our high achievers an environment where they could thrive. In so many high schools, kids who are academically inclined are made fun of and/or not given the kind of classes that would challenge them and help their advancement. An academic high school could help remedy that. And we certainly envisioned it to be inclusive in that students would not only be pre-selected by their school, but all would be given an opportunity to apply and then qualify.

Once again, the fight was made racial. Some members, led by Barbara Lett Simmons, thought an academic high school was too elitist and might only cater to white students. With white kids making up just a couple of percentage points, our African American Superintendent and I exposed the ridiculousness of this charge: We said we could take every white student—eligible or not—in the D.C. public secondary schools and they would not fit into two classrooms, so what were they talking about? This was a slight exaggeration, but not much. In addition, Barbara herself had gone to nothing but "elitist" schools and I pointed that out as well, saying, "Why shouldn't our students get the kind of education you had?" It was so aggravating that charges of racism were again used to argue against something that would primarily help black students, who made up 95% of our student population.

I chaired the Educational Programs Committee, which brought the model academic high school proposal forward. After much debate and several sessions, it lost by one vote and thus, did not get approved. This episode was so maddening that after five years of service, and struggles like this one with the Board, Superintendent Reed resigned. The arguments and votes against the academic high school appeared to be the last straw for him. I could relate to that. Vince went to the U.S. Department of Education where he served as Assistant Secretary, and then on to *The Washington Post* where he was Vice President for Community Relations and later, for Communications. At least he sure landed on his feet.

Later, I still chaired the Educational Programs Committee and once again, even in Dr. Reed's absence, I brought forward the model academic high school proposal. I knew I would walk back into that same hornet's nest, but I had to do it. This time, thank goodness, it got approved. Banneker Junior High School became Benjamin Banneker Academic High School, both named after the 18th century African American scientist, surveyor and author. It has been a great boon to our school system in its 35 years of existence. Banneker has been continually named one of the top high schools in the country according to the annual list in *U.S.News & World Report*; and in the newly released 2016 D.C. scores, which included public and charter schools, Banneker ranked the highest. I am so proud to have been a major part of bringing it about. First it was Vince and I. And then just me. But it happened. (And P.S. Banneker has always been made up of at least 80% African Americans, including now 81%, 14% Hispanic, and 2.2% other.)

Many years later, after Vincent Reed had suffered a stroke and was wheelchair-bound at home, and I was on the Council, I came up with the idea of having him honored at Banneker. After all the necessary approvals—and there were many—Vince and Frances Reed came to the school for a ceremony to celebrate him and one of his dreams. A huge plaque with his picture was unveiled that day. Frances said that it was the happiest she had seen him in the many years since his stroke.

To the White House—and Back

Alan Woods, who I worked with on the National Advisory Council on the Education of Disadvantaged Children, and who helped in my School Board campaigns, asked me to do some work for the Reagan Presidential Transition Team, which was being run by Pendleton James, at the end of 1980. After that, I received an appointment to be Associate Director of the Office of Presidential Personnel, even though I had not put my name in for anything. It was certainly not something I sought out as I was still so busy on the Board of Education, and planned to continue there until the end my term in January of 1982. But it was an honor to be asked to do that weighty job. And after all, it was the White House.

Even though I told very few people, the appointment was announced in a small article in the A section of *The Washington Post*: "School Board Member Named to White House Job."[32] I don't know why, but the news even reached the *Lake Charles American Press* in Louisiana with the headline: "Ex-Teacher Fills White House Post."[33]

I received many notes of congratulations, from friends and even Senator Tom Harkin of Iowa and Washington Teachers Union President Bill Simons. I'm sure Bill was just glad to see me get another job away from the School Board. (Unfortunately, I just read that Bill passed away on December 7, 2016 at the age of 92.)

The Office of Presidential Personnel vetted all candidates for the enormous number of positions in the new Administration. I had responsibility for helping to select potential hires for the office of the Attorney General/the Justice Department, and other similar agencies. I became aware immediately that it was going to be a very time-intensive job. I went to work both days on that first weekend starting at 7 a.m. and didn't get home until 8 p.m. Most of the time was spent with William French Smith, who would be appointed Attorney General, and some of his staff.

One weekday, I interviewed a woman I got a strange vibe from, like she coveted my job. She turned out to be a close friend of the Reagan family and next thing I know, she had my job. Maybe they also found out I had been an elected delegate to the Republican Convention for Reagan's challenger, George H.W. Bush. I was given a note thanking me for my service—all two weeks of it!

I was really so relieved. I had no desire to work such long hours each day, including weekends, while being on the School Board and attempting to take care of a family. I felt so fortunate that I was quickly swept aside.

But it was also embarrassing. The congratulatory notes were still coming in since the appointment was announced so publicly. I was getting phone calls asking how the work was going. I had to say, "I was too busy with the School Board," or "It was a temporary thing." So that job not working out was somewhat humiliating—but I was still very glad to have been gotten rid of.

Alan tried several months later to again attempt to get me to work in the Administration, although I was not so sure about it especially after that first outing. However, now that I had decided not to run again for the Board of Education, I thought it would not only be good to get a new experience, but it would be nice for a change to make some real money, like the brief stint at the White House. I also thought doing so could allow David more freedom to pursue something he might really enjoy.

Alan called to say he had set up an appointment for me with the White House Press Secretary. He gave me a time and date, which was the first week of April in 1981. The meeting did not happen. That Press Secretary was James Brady, who was terribly injured in the Reagan assassination attempt on March 30th outside the Washington Hilton Hotel. That awful event happened just a block from where I live now.

Also sadly, a few years later, dear Alan Woods succumbed to cancer in his 40s. He was a great public servant, a wonderful friend, and I'll always be grateful for how he mentored me and tried to boost my opportunities.

Another Inauguration

David and I went to a Reagan Inaugural Ball with our friends Ann and John Wylie and Tay and Roger Hahn. Ann and John owned an old black limousine, which they used to take trips with their four children. It was their version of a minivan. John, a doctor, picked us up in that car and brought along a chauffeur's cap.

As we neared the Kennedy Center for the party, we got stuck in a terrible traffic jam that was not moving at all. If this kept up, we were going to miss seeing the President (as he and the First Lady only stop at each ball for about 15 minutes). Then David came up with a plan.

While John donned his chauffer's cap, David and Roger got out of the car and stood on either side of the limo, pretending to be secret service agents with one hand imitating listening on their earpieces and the other hand on the top of the car. Cars then started stopping to let us through. The guys were so convincing that the other vehicles just parted without question. It's a good thing no one saw us three girls in the car laughing hysterically as it might have blown the whole thing.

Middle East Trip

I was fortunate to have another interesting opportunity in September of 1981. (And these amazing experiences always seemed to luckily land in my lap—I never looked for them.) I was invited to be a member of a delegation to the Middle East co-sponsored by the American Council of Young Political Leaders and the State Department. It was exciting to be invited again by such a prestigious group and this time, to go to such fascinating places. (Perhaps most exciting to me now is to have ever been considered a "young" political leader.)

Previously, in 1979, I had been a delegate to the United States-Soviet Conference, co-sponsored by the same two entities, which was held in Colorado. It was a joint conference focusing on domestic social ills with 15 representatives from the U.S. and the same number from Russia. I was elected the discussion leader from our delegation and we presented an honest account of our social problems. However, regardless of the topic, whether it be drugs, teenage pregnancies, alcohol, etc., the Russian contingent claimed that they had "no problems whatsoever," adding, "We don't even know what you're talking about." The fact they were all totally drunk for the entire conference belied those assertions.

The Middle East trip was scheduled for three weeks and took us to Saudi Arabia, Jordan, Israel and Egypt to foster understanding of each other's political processes and cultures. It was interesting to be on the trip as a woman and especially as a Jewish woman. I had a difficult time getting a Visa for Jordan. I'm not sure if it was because I was Jewish or because my passport had been stamped in Israel four years earlier. Later, I received for the most part very cordial and warm welcomes everywhere.

We had been told by the State Department when we were briefed that we should not expect anyone in Saudi Arabia to invite us to their home and not to take it personally. It was just not done.

On our first night there, the Director of the Agency for International Development (AID) hosted a reception for us, where I met a young man named Talal who worked for the Saudi education department. Although there were many princes (literally) there, I spent most of my time talking to Talal about education. He had been schooled in England and spoke perfect English.

At the end of the evening, Talal invited me to his family's home the next night. The host for AID was shocked at the invitation I received as was the State Department when briefed about it upon our return. Of course I accepted the invitation and asked if I could bring several of my fellow delegates along, and he agreed to three others. So there we were on the second night in Saudi Arabia at a beautiful Saudi home with Talal's family.

I sat in the women's living room with Talal's sister, who spoke a little English, and a friend of hers who spoke a little more, as well as a female member of the delegation I had brought along. Talal and his brother-in-law were in the men's living room with the two male delegates. In Saudi culture then, men could come into the women's rooms, but not the other way around.

In conversation with Talal's sister, I asked if she had ever been out of Saudi Arabia. The gist of what she said was, "Yes. Once I went to England." I asked, "How was your visit there?" She said, "I was staying with a Jewish family and I was so scared I just wanted to run away." I said, "Did they hurt you?" She replied, "No, they were nice but they were Jewish and that's a very bad thing."

Now here I am, Jewish, sitting in her living room across from her. But I didn't want to say anything because I didn't want to scare her. It was so awkward. But I continued conversing while we had dinner and until it was time to leave, when I thanked her very much for her hospitality. On the way home, I told Talal about the incident and asked him to please tell her that I so wanted to let know then that I was Jewish but did not for obvious reasons. He did tell her and she said she liked me anyway and was not scared. Talal and I stayed in touch for a while.

Another interesting experience also occurred in Saudi Arabia one day when we visited a souk (outdoor market). There were only three women in our delegation and we had been told to cover our arms. We thought we had done so as we headed off to the bustling marketplace. Upon arrival, each of us got hit by a stick on our arms (not hard, but it did sting) by an official policeman because the bottom portion of our wrists were showing. So we kept trying to hold the material down to our wrists with our fingers. On a more positive note, even though I left my big wallet with all my money sitting on a display counter in one of the booths and did not discover it missing until 30 minutes later, when I ran back, it was there where I left it, totally untouched.

I also made other friends during my travels: a military man named Shmuel Limone, who briefed us in Israel, as well as Mohamed Abdellah, head of the Egyptian Parliament, and Dalia Talaat in Cairo. Years later through Shmuel, we became friendly with a nice couple, Dalia and Amos. We all kept in touch for years as well. Both Shmuel and Mohammed were very handsome and I admit I immediately developed a mini-crush on both of them—as did the other women in the delegation. Those innocent crushes sure perked me up—and did help me get through my continuing challenges at home.

Upon returning home, I went to the family room where David and the kids sat victim to my telling the details of every minute of every day of that trip. I loved telling the details (in case you haven't noticed). I'm not sure they loved listening, but they were good sports.

Springland Lane

David and I occasionally would go to open houses just for fun. We enjoyed looking at homes and if you didn't buy, it was free entertainment. Occasionally we thought of buying one of those homes, like a beauty at Reno Rd. and Huntington St., but my children would have had to cross two busy streets to get to school, so that was out in my book. And besides, I really loved our house on Cumberland Street. We enjoyed our neighbors, and it was a short walk to the schools. The house had a great family room, which was my favorite place, where we'd gather to have Sunday dinners, play cards, watch football games, and listen to music. I kept wondering why destabilize something that at least offered some stability.

David, though, was serious about moving on. What I thought was a recreational activity was real to him. I think he wanted to show off the fruits of his labor by having a more glamorous home, and perhaps the thought of a new place was a salve for his depression. I also think a motivation was having a larger mortgage for tax purposes as he went up the financial ladder.

But a practical reason may have been our kitchen, which was so small. We had tried to expand it to get a little eat-in space, but could not get a permit to do it. But I had lived with that for over eight years and was glad to continue to do so.

One weekend day in 1981, David, returning from doing errands, came running into the house and said, "Come on, you have to see this house. It's on my favorite street," which is the first time he ever even mentioned Springland Lane. I had no idea where it was, although it turned out to be only ten blocks south from where we then lived. I went to see it with him, and as we approached David's "favorite street," I had a déjà vu moment. The one-block cul de sac of Springland Lane begins at the bottom of a hill on Reno Road. I recalled riding by the same intersection 16 years prior on the back of my friend Ben Noble's motorcycle, and had thought at the time that it was one of the prettiest spots I'd ever seen. With the curve of the road, the canopy of big, luscious trees, and a few darling houses abutting, I thought then that I was in heaven. But now, even revisiting "heaven" did not make me want to move.

The for-sale home was at the top right of the cul de sac, next to a wooded area, below Hearst Recreation Center and School. The minute we walked into the house, David started praising it. Normally, David would know, as a real estate lawyer, not to be overly effusive in front of the agent in hopes of getting a better deal. But David was lost in love, going "Isn't it fabulous? Isn't it beautiful? Isn't it the best house you ever saw? And it's my favorite street!" He would never have let his clients do that.

I liked it but thought of it as just a better landscaped version of our Cumberland St. house with an eat-in kitchen. This new house didn't even have the appealing large family room. And I also didn't like that the location was further from the kids' schools.

But David was dying to purchase it. Nothing I could say could stop it. I even brought up the fact that I had been looking for a well-paying job which would allow me to carry the mortgage myself on the house on Cumberland Street (that had been purchased for $80,000 eight years earlier). But I certainly couldn't make a dent in the new house he wanted to buy (and they didn't budge a penny on the asking price). I felt he was financially locking himself into the track he was on, which did not fulfill him.

Regardless, he wanted that house. I had no choice but to go along. If it was something that he thought would make him happy, it was hard to stand in his way. The kids were very disappointed. They were really attached to the old place and especially our neighbors, who they had played with since they were young. But there was no turning back. David was on a mission.

We had signed a contract with no contingencies—they wouldn't allow one—so we had to pay for the new house before selling our old one. It was a tough market—and it didn't sell. Therefore, David had to get a bridge loan, which he so dreaded before, in order to be able to make the payments on the two houses. This financial crunch went on for about eight months, which added to his depression. We kept reducing the price to get a buyer. Finally, we did—but quite a bit below what we needed to help carry the new house. Then we moved to Springland Lane. Even though it was about half a mile from our other place, it somehow felt like a bigger move.

(The one consolation about the move was that we had finally landed in Cleveland Park instead of North Cleveland Park. No more than a year later, a sign was put up one block south of our house which said, "Cleveland Park." Once again, missed again.)

Continuing Education

The public had been very concerned about the school system for a long time. In order to give people a chance to air their complaints and ideas close to their homes and to get them more involved, we began to do a series of Board meetings around the various communities. But after all that, and with good notice, not many showed up. I stated on the record that, "If we met in people's living rooms, they wouldn't come out of their bedrooms."

I wanted to serve more directly in the community and spent time as a volunteer tutor at Malcolm X Elementary School, which is on Mississippi Ave. in Southeast D.C. It was rewarding, and reinforced what the time on the Board of Education was all about—serving kids like those at Malcolm X. It also kept me grounded as the battles for improvement continued.

Trying to make a better public system is a long-term journey with no short cuts. During my time on the School Board, there were many examples of people trying to take the easy route. For instance, the Principal of Oyster Elementary School called me to ask for my help in transferring an incompetent teacher to another school. I told him that I would not help him transfer her, which would lay the problem at another school's doorstep, but I would help him go through the proper protocols for dismissal.

But he took the easy route. He transferred her somewhere else. A couple of years later, he called me again, complaining, "They transferred that teacher back!" I said, "Good. You deserve that. Now deal with it. This time go through the proper procedure." And thank goodness, he finally did.

Preparing to Leave the Board

After the struggles on the Board through the Barbara Sizemore episode, the strike, the fight over Banneker, the squabbling among Board members, and my not being elected President because I am white, I was ready for some relief and a new chapter. But first, we needed to find a new, highly qualified Superintendent, and I was chairing the Selection Committee.

I picked up the phone and called the Deputy Superintendent of the Montgomery County Schools, Floretta Dukes McKenzie, an African American woman who lived in the District, and I asked her to apply, which she did. She might have applied anyway, but I'm sure my call did not hurt. In 1981 we offered her the position. She accepted it, and went on to do a superb job. After leaving in 1988, Floretta started an education consulting practice and remained living in D.C. until she sadly passed in 2015.

And I also wanted to leave the Board of Education itself in good hands, I started the non-partisan Citizens for a Better School Board, and invited former Superintendent Vincent Reed and former Acting Superintendent Benjamin Henley to co-chair it with me. The three of us selected a diverse group of citizens to join us in our effort to find and support candidates who we knew would serve the school system well. A few of our candidates did win in the next election—50% of those we endorsed— including the person who succeeded me in the Ward 3 seat, Wanda Washburn. Reverend David Eaton of All Souls Church, who we also supported, defeated Eugene Kinlow, and then David went on to be President of the Board.

Leaving the Board of Education

In 1981, I announced I would not seek a third term on the Board of Education, but would complete my term which ended January 2, 1982. I said: "It was an extremely difficult decision to make because I can think of no greater cause than the education of young people ... but there comes a time to move on. My oldest child had just begun first grade when I went on the Board. She is now completing her first year at Deal Junior High School. That is an undeniable gauge of the years I have devoted to the Board ..."

My announcement statement also summarized the achievements about which I am still proud: "I have loved having an important role in seeing a school system go from nonexistent management, no testing, social promotions, no volunteer program, the least number of courses required for high school graduation in the metropolitan area, no standard curriculum, no true academic model high school, poor personnel evaluation procedures, no recertification requirements for teachers, to a school system which has reversed all of these inadequacies and is on the road to improving itself as evidenced by increasing test scores."

We did make improvements in many areas. But it is the nature of the school system that improvements must be improved upon.

The things we were on the forefront of are still being talked about and worked on today, such as stopping social promotions and improving teacher evaluations. I was so proud to have been advocating for these things 33 years ago when they were far less discussed and took far more courage to take them on. And thank goodness the needle has moved some more, and I do applaud the continuing strong efforts.

In *The Washington Star*, a major newspaper then, I added to my comments about why I was leaving and chose to be honest about the battle wounds I had been through and the scars that remained:

"I have loved my time on the Board ... I have loved the cause. ... I have loved the advancements we made ... I have loved the many friendships I have developed through this position. ...

But I have hated the counterproductive viciousness of some of my fellow board members whose only desire is to create chaos. ... I have hated the naivete of some of the media who cannot make a distinction between good and bad public servants and who do not appreciate that it is harder to change entrenched policies than to write editorials which criticize those who try.

I have hated the city government which treats the education of our children as just another pawn in its game of political posturing. ... I have hated the selfishness of special interest groups who would destroy the forest to save the trees. ...

I wish my successor a strong commitment, courage, fortitude, a sense of humor, patience, a stomach of iron and an ability to keep on trucking in the best interests of children while ducking the slings and arrows of those who second guess from the sidelines."[34]

Despite my mixed feelings about victories and disappointments, I was so pleased to get many beautiful notes and words of support. For example, the former Chair of the D.C. Council, John Hechinger, a Democrat, wrote me a lovely note: "A beautiful swan song. Thanks for your great service to our city." The *DC Gazette* wrote on May 1, 1981 in their "Roses and Thorns" section: "Roses to Carol Schwartz who has announced that she will not run for reelection this year. We've had a fair number of differences with Carol over the years but she's done her School Board job seriously and with considerable skill."

RNC softball team in 1974
(George H.W. Bush, Chair, is in back row with a person
on his shoulders, and I am in first standing row,
center-right with my hair pulled back.)

At the White House as the Vice Chair of
the National Advisory Council on the
Education of Disadvantaged Children,
with Chair Owen Peagler,
and on right, with our staff

1974 Board of Education campaign
picture (below) and handout (above)

School Board President Dr. Thurlow
Tibbs and me as Vice President,
enjoy a light moment after being
elected as officers in 1977.

Board of Education meeting
(from left, Conrad Smith, Barbara Lett Simmons, Board Secretary Dwight Cropp, me, Alaire Rieffel, and Calvin Lockridge)

Superintendent Vincent E. Reed and Board Secretary Dwight S. Cropp

Board members Hilda Mason and Julius Hobson Jr. and me on the left

Greeting First Lady Roslyn Carter, the only First Family to send a child to the D.C. Public Schools

A reunion of Board of Education members in the late '70s
(Superintendent Vince Reed far right)

Cute Kids Continue to Cutely Grow

Cumberland Street with Candy

Doug imitates his Dad

Mrs. Riston, our
longtime babysitter

  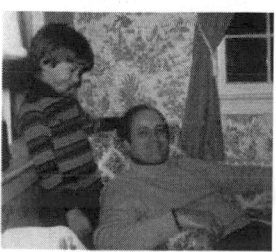

Doug
and
"Uncle"
Ed

David's 39th
birthday

Grandma Carrie (left) and Aunt Betty Jane,
who gave me unconditional love all my life

A holiday card

David and me
out and about

A haircut
in the late '70s

David's 40th with kids and Ma

Visiting Grandma C in
Greenville
before she passed

Middle Eastern
Young Political
Leaders trip
(Saudi Arabia
on left
and Egypt
on right)

CHAPTER 14

Becoming Queen

After more than seven years of 50-hour weeks, I had left my elected position on the D.C. Board of Education. Little did I know my days of victory were not entirely behind me.

My dear friend Tay is so talented at everything she does. She's so smart and capable. When she plays bridge, she's the best bridge player. She's the best cook. When she bowls, she's the best bowler. And now Tay was a big mover and shaker in the bowling league. So in January of 1982, Tay asked me to join her bowling league at the Bethesda River Bowl. I had gone from working all those hours to doing not much, so I gladly said okay.

I went there the first day having not bowled in a long while and when I did bowl some, I was inconsistent. That first week, I bowled an 80—not unusual for me. The next week, I miraculously bowled a 180—quite unusual; in fact, my highest score ever. (I told you I was inconsistent.)

But because the Bowling Association of America gave awards based on beating your average and since I scored 100 points over my "average" of 80 (from just one game), I was named "Queen of the Week" for the whole bowling alley. It was a real loophole in their system that I could gain such a title, but being a person who likes awards and attention, I took it anyway.

Then, because the 100-point differential was so enormous and so hard to beat, I was named "Queen of the Month." My name was featured in bold letters on the wall above the counter of the bowling alley, so anyone renting shoes got to see it. Meanwhile, my friend Tay, who had been bowling for years and is consistently great at it, had not received any such honor and here I was on the verge of becoming Bowler of the Century my first month there. I felt terrible about it for Tay's sake, but Tay of course never made me feel bad. She was such a good sport.

At the end of the year, the Queens of the Month did a bowl-off to see who would be crowned "Queen of the Year" and then get to compete in a huge regional bowl-off near Richmond, Virginia.

That big trip to the Richmond metropolitan area was so close within my grasp, but sadly I did not win the title. At least I did bowl well enough to become the runner-up. However, miraculously, the Queen of the Year was not able to fulfill her duties as she came down with a bad back. I'm sure my pushing her down the stairs had nothing to do with it. (Just kidding, of course.) But here I was Queen of the Year at Bethesda River Bowl, and my name became even more prominently displayed behind the counter for the whole next year. (I guess the palm reader was right! Maybe I don't even need this book.)

And off Tay and I went to the big bowl-off near Richmond. There, out of 17 contestants, I came in 14th. Frankly, I choked. Queen of the Day, Queen of the Week, Queen of the Month, Queen of the Year. The stardom was coming too fast, I guess. My bowling glory days were now behind me. But at least I have a three-inch "Queen of the Year" trophy to remind me, which I proudly display in the bottom of one of my closets—I think.

From Bowling to Badgered

After I left the School Board, I met a man named Charles King from Atlanta when I got invited to be part of Channel 7's televised version of Charles's "workshop" where he put black and white people together to talk about racism. In reality, he would badger the white people in the group to confess to being racist and to promise to be better in the future. I agreed to do this because I always wanted to advance racial causes and initially I didn't know what the true intent was. But it became obvious pretty quickly.

During the taping, Charles kept getting in our white faces, saying, "Deal with it. Admit you're a racist." All the people buckled, one by one, except for one. I said, "No, I'm not a racist. I have never been a racist. I am guilt-free there. You can't make me apologize for something that I am not."

Afterwards he told that in all the workshops he had done for decades all over the country, I'm the only person in his history who did not "yield." I just refused to say something that was not true. You can beat me up about lots of things, but not that. I would hear from Charles on occasion for a while before he died in 1991.

A First Non-American Car

Around this time, David and I had a fun experience. We attended the American Cancer Society Ball at the Washington Hilton as the guest of friends/clients. The grand door prize at the event was a Mercedes-Benz. There were a few other prizes, but everyone wanted that one. We had to leave early before the drawing as our hosts, who were dropping us back home, were ready to go. As we left, though, I told many friends who were there to call us *when* we won the Mercedes, jokingly of course, as there were about 2,000 people at the event.

When we got to the house and David left to take the babysitter home, friends did call from a pay phone at the Hilton to say we won the Mercedes. "Ha Ha," I laughed and hung up. After three or four calls from several more friends who I blew off, Tay called and said, "Carol, you really did win the Mercedes. Now get your butt down here and pick it up."

First thing I thought is that *we* didn't really win it. The friends had bought our tickets. I immediately called them and said they should take the car. They insisted it was ours—thank goodness.

When David got home, I went back to the hotel. They had moved the car from the dance floor to the stage, where Tay and I got in. Then they started lowering the stage to go to the basement and it got stuck. A little drama. But finally we made it to the lower level and I drove the car out and home. It was a great thrill.

David and I woke the kids up to show them the new car parked out front. With now having two cars, we decided it would be David's as I preferred to drive an American vehicle. (Full disclosure: I do have a used 1994 Jaguar now, bought in 2004.)

It turns out there's no such thing as a free car. What you got was a one-year lease for free and then at the end of that year, you received a good price to purchase it, or you returned the car to the dealership. Of course, most do buy as did we.

Janie Burka

Janie Burka was a good friend. We were in a bridge group early in our marriages along with close friends, Tay, Carol Schuman and Judy Irwin. Judy had gotten us all together in February of 1968 for a luncheon and we all became friends. Janie was married to David Burka, an accountant and businessman, and they had two sons and had just adopted a baby girl.

We and the Burkas sometimes went out as couples or as families. And every July 4th, when the kids were little, we got together with five or six other couples, alternating houses, for a cookout and small fireworks display. As we were leaving the party one year at 9:30 p.m., the Burkas and we decided since it was a beautiful weekend, "Let's go to Ocean City," where David and I had never been. After quick stops at both homes to get some necessities, off we went, getting to Ocean City, Maryland at about 2:00 a.m.

We spent a couple of nights and since I had not numbered clothes among my "necessities," I remained in the same Montgomery Ward flowery pink pantsuit the entire time—which became a running joke. The day we returned, David and I decided to continue it. He drove up to their house and honked while the kids and I hid in the convertible's backseat. Janie and David came out to see our car driving by with a shovel propped up in the passenger seat, dressed in that pink pantsuit. They seemed to enjoy our stunt, but I'm sure not as much as we did.

Janie was a smart, serious and lovely woman. Aside from bridge, she also liked to read and play tennis. She was a natural born leader. In the early 1980s, Janie was the President of the Sisterhood of Washington Hebrew Congregation.

On January 13, 1982, Janie was flying to visit her ailing mother in Florida near Miami. It was a snowy, icy day. The Air Florida flight #90 she was on crashed into the Potomac River on takeoff, killing 78 people, including Janie. It was so shocking. I felt so terribly sad for her family. And for those of us fortunate enough to be her friends, it was a huge loss as well.

That Sunday, when the roads were still snow-covered and icy, David, the children and I went to two homes to pay our respects: first the Burkas and then to the Pensky's because Carol's mother, who was a dear lady I had known since college, had also died. David was driving the Mercedes as we were coming back via Falls Road in Potomac, Maryland. As he rounded a curve, we saw a big truck coming toward us. He put his foot on the brake. We slid, the truck hit us, and we ended up in a fence. The whole front end of the car was totaled. David had a small cut on his nose, but we were so lucky that other than that and some bruises, nothing worse happened. After that episode and that week of losses, I became much more grateful that my family was intact.

A Two for One

On February 6, 1982, our daughters Stephanie and Hilary had a joint Bat Mitzvah. Stephanie had turned 13 that past August and Hilary was just 12 at the time, but our Reform temple was cooperative. Washington Hebrew, as it had such a large congregation, always had Bar/Bat Mitzvah services for two children each Saturday, so it was really nice to have two sisters do it together.

It was such a fun party, which we had at the temple's Ring Hall, and so many of the family came in for the event, including my parents, Ma, Johnny, Aunt Betty and Uncle Seymour from Denver, Uncle Albert from New York, and Aunt Betty from Baton Rouge.

Hanging out with friends and family as well as opening up the presents in our living room did create some good memories in our new Springland Lane home.

The girls immediately wrote thank you notes for the presents, as that is something I totally ingrained in them and their brother Doug. I still joke that I don't care if my children are serial killers as long as they write thank you notes. (I say this often but now I think it sounds better than it reads—and may stop using it.)

Preaching Judaism

When I told my folks about the girls' Bat Mitzvahs so they could arrange their travel, my father said, "Nobody in our immediate family has ever done anything that Jewish. That's silly."

My grandparents had pride in being Jewish as long as it wasn't too Jewish. My parents had no pride. They did not deny being Jewish, but they did not make a point of telling people nor did they participate in any of its traditions. There was no religion at all in my house. The only time God was mentioned was when my father said "G-d damn it." And that was a lot.

In the next generation, my brother Johnny and I took particular pride in being Jewish. I knew Johnny would enjoy going to temple, and after my talking with the administrator at Marbridge, they arranged for him and the few other Jewish residents to go to Congregation Beth Israel in Austin on Friday nights. Although in December when the Rabbi would ask for announcements, Johnny would jump up and say to the whole congregation that Christmas poinsettias were now on sale at the Marbridge greenhouse.

But many in my family either actively ran away from Judaism or just gave it up. Of my 12 first cousins, with 19 known marriages among them, not one of them was to a Jewish person, but who cares. In fact, I always said to my children when they were quite young, "I don't care who you marry or how dark-skinned my grandchildren are. But I do hope you will raise them as Jews."

Yet none of my cousins raised their children Jewish with one partial exception, although a few have some identity. (This is despite the fact that in the case of my maternal cousins, their fathers, my uncles Seymour and Joe had both been President of their temples in Denver and Baton Rouge respectively.) Now, though, I sometimes feel a little like a minority in my own family. And it makes me feel somewhat sad. (Oh by the way, the one partial exception: My cousin and eight-month boyfriend Andrew did raise his two boys Jewish while the two daughters he had with his second wife were raised Christian.)

My children have gone out with many non-Jews but have mainly had relationships with Jewish people and in some instances, the person had just a Jewish mother. I never pushed for it to be a Jewish person, but I must admit when it was, it made me glad—as I felt that our religion might at least have a shot at continuing in those cases.

Judaism is the world's oldest monotheistic religion still in practice, and this year in September of 2017 at Rosh Hashanah, we mark year 5778. However, the number of Jews in the world and this country is exceedingly small. Jews account for about 2.2% of the U.S. population and .2% of the world population. In America, 71% of Jews intermarry,[35] and those who do have been less likely to raise their children with a Jewish identification. I so worry about the Jewish religion dying out.

Although I am proud to be Jewish, I believe in an inclusive life and practice it. I am not at all against intermarriage. Everyone should be able to marry who they want and be with the person they love. Many if not most of the close people in my life, in fact, are not Jewish. I have often taken opportunities to expose these non-Jewish friends to Judaism. In the spirit of inclusion, one Passover when my kids were young, I invited three guests: a Muslim couple I was friendly with and a young man whose family was German Catholic and were in Germany during the Holocaust.

My maternal grandparents, temple-going Jews that they were, had a Christmas tree. My parents, non-temple-going Jews, had a Christmas tree. I, still a proud Jew, put up a Christmas tree when my kids were growing up because I wanted them to have the fun and warmth of that tradition that I had experienced. But I also had a Menorah on display in the house. I believe you can be inclusive and multicultural while also retaining your identity.

And you can live a diverse life, while still being sad to see your people diminishing. But too often Jews who intermarry don't fight for their children to retain some identification with being Jewish. They just let it go. I carry real disappointment about that, especially since I had to fight against prejudice for that open pride in my upbringing, although it was nothing compared to what Jewish people throughout history have had to fight against. In fact, many who survived fled the religion in order to live in peace. We know about Madeleine Albright's family. I recently met on different occasions an Italian woman and a man from Spain, both of whom were also raised Catholic, but just found out their families had actually been Jewish, and are now pursuing some identity with Judaism. I bet much of the world's population is somewhat Jewish.

In intermarriage, at the very least, the Jewish partner should advocate that the children practice both religions or certainly at the very least, be exposed to both. Why should they just give it up so easily and let their own heritage be erased? And what about the Jewish extended family and their feelings? Do they hate themselves and/or their families of origin that much?

I also understand that a lot of people are non-religious these days, and that applies to many in my own family. But if you're nothing, then be nothing. Don't just only celebrate the Christian holidays. Don't still have a Christmas tree, which recognizes Christian-associated symbols in your home, while totally ignoring anything Jewish. If you're going to throw up a Christmas tree without any religious intention, why not also put up a Menorah?

Traditionally, unlike other religions, Jews have not actively tried to convert people to Judaism. In fact, we have helped in some ways shrink our numbers. It used to be that Rabbis—even some Reform ones—would not marry a couple if the non-Jewish partner had not converted. Thankfully that has mostly changed. Now at least the door is open, which helps those families feel more welcome and thus, more inclined to participate.

Even so, the population in the Reform and Conservative Jewish categories continues to diminish. That raises questions in my mind, such as why shouldn't we proselytize and actually grow our numbers? We get all this credit for being good salespeople, meanwhile most of the religion is not even attempting to expand its customer base. Maybe it's about time we did. Many of the best Jews I have ever met are converts. I would certainly welcome others joining us, and religious leaders should as well.

Those who adopt Judaism seem to understand its magnificent positives—the emphasis on learning, love of family, helping your fellow human being, working toward social justice, and doing so without the fear of "hell" in the afterlife. The Jewish community has a lot to offer and we should enthusiastically and actively communicate that message, not only to our own but also to others who may wish to join us.

My Greatest Blessings

I've been blessed to have very smart and talented children. But when Stephanie was a little over two years old, I started having some concerns. She didn't really talk. All my friends' kids were saying different words, most of them understandable. Stephanie rarely said anything. One exception is she would point to the sky when a plane flew by and say, "amee." I was really getting worried.

One night, while David and Stephanie were out, the Burkas came over. Janie put her son Jeffrey in Stephanie's highchair. Stephanie then walked in and said, "That is my highchair." Exactly like that—clear as a bell. Janie and I looked at each other quizzically. We could not believe what we heard. So I said, "Stephanie, what did you say?" And she repeated, just as distinctly, "That is my highchair." It wasn't baby talk; it was like hearing an adult. So she went from not speaking at all to using full sentences and became the most verbal child imaginable—and the most articulate adult. I guess she was just taking it all in until she really had something to say. And she obviously didn't appreciate having Jeffrey in her highchair.

Stephanie also has a wonderful speaking and singing voice, but it was hard to get her to sing, especially upon my request. Steph did have enough desire to perform in public to have one of the starring roles in *The Pirates of Penzance* at Deal Junior High School—probably because I didn't ask her to do it. My daughter Hilary was in the chorus in that production. Not only was the show great, but it was amazing to see the commitment of the public school teachers who make those things happen.

Steph has attracted a lot of friends due to her spirit and magnetic personality. I've often described her as a pied piper. People just naturally follow her. She also loved to write poetry and read—still does.

Hilary is among the smartest and nicest people I have ever known, but tended to be more introverted. She was also stubborn. Both Steph and Doug had been easy to toilet train. With Steph, I bought pretty panties to bribe her. Doug, who tended to emulate his sisters, just followed along. But Hilary would not budge—so in diapers she stayed.

There was a little boy who lived across the street who I think Hilary had a crush on. He was about four and a half and she was two years younger. He gave her his baseball cap, which she wore every waking minute with great pride. Then one day, a light went off in my mind. I put the baseball cap on top of the refrigerator. So when Hilary was looking for it, I just nodded my head and eyes toward the ice box. She said, "I wan' my cap." And I said, "Only big girls can wear a cap. And big girls do not wear diapers." She became trained that day. And I gave her back her cap.

Hilary had an artistic bent. She wrote beautiful poetry at a young age. She also showed a real flair for humor starting at 7 years old. She began writing a newspaper for dogs entitled *The Bow Wow Times*, which even had a take on my own regular column with "Midget Schwartz Reports," from the perspective of our dog. She also loved to play the guitar and later added songwriting.

Hilary was a good student. In 12th grade she was the only person in the country to earn a perfect score on the National Latin Exam. And the beat went on. Just a few years ago, Hilary took a bartending class in New York and was told she got the highest score any person had received in years on the written test. However, when the actual drink-making test came about, as she tells it, all her drinks turned out green. But even today, whenever I need information of any kind, I call Hilary (and that's not just because she's my only kid who answers the phone). I think she likes to be of help, although she does remind me often that there's something called the Internet (and sometimes I even use it).

My son Doug as a young boy was so loving and lovable. He was adorable with his blonde curls and a smile that took over his face. As he grew older, he became gregarious and quite a performer in every area. He won the major school involvement award at the Murch Elementary School graduation. It was no wonder he won because at the ceremony itself, he was in every skit, sang every song, and basically stole the show. He's been doing that ever since. At his Bar Mitzvah in early 1985, he kept the temple in stitches between prayers.

Doug was born on December 30th, which made him the youngest kid in the class. I was torn. I thought it may be too hard being the youngest, especially for a boy since they tend to mature more slowly. When he entered pre-k, I shared my concerns with the teacher, "Tell me honestly. If you feel he should do another year of pre-k, let me know." At the end of the year, she said, "He's smart and has good social skills. He should go on." I did the same thing with the kindergarten teacher who made the same assessment. I was happy with my decision to push Doug forward until he got to 6th grade and was by far the shortest kid in the class. I think experiencing being small then as well as not anticipating being tall since his parents were not, he developed an even more "towering" personality. A few years later, he grew to be over six feet tall, and with that as well as his charm and good looks, was very popular with the girls.

Doug also has a really good singing voice. He plays the guitar and harmonica well and basically taught himself piano in his 30s, even though we did give him some lessons when he was younger. He's also an excellent photographer and a thoughtful writer.

The kids are all very funny, as was their father—and me sometimes. A sense of humor has been a thread that has tied us all together—and has helped us get through some very difficult times.

All the kids were also good athletes. David actually had good eye and hand coordination and would often hit the batting cages with Doug when we were in Rehoboth Beach. I was okay in that area as well. I was even able to beat all my kids in ping pong up until a few years ago. (And they had to practice real hard to bring my reign down.)

Doug was first baseman on the Wilson High School baseball team that won the city championship each year he was there (and mostly before and after) and was wide receiver on the Wilson Tigers, a team not quite as successful. He also played a lot of basketball. Stephanie and Hilary were both on the soccer and volleyballs teams at school. In addition, Hilary was on the basketball and swimming teams at different times, and she got "rookie of the year" on the softball team.

While at Deal on the volleyball team, the girls would travel to many schools in the city to compete. There was one time when the kids in the opposing team's bleachers were yelling at the few white kids on the Deal team and calling them "honkey, cracker," even "white bitch." Stephanie ran up into the stands and got right in their faces to lecture them on how prejudiced they were. Deal's African American female coach told me about it—not Stephanie— and she was as proud of her as I was. That's my daughter. And those are my children.

Blessings Sometimes in Disguise

As I mentioned earlier, both Stephanie and Hilary went through puberty early—really early, 8 and 10. With puberty comes a difficult time for most girls, but when it comes so soon it makes it even more troublesome. It's normal to have mother-daughter tension in adolescence. As I had two daughters so close in age—only a year apart in school—I got a double-whammy.

I always loved my daughters very much and it seemed to be for the most part reciprocated. But as they were going through the prime of their adolescence, I saw our relationships deteriorate. I'm sure my experience was exacerbated by my working so hard and not always at home. They just seemed mad at me about everything. (I bet they would have been madder had I been home more.) Since I want to be liked by everybody, even strangers, having my two daughters not like me at all was very painful. I now often joke that as we went through that phase when my daughters did not like me, I did not like them any better.

But when it was happening, it was no joking matter. It really hurt. Stephanie gave her love and affection to David, and Hilary just kind of took to herself. I know it's a hard time for girls normally, but with a depressed father, a distracted working mother, and no nearby family presence, I'm sure all of it was made harder still. But at least Doug was a doll in those days, and we had a good relationship, which did help some.

I also had to be the disciplinarian, which was not always fun. And I'm a perfectionist, so I'm sure my kids found me not that easy. In addition, being the mother, I was in charge of all the more annoying tasks. One was getting new clothes, which with our different clothing tastes made for tense outings and sometimes ended in tears—from all of us. And being the woman, I had to make sure the house ran efficiently, gifts were bought, notes were written, guests were entertained, appointments were made, etc., etc.—and all while working full-time. I did not find all that very easy either.

(So many women I know seemed to favor their fathers while growing up—and even as grownups. I find that disruptive to the feminist movement. Girls are harder on their mothers beginning in adolescence and ending probably never. It seems everyone expects more of us, especially our daughters. And boys/men are watching—certainly not a good start or example for them.)

Stephanie and Hilary were very close to one another naturally and made more so by having shared a room until they were 13 and 12. I think a part of me envied their closeness as it would have been nice to have had a sister. Sometimes it made me feel even more left out, but these thoughts only happened in the bad times. Before and after, I have always loved, encouraged, and been proud of that closeness.

A fun bonding experience, though, occurred in the early 1980s when my daughters took tap dancing lessons at Chevy Chase Community Center. It inspired me to sign up for my own class. So some evenings when I wasn't at a School Board meeting, I was shuffle-ball-changing it up at a D.C. recreation center or at home with the girls. It was also a good stress-reliever.

(Speaking of stress, Stephanie has some anxiety issues. One time when she was visiting and the two of us left the house, she said, "Oh no, I think I left a cigarette burning," always thinking she left something on. I said, "Well you probably left the water on as well, so that will take care of it." I have my own issues relating to stress: a hiatal hernia as a teenager and then acid reflux in my 30s. Stephanie, when she was about 14, gave me a horoscope book for Aquarians. When I got to my birthday, the only thing it said was I would have stomach problems. Not that I'd save the world or have a good year or hit the jackpot. None of that—only the stomach problems, which I already had. Now I had nothing to look forward to—except more stomach problems. Regardless, I just keep eating. And like Scarlett O'Hara said: "I'll worry about that tomorrow.")

Underlining the Undermining

I know I write a lot about my issues with David relating to his depression and drinking. I also know that the many people who knew him will probably take umbrage to much of it. David was universally loved by our friends, his clients and co-workers—and well he should have been. He was a great guy. And they also always saw the best of him. That's true of most of us. But because of his ailments, the difference between the outside David and the inside David were stark and dramatic. I fell in love with the outside one. I lived with the inside one.

In writing this book, I hated the thought of in any way raining on David's name and reputation. But then I realized that not being honest about my reality in my 22-year relationship with him made writing my life story sort of pointless. It would be like leaving my reality with my father, Stanley Levitt, out of the equation. So I had a choice of writing a history of my span in D.C. politically—or really writing about my life. I have chosen the latter.

When the kids were children, David and I were on the same page about discipline and keeping consistent rules. That was very helpful to their formation. But as the children went through their adolescent stage and needed boundaries and discipline more than ever, I found I always had to be the bad guy, even in fighting for David's own demands.

For instance, although David was not a big eater, he was adamant that he always have hard pretzels and Cokes in the house and told me that no one should be allowed to touch them. He would get furious with me if stuff was missing, but never said a word to the kids. Instead I had to always be the one to deliver the edict. But the kids did partake and when I firmly told them not to, he would then totally undercut me and say to them, "Don't worry. It's okay." Soon after, he'd again say to me, "I want my Cokes and pretzels where they should be," expecting me to enforce it again. This went on for years. (And by the way, at that time, I personally had no interest in pretzels—in fact to this day, I would have to be starving to death to eat a one, although I must admit I gladly take the free little ones on the plane.) I tell this story specifically to illustrate how David expected me to just take care of bad news things for him—basically set me up—and when I did his bidding, just left me twirling out there by myself.

And this went far beyond Cokes and pretzels. He wouldn't disagree with me in private; he'd do it in front of the children. And yet, sometimes when one would commit a minor infraction, he would say, "You're grounded for a month"—a ridiculously out-of-proportion punishment. But I wouldn't undercut him in front of them. I'd wait until later and say to him privately, "Don't you think a week or a few days is more reasonable considering the minor offense?" Next thing I know he'd walk into the kid's room, say sorry, and suddenly they weren't grounded at all. No learning experience went on, except the kids were smart enough to know just wait and it will all go away. Regardless, even in extreme cases, I never undermined him in front of the children and I did not like him doing it to me. I did let him know how I felt, but to no avail.

David and I didn't grow up with money—and then we started to become people who had some. But we decided early on that we didn't want to raise "princes and princesses," and that we would try not to make our children feel entitled. Thus, we jointly came up with a reasonable, but not overly generous, allowance.

I found out many years later from the kids that he used to hand them, when they were in about the 5th grade and through high school, $50 or $100 bills—or his credit card—just randomly, not even for special occasions, and then would say, "Don't tell your mother." It really was illustrative of the good cop/bad cop setup that was taking place. I became the perennial bad cop. I'm up to the task but I resented being put in that position. It was not fair.

A Lesson (I Mean, a Lecture) in Raising Daughters

Daughters, as I've said, can be challenging especially during their pubescence. But I found when I would finally work up the nerve to confront them on some important issue—an issue which David considered important as well, and one which was difficult to tackle considering their teenage sensitivity—things would inevitably go awry. I not only didn't get support from David, but when they cried and ran away from me, he was waiting with open arms and great sympathy. Not only did I feel sabotaged at that moment but I was growing more and more bitter as the years went on because of those kinds of actions.

I try to impart lessons from this when I meet younger people. It may be a stranger on a plane. If I learn that he has a teenage daughter, I jump in and say: "If you like your wife and want to keep your marriage together, I'm going to give you some advice. As your daughter goes through her stage of hating and disrespecting her mother, which she most likely will, don't allow it. Say, 'You're not going to talk to your mother that way' instead of what normally happens which is the daughter comes running to the father for aid and comfort against the mean, awful mother, and receives it. It's not healthy for your daughter and it's certainly not healthy for your marriage. Because a few years later when your daughter leaves home, your wife may still be mad at you whether she talks about it or not. And your marriage may be in trouble as a result." (Meanwhile the guy sitting next to me on the plane is thinking, "I should have bought the headphones"—as if those would have stopped me.)

New Opportunities Knock

Within a couple of weeks of leaving the Board of Education in early January of 1982, I was having lunch at a restaurant with a friend when I ran into Terrel Bell, Secretary of the Department of Education, who I had met several times in the past. He said he had planned to call me after he learned I was leaving the Board of Educations, and then asked me if I would be interested in coming to work at the Department. I was flattered at his overture and pleased with the offer from someone I admired.

I started soon thereafter as a full-time consultant at the U.S. Department of Education and worked directly with its Deputy Secretary. It was an interesting job where I helped coordinate the various educational functions within the Department, and it also paid a good salary. I made some lasting friends there—Bob Lewis and Peggy Monahan. The latter had been a nun and then married a former priest.

Several months later, around May of 1982, David and I had dinner with Dorothy Fleegler, who was visiting from Florida and was one of my former colleagues on the National Advisory Council on the Education of Disadvantaged Children. (I know this is a long title and though I loved the work we did, I always dreaded having to say the name.) Dorothy had also invited good friends of hers— a Congressman from Pennsylvania, Marc Lincoln Marks, and his wife Jane. We all hit it off and Marc, who said he knew of me from my recent Board of Education days, asked me to become his Press Secretary soon thereafter.

Even though I never worked on Capitol Hill and envied those who did, I wasn't sure at first. But when Marc said he had recently announced he would be leaving Congress in January, and thus, it would only be short-term, that helped. And when he agreed to my taking the month of July off as I had a trip planned with my kids, that sealed the deal. So after giving a couple of weeks' notice to the Department of Education, off to Capitol Hill I went.

It was one of the most fun experiences in my career. It was a busy job, but since Marc was retiring, not crazy. He often took me around with him to hearings and onto the floor of the House. I really had the feeling of what it was like to be a Congressperson. Marc was a maverick Republican from a working-class district outside of Pittsburgh. He was also a member of the House Commerce and Energy Committee, chaired by Representative John Dingell (D-MI), and that was during the breakup of the Bell System (the telephone conglomerate). So it was such a momentous and exciting time until it ended at the end of December.

Westward Bound with the Kids

That summer of 1982, I took off the month of July and went away with my children—ages 13, 12 and 10—on a trip to the West. We flew to Oakland where we rented a car, drove up to Yosemite and then back down the whole California coast to San Diego, spending time along the way in San Francisco, Monterey, Carmel and LA. From San Diego, where we spent a whole day at their fabulous zoo, we drove to Arizona, saw the Grand Canyon, then headed up to Las Vegas for a couple of days, and finally arrived in Denver, where we met up with David to visit family there.

I was excited about the trip but had some trepidations as I was flying a bit by the seat of my pants. I chose not to make hotel reservations, except in a couple of major cities, so we could stay longer or leave earlier, all depending on our fancy. I was also driving on my own for hours, often through winding mountain roads next to steep precipices where the drops were thousands of feet— all while being terrified of heights. And during the Grand Canyon portion, we had an axle issue with the rented car, which was terrifying in and of itself. But thank goodness, we were lucky.

(I really do like to drive and always have since I learned, as you may recall, at age 12. So this trip was not a hardship for me. I taught all three of my children to drive when they were teenagers, as my dad had me. And I don't want to be too braggy, but all of them are really good drivers.)

Even with axle issues and steep heights, it was all worth it because I so wanted my kids to have the experience—as I had never been to California until I was married and had a child—and I really wanted to spend some special time with them. When we were at home, since our house was residence central for their friends, I had little time with them even when I wasn't working. So it was great to leave that whole scene and have the kids all to myself during such an enjoyable journey. I loved every minute of it except for the axle incident and the following story:

On one particular day on the trip, after the Grand Canyon, we headed for Durango, Colorado to spend the night. We got to Durango after dark and there were no hotels available. I went to every single place. Nothing. I remember joking that I should drive erratically so the police would arrest us and put us all in jail to spend the night. We were laughing, but it was really getting nerve-wracking continuing to have to drive through the mountains of Colorado with three kids, tired, and nowhere to stay.

Finally, we came upon a semi-resort-looking place at 11 p.m. I asked if they had a room. They said, "We have one room for $250." It should have been $75 in those days! At most $90, but never $250. I said, "I'm here with three children and it's so late. Why are you trying to sock it to us?" They didn't budge. So I said, "I'd rather sleep in the car than spend that kind of money."

So that's exactly what we set out to do. I parked the car in front of a busy restaurant/club. There were lights so we felt pretty safe. I got clothes out of the trunk to create pillows and blankets for the kids on the seats and floor. I then locked the car doors and we all shut our eyes for a relaxing night of sleep in a parking lot in the middle of nowhere. About 20 minutes in, we heard noises. The car next to us was actually bouncing. There was a couple inside "doing it." Steph, Doug and I started giggling as it was obvious what was happening. (Hil recently reminded me that she disappointingly slept through it as she can sleep like a rock anywhere.) I thought, "Oh my God, I can't have my children listening to that all night." So I just pulled the car out of the parking lot and kept on going.

Next thing I know, I found myself on this narrow, circuitous Colorado road which was leading us to the top of a mountain. By then it's 2:00 in the morning. It was so scary. And I was exhausted. My back was killing me. But I kept on trucking. What was the choice? We were even too far away from the $250 hotel, although at that point I probably would have paid $1,000. When we reached the mountain top, I found a store and went in to get some coffee.

Then a gigantic 18-wheeler drove up, and the driver came into the store. I wasn't crying but I looked like I was ready to. This truck driver took such sympathy on me standing there with three kids in the car. He said, "Ma'am, I don't think you should go down by yourself. It's too treacherous. You're going to follow me. I am going to go nice and slow and we are going to go down that mountain together. Just keep your eyes on the red lights on the back of my truck." I kept both hands on the wheel, and followed as he inched me down that mountain. It probably took him double the time it would have normally. When we got to the bottom, dawn was coming up, and we were safe. Thank you, Mr. Truck Driver.

We found a fleabag motel at 5:30 a.m., which cost around $2.50, and slept four hours. We got up, showered, and drove to Denver to see my Aunt Betty and Uncle Seymour, and David who arrived soon thereafter. We spent several days in Denver and then flew to Midland to see my folks and Johnny before heading back home after a memorable month away.

Home Town Happenings

On January 30, 1983, the Washington football team (I've refused to say the team name since 2001) won the Super Bowl. We were big football fans (although David less so). I had taught the kids the game when they were very young. The big win was thrilling for our family and the city. Cars were honking in celebration for hours after. The day of the victory parade actually became a school holiday. I took my children and a large group of their friends (it must have been 25 of them) to the parade. What was to be a really fun day, though, took a turn as it was rainy, cold and simply awful out. We got up at the crack of dawn, had to fight the unbelievable crowds on the Metro, and there was no relief on the streets. And of course, I had to keep track of nearly 30 adolescents.

After many hours of waiting in the rain, the parade finally started. We could see *nothing*. The players rode by in buses because of the weather—and we could barely even see their waving hands through the rain-drenched, foggy windows. It was just hours and hours of crowds and misery. I remember finally sitting on a curb and crying—which was the most fun I had all day. At least I made sure all the kids got home safely. I was sad when the team lost the Super Bowl the next year—but not that sad!

(Speaking of our football team, it reminds of a story which took place at the end of 2013. Hilary and I were at the Prime Rib celebrating her birthday. Directly behind us at another booth was a group of men including former Senator George Allen Jr. (son of a former coach) and former Washington football team running back, John Riggins. I turned around and tapped John on the shoulder and told him that my other daughter was a huge fan since childhood. I then asked if he'd be willing to talk to her and when he said yes, I called. To my surprise, Stephanie answered—unusual for her—and I said hi and gave the phone to John who introduced himself. She started screaming—the happiest scream I ever heard. Thank you, John.)

In 1983, I had a little more time on my hands. I was able to play some bridge, spend more time with my family, and got even more immersed in volunteer work. I devoted a lot my time to the Board of Directors of the Metropolitan Police Boys and Girls Clubs, which I had joined in 1979 when Richard England recruited me. (Richard and his wife Lois were the most loving and giving philanthropists in a town of many.) I became more involved as Chair of its Membership Committee for many years, and then I started going up the leadership ladder.

Our friend Ed Morgan would continue to hang out at our house often as he lived only five minutes away. It was great having him around as he was so helpful for David's mood. He liked Ed, who was such easy, good company. The three of us played cards (three-handed canasta, gin, hearts, etc.). I would even ask one of my kids to delay homework if we needed a fourth. I kept scores from those games in my scrapbooks, as I've done with my bridge games since forever. And there is a ridiculous number of them. David really enjoyed playing cards and we often played bridge with our new friends, Jane and Marc Marks as well. He would often ask, "Do you think Marc and Jane may be available to play bridge tonight?" Such pleasurable times costing little to no money.

Eastward Bound with the Kids

As I had not gone to Europe until I was married, I wanted my children to be able to experience something like that earlier. So the summer of 1983, a year after the western USA trip, I took the kids on a six-week excursion to Europe—London, Paris, Baden-Baden in Germany for lunch (because we got on the wrong train), Barcelona, Marseilles, Saint-Tropez, Cannes, Nice, Monaco, Venice, Florence, Rome, Naples, Athens and six Greek Islands. David joined us for eight days for some of the latter portion, but most of it was just me and the kids. We each took only a backpack and no other luggage. I knew we would be traveling by train, moving from place to place, and should not be weighed down. Whenever we had two days in a hotel, early the first day we would wash our clothes as we had so few.

I did make reservations ahead of time in the various cities as I felt it would be too challenging to wing it with the language barriers. Doug, then 11, took responsibility for the money exchange rate and did a yeoman's job. We traveled by Euro rail (on those unlimited passes) and often slept overnight on the train to avoid hotel costs. We slept on the deck of a boat from Brindisi, Italy to Corfu, Greece—our jackets as blankets and backpacks as pillows.

We visited all of the big museums in all the major cities. I happen to be pretty knowledgeable about the Impressionist painters, and loved enlarging the children's exposure to them. By the third city, they could spot across the room a Degas or a Manet. And speaking of museums, when we were looking at the impressive and magnificent nude David statue by Michelangelo in Florence, in walked someone impressive and handsome himself: Richard Chamberlain (of *Dr. Kildare* and *The Thorn Birds* fame), with his equally handsome and demonstrative boyfriend.

And speaking of nude, there was a very famous nude beach in Mykonos, one of the Greek islands we visited with its beautiful white stucco homes nestled on the green hills overlooking the Aegean Sea. Quite fabulous! Well, maybe the nude beach was fabulous too, but I never got to see it as I did not know it existed until I got back home and everyone asked how I liked it. That was one of the real "oh darn" moments of my life. I guess it's just as well as the kids at 14, 13 and 11 may not have handled it so well as they were still recovering from the topless beaches in Nice.

Although we ate lots constantly, the kids and I ended up losing weight because we walked probably ten miles every day. We did the most walking in Paris and the most eating in Italy. The best hotel view we had was in Naples and the best overall view was from the Acropolis of Athens.

What an adventure with three curious children, who were such good sports. On this trip, I did love every single minute.

Skiing: Who Needs It!

On another trip not long after, David and I went on a week-long vacation with Herb Miller, a close friend and client of David's, and his wife Patrice. The four of us went to one of the fanciest ski resorts on earth, located in Northern Italy. We had to dress in black-tie for dinner every night in a room that looked like it belonged in a palace. The place was filled with princes, princesses, and other international aristocracy to whom we nodded as we passed. It was like nothing I had ever seen before—or since.

Patrice and Herb went skiing every day. David from the Bronx and I from West Texas were not skiers. We tried. We took a skiing lesson, but David was on his butt most of the time. I stayed on my feet but was scared to death. Then came the ski lift and my fear of heights kicked in big time. At the top, we needed to jump off, but David's skis got caught in the lift. I thought he was going to be swallowed up by the mechanism. I screamed, "David!! Watch out!" He managed to escape with my help, but it was so terrifying.

Between the ski uniforms that weigh a ton, the freezing cold, the heights, the expense, and the lift that nearly devoured David, I found that skiing combined everything I hated into one sport. If they threw in snakes and fire, it would have been complete. (Well, at least the fire would have been warming.) You can't breathe or move and then you're expected to fly down a mountain, breaking many bones in the process, all while spending a fortune to get this privilege. Why would anyone do this to themselves?

Every day for the rest of the trip, we just went downtown and walked around browsing in the stores. Not that we bought anything. I remember seeing a pretty blouse in one of the boutiques on sale for $400—and this was 34 years ago! In the end, I'm not sure if the ski lift or that price tag was more traumatizing. (Okay, the ski lift was worse.)

CHAPTER 15

I have dreamed of seeing the reversal of the grave injustice of D.C.'s lack of voting rights in Congress in the nearly 52 years I've lived here. Now, I'm not sure that dream will come true in my lifetime, though I will continue to fight for it for the rest of my days.

I have often wondered how members of Congress and our Presidents can get up in the morning and preach democracy, then work on expanding it around the world, putting money in the national budget to do just that—and some of it coming from federally tax-paying D.C. residents—while ignoring our lack of democracy here in the Nation's Capital. Those individuals go on to brag about all they are doing to bring liberty to people around the world, while at the same time, totally ignoring the 680,000 people who live right next to them, who are denied that same liberty—the right to vote in their national legislature, meaning we have no Representatives or Senators who can vote. We are the only democracy on earth that denies that right to citizens of a national capital. If you don't believe me, look it up. It is so hypocritical. Truly an abomination that must end.

Speaking out against this ongoing hypocrisy and injustice has been one of my motivations for writing this book. So I *beg* you to read these next several pages—even if nothing else.

Taxation Without Representation

It's amazing to me that in talking with a number of members of Congress that many of them don't realize that D.C. is not like the Virgin Islands, Puerto Rico, American Samoa, Northern Mariana Islands and Guam, which are territories that do *not pay* federal income tax and their citizens were not eligible for the draft when there was one. Unlike those territories, the citizens of the District of Columbia have *always paid* federal income taxes and were eligible for the draft. In fact, we pay more total federal income taxes than 22 states;[36] and per capita, District residents have the second highest federal tax obligation in the country.[37] And we have had more citizens die in wars than many states. On top of that, we have a bigger population than two states—Vermont and Wyoming (and that's been true for a while). The District of Columbia now has over 681,000 people[38] (50% of whom are black, 38% are white).Vermont has under 625,000 (1% of whom are black, 95% white), and Wyoming has under 586,000 now (1% of whom are black, 90% white).[39] It's *time* for D.C. to have votes in Congress.

When I was "lobbying" for D.C. voting rights, some members of Congress said, "Well, if we give you the right to vote in Congress, then we will have to give Puerto Rico and Guam the same." And I would say, "Well, tell them that after they pay federal income taxes for 100 years like the District of Columbia, and make themselves available for a draft if we reinstitute one, then you'll consider it." (I actually believe they should get votes immediately after starting to pay federal income taxes, because I think there should be *no taxation without representation*.) These discussions were with members of Congress who obviously did not fully understand the distinction between D.C. and territories. If they don't know, what about the rest of the people in the country?

Most regular citizens of the United States have no idea of the injustice that is being perpetrated on the residents of D.C. When people around the country become aware of the issue, where they stand is clear. A poll done by DC Vote in 2005 found that 78% of the respondents had "serious misunderstandings about the rights of people living in D.C." But when informed about the lack of voting rights, 87% of Democrats and even 77% of Republicans supported full voting representation for the District.[40] It's obvious that we have a lot more educating to do, and I am hopeful that as Americans become informed, they will help us in this fight by letting their voting Congresspersons know that they expect them to do something right away to rectify this terrible injustice.

We residents of Washington, D.C. have tried various methods to raise awareness of our lack of full voting rights. In 2000, an excellent idea was conceived by Sarah Shapiro, which called for using the slogan "Taxation Without Representation" on our license plates, to help publicize our plight. Commentator Mark Plotkin was involved in promoting the idea. As then Chair of the D.C. Council's Committee on Public Works and the Environment, I got their ball rolling by engineering it through the Council as swiftly as possible. It has been on our license plates for over 16 years now and still there has been no progress. But at least President Obama put our license plate—"Taxation Without Representation"—on the Presidential car in 2012, as had President Bill Clinton in 2000, and as has Donald Trump. But still no voting rights, and it's so frustrating. We had one good chance—nearly 40 years ago. Here is that full story—and it is an important story:

The Voting Rights Amendment of 1978

Back in 1978, D.C. had a great opportunity to get full voting representation. The United States Congress put forward the District of Columbia Voting Rights Amendment (while I was on the School Board), which gave us D.C. residents, who had no voting representation in Congress, two Senators and one member of the House of Representatives, which is the number we qualified for due to our population. As it was an amendment to the Constitution, it had seven years to be ratified by two-thirds of the states for it to be official; thus, it would expire in 1985 if not ratified. I was thrilled when Congress was finally taking on this injustice.

Here's how it came about: In 1977, President Jimmy Carter, in his first year, appointed a task force on D.C. affairs headed up by Vice President Walter Mondale. It came up with the Voting Rights Amendment, which was introduced in the 95th Congress in the House of Representatives by Don Edwards (D-CA). The Amendment passed in the House on March 2, 1978 by a vote of 289-127 (with 18 not voting). On August 22, 1978, it passed the Senate 67-32 (with one not voting), and then it was signed by President Carter and went out to the states.

Walter Fauntroy, who was D.C.'s non-voting Delegate to the House of Representatives in the 1970s, was leading the effort to get the Amendment passed in the states. In late 1978, I called up his office. Walter knew me, but I reiterated, "I'm a Republican. I'm Vice President of the Board of Education. I will go to any of the state legislatures that are controlled by Republicans to lobby for the Amendment. I will pay my own way to do so. Just call me." I never got that call.

Every six months or so I would call his office, as well as the Voting Rights Amendment local office which was led by Richard W. Clark, and I would leave messages asking to be sent somewhere. Meanwhile years went by with no call. In 1985, nearing the seven-year deadline, when I had just gotten sworn into the D.C. Council, I finally got the call: "Please contact the state legislatures. We're down to the wire." Of course I did, but most of those legislatures were not even in session or agendas had already been set. It was too late. Only 16 states had ratified the Amendment when the deadline came: New Jersey, Michigan, Ohio, Minnesota, Massachusetts, Connecticut, Wisconsin, Maryland, Hawaii, Oregon, Maine, West Virginia, Rhode Island, Iowa, Louisiana and Delaware. Bless those fair-minded states.

It's not like I alone could have gotten the ratifications from the 22 other states needed, but I could have tried and I bet I could have moved the needle in a couple of instances. And I bet there were plenty of others like me willing to try as well. It really was a good amendment, which gave us what we wanted voting-wise: the ability to vote in both houses of Congress. But unfortunately, the amendment pursuit did not have enough money and organization to get the job done. Little did we realize then that it would be our one and only chance. Now here we are, nearly 40 years later, with absolutely nothing.

Other Attempts

In 2007, though, 39 years later, Congressman Tom Davis (R-VA) and our current *non-voting* Delegate to Congress, Eleanor Holmes Norton, introduced and shepherded a bill through the House of Representatives to give D.C. one voting Congressperson and an additional one to Utah, which was due for another representative as determined by the population results of the 2000 census. This would have politically neutralized the issue and offset any Republican resistance as a Representative from Utah would likely be a Republican, while the District's seat would likely be a Democrat, considering the registration ratios of the two districts.

It passed the House Government Reform Committee on March 13, 2007, by a vote of 24 to 5, and the full House approved the bill on April 20, 2007 by a vote of 241 to 177. Even though I definitely preferred the 1977 Voting Rights Amendment which gave us full voting rights including in the Senate, at least the one voting representative this offered was better than none. I did spend days on the Hill lobbying along with many others, led by Delegate Norton, DC Vote, and DC Appleseed Center for Law & Justice, and we were excited to see its passage in the House of Representatives.

Senator Joe Lieberman (D-CT) and Senator Orrin Hatch (R-Utah) then introduced the same measure in the Senate on May 1, 2007. There again, I did some lobbying, but unfortunately, it only got 57 of the 60 votes needed to break a Senate filibuster (which was likely)—close, but it failed.[41] After all these years of nothing, to not even get a little of what we wanted—which would not have cost anybody anything—was maddening and so unfair.

Then, two years later, in 2009, Senators Lieberman and Hatch introduced a similar proposal. It passed the Senate this time 61 to 37,[42] but numerous amendments were tacked on by Republicans, pressured by the National Rifle Association (NRA), which dramatically curtailed the District's gun control laws.[43] The Mayor and Council decided to refuse the deal of one vote for us, counterbalanced by one for Utah, because of this new egregious affront to our self-determination by altering our own law. And we were right to do so. One hand giveth a little while the other hand slaps you across the face. Shame on those who followed the NRA and stomped on democracy for District residents once again.

Statehood: To Be or Not to Be

I've always believed that full voting rights is the primary goal. If we add to that legislative *and* budgetary autonomy—instead of constant interference by Congress and the President—we really have, in my estimation, the right package.

Many, though, over the years and now, have instead advocated for statehood for the District of Columbia. They feel this would be the clearest route to full representation and other autonomies. When the Voting Rights Amendment of 1978 seemed to be going nowhere, District voters in 1982 ratified a proposed Constitution to become a new state which would be named "New Columbia," and which would divide up the city with the federal government. "The District of Columbia" would take jurisdiction over land used for federal functions, and the state, "New Columbia," would take the rest. The proposed Constitution also called for a pretty large local political bureaucracy. Then in 1987, another state Constitution was drafted which simplified the bureaucracy somewhat.

Since 1983, at least a dozen statehood bills have been introduced in Congress with only two making it out of committee. The second one got to the House floor in 1993, where it was defeated 277 to 153. There have been no other statehood bills since, either debated or voted on in Congress.

Last year, on April 15, 2016, Mayor Muriel Bowser called for a citywide vote on a referendum on the day of the general election, November 8, 2016, to push for the District of Columbia becoming the 51st state. I applaud her and those working with her for this organized effort.

The Mayor along with DC Vote hope to follow a process known as the "Tennessee model," which I think has a lot of merit. Congress admitted Tennessee, which was a federal territory, into the Union in 1796 without requiring ratification by the existing states. The thinking is, if Tennessee can do it in 1796 without a Constitutional amendment—and a seven-year process—why can't the

District of Columbia do it now? (In the early 1980s, Mayor Barry suggested this same route, but it never went anywhere.)

Under the newest proposed state Constitution, modeled somewhat after the 1987 one, the Mayor would be the Governor, the Council would become a 21-member House of Delegates,[44] with the independent office of the Chief Financial Officer and the elected Attorney General remaining in place. Under the proposal, the new state would take over paying for the judicial branch from the federal government, which currently costs about $274 million a year. The authority to appoint judges, which now rests with the President, would be shifted to the Governor.[45] As stated, the city would be divided up with the federal government taking federal portions and the new state getting the remainder. Residents were given several opportunities to weigh in on and suggest changes to the proposed Constitution through community meetings, a Constitutional Convention, and online and by mail.

The new Constitution was written in the early fall of last year.[46] Afterwards, as the *Washington City Paper* reported on Tuesday, October 18, 2016, the name "New Columbia" has been changed: "... the D.C. Council approved a proposed Constitution for the 'State of Washington, D.C.,' where the 'D.C.' would stand for 'Douglass Commonwealth,' named after abolitionist Frederick Douglass."[47] The Council also decided there would need to be another Constitutional Convention within two years of becoming a state. All the old and new provisions were placed on the ballot for the November 2016 general election, and it passed getting 78.48% of the vote.

I have never preferred statehood even though it would give us full voting rights and autonomy because of the problems which would result: name change (and new 'D.C' name probably will not fly as the feds want Washington, D.C for their portion), division of our city, and possibly exploding expenses.

I moved here nearly 52 years ago to live in the Nation's Capital, not one of the smaller states. I'm sure those who were born and raised here take pride in that uniqueness as well. So my desire is to retain our unique non-state status and not carve up this beautiful, diverse city into a complicated maze. Let's just think about Embassy Row—which is lots of places—and Capitol Hill and Southwest near the federal buildings. Will you walk across the street and suddenly be out of the state? And who's going to do this carving up and how long will it take? There would also be the confusing matter of who would provide road work as well police and fire support, or would both entities do so?

Furthermore, statehood may eventually lead to counties, cities, townships, etc., like every other state. Then, each of these jurisdictions would have to have their own government entities with their own elected bodies, and each would have their own staff. That's what other states have. The fact that most states are bigger than 68.34 square miles in total may not be considered. (And that size is pre-statehood; it would be even smaller when the federal areas are taken out as statehood envisions.)

Also, history has shown that we like bureaucracies. So we could end up with a lot of that, which costs a lot, with few remaining residents to pay for it as many may have gotten the hell out of Dodge and moved to a cheaper, bigger state. We already pay among the highest taxes in the country. Can you imagine what we might have to pay for this kind of new scenario?

Another Solution

I would rather gain full voting rights in the House and the Senate, as well as fiscal and legislative autonomy, another way. The 1978 Voting Rights Amendment, which gave us full voting rights, could be the basis for a new proposal. We would need to add budget and legislative autonomies, and try a better and quicker avenue than the seven-year ratification period, which in reality could take up to 10 years. This would get us most of what we want while retaining our name, Washington, D.C., and its unique status as the Nation's Capital while not slicing up our wonderful city.

This better and quicker avenue would be an Act of Congress, which when passed could soon be put into law. The Constitution of the United States says that Congress has ultimate authority over the affairs of the District of Columbia. Why can't some members of Congress use that authority on our behalf, and take the crux of the 1978 Voting Rights Amendment giving residents of the District full voting rights, add in budget and legislative autonomy, and maybe even judicial, and then work to get it passed?

Some people say it's better to become a state, because if Congress alone gives us voting rights and autonomy, it can take it away. But remember, it alone gave Tennessee 221 years ago those rights, and didn't take them away. And today, it should be even more assured. How could Congressional members who go around the world promoting democracy have the gall, if once finally given, to take those deserved and paid-for rights away from us?

Now I know people will say that the Constitution also says that only states get full voting representation in Congress. But, as I just said above, that same Constitution also says Congress has control over the affairs of the District. So we may have an inherent contradiction in these stipulations of the Constitution. If that be the case, let the Supreme Court decide. Congress passes laws all the time that the Supreme Court needs to weigh in on.

This Act of Congress I am proposing—even if it's challenged and taken to the Supreme Court, which may or may not decide to weigh in—could take only a few years. And if that Congressional Act fails, we still have the choice of taking its contents or something else to the states in that longer amendment process.

If statehood—either using the Tennessee model or a Constitutional amendment—proves to be the only alternative, I may end up supporting it, in spite of the above concerns. That's how strongly I feel about our voting rights. But I believe those deserved rights can be realized better and faster by re-enacting and expanding the 1977 Voting Rights bill, and then having sane and well-meaning people sit down to get it accomplished. (Maybe we can call in Jimmy Carter and Walter Mondale to come to our aid as they so ably did in 1977—and thank goodness they're still here, knock on wood.)

I do not believe that the residents of this city or the President and members of Congress want to see such a dismantling of the Nation's Capital as would happen under statehood. So I think they would join us in helping to find a resolution to this abominable disenfranchisement of over 680,000 citizens of the United States of American which has gone on for far too long—and which undermines America as a beacon of democracy around the world.

Regarding the November 8, 2016, statehood initiative vote, with Bowser's strong push as well as the October 18th action by the Council which called for a Constitutional Convention in two years before enactment, I voted "yes" to keep the ball rolling forward and all options open. I agree with the headline of *The Washington Post*'s editorial on October 21, 2016: "The District Vote Is About More Than Statehood," as well as its subhead: "A new President and Congress should find ways to remedy D.C.'s chronic lack of representation on Capitol Hill."[48] Now let this important discussion of D.C.'s full voting rights and needed autonomies—regardless of its iterations—continue!

Enough Is Enough

I know past experience should make me, even optimistic me, realize that the chances of Congress or the President doing what's right for District residents is nil to none. And it does not seem to matter if it's a Republican or Democratic Congress or a Republican or Democratic President, or if the Democrats hold it all. In the last 30+ years, *no one*, other than former non-voting Delegate Walter Fauntroy, present non-voting Delegate Eleanor Holmes Norton, President Carter, Vice President Mondale, members of Congress who introduced the Amendment in 1978 and the Democratic Congress that passed it, and more recently, Senator Joe Lieberman (D) and Congressman Tom Davis (R), ever lifted a finger for us.

I've so often wondered why that is. I know some members of Congress enjoy having D.C. as a whipping post and guinea pig for pet projects that they don't even have in their own states—and that they impose on us through the budget or riders (which is language added to legislation). Those who do that should be ashamed of themselves. But that's not all 535 members of Congress. That's just a few—maybe 10. Where are the 525 others? I keep hoping they will wake up one day and do something to rectify this wrong. Maybe if we just acted like we're Croatia or Chile or Afghanistan— places where they seem to care enough to advance democracy.

Now how about looking at us? We're black. We're white. We're rich. We're poor. We're young. We're old. We're religious. We're not. And we're all the in-betweens. We have children who died for our country. We work. We're retired. We volunteer. Just look at us. We help keep the restaurants you enjoy in business. We primarily pave your roads and fund your buses. And we pay federal income taxes. Just look at us. And once you do look and finally see us, please do something. Enough is enough.

But if you choose to do what you and others have done before you, which is basically nothing, I think we in D.C. have to really get organized and act on our own. I've never been arrested for anything. But I'm ready to get arrested for this.

In fact, I was so frustrated—and ready to get arrested—that a few years ago after I wrote my big check to pay my federal taxes on April 15, 2011, I also wrote a piece for *The Washington Post*, which it ran. It said that I'm sick of taxation without representation, and that I was not going to pay my federal income taxes in 2012 unless we had action on our voting rights, and invited others to join me. I did get some calls, but soon realized that this action needed a real concerted effort before attempting such a project. But that effort may not be so hard these days as so many of us are sick and tired of the abuse and neglect. In 2011, I had the feeling I might be the only person in jail. Now I know I would not be alone.

And maybe the Supreme Court, which appears to be a fair-minded group, may want to weigh in on this matter directly, even without the passage of statehood or any Act of Congress. There are Constitutional rights at stake right here and right now. Is not denying D.C. taxpaying residents full voting rights and autonomy a violation of the intent of the Equal Protection Clause of the Constitution? It reads that no "state" shall deny to any person "equal protection under the law." The federal government is using the loophole that D.C. is not a "state" per se to deny District residents equal rights protections. Meanwhile, that same federal government treats D.C. like a "state" in many other ways—e.g. Medicare, taxes—but only when it suits them, and we can prove that is often.

Or maybe we should use the argument that we are denied the basic tenet our democracy was founded upon: "life, liberty and the pursuit of happiness." I believe the other basic tenet is "no taxation without representation." How's that for double jeopardy? I know I certainly don't feel liberated nor do I feel happy about being screwed out of a basic right of votes in Congress—being taxed without representation—for the nearly 52 years I've lived here.

I believe the Supreme Court will see the irony and injustice of all this, as well as the conflicting Constitutional issues, and clean this unfair baby up if others don't. Or at least not require us any longer to pay federal income tax. If we are not a state and have no protections as residents of a state, yet have the responsibilities (federal taxes, military draft), then make us a territory. Then we will not have those responsibilities—and the federal government will not have the benefit of our federal taxes. They've had it both ways for far too long.

When I hear people in Congress say, "It's not Constitutional to give you voting rights," I say, "Stop the lame excuse. Try it. Let the Supreme Court decide. You do that in lots of other cases. And just maybe the Supreme Court will decide what you're doing to D.C. is not legal." Maybe the Supreme Court will side with *Post* columnist Petula Dvorak, who stated June 30, 2016: "... what's been going on in a city more populated than two states and full of everyday citizens for more than 200 years is Unconstitutional."[49] I certainly agree. Unconstitutional. Unconscionable. And just plain wrong.

CHAPTER 16

First Council Run

The Council of the District of Columbia is made up of 13 members. Each of the eight Wards in D.C. elects a representative. In addition, there are four at-large members and a Chair elected citywide. The Home Rule Charter designated that two of the four at-large seats must not be held by the majority party.

In 1983, Reverend Jerry Moore, who was a Republican, occupied one of the non-majority at-large seats on the Council. Jerry Moore was extremely well-liked and was the pastor of one of the biggest and most renowned Baptist churches in town. David and I had supported him in the past and we were fond of him as well. David, although still a Democrat then, had even been Treasurer for one or two of his campaigns. But by late 1983, Jerry had been on the Council for 16 years (a combination of appointed and elected) and had become somewhat of a rubber stamp for the other Councilmembers and the Mayor. He voted for every tax increase, although we were already the most highly taxed residents in the region. And unfortunately, he also had a reputation at that point of nodding off occasionally.

I felt it was time for a true alternative voice—and new energy. And I had started to miss the ability to directly improve people's lives as I had been able to do on the Board of Education a couple of years earlier.

I went to Jerry personally toward the end of 1983 and told him that I would be running against him in hopes of his deciding to bow out gracefully and giving us supporters a chance to fete him for his years of service. He then became the only person other than David and a couple of friends who knew that I was even considering running. But I did feel I needed to give him the heads-up out of respect, though I was smart enough to know he might take full advantage of it.

And take advantage of it he did, with great aplomb. He got all his ducks in a row. He immediately got the unions, the Board of Trade, the Chamber of Commerce, the local Republican Committee, the Mayor, and all his fellow Councilmembers to announce their endorsements for his reelection—all before I even announced. Jerry Moore was friendly with then Vice President George H.W. and Barbara Bush. He invited the D.C. Republican Committee for a special service at his congregation, the 19th Street Baptist Church, with the Bushes in attendance. Rev. Moore hadn't received much of a challenge in the Republican primary in past years, so he was pulling out all the stops. And good for him. I had not seen him so energetic in years.

Many months later, in May of 1984, I made my formal announcement and expressed the feelings behind my run:

> "I'm sick of people leaving our city in search for affordable housing ... I'm sick of reading about nursing home deficiencies, libraries cutting back their hours and recreation fees for our children and youth while millions are squandered daily on fat administrative staffs. I'm sick of our snow non-removal ... I'm sick of practically everyone—in all sections of our city—making jokes about our city government. And it doesn't have to be this way. There is nothing sacred about the status quo. ... I cannot sit by and not try to change things for the better ... by having the courage to deal with our city's problems rather than ignoring them." I hit on a theme I would use often during my runs and time in elected office: "The fact is that we have one of the highest tax burdens of any citizens in the country and very little to show for it."

I was determined to protect the interest of the taxpayers and to ensure they at least got the services they were paying highly for. I sincerely felt that the residents of the District of Columbia were being taken advantage of by the system, and had just gotten used to the bad treatment. So I came up with the slogan of this campaign: "Wake Up, Washington."

Mayor Barry was not happy with my taking on Jerry Moore and he actively helped him in this campaign. When I decided to run, Marion asked, "Why are you running against my friend Jerry Moore?" I could hardly wait to remind him of something that occurred a year or so earlier when I had bumped into him at Eaton Elementary School. I had requested at that time that he appoint me to the Board of Trustees of the University of the District of Columbia (UDC). I even followed up with Dwight Cropp, who worked in a high-level position for Marion at the time, about my interest in serving in that non-paying but important capacity. But nothing ever happened. So when he asked why I had the audacity to run against Jerry, I said, "You know, Marion, if you had put me on the UDC Board as I had asked, I'm sure I would have been too busy contributing in that way to even think about running against your good friend."

The primary for the at-large Council seat was set for September 11th and the campaign got well under way in the summer of 1984. But it was David and Goliath. We were doing okay in fundraising, but Rev. Moore had money pouring in from all the unions and business groups. They also had all their workers campaigning for

Jerry as well as D.C. government workers on their "off" time, and possibly even their "on" time. In addition, during that election, I was the only person running against an incumbent, and the Councilmembers and those connected with them were fighting to keep their team/the status quo entrenched. It was overwhelming.

Some of the establishment had no qualms with using their positions and power to try to help Jerry. For instance, Jerry was Chair of the Public Works Committee, which had jurisdiction over alley closings. Interestingly, during the election, on Friday nights, Council Chair Dave Clarke, from his office, would call developers who had alley closings pending before Jerry's Committee and blatantly ask for a contribution to Moore's campaign while mentioning their alley closing request. We were told of these calls by many of the developers who received them.

But I was determined to fight in my own less powerful way. I set up my usual all-volunteer campaign. One of the great things about these campaigns has been the people I've met, some of whom have become dear lifelong friends. One of them was A. Cornelius Baker, a recent college graduate from upstate New York, who came in and volunteered for the 1984 campaign. Corn said he had watched the race, liked me, and didn't like the way the insiders were trying to keep the power to themselves. It's a good thing because I immediately took to him. He wound up initially working with me on the Council, and subsequently has had his own stellar career working primarily with AIDS-related organizations. And he's remained one of my most treasured friends—well, more like family. In fact, his grandma Fannie Baker, I have adopted as my own (even though she's too young for that).

As mentioned, the slogan was "Wake Up Washington" with a rising sun logo. (It looked a lot like the Day's Inn insignia, which I noticed later.) For the first time I used my signature campaign colors, yellow and black (which I continued to use in all my campaigns) to signify a new day a-dawning.

My husband David switched from Democrat to Republican in 1984 in order to vote for me in the primary. After being a lifelong liberal Democrat, he had actually started thinking about becoming a Republican since working for the D.C. government in the early 1970s. But like so many others, he stayed a Democrat because that primary is where all the action is in D.C. His switching during the campaign was not unusual. Jerry Moore and his supporters asked everyone to do it, and we started doing the same. In fact, to this day, I still have several liberal Democratic friends who remind me that they made the ultimate sacrifice—becoming a Republican for a day—for me. And let me say back to them once again, thank you.

During that first Council run, I felt all the odds were against me—and they were. And those ingrained powers were united in their determination to remain in charge. How could I possibly change that, especially with only volunteers, little money, and myself as candidate and campaign manager?

One night, I found myself lying in bed thinking, how could I get my point across? What can I possibly do? It was the middle of the night, which is when I usually get my best work done. With David sound asleep, suddenly, I sat up and started writing something. I just knew it was the answer. It was a radio ad because we couldn't afford television. This is how it went: First there was the sound of a phone ringing. A person answers and says, "Hello, this is the D.C. Council." I say, "Hi, I'm Carol Schwartz and I would like to become a member of the D.C. Council." And she responds very firmly, "Sorry, Mrs. Schwartz, the D.C. Council is a closed club." Then you just hear the phone slam down and a dial tone.

After that, I would say at the end of forums and speeches: "Open up that closed club by giving me your vote in September."

To this day—33 years later—when my now friend Jeffrey Slavin (who then worked at the Council and was a huge Jerry Moore supporter) calls me, he announces himself as "This is the closed club," in honor of that ad. Jeffrey told me many years later that when they in the Jerry Moore circle first heard the ad, they all went nuts because they knew it would be extremely effective.

The ad was effective, but *The Washington Post* endorsed Jerry Moore anyway. I am sure the Board of Trade and the Chamber of Commerce helped. I was happy to get the endorsement of the *Northwest Current*. They supported my "stronger more aggressive point of view," and said, "There are and will always be a few dark corners in any government that could stand a little more light of day. We believe Mrs. Schwartz would shed that light."[50]

I also received the nod of *The Georgetowner*, which recognized my unorthodox approach to politics: "Talking with her, you often have to remind yourself that she is a Republican, in the way she talks about people-oriented issues ... Her Republicanism, however, is of the pragmatic kind." As the paper quoted me, "I believe in being frugal. I don't believe in waste."[51]

In the end, against the odds, I won the Republican primary for an at-large seat on the Council with 57% of the vote. I was thrilled and excited at the prospect of being a real alternative voice in government. However, my battle was not over. The general election still faced me. And it was going to be quite a challenge.

Josephine Butler, who represented the Statehood party, was a candidate. Two Independents had signed on, Brian Moore and Maurice Jackson, but soon dropped out with Brian endorsing me. Since Jerry Moore had a lot of support from Democratic voters as well as establishment backing, he decided to stage an orchestrated and well-funded write-in effort in the November general election. Barry ally and former Campaign Manager Ivanhoe Donaldson, as well as many others, gave Jerry a lot of help.

I got some too: *The Georgetowner* endorsed me in the general election, echoing, "It's high time to break up the closed club." I was grateful and flattered when the paper stated, "Carol Schwartz is an outstanding candidate who has offered us her service; we would be foolish to refuse."[52] I was on a roll when the *Washington City Paper* threw me its support: "We believe Carol Schwartz will be an independent voice on the D.C. City Council."[53]

In the November general election, I wound up breaking into that Council "closed club" as an at-large member representing the whole city with a margin of 10,000 votes. I am grateful for getting support from a lot of gay voters, which may have helped push me over the top.

We had our victory party at Herb's on P St., N.W., which was owned by friend and supporter Herb White, and it was an electric night. Gary Tischler of *The Georgetowner* described the diverse crowd: "... there was so much cross-pollination that the gathering looked like a varied field of flowers in a windstorm. ... Schwartz's election and party gave off emanations of what a rainbow coalition, District-style, might really look like." He ended with, "'It's the story that goes like this: Can a nice Jewish girl from Texas find true love and happiness in Washington, D.C. politics?' You bet."[54]

Even though Jerry Moore and I battled during that campaign, as with many of my adversaries, we've remained dear friends—and I made sure that his wife kept her valued low license plate number. Jerry was a volunteer in my last three Mayoral campaigns and I will always appreciate his good advice and help on the ground. Several years ago, when his family and church celebrated his 90th birthday on June 12, 2008, I, along with former Council Chair Sterling Tucker, was asked to do the video tribute.

I was especially close to Jerry's beautiful wife Attyce, who never didn't say "I love you" to me. Attyce sadly passed away in

2014. She had gotten shingles several years earlier, which had made her life so miserable that I think she was glad to go. (I've known many people who have had similar circumstances with shingles—men and women—so I would like to suggest that everyone over 35 years of age get a simple shingles shot to avoid this vicious illness.)

Jerry and I still talk on the phone often, and I go by for a visit at least every couple of months, including today. Jerry, pushing 100, is such a dear and of sounder mind than most people I know.

'Welcome' to the D.C. Council

After winning the at-large seat, the other Councilmembers and the Mayor were not so warm in welcoming me. When I went on the Council in January of 1985, the first thing I tried to do was break the ice as I knew people were upset about Jerry Moore and disliked me for being responsible. Thus, I invited the Councilmembers and staffs to an open house in my office with coffee and cookies. Most did come. Ward 3 representative Polly Shackleton did not, and had told her staff, "You are not to speak to Carol Schwartz or her staff. I don't care how nice they are to you. Don't speak to them." It was hard to deal with, but my staff and I kept trying to rise above.

That first term I did not get to chair one of the Council committees. This was normal for a freshman Councilmember. But two years later, Councilmember Bill Spaulding lost and Polly Shackleton retired, so there was a committee chair opening. And one of the great things the Council always did (even though it was consistently made up of 11 Democrats and two non-majority party members) is treat everyone the same when it came to chairing committees and office space. I always found that to be especially generous and exemplary—and still do. It went by seniority and everyone went up the ladder—until me.

When it was my turn due to seniority, Council Chair Dave Clarke shrank the committees from 11 to 10 in order to deny me one. He was still mad about his friend Jerry Moore, I guess. There were other Councilmembers like my friend Betty Ann Kane who said, "That's not fair. We've never done this before." But Dave was adamant and as Council Chair, he could do it. So I was really the odd person out. I commented that our staff could barely get a typewriter. (Now remember, this was back in the dinosaur age.)

Due to my lack of a committee throughout my four-year term, I had a small staff (three positions budgeted, which I spread to three and a half) but they were great. Gloria Strickland from Ward 7, who had been Deputy Executive Director for the National Advisory Council on the Education of Disadvantaged Children, was my receptionist and scheduler. Bob Richards became my Executive Assistant/Legal Counsel. He also lived in Ward 7 and was a lawyer and the husband of Laura Murray Richards, who had been a *Washington Star* reporter when I was on the School Board. Ron Cocome of Ward 2 was my Legislative Assistant. Cornelius Baker lived in Ward 4 and worked in my office part-time at first, then full-time. I was glad to have such a highly competent and diverse staff of four, made up of three African Americans, two gay men, and a woman ranging in age from the early 20s to the mid-60s.

During the first meeting with my staff, I got down to crucial business. I had to mark down everyone's birthday. I was not going to let those go by without celebrating them. Gloria said her birthday was December 24th. I responded, "I'll be darned. That's my father's birthday!" Then I asked the other two and wrote the dates down. When it came Corn's time, he said, "September 30th." I became momentarily speechless and then said, "That is my mother's birthday." I still find it astounding to this day that two out of my four staff members had my parents' birthdays.

A strange incident occurred right after I got on the Council. Several local Asian businessmen came to my office for an introductory meeting and handed me a small paper bag, which I thought had some candy or such in it. I gave it to a staff member, walked into my office, and we started to talk. Within minutes, the staff member opened the door and said, "I must talk to you." I went out and he opened the bag, which had cash. I immediately walked back into the office with the bag and said, "Get out," while pushing the bag into the same hands it arrived in, "And don't ever come back." They said, "That's not how [blank] reacted." (I never had to deal with that kind of issue again. Maybe my scaring them stopped it and/or maybe word spread.)

I had a different kind of strange start with one of my older male Council colleagues. For the first couple of years we served together, he never said anything to me except things like, "Did I tell you I have a Jewish lawyer?" Or "When I was growing up, I had a friend who was Jewish." I don't care if we were stuck talking a while or we were just on a minute-long elevator ride, the only thing he could think of saying to me was something about being Jewish. Finally, after one of the numerous instances of these routines, I walked into his office and said, "Can I talk to you a minute just on our own?" He said yes. I told him, "You never have anything to discuss with me other than the fact I'm Jewish. What if I kept only saying to you, 'I have a black friend. I went to lunch once with a black person.' What would you think about that?" He said, "I think I would find that annoying." I said, "What you're doing is annoying me. So I would prefer that if that's the only thing you have to say to me, let's not talk at all."

We actually ended up being really friendly. Several months ago, now four decades later, I called to check on him—and to get a phone number of a mutual friend who I heard was ill—and we had a lovely conversation about the old days for about 10 minutes. And then he said to me, and I swear this is the truth: "Did I ever tell you that my first job was with a Jewish man who was a diamond dealer who was very kind to me?" I said, "Isn't it wonderful that you can find good people everywhere?" I then hung up with sort of a smile on my face. Some things just never change.

Being a Councilmember was considered to be a part-time job, even though the salary was comparable to a good full-time job. Some Councilmembers, though, did have other employment. I not only made it full-time, but usually worked 50 to 60 hours a week, including evenings and weekends. I also wouldn't take honorariums. When I received a $400 one for speaking from Dr. Edward Mazique, Chair of D.C. PAC, I returned the check and wrote on July 25, 1985: "Although I appreciate ... I do not accept honorariums for speaking before public groups. I see that as part of my position for which I am paid by the taxpayers. If you wish, I would accept a contribution to my Constituent Service Fund which allows me to use the money for the benefit of D.C. residents. Please note that the legal limit is $200."

My small staff and I took constituent service needs very seriously practically 7/24/365, answering every phone call and letter. And the more you get known for that, the more you get. We also tried to get to as many community meetings as possible, and would find all types of ways to help our citizens. An example is when the C&P Telephone Company applied for individual user increases and I made sure we presented specific testimony:

> "The size of the increase, considering recent increases and the decrease in the rate of inflation, would argue against the need. ... I object to the introduction of a separate and glutinous dial tone charge ... raising individual phone rates 88.5% to 210%." I also objected to raising pay phone costs, saying: "Many people, who are among the most needy in the community, use coin phones exclusively by necessity ... which would add insult to injury."

Schwartz with Warts

Being on the Council brought many welcome opportunities and sometimes a bit of embarrassment, like the experience I am about to describe.

Some background: When I was in high school, I got a few warts on my hands and had to have them burned off. My hands were always very small and childlike and I didn't like them very much—and the warts did not help. (Interestingly, when I got in my 30s and 40s, people used to comment on my pretty hands. I guess those chubby little warty things matured nicely.)

Now on the D.C. Council in the mid-1980s. The League of Republican Women sponsored a blood drive at the National Presbyterian Church on Nebraska Ave. in Northwest D.C.; and they had asked me to be its Honorary Chair. The big day arrived, and it must have been a very slow news time as some media (print and TV) followed me from my Council office to the church where the drive began at noon. When we arrived, I went back to be the first person to give blood that day.

I sat down at the desk where you are required first to answer some questions. I was fine up until this point: "Have you ever had warts?" Oh dear. "Warts, but infrequently." The response: "Thank you, but we cannot take your blood as a precaution against staph infection." I said, "Can't we fake it? Just take it and throw it away?" The answer: "No." Oh dear. What to do? All the media was standing there with baited breath and their cameras pointed, waiting for my blood to be taken—and now it couldn't be. They're going to think I have syphilis or something. But I realized that if I clarified, warts sounded even worse. So I just picked up my purse from that desk, walked back to the media, and said, "They could not take my blood today because I had to admit I had the flu just last week." Sometimes you have to improvise, but now I'm fessing up—and my wart scars feel better already.

Meanwhile on the Home Front

At home, there continued to be moments of fun. The holiday open house parties and the rolling of hundreds, which felt like thousands, of meatballs and rum balls continued, along with preparing shrimp mousse, green goddess dip, marinated mushrooms and more. Aren't you sorry you weren't invited? Lots of people came—by that time, the party included several hundred people. David enjoyed those events as much as I did, in fact even more, as

I, being such a perfectionist, was always running around filling the platters and clearing plates before people were even finished.

Speaking of parties, David and I had a spring bash on Springland Lane in March of 1985. We invited friends and all of the volunteers from the winning Council campaign. Since it was a pretty day, we used the circular area of the cul de sac to hang out, grill hot dogs and hamburgers and dance. David even sang a few songs into the standing microphone.

In the middle of the party, two partners in a real estate company David represented arrived with a beautiful car they had leased for their "brilliant lawyer" and presented it to him. It was very exciting. But afterwards, David and I discussed it and said, given my Council role, it would be inappropriate for him to take the gift. So it was returned that day. It was a generous gesture, but one we chose not to accept—and I'm sure they understood. Around that time, they had also asked David to head up the company, but he preferred being its lawyer, and declined that as well.

Speaking of clients, another of David's, Cy Katzen, told me this story: They were negotiating a real estate deal for property Cy owned. In the middle, David just jumped up from the table and said, "We're finished. Let's go, Cy." Of course Cy got up, but was scared the deal would fall apart and kept saying, "David, what are you doing?" David's response was, "Just keep walking." The people at the table came running after them and Cy got a better deal.

Other interesting times: Back in the early '80s, David and I took a trip to Europe with a friend/business associate who was traveling with a woman who was not his wife. One night at dinner, someone he knew came over to the table. Our friend decided to introduce his girlfriend as my roommate from college. That was already a suspicious-sounding story to begin with, but it was made far worse due to the fact that my "roommate" was at least 10 years younger than I am and looked about 20 years younger. I don't think the lie had credibility, but unfortunately since he and David worked together, I had no choice but to play along.

A similar thing happened another time. David had been on a business trip with an associate and came home after several days away. He was sleeping in the bed beside me and the business associate's wife called. She asked, "Do you know where David and my husband are staying in Chicago?" I immediately got the drift and chose not to say that my husband was here at home. I just said, "I don't know." She called back soon thereafter and said, "My husband told me David was coming back to D.C. earlier, but I just wanted to see if you would be honest with me," of course connoting to me that she knew that her husband was running around. I then said, "These things are difficult, and I'm sorry." After I hung up, I thought, "What if my husband wasn't home?" Maybe misery wanted company. Thank goodness, after they divorced, she and I were able to keep a cordial relationship.

David, over the 22 years we were together, was often so unhappy that I even suggested on several occasions later in our marriage that maybe he should get a girlfriend as well. This was really hard for me as I am insecure and jealous with someone I love, and I did love David. But I seriously suggested it as he was so miserable and I was so miserable living with the misery. Fortunately, or unfortunately, I don't think he ever did.

David's depression and drinking persisted. I did marvel at his still being able to function so well at work, which was obvious from his rave reviews and the money he was earning. People loved and respected David tremendously—and for very good reason. He *was* a brilliant lawyer. Colleagues and clients speak of his brilliance to this day. He was quite well-read. He could quote soliloquys of Shakespeare. It reminded me of my father who could multiply seven-digit numbers by seven-digit numbers in his head.

David was a dichotomy. He had great confidence in his brains, but suffered from such deep self-doubt. And he had terrible depression, but was so productive despite that. There was darkness displayed in his sad eyes, even when he was smiling, but he had such a terrific sense of humor and sense of fun as well. He was also such a good actor that he was able to disguise what was really going on. So much talent. So smart. So many successes. Yet so sad. Such a dichotomy.

CHAPTER 17

First Legislative Battles

Early in 1985, the D.C. Council was in the midst of a major rent control battle. The city had very strong rent control laws, which were important, especially to protect low-income and senior tenants. However, as a result, no new rental units were being built. And existing rentals were being converted to condos, which limited the number of rental apartments on the market. This law was having the unintended consequence of exacerbating the severe shortage of rental units, and resulting in the few units remaining being exorbitantly expensive. While helping some existing tenants, these tough provisions were hurting many potential ones.

New rent control legislation had just been introduced. There were two competing bills—the Dave Clark bill, which simply extended what we had, and John Ray's, which loosened rent control too much. In the end, Ray's bill was amended to achieve a two-pronged goal: continuing the protections for renters while also stimulating new rental housing development. We had our compromise and it passed 10 to 3 with my support. [55]

I was also successful in putting in a provision that helped guarantee the development of more rental housing. The developers had no trust in the D.C. government and its promise that any new housing built would not be subject to our stringent rent control laws. They felt the government would simply rescind on its commitment after they made the investment. I saw their point, and one of those nights when I was lying awake worrying about this issue, I came up with the idea of penalizing the government if it changed its mind. In that case, the city would have to pay the difference between what the property was worth before rent control and what it would be worth if rent control was imposed. [56] That made it fair.

The bill with my added provision was exactly what was needed. But as was typical, the Council was greeted with protests and inflammatory rhetoric that falsely claimed we were gutting rent control. It's always difficult to battle inaccurate assumptions, especially when your intentions were to not only preserve rent control, but to provide additional housing opportunities for all renters at better prices. Thankfully we did both.

Then the Council started working on strengthening our no-fault auto insurance, which had become the norm around the country. The insurance companies went ballistic and started sending out costly mailings against it. I ultimately voted for the new law in November of 1985, but only after putting in a series of amendments which I felt were needed: providing mandatory fines for uninsured drivers—$500 for a first offense and $1,000 for any subsequent offenses; strengthening the process for cancellation of insurance; increasing the amount of collectible damages from an uninsured driver; as well as requiring more information be given to consumers from insurance companies on the cost of premiums.

Budget Battles

Since the start of Home Rule, D.C. government expenses outstripped the rate of inflation by 78%—a staggering $900 million. Each year, the Mayor would increase spending by $100 or $200 million, which we could not sustain and which just increased our enormous deficit that was $1 billion in 1984.[57] The size of government was ballooning. At one point, the Mayor could not even account for how many employees were on the payroll. Moreover, basic services were not always provided adequately, while the money instead was given to consultants as well as salary increases to high-ranking staff. Outside voices agreed that it was reckless. On May 9, 1985, the *Current* newspaper said, "Our government is on a spending binge which is not necessary and not responsible."[58]

I felt one of my most crucial purposes as a Councilmember was to protect the District taxpayer. For me, this means responsible budgets with the right priorities, good services, reasonable tax rates, and safeguarding dollars from being given away to bad deals or lost to corrupt practices. In D.C. in the mid-to-late '80s, that was quite a daunting task to achieve.

But I took it on anyway with first concentrating on what I named D.C.'s "bloated budgets." On March 19, 1985—just two and half months after being sworn in—I released a statement on the proposed Fiscal Year (FY) '86 budget, (that ended up passing 12 to 1, with me as the sole vote against):

"During the eleven years of Council budgets, operating costs of our government has increased by over 250%. Overall taxes on our people are now the third highest in the nation ... In bad times taxes rise. In good times taxes remain even—evenly high. This year we are asked to approve an increase in the operating budget of $168.5 million ... a year in which inflation is projected between 3 to 4%, the increase now before us is at 8%. ... Earlier I proposed to you that during committee markups $100 million be found for budget reduction: half used toward deficit reduction and half in personal income tax cuts, including an increase in personal exemption from the current $750 to $1,000 ... Unfortunately, our markup sessions did not produce substantial cuts. Where cuts were found at all, for the most part they were gobbled up to be spent elsewhere. ... The budget before us is one in which no serious attempt has been made to cut outrageous excesses of government. I take no pleasure in having to do so, but I will vote against approval of this budget."

Then came the FY '87 budget request from the Mayor, which was no better than the '86 request; and in fact, worse. My concerns about budget issues, specifically regarding the FY 1987 budget, were best explained in the op-ed piece I wrote which was published in *The Washington Post* in March of 1986. I will quote liberally from that op-ed piece below. (Now keep in mind that I am, at this point, a junior member of the Council, the only Republican, already disliked by my colleagues for even being there, and in a group that, for the most part, just went along to get along):

'D.C.'s Dead-End Budget'
(renamed by the *Post* from my 'D.C.'s Bloated Budget')

"On Feb. 3, Mayor Barry submitted to the D.C. Council a fiscal year 1987 budget request of $2.4 billion. Including grants and other funds, his proposed operating expenses for the District totaled $3.35 billion—an astounding $5,400 for every resident of our city.

On March 18, not to be outdone, the Council—with my lone dissent—adopted a budget greater by some $20 million than that proposed by the Mayor ...

Funds for improving vital services could have been provided, long overdue tax relief could have been given, and our city debt— the borrowing of money from our children—could have been reduced. The only casualty would have been the enormous waste in non-essential government services and reprogrammed slush-fund monies. ...

The budget submission was the 13th under Home Rule. The first, for fiscal year 1975, provided for operating expenses of $1.19 billion. This year's budget, at $3.35 billion, is an increase of almost 300 percent ...

Bad as that is, the news is far worse: increases in the cost of this government in these 13 years are all in the wrong places. ... while the budgets of the Board of Education and the police and fire departments have been no greater than the rate of inflation, the personnel office has increased by 900%. ...

While government and its cost have expanded dramatically, vital services to our people have not increased; only the size and cost of the bureaucracy have increased. Our tax burden is among the highest in the country, while our services are dreadful—and still, few in the government seem to care ...

Where are the government's priorities? ... bridges themselves and sidewalks and roadways are falling apart ... Businesses continue to leave the District ... Our public housing projects fall down around our most needy citizens, while federal money to prepare those projects lies unused in banks ... We do not fund adequate prison facilities, but the Barry administration can find money to renovate a building to house convicted felons next to a public school. ...

The cost of our government has increased wildly to be matched by wildly increased taxes but not matched by better services—not for the wealthy, not for the poor, not for anyone. A budget has been characterized as the road map for government. By that standard, we have taken too many wrong turns and are clearly heading toward a dead-end."[59]

Since those who defended our spending used the fact that we operated like a county and a state, as well as a city, I did a comparison of several cities, incorporating respective county and state per capita spending, and released it in my statement on the FY 1987 budget: per capita operating budget for San Francisco was $2,711, for Milwaukee $2,729, Portland, Oregon $2,406—and D.C. $3,852 (not including grants and other funds)—38% more than the average. San Francisco had one public employee for every 22 residents, Portland had one for every 37—and D.C. had one for every 15 residents for a grand total of 41,308 city employees.

(I recognize I just put you through a litany of facts and figures, which I found to be very interesting, but may be of no real interest to you. I still did it because rather than just speak in what might be considered hyperbole, these facts and figures back it up. Now for the most part, as we continue this journey, I will try to do less of these facts and figures so your eyes won't glaze over. But know that these types of researched facts and figures were ever-present in my thinking, whether spelled out or not.)

If the lavish spending had been on needed programs like crime prevention, education, and drug abuse, it might have been tolerable. But instead, consultants were raking it in. Although I could not stop such shenanigans, I did try to bring in some accountability. In September of 1985, I successfully put forth a requirement in the Budget Support Act that the annual budget include a breakdown of what agencies planned to spend on consultant contracts, hoping that public exposure would curtail those practices. Unfortunately, the Executive basically ignored that requirement so on January 20th of that year, I introduced the "Budget Accountability Amendment Act of 1987," which by law required the Executive in all future budget submissions to treat as a separate line item all monies expended for consultant contracts for each agency, department or board.

But the beat went on. The FY 1988 budget request by the Mayor provided for a total operating cost of $3.6 billion, nearly $6,000 for every man, woman and child—and one employee for every 14 District residents. In my statement on that budget request, I said: "This dangerous and foolhardy waste must come to an end. I prefer that it come to an end because we, as legislators, sensibly and intentionally end it, rather than because the cost of such wastefulness drives our middle-income tax base out of the District and the whole government down." (These statements made in the late '80s were an attempt to keep our limited Home Rule surviving and thriving.)

I found it hard to believe that I was the only voice speaking up against these reckless budgets in the mid-to-late '80s and the sole vote against them (with one exception one time described below). The Council served unfortunately as just one big budget rubber stamp. I became like a broken record, but someone had to be the voice of reality. It was hard to go it alone. Life would have been so much easier for me if I had just gone along like the others. But I could not in good conscience refrain from using my elected position to make things better.

I also tried to get Council colleagues on board behind the scenes. After I did all the above research with, at that time, just three and a half staff positions, I shared the findings with them. When I couldn't prevail upon my fellow members to start making cuts and adjustments in the budget, I spoke out strongly in public, including in such opinion pieces as the one redacted above.

Fellow Councilmembers did not take well to that. Several, as reported in the paper, actually walked out of the Council chambers as I read my statement condemning the irresponsible budget of FY 1987, which I went on to vote against due to the dire financial state it led us toward. They should have sat and listened. Because the warnings I was giving were not heeded at that time, we in the District paid a big price with a Control Board six years after I left the Council. They really should have sat and listened. Thank goodness a majority of officials in succeeding decades have had a different attitude regarding fiscal responsibility, encouraging business, and ensuring tax parity with the region—but I do not know if it will continue. Yet I was proud to be at the forefront of those causes back in the '80s when it was hard—and certainly not popular among D.C.'s elected leaders—to take on that out-of-control spending.

I did finally win over one convert during my fourth budget year. John Wilson, the Ward 2 Councilmember and Chair of the Finance Committee at that time (who went on to be Chair of the Council), and who helped design those budgets, got up from his chair, came up behind me, poked me on the shoulder, leaned over and said, "Carol, you're absolutely right. I'm joining you this year and voting no," thus voting against his own budget. But unfortunately, he was the only one who ever joined me on this important issue during those four years.

Tax Battles: Several Important Wins

In the 1980s we had the third highest overall tax rate in the country. And even so, our financial house was completely out of order. While already taxing our businesses and residents so much that they were leaving town, the Mayor and my colleagues on the Council were always finding new ways to tax more.

For instance, a tax increase on lottery tickets was put on the table. Though I was not there when the lottery came in and generally dislike gambling of any kind, I fervently opposed this tax hike as it would just reduce ticket sales, driving people to buy in competing jurisdictions. A similar measure that passed a couple of years before, a gasoline surtax, just ended up reducing gas revenues in the city by 27%, permanently cutting hundreds of jobs, and closing too many of our needed small businesses. These kinds of tax gimmicks were counter-productive, resulting in driving out business and citizens and ultimately leading to less tax revenue for the District.

Of course some flight from the city was due to schools and crime, but many were also leaving because of the tax burden. The District income tax rate was 11%, widely surpassing neighboring jurisdictions which were at about 4% to 6%. Our sales tax was 6% compared to Maryland's 5% and Virginia's 4%.[60] To be so out of proportion to our surrounding jurisdictions, in some cases extremely so, was illogical and self-defeating.

Not only were we overtaxed but as I have continually emphasized, we were underserved. I was really struck by that fact one day when a snow plow finally came to my street at midnight, days after the snowfall. I was so excited that I ran outside and yelled, "Thank you! Thank you!" Afterwards, I realized how ridiculous that whole scene was. I then wrote a "For the Record" piece in *The*

Washington Post, which ran it. It discussed how we pay such high taxes and yet when we finally get *any* service, we feel so grateful that we want to write a thank you note. How pathetic is that![61]

I made proposals to alleviate the tax burden: A "Sales Reduction Amendment" to reduce our sales tax by 1%, from 6% to 5%, in order to make us more competitive in the region and to help our remaining businesses and to attract more. Another, as mentioned, called for taking $50 million in budget savings to cut income taxes. I also urged the raising of the individual tax exemption from $750 to $1,000 and the standard deduction from $1,000 to $2,000—both mirroring the federal levels.

Additionally, in the mid-'80s, I called for eliminating all taxes for persons whose income was under $3,000 and for those filing joint returns under $4,500. I said at the time, "There are reasonable limits to the tax burden which wise governments place on their citizens. The District has gone well into the outer limits."

Because of the lack of similar thinking by Councilmembers at the time, many of my proposals languished in committee. At least I received an occasional pat on the back, such as from *The Georgetowner* which named me the "Most Outstanding Member of the Council" in 1985.

And when proposals did not go through, I just kept coming back with more. In 1986, I brought back increasing the individual tax exemption and the standard deduction to closely match the federal level in two pieces of very long-winded-titled legislation, which I'm sparing you. Tax relief, more often than not, increases spending by consumers which offsets any revenue losses from that tax relief.

Some years we had extra revenue anyhow. Unanticipated revenues for FY '86 amounted to $169 million, and in FY '87 were projected at $131 million. Unfortunately, we returned none of this money to over-taxed taxpayers, even though I tried. And we could have so easily done so with tax breaks, and with no jobs or programs needing to be eliminated. What a missed opportunity!

In 1987, the federal income tax code was changed to provide tax relief to enhance economic expansion and job creation. It brought a so-called "windfall" to residents in the District, as well as to other jurisdictions. However, Mayor Barry decided to use that federal relief to pile on additional local taxes, which made the "windfall" disappear. As a result, many lower-income taxpayers would pay more in taxes to the District than to the federal government. And many of the lowest taxpayers, who now would not even be required to file federal income taxes, would still be taxed by the D.C. government under Barry's plan.

In order to rectify the Mayor's proposal, I offered an individual tax conformity plan, which would have simplified the filing of individual income taxes by mailing in a postcard (that also would have saved some of the government's administrative costs), and would state that any amount owed to the federal government, 33% of that would be the District tax obligation. If your income was too low to file with the feds, you also would not owe D.C. anything. My legislation on simplification did not pass– another missed opportunity. My wake-up call did get the attention of my colleagues and the Council did stop the Mayor's plan to take the tax "windfall" from residents.

Then, the tax proposal that came before us in the Mayor's FY 1988 Budget Request Act allowed our citizens to keep the federally-created "windfall" in FY 1988—as the Council had done in FY 1987—*and* it also included *my* proposal for an increase in the District's individual income tax personal exemption from $750 to $1,000 and an increase in the standard deduction from $1,000 to $2,000. Therefore, in spite of not seeing the cuts in government spending and waste which I wanted, I voted for the FY 1988 budget as it included my own various tax cuts. It became my one and only "aye" for a budget in those four years on the Council.

During my first term on the Council, we did make a difference when it came to taxes for seniors as well, who were having trouble staying in their homes because of rising property assessments. I introduced the "Senior Citizens Realty Tax Deferral Amendment Act" and it passed in 1986. Such a great victory! This allowed individuals 65 years or older, who had lived in the property at least five years, the option to defer payment of increases in their real property taxes—with a low interest rate—as long as they maintained the subject property as their principal place of residence until the property was sold or transferred to a third party. It passed unanimously and helped seniors remain in their homes without additional tax worry. It's done standardly now in most places, but in 1986, it was quite novel.

I continually tried to decrease such taxes for all regardless of age. I introduced legislation to limit tax assessments on real property to the most recent purchase price plus cost of structural improvements—and this tax relief would apply to only owner-occupied homes and not to landlords. I gave reasoning for this in my introduction statement on February 15, 1988:

"Increasing tax revenues to the District government through the reassessment process has gotten out of hand—it is a cruel, dangerous and irresponsible way to collect more tax dollars. This is especially true as it affects our homeowners.

As assessments rise, all that this body of government—the Council—must do to raise taxes is to keep the tax rate constant. So, if this body does not actually act to lower the tax rate, taxes continue to rise. That is exactly what has and what is continuing to happen. What I propose is that, as a body, we should act directly and responsibly. If any of us believes more tax revenue is needed and that taxes on homeowners should be increased, let that Councilmember stand up and vote to increase the tax rate, not hide behind the Mayor's skirts through the creative raising of taxes by reassessment.

I ask you to look at the unfairness of the practice of taxation through reassessment. Take this example: ten years ago a middle class family buys a home for $40,000; today that same middle class family, whose members have the same jobs and the same relative earning power, live in a house no longer worth the $65,000— which is the inflation adjusted purchase price of their $40,000 home—but, now their home is appraised by the District at $200,000. How can that middle class family be expected to pay taxes on the home in which they live but which is now valued at what only a wealthy family could afford to buy? Through no fault of their own, this family is now priced out of their home.

No other taxing mechanism we, in the District, have is quite so cruel or destructive. If someone invests in a bond or owns stock or jewelry or works of art, and if those assets increase in value, no taxes of any kind are due on that appreciation of value until the time of sale. Yet, a home—an individual's or family's most important possession—can be, in effect, taken away by drastic reassessments in value and the resulting tax increases. How can anyone intelligently plan for their financial future and well-being in such an unstable climate?

While the relief provided to District homeowners accomplished by this legislation would be substantial, the effect on the District treasury would not be as severe as it might appear, because the annual turnover of residential property in the District is approximately 6.7%, which statistically results in complete turnover every fifteen years. ... In addition, the District will get its capital gains share of taxes on the full value of the house when it is sold ... And, if the District government decides it needs more revenue from homeowners' property taxes, it can raise the Class 1 rate, but a full and open discussion with public votes will be needed—not just waking up one day to receive a 60% increase— all done by non-accountable, non-elected people."

The above proposal never passed, but it did start a discussion. In the latter part of the '90s, we did cap the assessment increase to 25% in any given year, which then went to 10% which did help.

Tax Battles: Two Amazing Victories

I did have some tax successes that benefited residents, mentioned above. But the two toughest and most significant are these:

In January of 1986, I put forward with Councilmember Nadine Winter, legislation to make our estate and inheritance taxes, which were among the highest in the nation, less onerous by coupling them with the lower federal government's rate. It passed and was a step forward in trying to keep residents who were leaving for states that have better inheritance tax rates. (Unfortunately, they were uncoupled years later by Councilmember Jack Evans, with me opposing—and then trying to bring the coupling back.)

And in 1988, the last year of my first term, I was able to get the top marginal income tax rate reduced from 11% to 9.5%. I took the coupling of the inheritance tax as an opening and pushed through tying our income tax to the federal level as well. Other than getting John Wilson's buy-in, which was very helpful as he was Chair of the Finance Committee, it was a non-fanfare move on my part. Of course it went through the normal open process, but I didn't draw specific attention to it for fear that it might not pass.

What the city had been doing for years in setting our top income tax rate so high was helping force out not only our most affluent residents (who either left entirely or chose to set up their residency elsewhere), but our middle-class residents as well (with Virginia and Maryland only being 4% and 6% respectively while we were 11%). I wanted to make sure we were at least becoming more competitive in order to keep those residents and their considerable money in our treasury. That, too, was included in the one budget—FY 1988—I voted for in that four-year term.

As I look back on those tax-cutting accomplishments during that time of our history, I still feel great pride. And when you consider the fact that I chaired no committee, a perch from which you can wheel and deal to get your agenda through, I have more pride.

Other Fiscal Battles

Protecting taxpayers and District resources meant constantly being a watchdog. This often caused me to be the lone no vote against suspect deals when others were rubber-stamping them.

This was the case when Bob Johnson won the cable contract for D.C. in a competitive bidding process. (Actually, I think it was a company from Indiana but Bob was its local partner.) The company offered a good proposal—and fair for both D.C. and its local partner, which we signed onto. But a few short months later, Johnson came back demanding huge financial concessions. It was a bait and switch after awarding the contract. "How do we go in four months from being promised the world to getting not hardly the world. It's really disgusting," I said in *The Washington Times.*⁶²

The vote on the Council was 10 to 1 to approve the modification. Again, I was the sole vote against—all in the name of protecting taxpayer interests and to disapprove the bait-and-switch tactics which occurred on a competitively bid contract. What was going to keep other companies from following that precedent of getting a contract based on best bid and then just redoing it afterwards?

I was also the only Councilmember to vote against a $9 million revenue bond application for developer Jeffrey Cohen, and asked why the city did not do its own appraisal of the property instead of relying on one done by the developer. Why should the District be subsidizing a very wealthy businessman? My questioning spearheaded an independent appraisal.

And in 1985, when it was found that the President of the University of the District of Columbia was using the institution's funds to buy personal treasures, including a decorative hummingbird for his office for which he spent $102,000, I helped call for hearings and asked pointed questions, along with others. After those hearings, he resigned.⁶³ I wonder where that decorative hummingbird is now.

Battles Against Crime That Pays

The Council passed the "Youth Rehabilitation Act of 1985" in June as an emergency, without prior notice to Councilmembers I protested the emergency, and therefore, it was removed from that category. The legislation allowed, even encouraged, a convicted felon between the ages of 18 and 22 to get different and preferential treatment. It included murderers until I was successful in getting that taken out in an amendment on first reading.

The preferential treatment would give these individuals free education, job training, job placement, and the ability to have their felony conviction expunged from the record. I said at the time,

"Who is giving free education, free job training and free job placement to our law-abiding 18 to 22-year-olds?" Of course, we should do rehabilitation for those convicted of major crimes, but this went beyond the pale. Talk about crime paying.

On July 9th, I proposed a series of amendments to help rectify some of the damages of this legislation as it had been passed two weeks earlier on first reading. I said in the cover letter of my second-reading amendments that I would introduce them individually and ask for a roll call vote on each. Here is a paragraph from that cover letter:

"Legislatures should at least on occasion look beyond the specifics of a given piece of legislation to its broader implications. I ask that before voting for this legislation, each of us ask ourselves what kind of message would we send to the community? To those who commit crime, we would send a message of indulgent weakness. To those who do not commit crime, particularly law-abiding 18 to 22-year-olds, we would send a message of why bother. To the victims of crime, we would send the message of who cares. To a judiciary already under attack for coddling criminals, we would say lawmakers want more of the same. To the police, who we ask to risk their own lives, we would thumb our noses. To the citizens of Washington who voted for minimum sentencing and who want punishment certain as a deterrent of crime, we would say that's tough."

On December 4, 2016, over 30 years after this Act's passage by the Council, *The Washington Post* reported on the failures of the D.C. Youth Rehabilitation Act in an article, one of a series, entitled "How a Mercy Law Enables Criminals." The article concluded:

"Hundreds of criminals sentenced by ... judges under an obscure local law crafted to give second chances to young adult offenders have gone on to rob, rape, or kill residents of the nation's capital.

The original intent of the law was to rehabilitate inexperienced criminals younger than 22. The District's Youth Rehabilitation Act allows for shorter sentences for crimes and an opportunity for offenders to emerge with no criminal record. But a *Washington Post* investigation has found a pattern of violent offenders returning rapidly to the streets and committing more crimes. Hundreds have been sentenced under the act multiple times."

A December 12, 2016 *Washington Post* editorial further said:

"... instances of the law giving licenses to some hardened criminals are startling. At least 121 defendants sentenced under the act went on to be charged with murder since 2010 with 30 of the killings taking place while the suspects were on probation and four occurring while the defendants would have been incarcerated if not given a sentencing break."[64]

My warnings about the Youth Rehabilitation Act may not have been popular, but 31 years later my warnings proved prescient.[65] There again, the Council in the '80s maybe should have listened. (P.S. I was so pleased to read this morning, September 19, 2017, the headline in the Metro section of the *Post* that read, "Youth Act Rewrite Has Support on Council." And according to the article, Mayor Bowser had signed on to such an effort last December after the *Post* articles ran. It is good that even after three decades, the problematic aspects of this legislation will be hopefully rectified.)

Battles for Rights

We stood up against discrimination often on the Council. For instance, we passed a bill prohibiting companies from using an AIDS antibody test to deny insurance. It was legislation we were proud of supporting. Unfortunately, insurance companies ended up just leaving the market as they had threatened to do, so a couple of years later, after I left the Council, the law was repealed.

Around that same time, there was a bad incident when a gay citizen got punched in the face and was called a "faggot." To add to that, the police did not even take a statement. After we on the Council stepped in, the police finally did take that statement.

My concern for gay rights made me an activist in this cause. Members of Congress, as mentioned, would sometimes try to overturn laws we passed and install riders to impose their own will on the city. It was so anti-democratic and often targeted toward our LGBT population. I tried to use my influence to get members of Congress to back off on many occasions and have copies of lots of letters to prove it.

Then, in 1988, Congress tried to erode the District's human rights law through the D.C. Appropriations Bill. Specifically, they attempted to cut off all $3.2 billion of federal funding for the District unless we revised our human rights law to allow religious schools in the District to discriminate against gays and lesbians. We decided enough was enough.

As our lobbying efforts usually just fell on deaf ears, we determined it was time for bolder action. Several Councilmembers, including me, joined Chair David Clarke in filing a lawsuit. As I stated at the time, "The lawsuit is one of the few recourses that we have. We've got to exercise that recourse if Congress does not re-think their position. The only other solution is to pass laws the Council believes Congress will approve, which means not always voting one's conscience and I don't have the stomach for that."

In December of 1988, the judge sided with the District on this issue. It ruled that Council votes are free speech and protected by the Constitution. It was a true victory for Home Rule. I was glad to see that Judge Royce Lamberth appointed by Reagan backed our position. I said at the time, "We felt very strong about defend-ing our human rights statutes. It was very gratifying to have been vindicated by a judge who obviously believes in the Constitution."

Being the lone Republican on the Council then, I was busy. I wrote letters relating to human rights, for instance, urging Con-gress to vote to override President Reagan's veto of economic sanctions against South Africa to protest Apartheid.

In a November 24, 1987 statement in support of the "Secretary General Mikhail Gorbachev Welcoming Resolution," I joined my co-introducer Councilmember Hilda Mason in commending "both world leaders [Gorbachev and President Reagan] for taking the initiative to consider an agreement to reduce nuclear weapons." I continued, "Mr. Gorbachev is indeed welcome here as would be any leader who desires peace and an improved relationship with the United States. ... I would, however, consider myself to be re-miss if at this time I did not also urge that during this visit serious dialogue take place between the two leaders on the issue of con-tinuing human rights violations by the Soviet Government."

And here at home we had our own battles. In the mid-'80s, some residents protested outside a market in Ward 8 owned by a Korean man after an alleged incident of mistreatment of a black customer. Reverend Willie Wilson led the boycott of the store. That was okay. But then he went on and made some inflammatory remarks such as, "If they really wanted to punish the shopkeeper, they would have cut off the owner's head and rolled it down the street."[66] The statement was incendiary, especially coming from a religious leader—and not okay. I spoke up against it.

On Rosh Hashanah of 1985, I introduced a Council resolution condemning those who breed hatred on any group. Then on De-cember 3, 1985, I introduced and the Council voted unanimously for the "Condemnation of Violent Acts Against Our Korean-American Business Community Resolution." I said at the time, "The District of Columbia must remain a place where all people of good will can live and work together."

I wish others would put themselves out there to protect all minorities, and not just their own. For instance, speaking at Howard University, Louis Farrakhan expressed very hateful things about Jewish people. He has done so often through the years. I was not only distraught by his statements but the fact that so few non-Jewish people spoke out against his bigotry.

Two exemplary exceptions were civil rights leader and Congressman John Lewis and Howard University President James E. Cheeks. I was so touched by the articles they wrote condemning Farrakhan's words that I wrote each a thank you note. After many Jewish Americans stood up to fight against racial discrimination, I wondered why there weren't more African Americans raising their voices against Farrakhan's bigotry and hatred. I still wonder.

Battles for Economic Opportunity

We on the Council fought for economic opportunity for all, making needed changes to procurement rules to open doors for more minority contractors, who had been previously frozen out. Unfortunately, this good intention became abused by the Barry Administration and led to favoritism and gross contract overspending. These programs, though, can be done well with added points in a competitive procurement process, which doesn't include, "Hey, buddy, come and get it—and for even more money."

I also led the way with the "District of Columbia Enterprise Zone Study Commission Act of 1986" in order to look at creating development zones in underserved parts of the District. The Act encouraged replicating programs that had been successful in other cities through a new federal initiative. I pointed out that these zones had benefitted other local economies and that according to HUD statistics: 23 states were successfully using enterprise programs in over 1,400 zones; 80,000 jobs had already been created or saved; and $3 billion in capital investment had been generated. The Act passed, and thus got this worthwhile program with its federal dollars started. Then Mayor Barry in October of 1986 established three development zones east of the Anacostia River, which I was thrilled to see him do.

Battles of Practicality and Independence

Only Councilmember Betty Ann Kane and I voted against a University of the District of Columbia and Antioch Law School merger—which was really a "bail-out" proposed by Councilmember Hilda Mason to help her friends who ran the Ohio law school that was about to go under—at a cost to D.C. of $3 million in public funds each year. I said in my statement on July 8, 1986, "If we are going to spend $3 million on legal education, we could send 200 to 300 of our young people to the best law schools in the United States for that same $3 million." (Remember, this was 1986.) And on September 23, 1986, I said, "I am convinced the $3 million authorized ... is insufficient ..." and "the ultimate cost will be many times that amount." And it was.

Whereas other members rubber-stamped the deal, I knew the school was just an extra expense being placed on our already challenged public university—which did not want it, and said so. I stated at the time: "We are forcing UDC to take on the burden of a law school, when they already voted responsibly in the spring that they had enough to do trying to bring our public university to the standards we would like to see it have."[67]

I also pointed out that Antioch had only 10 students from the District of Columbia out of its enrollment of 328. In addition, I noted that "Washington has more law schools than any city in the United States other than New York."

The overwhelming majority of the Council took a different position on the merger and approved it along with funding. Mayor Barry did *not* veto the law, but then later refused to release the funds. I was perturbed by his action, as the law—one I didn't even vote for—should always be followed. And therefore, I spoke out for releasing those authorized funds. Here I was fighting for appropriate follow-through on a merger I was against in the first place. But in my book, right is right.

The merger did cost more as I had predicted. (It was a long struggle at the beginning for it to work. But in the last 15 years or so, the University of the District of Columbia Law School—renamed now the David A. Clarke School of Law and ably led by Shelley Broderick—has graduated many good students, most of whom have gone into public interest law.)

I have always exerted my independence and tried to protect others' independence as well. My concern for civil liberties also influenced some of my votes. Council Chair Dave Clarke and I were the only Councilmembers to vote against the seat belt law. It may now seem antiquated, but at the time my view was that people even had the civil right to put themselves in danger—even though I always have my seat belt on!

There was one vote where I wished I followed my independent voice. I initially voted on the first reading *against* raising the drinking age from 18 to 21, even though it passed soundly without me. I thought it was not fair that young people who can marry and die for their country at age 18 would not even be able to toast their wedding or their survival from war. We all know that every young person 18 to 20 has a fake ID. I dare you to find one who does not. However, that's unfortunately what an unfair law can get you.

Yet, because the federal government threatened every "state" (see, another example where we were treated as a state) with taking away highway funding unless the drinking age was raised, I felt my hand was forced. Thus, I silenced my independent voice and cast a vote for it on second reading.

But my true conviction never supported it—and still doesn't. Even though I'm a non-drinker, it's the only vote I ever regretted. Right is right, and in my estimation, if you're allowed to die in service for your country at 18, you should be allowed to buy a beer. I hope this will be rethought—not only locally, but also nationally.

Battles Which Don't Fit into Any of the Above Categories

On June 25, 1985, I introduced legislation called the "Child Stealing Act" that would make abduction of a minor child by a non-custodial relation a felony, punishable by up to three years in prison and/or a fine of up to $2,000. This felony status was needed to ensure that federal agencies would aid in the search for a child which they would not have done without that status. All states, except West Virginia and us, had already enacted it. Then on September 12, 1985, Wilhelmina Rolark, the Chair of the Judiciary Committee, introduced my same bill with a new name, "Parental Kidnapping Prevention," which passed. Talk about kidnapping! But it—they—did thankfully become law.

On December 13, 1988, I introduced legislation to rename the Southwest Expressway (Interstate 395), the Eisenhower Southwest Expressway. I did so then because 1989 would mark President Dwight D. Eisenhower's 100th birthday. He had not only served the nation for all of his adult life—much of it in Washington—but he was also the father of the Interstate Highway System. It seemed a fitting tribute, especially since there was no national monument for him in the works at that time. (Now 30 years later, there is.) The legislation unanimously passed the Council.

Battling Concerns at Home

I remained concerned about David's not-so-healthy habits. He usually got up at 5:00 in the morning, drank coffee and chain-smoked cigarettes for several hours before going to work about 8. He would eat no breakfast. At work, according to his assistant, he continued doing the same—coffee and cigarettes—all day long (you could smoke in your office then), and he rarely had lunch. His assistant even told my daughter much later that she was so concerned about the caffeine intake that she began to sneak in de-caf sometimes. At night, he headed straight to the liquor cabinet and usually ate very little dinner except on Sunday nights when we had Chinese food or pizza. My occasional brunch on the week-end or spaghetti dinners could be winners as well as bringing in lox and bagels from Posin's Delicatessen on Georgia Ave. But for the most part, food was of little interest. David did exercise once in a while, playing racquetball with Doug or one of his associates.

His smoker's cough, which was there when I met him at age 26, became worse and worse. The kids and I could even find him in a department store by that cough. Hilary recalls that when she was in a program at Murch in the 6th grade, she heard it and knew that her dad was in the audience. I tried to get him to cut back on his drinking and smoking, even though I certainly did the latter, and to eat more, and I certainly did that as well. But David marched to his own drummer, so it was a losing battle.

At home, David also would purposely annoy himself. Right after getting his Jack Daniels when he returned from work, he would go into the breakfast room by the kitchen, turn on the television, and watch Dan Rather every night. By this point, he had gone from being a liberal Democrat to a quite conservative Republican, far more conservative than I had ever been.

David hated Dan Rather and his views, and yet he would tor-ment himself by insisting on watching him every single evening. At least two nights a week, he would call CBS and complain about something Dan Rather had said. I used to say to him, "David, why don't you *not* watch Dan Rather who you find so aggravating?" But he continued watching—and calling. Around that time, David also started writing letters to the editor (which were quite good, by the way) on a regular basis whenever he read things that irked him, which was often. But who am I to criticize letters to the editor?

Battling to Put Republican to Work

In very Democratic D.C., I had to rigorously defend myself for being a Republican. But my registration had a benefit for the city in that it allowed me to be a more effective advocate on our behalf in Congress. I could get appointments with non-Democratic members that others could not. And sometimes it made a difference.

One example: In 1999, I and my good friend Carl Schmid were successful in getting a meeting with Todd Tiahrt, a Republican Congressman from Kansas, who had put a rider into the D.C. Appropriations Bill that banned adoptions by unmarried couples, which seemed to be targeting the LGBT community. In the meeting, I talked about my lesbian and gay friends who had adopted children and given them stable and loving homes. I actually got teary eyed when relating some of the experiences I had personally observed with these families. I can't cry on command, but I do believe my tears helped the cause because soon thereafter, the rider was withdrawn—and those needed adoptions continued.

Now I want to address an issue regarding this, which I can speak about with real authority. I ask you to bear with me.

While living and running for office in Washington, D.C., I have been put on the defensive about being a Republican—and that all started decades ago, long before the party went so right-wing, and 40 years before Donald Trump, when people like Everett Dirksen, Nelson Rockefeller, Jacob Javits and Mark Hatfield were prominent leaders, and even with notable good guys later like Olympia Snow, Jack Kemp, Charles "Mac" Mathias, Connie Morella, Jim Kolbe, Arlen Specter, Richard Lugar, John McCain, and others.

In this overwhelmingly Democratic city, the word Republican has always been objectionable. The intolerance was strong and ever-present, even among the most liberal of liberals and sometimes especially among them. I understand intolerant people not wanting to hear other views and I expect them to be narrow-minded. But liberals?

As said, even my own mother-in-law hated the fact I was a Republican. Ma, who was born and bred in New York and considered herself a liberal, was almost merciless in her judgment of my politics—even seemed embarrassed about them. Thank goodness she ended up loving me despite my voter registration, though it took a long time. But why should we have had to go through that?

I used to joke that lepers got better treatment than Republicans in D.C. where Republicans were outnumbered 77% to 7% then and presently 76% to 6%. (Now I feel badly that I demeaned lepers, so please forgive.) This dismissive or worse treatment always bothered me as I feel that if you pride yourself on being a tolerant person that should extend to political tolerance as well. Why judge a person fully on a label unless it's something like Nazi or the Ku Klux Klan? At least reserve your judgment until you've heard the breadth of their viewpoints. If they are intolerant themselves, judge away. But don't just fill in the blanks based on your own worst assumptions. That in itself is prejudice and something we should all abhor.

When I was confronted with these disparaging attitudes, it actually made me want to hunker down and remain a Republican forever just to be back in those people's faces. I wanted to be an example to expand people's perceptions. I am a sort of rebel with a cause in that way and maybe it's the teacher in me who wants to open people's minds—and this pertains to my own mind as well. We should reserve our criticism for those whose thinking and actions really deserve it, rather than just on a label. These same thoughts pertain to all—regardless of party or non-party.

Many people have told me, "You're the only Republican I ever voted for" (and lots of them are my age or older), and I still hear it practically every day. Though happy to hear it and even feeling special at that moment, I have often felt, "Why only me?" But that comment is perfect compared to the one I got just a few months ago at a charity fundraiser. I was sitting next to a lady who said to me, "I have always admired you but must admit I didn't vote for you." I stupidly asked why, thinking she would probably say a vote of mine she didn't like. She responded, "I'm a Democrat."

I try to vote for the person and not the party, though I understand concerns about who's in control of Congress and who gets to pick Supreme Court Justices. And I am certainly grateful for the huge number of Democrats who have voted for me over the years. I would never have been able to be elected without them.

But for those of you who remain closed even to the thought of voting for someone not of your party. I hope you will realize that there are plenty of varying views out there. I recognize some are not worth the effort, but others are. Why not take the time to look and study the options, where possible? Has limiting those choices in the past really served us so well? Did that woman at the fundraiser who admired me so much that she mentioned it gain anything because she wouldn't vote for a Republican who might still be in office if she had? At least, I hope you'll think about it.

CHAPTER 18

Barry Administration

I always had mixed personal feelings about Marion Barry. As I mentioned earlier, I met him in the early '70s when he was heading up, along with his wife Mary Treadwell, Pride Inc., and I was a volunteer at the drug treatment center. Although I thought Pride Inc.'s mission had merit, there was public discussion that both seemed to be living pretty well off of a non-profit organization.

After Marion became Mayor in 1979, I did develop a real respect for his intelligence as well as an appreciation of his undeniable street smarts, his engaging personality, and his extraordinary connection with people. Marion's background was impressive, having been a civil rights activist as well as acquiring a master's degree in organic chemistry from Fisk University. As Mayor, he started tackling at least some of the issues I cared about: for example, his enduring youth summer jobs program and bringing more African Americans into government. He also had a very strong record of hiring women and members of the LGBT community early on.

In the mid-'80s when I was an at-large member of the Council and he was Mayor, we became friends. We shared similar beginnings, both of us having been born in Mississippi and then moving to Tennessee. We also faced financial and prejudicial challenges, although his far more. I believe those beginnings helped our bonding. Marion and I worked mostly well together during that time.

However, I became more concerned about the looming budget deficits due to the bloated bureaucracy he as Mayor created even while our population and revenues declined. I was also concerned about his crony contracts, his well-known drug use, and his indiscreet womanizing.

There was just no accounting for the future and who would eventually need to pay for this irresponsible and even glutinous spending. While the Mayor's office received a 30% increase from '83 to '86, other crucial areas of government suffered:

- School Superintendent Floretta McKenzie threatened to quit if the Mayor didn't give the ailing school system enough money, and over 44,000 parents signed a petition requesting the same.

- In 1986, the U.S. District Court took over local jails because of D.C.'s failure to deal with prison overcrowding in spite of all the money being spent. Instead of fixing the problem, they tried to sneak prisoners out the door to Pennsylvania and to an old police station in a residential neighborhood, according to Juan Williams in a notable 1986 article entitled "A Black Mayor Betrays the Faith" in the *The Washington Monthly*.[68] I spoke about the prison overcrowding and the lack of action by the Mayor and Council in a statement I made on February 25, 1986. But it was said best by Judge Bryant, who was the presiding judge on this issue: "I need a Geiger counter to detect any activity of the government in dealing with the problem."

- The city also failed to improve its deteriorating public housing projects. The District had been sitting on $8.8 million in federal housing money instead of spending it. Units remained vacant waiting for renovation while the waiting list grew. Because of these failures, the Secretary of Housing and Urban Development (HUD) directed an aide to oversee public housing in D.C.[69]

Several people outside Barry's Administration—but with close ties to him—also got in real trouble with the law:

- His former wife Mary Treadwell, with whom he founded Pride Inc., was found guilty of conspiring to defraud the federal government as well as tenants of Clifton Terrace Apartments for personal gain. Pride Inc. had spun off a real estate company, P.I. Properties, that bought Clifton Terrace from HUD, but had made only four monthly payments—much fewer than required. (Marion was married to Mary and co-ran Pride Inc. with her during the time of the spin-off.)

- Ivanhoe Donaldson, a noted civil rights leader in the '60s, was one of Mayor Barry's closest friends and most trusted aides. Donaldson was often credited with orchestrating Marion's victories in 1978 and 1982. He left the Administration in 1983 to work for EF Hutton's municipal bond division. But in January of '86, Donaldson pled guilty to stealing $200,000 from the city (though the feds said the amount may have been as high as $1 million), obstructing justice—by trying to get four people to submit false affidavits—as well as income tax evasion. He was sentenced to prison. (Memorably, around the time, Marion was asked by the press about the situation with Ivanhoe, and he responded, "Ivan-who?" That became a running joke in our family and we even named our talking myna bird, "Ivan-who.")[70]

(I actually got to know Ivanhoe a little better in the last several years as we both liked a restaurant called the Dancing Crab in Tenleytown. I would often go to it when my kids were in town and he was always there. We had some good conversations about D.C. and people we knew from the past. A couple of years ago, Dancing Crab closed and about a year ago, Ivanhoe passed away.)

In the 1980s, the list of ethical lapses surrounding and in the Barry Administration went on. (These were amply described in in-depth articles written in 1986 by Juan Williams in *The Washington Monthly* as well as by Anne LaLena in *The Washington City Paper*, which were invaluable resources.)[71] In one such article, Juan Williams scathingly pointed out that the minority set-aside program had turned into a treasure chest for the Mayor Barry's friends; specifically, he said that 40% of the city's housing acquisition money from 1979 to 1981 went to builder Theodore Hagen, Chair of the Mayor's Inauguration Committee.[72]

And several officials were indicted and many resigned due to misconduct:

- A lobbyist who bought Marion's then wife Effi $1,150 worth of merchandise from a Georgetown shop; a lottery official who was paying his deputy for 17 months for doing no work; a Director of Human Services who paid his full home rent with city funds; a city permit examiner who was indicted on charges of soliciting and accepting bribes; a D.C. Elections and Ethics Board Chair (also President of D.C. Chamber of Commerce) who resigned after being charged with misusing thousands of dollars of Chamber funds; a supervisor at the Department of Public Works maintenance warehouse who was arrested on bribery charges; a Public Health Commissioner who agreed to repay the city for personal trips and hundreds of long-distance phone calls from his business car; a Chief Account Officer of the D.C. Corrections Department who pled guilty to taking more than $22,000 from an inmate trust fund, and who already had a prison conviction for embezzlement which corrections department officials knew about when they hired him; an Executive Director of the city's Commission on the Arts and Humanities who resigned after it was discovered she had stolen $16,000 worth of funds; a D.C. Public Works Director who admitted that he and an aide accepted free travel and accommodations from a D.C. contractor; a Deputy Mayor for Finance who resigned after admitting receiving an illegal referral fee and gifts from contractors; an electrical inspector for the Department of Consumer and Regulatory Affairs who was charged with bribery; an accounting clerk for the Department of Human Services who was arrested for dealing cocaine; an Executive Assistant, in charge of marketing and advertising, who pled guilty to accepting $5,500 in payoffs; an Executive Director of the D.C. Housing Finance Agency who repaid $2,500 after it was discovered he used an agency credit card for personal use. And there was much, much more. In all, the FBI subpoenaed nearly 500 people in or involved with D.C. government for various investigations.[73]

During this time in the mid-1980s, government sweetheart deals for developers abounded. In February of 1985, developer

Jeffrey Cohen assessed his own Shaw property in D.C. for $11 million for which he had recently paid about $8 million and planned to lease it back to the city. Public outcry ensued.

In June of 1986, a new appraisal took place showing the city paid $1.5 million more than what the land was worth. It was determined that the city had violated HUD procedures by not having an independent appraisal.[74] Barry claimed his friendship played no role in the overpayment. I was the lone vote on the Council against that deal.

Instead of taking stock and correcting the abuses in government, those who blew the whistle on corruption were punished.

In January of 1986, Alvin Frost, a financial analyst, charged in an eight-page letter to Barry that the operation of the cash flow accounts at the Financial Management Office "is rife with incompetence, mismanagement, negligence, political favoritism, intimidation, indifference." Instead of initiating an investigation, Barry fired Frost.[75] This was after a budget analyst was fired in November of '82 for disputing Barry's budget figures in public.

In April of 1986, Benjamin H. Johnson, a social service representative with the Department of Human Services was suspended for 10 days without pay after writing the Mayor that his office was badly managed and that the department "allow[s] employees to work part-time for full-time pay."[76]

Two city officials lost their jobs after complaining of illegal practices in the minority contracting program: A top purchasing officer named Jose Gutierrez said Barry was paying millions more than necessary for goods and services provided by contractors. He balked when he was directed to award contracts to Barry associates. Instead of following up on the allegations made, Gutierrez himself was investigated by the Mayor's office and made to take the fall. He was demoted for showing "lack of respect for the family creed," as Marion said. Then he was fired.[77]

Watching Government Work—or Not

On July 17, 1985, I wrote a memo to the Chair of the Council's Committee on Government Operations on which I served, about the dismissal of a possible whistleblower—Jose Gutierrez, a top purchaser of minority contracts. The memos below illustrate the workings—or non-workings—of government. Or let's just call it what it is: the habitual B.S. of government. Here's such a great example of "sound and fury, signifying nothing":

In correspondence to the Chair, I stated that our Committee should hold an investigation on the Gutierrez firing. I wrote: "While the Mayor's office has conducted an investigation, I believe that our Committee should conduct its own full investigation of the charges made by Mr. Gutierrez, as well as those made against him. I am certain that you will agree that we on the Council can bring a greater sense of the public's concern and impartiality to such an investigation."

On July 26, 1985, the Chair responded that he had monitored the Gutierrez situation very closely and then said: "I am convinced, more than ever before, that this matter was simply a symptom of the major ailment that this city faces—that of a procurement system that is simply unable to buy materials of the right quality, in the right quantity, at the right time, at the right price, from the right source. The procurement system itself just doesn't work and I have made its overhaul the major priority of the Committee ... and we are now working on a bill." *(My take: He was not going to hold an investigation. But he was certainly touting his strong support of a procurement bill.)*

On August 2, 1985, I wrote: "I am sorry you have decided not to call for a public hearing ... I certainly support your avowed effort to straighten out the District procurement system ... I note that in 1983, you submitted a procurement bill ... Yet, in December of 1983, when the Committee voted overwhelmingly to approve the bill (4 to 0) and it went before the full Council that same month, you withdrew the bill from the dais. Then in the next Council two-year period, you offered no procurement bill. Now there is a bill in your Committee that has 10 co-sponsors that was submitted in March and now, five months later, you have still not brought it before the Committee for a vote." *(My take: So, not only was he not holding a hearing on alleged procurement abuses and possibly a wrongful firing, he had no intention—before or now—of bringing a procurement bill forward that would dissipate Mayor Barry's unfettered control of the total procurement system.)*

On August 6th, the Chair wrote back, "I am concerned ... that you have apparently either misunderstood or misinterpreted my memo of July 26th regarding your request for a timely investigation of the Department of Administrative Services (DAS). My communications to you have indicated no decision on my part not to hold a public hearing. This Committee will be holding such public forums as are appropriate and necessary to fully restructure the District-wide procurement system into one that is second to no other. I hope this clarifies my position on this issue." *(My take: In spite of all the above, no hearing was ever held by that Committee on anything related to Gutierrez or the alleged abuses at DAS. And my remembrance is that the procurement bill to improve the system once again went nowhere.)*

Trying to Make It Better

I was deeply disturbed by these episodes where public servants who spoke out about government abuse found themselves disciplined or fired. This, of course, only discourages others from speaking up. I wanted to try to make it better. But when you're a junior member of the Council, it's not so easy. You have fewer staff and even more importantly, you have no Committee and therefore, no ability to really negotiate—like in the situation with the Committee Chair above. If he had a bill in my Committee that he wanted voted out, he might have been more amenable to holding the investigation or at least a hearing on these issues.

I was still not going to let the barriers stop me. So on June 2, 1987, I introduced the "District of Columbia Anti-Corruption and Fraud Act." This legislation would help deal with internal investigations of corruption and fraud in the government by adding subpoena power to the arsenal of the D.C. Auditor. That position is appointed by the Council Chair with Council approval for a fixed term of seven years (Councilmembers' terms are for four), thus giving the Auditor needed independence.

The legislation also added protections to District employees who report wrongdoing, and provided an easily accessible and confidential hotline into the Auditor's office. I wrote then, "It would effectively deputize all 42,000 government employees as investigators, by guaranteeing to those employees protections against retribution and/or harassment by their employer."

As I said at the time of the introduction: "The District government today has an Inspector General, a Police Department Integrity Unit, an Ethics Ombudsman, Department of Administrative Services' procurement monitors, Office of Personnel ethics counselors, and an Office of Campaign Finance; all of these are Executive branch agencies and therefore, lack true independence." I'm proud to say that the independent Auditor's office got that subpoena power and the hotline. Needed teeth were added.

(Then many years later, after an eight-year break from the Council, one of the first pieces of legislation I wrote, introduced and got passed upon my return in the mid-'90s, gave us the strongest whistleblower's protection law in the country. It not only protected whistleblowers but required supervisors to report wrongdoing, while also ensuring that employees who were in the midst of being fired could *not* cloak themselves in the protections, among other provisions. The federal government later used this law as a blueprint for its own.)

The Personal Is Political and Vice Versa

By this point, things in Barry's personal life were also providing distractions, harming not just his reputation but the city's as well.

A story broke regarding Marion trying to pick up a woman while riding in his Mayoral limousine. To complete the picture, he was wearing a baseball cap with Mayor written on it. It was reported that the woman rejected his advances but that he persisted, even knocking on her door. Later, when he was asked about the incident, Marion said that he was just trying to teach politics to her young son. The son was three years old.

I as a Councilmember and friend confronted him soon thereafter. I said, "Marion, no one cares what arrangements you and Effi have or do not have. But you're the Mayor of the Nation's Capital and you have to be discreet. You can't go around acting like a horny teenager." At the time he seemed to appreciate my honesty—not that it really helped.

At the beginning of his second term, he spent an evening at a nude bar called "This Is It." That didn't bother me. Marion claimed he went to the bar to either pick up or seek a campaign contribution. That also didn't bother me. Reports were that he had taken cocaine at the bar. Now that bothered me.

The Mayor's drug use was an open secret. Everyone knew of his cocaine abuse at a time when the crack problem in the District was about to explode. A former girlfriend, Karen Johnson, was indicted on charges of selling cocaine in 1984. A former boyfriend of hers was wired with a secret recorder in 1983 and she allegedly boasted that she sold cocaine to Barry on 20 or 30 occasions. Yet Ms. Johnson refused to answer questions to the grand jury regarding selling the Mayor drugs and was sentenced up to 18 months in prison for contempt of court.[78]

Maybe the drugs were clouding Marion's judgment at times to the point where he started to sound insensitive, which he usually was not. There were consistent troubles with snow removal. In the winter of 1979, snow blanketed the city while Marion rode to work in a limo. "There are more things for me to worry about than snow," he said at the time. And when people couldn't drive to work due to lack of snow removal, he retorted to the media, "They can walk!"[79]

These problems continued. In 1987, while he was in California for the Super Bowl, a blizzard hit D.C. The city was at a standstill. But Marion remained on the West Coast, neglecting the trouble back home. It was said that out there, he was found sitting on a curb and had to be rushed to the hospital.[80] There were reports it was an overdose—but were not confirmed.

It was obvious Marion was suffering gravely with these addictions for a very long time. And I would have been glad to help if he wanted to do something about it. But he didn't, and I couldn't bear watching the city suffer as a result of his negligence and the ethically challenged behaviors that were looming around his Administration. My worry was made more pronounced because of the drug problems that affected too many of our citizens and contributed to the violence which made the District be called the "murder capital" of the nation by 1990. Unfortunately, at the time, the Mayor did not have the state of mind or moral authority to tackle these problems.

At the then called District Building, it was a troublesome time for our Mayor—and for all of us in the District itself as a result.

Back at Home

Meanwhile, my kids were growing up fast. My son Doug had his Bar Mitzvah in 1985. We had a fun party at the Vista Hotel with no sit-down meal, having food stations instead so the group could circulate. There was lots of dancing (one of my favorite things to do) and a great band whose leader and singer was a boyfriend of Stephanie's.

The kids attended Alice Deal Junior High School and then all went on to graduate from Wilson High School—both D.C. public schools. David and I certainly felt it was important to send our kids to our public schools. We had both been educated ourselves by them in distant parts of the country. So initially it was our decision to send them there. However, it soon became theirs as well. It got to the point that our kids were so attached to their schools that to punish them, we would threaten to send them to one of the fancy private schools.

In fact, I think all people should, regardless of their income, at least think about sending their children to public schools or just try them, whether traditional or charter. Many don't have a choice. I believe people who have a choice should start feeling an obligation. Although there may be some challenging experiences, what in life worthwhile isn't challenging? Public schools are a great equalizer and should be used to expose our kids to diversity, including economic, instead of running away from it.

If children got to know each other at an early age, the chances of their feeling comfortable with one another even if from different backgrounds would be enhanced. Just go into a racially and economically diverse pre-school program and you will see kids playing together with no hesitation and with great enthusiasm.

It is only the delay in socializing that can lead to self-imposed segregation where divisions and everyone else's agendas take hold. It's like one of my favorite songs from one of my favorite musicals, *South Pacific*: "You've Got to Be Carefully Taught ... to hate and fear." Young kids on their own are great, loving and welcoming. My philosophy is that if everyone sent their kids to public schools starting in pre-k programs, it would certainly improve not only our community and our ability to interact, it would also help society as a whole.

In the fall of 1984, our daughter Stephanie received an honor. Wilson had a class called Youth Awareness (and by the way, when I chaired the Educational Programs Committee on the School Board, I helped lead the way in passing this required class for every D.C. high school sophomore). This program gave students information about real-life issues like bullying, sexual harassment, drugs and crime. The students even took a field trip to Lorton, our then prison in Virginia, to build awareness of the things too many teens have to face—and the dangers of making the wrong choices.

Through her active participation and commitment to the class, Stephanie received the NAACP Lorton Chapter Youth Leadership Award, which was very exciting. The ceremony and celebration took place at Lorton Prison on a Sunday. Our whole family joined the families of honorees from other schools, and we all rode on a school bus out to the facility in Virginia.

Once at Lorton, after being frisked, we were led to the cafeteria for the ceremony and dinner. The band, made up of inmates, was fabulous. The meal of fish sticks, rice and green beans, not so much. Stephanie, Doug and David barely touched the food. But both Hilary, always an avid eater, and I, every much the same if not more, licked our plates clean. We even asked for seconds. The rest of the family never let us forget it. As we took the ride back to the city after the very long full day's excursion, David joked to Stephanie, "Please don't win any more awards." After leaving the bus, we stopped by Roy Rogers to get dinner for those who hadn't eaten much earlier. Hilary and I probably ate there too.

David by that point was doing quite well as a partner at Willkie, Farr and Gallagher. He was the lawyer on some major development projects in D.C., including Georgetown Park, Washington Harbour, and in Virginia, Potomac Mills. David, who grew up with little money, really enjoyed spending it once he started making it. I, on the other hand, having grown up similarly financially, was afraid of being poor again and preferred saving money.

Even when he first started buying me nice pieces of jewelry on special occasions, I had a hard time being gracious. In fact, initially, I took a pretty gold and pearl pin that David had bought me back to Garfinckel's and headed to Sears on Wisconsin Ave. to buy much more needed household items as well as clothes and shoes.

When I saw that it hurt his feelings and when my friend Tay counseled me to just say thank you "or he'll find someone else to buy jewelry for," I became a better recipient. In fact, as the years went on, I really developed a true appreciation of the lovely things David gave me.

My father remained the father I knew. Instead of being proud when David started to make really good money, my father resented it. My parents usually sent $100 to each of us for our birthdays and some gifts. I reciprocated similarly. Then not long after David told Dad about getting a nice raise, their presents just stopped coming. Dad said, "You all make enough money. We're not going to give you anything else." I continued to send checks to my parents and Johnny for their special occasions, and Dad finally loosened up some years later.

David and I did have a wonderful opportunity in 1985 to give time and money to a cause we really cared about. The Kennedy Center asked us to serve as Chairs for "Memorial Candles," a symphony performance and gala to honor the 40th anniversary of the Holocaust. It was sponsored by the Friends of the Kennedy Center and the American-Israel Cultural Foundation. It was a well-attended, beautiful and touching event.

Speech to B'Nai B'rith

On May 15, 1986, I received the Woman of Commitment award from the B'Nai B'rith organization, which really pleased me. I was equally appreciative of getting a chance at the event to express what being Jewish means to me:

"In the 11 and a half years since I first got elected to the Board of Education in 1974, I have always been conscious of the fact that I am the only elected public official in the top levels of the D.C.

government—out of those 26—who is Jewish. When I married my husband 20 years ago, I certainly did not do so because of his name, David Schwartz. But I have grown more grateful for that name because it is undeniable evidence of my heritage—a heritage which I am very proud of. I talk about it. I brag about it. When I visited Baptist churches in every part of this city during my campaign for the Council a year and a half ago, I mentioned it in case the congregations did not know.

I was not always so proud. I grew up in a town in Texas where we were one of a couple of Jewish families and I experienced many unpleasant situations due to my religion. Those things are hard when you're young. But as I grew up, I grew stronger and I grew prouder, and I have not stopped growing in those areas, even at the age of 42. So much of that pride and strength have grown from the need to overcome people's limited and prejudicial perceptions. Overcoming has been a great motivating factor in my life. I often wonder how people who do not have something to overcome—whether it be a minority race or religion, a handicapping condition or poverty—succeed. But maybe they were short or unattractive, unloved, or insecure. We will never know the motivation for each and every person.

But I do know my own—a real commitment—which I share with this organization—to promote familiarity and understanding of each other so we can alleviate prejudice once and for all and a great commitment to give back to society so much of the pride and strength I have gained through the years. Your recognition of that commitment will serve to spur me on. And I thank you for it."

CHAPTER 19

First Mayoral Run

In 1986, Marion Barry was preparing to run for his third term as Mayor. Barry's most credible opponent in the Democratic primary was Mattie Taylor, a former School Board member and D.C. employment services official. Mattie was a wonderful and smart woman, but she had been out of political life for some time.

Barry won the Democratic primary, with nearly 71% of the vote. And in D.C., winning the Democratic primary is tantamount to winning the general election with its 11 to 1 voter ratio.[81] But with so much fiscal irresponsibility, inadequate services and ethical breaches pervading the Administration, I couldn't bear Marion having a free ride to a third victory in November. So I begged others to run—all prominent African Americans, mostly Democrats. I even said that I would help them with the campaign and raising money. (And in those days I could do some money raising, especially if it wasn't for myself.) All refused, reluctant to take on the Barry machine and certain that Barry would win by a landslide.

I really didn't want to do it either. But in June of 1986, a few weeks before the petitions were due, I announced my candidacy for Mayor simply because someone had to step up in the general election. (I had been proud of Mattie for doing so in the primary.) Knowing that I was basically signing up to become a sacrificial lamb, I was willing, though, to do so because I believed our citizens deserved better than the aforementioned status quo. Just like in the 1976 movie *Network*, I felt that we should all open our windows and yell out, "I'm mad as hell and I don't want to take this anymore!" Thus began the first of my Mayoral bids, and one of a couple where I really didn't even want to be in the ring.

Once I decided to jump in, it was not hard for me to get into it. I immediately sat down and started writing my announcement and the words just flowed. Here are a couple of quotes (not necessarily in order) which I recently found in a *Washington Post* article on my announcement, dated June 25, 1986—31 years ago:[82]

"I am running because I cannot accept an Administration which spends millions of dollars on consultant contracts with cronies, but cannot find the money to answer the police emergency phone lines.

I am running because during a time of economic boom, the current Administration has spent eight years studying and restudying how to develop the New York Avenue corridor, and has done nothing to implement one word of a study report; the current Administration has used our minority contracting program to reward rich friends, not to encourage and stimulate small, minority-owned businesses; the current Administration has done little to promote the economic development of our neglected neighborhoods, which remain largely unserviced by supermarkets, drugstores and transportation.

I am running because eight years after the 'boards were coming off' our vacant housing units, the housing shortage has reached crisis proportions.

I am running because I intend to attract to our government people in high-level positions who believe that public service means just that—serving the public, not serving yourself at the public's expense.

I am running because I am tired of an Administration which loudly proclaims that it is not increasing our taxes, while it institutes a program of creative property tax reassessment which is extracting millions of additional dollars from our already over-burdened taxpayers.

I am running because I have had enough of an Administration which spends all of its time taking credit for what it has not done and seems incapable of doing what should be done.

I am running because as a citizen and taxpayer, I am tired of footing the bill for the waste, incompetence and inefficiency which is rampant everywhere you look in this government.

Please join with me as we work together to create a government which is concerned about all of us—black and white, Hispanic and Asian, rich, poor, and middle class—a government of which we all can be proud rather than ashamed—a government which is as good as its people!"

In addition to all those mentioned, there was another big reason I ran: fear of regret. More than I feared going up against insurmountable odds and failing, I feared that same old regret. And still do. I just never wanted to be that old woman sitting in the rocking chair on the nursing home porch, rocking back forth, thinking, "I could have. I should have. Why didn't I?" That fear has been a primary driver for me always. Maybe it became more pronounced because of seeing so many people in my life depressed because of, among other things, not doing what they wanted to do—and regretting it.

Though in this case, regret for my own sake was far less pronounced in my mind than the fear I felt for the city when I knew that our only available other choice would be disastrous.

The media at my announcement questioned my shot at winning: "How can you do it—you're white, you're a woman, you're a Republican. How do you stand a chance?"

Knowing that so many in the city would balk at voting for a Republican, even a more than moderate one, I emphasized how the Mayor was not a partisan position. Nor was it a racial one, even with the city being then 70% black. Thus I said in my announcement statement: "There is no Republican or Democratic way to pick up trash, no male or female way to do something about our housing shortage or to stimulate economic development of our neglected neighborhoods. There is no white or black way to fix our potholes or to create work for our youth. The issues which confront this government are not racial or partisan issues—they are people issues."

I knew I would also face a huge money disadvantage. I was running with the help of one paid staff member and the rest were volunteers. We ultimately raised and spent $260,000 to the $1.2 million that was reported in the incumbent Mayor's coffer. I'm sure there was far more in the latter.

My announcement for Mayor did stun my colleagues on the Council. A few, as I anticipated, emphasized my party affiliation drawbacks. Councilmember Frank Smith said, "Ward 1 has 30,000 registered Democrats and 1,100 registered Republicans. You figure out if she has a chance." Hilda Mason stated, "I don't know what to say. Maybe I'll announce." John Ray was more generous: "She certainly doesn't have anything to lose and everything to gain. If she makes a good showing, she's a winner."[83]

The Washington Post declared in a headline, "Schwartz Candidacy Livens Mayoral Race in District."[84] I think my purpose in life has been to enliven D.C. Mayoral races. The paper did state, though, that I was "a challenger Barry won't be able to dismiss lightly." In 1978 and 1982, Barry faced his strongest competition in the primary. This year was different, as the *Post* acknowledged, that even the primary "contest may well take a back seat to the November 4th general election."

My friend and former colleague from the School Board, Conrad Smith, an African American Democrat from Ward 1, was quoted as saying that I may have a chance and added, "The best politician that D.C. ever fostered was Marion Barry, and the second best was Carol Schwartz." As I recognized the political skills Marion had, I was very flattered then and remain so today by that comparison.

But I was realistic. The racial and political demographics were really against me. There had not been a female D.C. Mayor before (and if women have trouble breaking through glass ceilings today, it is nothing compared to what we faced in the mid-1980s). And being Jewish was not exactly an asset in a very church-going town.

David's Steadfast Support

My husband David was there as he had always been in my political career. I know he was proud of me and enjoyed my being a voice of reason in public life. I also believe David got a great deal of satisfaction out of supporting me through these kind of endeavors. It was an escape from his normal work routine as well as his way of contributing to the community around him. And we both, who felt frustrated and offended by *any* corruption in government, felt particularly so with the rampant amount that we in D.C. were experiencing.

The Washington Times published an article on David entitled "Scaling Mountains with Mrs. Schwartz." In the article, our friend Congressman Marc Marks said of David, 'I know of no one else who has a better reputation for excellence and for being ethical.'"

David for his part was quite generous in his descriptions of me: "She is a very courageous woman—really and truly the most remarkable person I've ever known," although he compared my race against Barry to "climbing Mount Everest with one leg." And he added, "Although I've always been behind her, there were times in the past when I've told her to slow down—it's too tough ... She never listens." He went on to say, "I think Carol's public life has really benefited the children rather than hurt them in any way. It has taught them that any person who has a goal or sets out to accomplish something never loses."

I loved this *Times* article, especially because it was nice to see David get some credit for helping with my career and for himself. I talked about him in the piece as well, saying, "He's much more reserved than I am, and it takes some time to discover what a good sense of humor he has, and that he is a strong-willed, determined and opinionated man ... He's been so supportive throughout everything I've chosen to do."[85]

Always Honest

In March of 1986, I was at a reception at the Kennedy Center and I ran into a bunch of women I knew and we were just standing around making small talk. One of the gals was Diana McClellan, who had been "Ear on Washington" for *The Washington Star* several years earlier. Our conversation centered around what we were up to, what TV shows we liked, what the kids were doing—just general stuff.

Then in August of 1986 in the midst of the campaign, David, the kids and I had taken a long weekend to go to Rehoboth to get some rest. I was perusing *Washingtonian Magazine* and there was an article entitled, "TV Shows Celebrities Like to Watch." I'm just reading away enjoying it and toward the end, it said, "Marion Barry when asked what TV shows he liked to watch responded, 'I'm too busy running the city to be watching TV.' His opponent, Carol Schwartz, on the other hand said, 'I like *Jeopardy* and *Divorce Court*.'" How embarrassing, but honest. Also honestly, I wanted to yell, "He should have said he was 'too busy running the city into the ground!' And I should have added *The Golden Girls!*"

Campaigning, Coverage and Company

Despite the problems including some criminal-type in the Barry Administration, during the campaign I purposefully avoided the term "corruption" because I did not want to run an inflammatory race. I stuck to the issues and the real failures of the Administration in providing for the needs of our residents.

I enjoyed the campaigning. Although before entering the public arena, I never thought of myself as much of a politician. As I told *The Washington Post*, while running for Secretary of the Freshman Class at the University of Texas, "I was no more of a politician than a fly on the moon," scrambling my idioms as usual. In the same article, I said I wanted to "strike while the lightning is hot" and then wondered aloud why I use such phrases.

I did get a good amount of encouragement throughout the race. Most of my friends were Democrats and they signed on early in the effort. And many calls and letters came in from strangers. One said, "Don't be intimidated, Carol Schwartz. Instead, be inspired." It was signed, "a concerned Democrat." And on the campaign trail a black voter, according to *The Washington Times* remarked, "Her being female and white should have nothing to do with the way people vote."[86]

It was good to see former colleagues recognize some merits. Ward 8 School Board member R. Calvin Lockridge remarked to *The Washington Post* that "Carol has suffered some of the same discrimination that black people have," referring to my upbringing in West Texas. "I found we could disagree on ideology on certain issues ... she is a person of substance in regard to education—someone you could disagree with and still be friendly."[87]

(Calvin, who became directly involved in several of my later Mayoral campaigns, passed last year. Bless him.)

I used many of what would become my usual lines while campaigning. If I was passing out literature to someone who said, "I don't live in the city," I'd respond, "Well, give this to a friend who does, and I'll forgive you for not living here."

The Washington Times profiled my campaigning. In between stops I'd munch on a candy bar and then light a cigarette. (Thank goodness I quit that nasty habit—the latter one—in 2001.) I implored voters to "Give me a chance. And if I don't do a good job, get me out of there. No one has a God-given right to be Mayor."

I did receive resistance from people. Of course, there was blowback about being a Republican. "Yes, but it doesn't matter," I would say. In another exchange, the *Times* highlighted a little boy outside a Safeway store where I was campaigning. The boy said, "My mother always votes for Mayor Barry. She told me that when she was little, white folks used to beat up on black folks." I said, "Well, that's true. But that doesn't mean everybody was bad."[88]

Some accused my campaign of being a brilliant but cynical career move.[89] But no one would go through a grueling five-month campaign for just that reason. Besides, if you lose, you're a loser. Up to that point, with two successful School Board runs and one victorious at-large Council race against a popular incumbent, I was a winner—so I was taking a real chance.

I even got coverage in Texas newspapers for being a girl from the state who made her stake in the Nation's Capital. The *Dallas Times Herald* in October of 1986 said, which I believe is apt, "Those who know her best will tell you it was the oil-rich city (Midland) and all the heartache she learned there, that created the core of the woman she is today."

In that article, my friend Ann Wylie gave insight: "Her childhood gave her tremendous drive to show Midland—and the world—that she wasn't just a no-account from the wrong side of the tracks ... [Carol] was a cheerful, outgoing girl ... She wanted to do good and to help people who she perceived as getting a raw deal from life." The journalist even talked to my beloved Aunt Doe, who was straightforward as always: "She was humiliated many, many times. Life was very unpleasant for Carol," said Dora Faye Garmon.[90] I felt these were on-target descriptors of me and the drives in my life—and they were their descriptions, not mine. But they were aware as they had lived through some of it with me.

I have always loved the way campaigns brought new wonderful people into my life. Dennis Brickhouse, a volunteer who had delayed law school to work on the campaign, insisted on being my driver, and he was really good company. We had a number of wonderful volunteers who I became very friendly with. Joe Albanese was one. During and after the campaign, he would come to our house on Springland Lane, and we would have great conversations while he sat on the couch and I sat in bed in my granny gown, with David visiting for a few minutes and then snoring away next to me. Joe was very active in politics and served as President of the Gay & Lesbian Community Center in D.C. He died from AIDS in 1992. I still miss our visits and have thought of him often over the past 25 years.

As I campaigned, many said I reminded them of two people: One was Elizabeth Dole (when she was a plumper brunette and who was then Secretary of the U.S. Department of Transportation) and the other was Connie Morella, who was a Member of the Maryland House of Delegates and running for Congress to represent Montgomery County, Maryland. I have gotten to know both and am flattered by the comparisons.

My first meeting with Connie was special. It was during this 1986 campaign and I was attending a large dinner sponsored by the Bar Association of the Metropolitan Area. They introduced the politicians who were present and running for office. I heard Connie's name and thought I would try to find her later. But before I could do anything, a beautiful, petite woman taps me on the shoulder and says, "I was dying to meet you as everyone says I remind them of you." Size and beauty-wise—not even close so I can't take the compliment. But warmth and personality, I'll take gladly. We have been friends ever since. She and her husband Tony have been to my home many times and we often meet up for lunch. I adore her and she is the kind of Republican who makes me proud.

In that election, I did get an awful lot of support. Nineteen of the 28 Co-Chairs of my Campaign Committee were Democrats, 18 were African American, and they were from all eight Wards. Some well-known names were: Harold Bell (sportscaster), Ed Hancock (former Board of Education member), Ben Henley (retired D.C. Vice Superintendent), Philip Pannell (former D.C. Human Rights Commissioner), Minnie Woodson (former Board of Education President), Paul Hays (former President, Capitol Hill Restoration Society), Manuel Lopez (ANC Commissioner), Marjorie Parker (former Chair of the UDC Board and wife of Judge

Barrington Parker), and Reverend Nathaniel Thomas (President, Far N.E./S.E. Council).

Mattie Taylor (former Board of Education member), who ran against Barry in the Democratic primary, endorsed me and was a Co-Chair. She said, "I am a totally black woman and if I ever had the choice of supporting a white woman over a black man, I would have chosen the black man—if he were doing his job. But he is not. Instead he is selling my people down the drain." As I was such an underdog in this race, I was—and remain—grateful for those who stood out there with me in a very visible way.

Taking on Barry

Here are other issues I raised during the campaign—both directly to Marion in debates and behind his back in other venues:

- I reminded voters that our housing shortage was at such a critical level and getting worse while an appalling 20% of our public housing sat vacant due to disrepair. And all this with millions in federal funds for repair purposes laying unused.[91] In addition to urging the use of the money, I made suggestions, such as establishing mandatory adult apartment maintenance training programs and making sure there were tenant boards to oversee that maintenance.

- As a public official on the D.C. Council and formerly the Board of Education, I felt a real duty to walk the talk. As my three children were public school students, I called out the Mayor on his hypocrisy on this issue. Back in 1978 when he was first running for Mayor, Barry said that elected officials have a "moral responsibility" to send their kids to public schools. Yet by 1986, Barry's only child was in a private school and he admitted that his 1978 statement was just said for "tactical purposes." Tactical be damned. I just believe you do what is right—and stand by your word.

- I reminded voters about how Barry said he was going to fire the many wrongdoers in his Administration, but his record certainly showed otherwise.

- I also took the Mayor on for imposing tax increases *only* in non-election years.

- And I challenged him for not taking any stand against Farrakhan's hateful comments toward Jewish people, even when other African American leaders like John Lewis and James Cheeks did so.

The Washington Post Endorses

During the campaign many of my supporters, and especially my husband, anticipated my getting the endorsement of *The Washington Post*, which could have really made a difference in the race. I did not expect it, but still hoped for it. The night the endorsement was due to come out, David and I waited outside the *Post* building on 15th St. for an hour. When it finally came, we opened the paper and there it was, called "The Mayor's Race." And it was long. It took at least two-thirds of the editorial page. It was the longest editorial I ever saw before or since (except the recent one about Clinton-Trump).

Some kind things were said: "She has run a very dignified, responsible campaign and an extremely combative one—attributes that don't usually go together. Mrs. Schwartz has campaigned earnestly and unselfconsciously in every section of the city."

About him: "In spite of some grave failures and derelictions—including the conviction of a Deputy Mayor on corruption charges and the departure of other top aides with something less than high honors ... The prison system needs new management, new prison space and new commitment to maintain Constitutionally humane facilities as ordered by the courts. Housing, too, suffers from poor management, from the condition of public housing to the maintenance of city-owned properties generally. Emergency services—from 911 to ambulance crews—still need attention .... drug programs still aren't making a dent in the problem. The planning and development of areas beyond the city's center need overhaul, to control growth ... while attracting development in those parts of the city where it would be welcomed."

Despite all that, and having had eight years as Mayor to tackle those problems with a mostly compliant Council, the *Post* gave the endorsement to Barry, but with "reservations and misgivings."[92]

I really wasn't surprised, but certainly was disappointed as it might have been my one chance for victory. I have often found that the *Post* editorials are hardly cutting edge—timid about the racial issue and usually backing the business community's pick. And why not? They buy the ads. And I sure couldn't afford to.

I think the *Post* knew it did not make the right choice. Ten years later, editorial head Meg Greenfield was asked by *The New Yorker* (which did a long piece on *The Washington Post*) what her biggest regret was during her 20 years as the *Post* Editorial Page Editor. She said it was endorsing Marion Barry over Carol Schwartz in the 1986 general election.[93] I happened to be reading the article—with no advance notice of its content—when I came across those words. I smiled, cried, and looked up at David, saying, "See ... sometimes there is justice."

An End—and an Awakening

In the end, I received 33% of the vote, the highest of any Republican Mayoral candidate up to that point. That certainly was impressive considering the demographic disparities I often mention. And though I was outspent 5 to 1, I still received one in three votes.[94] Afterwards, I was pleased that *The Washington Post* said I ran "an exceptional challenge—a campaign that was dignified, straightforward and tough."[95]

I also witnessed, in this campaign, an awakening of support in the gay community, which had started somewhat in the 1984 Council election. I carried the so-called "gay" precincts in Dupont Circle, Capitol Hill and Adams Morgan. And a *Washington Blade* exit poll indicated many gays switched their support from Barry to me. *The Washington Post* said on October 12, 1988, "Even some of the Mayor's supporters concede that Schwartz has taken popular stands on gay issues."

In fact, *The Washington Blade* remarked that in the 1984 Council election that I "received a much larger share of the gay vote than many gay leaders expected ..." And in 1986, a gay Republican Club official, Peter Wey, said, "She could have drifted away from the gay community after she was elected [for at-large Council]. But if anything, she's drifted more toward the gay community."[96]

I had a real history of support for LGBT issues and appreciated the recognition. That support, though, got me in some hot water as well. Remember, this was 1986. I had a *Post* reporter follow me as I campaigned one night and I took him to both gay and lesbian bars, among other nightclubs. A big picture of me dancing with a lesbian appeared in the paper. I did hear from some people that they wouldn't vote for me because of it—even though I thought we looked cute. But my feeling was—and remains—if that was their attitude, those were *not* votes I wanted anyway.

In that 1986 election, I was pleased to also get the endorsement of 125 black ministers. All in all, I had a lot to be proud of. And I was satisfied knowing that by challenging the established regime, I and those who supported me would not be responsible for the next four years. And as it turned out, thank goodness!

Midland High School Reunion

I lost in more than one way. Even though I ate candy bars to keep myself going on the campaign trail, I lost weight. That came in handy as my Midland High School 25th Reunion took place in the midst of the race at the end of July of 1986. If I could have written a script about the poor girl discriminated against from the south side of Midland, Texas, going back for her 25th reunion, I would have written my story. I was proud of my husband, who was attractive, a successful lawyer, and looked it. I had two pretty daughters, age 17 and 16, and an adorable son, age 14. And here I was, a sort-of normal-sized at-large Councilmember in Washington, D.C. who was running for Mayor. You kind of dream of going to your high school reunion in circumstances like that.

At the reunion, I wore a white dress that surprisingly showed off my thinner figure. The dress had short sleeves and my arms didn't even look bad. Usually I found short sleeves to be the bane of my physical existence. I came in second for "Least Changed." Always the runner-up but I was still honored. The winner was Bea Ann Smith, a judge in Austin, who had a leg up because she had the exact same hairdo. Plus, she had changed the least.

The one thing that did bother me during that trip to Midland in late July was that my mom didn't look good. Mom had always been a little hefty. But on that trip, she looked awfully thin to me and her coloring didn't seem right. I expressed my concern, "Mom, are you okay?" She said, "I'm fine." I asked, "Have you been to the doctor? I don't like the way you look." She said, "I've been to the doctor, and everything's just fine. When you get older, you just get thinner," she insisted.

Other than that worry, which Mom did dispel somewhat, the weekend of the reunion was a glorious time. David was in such a good mood, and I always tended to be happier when he was. It was also nice to have a very long family weekend together before our eldest daughter Stephanie went away to college that fall. As soon as the plane landed in D.C., I returned to the campaign trail and Stephanie to her packing.

Flying the Coop

I had wanted Stephanie to go to a college that was more like the University of Texas or the University of Wisconsin. Steph was always a little hippy-ish and I thought that in those schools, she could still fit in, but also have other types of experiences like rooting for sports teams as she loved to do in D.C. Instead, she chose the artsy Bard College in Annandale-on-Hudson, New York, a couple of hours north of New York City. Bard happened to be the second most expensive college in the country at that time, only behind Bennington. David was doing well then so we could afford it. That was not my objection anyway. I just saw her surrounded by people like herself or worse. David was encouraging her choice, saying he loved the idea of a small liberal arts college.

As I was driving Stephanie up to Bard, I remember saying, continuing my displeasure with the selection, "I bet all the guys wear earrings," one of my pet peeves. As soon as we arrived, Steph elbowed me and pointed to a guy, "Look, Mom! He doesn't have an earring in his ear." She was right. He had the earring in his nose. In fact, all the students seemed to have piercings everywhere and seemed a little edgy—just as I predicted. There's nothing better than rebellious rich white kids! If they would just go to a reasonably priced city or state school, they might actually run into a few of the people on whose behalf they say they are rebelling. Annandale-on-Hudson was just not that place.

Stephanie did benefit from the rigorous academic curriculum as well as the enormous amount of writing required. She also had the treasured experience of participating in a writing class taught by Mary McCarthy, the author of *The Group*, the groundbreaking bestseller from the early '60s which was made into a film with Candice Bergin. In fact, Professor McCarthy hosted the class at her home for a pre-Christmas dinner that year.

Some Honors Along the Way ...

In 1987, I received the Woman of the Year from the Capitol Hill Kiwanis Club. Then in 1989, I was happy to get the Mother of the Year Award—not from my children who probably would have voted no—but from the Cleveland Park Citizens Association.

After the Mayoral election, the White House called in early 1987 and said that President Reagan wanted to appoint me to the Board of the Pennsylvania Avenue Development Corporation (PADC), which was totally unexpected, especially since I did not have any friends that I knew of in the White House. The caller, a fairly high-level official, said that the President had been very impressed with my run against Barry.

PADC was the organization that did all of the planning and approval of projects on Pennsylvania Ave., N.W. between the White House and the Capitol. It was a real honor and I would have loved to have served in that capacity. However, I had a conflict of interest with my husband's law practice. David represented the developers of Market Square, which was one of the few remaining undeveloped properties on the Avenue. The need for me to abstain on that project would have diminished my contributions.

Therefore, I declined. Right away we got an unsolicited invitation to a State Dinner at the White House—a bucket list item of mine.

Opportunities Not Taken

Soon thereafter, the General Counsel to the President called me and said, "Carol, we're so sorry you couldn't take the other appointment. The President likes and admires you so much. What can we do for you?" As you know, David did not like practicing law though he was really making money then. About four years earlier, he had been asked to be a partner at Willkie, Farr and Gallagher, a very prestigious Wall Street firm started by Wendell Willkie (the 1940 Republican nominee for President)—an offer he took gladly. But it still didn't make David happy. And he seemed even more depressed after the Mayoral election loss.

I thought this White House offer might deliver a change to David's life. I said to the General Counsel, "I'd like a federal judgeship for my husband if possible. He is more than qualified—with his successful law career in prestigious firms, his high-level experience with the D.C. Council, and for many years, as an adjunct Professor at Georgetown Law School. He'd be an excellent judge."

He got back to me immediately and said, "We would love to meet him. There are vacancies, and we are very prone to move ahead with the process," So I told David right away and asked him to call the President's office as it looked like he might be able to be put forward as a judge for the D.C. Court of Appeals. But unfortunately, David never called.

Then here came another interesting and sort of glamorous opportunity that did not present an obvious conflict of interest—but I thought could in the long run. John McLaughlin, whose *McLaughlin Group* had become very successful, called and asked me if I would come and be a guest panelist with maybe more to come. He said he watched me on the Council and I had just the kind of spunk and intelligence he wanted on the show.

The offer did appeal to me as I do like to talk and I sure like to give my opinions. And here was a chance to do it not just locally but nationally. However, John himself was very conservative and many of the views expressed on the show were as well. I felt the connection would only play into the broad-brush Republican angle that would harm, not help my career in D.C., which was my real passion, especially if I wanted to run for Mayor again. Thus, I did—sort of regrettably—say no. (John died on August 16, 2016 at age 89, and did his signature show practically up until the end.)

Edelman and Hahn families
hanging out with us

Family in Midland
(at apartment complex pool)

I told you we had Christmas trees.

Steph and Hil visiting their
grandparents on their
own for two weeks

Note kitchen jungle wallpaper.

Dad and Uncle Earl
doing their favorite

Out with the Hahns and
Wylies: Tay, Roger,
Ann, John (left to right)

The Kids' Bat and Bar Mitzvahs

Aunt Bettys, Uncle Albert
and Mom (below)

Elsie and Conrad(s) (below)

Me doing
my favorite (below)

Running for Council and Winning

People used to think I was Elizabeth Dole and she was me. I wish!

A group of supporters

Chair David A. Clarke swearing me in

First Council meeting

Reception (Mayor Barry in front)

General Hassan & Johnny

In 1984, the D.C. Council was the only "state" legislature in the country that was majority women.

Councilmembers and Mayor Barry
and his wife Effi (left)

Florida Avenue Grill with Bob
Richards, staff lawyer and friend

Cornelius Baker at beach,
friend and staff member

Gloria Strickland and Ron Cocome,
friends and staff members

Springland
Lane house

Meeting Soviet dissident
Natan Sharansky

Marion Barry and I at
Camp Brown for D.C. kids

Running for Mayor
(and it won't be the last time)

Campaign Committee: me kissing Mattie Taylor, one of three chairs

Supporters Cornelius Baker, Joe Albanese, Rick Pillsbury and Bob Roehr

Post-Mayoral Race/Still on Council

Marla Gibbs & Hal Williams from "227"   Groundbreaking ceremony

Jean Kirkpatrick and husband Evron

Jim Nathanson and me at a Bar/Bat Mitzvah
for special needs individuals

Going to a State Dinner
in 1987

George H.W. Bush

1987 State Dinner

Bob Dole and Maureen Reagan

Congressman Jack Kemp

At a brunch at Vice President's house

Doug and I
with Lena
Horne and
Patti LaBelle

CHAPTER 20

Losing Mom

My mom had been even-tempered most of her life. But then she went through a very bad menopause. And her personality just sort of changed, becoming more irritable. In her case, it probably wasn't just about the change of life. She actually had good reason. Few people had better reason than that woman, with her many aggravations—being responsible for Johnny, working on her feet on a concrete floor full-time six to seven days a week, but mostly because of her having to put up with my father. It was still difficult to see her change, albeit understandable, because she had always seemed like "whatever" and just took to herself. Now she seemed so tired, was starting to be bitter, and just wasn't a happy camper.

Contributing to the difficulty is that she quit smoking. Mom was practically a chain smoker since the age of 16. I never remember my mother without a cigarette in her mouth. And with my dad smoking cigars, I guess it's no wonder I became a smoker. But when she was about 46 she quit smoking. She had developed a smoker's cough, which sometimes affected her continence (which she talked openly about).

She finally decided to act. So she quit cold turkey—and both issues went away. Soon after, she went through this very emotionally trying menopause period, which was exacerbated by going through nicotine withdrawal from a lifetime of smoking.

She finally got through those life-changing experiences and was feeling so much better. It seemed like the mom I knew was back. In fact, even better. She lost weight and started dressing up and wearing some makeup. She even took a belly dancing course to add to her swimming. She actually seemed to be finally enjoying herself. That's when her doctor said, "You should do a hysterectomy now because there's a lot of ovarian cancer out there, even if not in your family. And if we just remove it, you won't have to worry." It was the "in" operation. It was like the tonsils of its day. So Mom did the hysterectomy, which was not even needed.

Then about seven years after the surgery, Mom buckled over. I wasn't there, but I heard all about it. She released a blood-curdling scream. Dad got her to the hospital. They said she was dying, but they had no idea what she was dying of. So they did exploratory surgery. It turned out that the scar tissue from the unnecessary hysterectomy had come away from the surface and the large intestine had gotten caught up in it. It was strangulating and black with gangrene.

Fortunately, her large intestine was unusually long, and they were able to cut off the huge gangrened part and sew it back together. She didn't even have to wear a bag. Thank goodness, once she recovered from that long and dangerous surgery, things were back to normal—or so we thought. And we were very grateful.

We didn't find out until much later that during the large intestine operation, she received bad blood and contracted Hepatitis C. If she had gone to the doctor early, it probably could have been managed. There wasn't a cure then, but she could have gotten medicines that would have helped enormously. But Mom totally went untreated. She was fine after the surgery for a while, but then she started losing weight and energy. Unfortunately, she didn't go to the doctor for years (although she told me she had)—until it was too late. And then, when she finally went, they gave her the wrong medicine. Dad talked about suing, but didn't. I guess he realized that she was so weak by then that she probably would not have survived even with the right medicine. It was so sad.

I had not seen Mom since the reunion, when I thought she didn't look good. But I had no knowledge of the seriousness of what she was going through. When we talked, she always said she was fine. She intentionally hid it from me because I was in the midst of the 1986 Mayoral campaign. The week before election day, she went into the hospital. I had no idea. She forbade Dad from telling me, which was highly unusual for her as she never took him on. But this time she told him, "Don't you dare tell Carol or else." My mother rarely would talk like that. She followed up with: "She's right at the end of a campaign. There's nothing that can be done for me. I know her, she'll come running down here. I do not want her to know." She just put her foot down.

Then the morning of the election, Dad called and said, "Your mom has been in the hospital for five days. She wouldn't let me tell you, but I need to tell you now." So I went through election day worried sick about Mom.

Then David and I flew down to Midland. Before going to the hospital, we went to my parents' apartment to leave our stuff. And David just got into bed. He stayed in bed the whole time. He never went out to eat. We'd bring him in food. I asked him to please come to the hospital with me to see Mom, but he just wouldn't. It was so awful.

His depression was worse than usual, maybe exacerbated by the results of the election. Occasionally, when we'd go to the beach during the summer, he would do the same thing. Typically, he was so fastidious about his personal being, but when going through those episodes, he'd stop shaving or bathing and just stay in bed, debilitated. This time was one of those. Although I always tried to be kind to him, now I was so mad thinking, "What about my mom? Couldn't he just pull himself together long enough to say hello or ask how she was doing? He sure always managed to get to work."

When I got to the hospital that first day, I learned that Mom had been telling the nurses that "My beautiful daughter is coming to town." My mom had never been effusive or demonstrative—never said I was pretty or anything like that, and rarely gave hugs. It was so nice to finally hear it coming from her, even at a time when I was so worried about her well-being.

I spent most of the days at the hospital with Mom, except at night when I would bring in food and stay with David. He did not see Mom the whole time, from early Thursday until Monday, when he had to leave Midland to return to work. As we left the apartment that morning to drive to the airport, I finally said, "You're going to see my mother." And we did.

I stayed in Midland for another week. I knew David was seriously depressed. Meanwhile my mother's in the hospital dying. I was so divided, but I had to stay with my mother. I was so glad I was there when Dad brought her home to their then small two-story duplex apartment.

We had set up a cot in the middle of the living room downstairs as we couldn't get her up the stairs to her bedroom. Mom loved to read so I moved a nightstand and lamp by her bed. Their small apartment was filled with lots of furniture and knick-knacks and everything was meticulously placed, under normal circumstances. But these were not normal circumstances. When Dad walked in, he yelled, "Get rid of that fucking table and lamp. I don't want them there. Put them back where they belong."

I admit I have that kind of anal-ness, but not in that kind of situation when someone is dying! Even knowing my father, his rage and need for control, I could not believe it. It was beyond the pale. He just went on and on about not wanting the lamp and table out of place. But I refused to move them. My mother in her weak, docile way stated, "It's okay, Carol. Just move them back." But I would not do it. I also suggested getting her a TV. But Dad said he would "not bring a TV into the house," even when she was weak and dying. It was horrible. Mom said, "Don't worry. I'll just read."

Then Dad and I went into the nearby kitchen area while my mom was lying in bed about 10 feet away. He continued screaming about the moved lamp and table. As I was unloading the dishwasher, I took one of those aluminum foil pans (one you can crumble up and throw away) and hit him on the head with it, and said "Stop. Enough." We were out of Mom's view, although she could hear him yelling. I knew the pan wouldn't really hurt him. I had always been scared to death of my father, for good reason. But this time, I just had to make him stop, and finally he did.

I sponge bathed Mom. She was just too weak to do anything else. She had dwindled to 85 pounds when she used to weigh double that. But Mom would insist upon writing her own thank you notes to the few who had visited, and sent flowers or cards. I will always remember that even as she was dying, she was trying to do the polite thing. I would sit next to her and write the envelopes.

After ten days in Midland, I didn't want to leave Mom but David just sounded so awful over the phone; and I was still on the Council, so I had to work as well. I flew back to D.C. on November 13th to be there for David's 47th birthday the next day. I told Mom I would come down in a couple of days, but Mom said, "No, you work and besides, David didn't look so good. You should be at home." I did plan to go back in two weeks despite her objections.

But then on November 23rd I got a call that Mom had been rushed to the hospital. She was shrieking in pain, and then she just blacked out. I think her liver had erupted. I begged for David to come with me, but he would not. He said he needed to work. My daughter Hilary flew down that day with me instead, and I was grateful to have her there. But I was so mad that David was once again nowhere to be found for me personally. He was there for campaigns—mainly because he enjoyed them. But personally, I was always on my own.

The hospital immediately put Mom on a breathing machine, although she was unconscious and probably gone. She was bloated from all the intravenous liquids they were giving her. She didn't look like herself. And we never saw her awake. Dad made the excruciating decision to pull the plug, as the breathing machine was the only thing keeping her alive.

I'm four years older now than my mother was when she died. She had just turned 69 on September 30th and she died on November 25th. Too young. Her mother had lived to 88 and her father, 83. So she was really robbed. And we were all robbed. In a way, I think she committed her own form of suicide by not going to the doctor until it was really too late. I think she just wanted to get the hell out. Between the responsibility for Johnny, my tyrannical father, so few friends because of him, and now not feeling well on top of it, I guess she felt like life wasn't worth living.

David and Doug came down after Mom died. Stephanie flew in from college. The most difficult thing was telling Johnny. We waited until he arrived from Austin to tell him in person. It was heartbreaking to give my brother the sad news that his beloved Mom was gone.

My father, never very Jewish, actually selected a minister to lead the memorial service in Midland, because he had been there for him in the hospital. Aunt Betty and Uncle Seymour flew in for the service from Denver. Aunt Betty and Uncle Joe in Baton Rouge were meeting us in Greenville, Mississippi for the burial. Hilary remembers the minister calling Mom Hilary instead of Hilda during the funeral in Midland. I was too sad and numb to remember anything. I had always felt that Mom deserved so much better than she got often in life after she married. My only consolation at this devastating time was that now she at least was out of pain and aggravation—and was resting.

We then went to Greenville to bury Mom next to her parents in the Jewish section of the cemetery on Main Street. Johnny, who was weepy all day, broke down, sobbing in Uncle Seymour's arms.

Mom, a good writer and a poet in her youth, in recent years had taken poetry classes at Midland College. I love this one, which I think speaks for itself and her life:

Fun
It's tanning lazily in the sun
It's energy to dance – to run
    across tickling cinnamon sand
It's pride – challenging tide
      to fill in footsteps
      to try to hide
      tracks across ocean side
It's a beach ball tossed by active hands
It's a day at the beach, a succulent peach
It's laughter – after
It's youth
It's fast
Too soon it's past

Early 1987

After my mother's death, I went back to my Council job, which I loved doing but as I think most people know, while those positions are interesting, they are also difficult and stressful. And my father had become another full-time job. He was in emotionally horrible shape after Mom died. He would call me literally every day. I'd be on the phone with him for hours every night because he felt so guilty that he hadn't been nicer to my mother. He was justified in feeling guilty but I never told him that. I just said, "She loved you and I'm sure she knew you loved her," whatever I could think of to try to console him without saying he was a wonderful husband, which he definitely wasn't. I feared he was going to commit suicide and he often threatened to.

My father went to an extreme in his mourning, I suppose, in reaction to that guilt. He set up shrines to my mother by scotch-taping many pictures of her over most of the walls in his apartment and covering the dashboard of his car with beautiful photos of her from her younger years. And beautiful she was then. The dashboard was blanketed. He even pinned an old laminated photo ID of hers onto his shirt pocket over his heart, and wore it every day and everywhere for several years. It was Mom's ID from the Manhattan Project where Dad had worked 40 years earlier.

Dad's behavior was so worrisome that sometimes when I called and could not reach him, I was afraid he had lived up to his threats of many decades to "blow his brains out." Sometimes I would even have a friend of mine go over with some food or ring the doorbell for a "visit" just to make sure he was still there and alive. This especially happened every Thanksgiving after Mom died. I would invite him up but he would say, "No, I'll come at Christmas with Johnny." And then he would never answer the phone that day— and I would usually put my friend into action. Thanksgiving was a big deal in my house. I cooked for days, the kids were always there, and usually I invited in good friends and others who might have been alone on the holiday. Having the additional stress of not being able to locate my father was distracting and maddening. Maybe he meant it to be so.

I was so sad about my mom being gone, and on top of that, was feeling overwhelmed with responsibilities for my father and brother. Because of Dad's enormous grief which rendered him nearly incapacitated, I had to take over even more responsibility for Johnny. Although Johnny was and is the love of my life, the added burden of his care and school activities was becoming too much for me to handle with work, husband, kids, etc. Meanwhile, David's depression never got any better. It really was overwhelming, and I was starting to get extremely depressed myself.

I had also forlornly anticipated the day my kids would leave home—and here it was. Stephanie was away at college, and Hilary was to go the following fall. I had always rued this day. In fact, the September before Stephanie went to college, the five of us were driving up to New York for the Jewish holidays. I looked back at my children in the backseat and thought that this was the last year we would all be together at this time. Tears started rolling down my face, but I didn't say anything and no one saw. As much as I'd miss my children, I guess I was also aware that soon we wouldn't have the kids at home to be a buffer for the unhappiness in the marriage. Finally, I who had always looked at life as the glass half-full saw only unhappiness—and an empty glass.

It was at times like this—though this was the worst of times ever—that I wondered why did I stay? Since the 20-year refrain of "At least he doesn't beat me and I can talk on the phone" wasn't working anymore, the answer was always the same: the children. And there was another answer: my always being responsible and dependable, as well as loyal, even when I didn't want to be or it was not deserved. My mom called me capable, responsible, lots of -ables, which can sure tie you down. And it did.

Instead of leaving, I just stayed busy. I would write letters. I would clip articles. I would do legislation—anything to just stay busy and not think about my home life. I would straighten pictures and knick-knacks. If I could not control other things, at least I could control my stuff. Many times I'd be hysterical, crying (and always late at night when everyone was sleeping) and then I would start cleaning and straightening. That would keep me sane enough to stay—and function in the roles I had to play.

Issues with my Daughters

Although this sounds like a blip in comparison with the other drama, we also had some tension with our daughter Hilary over her school choice. She was determined to go to NYU. She was a young 17, not very mature, and both David and I were really scared of her going alone to New York City. David was just as adamant as I in forbidding her to go. When she was filling out applications, we said no to NYU and when she was so upset about it, we finally said, "Go ahead and apply, but even if you get in, you're not going," both of us thinking that despite her good grades she probably wouldn't be accepted anyway. And then the decision would be made—and not by us. But she did get in. (I remember thinking at the time that I wished David had used his alumni clout there to call and request the opposite of what most parents ask: "Do *not* accept my child.")

After that, we had a screaming fight with her over it. She was crying. I was crying. She ran upstairs to her room. I finally turned to David and said, "If we don't let her go to New York and her life does not work out, she will always blame us and I don't want to carry that load." He agreed. I opened the door to the upstairs to let her know she could go. Just then Hilary was coming down the stairs to tell us she was okay with not going as she didn't want to make us be so unhappy. But we gave her our permission. And off to New York she went and she is still there 30 years later. As an aside, one of my cautions to her was to never ride the "dangerous subway." Now, along with the bus, it's been my own favorite way to travel in New York City.

Then Stephanie came home from college for the summer. She had lost a huge amount of weight, and I even commented about how great she looked. Then, a boyfriend of hers wrote David and me a letter, telling us she was bulimic. In it he said, "Haven't you noticed her running the shower upstairs a lot" to cover up the sounds? It was a courageous and responsible thing for him to do and I was very appreciative. But at the time, I was panicky. David read the letter first and in his typical way, handed it to me to deal with. I immediately ran upstairs and started yelling at her, crying as I did so. I begged her to stop and to get help if she needed it. I was hysterical at the thought of my beautiful daughter hurting herself. I even ran to the office of a friend who was a psychiatrist— my first and only initiation of a session in all those years—to tell him how I had reacted, and I guess just to get some comfort.

Afterwards, I often checked in with Steph to see how she was doing in her efforts to stop. And she was very honest, saying, "I did it two nights ago, but I haven't since." I later learned that expensive Bard must have had to use a lot of its money to buy bathrooms, as an unusually large proportion of men and women were lined up to throw up at that small school. Since many young people have died from eating disorders including bulimia, it would have been nice had the school's administration told the parents instead of our having to find out on our own or through a friend. Regardless, that just added to the list of reasons why I felt it had not been the right choice in the first place. Thank God she did re-cover in a few years—but only after going through more trying times.

Losing Ma

David and I always talked to his mother on Sundays, but she and I often talked a time or two in between about our activities. Each year, Ma looked forward to her reunion with friends from her youth during the summer at a small inn in the Catskills near New York City. I talked to her on June 29th, the day before she was leaving West Palm Beach to go up North, and even though she was excited about her trip, she wasn't feeling her usual self. I said, "Have you gone to the doctor?" She said, "I don't feel that bad." And she did sound okay. Her friends, who lived in New York City, were arriving on July 1st. Since she had further to travel, she went up a day earlier. Ma called me once she got to the inn and said she was fine but tired and was going to bed.

The morning of July 1, 1987, we received a call from the inn that David's mother had passed away. David and I both took the news hard. We did get some information first-hand which gave us some solace. When Ma had not come down for breakfast that morning, someone opened the door and found her in bed with no signs of pain or struggle. It appeared she had just closed her eyes and passed away in her sleep.

Our original thought was to fly up to the Catskills to take her to the city, but the funeral home was already at the inn. So we called their sister funeral home in NYC, made arrangements, con-tacted family and friends, and had the funeral in Manhattan the following day. My dear mother-in-law is buried beside her hus-band Herman in a cemetery in New Jersey.

I had grown to not only like Ma, but to love her very much. Especially after my mother died, I felt even closer to her and really needed that relationship. Her passing created an unfillable void—made worse by the fact that it occurred less than eight months af-ter my own mother's.

The Aftermath

After her death, David was a wreck. Maybe some of his reac-tion was out of guilt. He never paid much attention to his mom and maybe he felt badly about that. But I don't know. David never really discussed his family even though I sure tried to get him to, especially early on. I am curious about everybody, even strangers, so it was hard to know so little about the man I married and the father of my children.

All I knew at that time was that he was really suffering and even becoming somewhat catatonic. I remember a month or so later, being in Rehoboth Beach and walking on the boardwalk, holding his hand. But it was different than normal. I was basically holding his hand to lead him. That's how out of it he seemed. It was actually reminiscent of Johnny and my taking care of him. His condition was scary. He was drinking more than his usual too much. His drinking, which had always been prevalent, now was growing out of control.

Over the years, I would mention his drinking occasionally, especially if it seemed extreme. Sometimes I would talk about his drinking after we were out playing cards with people we knew when he'd get sloppy and constantly expose his hand, which then made it obvious to them. On the way home, I would share my concerns as I was worried about his reputation. His response was always the same, "You don't even drink at all, so what do you know about drinking too much?" I did know enough to know that drinking was exacerbating his depression. I guess it always had. Later, I learned that alcohol is actually a depressant itself and drinking is like rubbing salt in a wound.

There was other disturbing behavior. He started doing stock options (very high-risk stock purchases). David had always taken care of all of our finances, and even when I asked about them, he acted like it was none of my business and kept me in the dark. But now, he started saying to me, "Oh, today we made $35,000 with the options." Then other days, he would complain, "Oh, those options are terrible. I lost a lot today. They're driving me crazy." I would recommend, "Then don't do them." And he'd answer, "But some days, I make a lot of money." I'd say, "If it's making you nervous, it's not worth it." (In the end, it turned out that he had lost hundreds of thousands of dollars on those damn options.)

He also started having issues with one of his longtime clients, who was also a friend. He was having a hard time getting paid for his work; and although he was a partner, the firm was bugging him to collect the money—not his strong suit. He also feared he might get sued by the same client. I'm not sure if that was real or imagined, harking back to those daily dinner conversations during our early marriage when he felt he was going to get fired five minutes after getting a big bonus. But it seemed to really worry him.

David also started declining to ever go out with our friends. We'd make plans after he had said, "Fine" and then when the day—or usually night—came, he would back out. I would have to go alone, arriving with one excuse or another: "He had to work late," "He has the flu," "He was called out of town on business." Meanwhile, he was home depressed. I actually had this go-it-alone experience with one couple who lived in Bethesda twice in a month's time. One was a brunch and one was a dinner party. I'm sure they thought we were separated or something. Yes, we were separated—I was where we were supposed to be and he was home in bed. It felt so awkward on top of the loneliness I felt.

David was clearly very depressed and in pain. But what was so infuriating is that I could not get him to seek help then or in prior years. The one time I did, which was about seven years earlier, he did go to someone we knew for one session. The doctor gave him some pills that he said were mild but effective. He called them "Muzak for the mind." Soon thereafter, we went to Rehoboth for a week, David's favorite thing to do—or so he said. David just got in bed and stayed. This was the first time that he stopped bathing and shaving. I asked him then if he had taken his pills and he said, "Yes." I remember thinking they don't seem to be helping much.

Probably a year later, I found the bottle with the number of pills listed on the outside, and only two were missing. I questioned, "Why didn't you take the pills? Why don't you at least try to get better?" And he replied, "When I took them, I did not feel like myself." (I thought that was the point of the pills—not to feel like your depressed self!) Now, seven years later, he wouldn't even go to the doctor once—or even take two pills.

(This is an aside, but maybe not. David said going to Rehoboth in August was his favorite vacation. Yet when we went for more than a week, David would always return to D.C. to work. I would say, "You're having fun with the kids, and most of your clients are here. Why don't you stay and relax?" But he'd go back anyway. Years later, a friend/associate of his told me that he asked David, since the office was so quiet, "Why don't you just go back to the beach with your family?" David answered, "I get bored there.")

While I'm trying to help David with the emotional aftermath of his mother's death in 1987, I was going through my own very dark period. My mother's death was devastating for me. I was also so sad for the tough life she had and how much crap she put up with. Then Ma's death. And David's state of mind and neediness, as well as my father's. I felt like I was drowning. I would just sit in my office and cry.

My Administrative Assistant and friend for years, Gloria Strickland, would come in and tell me to go shopping. I was then not at all a shopper. But she just wanted to get me out of the office and make me feel better. I would sometimes follow her instructions, but there was no escape. I, who always valued life, and could find something positive to zero in on, could not anymore. I would never have committed suicide, but must admit at that point I was wishing a bus would just jump up on the curb and hit me.

I also began to really resent how David, who never showed his mother any attention or affection, mourned her death and expected me to be there soothing his pain. When my mother had died eight months earlier and I was constantly crying, he never once even patted my arm much less put his arm around me or gave the hug I so desperately needed. And then every single night, in spite of that sorrow, and in spite of working all day, I would have to have at least a 45-minute conversation to ease my father's grief. My dad and David were friendly, so I asked David on several occasions if he would make the call to Dad, or even just take over a call for fifteen minutes, just to give me a break. Never happened.

Fall of 1987

Hilary now went off to college—joining her sister in leaving home just one year later. My sadness at becoming an empty-nester was now being realized, adding to this mournful time. With the tension at home on top of the stress at work, I was overcome with unhappiness. And I continued feeling like I was drowning.

At the end of October of 1987, my friends Carol and David Pensky had a party at a wonderful downtown Italian restaurant on I St., N.W. As usual, although we had RSVP'd for two, I went alone—and actually had a nice time for the first time in ages. On the way home, which probably was only a ten-minute ride, it hit me like a ton of bricks that here I was alone again and heading home to misery. With no more thought than that, I walked in the door, went upstairs and said to David, who was sitting in the bed, "I can't take this anymore. I am always alone so I might as well be alone." He started crying. Doug, who was across the hall in his own bedroom, came in and said, "What's going on?" I told him what I had said to his dad, basically that I wanted to separate. Doug started crying and laid on the bed. I then joined them, crying as well. Moments later, I looked over at two of the three most important men in my life (the other being Johnny) crying, and knew I could probably never leave—even as much as I wanted to.

Soon thereafter, David started seeing a therapist in Georgetown. He didn't talk much about it, but he did tell me the doctor wanted to have a session with me alone, which I immediately followed through on. I was so glad that he was starting to seek some help.

And I never actually left David, not even for one night. I doubt if I ever would have because of his neediness and because of my children and their love of their father. I did so want to leave by this point and finally had the courage to say so. But I think it was my daughter Steph who said, "Mom, you'll never leave. You don't leave people who really need you." I'll never know because as the holidays of 1987 approached, the crisis at home grew.

CHAPTER 21

Winter of 1987-88

A little before Christmas of 1987, I went up to New York for a meeting of the President's Conference for a Drug Free America. I was a member of the Board, having been appointed to it by President Reagan. The symposium started Monday evening and ran through Wednesday. David was due to come in to New York Thursday for his law firm's holiday party that night (Willkie, Farr and Gallagher's main office was there). We had planned for me to stay Wednesday night rather than my going back to D.C. one day and coming back to New York the next, and I had already arranged to have dinner with Hilary that night.

When I talked to David on Wednesday, he sounded depressed and I said, "Honey, are you feeling alright? Are you coming up tomorrow?" He said, "Yes, I'm just going to relax and go to bed soon." On Thursday, I kept calling David to find out the exact time he was arriving in New York, and could not reach him, either at home or at work. I started to get worried as the afternoon passed, and then I got a call.

Unbeknownst to me, David had contacted John Wylie, the husband of my childhood friend Ann and a friend of ours, who was a respected psychiatrist, to finally deal with his alcoholism. I had again once or twice over the last two months brought up a separation because of the ongoing drinking and depression. I said such things as, "Maybe I will get an apartment nearby or you will, whichever is your preference. Of course I'll decorate it for you as I have your offices." Other than those few mentions, no one made a move. But maybe the threat of leaving was the motivator for him to finally seek some real therapy for his drinking.

David had gone to John's office Thursday afternoon and asked for his help. He said, "I want to check into a clinic for alcoholism today." John said, "If you want to go to the really good ones like Betty Ford, you have to book at least a little ahead of time." But David insisted he wanted to go right then. John tried various facilities and there was one in Pennsylvania, about three hours north of Washington, that would take him that night.

John was firm: "You can't drive up there by yourself. I'll take you if you want." David said, "No, I'm going to ask Tom." Tom Kaufman was an associate of David's and someone he trusted deeply. Tom's then wife Debbie had worked at one point as a counselor so had some experience in this area. David felt he would be in good hands with them. Tom and Debbie agreed to drive him up that night, for which I will always be grateful.

David called me from John's office and told me his plans at around 6 p.m. just as I was panicking about the 7:30 firm party in New York and his whereabouts. I commended him, and told him I would come home right away and would drive him up to Pennsylvania early the next morning. But he replied, "I want to go now before I change my mind." I said "Okay." Needless to say, I didn't go to the firm party, just worriedly went to sleep and then went back to D.C., at least happy that David was serious about recovery.

I know that John too was happy that David was willing to confront his drinking problem. I remember hearing he even said to Ann that night, "I have an early Christmas present for you. David Schwartz is going to a clinic for his alcoholism."

The clinic had a four-week program. There was one visiting day in the middle, and the kids went up to see him over their winter break. The counselors at the facility did not want me to go up. They thought he was too dependent on me. In fact, David was not permitted to call me nor was I to call him. John was also firm in his advice that David needed to become a little independent of me. And I know John wasn't saying that to be mean. He was trying to be helpful to both of us.

But meanwhile, David called me every day even though it was against the rules. Counselors would come up and tell him to get off the phone. He was supposed to be isolated in his program, other than that one special visiting day. But he kept calling me. I would say such things as, "I'm proud of you. Keep with the program. It'll be a good thing." I didn't say I was leaving him. I never discussed that, and was even hopeful that things could be better with us as well. I just talked to him on the phone and tried to be comforting. I would say, though, sometimes, "You're breaking the rules. You need to complete this and invest time and energy to it."

Three weeks into the program, on Friday, January 15th, David arrived home totally by surprise. He had gotten kicked out of the clinic, maybe for his phone calls to me or maybe for something else. I was never quite sure and he didn't say. But I got home from work and there he was. It shocked me because I knew he had about 10 days left in the program. I just gave him a hug and some food, put him to bed in our bed, and slept there as well. I tried to comfort him. He seemed so zombie-ish, really out of it. On Saturday he just stayed in bed until late afternoon.

Early that evening I was going to a candlelight vigil in Southeast D.C. for someone who had been shot in the streets in a gang-related incident. I not only wanted to go but felt I needed to for my official Council duties. Of course, Doug was home as he was a junior in high school. And Stephanie was now back in D.C., having left Bard at the winter break time. Unbeknownst to me, David had actually asked her to take the semester off and come home. As Steph was worried about her father, she complied. (I thought she was just having issues of her own at school and needed to take a break.) Hilary was back at NYU and had to be there for her end-of-semester exams, which were in January.

Steph and Doug had planned to go with me to the vigil, but they could have stayed home with their dad if need be. However, David said he wanted to go as well. And although he seemed dazed at the event and afterwards, he said he liked participating.

He did tell me that weekend, "I'm on a medication that won't let me drink. If I drink, I'll get sick to my stomach." In the next breath he would say, "I can't imagine a life without drinking." So I said, "Maybe you can go off the medication and have a drink a day." It was naïve to think he could drink moderately, but I was so desperate for him to feel better.

After the vigil that Saturday, I called John Wylie because of my deep worry about David's zombie-like state, and he came over. He and David sat all night in the kitchen, talking. Throughout the night, I went down to the kitchen to see if they needed anything. But other than that, I just stayed up in my room and left them alone so they could have a confidential conversation. I don't know if they ever slept. I know I didn't.

The next morning, I made the three of us a little something to eat, and then John announced, "I'm taking David to my gym in Chevy Chase. I think it would be good for him to get out and do a little exercise." I watched them walk slowly to the car and wondered how David in his state, when he could barely walk, could do any exercise. But I agreed it was a good and loving idea to try. John and David were at the gym for a few hours and then came back and talked on their own some more.

While David and John were at the gym that Sunday morning, I started thinking about ways to cheer David up. As the next day was a Monday holiday, Martin Luther King's Birthday, I called up a few of David's associates/friends of many years—Tom Kaufman, Larry Atlas and John Ratino—and told them that David was now back and seemed awfully blue. I asked them to come over for a visit the next day since the office was closed. I booked them in at different times. They came. I provided some food to each and then just went upstairs so they could have their own time.

On Tuesday, January 19th, David went to work. It was his idea, even though I wasn't sure it was a good one. He dressed and said, "I'm going to work today." I think he was embarrassed as he had found out over the course of the month off that everyone at work knew he had gone away to the clinic. Unfortunately, the administrative partner at the firm's New York office, who had been told about David in confidence, had made it her business to spread the word. Unforgivable! I and our very few close friends who knew had not said a word to anyone, which is certainly the right and humane way to handle such personal—and personnel— matters.

I talked to him several times during the day to see how he was. On Tuesday night, I arrived home from work and he was sitting in bed. My birthday was the next day. A couple of months earlier, I had made a reservation for myself to go to a spa in Florida over my birthday because I was going ape-shit at the time and knew I needed a getaway. It was my first spa retreat ever in my soon-to-be 44 years. Even when David went away to the clinic, I didn't change it because he was not due back until after I returned. But I had to go. It was really my lifeline then, getting away to that spa. And besides, Steph and Doug were going to be there with David.

So I reminded David (and the kids were there), "Tomorrow is my birthday and the next day, I'm going to that spa for five days." David just sat there, staring into space. The kids said, "Do you have to go?" I raised my voice, "I can't take this any longer. I've got to get away." I then walked across the hall from our bedroom to the little den and shut the door hard. I was also mad at the kids for not understanding how I felt, as I was going crazy as well at that time.

In the den, I started calling some friends and family, not mentioning the nightmare I was going through, but just needing to hear some loving voices and to have some distraction. I ended up falling asleep on the daybed there, where I had made my calls. It was the only time I remember not sleeping in my bed when at home. It was not a conscious decision. I was just so exhausted from all the turmoil that I closed my eyes. The next thing I know Doug is waking me up at about 7:00 a.m., saying "Mom, where's Dad?"

Doug and I started looking around the house and then Doug opened the front door and walked outside. I went to the kitchen to look in the backyard and then I heard Doug yelling hysterically. He had found his father in the wooded area right next to our home. I ran to the front. Doug screamed, "Dad's outside. He killed himself." I fell to my knees and cried, "David, no!" Stephanie heard the commotion from her bedroom further up, and ran downstairs to the entryway. She then rushed outside to see her father. Even though she was hysterical as well, she came back in to grab a prayer book so that she could read the Mourner's Kaddish over his body. David was only 48 years old.

I could not go outside. I did not want to see him like that. I just couldn't do it and I'm so glad that I did not. My two babies have had that vision for nearly 30 years now and I feel so terrible for them. I do imagine it, but at least there's no real vision.

Then I called my daughter Hilary in New York. I left a message at the dorm's front desk to call home immediately. She did so right away and I had to tell her, "Dad killed himself this morning." No one was there to hug her, and then she had to take a lonely trip home, knowing what awaited her. Poor baby.

The police soon arrived. They asked if David had left a note or anything. I said that I didn't know. I certainly hadn't looked for one as I was so devastated, in shock, and trying to comfort my children. I hadn't even thought about that yet. We went upstairs and there was a page ripped out of a yellow legal pad, which we found in a dressing room off the bedroom. It read only, "I'm sorry. I screwed up everything" in his distinctive handwriting.

The Ensuing Pain

David had never said anything about suicide in all the years I had known him. It never occurred to me that he might do such a thing, especially because of his love for his children. It was so shocking and so unbelievable. Over the years since, I have often thought that here I had a father who all my life would say, "One of these days I'm going to blow my brains out," and then my husband, who never said a word, did exactly that in that way. And my next thought is always a woe-with-me one: "Why me Lord?"

I do know that many years before, David bought a gun saying that he wanted it for our safety, and that he needed to get it right away as the D.C. Council was talking about doing a gun control law and he wanted it to be grandfathered in. The children were still young then and I did not want a gun in the house. So I insisted that he put it in the bank deposit box. I thought he did. And we had a running joke afterwards that someone would break into the house and we would call out, "Wait! You have to come back tomorrow after the bank opens!" We would both laugh.

But apparently he kept a gun, whether it was the same one or not I do not know, in his bottom dresser drawer. My daughter Hilary told me recently that she found it while trying to locate clothes for a dress-up game when she was about 10 in 1980. She said she never told anyone and thought it was just there for protection. I wish I had rummaged, but stupid me always respected people's privacy—and took people at their word. I just wish I had known about it. It turns out David did know that she had found it. When Hilary came downstairs to show off the funny shorts she found in his drawer (the very garment the gun was wrapped in), she said her dad's face collapsed—and they both avoided the topic afterwards. Was the gun really there for protection? Or was he thinking of suicide even then? We will never know.

Sometime later that decade, around the time the girls were going off to college, David announced to me that he had brought the gun home from the bank deposit box. I was unhappy, but he was adamant. I did ask him to at least hide it way away so the children or their friends could not find it, and to not tell me where it was.

I also learned from the police later that he had bought another gun after he had left work on Tuesday, January 19th. When he was discovered on the ground, one gun lay next to him and another was in his pocket. He was obviously determined.

Of course, one of my initial thoughts was that David killed himself on my birthday to get even because I wanted to leave him. Then I realized that he had been at his office on Tuesday and his will, which left me everything, was in his desk drawer and appeared totally unchanged. So how mad at me could he have been? He also left that suicide note which said, "I'm sorry. I screwed up everything," obviously putting the blame on himself, not me.

All the things I considered as reasons for the timing were: 1) mad and getting even, which was basically dissipated because of the above, or 2) so out of it, he didn't know what he was doing or that it was my birthday, or 3) just in pain and wanting to get the hell out, or 4) maybe in his crazy way, thinking it was a gift to finally set me free, especially knowing how loyal I am and that I would probably never leave on my own. But we'll never know the reason. (And by the way, it was certainly not a gift—having to live with that horrible death and its aftermath each birthday forever.)

I do know that right after David died, a cousin of his told me that the whole family, when he was a child, called him Hamlet because he was so melancholy. Throughout our married life, I found him to be that way, although I never thought of it as "melancholy";

now I think that was the perfect word. Also her words made me realize that instead of saying to myself, "Maybe I could have kept him alive," I should be saying, "Maybe you *did* help keep him alive for all those years."

Regardless, I still think to this day how extraordinary it was that David became so successful and was so functioning while obviously going through such inner upheaval constantly during his life, all the while untreated except for my untrained "counseling" and the alcohol. In addition to his nice singing voice, David was also a really good actor. I'm sure the latter is what enabled him to mask his depression, both professionally and socially, with only a few of us being aware. Given this terrible burden he must have carried all of his life, I guess we were lucky to have him for as long as we did—and to have gotten as much out of him as we did.

The more I have lived and the more I have seen depression in family and friends, the more I realize what a superstar my husband was. I see so many people wallow, cry, so down they bring everybody else around them down, talk about their low thoughts constantly to anyone who'll listen, many incapable of doing hardly anything, some just taking to their beds, and not just occasionally.

Then I think of David with his what I know now was clinical depression—probably a lifetime of it—and how he got up most every morning and just kept going. Not only just kept going, but was enormously respected and rewarded in his work, a great dad to his children, often the life of the party. What an accomplished life, especially when you consider the endless inner doubts and pain. He really was a superstar. Kudos to you, David Schwartz.

The Loving Support

That morning, January 20, 1988, local television and radio stations interrupted their programs to report: "Councilmember Carol Schwartz's husband committed suicide early this morning." Because of all the calls from media, later that afternoon, we released a statement from the family in which we called David a "dear husband" and "loving father," and expressed gratitude for the outpouring of sympathy and support. That evening it was the lead-in to the news, and the next day, on the front page of various sections of the major papers.

And that first morning, friends and colleagues who heard came running over to our home immediately. My dear friend Tay heard the news on the radio while driving to work. She turned around and headed to our house. She rushed through the door and hugged me. We fell to the floor crying.

Our close friends, the Myersons, flew right in from New York. We all ran out the door to them, hugging and sobbing. My colleagues on the Council came in the morning as a group and could not have been more consoling. Many stayed and continued coming back throughout the rest of the week. I especially remember Charlene Drew Jarvis and Betty Ann Kane working in the kitchen for hours. Mayor Marion Barry rushed over that first day and stayed for a long time, sitting in the living room. He returned, I remember, at least two other days, each time staying for a lengthy period. In fact, Mattie Taylor put him to work. She said, "Look at the trash accumulating. Can you get some help?"

The house was full for days. Hundreds and hundreds of people arrived from early morning until late at night. So much food, so many flowers, letters, cards. The support we received was just unbelievable. Each night, Rabbi Weinberg or another Rabbi from our temple would come to say prayers, and the large number present, mostly non-Jews, would reverently participate. It was quite touching—and memorable.

The many people there for us really helped, all the hugs, the kisses and the kind words. And it was not just that. It was the many people who revealed their own experiences with suicide. Individuals I'd known for years would whisper in my ear, "My sister committed suicide" or "My father did the same." I never knew that about them. It was amazing the number of people who have had suicide touch their lives, but who had never talked about it before.

It is sad that the too-often atmosphere of shame surrounding suicide may prevent people from disclosing it and/or talking openly about it. In fact, it is so hidden, you think that you are the only person in the world who has gone through a suicide death. Actually, there are many. And keeping it under wraps is really a disservice to yourself in that it deprives you of the ability to have friends and others embrace you literally and figuratively in a loving way that is so desperately needed at that time. It is also so unfair to those who actually expose it and who then feel so terribly lonely and unique when it happens to them.

My own husband's death was broadcast widely because of my elected public position. Therefore, we did not have the chance to make a decision on this issue in the obituary. I do believe, however, that we would have told the truth that he died of suicide. But that would have been rare. Usually it's "undisclosed causes," "not known at this time," or other such nebulous words. A colleague of my husband died several months later in similar fashion, but with pills. However, we read in the *Post* that he died of "cardiac arrest." That's true. Your heart does stop when you die, but it's not the whole truth. Having lost many dear people in my life, I certainly know that suicide is among the hardest. Why add secrecy and loneliness to that painful equation?

At this point, I do want to say something additional about suicide. In the 29 years since David's death, in talking to someone on a plane, when asked if I'm married, I say, "No, I'm a widow." (Now this following response is becoming far less frequent as I age): "But you're too young to be a widow. How did your husband die?" I have always responded, when asked, "Suicide." And too often, the next question is, "How did he do it?" I am always taken aback by that question. At first I would try to answer. But then I started saying, "That's just too hard to talk about." Now I say, "I'm sorry but that question is just too painful for me to answer to satisfy your curiosity" or "for your listening pleasure." I know that's sharp, but I want it to be a lesson and a wake-up call so that they will not do it to others.

I know it's hard not to ask, but please do not. Occasionally I've met someone and have asked, "Do you have children?" A response has been, "I had three, but one died." I don't think I've ever asked, "How?" But now having gone through this experience, in spite of being curious, I always just say, "I'm sorry." By the way, I've actually had some people, including a former First Lady who's in her 90s now, ask me decades ago, "Why?" Answering "How" is a heck of lot easier than "Why," but both are inappropriate questions.

After David died, my friends Tay and Joy Safer, each took turns spending the night just to watch over me. Initially I couldn't sleep at all so the doctor gave me Halcyon, which even stubborn me could not fight.

There were two really absurd things that happened the day David died. At about 11:00 a.m. that morning I received a phone call from a much older married Congressman, who had been a client of my husband. He said, "I'm so sorry to hear about David. I'd like to take you out to lunch today." Obviously I said no. And then, in the mid-afternoon, a letter was hand-delivered from a well-known married journalist, who I knew casually, expressing sympathy and going on to say, "I'd love to come over and hold you in my arms." Bizarre! Needless to say, I never followed through on either of their offers or anything else.

Of course, even in those tragic circumstances, you have to jump in and make immediate decisions relating to a service and burial. The only thing I knew is that David wanted to be cremated, as I do as well. He had never talked about where he wanted to be buried. I had always said, as we drove down Rock Creek Park near Massachusetts Ave., that I wanted to be buried in that cemetery on the hill on the right. I thought it was so beautiful. David didn't say, "Me too," but he also didn't say, "I don't want to be there."

I had no idea of the name of the cemetery or whether it was a place where Jewish people could be buried. I knew nothing. I quickly and luckily found out it is Oak Hill Cemetery, that its entrance is on R St., N.W. in Georgetown, and that it is non-denominational. I found a beautiful burial spot and bought a step that would house David's urn and ashes, overlooking Rock Creek Park and the road below. I also bought two other adjacent steps with each step accommodating two urns for myself and our children as an option.

Well over a thousand people came to David's funeral at Washington Hebrew Congregation, where we had been members for about 15 years. In the announcement of the funeral, I asked that contributions be made in his name to two charities—one in D.C. benefiting children and one doing medical research in Israel.

Stephanie, Hilary and Douglas planned the whole service, and Rabbi Joseph Weinberg willingly and lovingly allowed them to do so. My children, who were 19, 18 and 16 at the time, read poems. Stephanie read a piece by one of David's favorite poets, Edna St. Vincent Millay. ("I miss him in the weeping of the rain ... And entering with relief some quiet place, where never fell his foot or shone his face, I say, there is no memory of him here! And so stand stricken, so remembering him.") Hilary read a poem by one of David's favorites, Dylan Thomas, entitled "Lie Still, Sleep Becalmed." And Doug read Robert Frost's "Nothing Gold Can Stay."

Herb Miller did a lovely eulogy and said something like, "friendship is a pure love." Tom Kaufman called David "an irreplaceable friend," and added, "There was no better problem solver than David." Tay Hahn read a piece from *The Prophet* by Kahlil Gibran (one of my favorite works). David Myerson also did a eulogy, beautifully quoting Kierkegaard: "Life can only be understood backward, but it must be lived forward." The kids selected two songs for the service: Don McLean's "Vincent" (about the sensitivity and depression of the artist Vincent Van Gogh, who also died of suicide) and Judy Collins's version of "Who Knows Where the Time Goes."

During the service, Rabbi Joe Weinberg said, "Each of us is responsible for our own lives." For me, those words were the most comforting ones uttered during that whole terrible time and they still comfort me today. Unfortunately, we lost dear Joe at only age 62 in 1999. Rabbi Weinberg also told my children that "Your dad died from a disease," which seemed to really help them as well.

After the funeral, we had a private burial—with only a few of us—at the cemetery. At the end of the short ceremony, Alda Douglas, David's Administrative Assistant and a friend of both of ours for many years and who has a lovely voice, sang a beautiful gospel song and we all broke down. We then put the urn with David's ashes in the step. I had chosen "David Schwartz at Peace" to be engraved on the urn. Rabbi Weinberg concluded with a fitting lament: "The memory of a righteous man lives on."

A year later was the unveiling of the stone. It reads, "David H. Schwartz ... loved ... respected ... missed."

CHAPTER 22

Picking up the Pieces

Five days after David died, my friends Joy and John Safer flew me and the kids down with them on their private plane to their place in Nassau, Bahamas, so we could get away from D.C. By that point, exhaustion from the emotional drain, as well as the commotion of that time and the reality of David's death had taken hold. We desperately needed that three-day break. And I will always be grateful for their loving kindness. While in Nassau, we just slept and rested, but we did watch our Washington football team, led by quarterback Doug Williams, win the Super Bowl, which did give us all a lift.

It was hard to start picking up the pieces after returning to D.C. because only a few weeks later, my beloved friend Gloria Strickland died. She had some type of heart disease since childhood. As you may recall, she worked on my Council staff for years and was a wonderful, caring human being. Her picture has been in my bedroom ever since.

In the course of 15 months, I had lost my mother, my mother-in-law, my husband and a dear friend. I felt like I had been run over by a truck—or that bus I used to think about.

The immediate aftermath of David's death brought tumult in every way, including financial complexities. David had handled all the financial affairs and he left those matters in a mess. His filing system consisted of two large paper bags in the bottom of his closet. I found unpaid bills stuffed in his nightstand drawers. I was overwhelmed. I had to navigate through all the accounts, unpaid bills and insurance matters. Thank goodness our good friend Marc Marks was there to help as he had been immediately after David's death with making sure the obituary got done and the funeral home got paid. He handled phone calls, even contacting Hilary's college professors to notify them that she would have to delay her final exams.

Marc was invaluable at that time. I was not only devastated but scared. Would we be financially okay? How would I manage all the stocks and accounts I had known nothing about before?

We addressed the life insurance. Years ago and once we started a family, David would mention that he bought some life insurance policies, such as a small one with the American Bar Association. So I knew that there was some protection. However, when it came to collecting, it turned out that all but one would *not* be paying. I eventually learned that a year and a half earlier, the human resources officer at David's firm had recommended to him that he consolidate all of those small insurance policies into one, and David gave his approval. So we couldn't collect on that large consolidated policy (made up of decades-old ones) because it had been joined together so recently, and the two-year anti-suicide clause was still in effect. I received only a few thousand dollars for the premiums that had been paid to all those policies. Thank goodness we did find one policy of some size that had not been consolidated and which did pay. It really helped us, and we needed it as the firm, although David was a partner, gave us nothing except for some token pay for untaken sick and holiday leave, which Marc had insisted it pay.

I was worried at first. Here I had two kids in college and one ready to go in a year and a half, and a big house which had been easy to carry with David's salary—but now?

I did receive a little Social Security for Doug for 21 months until he turned 18. I also had my job, which paid around $50,000 a year. And I was relieved that I had made a point of saving money over the years, which did help. And thankfully, David had made some good stock decisions other than those hurtful options. Many years earlier, David told me if anything ever happened to him that I should use a certain firm for financial management, which I did. With the help of Marc and others, I secured a solid accounting firm. I knew then that if we weren't excessive, we'd be okay.

Returning to Not Normal

The kids' adjustment was a rocky road. Even though my two daughters were of college-age, they were still teenagers, and with the emotional struggles of David's death, their challenges grew.

Stephanie was home now, in deep mourning, drinking to a degree that disturbed me greatly. She enrolled in some classes at Georgetown until deciding her next move. Meanwhile, after only two weeks at home, Hilary went back to NYU to resume her freshman year. Although she wanted to go back, the separation was jarring for her. Added to that were her guilt feelings about being absent during the last months of her father's life. I tried to tell her that we all understood that she was in college.

But in her emotional distress, Hilary became anorexic. I was petrified. I asked her to come home, but she wouldn't leave school. I called friends who lived in New York, and they suggested a psychologist they knew, who she started seeing right away. But her weight continued to dwindle to the point where the doctor and I thought of institutionalizing her. When we threatened her with that, she began to really work on getting better, and thank God, she eventually did.

I got Stephanie to go to the St. Francis Center (which is now the Wendt Center for Loss and Healing), which I knew about because I was friendly with the founder, Bill Wendt, and because of Carol Pensky's involvement there. Doug started going to a counselor as well and certainly cried a lot initially about his dad's death. Then he seemed to immerse himself even more in normal high school activities—a girlfriend, playing football and baseball, and hanging out with friends. I learned later, though, that he was also drinking after his father died. I wished I had known then. I did, though, catch him and a friend smoking pot in the house upon coming home before expected and reamed him out about that. At least I never smelled that smell again at home.

Instead of turning to counseling, drinking or drugs, I turned to shopping for distraction and comfort. Gloria Strickland, who had pushed me to shop during those painful days after Mom's death and who was now gone herself, would have been proud. I also didn't turn to eating. Instead, I could not eat during that period—a one and only time—and lost 25 lbs. As I came back, so did they.

Before David's death, we kept pretty strict rules—or at least I did. After his death, I admit I did let some things go. I had become aware after David died of his ongoing habit of slipping the kids money or just handing his credit card over to them after we had agreed upon a set allowance, and then saying, "Don't tell your mom." In addition, as you've read, I had always been the consistent disciplinarian parent.

So here we are in early 1988 with three vulnerable teenagers having lost the one parent who was more lenient and generous, and getting stuck with the cheap disciplinarian. (This is my assessment, not necessarily theirs.) I really felt badly for them, so I loosened the purse strings—and tough enforcement of the rules didn't seem that important anymore. I guess I just wanted life to get better for my three children to compensate for all that they had recently gone through.

But sometimes I still had to draw a line, or at least try. Three weeks before David died, Doug had turned 16 and gotten his driver's license. Several weeks after the burial, when snow and ice covered the ground, Doug asked if he could take the car (a Chevy Malibu from Curtis Chevrolet on Georgia Ave., which had been passed along from Steph to Hil to Doug). I immediately and firmly said, "No. It's dangerous out there." "But Mom," he responded, "I just need to get out of the house. Some friends are getting together. Please let me go. It's only a short ride away." This went on for about 20 minutes. He finally wore me down, something he could never have done pre-David's death, and off he went, much to my chagrin and defeat.

About five minutes later, Doug appeared back in the house. We lived on a hill and when Doug got to the bottom of Springland Lane at the light, the car did not stop even though he was trying to brake as hard as he could. He just slid all the way across to the other side of Reno Rd., where he wound up in a shallow ditch. He was able to turn around and drive back up the hill. He then came inside and said, "I think you were right about the ice." Thank God no one was hit or hurt and the car was even okay. And I had scored, in losing, a victory.

All the while, my work on the Council continued. During my first term, my small staff answered literally a thousand constituent service complaints. I made a point of responding to all of them. The complaints regarded water bills, trash pickup, taxes, traffic signals, etc. and came in at a break-neck pace. I guess that's your reward when you get a reputation for actually responding.

On that subject, over the years, I have had so many people say thank you to me for being one of the few people on the Council back then who followed through on their questions and issues. I don't know if that's true or not, but I do know that my response to them was always, "I appreciate your thank you, but please know that I was just doing the job you were paying me to do." I also tried to write high school graduating classes a special congratulatory letter as well as sympathy notes to people I was aware of who had lost a family member. So many over the years have mentioned how much they appreciated those remembrances

Some constituent service matters were particularly memorable. One was a hysterical call to my Council office from a senior citizen who had walked into her living room to find a rat chewing on her sofa. A call to the Mayor's War on Rats Office (yes, there was such an entity) elicited an offer not to exterminate the rat but to send a "rat counselor" later to work with the constituent on her problem—an offer they kept repeating. I finally became hysterical myself and yelled into the phone, "She doesn't need a counselor! She needs the rat gone!" I, though, by then, *did* need a counselor.

Coming to a Sad Decision

Even before David died, Bill Lightfoot, a Democrat who had just become an Independent and who was a successful personal injury lawyer, was orchestrating a "draft movement" to try to take my minority party at-large seat on the Council. I use the term "draft movement" loosely because Bill did attend the meetings, even though draft committees are supposed to be arm's length from the candidate; and there is supposed to be no communication between the two. Bill, as a lawyer, knew the rules but just wasn't abiding by them.

(By the way, many consider a draft committee very appealing—although I never did one—in that it allows a candidate to raise additional money, i.e. a donor can give whatever to the draft committee and then also give the maximum to the campaign committee separately. I never liked them because I always felt that the candidate who went that route was either not serious/driven to run, or just wanted to skirt the campaign limits—neither of which I would find appealing in a candidate.)

I had met Bill several times over the years, and decided to call him directly to protest. I said, "I am very aware that every meeting of your draft committee is being attended by you. I know you know that is not how it's supposed to work. So stop immediately or I will report you to the Board of Elections and Ethics," which I could easily have done without bothering to make that phone call.

After David died, Bill did set up a real campaign. But I had a decision to make that had nothing to do with any competition, and only had to do with my own personal issues. I was up for reelection in November of 1988 with a primary in September. I really wanted to continue serving. But the devastating blows of my mother, my mother-in-law, David and Gloria were just too much. I kept thinking and even saying, I needed time for my own healing and to be there for my children as they went through theirs.

But I was torn. Then the decision came pouring out of me through the writing I did in the middle of the night. I soon called a press conference in my office. On June 5, 1988, with my three children standing behind me, I sat at my Council desk and read that statement to the public and press, which said it all:

> "I am announcing today that I will not seek reelection to the Council of the District of Columbia this year. It is very difficult to leave something you care about so much but sometimes in life you find that it is harder to stay. I'm at that point in my life. In this business—politics—in the public eye—you need a stomach of iron,

nerves of steel and the thickest skin in the world. Yesterday, I had those things and I anticipate that I will tomorrow but in all honesty, I do not have them today—today, when I need to make a decision. The petitions for candidacy are due in by July 6th—just five weeks away—and I cannot delay a decision any longer. And certainly I cannot delay a decision not to run any longer because it is too important a position for there not to be the best competition for it possible.

I had wanted to run and had hoped the strength to do so would come as these last few months have passed. But it hasn't come to the degree needed to go through a grueling campaign—and make no mistake about it—campaigns are grueling even when you're the incumbent and expected to win. You have to always be "on," perfect, sharp, articulate. Not an easy task under normal circumstances but certainly an impossible one when you have experienced four great personal losses—my mother, my mother-in-law, my husband and one of my best friends—in the past eighteen months and the last two just four and a half months ago.

Those who know me—both casually and well—know I hate to admit defeat—not losses such as the Mayor's race or legislative issues—I'm a realist—but I hate to admit defeat where I'm in total control of the decision as I am in this case. But I must this time—the thick skin on this "tough, strong woman" has been rubbed raw by the unforeseeable events of the past year and a half. The skin needs time to mend and the woman needs time to heal—away from the microscope of a campaign.

Good souls—both friends and foes—throughout this city have been wonderful to me and my children during an awful personal time of our lives and I will always be grateful to them. Their concern, love and prayers have helped to bring us through the last four and a half months. I have also been blessed with loyal supporters since I first ran for the School Board in 1974—supporters which have grown in number each year as I have tackled first the educational—and now the total governmental—problems of our city. The worst part in making this decision was feeling that I was letting them down. But I am not going away. I'll be on the Council until my term expires in January—fighting for important issues until the end—and I plan to remain an involved citizen in our city for many years to come. Have no fear—or in some cases, jubilation—I may be down but I'm not out—I'm just taking a much-needed break from campaigning."

I did add that "My children have stuck by me through thick and thin and have helped me and will continue to help me. They're troopers in politics, and in everything they do."[97]

My colleagues gave encouraging words. Council Chair David Clarke said, "I'm very, very supportive. I had not expected it, but I understand, and I'm sympathetic ... few of us have been in the position she's in." And Marion Barry said, "Carol and I are probably closer than most people think in our personal relationship. Although we differ politically, as human beings we understand a lot about personal tragedies and how those kinds of things make you want to stop for a while and leave office."[98]

Even *The Washington Post* had some warm words: "Surely we have not seen the last of Mrs. Schwartz's hard work on behalf of all corners of Washington ... nor can we believe her forceful voice of loyal opposition will not return to deflate, deride, annoy and otherwise shake up the lopsided one-party domination of local government. ... she has proven her dedication to public service and has transcended racial and partisan barriers with disarming openness. ... best wishes of a sympathetic community."[99]

As hard of a time as I had in 1985 when I entered the Council, the opposite occurred on my way out four years later. By then, it appears, I had earned my colleagues' respect and even affection. At the last legislative session of my tenure, the Councilmembers spoke one by one. I hear it had not happened before nor do I think since. It was quite a tribute. Wilhelmina Rolark even said, "When you came to the Council, replacing my friend Jerry Moore, I didn't like you very much. Now, I can honestly say, I love you, Carol Schwartz." It was more than I could have imagined, and I was touched by—and grateful for—all their kind words.

Honoring Women—Finally!

Whenever David and I passed the Cosmos Club on Massachusetts Ave. between 21st and 22nd Sts., N.W., which was often as it was a route downtown, David would always point it out: "That's the Cosmos Club. There's no amount of money or family connections that can get you in. It's only based on accomplishments." Though David was not a club person and we had never belonged to one, that club really enthralled him.

Then in the fall of 1988, after David died and I announced I would be leaving the Council, I got a letter from a man named Willis Armstrong, who I did not know. It was a beautiful note stating that the Cosmos Club had just voted to allow women members and that he had been one of the advocates for that change for years. In his letter, he, an older D.C. resident, said that I was one of the women he was thinking of when he argued the point. He wanted to sponsor me to be a member, which would have put me in the first crop of women. I was very touched and actually thrilled at the time, but was so distracted due to other circumstances, including moving out of my office, that I just stuck the letter in the back flap of my briefcase.

Six to eight months later, I discovered the letter in the briefcase in my closet. I was mortified that I had never answered it, so I called Mr. Armstrong immediately and profusely apologized. Willis was very understanding, but said he so wanted me to be in the first class. I told him that I was happy that he nominated me and would be proud to be in the second crop of women, which I was.

Willis, a retired foreign service officer and next in line to be President of the Club, presented me with one of the nicest honors of my life. And he and his wife Louise became friends. (When Willis had a stroke while on vacation soon thereafter, he was unable to fulfill his duties as the incoming elected President. However, when the Club refused to put his name in the board meeting room along with other elected Presidents, I, only then a year-long member, fought on my own initiative to overturn that decision, but unfortunately was unsuccessful. It would be nice if they would add Willis Armstrong's name now.)

I always remember thinking (and this is the only time I've thought this), "Thank goodness David is not here. He would be really envious." David was never jealous of my accomplishments. In fact, I think he took pride in them. And he certainly had accomplishments of his own. But this invitation—not my elections, not my awards—would have made him jealous as hell.

Now to a connected and important aside: I often thought people believed David was the brains behind my career and that he wrote my stuff—which he did *not*. This is not an atypical way of thinking when a woman is partnered with a smart man: everyone assumes it's all him (or at least they sure did in that day). In fact, several months ago, when I brought up this issue, a good male friend actually confessed that he did think that David wrote my op-ed pieces and campaign speeches. And his wife resented his saying that as much as I did. But I always suspected that was the case. I was right. It was those people over the years who were not.

When I kept writing, after David was gone—the speech above and all the others, including my op-ed pieces, my columns, and subsequent campaign materials—maybe many of them finally realized that I actually had some brains and writing ability of my own. And I hope this book speaks volumes.

Life Goes On

In October of 1988, I was asked to be a member of the United States official delegation of 12 people to observe the plebiscite in Chile, which marked the end of Augusto Pinochet's reign of power. It had been organized by the National Democratic Institute (NDI). I was one of just two Republicans picked to go and then was made a team leader with the responsibility for a portion of the final report. Senator Bruce Babbitt, former Governor of Arizona and later Secretary of the Interior, led the delegation and was joined by his wife Harriet, who's a doll. Another lovely person on that trip was co-delegate Barbara Boggs Sigmund, Mayor of Princeton, New Jersey and daughter of Lindy and Hale Boggs, as well as sister of Cokie Roberts. Barbara lost her eye to cancer and was quite a knock-out with her printed eye patches that matched her fabulous clothes. Unfortunately, she passed away in 1990.

We were there to ensure the credibility of the democratic process and thus observed the voting at the polls on election day. I asked to stay in Santiago, while a few went out to other parts of the country in small planes (I felt I had been traumatized enough that year). It was a thrill to see the excitement and emotion people felt while exercising the basic right to vote—which most of them had never experienced. Our Chilean driver, who was in his mid-40s, was one of those who had never voted before. I actually cried as I watched him walk into the ballot booth.

On the way home to the U.S., I wrote a piece about how emotionally moving it was to see democracy come to Chile after all those years, and how sinful it was that it had not made it fully to the District of Columbia. In addition, I talked about how so many citizens of the U.S. who have the right to vote don't even exercise it. The trip was therapeutic in many ways, both in the experience and the writing I did, as well as in the camaraderie of the group.

Meanwhile, Stephanie had taken some courses at Georgetown University in the spring even though she was distraught and distracted. But then the University of Wisconsin accepted her as a transfer starting in the summer. She was happy—and I was thrilled as I always thought Wisconsin would be a good choice for her. So off she flew to Madison in June. The next day, though, she was on a flight back. Wisconsin had just received her grades from Georgetown and would not admit her that summer. Even though the whole family was in terrible mourning and Stephanie's situation was far from a good one, humor was still invoked. All summer long, Doug and Hilary would pantomime a plane taking off and then turning right around to come back, just to needle their sister about the Wisconsin debacle. Steph then took courses at American University to lift her grades enough to enter Wisconsin in the fall, which she did. She was always very smart, but during that period, she was understandably having a tough time.

In October of 1988, just months after David died, I went to see Wilson High School play Cardoza High School as Doug was a wide receiver for Wilson. It was a chilly day. I sat in the bleachers thinking how nice it was to see my son playing football and how much David would have liked it if he were here. And I was also glad to be back to some normalcy. Just when I was thinking everything was pretty good and normal, Doug's hand got sliced in the game. I watched him rushing off the field, clenching it. The coach and medical person, both African American, were convinced that his hand was intentionally cut by someone on the opposing team with a blade or some sharp object. It was so scary. I rushed him to Washington Hospital Center. We waited and waited while his hand was bleeding profusely. I begged the nurses to please take us. He was finally seen—though it seemed like hours—and treated. To this day, he doesn't have feeling in that part of his hand, poor baby. And earlier Doug had a bad experience when a big guy knocked him off in his bike in Rock Creek Park, and rode off with it when he was 13. Pretty scary stuff for a kid.

When I think of Doug, I feel empathy for him because of those things. I especially feel a great deal of empathy for him as he was the one who discovered his father out in the side yard and was the only child at home when his dad so obviously deteriorated that fall. But I am proud of the way he has gone on with such perseverance and strength. I feel the same way about my daughters. No child should have to go through such a violent death of a parent added on to the normal—or not so normal—pains of growing up.

I want you to know that all three of my children, in spite of the wretched pain that happened to us on my 44th birthday, have since made a big loving deal of my subsequent birthdays, now numbering 29. Friends and family alike have done the same. For nearly three decades now, so many have always kindly tried to distract me by showering me with calls, cards, flowers. How blessed is that? I will always be grateful, especially to my children who, in spite of their own sorrow that day, try to make it special for me. And I try, in return, to acknowledge their own pain, as well as their self-sacrificing thoughtfulness of me each January 20th.

Seven years after David died, I was in Palm Beach on Worth Ave. the week of my birthday and saw a pretty large-bead necklace, which cost $400. I loved it, but walked away, and back the six blocks to the rental car. As I was opening the door, I thought, "If David was here, he'd buy me that necklace." Then I thought, "Carol, why in the hell can't you buy that necklace for yourself?"

I locked the car, walked back, handed the lady my credit card and sang "Happy birthday to me ..." I've done that exact same thing for the last 22 years, and I certainly have some beautiful things to show for it. I would suggest that any of you out there who are alone, or not, gift yourself now and then. (By the way, I donated that necklace to the Whitman-Walker Clinic as an auction item 12 years ago, so it's now been "gifted" elsewhere.)

A Bad Start

One of my least proud episodes was taking up with a married man at this time. I could blame my sadness and desperation but that's no excuse. He was a friend, and was successful and charismatic. And I admit I needed the attention and affection after the trauma of my husband's death and the years of an unhappy marriage. I tried to keep the affair secret, especially from the kids. One weekend, I told my daughters I was going to visit an old friend in Pennsylvania. Since it was a friend I hadn't seen or mentioned in years, they were immediately suspicious and called information to get her number. I wasn't there and then they called another close friend to feign worry about me—who got in touch with me right away. I came home immediately and confessed.

The man I was involved with said he had always loved me and was going to leave his wife and start a new life with me—the typical stuff. But after a short while, I grew weary of the false promises. I also never liked the idea of breaking up a marriage or really hurting another woman so it was one of those cases of "be careful what you wish for." What if he really left her and came to me? I wasn't sure if my guilt feelings and his could ever be overcome. (His guilt and her hurt should have been lessened by the time I arrived, since he was a known gallivanter forever, from college on.) However, between my weariness with the situation and my conscience, I'd break up with him. And being the loyal person he was, he would immediately take up with an old girlfriend.

One day, I just knew he was at the old girlfriend's apartment (as he had told me all about her and others) so I decided to check it out to confirm my suspicions. Meanwhile, he was still calling me constantly and saying, "I can't possibly live without you." I drove over there and circled the street. And sure enough, I spotted his car. While driving around the block, I saw another familiar car. It was his wife, circling the street as well. Here were both his wife and most recent mistress circling the block of another mistress's residence. How pitiful is that! Thank goodness I recognized it for what it was—and have never done anything like that again.

Full disclosure: there had been a drive-by once before. When he told me that he had moved out of the house and was staying in a hotel, I did not believe him. So I drove by his house late at night and saw his car was not there. Could he possibly be telling the truth? But knowing him, I decided to check further. I found his car parked three blocks away. (In his residential neighborhood of large properties, there was hardly a dearth of parking in front of one's own home.) It wasn't just the deception that finally ended things. It was my ultimate relief that his car was still in the vicinity of his own house—and my hope that it would stay there for good.

So I did really break up with him. I truly meant it this time and he knew it. In spite of his calls, which I wouldn't answer, or his dropping by my house, where I wouldn't open the door, this time I was firm and serious. I had told him for months that if he really loved me and was my friend, he would leave me alone and let me go about my life. But selfishly, he was intent on winning me back.

Six weeks into my refusing contact, it was my birthday and dear friends and my children had come into town to be with me. At that point, they all knew about him. As we were visiting, a magnificent array of tropical flowers arrived with a beautiful love note from him. By then, I was done and mad about his continued attempts at manipulation. I knew him well enough to know that he would never stop unless I scared him into stopping. So I went into action—and we actually had fun doing this. I took a card and had my girlfriend write to his wife, "Thinking of you with love," from him. I had the new note and same flowers delivered to their house.

It worked. That part of our relationship was over. We were occasionally in touch as friends, but only rarely. I did appreciate that when my brother would visit, he would make a point of seeing him and taking him to lunch or out for a drive. I do not regret that experience as I think that each one that gets you from here to there—to a better spot—is valuable, as long as not too much chaos is created in between. The experience did keep me from ever getting involved with an attached man again, even though I have found that sadly those, for the most part, are the most available.

General Clothing Store Is Gone

But Much More Sadly and Importantly, Major Loved Ones Are Gone

Trying to Keep Life Going for Me and Family

My first cruise, taking kids to the Caribbean over holidays end of 1990

Planting a tree
for David in Israel

Visiting Steph in Seattle,
where she worked with
individuals who had
cerebral palsy,
like Lori (below)

Israel 1992

My favorite
photo is this
passport picture.

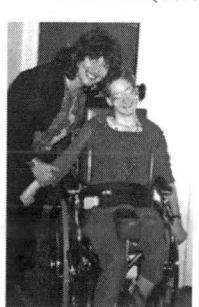

Taking Johnny to visit
Linda and Aunt Doe in
San Antonio

With Doug who
as first baseman for
the Wilson Tigers
won citywide
championships

CHAPTER 23

Starting Over

I had met Larry King, the TV and radio personality, several times over the years at Duke Ziebert's, a restaurant frequented by politicians and notables. (I had become friendly there with the Speaker of the House for 18 years, Tip O'Neill.) Duke reintroduced people over and over again, which was really endearing. Larry and I would always just say hi with no extra conversation.

However, in the spring after David died and I had lost about 20 pounds (not by effort, but just by lack of appetite), I ran into Larry at a Whitman-Walker Clinic fundraiser, which I was on the Board of and he was the master of ceremonies for. It took place at the Kalorama home of a dear friend Bob Alfandre (who we unfortunately lost a couple of years ago). We were out by the pool and I noticed Larry King looking me over. So I really wasn't shocked when a month or so later at the end of June, I ran into him downtown and he asked, "Have you started dating yet?" I responded, "No, but it's been five months now and I've begun to think about it." He asked for my number and wrote it on his *New York Times.*

About 20 minutes later, I arrived at my Council office and my staff was all in a tizzy: "Larry King just called you and asked that you call him right away." I did, and his first words were, "After I ran into you at the fundraiser, I have not been able to get you out of my mind. So it was just fate that had us bump into each other today." Since I was busy and he was going down to Atlanta for the Democratic National Convention, we made a date to meet at Paul Young's restaurant on a Saturday at 8 p.m. two weeks later.

As I was vulnerable at this stage of my life and he was who he was, I decided to be overly cautious after his effusive come-on. So I picked up the phone and called a girlfriend who had been an attractive divorcee in D.C. for years, and asked her if she had a Larry King story—and gave no reason. She said yes and remembered being at the Lincoln Memorial at night with him and he said, interestingly enough, that he had not been able to get her out of his mind. That's all I needed to hear. Although I was still vulnerable, I was not that vulnerable anymore.

I read about him a lot in the newspaper during the Convention being at this party and that party. He called and said, "I'm here at the Convention and I just can't get you out of my mind." I said, "I'd love to hear more about that this weekend when we're together, but right now I'm rushing to the tennis tournament."

The day of my date, my kids happened to be home from school and a cousin, Ross, was visiting from Cleveland. They were all excited that I was going out on my first real date, and especially because it was somebody they had heard of. That day, the phone rang and it was Larry. I thought, "Oh dear. Me and my cute short shrift to him earlier in the week is resulting now in a cancellation"—and I won't be able to relate this story. It turned out that he was just offering me a choice: our plan for dinner out OR a dinner party for 12 at Lynda Carter's ("Wonder Woman's") home to celebrate her 40th birthday. Duh ... I chose the party.

Larry picked me up and the family enjoyed meeting him. When we got to Lynda's, she was very friendly and seemed to know me from my political life. She gave me a tour of her beautiful home and then I got to greet the other guests, who included Congressman John Dingell (who I knew from my time on the Hill) and his wife Debbie, who was a successful political and government relations person and now a Congresswoman herself; as well as a society writer for the *Post*, Chuck Conconi and his wife Janelle Jones, a darling couple who later became supporters of mine. Lynda sat the couples apart at the table and later in the meal, Larry came over and said he wanted to show me the pool area. I had already seen it with Lynda, but of course didn't say so.

As soon as we got out there, he grabbed me and gave me a passionate kiss. I pushed him away—he was lucky he didn't land in the pool—and said, "This is my first real date after a very traumatic experience and I am certainly not ready for this so soon," and I walked back inside. On the way home, he handed me his private phone number and said, "When you are ready, give me a call." I never called. I read a year or so later that he met someone on the train heading to New York, proposed on the first date, quickly got married for his 7th time, and then separated less than a year later. He married for the 8th time at age 64, and then had two children with her. I wonder if he still can't get me out of his mind.

Once I decided to start dating, for the second time in my life—remember the 25-pound weight loss from ages 16 to 18—my dance card was full. I was only 44 and was fairly well known from having run for office several times. Friends would call and say that someone they knew had asked them to make an introduction so the person could take me out. I remember there were probably at least 20 people I went out with over an eight-month period. Most were just one-date things. Some were several dates like Tom Fichandler, co-founder of Arena Stage and ex-husband of Zelda.

None ever progressed intimately. They included several friends who were widowers, and new people like Fred Singer, a well-known scientist—those were my favorite dates. And friends they remained—and I really like the women they later married.

When a longtime friend Jim Smith [name change] would have a girlfriend, he would tend to fade away for a while. But he was a loyal friend to David and me in the tough times. In February of 1989, 13 months after David died, Jim came to the house to take Doug to dinner as he was the only child at home then. I hadn't seen Jim for some time and came down to say hi. I asked how his kids were doing, and he filled me in. Then I asked about the woman he had been dating for several years. He said, "Well, actually we broke up recently."

I then remember watching him walk down the pathway with Doug and thought, "This is someone I know so well, someone I have always liked and found to be smart and attractive, and now, here he is—and available." I also thought that I had all these functions to go to and maybe he could accompany me sometime. And not just that. I had been dating for a while and nothing had clicked. Jim had always been fun and comfortable as well as a rock-solid guy and one of the best people I knew. Why not? The next day, before I could make a move, he called to ask me out. That began a many-year relationship. And it was quite a good one for a while.

Post-Council Work

During the time off the Council, which started in January of 1989, I continued to devote myself to volunteer work—some old, some new. My work with the Metropolitan Police Boys and Girls Clubs spanned 25 years from 1979 until 2004. I had been the Board's Membership Chair for over a decade and brought a lot of people onto the Board, including some who went into leadership roles. Then in 1994, I became its first woman President in its then 62-year history.

I remained an active member of the Community and Friends Board of the Kennedy Center, which I had joined in 1984, brought in by my dear friend Tom Mader, who was the Executive Director. I was Chair of the Board's Education Committee for many years and worked with the then President of the Kennedy Center to grow its outreach to regional schools.

But when the education staff told us they were having a hard time getting a call-back from the Superintendents' offices around the region, I then had an idea. I suggested we have a Sunday brunch at the Kennedy Center and offer two tickets to the matinee afterwards. Because of being known from my School Board years, the invitation came from the President of the Kennedy Center and me as hosts. I also followed up with phone calls. The idea worked. We had practically every single Superintendent from the entire region there. At our brief remarks at lunch, I said, "There's no such thing as a free lunch. We need a name from you—a contact in your office—so we can start bringing your students here for free and help your teachers by giving them free training in the arts." Today, the Kennedy Center, among other things, is known for those arts education programs which have been enormously successful.

Although we were only an advisory board, the President of the Kennedy Center came to our quarterly meetings. At one of those, I brought up something that had bothered me for years. In order to purchase anything at the Center, you had to line up at one large glass case which had only a few gifts to buy in it. (It's now the area where volunteers sit to welcome people.) Obviously that system did not encourage business. I pointed out other gift shops in museums around the city and how they were large and inviting, allowing you to just browse—and also how they were big money makers for those museums. Not long after, here came the first-floor gift shop and then later, the lower-level one.

After leaving the Council, I was appointed Co-Chair of the D.C. Drug Strategy Task Force in 1989 and served for two years. Also in 1989, I was elected to the Board of the Whitman-Walker Clinic. In addition, I was asked to be on the Regional AAA (American Automobile Association) Advisory Board, as well as the Boards of the St. John's Child Development Center, which served special-needs students, and the Board of the Jewish Council for the Aging.

In 1990, I was named Vice Chair of the National Education Commission on Time and Learning, a nine-member group that was appointed by the Secretary of the Department of Education Lamar Alexander, and I served for the three years of its existence. We studied the effect of time on learning and looked at the then few examples in the U.S. of lengthened school days as well as practices in other countries such as Japan, which we visited. When the Commission ended in 1993, we delivered a cogent and well-publicized report which recommended both a longer school day and year, especially for disadvantaged children who were underachieving. (Remember, that was an issue I had promoted on my own for D.C. back in the mid-'70s.)

I was also a member of the Advisory Board of the Children's Education Foundation from 1989-92, and the Advisory Council of the National Council of Girl Scouts from 1988-90.

Later, in 1994, I was asked to go on the Board of the Hattie M. Strong Foundation by its Chair, Hank Strong. I was very flattered as it was basically a Board made up of family members with only a couple of non-family participants, including Vincent Reed and later, Togo West. The Foundation was known for its no-interest loans to college students, which they usually paid back over many years so that others could have the same opportunity, as well as for its educational grants to worthy local educational programs.

So time was consumed with all that volunteer work; and by the way, I never joined anything that I didn't truly engage in. I also wrote occasional op-ed pieces and served as an intermittent political commentator for WAMU radio.

In addition, time was spent with Johnny and my kids (with their coming here or my going to them). By then, Doug was also away at college, Cornell University, where he had been accepted into an exclusive class with astronomer and writer Carl Sagan.

I have been blessed with a lot of good friends—and I finally had some time to spend with them. And I even got a chance to play bridge once in a while. I had always enjoyed hosting parties and it was fun to do it in a less hectic way now that I had more free time.

Standing Beside My LGBT Friends

I seem to gravitate to people who are gay. I think it all began with two of my friends in high school, who I later believed were gay but who never outed themselves. Maybe on some level, I knew at the time. Lionel was one such friend. We hung out a lot in school and shared a similar sense of humor. After graduation, he rarely kept in touch, but I do know that he left Midland and became a hairdresser. Sadly, not many years later, he committed suicide. Another friend was Bill. I was fairly close with him and his twin sister. Bill was a great dancer and he made me look like I was one. In our high school years at the Friday night dances at the Youth Center, we often won the jitterbug contest. Unfortunately, in his college years, he too committed suicide.

In the subsequent decades, I have thought of Bill and Lionel and how terrible their struggles and ends were. It must have been particularly hard for them, given that time, the late 1950s and early '60s, and given the place.

I have tried to be of help to the LGBT community in various ways and in various positions for a long while without even thinking about it in those terms. When I was on the D.C. Board of Education in the 1970s, I helped get a rule passed to ban discrimination against teachers and other employees based on sexual orientation. And when I went on the Council in January of 1985, two of my four staff members were gay with many more to come, including my Chief of Staff and Deputy Committee Clerk in my last years on the Council. And I rarely missed Pride events.

In the 1980s, '90s, and 2000s, while on the Council, I supported all legislation proposed that benefited the community. I was particularly proud of the law suit we filed against the feds, who were trying to force us to allow religious schools to discriminate against gays and lesbians—a suit which we won. I also, along with my friend Carl Schmid, got the rider in the D.C. Appropriations Bill, which would have banned gay adoptions, taken away and was an active promoter and defender of our Domestic Partnership laws in all their iterations. I have copies of many letters I wrote to various Congresspersons like Senator Trent Lott in efforts to stop their attempts to prohibit our enacting those partnership laws. I also have copies of letters that I wrote to Pepco Holdings Inc. and Washington Gas on September 6, 2006, expressing my concern that they did not offer domestic partnership benefits to their employees, and urging them to do so. In 2000, I introduced a bill to prohibit harassment of all types, including on the basis of sexual orientation, to protect students in public and private schools.

When the crisis of AIDS hit in the 1980s, I increased my involvement directly with the community. These were days of such tragedy for too many, including so many dear friends. I found the inaugural display of the AIDS Quilt, which came to D.C. in October of 1987, to be therapeutic. It covered more than 100 yards on the National Mall and was a beautiful tribute to those gone. It was also a stunning effort to shatter prejudice while calling attention to this dreaded disease. Officially called the NAMES Project, it was brilliantly conceived in 1985 by Cleve Jones, an AIDS activist. Each panel memorialized a person who died. I recalled those I had lost so far, and friends who were then sick and may grow sicker. I walked alone across the mall for hours, looking at each panel, crying. (The AIDS Quilt now has 49,000 panels.)

A year and a half later, in 1989, I was proud to be elected a member of the Board of Directors of the Whitman-Walker Clinic, and was reelected many times—the one year my name was not put in for election, the Board appointed me. I served for 17 consecutive years in all (1989-2006) and was elected one year as Vice President by the Board. The Clinic started as a health center for gays and lesbians, but quickly became the center for fighting HIV and AIDS, both with prevention and treatment.

The Whitman-Walker Clinic named one of its facilities after Elizabeth Taylor, who was an outstanding benefactor and crusader against the disease starting when her dear friend Rock Hudson passed away from AIDS. I got to meet her several times and was surprised that she was so much shorter than not-tall me. (Elizabeth Taylor meant a lot to me, especially in my obsessed-with-movie-stars youth. I was fascinated with her career and life, and thought she was so beautiful with her violet eyes. I could always name her seven husbands, eight marriages [Richard Burton was twice] in order. My kids have promised to check me for dementia with one question: name Elizabeth Taylor's husbands.)

In June of 2002, I introduced the "Surname Choice Act" on the Council. Before then, the law, as interpreted by the Bureau of Vital Statistics, prevented parents from giving their child both of their surnames or the surname of either parent. That prohibition applied to all parents, but particularly impacted gays and lesbians. Once the Act I introduced passed unanimously and was enacted into law, that changed.

I sometimes worked with the Gay & Lesbian Activist Alliance (GLAA) and its leadership, which most of the years were Barrett Brick and Rick Rosendall—two strong activists who became dear friends—on these issues of importance to the community.

Due to my involvement with these causes, I have had many disagreements over the years with some religious people, even friends, who claim that homosexuality is condemned by God in the Bible. Sometimes I say, "Well, things change. Slavery appeared to be an acceptable state in the Bible. And we certainly don't accept it now." I mostly have countered with, "If God didn't want gay people, why did he create them? We are all God's children." And these children have been especially close to my heart—and long before I had a child who became one of them.

Dad and Johnny

I still had my hands full with Dad and Johnny. I visited both several times a year. I also usually brought Johnny up to Washington to spend time with me for a week or so twice annually as well. (Dad was invited but often passed.) Johnny loved coming to D.C., but the anxiety he experienced when it was time to fly home became too much. Signs of the problem started many years before. One time, the kids and I took Johnny to the airport (Dulles, as it had the only non-stop to Austin). I let them off, and went to park the car. Right away, Johnny complained of terrible stomach pangs and Stephanie called for help. When I arrived from parking, an ambulance was there to take Johnny to a hospital. Although he was fine shortly thereafter, that delayed his trip back for several days.

Johnny credited Stephanie with "saving him," but it was never very clear whether Johnny was actually sick or suffering from anxiety about flying, or separation, or both. Or was it just manipulation to extend his stay? Since it continued to occur—and only on his way home—it became obvious that it was more about separation and manipulation than flying.

Johnny's separation anxiety got worse after the deaths of Mom and David. It started reaching a breaking point. After one particularly long and stressful visit with both Dad and Johnny in D.C., I was very relieved as I saw them off at Dulles. I then drove home in the pouring rain, looking so forward to just collapsing. As soon as I reached the house, I was told by one of my children that Texas Dad, which is what the kids called my father, had just phoned. He said that the pilot turned the plane around on the runway because of Johnny's vocal anxiety, and they were at a hospital in Leesburg, Virginia. I drove there immediately, again in the pouring rain. So much for collapsing. Johnny stayed there overnight and I checked Dad and me into a nearby motel so that we could be near him.

Another time, I led Johnny to his seat in coach and then waited at the gate for the plane to take off—as I had learned to do after the Leesburg experience. I was relieved as the plane started taxiing out. Next thing, the plane is turning around on the tarmac and heading back to the gate. Apparently Johnny had started screaming, which prompted the turnaround.

And another time, the pilot was forced to turn around *after* take-off because of Johnny's screaming. It turns out that the daughter of a family friend was also on the plane, recognized Johnny, and told her family about the incident, which then made it around town pretty fast.

And yet another time, the plane took off toward Texas. But in mid-flight, Johnny began to shriek until this pilot—or maybe the same one—had to turn around and head back to Washington. Soon after, my daughter's good friend Jennie received a call from her sister who said, "You can't believe what happened on my plane.

This mentally disabled man in a cowboy hat started yelling and the plane had to turn back." Jennie, who had already heard the story from Steph, yelled, "That was Uncle Johnny!"

Poor United Airlines. I'm sure they were ready to drop their non-stop flight to Austin. I was surprised they didn't ban us. I would always say to Johnny that if he did it again, he could not come for a visit anymore. Obviously the threat was not working. So after that last experience, I showed him I meant what I said. No more visits to D.C. I began just traveling regularly to Austin and Midland. And United Airlines was able to restart non-turnaround service to Austin.

For my dad's 75th birthday, I arranged for Dad to come to D.C. to stay at the Cosmos Club, which he loved as having breakfast in its dining room and spending time in the library was a real treat for him. Johnny came in with him and stayed with us as Dad usually did. Dad's brothers Albert and Earl came in and treated us to the Prime Rib restaurant for the birthday dinner as Uncle Earl was a pal of the owner. We were so distracted with catching up with each other that we didn't notice that Johnny had ordered and drank at least 10 Cokes. He got chest palpitations and it was another rush to the hospital. Thank goodness, he was soon fine again.

Dad wrote often to me in between visits. He would mostly talk about the meals he had and how much they cost—usually less than three bucks with senior discounts including the tip, at places like Pizza Hut. Dad was always fiscally conservative, but as he got older (and actually had some wherewithal because of his savings and investments), he often became even more extreme in his frugality. In comparison, back in the old days he had actually splurged—sometimes spending as much as $5 for a meal.

At one point, Dad wanted to take Johnny out of school, just to have him as a companion. I convinced him that removing Johnny from school was not in Johnny's best interest as he had activities, friends and animals at Marbridge. And besides, Dad, because of his mercurial temperament, always made Johnny nervous.

But even in his loneliness, Dad found enjoyment traveling by car to different places, mostly old battlegrounds (mainly Civil War as he was an expert), sometimes accompanied by Johnny.

Soon after Mom died in 1986, Dad started, with Larry Griffin, then head of the English Department at Midland College, the Hilda Simmons Levitt Poetry Contest. It became an annual contest that brought a noted poet in to judge the entries, and gave monetary prizes to the 1st–4th place winners. Dad seemed to enjoy the planning as well as the spring event itself. The contest immediately became well-publicized and successful, and has been such a fitting tribute to Mom. I was proud of Dad for doing that—and he was proud of himself. I have continued it since Dad's passing, and go to Midland every other year to be part of the annual presentation in April. The Hilda Simmons Levitt Poetry Contest remains the largest poetry competition in Texas, both in its prize amounts and the number of entries. And I just learned this year that it is also the largest poetry contest in a community college in the country.

After Mom died, Dad's many letters became more effusive with words like, "Thanks for being a loyal and loving daughter." I think he appreciated my being there in every way after Mom's death. And I was glad finally to be appreciated by my father after all those years, for whatever reason.

Dark Days in D.C.

Though I had gone off the Council in January of 1989 and was just active in the community, I did keep a close eye on what was going on in D.C.—and much of it was disturbing. As the crack epidemic rocked the city, D.C. became known as the "murder capital of the country" in 1990 with 474 homicides.[100] All the while, the unemployment rate and deficits grew. And the federal government continued to investigate Mayor Marion Barry for drug use.

In 1989, a friend of Marion's, Charles Lewis, told federal authorities that he and Barry smoked crack at the downtown Washington Ramada Inn on several occasions and that they also used cocaine together in the Virgin Islands. At least one witness had corroborated that. Barry testified that he knew of no drug activity at the Ramada, so the possibility existed that he could be brought up on perjury charges as well. At a news conference Barry asserted that, "At no time did I see any drugs, use any drugs or have any knowledge of any drugs ... I fought all my life to make this society a drug-free society."[101]

Then came the infamous day of January 18, 1990, when Marion met up with a girlfriend Rasheeda Moore at the Vista Hotel. What he didn't know was that Rasheeda was now an FBI informant and that this was a sting operation. Marion was caught on tape smoking crack, and federal agents rushed into the room. The memorable words from Marion were captured on tape: "The bitch set me up."

Marion was arrested, and throughout the city, there were strong feelings on both sides about the arrest. Many were glad.

Others were resentful. I, as a private citizen at that time who knew him well, was relieved that he finally did get caught doing what we all knew he was doing and had been doing for such a long time. It was sad to see him damaging his health so severely. And with all the drug use in our city and problems in our government, including those relating to it, seeing the Mayor of D.C. smoking crack on camera, whatever the circumstances—bitch or no bitch, set-up or no set-up—was seriously damaging to our reputation.

Despite all that, Marion continued on as Mayor until January 2, 1991. He did, though, in June of 1990, declare he would not seek reelection. Instead, that year he ran for the Council as an Independent against 74-year-old incumbent Statehood Party Councilmember Hilda Mason, who was a dear friend of his for 30 years, for her at-large minority party seat. So here he was, the sitting Democratic Mayor, now registered as an Independent, running for the Council when he should have been in a drug treatment program instead. Obviously the electorate agreed—he suffered the only defeat of his career.

On January 2, 1991, Sharon Pratt Dixon (who married later and became Kelly, and is now back to Sharon Pratt) was sworn in as our first woman Mayor. A former PEPCO executive and an attorney, who had never held public office except as Democratic National Committeewoman, Sharon beat out veteran Council Chair David Clarke and Councilmembers John Ray and Charlene Drew Jarvis in the Democratic primary. She then won handily in the general election against Republican Maurice Turner, who was a former D.C. Police Chief.

In June of 1990, while he was still Mayor, Barry's criminal trial began. He was charged with three felony counts of perjury, 10 counts of drug possession, and one misdemeanor count of conspiracy to possess cocaine. Two months later, he was convicted for one possession incident and acquitted on another. The jury deadlocked on the rest. A *Washington Times* article stated, "Six or seven jurors (of whom two were white and the rest black) believed that the evidence against Barry was overwhelming and that he had displayed 'arrogance' during the trial. Against these, five African American jurors were convinced that the prosecution had falsified evidence and testimony as part of a racist conspiracy, and even disputed factual findings that had not even been contested in court. After scolding the jurors for not following his instructions, the judge declared a mistrial on the remaining charges."[102]

Marion was sentenced to six months and reported to prison in October of 1991. The news did not end there. Stories ran amuck saying such things as he had inappropriate contact with a woman in the prison's waiting room while other inmates visited with their kids and families.[103] He was released in April of 1992. That June, after moving from Ward 7 to Ward 8, he announced his candidacy for the Ward 8 Council seat which he won, beating another of his good friends, long-term incumbent Wilhelmina Rolark. In 1993, Marion married his fourth wife, a friend of many years, Cora Masters, who organized a homecoming upon his return from prison.

More dark days for D.C.: In July of 1990, Mitch Snyder, a legendary homeless advocate, who ran the Community for Creative Non-Violence (CCNV) with his girlfriend Carol Fennelly, hanged himself at the shelter. There were echoes of my own story, but unlike David who only said, "I'm sorry. I screwed up everything," Mitch unfairly left a very long letter in which he tried to pin the blame on his CCNV co-founder/partner and companion of 15 years. My heart went out to her. I remain friends with Carol, and she's continuing to do good work with an organization called Hope House, which brings prisoners and their families together.

And in 1993, my friend and Council Chair John A. Wilson also hanged himself at his house. He had been pretty open about his depression, even talking about it in speeches. In one speech, he mentioned a friend who had shot himself in his yard and I knew he was referring to my husband David. John was a brilliant legislator, but his alcohol and drug use exacerbated his well-known depression. I still miss him, but am glad that occasionally I see his lovely wife Bonnie around town. In 1994, the District Building was rightly renamed the John A. Wilson Building in his honor.

CHAPTER 24

Searching for Home

Jim and I had a good start in our relationship after he asked me out in late February of 1989. Having known each other for many years, it felt so comfortable, and since he was fond of David's and my children and they him, they seemed pleased as well. Because Doug was still at home, it seemed more appropriate for me to go to Jim's place, even though he did stay over once in a while. After Doug left for college in early September, Jim moved in with me.

During all those years before, I thought Jim was smart, attractive, fun and easygoing. And now I became very attracted to him. It was a sweet, loving relationship. Jim played the piano beautifully. He was very smart, talented and very modest—all lovely characteristics. He did nice things like always making coffee in the morning, and even brought it to me sometimes in bed. Guys or gals, that's a winner! There were some really wonderful times.

Then after we began living together for about seven or eight months, he remained smart and attractive and even sexy, but fun, not so much. And the easygoing part was taken to an extreme. He really didn't like to go out. Instead, he just wanted to stay home and read. So here I was going out alone as usual. He was very handy and had always been so helpful to David and me around the house, e.g. painting some rooms when we were putting our house on the market, always repairing something. But now years later as a couple, I had to practically beg him to change a lightbulb.

Also indicative was the following: I am superstitious. It started in childhood. I also think it's a Southern thing, which was just a part of my life. Here's one that has stuck with me to this day: When you are walking with someone and something comes between you, you both always have to say "bread and butter" or else it could be bad luck. I do not insist upon it every time it happens as I have decided that just one time per walking experience will do as a compromise. When we were friends, Jim would always accommodate this need by saying "bread and butter," often without even being asked. However, when we became a couple and were living together, Jim refused. He said it was silly and ridiculous. Maybe so, but superstitions can be real to people who grew up with them. And why did he do it before and then suddenly stop—especially since it only had to be said one time—and then have to be so stubborn about it? That was silly and ridiculous to me. And worse, it was just not caring or even nice. I would certainly have said "bread and butter" for him.

(Now 37 years later, I am aware my superstitions are some-what silly and I should get over them. But just this week, two things happened: 1) On Monday, Aleida [who helps two days a week with the house] and I were just commenting about how un-believable it was that the vacuum cleaner was still working well after 22 years. No more than five minutes later, it blew up. And why? Because we didn't knock on wood. 2) Just tonight, Friday, I accidentally put my shoes on the bed, something I never do be-cause it's bad luck. Then I said, "Carol, stop being so ridiculous." I put those shoes on and went to an event which had valet parking. Soon after, the valet guy came to find me as my car couldn't be started again, totally blocking the route where all the other cars were trying to get to the garage. Since it was not a battery problem, I spent much of the evening trying to get the car rescued, which it finally was. Moral of the story: I'm keeping my superstitions.)

Jim had been in political life for decades. When we started da-ting, Jim worked for a foundation and had been doing so for several years. But not long after he moved in, Jim found out that the foundation would be dissolved. So that spring he was going to be out of work. Even though he knew it would end six months prior, he refused to financially plan accordingly. And I knew from past patterns that he usually took some time between jobs because he would never settle for less money. (In fact, David and I had given him loans a couple of times during those periods, which he always paid back.)

In February of 1990, his foundation had a conference in San Francisco, which he needed to attend, and which was right before his job ended. I joined him there for several days. Then from there, he decided to travel on to Hawaii as it was the one state he hadn't visited, and he wanted me to come along. I really wanted to see Hawaii, but instead, I begged him not to go as I knew it would blow his little savings—and said so. I even chose not to go myself, always wanting to lead by example. He went on the trip anyway, and that really aggravated me because now I knew I would have to support him financially, at least for a while. And I did. Not a good place to be in a new live-in situation.

I started wanting to be away more. David and I had rented a condo in Rehoboth Beach, Delaware every August for several weeks since 1976. After he died, I rented a two-bedroom condo for two summers with three of my friends who didn't know each other. It was an interesting combo—me a widow, one a divorcee, one who never married, and the fourth, separated. Sharing the cost for a place a few blocks from the ocean Memorial Day through Labor Day four ways was about the same amount David and I had paid for only a few weeks, ocean-side.

I did much of my healing then and there. I've often said Rehoboth is my therapy. One of the most special things about Rehoboth is its precious downtown area with its small mostly independent shops. Of course there are some t-shirt stores and a couple of fast food places, but it's mainly lovely boutiques of all kinds and fabulous independently-owned restaurants, probably more per square foot and population than anywhere I know.

There are also a huge number of discount stores at the three Tangier Outlets on the highway, which are a huge draw. But I often tell people who live and vacation there that they should make sure they shop downtown too because if they do not, one day they will wake up and all those boutiques will be McDonald's. And then they will be sorry they didn't because they will miss those darling shops—and their property value may go down with them gone. I believe the same to be true about those who only shop online. Convenient yes, maybe a little cheaper, but why not also walk into a department or small independent store in your town or neighborhood and give it some business as well. I have a feeling if those stores end up being boarded up or become banks because you didn't walk in and buy something, you might wish you had.

In *Delaware Today* magazine in the late '80s, both Lynda Carter and I were quoted as saying Rehoboth Beach is our favorite vacation spot. So given that, the fond family memories, and the fact that the home prices were lower then, I decided to buy a house there. I also knew that it would be a good investment. And it is.

I looked during the summers of 1989 and 1990 with my agent Betty Anderson. She had become used to having to answer one of my most quirky questions: "Does the address of the house have the number three in it?" I had developed an affinity for that number after having a trio of children and then realizing that uncannily every single home I had ever lived in had a three in its street number. (Many years later, after having this three fixation for a long time, Johnny and I went to Greenville, Mississippi and drove by the hospital where we both were born. Guess what? Its address: 300 S. Washington St.)

Regardless of the street address, I had not found the right place for me after two summers of looking. Then one day in late July of 1990, my daughter Stephanie and I met at our then favorite restaurant in town, Camel's Hump (which is gone now). She had just driven in separately, parked a bit away and had forgotten to bring my parking pass. As I drove her back to her car to get it, that sidetrack took me onto a street I had never been on—and improved my life forever. (Thanks for your flakiness that day, Steph!)

Right there, on the left as we were driving back on this one-way street, I saw an adorable Cape Cod house with a new for-sale sign. Sitting on the stoop was the owner of the house, an older gentleman smoking a cigarette. I jumped out of the car and asked him when the house had gone on the market. He said, "Just a few minutes ago." I asked, "What is the price?" He told me he was told he couldn't say and I'd have to call the number on the sign. I ran to my rented condo and called Betty. I let her know a great house had just gone on the market and said, "Let's go see it right now." We did, and I put in an offer for the asking price as I knew it was the perfect house for me, that it was well-priced, and would be gone in a minute if I didn't act. Of course, he and his agent took the full offer and we signed a contract. Since I said, "Pretty mirror," as I was touring the house, right after signing, he said to me, "The mirror is yours as a new house gift." And there over the fireplace—27 years later—it remains.

I was so happy and went back to the apartment to just relish the moment. I then thought, "Oh dear! I forgot to ask the most important question: Does it have a three in the address?" I called Betty and said, "What's the address?" She said, "Let me check." She came back a minute later and said, "Carol, [pause] sit down. The street address is 33." It was meant to be.

The house was right downtown, a block and a half to Rehoboth Ave. (the main drag) and three blocks to the beach. The man on the stoop I had bought it from had worked at Quillan's Hardware Store a block away for 45 years and had actually built the house himself with a friend in 1955. Now, in 1990, 35 years later and a widower with emphysema, he was moving to Georgetown, Delaware to live with his daughter. But he never made it. A few days later, the former owner ended up in the hospital in Lewes, Delaware and died there. I went to visit him several times before he passed away and took him a shirt for his birthday. Although we only knew each other briefly, I think of him sometimes as I sit in that solid wonderful house he built looking at that pretty mirror.

Immediately after purchasing the house, I began making improvements. Because I had gotten a far better price than I had planned on spending, I had the money to do so. Since I was not working then, I decided to be my own contractor and also do the design myself. I lived in a small room upstairs, and went about hiring people to put in central air conditioning, rooms (including a bathroom) in the unfinished basement, a large enclosed back porch-type room, and an outdoor shower/dressing area.

One of the people I hired to do much of the building and carpentry work was named John. I got a landscaper to do the front and backyards including a small patio and a little fountain, and I also bought a shed for the backyard. That small backyard is mighty crowded. Within two months, all the construction was completed and a month after that, the entire place was decorated. I had such fun running around to the furniture and antique stores in the area. My goal was to have it totally done and ready for all of us to have Thanksgiving there. That was accomplished with one exception.

John did a good job but he was very difficult to work with. I don't think he had ever worked for a woman before and wanted to do things his way—and not mine. I knew exactly how I wanted the finished house to look and resented having to fight for that while paying for it. Jim mostly remained in D.C. during that time. But he did come in to help do the basement ceiling, where he had the ingenious idea to use a canvas fabric nailed up as high as could be to cover the pipes and to keep the ceiling from being too low.

Jim was very aware of the tough issues I was having in working with John—and he found him difficult as well. Although John and I had become friendly and I had even had dinner with him and his wife several times, the tension regarding my giving any directions to him remained.

One weekend Jim came for a visit. John was there working and he and I got into an argument, which Jim knew was not unusual. But Jim immediately walked in and said, "I think John is absolutely right." That's when I knew for sure that Jim was not right for me as a lifetime companion. Coupled with the ongoing financial and couch potato issues, his throwing me under the bus that day was kind of the last straw. We had a talk that night and I asked him to move out by Thanksgiving, which was about six weeks away. The family and the Myersons did celebrate the holiday in Rehoboth, and the house looked exactly then as it looks today. I was really proud. Also, Jim and I knew after those 21 months together that parting was better for both of us. And I knew then I was in the right place—literally and personally.

Although Jim moved away, we continued on and off for many years. We really loved each other, but we were just not the right fit for the long run. There again, another strong, smart and attractive man had not worked out, mainly because he was an independent, stubborn loner—which I later became. Unbeknownst to me, Jim kept track of the expenses I covered for him during the time we lived together, and dropped the money off years later at my building's front desk. Jim is a good guy, and our relationship was a very special one.

He started out as a dear friend of David's and mine many years earlier, and here we are in 2017—decades later—still good friends.

Carol's Choice

I'm not into naming houses, but I decided to name this house and you will soon see why. When Mom and Dad got a car supposedly for me to use to visit Johnny when I went off to college, Dad picked it out and I wasn't even asked to go along. When I got married, David's choice was that we get rid of my paid-for car and keep his unpaid-for one. And each car after that, David waited until I was out of town to pick out one for us and/or me. I never even got to participate, and it was my money too. And it's not like it was a one-year rental. In each case, it was a car I would keep for years.

The same was true as David generously gave me jewelry and furs over the years. I know it's hard for anyone to sympathize with me here, but it would have been nice to go to the store and try on earrings or coats to get the most flattering, or just go for the fun of it as I too, like him, grew up with no money so buying expensive purchases would have been a treat for me as well. I suggested that maybe occasionally I could go with him to share in the adventure, but it didn't happen. So I just shut up and was grateful to get what I got, which was usually nice, even if I got no choice in it.

Sometimes I did wonder, though, was this about love and generosity or more about showmanship and control? During my first election for the Council, David showed up at the office with a red Plymouth convertible for all to see, which became my car until it wasn't. Then I went to Rehoboth for a girls' weekend in 1986 with my friend Joy Safer on our own. When we returned that Sunday, there sat a red 1986 Chrysler LeBaron convertible from a Maryland dealership. David said in front of Joy that he had made no commitment to buy it.

After Joy left, I said, "If that's the car you now want me to have, at least let's buy it from the Chrysler dealership in Anacostia, especially since you said you made no commitment, and since I am a Councilmember in Washington and like to promote D.C. businesses." Then he started his usual pouting: "But this is what I picked out for you." I said, "Okay, we'll order the same exact car from the D.C. dealership." He continued pouting. I was furious, but as usual gave in. I did take the car out to Wheaton to have the Maryland emblem taken off. Again, no choice. Same was true of our house on Springland Lane.

Thinking back now, how happy would David have been if I just went out with no discussion beforehand, traded in his car and picked out a new one, and then got upset if he even dared to mention that he would like to look himself, join me in the search, or at least pick, if he was on the Council, the politically correct dealership? I don't think he would have been very happy or considered himself very fortunate for my generosity at that moment. In fact, he would gone friggin' ballistic! I didn't go ballistic then, but obviously I am now. I know I shouldn't sound off all these years later. I should just move on, and I pretty much have. But writing a book does cause you to relive your life. It is also supposed to be therapeutic—and discussing this with you here has certainly helped.

All this is a roundabout way of saying that this Rehoboth house in 1990 became my first materialistic choice of any real expense. So I named it "Carol's Choice."

Trips with Kids

In order to keep us busy—and not at home—I planned new experiences with the kids out of town. For Doug's high school graduation in 1989, I took my three children to Santa Fe, New Mexico—their first time, my second—for a week. It was, and remains, one of my favorite places. Then over the holidays in 1990, off we went on a Caribbean cruise—a first for each of us. We had a great time, especially dancing to "Feeling Hot Hot Hot," which played constantly on the deck. After the shows, we would dance to a band or DJ, and I taught the kids to jitterbug. We ended up sort of "adopting" another passenger in his 30s. He was there with his wife and in-laws, but every time we turned around, he was nearby wanting to talk to us—and not in a flirtatious way. It turned out that he and his wife were in the throes of a divorce, but the in-laws did not know and the trip had already been booked. (Interestingly, he was a diamond dealer and put together trips to Asia for dealers. I guess in appreciation of our "adoption," a couple of years later, he invited me to join them in going to Hong Kong and Thailand [Bangkok and Peugeot] at a low cost to me.)

During that Caribbean cruise, we stopped at one of the islands where I had heard about a recent insurrection. In making conversation with the local jeep driver, I asked about the "resurrection" in my quintessential flub-up-the-word fashion. My kids never let me forget about that one either.

I took another fun trip when Doug did a junior semester abroad in Seville, Spain in the spring of 1992 and stayed in this wonderful little apartment with his host family, who spoke only Spanish. In my elementary way of putting together a few words I learned in high school, the family and I were able to communicate some—and we hugged a lot. Doug, on the other hand, who had taken a couple of courses, was totally fluent, to the degree that most Spaniards thought he was one of them.

When I got there, Doug was sick, but he generously made sure his friends were available to take me out to the festivities of Carnival, their Mardi Gras. I had such a nice evening with them. Thank goodness he did get well in time for the World Expo that opened in Seville that spring. We spent several days there at the various countries' exhibits.

As we were leaving the Japanese pavilion, a man with a camera walked up to us and asked if he could take our picture. We said sure, and he gave us a form to sign. Months later, a friend from D.C. called to say how thrilled they were to see a big picture of me and Doug in a full-page ad for a camera company in the international edition of *Time Magazine*. Another friend sent me the ad. It's a cute picture, and we were pleased to be picked. But we're still waiting for the check—in spite of those damn signatures!

Then in December of 1992, I took the children to Israel for 10 days—their first time, my third. The first thing we did was plant a tree in memory of David. Then we toured all over the country. When we went to Masada, it was a very windy day and the tram ride up was really scary. Little did we know that they would soon thereafter close the tram for the day and that we would have to walk down that big mountain.

I am scared to death of heights—which I think I've mentioned a time or two—so I scooted down most of it on my rear end. I had just said to the kids as I was holding up other walkers and was so embarrassed, "At least no one here knows who I am." At that very moment, Rabbi Bruce Lustig from Washington Hebrew Congregation, who was walking up the mountain with a large group of students, said, "There's Carol Schwartz from our temple and she used to be a D.C. Councilmember." From my seat on the ground,

I waved. By the way, not long ago, I ran into Bruce at the temple as he was in the midst of telling someone that 25-year-old story.

It is hard to say, after the devastating loss of David, that some good things happened. But they did. The kids finally got the help they probably needed anyway, and we became closer as a family. We felt that we were there for each other more—and we were. At one point, I had a growth removed from my shoulder and my son Doug lovingly nursed me as I recovered. The fact that I was drugged and too out of it to talk may have helped with the "lovingly" part. Later, that poor baby was traveling in Europe and got a hernia, and kept on traveling anyway. But upon his return to D.C., I got to reciprocate a little during his post-surgery recovery.

Steph Takes Off

Stephanie graduated from Wisconsin in the winter of 1990, and soon came back to Washington with her friend Gwen for a visit before moving out to Seattle. Gwen was trying to figure out her sexuality at the time, or at least that's what she told me. In case she wanted to date men, I decided she needed a bit of a makeover. I took her shopping and tried to put her in a skirt. The best she would agree to was a long skirt and boots, even though I recognize from experience that long skirts don't bring the boys a-running.

Steph had primarily been with men, but she had told me about an experience with a woman in college. I remember watching Stephanie and Gwen driving away down Springland Lane to begin their journey across country. I thought at the time that they might become a couple (and I liked Gwen a lot), and another new chapter would begin. Not long after, I visited Steph in Seattle. Gwen had a cute girlfriend—and Steph was with a cute guy, who she ended up being with for three years.

They had met working in a group home run by United Cerebral Palsy. Both of them took care of those adults in every way—changing their diapers and spending an hour or so feeding each one—and became supervisors. Steph did a lot of heavy lifting, literally, which unfortunately likely contributed to her back issues. She also advocated for those individuals who lived in the home by trying to get the services they needed. I was so proud of her for doing that kind of work, which I call "God's work." Steph became so impassioned about her patients' well-being that it drove her to law school to study public interest law. And she has spent her legal career with that concentration.

Personal Life: Still Trying ...

In the spring of 1991, I was browsing on Rehoboth Ave., and walked into a store with lovely antiques. The owner was there. He was a bald guy around my age, nice looking. But I didn't notice that then. I was only paying attention to the bronze artifacts and the pretty paintings. He came over, said his name was Robert [name change], and started talking to me: "Do you live in Rehoboth?" "In D.C., but vacation here." He started flirting with me and asked me for my phone number. I said, "I have to think before giving it," and left.

I thought he was interesting, but rarely gave out my phone number, especially to someone I didn't know. So I asked a couple of store owners I was friendly with down the street about him. They said that they liked him. So I went back and gave him my number. That very day, he called, asked me out, and started pursuing me. We had a fun summer/early fall romance. Robert was a Syrian Jew from an Orthodox family who lived in Deal, New Jersey. We spent a weekend there. He actually lived in Ft. Lauderdale on the intercoastal. I went down in early September for about four weeks. My father even called me at the time and said, "When are you going home?" I didn't know. I was having such a good time.

Robert was a man who liked to spoil people—me, his son, his mother. He had an ex-wife who came over to his place in Ft. Lauderdale probably every other day. She was very dependent on him and he spoiled her as well.

I did enjoy the exposure to his life—religious and otherwise—for the most part. Robert was really smart and appealing. Unfortunately, he was also a gambler (and did well gambling on football), owned a store that was always "going out of business" but which always reopened the next year, and was a big marijuana smoker—things I did not like so I knew he was not the one for me. And besides, I was too much of an independent career woman who wanted to live in D.C. But it was interesting while it lasted.

Not long after we broke up, he met a lady on the Internet, who is very nice and they have been together since. We check in with each other every few years.

Then after that, around 1992, I went out some with a guy named Frank. It never got serious but I would see him every so often. We had served together on a board. He was a born-again Southern Baptist from a small town in Georgia who taught Sunday school. He was very tall and attractive, and had a great combination of being a good ole Southern boy and a real intelligent, successful businessman. And I liked that Frank was a take-charge kind of person. He was also a good dancer, and several friends who met him were impressed. One of our most fun times was going to Daytona for the auto race. It was my first opportunity to see such a race. I'm still dizzy from watching those cars speed around.

I went out over the years with two men who were older and had been separated from their wives for a long time, even decades, and outwardly dated others. One was Frank. Another was Mike, a doctor who lived in Maryland and who I met in 2002 through a person I met on a plane. On one of our few dates, when we were talking about our outside social life, he whipped out a provocative—but at least she was dressed—picture of a gal who looked like she could be my—or his—granddaughter. That took care of Mike.

All these openly separated-for-years men seemed to maintain good relationships with their kids and cordial ones with their virtually exes. They were usually wealthy and I guess that played into these arrangements as money can make things more complicated. But I did find it awkward going out with guys who were still legally married, although separated. But since I really never wanted to marry again, it should have been perfect, though it wasn't.

Snowbirding

I had often visited Florida when Ma was alive. I had earlier experiences there visiting my paternal grandparents in Miami Beach, where they spent their last years. After Ma and David died, I started renting out Ma's place in Florida during the winter season. It was small and not glamorous but I made enough to help with its costs. I did that for about four years and then realized how stupid it was. Here I was in D.C. in January and February—not working except for my volunteer activities—and very cold. So the winter of 1992, I decided not to rent the place out, but use it myself. I drove 14 hours to get there, stopping in Charleston, South Carolina the first year and the next in Savannah, Georgia to see both for the first time and to break up a long trip, longer when you're alone. They were the beginning of my journeys to Florida in the winter—for one and a half to two and a half months—and obviously when I'm not working.

Ma had a lot of friends who I had become friendly with over the years and they took up a lot of my time. No complaints as I enjoyed them immensely: Miriam Jacobs, Bert Keller and Sonia

Gold especially, and Charlotte Garland, who I met on my own. I am only complaining now that I lost them all years ago and still miss their company when I'm in Florida—as I do my mother-in-law. But thank goodness I have many new friends, as well as D.C. friends who are there when I am.

What I don't miss are people like this guy I'm about to describe. One time when I was down in West Palm Beach, I was meeting a male friend from Miami at a restaurant halfway in between, near the turnpike in Boca Raton. I arrived a little early and was sitting at the bar waiting. A nice looking blonde man, younger than I but not too young, sat down next to me and started chit-chatting. It turned out he was a cousin of one of the D.C. football team's major players and said he went to Washington often. He also said, when asked, that he had been separated from his wife for a while and had several young children. He wanted my phone number for his next trip to D.C. I gave it to him and got his card. He called soon thereafter and we made a date.

A few days before the big day, I decided to trust my "not-born-yesterday" instinct. And rather than call the office number on the card, I called information and asked for his home number in the small town where he lived. (It was helpful that he had an unusual name). I called the number and not surprising to me, a woman answered. I asked for Mr. Blah-blah, and she said, "He's not here." I said, "Are you Mrs. 'Blah-blah,'" and she said, "Yes, and you can find my husband at his office," and gave me his number. I immediately called Mr. Blah-blah, and he came right on the phone and said he was so looking forward to our date in a few days. And I said, "I just talked to your wife. We had such a nice conversation. And I have no intention of meeting a married man for a date in a few days or any day. Goodbye." I so enjoyed thinking about him walking in the house that evening, anticipating what I had said to his wife. Hopefully, he learned a lesson—but doubtfully!

Personal Boycotts

I tend to boycott movies or TV shows which idolize or even attempt to humanize villains. An example is *The Sopranos*, which I know was one of the most watched and awarded TV series in history. I watched it once and when I saw that these murderers were also husbands and fathers who I was supposed to care about, I couldn't—and wouldn't even if I could

Similarly, but certainly not in the same category, I refuse to watch *The Real Housewives* ... of anything. I do not like shows that depict women as just catty, gossipy, unnatural looking, ostentatious people. I know there are a few like that, but in my mind, those are not the real housewives. Even though I am not above junky shows—for example, I like *The Bachelorette*—those others, though, are just beyond the pale and demean women, even if that's not their intention. (But speaking of *The Bachelorette*, why do all these attractive brunette women—and men—have to become fair-haired during the course of the show?! Can anyone answer that for me please? At least they didn't do that with Rachel.)

In the early '90s, as I was driving those 14 hours to West Palm Beach, one of my favorite things that I *really* looked forward to was eating at a very special place—Cracker Barrel. (And in those days, you could not find them up North.) Being a Southerner, I could hardly wait to have either the chicken and dumplings dinner or the turkey and dressing one with my favorite sides, collard greens and fried okra or fried apples.

And then I heard about Cracker Barrel not hiring gay people. My personal boycott began. It was so hard to drive by the many Cracker Barrels that are along I-95 in the South and not allow myself to stop, especially if I was hungry. I did *not*, but I had to argue with myself: "No one knows you're doing the boycott, so it doesn't matter if you stop." Another argument: "They only charge $6.95 for the meal, including two sides. So it's not like you're keeping them in business." The last: "No one will see you way down here anyhow." But I could not talk myself out of the boycott. Boy was I glad when I heard their hiring practices had changed. I celebrated with the chicken fried steak dinner with three sides for $8.95 that first time back.

Boycotts continued. Denny's got my same treatment for their discrimination against African Americans, but it was, honestly, less of a sacrifice. Mel Gibson has become a perennial boycott. I used to think he was a cute, decent actor until his blatant and numerous anti-Semitic remarks. I then decided to not only never buy a ticket to one of his movies, but to not even watch one for free on television. Just a warning! And I had not even slipped up once until just this weekend when I saw the movie he directed was on for free. It was good, so I am willing to reform—but only if *he* is.

CHAPTER 25

Goodbye to my Formidable Father

Although Dad was still very handsome and energetic, he had a lot of health issues. He had a hole in his heart or some sort of heart murmur since he was a child. (I know no more details as that's all he ever said.) On top of that, he had really bad hay fever. He could barely breathe and always had to breathe through his mouth. I think that's another reason why he was in such a foul mood all the time. Then he had a lot of circulation problems with very little feeling in his feet and legs—probably because of the bad heart and likely a diabetes condition on top of it, even though all were untreated. He refused to go to the doctor or take any medications. He ate constantly and rapidly, and certainly not healthily. He would eat steak for breakfast and drink cream from the container. I understand he had those eating habits since he was a child, but remained slim then. As he got older, he developed a barrel chest, which I'm sure added to the heart problems.

The numbness in his legs kept getting worse and made it harder for him to walk, and certainly climb stairs. He lived in a rented apartment with metal stairs going up to his bedroom on the second floor. Several years after Mom died, he started staying at a motel where he could avoid those stairs. He could also park right outside his room. The motel had a restaurant where he could eat his meals and not have to shop or cook. Some might ask, "Why did he keep the apartment?" Answer: 1) He didn't want to have to go through his stuff there, and 2) he could now afford to do both.

I then started going to Texas pretty often as he didn't feel well enough to come up. I'd stay at the apartment—the #3 answer above—and visit him at the motel. He even talked of going into a nursing facility, which I thought he'd never do, and we did look at one place. Instead, he decided to move into the Midland Hilton downtown at the end of 1993. There, he could order room service for his meals. It was interesting to see my very fiscally conservative father at the end say basically, "To hell with what it costs. I'm just going to be comfortable." I agree that is exactly how he should have felt. He also started watching TV, which I really resented because I never got to have one in Midland, and felt even more sorry for my mother, who would have loved it. Big ol' hypocrite!

Even though he never left the room at the Hilton except for the hospital, his second-floor room at that point looked across the street at City Hall, so at least he had a view of some outside activity other than the caregivers he would call in. One of these was a social worker named Lettie England. On her first day there, she asked Dad if he was Carol Levitt's father. We had gone to junior high school together and had not seen each other for decades. We reconnected when I visited and have remained dear friends since. In fact, I was just with her in Midland recently. Lettie was enormously helpful to Dad during that difficult time.

His health just kept getting worse. He developed congestive heart failure and time after time, he would be rushed to the hospital where they would restart his heart and get him on medication, which would work until it didn't work, which was usually the next week or so. Each time he ended up in the hospital, he would call me and S.W. Other visitors were Vernon and Shirley Gilbert, who owned the security company he and Mom used for the house and store, and who had become friends over the years.

Vernon and Shirley were born-again Christians and every time they went to see Dad in the hospital, they would browbeat him to accept Jesus as his savior. He told them, "I'm not going to do that. Now just leave me alone." But they would not leave him alone. When I was there, I tried to get them to back off and said, "Dad is a good person. He'll be fine in the afterlife." But nothing would stop their pressuring him to convert.

I had watched similar experiences before. My grandma in Greenville had worked selling notions (merchandise like pens and calendars) for a company that was owned by born-again Christians. The owner, P.T. Johnson, had asked Grandma to work for him as she had been kind to his mother. P.T. and his wife Mary also badgered Grandma to convert, which she always refused to do. Then when she got very sick with Alzheimer's, she was cared for in her home around the clock by the Ford family—a mother, daughter and a sister-in-law. They also tried to get my grandma to do the same. I don't know for sure what happened, but she probably did due to her senile state. Regardless, I know that good soul is in a good place.

I believe the Johnsons, Fords and Gilberts were well-meaning. They genuinely believe that people who do not go along with their beliefs will go to hell. But I wish people like them would realize that other people are entitled to their own beliefs or lack thereof.

Nothing Dad or I said was getting the Gilberts off his back. Knowing Frank, the guy I was seeing at the time, was an avid born-again as well, I called him from a pay phone at the hospital. I said, "These people are driving Dad insane about converting. What can I do?" Frank said simply, "Just tell them [such and such] Romans chapter and verse." (I found out later that it refers to Jews being the "chosen people" and therefore being exempt.) Frank even said, "If they have questions or don't agree, have them call me to discuss it. Tell them to call collect." So I told Vernon and Shirley the chapter and verse and gave them Frank's number. They said they thought they knew it, but would go read it to be sure. They came back the next day and announced, "He's absolutely right." And they never bothered Dad on that subject again.

Practically every time Dad would go to the hospital, I would fly down. Each time it seemed like he was going to die. He would just be lying there with his eyes closed and with labored breathing. One time the doctor told me, "It should be any minute now. There's nothing we can do." I sat there alone, crying. Though Dad had always been so harsh (and I was still scared of him even then at age 50), the thought of losing my one remaining parent was heartbreaking. Suddenly, he bolted up from the bed and said, "Carol." He was back from near death. This time was the most dramatic, but he came back from the brink multiple times more.

Because he had so many of those instances of rushing to the hospital where they would restart his heart, he made a decision. He said, "I am not going to live like this anymore. I'm sick of dying and being revived." He brought in hospice care to his room at the hotel. He made Lettie as well as the hospice care workers sign a document promising not to try to have him revived anymore. And he made me promise the same.

I then moved into the Hilton and took the room next door to him for weeks. I sent for the kids. And I broke my promise. I could not stand to see him unable to breathe. So I called the ambulance. He told me that I would have to leave if I did not obey his orders.

When Doug and Hil arrived at the hotel, they saw their grandfather, aka "Texas Dad," strapped on a stretcher as they were bringing him out of the ambulance for the last time. He looked so weak and gaunt, but managed to firmly say, "What in the hell are you doing here?" That was my dad! Steph arrived soon thereafter.

The kids stayed at the hotel as well. We sat in Dad's room with him for days. Dad was uncomfortable. His skin itched so badly he would often rub a bathtub scrubber against his back and we would assist. Doug helped him bathe and go to the bathroom. We made sure he drank Ensure. Nurses came each day to check on him.

Our longtime friend Ed came down. My father always liked him so his presence helped boost Dad a bit. He even laughed a few times. But it was the calm before the end.

The next day, Dad was sitting, wrapped in a towel that was falling away. I held him and said it was okay. The kids sat there and hugged him as well. I said things to try make him feel better like, "You've been a good father. You've been great with Johnny. You've done a good job." Although I knew all wasn't true (except the Johnny part), sometimes you just do what you need to do and this was one of those times—just like things I would say to him to be comforting after Mom died.

A day or so later, the children had gone to the airport to take Hilary as she had to get back to work in New York. Since sometimes Dad would appear near death and other times better, I told her it was okay to leave.

Soon thereafter, Dad was sitting on a wing chair next to the window. I was leaning down, wiping his weeping legs. There was a sticky substance that was continually oozing out and which made him feel even more uncomfortable, so I often wiped his legs with a warm, damp towel. Dad's eyes were closed. He had his head to one side like he was dozing. Then all of a sudden, he bolted right up off the chair. It was like an electric shock had gone through him. For a moment he was suspended in the air. His face was right at my shoulder. His beautiful blue eyes were wide open and appeared to be staring at a light, just like people describe. It was unbelievable. It was semi-frightening, but it was also consoling in that I had never seen him look so calm. I had known him 50 years and it was the first time I had ever witnessed him look that peaceful, ever. Then he fell back onto the chair, and he was gone.

Ed was lying down on the bed in the room napping. I woke him and said, "I think Dad is gone." Ed went over, felt his pulse, and said, "He is." There was my father, the man who was so powerful and full of rage—the man I was so frightened of all my life—now sitting there with no obvious pain, power or rage.

We immediately called for an ambulance and I contacted the airport to page the kids. However, Hilary's plane had already left, and Steph and Doug were in route to the hotel. Hilary flew back to Midland the next morning.

I had immediate feelings of being an orphan. When Mom died seven and a half years earlier, I was inconsolable. Now losing my last parent, I had not only the feeling of aloneness but also the awareness of my own mortality. When you have parents, there seems to a buffer. Without them, you know it's you on deck.

The next day, we sat down at a fast food restaurant and started planning the funeral ourselves. I thought of the songs Dad would like to have played: "My Way" (Frank Sinatra), "Wabash Cannon-ball" (Roy Acuff), "Blue Eyes Crying in the Rain" (Willie Nelson), "I'm So Lonesome I Could Cry" (Hank Williams). By that point, we were becoming good at planning funerals. We assigned each of us topics to write about: his and Mom's relationship, his brilliance, his independence.

We flew Johnny in from school. When I met him at the airport, I sat him down and told him about Dad passing away. He knew he had been very sick so he was not too surprised. Of course Johnny was very sad, and talked often of what a good guy his dad was. And he was good to Johnny. But he didn't fall apart like he did when our mom died, nor did I.

At the service, the kids read their parts and then went back to the tech booth to cue the songs. They ran the whole thing and had planned it to a T. Doug basically MC'd. Hilary broke down during her part. It was quite emotional but all the while they had to carry on with what turned out to be a well-attended funeral. An acquaintance of my mother's from AAUW attended. She cried, and told my children, "I'm not surprised you outstanding kids are Hilda Levitt's grandchildren." It was good to know some people appreciated that my mother was as special as she was.

Then there was a lighter moment. After Stephanie spoke, she ran back to the booth to cue up a song, "Wabash Cannonball," as planned. When Doug mentioned the title, she was supposed to hit play. Instead of doing of so—because of her sometimes wicked sense of humor—she just let Doug stand there waiting. Doug looked back to her in the booth and she was just laughing. Again he said, "Wabash Cannonball," and she still made him wait. Finally, she did hit play.

Even with that, it was a beautiful and moving service that was a little out of the ordinary, just like Dad. I think that even he would have liked it, of course with some criticisms.

I'll never forget how Aunt Betty and Uncle Seymour came running in from Denver to help me, the kids and Ed with the daunting task of going through Dad's crowded apartment as well as through the house I grew up in, which had been used for decades as solely a storage space. There were Levi's and Wrangler's piled up nearly to the ceiling from the old store—much of which we gave to the Gilberts' charity.

The kids were so helpful during this whole time: being there for my dad—and me—those last days and afterwards, and putting that wonderful service together. Then they worked for days at the house, breathing in soot, going through that clothing as well as store receipts my parents had saved from the 1940s, along with old letters and photographs. It was a grueling job and they never complained. God bless them.

The rest of us concentrated on the crowded apartment. I would check in on the kids at the old house, and once found them all crying. I said, "What's going on?" Doug said, with tears in his eyes, "Mom, we were just talking about how you have not had an easy life." And I responded: "Yes, and you know what the worst part is? I've gone through the whole thing fucking sober." They then started laughing, which helped ease the gloom.

Despite the apartment and house packed to the rafters, Dad left things very organized: a trust for Johnny and his financial matters intact. My parents, who were able to get a loan decades ago after a failing business because they paid all their bills on time, were nothing if not responsible.

We took Dad to Greenville to be buried next to Mom and her family as Dad had wished. Aunt Betty and Uncle Joe and their kids from Baton Rouge came in for the burial. Dad was laid near the headstone that said Simmons as Mom had been over seven years earlier. A couple of years later, I had a separate Levitt headstone made, which matched the Simmons one. I also replaced and paid for all the various unmatched footstones with matching ones—of course, after getting the permission of my uncles and aunts first.

Rebecca Watson, a professor who was appointed the Hilda Simmons Levitt Poetry Contest liaison (after Larry Griffin went overseas to teach), painted a detailed portrait of my father in the Midland College literary magazine. She said she hadn't anticipated the barrage of calls from him, inquiring about every aspect of the contest. Soon she realized the calls would delve into other topics, like "the moral decay of the United States, or the solar system." She spoke of my Dad's incredible mind and how he was able to recall every price for each stock he had purchased and would delve into details about musicians and literary figures.

As Rebecca so perfectly recounted, as soon as you were sucked into that mind, he would hit you with something truly unexpected like, "The Great Depression never happened." (My take: Of course he thought so as he went off to MIT with a car during those years.)

Rebecca continued: "To receive a call from Stanley was to be drawn into another, fascinating world." Rebecca, in her piece, also recalled how when she messed up at a presentation, Dad was consoling telling her, "Everything was just the way it was supposed to be."[104] (I sure wish that I had seen that consoling side of him in the 50 years he was in my life. In fact, he was often the reason I needed consoling.) But I was glad she received it—and did appreciate her appreciation of him.

Rebecca did capture him. With my dad, you were bounced around from brilliance to craziness to meanness to sweetness. My father: formidable, charismatic, surprising, but unfortunately most of all, frightening.

It's interesting because as much as I feared my father and more adored my mother, I find that the memory of Dad sticks with me more. His presence was so vivid and undeniable. And because of him—and not wanting to be like him—I became the person I am. So in many ways, he defined me.

After Dad died in 1994, I let Johnny come to D.C. on a trial run. He boarded the plane back and it went all the way to Austin without incident. Following through on my threats for those years in between did the trick as I hoped it would. He continued to travel back and forth a lot after that.

An Interesting Plane Ride

Right after Dad died and we had cleaned out the apartment and house, Ed and I drove Dad's car back to D.C. and made sure everything was put into a storage space, including the shipped furniture, letters, pictures, etc. (I so appreciated Ed's huge help during that dreadful time.) By then, I was worn out physically and emotionally. So I headed to West Palm Beach for a respite.

I had my ticket, but there was a huge line at the airport to check in. The weather had been terrible and there were many stranded passengers. When I finally got to the counter, I learned that there was no room on the plane as they had overbooked. I was so tired and sad and ready to get away from the cold weather that I just started crying. The woman said, "I'm so sorry, it's our fault. We have a plane going out tomorrow morning and only one first-class seat left, so I'm going to bump you up from coach and give it to you." It made me feel better, and I thanked her profusely.

Late the next morning, I got on the plane and there was a middle-aged African American man sitting next to me. I said, just being my usual outgoing self, "Hi, how are you?" I could quickly tell that the gentleman did not want to talk, so I read my book.

A little while later, the flight attendant told us about the three different meal offerings. They were chicken, beef and shrimp. They sounded delicious. I really wanted all of them, but of course

I had to order just one. I chose chicken. And then she asked the man next to me what he wanted, and he said, "Just a drink." I jumped in, "Oh, you're not having your lunch? Would you mind ordering the shrimp or beef for me?" This way I could at least have two of the three I wanted. (I looked for a third passenger—just kidding.) I think my seatmate was astounded at my audacity in asking, but he complied. And then *he* started talking to *me*.

We made some small talk at first but we ended up having a serious discussion about Black-Jewish relations. I had been involved in many such discussions at Howard University and other forums. I reiterated the concern I had raised at those forums, which usually revolved around, "What can Jews do to improve relations?" I told him that I felt Jewish people were always being pressed to hold up their end in defending fellow minorities. But when a Louis Farrakhan calls Jews satanic or worse, most in the African American community remain totally silent with very few exceptions.

So I told my African American seatmate, who I didn't know from Adam, that I will not get involved in these public discussions any more until there is some evenness in help and protection, and not just one group aiding the other. He just looked at me like, "I can't believe you're saying all this." But we kept talking away.

At the end of the trip, he said, "I want to tell you, I've been traveling most of my life because of my career. But this has been the most interesting plane ride I've ever had in that long life of travel. I've just loved talking to you." And I said, "Well, thank you very much. By the way, my name is Carol Schwartz." Then he said, "I'm Hank Aaron." And I screamed, "THE Hank Aaron?" "Yes." We exchanged cards.

Our plane ride occurred on a Saturday. Over the weekend in Florida, I got really sick. Hank called me on Monday and asked me to have lunch with him. But unfortunately I was too sick to go; in fact, I went to the doctor instead. So ended my brush with a legend. But obviously, it was a memorable one.

Keeping Busy

In addition to my many volunteer activities, I also got involved with the Program Committee at the Cosmos Club where I and others solicited speakers and then introduced them.

One day, Nancy Schlossberg, also a member of the Committee, and I started talking about the Club's programs, which always had a format of a speaker with Q&A at the end. It was so obvious that the intelligent members were dying to speak themselves as they had both experience and strong views. Whenever one would ask a question they would give a long preamble, and that included ourselves. We realized there should be an outlet so members can air their own opinions—and not just in the form of a question.

Out of that came our idea for the Month in Review, a monthly discussion on various topical issues in the news. When we presented the idea, the Program Committee bought into it right away. Nancy and I were put in charge, and we got members of the Club who were journalists/commentators to do an overview, and then the discussion would open up to all in attendance. Nancy and I took turns moderating for the first six months or so. Decades later, the Month in Review is still one of the most popular programs, and is now in a bigger room due to demand. Several years ago, Nancy and I were honored by the Committee at the Club for its creation.

I continued to spend a lot of time with Johnny in D.C. or Austin, as well as taking him back to Midland where we hung out with S.W. and his wife Aquilla, Gary Thurman, Lettie England, Larry Griffin, Gwen Burns, the Gilberts, Jean and Buzz Banks (sadly Jean died in August of 2017), and Kathleen and Richard Brewer before they moved. We visited friends and relatives elsewhere, such as Denver and San Antonio. In addition, I took the time to visit my kids more as they were now living away. They were always a source of interest and entertainment in my life.

One story that springs to mind revolves around my son. Doug always enjoyed calling me up and putting on an accent to fool me into thinking it wasn't him—and was so damn good at it. He would ask, "Is Carol Schwartz home?" I'd say, "This is she." (Since I always had a listed number, I was used to strangers calling me up at home to ask about city issues.) Inevitably, I would be fooled into a full conversation until finally Doug would say, "Mom, it's me."

A while after my dad died, I got a call from someone with a very thick Southern accent. He said in that heavy drawl, "Is this Ms. Swaartz?" I wasn't going to be fooled this time. "Hi, Doug." The caller was a bit confused but pressed on, "Ms. Swaartz, I want to talk to you about your father's gravestone" (which Doug knew about). I said, "Okay, Doug. I got it!" This went on for a minute or two until he said, "Ms. Swaartz, maybe this isn't the best time for you," and hung up. Now *I* was confused. I called Doug and asked if he had just telephoned. "No." I then realized it really was the tombstone guy in Greenville, Mississippi. I called back and apologized profusely. Even though I found it hard to explain, I tried.

Interesting Outings

Although friends usually did not fix me up, a couple I like a lot got back from a trip and called me to say they met this fabulous man who was staying at their same very nice hotel. They said that he was single, Jewish, a theater director who looked a lot like my late husband, and that he was going to be in D.C. directing a play soon. They said they had given him my number so wanted me to know to expect that call. Sure enough, a week or so later, he did call and we made plans to meet at a Lebanese restaurant.

When I walked in, he was there. Wow. He did look like David, but taller and even handsomer. He was also charming, a great conversationalist, and some of his best friends were big celebrities I was a fan of. What a great date, and as we were saying goodnight, he asked me out again, but I was leaving for Florida the next day for a long weekend. He called as planned after my return. I recognized his voice right away but what he had to say on the phone was nothing like the conversation we had at dinner. It was actually obscene. I thought at first he was joking—though I didn't find it funny. He kept on and I then just hung up. He called back several times and I hung up again until I stopped answering. I'm still grateful that those dear friends tried.

Then I attended friends' daughter's wedding many years ago. They sat me next to a pal of theirs for many years who lived in New York. He is an appealing African American sculptor—and a great dancer. We did not sit down the entire evening. After that, we would call once in a while and hang out in either New York or D.C. We went together to one of his art openings, which was really fun. He was very interesting and good company, but no real romance. Recently he got married, but we still stay in touch now and then as we did become friends.

At various times over the years, I have also gone out with an interesting former elected representative of a major federal union, who was always a valued political supporter—and continues to be such a dear and special friend.

CHAPTER 26

1994 Mayoral Race: Setting the Stage

During this time, I had a good amount of creative and activist outlets, but I needed more challenges and I missed my first love—serving the city as a whole as I had been able to do both on the Board of Education and the Council. The year was 1994. It was a couple of months after Dad died. But, unfortunately for D.C., Marion Barry was again running for Mayor. And though there was strong opposition, my instinct told me that he'd win the Democratic primary that September as the oppositions' votes would be split. I'd taken him on before. I was prepared to take him on again.

Some background: In April of 1992, Marion Barry was released from prison. That same year he successfully ran against Wilhelmina Rolark for the Ward 8 Council seat with the very Marion slogan: "I May Not Be Perfect, But I'm Perfect for D.C." I'm not sure he was "perfect" for D.C., but he was the perfect candidate—so savvy (moving to Ward 8 where he was always popular and picking that clever slogan), so charismatic, and so personable.

In the 1994 Democratic primary, he faced a beleaguered incumbent Mayor, Sharon Pratt Kelly, as well as Councilmember John Ray (a strong candidate in a group which included a few other lesser known candidates). I knew that Barry would be the victor with Kelly and Ray splitting the opposition vote.

And I knew exactly how he would run his campaign: with demagoguery, rewriting history, and promising everyone jobs. We had been here before—for 12 years—and I felt we deserved more, especially when the most basic services and the finances of the city were still suffering so dramatically.

People would call me daily to ask me to run for Mayor. Even though I had been gone from elected political office for nearly six years, I got stopped on the street by strangers begging me to consider it. There was a growing sense of urgency, not only in my own mind but in others. I then decided this time to run *for* Mayor—and *against* Marion Barry—as opposed to just *against* him in 1986.

On June 28th, with Johnny (whose 52nd birthday was the next day) and my all kids there, I held a press conference with many media in attendance and announced that I would be running for Mayor. I stressed what I felt was the truth about city government: "I see impending bankruptcy—both financially and morally. I see frustration in the eyes of our people. I see hopelessness in the eyes of our children. How could I sit by and not try again?"

I knew the numbers were against me as a Republican (remember that 11 to 1 ratio—actually how could you not) as well as the racial disparity and gender issues. The latter had unfortunately and unfairly been exacerbated by how many viewed the performance of Sharon Pratt Kelly. Therefore, in my announcement, along with emphasizing my past experience and accomplishments, I again said: "There is no Republican or Democratic way to pick up trash, no male or female way to do something about our housing shortage or to stimulate economic development of our neglected neighborhoods. There is no white or black way to fix our potholes or to create work for our youth. The issues which confront this government are not racial or partisan issues—they are people issues."

Jonetta Rose Barras, of *The Washington Times*, noted about the announcement, "She avoided bashing her Democratic rivals, instead touting her record of service to the community."[105]

I defeated challenger Brian Moore in the Republican primary by 62 percentage points—but that didn't stop him from asking me out. (I told him I was too busy to accept.) Marion did win the Democratic primary in early September with 47% of the vote, besting the closest competitor John Ray with 37%, and Sharon with 13%. Prior to the primary, at-large Councilmember Bill Lightfoot, who had won my former seat after I announced I wasn't seeking reelection, had filed papers to run for Mayor as an Independent in the general election. However, soon after the primary, he withdrew his candidacy, claiming he did not want to be the "stop Barry candidate."[106] I *did* want to be that candidate. And I *did* want to be Mayor as I felt I had the commitment, experience and capability to be a good one.

Now Marion and I would basically go head-to-head in the general election. (A few lesser-known Independent and Statehood-Green Party candidates would contend, but each ended up receiving less than 1% of the vote.)

That primary night in September of 1994—in the middle of the night—I had volunteers blanket the city with my yellow and black campaign posters. So that Wednesday morning, the day after the primary Marion won, as everyone headed to work or out, there was my picture and my name: "Carol." I made a conscious decision to go simply with "Carol" and no last name. (And please realize that this was long before it became a standard in present day.) I did so for a couple of reasons: 1) I had been gone for six years and knew that just having "Carol" would cause a discussion and draw attention to the campaign, and 2) when "Schwartz" was on the poster, as it had been in my past four campaigns, the way the signs had to be stapled together around the polls only emphasized "wart" or "war" instead of the full name.

The signs with just my first name got quite a lot of notice and chatter. At the time, one journalist nastily chattered in the *Post* that I was just using "Carol" to try to deny I was Jewish, although I must give her credit for cleverly making her byline that day just "Cindy." But how wrong she was about me! If I had really wanted to do that, I would have changed my name years ago, dropped my temple membership, and not have been as involved in Jewish causes as I was. Actually, I was a smart Jewish person who got a big article out of her! Thanks for the publicity, Cindy.[107]

As always, I guided my own campaign, acted as my own Campaign Manager, and wrote much of the speeches and brochures. Yet, in this race. I was backed by the largest flank of volunteers in all my elections, and they helped in every aspect of the campaign. Our two-story headquarters on K St. next to a Burger King buzzed with activity day and night.

Ed Morgan was the Deputy Campaign Manager. Doug and Stephanie came home to work on the campaign full-time, and they were indispensable. My daughter Hilary came back many weekends to help, but was working full-time in New York as well performing in an off-off Broadway play.

1994 Mayoral Race: The Backdrop

Marion was brilliant in framing the election as redemption for himself and for the city. He tapped into the anger of many African American citizens who believed that he was set up during his arrest (which he was, but he didn't have to cooperate so willingly). He also tapped into concern about "the Plan"—the fear about white people trying to take over this predominantly black city, which many felt would be expedited by the election of a white Mayor. (The irony is that over 20 years later, the white population in the city is growing more and more while the African American population is more and more diminishing. And all of this has been under the watch of black Mayors.)

And Barry capitalized on collective amnesia. The Administration of Mayor Sharon Pratt Kelly had failures, but in many ways, the failures of the previous Administration—his—were just coming home to roost during her tenure. However, a lot of residents in D.C. looked back at the Barry years as a better time than it really was—the proverbial rose-colored glasses.

The election was racially and economically splintered. In the Democratic primary, in which there were no white candidates, Councilmember John Ray won Wards 2 and 3, the predominantly white Wards. Barry dominated in Wards 4, 5, and especially across the Anacostia River in Wards 7 and 8—and took two other Wards as well. One Barry voter expressed the feelings of many: "... he made mistakes a lot of officials have ... what he did was hurt himself." It was so maddening to see him constantly excused.

Ronald Walters, Chair of the Political Science Department at Howard University, summarized the sentiment: "Many blacks simply don't see Barry in the one-dimensional term of the crack-head the Vista video suggested." He said some residents were seething over the way Barry was brought down. Walters described the many black votes for Marion as strikes "... against the white power establishment attempting to dictate their lives."[108]

It was more complicated by the white leadership of Congress breathing down the neck of the District. That did not help matters and just further fostered the perception that the "white establishment" was out to take power away from a majority black city.

I can understand some of the sentiments expressed above, but it doesn't excuse turning a blind eye to: 1) what Barry didn't do for the city in the 12 years he was given three chances, and 2) not giving a person who had done as much or more good for the city one chance—and mostly because she was not born black.

But this was the backdrop against which I ran for Mayor. You can question my sanity, my sobriety, my self-punishment, but you can never question my commitment and courage.

How could Barry keep coming back like he did? Those still confused about Barry's appeal need only look at his incredible charm as well as the fact that during Barry's terms, the government became a major employer—supplying jobs to nearly a tenth of the population.[109] Most thought that would stop if he wasn't there.

Actually, I would have made sure that D.C. residents got our jobs—and not just government's—and those employees would be representative of our population. (All one had to do was look at my own Council staff.) I also stood on the side of D.C.—and good government. I believed that cause transcended race. I did recognize the fear of those in the African American community about losing black leadership. But had I been elected, I would have ensured that we had it at the highest levels of government, that we encouraged others to run for the Council, and that we educated our inner-city young people to be the leaders of the future.

As much as I appreciated the positive things Barry had done, I often questioned the undying love for him by the most struggling and disadvantaged of our citizens. Many of the problems that *his* Administration unleashed unduly affected them. From 1980 to 1986—under Barry's watch—the number of people living in poverty increased by 8%.[110] And the waiting list for public housing ballooned from 7,600 families in 1980 to nearly 13,000 families by 1987.[111] Underperforming schools, unsafe streets, and a housing program in shatters certainly more negatively affected those at the lower end of the economic ladder, most of whom were black. However, his message of redemption resonated with those same individuals. When it came to Marion, facts did not quite resonate in the same fashion.

The *fact* was that during his 12-year tenure as Mayor, government spending increased by $1.8 billion. As a result, in 1994, D.C. faced a dire financial situation which he certainly helped create. The city by then had a $40 million deficit from the prior fiscal year, and according to financial reviews, was likely to face a billion-dollar deficit by the year 2000. The city was ordered by Congress to cut $140 million in spending.

The *fact* was that in 1994, developers prospered as public housing languished with still 10,000 people on the waiting list—at least it was 3,000 better than under Barry. [112] The housing agency, in *fact*, was so poorly managed, it had nine directors in a 10-year period. The *fact* was the few units that were even renovated during all those years were done so at a cost of four times the national average.[113]

Some more facts: In Barry's last years as Mayor, we lost local autonomy to receiverships as the courts took over agencies from foster care to corrections. The repeat offender rate was at 95%. We suffered the loss of over 76,000 residents, and many of them middle-class African Americans, to Prince Georges County, Maryland. And I could go on and on ... and will.

Marion not only framed the race as his personal redemption, but also one in which *only* he had the experience to get us out of the mess he himself had created and fostered. While this ridiculousness drew many in, other voters, both black and white, were perplexed that a man who had not only embarrassed the city but helped lead it to the above financial brink would get such a pass.

1994 Mayoral Race: Fighting Again Against the Odds

Once again, with the city being 70% African American then, there was wide distrust among many of a white woman leading the city, and a Republican was resisted strongly too, with Republicans just making up 7% of the electorate. The total electorate numbered 330,571 registered voters with nearly 80% of them being Democrats. But I had fought against the odds most of my life. While others were reluctant to take on the juggernaut that was Marion Barry in a politically and racially fractured Washington, D.C., I didn't hesitate—and called the issues as I saw them.

If Marion had personally redeemed himself from drugs, I was proud of him for doing so. But this election was not about a single man's redemption; it was about the redemption of the city. The corruption and fiscal irresponsibility of his terms could not be ignored. If voters rejected giving Sharon Pratt Kelly another term, they should not give Marion Barry a *fourth*.

I talked about the black middle class flight to the suburbs under Barry's watch. When the debates came, I stressed the scourge of drugs in our town and the poor example Marion Barry had set.

As "Loose Lips" in the *Washington City Paper* stated, "Hizzoner has run into something he didn't encounter in the Democratic primary: a real challenger, in the form of Republican Carol Schwartz. During the primary, Barry's opponents seemed afraid to confront him; Schwartz shows no such trepidation, and has raised issues that previously got swept under the rug—issues that needed to be aired before the conclusion of this campaign."[114]

I called Marion out on his record, but at the same time I was determined to run an upbeat campaign with no unfair shots. Although my electoral strengths lay in Wards 2, 3 and parts of 6, I refused to target my message. My message was always my message everywhere. Even though I knew targeting could provide a better path toward victory, I just could not treat people differently—and surely not based on geographic location, economics or race. Even then such practices were the norm, as they are today. But they assault my basic values and I refused to use them—then and later. By the way, and not surprisingly, the Barry campaign did not follow that same philosophy—they targeted away.

1994 Mayoral Race: It Takes a Village

The significant backing I received in the form of hundreds of contributors and volunteers represented a diverse group. Along with the small local Republican organization—I never took money or help from the National Republican Party even when it was offered—I had in my corner many staunch Democrats. They included a large number of African Americans, many of whom had to fight the backlash for helping me and even described getting angry looks and comments for that support.

"You do feel out of place," said Charles Glover in a *Post* piece. "You get hostility." But he added, "[There's] too much at stake." Some of the supporters had to withstand cruel taunts like: "Man, how many times have you had to clean her house?" Charles went on: "It amazes me how people forget the bad things that happened when he was Mayor. But I can't, and I won't."[115]

I realize it took courage for African Americans to come out in support of me. But there were many black Washingtonians who thought that true equality meant thinking for themselves. Former D.C. Secretary under Mayor Pratt Kelly, Mildred W. Goodman, was eloquent in her description of the issues at hand in her endorsement statement at one of my "Women for Carol" receptions.

Mildred described the difficult decision, especially coming out against a fellow Democrat but declared, "I find the notion of drinking Jim Jones brand of Kool Aid far more reprehensible. ... At this time, I also wish to raise my voice in denunciation of the racially divisive tactics that have been and continue to be used to ostracize and to intimidate local voters." Mildred said, "There are people in the community who say those of us who are African American and who are not willing to vote for Mr. Barry are being disloyal to our race. This election must not be determined on the basis of race. If it is, we will all be the losers, blacks and whites. I cannot emphasize too strongly my resentment to anyone having the audacity to indicate that my membership in the black race requires validation based on their criteria. I need no one's validation. I am black and I am proud but let no one think that I am black and I am stupid." Mildred concluded, "And, the irony of all ironies will be to have black folks encouraging black folks not to think for themselves."

One of Marion's first statements after winning the primary spoke of racial schisms, which he not only played on, but helped cause. He said directly and explicitly to white voters, "Get over the personal hang-ups you've got. Get over it." (As if race was the only reason some white person would not vote for him now, even if they had before.) It was his mantra throughout the campaign.[116]

Regardless, many others planned to vote their conscience. A former Press Secretary for Marion Barry, Annette J. Samuels,

Another time Marion Barry himself told Aaron, "You must be brain-dead working for that white woman." At a debate when I brought up the incident, Marion asserted, "That's an absolute lie. You're lying." But Aaron verified the interaction, saying "I was shocked [by it]."[120]

1994 Mayoral Race: In His Face

In the September primary, both Sharon Pratt Kelly and John Ray had shied away from taking Barry on for his alcohol and drug abuse as well as his 1990 arrest. But at a nationally televised debate at the National Press Club in early October, I did not back off when Barry spoke of his ability to help youth. I said forcefully, "His addiction unfortunately compromised his ability to fight the drug-dealing that was killing our youth ... The police will tell you that most murders are drug-related in D.C. And under my opponent our murder rate rose a tragic 162% [from 1979 through 1990]. The national average was 9 percent ..." Members of the media called it the sharpest attack on Barry in the election. Marion did not respond to this accusation in the debate and would not respond to questions about it afterwards.[121]

That debate at the National Press Club inured a great deal of attention and support. Right after, I noticed a sea-change. People started saying that the strength I showed in that debate caused them to not only *not* want Marion Barry as Mayor, but to *want* me to be Mayor. More Democrats for Carol signs popped up in yards around the city and more volunteers signed up.

I persisted in debates: "We could forget about his drug problem if it were only a personal problem. If he has turned around his life I am there to support and commend him. But it is his proven record of broken promises and gross mismanagement that we cannot afford again ... I'm going to deal with the record, and all of this is part of the record. If people want to look back with rose-colored glasses they can, but I am not going to." The plain truth was the city would not be "in such dire financial straits if he had not brought us those bloated budgets."

Criticisms volleyed back and forth. While I accused him of failing, he presented me as a novice. I hit Barry back. I was putting out position papers on education, crime, and the city's relationship with Congress while Marion was on a "national tour congratulating himself and raising money."[122]

At one debate, Marion declared, "We ought to guarantee four years of college to our high school graduates." Of course, he backed away from the assertion after: "I didn't say we were going to do it next year." I came back swinging, saying he could never keep that promise, and that he was playing a "cruel hoax" on the city's youth with such empty campaign rhetoric.

Marion spoke confidently in the third person: "Added together, Marion Barry has the best possibility to reduce crime in this city." I retorted, "If you are the best possible, Mr. Barry, why did murders go up 162% during your Administration?"[123] One time, Marion said, "Stop pointing the finger and start pointing the way," a line he lifted from Sharon Pratt Kelly.[124]

Although we greeted each other with warmth as the debates started, I knew I had to go on the offensive, seeing the odds against me. Besides, he deserved it after three failed terms—and a jail term for drug use. Please! At our second debate, I said, "Our city is dying under the dead weight of my opponent's legacy—a legacy of fear, filth, frustration, financial chaos and flight." Good one, eh?

The fireworks continued at a luncheon with *Washington Post* reporters and editors: "You talk about [how] you're going to manage the city better; you had 12 years to manage the city better. What makes me have any more confidence that you'll do better this time around?" And after he accused me of having no budget experience, I came back with, "I had enough budget expertise to vote against your budgets." And I said, "What have you done about the budget crisis since you've been back on the Council the last couple of years?" I also expressed concern with his missing Council votes as a member and now forums as a candidate, which was a pattern similar to when he held the Mayor's office.

Barry's major attack at the *Post* meeting occurred when he accused me of being part of a scheme by Republicans to take over the U.S. House and Senate as well as cities across the country like Los Angeles and New York. I stated that I had never taken a dime from the National Republican Party or any of its offers of help, individually or collectively, so I could look anyone in the eye and state, "No help from national Republicans." So my campaign was hardly part of any nationally organized "conspiracy."

At that meeting with editors and reporters, I also expressed a deeply held viewpoint that would eventually in the years to come get me on the bad side of the *Post*. I said I would never consider "getting rid of the elected Board of Education" because of there being so few elected offices in our city. I'm in favor of more democracy, not less for our democracy-hungry residents. I still hold firm to that reasoning.[125]

My aggression against Barry seemed to throw him a bit off guard. "He doesn't look like he's having much fun," said political commentator Mark Plotkin. Barry even threatened not to participate in any more debates because of what he called my "below-the-belt" attacks. But he usually showed up anyway. Maybe he was having more fun than he admitted. I sure was some of time, despite the challenges.

1994 Mayoral Race: Pushing for a Fair Shake

Sometimes it was hard to get a fair shake from voters. A Republican, to many of them, meant someone who did not understand and back their interests. However, publications like *Roll Call* noted that, "Schwartz with talk of better services, housing is a liberal Democrat in tone," while "Barry says jobs will come from the private sector, like a Republican." How sad and counterproductive that voters just look at the party—and not the person.

I did feel frustration with some in the media who devoted way more time and space to Barry than to the alternative. Then when I did get some attention, it was really hard to get the reporting to be accurate and fair.

I had a memorable run-in with longtime D.C. political reporter, Tom Sherwood. Tom had written for *The Washington Post* for 15 years and then became an TV reporter for NBC4 in 1989. When Tom was writing for *The Washington Post,* I never thought he treated me as fairly as he should have. He always seemed to be enamored of Marion Barry. Maybe it had to do with his being a guy from the South, Atlanta specifically, and therefore having particular sensitivity about the racial issue. During the 1986 campaign, I got the feeling that when he saw me, he thought, "How dare she have the audacity to run against Barry!" And his reporting seemed to imply the same. He was clearly a good writer and very smart, but we had a tough time during that 1986 campaign.

During the 1994 race, when Tom was at Channel 4, I did a press conference on the budget, which I and everyone felt really good about. My son Doug had done a great job gathering all the information and creating visual aids. The presentation and the question and answer session, which lasted for nearly an hour in total, went exceedingly well with only the occasional "um" and "ah" that most people do when they speak—and certainly for that length of time.

On the news that evening, Tom Sherwood said, "Carol Schwartz did a presentation of her budget today," and the film cut to me saying not much more than "... ah." And that was basically it. The next scene featured Tom over at Marion Barry's headquarters. He said, "Carol Schwartz presented her budget today," and the two of them just started to laugh! That was the entire segment—the whole coverage of my very in-depth budget presentation. Doug, Ed and I, who watched the segment together, just looked at each other like, "What the hell?"

I had done my share of complaining directly to reporters about unfair coverage, but rarely went above anyone's head. Yet this was over and beyond even the pale. I had been friendly with Allan Horlick, who was then the Station Manager at WRC/NBC4. We had worked together on the Board of the Metropolitan Police Boys and Girls Clubs. In fact, soon after my husband died and I left the Council, Alan asked me to do a pilot for a talk show. I was hesitant, but did say yes. In one segment, I had Carol Fennelly come on, along with her daughter and son, to talk about her life at the Community for Creative Non-Violence (CCNV) and her partner Mitch Snyder, who had recently committed suicide. Our interview went fairly well, but Alan and I both felt that I was still too sad from my own recent experience—and certainly looked it.

Here, five years later, after Tom's piece on my budget presentation, I called Allan and said, "Would you do me a favor? I've never asked you to do anything for me. But Tom Sherwood was at my press conference and he taped the whole thing. Would you please view the presentation in its entirety? It's about 45 minutes. And then would you view the short segment on the evening news and what he chose to pull from that press conference." He said, "Sure." About an hour later he called and said, "Carol, I asked the News Director to go with me and we did view the tape in its entirety and then we watched what Tom used. I've been in the business for years. You are absolutely right. That was appalling. I apologize and I will make sure that nothing like this ever happens to you again."

A few days later, I was in the makeup room before taping a television debate between Marion Barry and me. In walked Tom Sherwood. He started screaming at me at the top of his lungs, "How dare you call my Station Manager?!" He was just shrieking. So I shrieked back at him, "How dare you take my solid press conference and try to make me look like a fool? How dare *you*? I don't ask for preferential treatment from you or anybody else. But I do ask for fairness. Do it again and I'll come back in your face *again*!"

The moderator Del Walters witnessed it all. In the 20 years since, Tom and I have become good friends. I can't say we haven't had some combative moments. But we've grown to appreciate each other—both personally and professionally.

1994 Mayoral Race: Some Laughs

The campaign was not without gaffes. At a debate, the issue of bringing the Washington football team back into the city was brought up. I suggested renovating the old RFK stadium and even adding levels. Marion mocked that idea, "You're going to need some super-duper binoculars." I laughed with Marion at that, as did my kids listening on the radio.

During another debate, Stephanie and Doug were listening on the car radio as they drove around doing campaign stuff. I was really landing some punches and Marion was using his usual "Get over it" line to me and listeners. My kids were excited about how well I was doing. So they turned around and drove over to WAMU to surprise and congratulate me when it was finished. About the time they arrived, Marion started whining as usual, saying that my legitimate points were mean-spirited. I decided to bring in a famous quote, and as you may have learned, I'm not great with repeating those verbatim. So as Marion was complaining for the fourth time, I said, "As a great Democratic President Harry Truman once said, [long pause] if you can't stand the kitchen [longer pause] get out!" I immediately realized how wrong it was and laughed as did Marion and the host. But deep down, I was saying to myself, "When will you ever learn?" I don't think my kids were laughing. I'm sure all they were thinking was, "Oh no, not again."

At one of the final well-attended debates, Marion kept saying about me, "Republican this, Republican that." I said, "Marion, is Republican the only thing you can say about me?" But he just kept it up with "Republican this, Republican that, Republican everything." Finally, I looked at him and said: "If you have problems with me being a Republican—Get over it!" He burst out laughing, appreciating that I threw his signature line back at him. Everybody stood up and cheered, including his supporters. That exchange was all over the 11 p.m. news.[126]

1994 Mayoral Race: In Profile

On October 17th, the *Post* featured me and my kids on the front page of the Style section. It was a good photo of us and we looked happy. My dear friend Tom Mader got a copy framed and gave it to us. It is still displayed in my home office.

The piece was one of those in-depth profiles of a candidate. "'I can't see this city going down the tubes. It hurts me,'" the writer described me saying in a "voice part Bacall ..." Reporters seemed to always get a kick out of describing my big hair, flowery dresses—which I get a kick out of wearing—and my voice. When asked what motivated me to seek making a difference: "... This is what gets me up in the morning. ... What gives me satisfaction and peace is working on problems. I'm also one of those people that need 100 problems to work on at once, not two or three."

And what makes me run? "Everybody that knows me really well knows that I have no choice. This was not a free-will decision here." That's at the heart of it. It's something deep inside me beyond my control that drives me when I see things that need fixing.

The article went on to say: "When she talks about her love of Washington's beauty, her many good works as a volunteer all over town, or the hazards of returning Barry to office, [she] does so with a full-throated vehemence born of long struggles against the odds ... Life has made her outwardly tough and given her a wide and diverse set of friends, but it has also left her a bit bruised, those friends say ... [She] has had more heartache than a lot of 50-year-olds on the planet." Not often did the media get the vulnerability that lies beneath my bravado, but that article did.

And it hit a point I often made: "She wears the fact that her children attended public schools like a badge of honor. 'I felt very strongly, if those of us who are committed to our city don't commit ourselves to our public schools, then who is supposed to? How many liberal Democrats do you know who have committed their children to where their mouths are?'"[127]

1994 Mayoral Race: A Glimpse of My Vision

My Administration would be devoted to social safety nets *and* fiscal responsibility. And make no mistake, both are possible. I'm sorry I never got a chance to prove that.

I wanted to continue commonsensical policies to combat AIDS, including making condoms available at schools and giving clean needles to intravenous drug users. (It's happening, so why not at least protect?) I pushed to explore creation of enterprise zones to give tax breaks to doctors who open practices in underserved neighborhoods.[128] I wanted to bolster citywide tutoring and after-school programs.

And unlike the precedent set by the previous Barry Administration, I was not about to let rich developers get a free ride. If a developer wanted a prime downtown location, I might consider it, but would first make sure we didn't want to keep the land for ourselves. And if we chose to sell—and only for very good reasons—there would have to be a competitive bid process. I would also push for benefits for the city, such as fulfilling affordable housing needs in places developers ignored, like Anacostia, asking, "What are you going to do for us across the river?"—and holding them to it.[129]

I would be tough on crime but would recognize that an ounce of prevention is worth a pound of cure. The key was to provide alternatives for our at-risk youth through partnerships with organizations like the Big Sisters/Brothers and the Department of Recreation. Meanwhile, Marion had voted on the Council to cut the recreation budget by 10% for the past fiscal year. I felt that government needed to provide leadership and support in reducing crime not only by an adequate and well-trained police force, but also by building relations between the community and police officers, who in my administration would spend time walking or biking the streets, and become even more involved with youth as some were with the Metropolitan Police Boys and Girls Clubs.

And of enormous concern to me was the fact that when people made crisis calls to Alcohol and Drug Abuse Services, they would receive a long and confusing list of telephone numbers to sift through, and once they finally dialed, no one answered. There was a critical need to give substance abusers one number—a single portal of entry—and decrease waiting periods. Drug treatment on demand was an urgent need, and I would have provided it right away by going out into the affected areas myself, asking people to come and turn their lives around. And I promised what should have been a simple thing—having government employees who actually like people answering the phones when residents called.[130]

Now remember, this was a "glimpse"—just some ideas—so obviously not all-inclusive.

1994 Mayoral Race: The Final Days

I was touched by the kind words which many of my former colleagues used, whether supporters or not. Councilmember Harry Thomas Sr. (D-Ward 5) called me "a beautiful lady, the only Republican I would talk good for." Conrad Smith, a Democrat, remarked that on the School Board I was a "very gutsy lady" who did an excellent job. She never had, he said, "a single enemy." Jim

Ford, another Democrat and clerk of the D.C. Council's Committee on Education, said I was "hugely popular with Council and School Board staff members. About 20 who worked with her are volunteering in her campaign. She was good at motivating people, fun to be around and fair ... she retained good relations with opponents by not personalizing debates or carrying grudges."[131]

Many in the business community and deep-pocketed political action committees, though, backed Barry. He won the endorsements of many business organizations, including the Apartment and Office Building Association of Metropolitan Washington, which represented owners of more than two-thirds of D.C.'s downtown commercial spaces, and the Board of Trade—most of whom lived in the suburbs. After all, business leaders usually bet on who is likely to win. But they should have been smart enough to know that Marion becoming Mayor then, having only been out of prison for two and a half years and having already served for three terms in a town that was consistently losing population, lacking adequate services, and not booming with business, could *not* be good for D.C.—and certainly not for business. My philosophy has always been that leaders should lead, not follow. But there they were, lined up at his trough.

Meanwhile, Marion continued to state his much-used line about the city's current problems: "What you need to be concerned about is not how we got here, but who can best get us out." I countered, "Let's deal with reality. Why would we look to the person who 'buried' us to undig the grave?" And I called him out on his divisiveness: "He tries to unify us one minute, divide us the next. I feel like a yo-yo ...." Another time: "It's almost laughable," I said straight to Marion. "The gap between your rhetoric and your record is almost as large as the deficit you left Mayor Kelly."

The campaign was growing more intense, if possible. In the last debates we accused each other of lying to voters and exaggerating each other's records. Marion said I would not be "received well" in certain parts of Washington. I interrupted him with a cry of, "That's outrageous." I added, "I was formerly an at-large member of the Council and I was welcomed everywhere in this city." And I called him on not taking responsibility for his record: "Every time I mention his record, he plays the victim. He plays the victim better than anyone. It's always a conspiracy, or somebody's always setting him up .... None of us has a God-given right to be Mayor, even though some of us act like we do."[132]

In the final weeks, Barry was doing a lot of polling. I have never done polls during my elections for several reasons: 1) They are expensive and since I actually get shy about fundraising for myself—and even somewhat for charities (and then can only do so through a letter or event)—I would rather reserve my limited resources for direct voter appeals. 2) I am too independent-minded to mold myself and my message to opinion polls. 3) If I found out I was by chance leading, I might have lost that extra motivation. And, 4) since I am often the underdog, why would I bother to remind myself—and just discourage myself—while paying for it?[133]

Barry's own polls must have shown I was doing well. A couple of weeks before election day, he made a promise to reduce the prison time for inmates, which was obviously a move to appeal to them and their loved ones. He gave no specifics on how this would be accomplished, but it was an effective get-out-the-vote tactic.

Of course, Marion would always continue resorting to, "She's a Republican." I urged Democrats time and again to "close your eyes, hold your nose, and just pull that lever for me."

I received the endorsement from "Loose Lips" (Ken Cummins) of the *Washington City Paper*: "There are two reasons to vote for Schwartz on Tuesday. The first is because she has the drive, the honesty, the commitment, the personality and the know-how to run the D.C. government for the next four years. The second reason to vote for Schwartz even if you still harbor reservations about her ability to govern a predominantly black city, is to send Barry a message that this time he can't take everything and everyone for granted. A large vote for Schwartz would remind Barry that a sizable chunk of the electorate will not be intimidated or rolled. Whatever your reasons, vote Schwartz."[134]

The most satisfying, though late in coming, was getting the endorsement from *The Washington Post*, who admitted regret for endorsing Barry in 1986. I wished my husband David were here to see it as he had been so upset back then about their endorsement of Marion. From the November 7, 1994 *Post*:

> "For those ready to throw in the towel after Mr. Barry's Democratic primary victory in the mistaken belief that the general election offered no practical alternative, Carol Schwartz has ably proved otherwise.
> On the Council her calls for financial austerity were unsuccessful only because they were ahead of its time.
> Anyone who doubts that Mrs. Schwartz has the political skill, the temperament, the intelligence and the guts to do the job today

need only look at the campaign she has been waging—both against the odds and conventional wisdom, and at a time when an awful lot of people who shared her view of what should happen were, for reasons of self-interest and expedience, in hiding. Schwartz, to the ridicule of some and the indifference of others, stepped up to the challenge and refused to let Mr. Barry get away with acting as if he were entitled to a free ride into office. She has turned tomorrow's voting into what it was supposed to be: an election. When Barry left office, the District was in deep trouble ...

As with his astounding proposal to trade leniency toward convicted criminals for the votes of their friends and relatives, Mr. Barry has, in this campaign, made it plain for all to see that this would not be a new improved Barry administration, far from it.

... a weighing of her proposals on the budget, crime and economic development, as well as her ability to put together a grass-roots campaign and army of unpaid volunteers across this city, says a good deal about her potential for mobilizing people to get the job done.

... her audacious campaign has certainly improved her standing ... She has a chance, though, only if people want her to win ... There is no excuse for those minded to stay home."[135]

Despite the tension of the campaign, or because of it, I wrote an open letter to Marion before election day:

"Dear Marion,

Often in this race, you have spoken eloquently about the need for healing. It is for that very reason that I write you today. You and I are old-timers at this—we have been battling each other professionally for 20 years. Yet, in fact, we have been friendly for all of those years.

As you and I both know, our similarities probably outnumber our differences. We were both born in small Southern towns as racial and religious minorities. We both worked our way up as activists, making D.C. our adopted home. We have both held elected office in this town since the beginning of Home Rule. And Lord knows, we have both had tough personal times. But perhaps more than all of that, it is our love for D.C. and its people that we have in common.

Our city is crippled by crises. A crisis of fear and a crisis of flight. A crisis of family and a crisis of community. If we are to emerge from these crises—if we are to save our city—we must all come together and join forces. And forever, you and I must instill new hope in our city.

So I reach out to you today as a long-time colleague and a friend—but more importantly as a Washingtonian. Together, we must ensure our people a fair election. Together, we must call for unity and healing, regardless of who wins. To this end, I intend to come to your election-night party if you are the winner, and I hope that you will do the same if I win. Marion, coming together election night is the least we owe the citizens and city we love."

Sincerely,

Carol Schwartz"[136]

I meant it. And we did. We would join hands on election night and eat lunch together the day after, in the spirit of uniting and healing our town.

The weekend before the election, volunteers and I traveled in a trolley through every Ward of the city. It was such fun. We danced the whole way to Melvin and the Blue Note's "Wake Up Everybody" blaring over the speakers. It was thrilling as we drove around to see the applause and cheers we received in so many places. It was a real high. Some people even chased the trolley down the block, and I chose to take that as a positive thing.

1994 Mayoral Race: Election Day

The morning of Election Day, I woke up before the sun rose and headed to an early morning interview at NBC4. My kids traveled with me all day to various polling places at churches, schools and recreation centers throughout the city.

The people who covered the polls, passing out literature to get those last-minute decisions, were emotional on both sides. We relied only on our enthusiastic volunteers (and had every precinct across town covered), while Barry had some energetic, vocal volunteers and many paid poll workers. It was tough on some of our people, who were outnumbered in many locations with lots of people shouting "Barry!" "Barry!" A classmate of Doug was so harassed at one polling place that we just had mercy on him and took him with us. Unfortunately, this was not an isolated incident. It happened to many of our volunteers all over town. At another polling place, our former neighbor, who was a teen then, shouted, "We need more people!" as we were forced to drive away to make the next stop. Our volunteers went above and beyond, and I will always be grateful to them.

Soon after the polls closed, the initial results came in. Ed, the kids and I were watching at my house. I was leading. My supporters were incredibly excited. I said to Ed, "It's not enough." He said, "You're right. It's not." We knew my support would be heavily tilted toward the morning count before Barry brought out his busloads of voters to the polls later in the afternoon and evening. And bus loads he did bring. We saw the count begin to inch the other way. In the end, Barry won 56% to my 42%. A loss, but called by the media a "surprisingly strong" showing. Not many expected a white, Jewish, Republican woman with 77% to 7% odds against her to come even that close. It remains the closest Mayoral general election result in the 43 years of Home Rule in Washington, D.C.

As was tradition, a police escort arrived at my home to take us to the Hilton, where we were having our election night party, to greet supporters. We rode with the top down in my red Chrysler convertible, (which people were used to seeing me in) with posters displayed all over it.

The ballroom was mobbed. Hundreds and hundreds of supporters—or more—crowded around the stage. It was hard for my kids and I to stay together as we waded through the crowd to get to that stage. I conceded at 11:20 p.m. I was not distraught. I felt proud. I said from the podium, "I thank each and every one of you for having faith in the face of cynicism, for having commitment in the face of intimidation. We have sounded a wake-up call that will ring throughout our city for years to come."[137] Then just as I promised, I went to Marion's victory party at the Washington Convention Center. Marion and I shared a hug. And we held our arms up together in unity.

1994 Mayoral Race: After the Results

Next came the post-election analysis from the media. The vote was highly splintered. I won 92% of the vote in predominantly white, affluent Ward 3, which had a particularly high turnout. Barry won 91% in economically disenfranchised, African American Ward 8. But it wasn't entirely split by race. My supporters also came from middle-class black neighborhoods that were Democratic strongholds. I also received sizable support from the gay community. *The Washington Blade* reported that Barry only received 4% of the white gay vote and we split the black gay vote 50-50.[138] Many voters claimed, "I voted Republican for the first time in my life." A group in Ward 3 threatened to secede from the city after the election, but fortunately that never happened.[139]

The *Post* declared that Barry "Failed in an effort to unify the city." Jeff Henig, director of the George Washington University Center for Washington Area Studies, stated that "For Schwartz to poll so well in a city that is two-thirds African American and where Democrats outnumber Republicans 11 to 1 shows that she won substantial numbers of black and Democratic votes."[140]

A *Post* editorial said, "Her percent vote in an overwhelmingly Democratic city was truly impressive ... She captured respectable total votes in middle-class black voter precincts east of Rock Creek Park. Barry's victory was minimal in those middle-class black neighborhoods. Her election-day performance demonstrated that she brought a much broader appeal ... than Mr. Barry or even some in the press had credited her with having."[141]

The day after the election, as also promised, I took Marion to lunch as that was the deal. (Again, if I could renegotiate this, I would switch it up as losing *and* paying for lunch is a real lose-lose proposition.) We were friendly during the meal and we both spoke openly and honestly. I told him he needed to be responsible with finances and his own behavior. I even warned him about his womanizing issue: "My daughter Stephanie noticed the way you look at her." He said, "Oh yea, Cora is always on me about that." Even through that sometimes tense race, we came out friends. We always liked each other personally—and did 'til the day he died.

I know there have been rumors for 40 years that Marion and I were involved romantically because we got along so well. Those rumors can't be further from the truth. We were always friends and never shared more than a kiss on the cheek. Not that he didn't come out with some proclamations. He'd say fairly regularly, "You know I've had a crush on you for 25 years." I had my stock answers: "Marion, who haven't you had a crush on?" Or, "Marion, of course you have a crush on me. I'm a female between the age of 9 and 90." Either worked. And off he went to the next female.

Johnny's Surprise 50th Birthday
with 50 Guests in San Antonio

Johnny's Surprise!

With Roxanne Block

Aunt Doe and Linda

Johnny, Uncle Albert,
Uncle Earl and friend Mary Ellen

Johnny, Aunt Betty Jane and Dad

Johnny with Uncles
Albert and Seymour

Linda greets Johnny

Aunt Betty and her
brothers, Elliot and Leo

Aunt Doe visits D.C.

My favorite garb: granny gowns (flattering, eh?)

One of Last Visits with Dad in Midland

Johnny and Doug:
Hook 'em horns

Three generations

Dad with S.W.,
his most long-term
friend

In Odessa with childhood
friend and Dad's caretaker
Lettie England

My childhood home in
Midland on the two main
oil truck roads

Time with Friends and Family

Hil and I visiting Doug in Spain
on his Fulbright

Ardith and David above
(I told you they were glamorous)
and with our families
below on Thanksgiving)

Steph
and
Doug

1994 Mayoral Campaign

From *Washington Post*, October 17, 1994
(framed, given to me by Tom Mader)

Great volunteers
Aaron and Nicole

My kids were a wonderful help in my campaigns.

Uniting our city election night
(Rock Newman on left, Cora Barry on right) *Washington Times* Photo

CHAPTER 27

Dawn of a New Day

I was still living in the house on Springland Lane where my husband had died outside nearly seven years earlier. I had wanted to move right away. But I knew it was important not to make rash decisions at that time. And I also realized that home meant stability to my children at a time they desperately needed it. After a couple of years, when I broached moving, they seemed sad about the idea. So although the house was isolated at the end of a cul de sac, and it clearly held some tough daily reminders of David and that tragic time, I didn't make moving a high priority.

In the last few years, though, I had occasionally looked around for an apartment which I decided should be the next step for me. But nothing felt right enough for me to make the move. I did put in several low-ball offers for a couple of units but never countered when they were happily rejected. Then I had a break-in at the house while I was out of town. One or more invaders came through the window of the side kitchen door facing the small wooded area. Thank goodness when they went into the entryway, my motion detector got them and they ran out the same way they came in. When the police arrived and called me, I was relieved that I wasn't there—and later, that nothing had been taken. But the incident did motivate me to start looking again more seriously for that new home I wanted.

I saw a lot of apartments in the fall of 1993. I had been looking at places like the Watergate, Foxhall, and 2101 Connecticut Ave. It needed to be a nice apartment because at the time, I was only 49 years old and if I was going to sell my house, I needed to get an apartment that was of equal or more value in order not to trigger a capital gains tax on our three former homes. (At age 55, it's a different story.) My realtor who I had worked with for a while, said the "to-die-for" apartment was at 2029 Connecticut Ave., and I should go see it. Unfortunately, it was nearly double my budget and I told her so. She said, "Well at least go look." I responded, "No." She kept at it, and finally said, "Why not?" I said, "I don't go looking for a Jaguar when I can only afford a Chevy. Because instead of being happy with my Chevy, I will long for the Jaguar I couldn't afford. I don't do that to myself."

Meanwhile, my dad was beginning to have a lot more health issues so I was spending most of my time with him in Texas. Thus, the apartment hunting was put on hold. After Dad died on March 12, 1994, I was very busy with moving all of his and Mom's things up North, and then running for Mayor June through November of that year, so that's where it stayed.

In early December of 1994, after the campaign ended and we closed the office, I decided to reactivate the apartment search. I called my realtor Teri and said that I wanted to concentrate on the Dupont Circle/Kalorama/Adams Morgan area because the campaign had made me realize I wanted to be in a more diverse, centralized location with restaurants and shops right nearby. She called right back and said, "That 'to-die-for' apartment I told you about last year just dropped hundreds of thousands of dollars today." Even though it was still above my budget, it finally had the right number of digits. And because both of my parents were now gone, I did have some additional resources.

Stephanie (who after the campaign had stayed in town as she applied to law school) and I immediately went over to look at it. The apartment had very little furniture with no pictures on the wall, but it had been magnificently renovated. Steph and I were pretty blown away by it. With beautiful marble and the most up-to-date kitchen and bathrooms, not to mention the enormous square footage, classic columns and large beautiful windows with wonderful views, it was impossible to walk away. I put in an offer immediately. Because of the new price, I knew it would go quickly. (And it was hard to believe that I made that phone call that December day—a year after I had abandoned the apartment search—and then coincidentally that "to-die-for" apartment had dramatically dropped in price that very morning. Still is unbelievable!)

But first, I did call the owner and asked if the price could possibly be any lower. He, who was a resident of Middleburg, Virginia, said, "I am taking a huge hit on what we use as a pied-a-terre apartment and wouldn't be selling at all if I didn't have to. But I've watched you from afar for years and have admired your work, so because I know and like you, I'm going to give you one lower-priced counter-offer. Now take it or leave it." I took it. I ended up paying less for the apartment than they had paid for the renovation alone. I felt like I had been given a gift, not just by the owner but from above. (Several months later, after I'd decorated their beautiful apartment, I invited him and his lovely wife over briefly to see the place—only briefly because I thought they might be sad—and then took them to the Cosmos Club for lunch to thank them for the "gift.")

I remember telling people about moving to an apartment and they would say something like, "It's good to downsize when the kids are gone." And then I would embarrassingly admit, "Actually, it's bigger than my house." I bought the apartment in the afternoon and that night, close to midnight, I wanted to show it to Jim, who I was seeing on and off. The realtor, a friend and a night owl like me, agreed to come with the key. As we were waiting out front for her to show up, I looked up and said, "See those windows right below the top ones. That's my apartment." Jim then said, "Which windows are yours?" And once again embarrassingly I had to say, "All of them." I still pinch myself about the good fortune the apartment brought into my life—literally and figuratively.

It was obviously not a great seller's market because I was able to get such a good price on the purchase. Now here I was in this bad seller's market, having to sell my house, which needed some work that I didn't have time to do. And of course, I hadn't asked for a house-selling contingency from the apartment owner as I was getting such a fair deal, actually a steal.

Two years earlier, when I had seen an apartment I kind of liked, I put the house on the market briefly. The only real interest came from a couple who lived nearby and who I knew a bit socially. She was a Superior Court Judge and he had a high-level appointment at the Justice Department in the Clinton Administration. They did not make an offer then so I took the house off the market right away with relief because I realized I was not that crazy about that apartment anyway.

Cut to present. The night before my open house for realtors, I got a call from that very same couple, asking if they could come in early and look at the house again. I said yes. They came and on the spot, made a lower offer. I responded with, "Because I know and like you, I'm going to give you one lower-priced counter-offer. Now take it or leave it." They took it. There again, I felt like I had been given a gift—selling my house that needed work for basically the price I wanted in a lousy market before it even went on the market. The settlements were within a couple of weeks of each other, and I moved into my gorgeous new apartment in mid-March of 1995.

Interestingly, I got a call right after the purchase of the apartment—and before the settlement—from a friend who said that George McGovern (former Senator and Democratic Presidential nominee) wanted to call me and asked if it was okay to give him my number. I said, "Of course. And besides, it's always been in the phone book." George called right away. He and his wife Eleanor had lived at 2029 Connecticut Ave. for many years before moving to Forest Hills, also in D.C., and they wanted to come back to the building. He offered to buy my contract and give me a large profit (I didn't even ask the amount).

I hated to say no to him as they had just lost their daughter, which I had learned about through a cover story about the family in *Parade Magazine*. I gave him sympathy, and then told him about my own situation in which I had lost my husband sort of similarly seven years earlier, and how this was a new beginning for me after all those years of wanting it. I, therefore, could not say yes. He understood. We went on to talk about our favorite topic—politics.

I actually knew George McGovern, having met him several times over the years and in fact, he had told me he had voted for me for Mayor. As pleased as I was to hear that news then, since he had been the Democratic Presidential nominee, I decided I should never share that information. Then one time I saw him at a large gathering with a group surrounding him, and he yelled out, "See that woman over there! That's Carol Schwartz. I voted for her for Mayor." And he came up and gave me a hug, and I said to him, "I had never told anybody about your voting for me." And he said, "Well, I've told everybody so you might as well start." So clearly, I've started telling people.

Next came the move, which was a massive effort. I've always been a pack-rat and since the house was big, it enabled me to be so. At first I tried to winnow things down there rather than just moving all that junk to the next location. And then I decided that I would spend all that time and effort when I unpacked instead. When that time came, due to the vastness of the apartment, I decided, "The hell with getting rid of stuff." So there it remains— only added to—23 years later.

It took a lot to pack up the house, and thank goodness for Steph's and my right-hand woman Aleida Lumbi's help. Whenever I have a big project before me, just like a campaign, I go into hyper-functioning mode, even more than my usual hyper state. It was like when I remodeled and decorated the house in Rehoboth in record time, but this unpacking and decorating effort, though so much larger and included incorporating my folks' stuff from storage, went at an even swifter speed. I would go for days barely sleeping. I would often just fall into a quick doze in my clothes and then get up to unload more. To fully illustrate, I moved in mid-March and had a house-warming party, with every picture on the wall and every knick-knack in place, in early April. And here's a shout-out to Steph, Aleida, Tom Mader, Heather Krebs, etc., who helped along the way. I have also always been grateful for the good and accommodating staff at 2029 for the 22 years I've lived here.

I really enjoy decorating. I kind of view a room as a blank canvas which I want to fill—in fact, overfill. I often say, "There is a thin line between good taste and overdone, and I crossed it years ago." Recently, a neighbor said she had just told someone that my apartment is a museum of treasures I had gotten from around the world. Maybe that is true of a small portion of my jewelry, but my paintings, furniture and knick-knacks are mostly junk—with some good things thrown in—and were all bought in the United States, mainly at flea markets and auctions, although some of the "good things" were from my folks and grandparents. I enjoy putting a painting I spent $3.50 for at a garage sale next to something I spent far more for—and dare you to tell the difference. My decorating is eclectic—like my friends, like my life.

I loved my magnificent new place with its beautiful views, so centrally located and so close to restaurants and public transportation. It really was a new beginning. Between the new home and the unsuccessful—yet successful—Mayoral effort, I felt on top of the world for the first time in decades.

Back to Reality

But as life has its way of giving you a reality check, mine came soon enough. I had met a man named Michael, who was a few years younger than I, through my Council work in the '80s, where he worked in a responsible position in the central office. He was very soft-spoken and nice, and we became friendly. He was raised in D.C. and I learned later, came from a fairly well-known family.

One day, several years after I had left the Council, I was walking in Cleveland Park and Michael came running out of an office. He said, "I'm so glad to see you. I've missed you." We had a good visit. At this point, he told me he had left the Council and was now selling real estate. Then he gave me his card and said, "If you ever run for office again, and I hope you will, I would love to help you."

People often would give me their cards in this manner and I kept them in a file. In 1994, when I decided to run against Marion Barry, I took out the card file and gave Michael a call. He said he was available to work full-time. He had great administrative experience, was an African American Democrat, a born and raised resident of D.C., gay, and a person I knew and liked—certainly all positives in my view. I brought him on board to run the office and started paying him right away. I was so glad to have someone of his caliber and background to help. He asked for my credit card information to get a computer and Xerox machine, which I gave in order to get the office up and running. Usually, right after announcing for office, I have (and I presume many candidates do as well) just used my own resources in the form of a loan to finance such items until a campaign finance form is filed, a committee with a bank account is established, and money is raised.

Michael was great. He worked from early morning until late at night. He ordered the supplies, t-shirts, etc. All bills would come to the office and be paid out of the campaign's account with checks written by Kathy, a financial expert and a volunteer for years. The only equipment charge on my credit card was for the original delivery fee and first month's rent for the copier and computer, which I reported as a loan. The subsequent monthly rental charges for those items were paid directly by the campaign.

When the campaign was over in November, Michael helped close up the office. Everything seemed fine. Soon enough, though, I noticed my Amex card was being charged around $800 dollars a month for a computer and copy machine. At first I thought it was a mistake and I didn't pay those expenses. I called up Amex and said, "These are not my charges." But those expenses kept being charged to my card. I thought, "What is going on here?"

It turns out that Michael had moved the office computer and copy machine to his home and charged the delivery and subsequent monthly rental fees to my personal credit card. Amex allowed him to do that—seven months after the original one-time charge, and with no call to me to verify. Just because he had given the company my credit card for that one-time delivery to my office and first month's rent back in June, did not mean that they could accept my personal credit card in December for equipment going to someone else's home, and then keep charging my card for that expense, even when I called to say don't. How dare them—and him!

Because of this deception, Kathy, Ed, who had helped me run the campaign, and I started to dig deeper. We discovered that Michael had also set up a fake t-shirt company early in the campaign, including a bank account in the non-existent t-shirt company's name. He would present receipts for t-shirts. Then the campaign would pay and mail the check to a Capitol Hill address, which happened to be the home of a friend of Michael's. Because there were so many t-shirts wanted and needed, especially in that 1994 campaign, and because Michael was the person who ordered and dispersed them, and because we were using many different t-shirt vendors, it was easy for him to just throw in additional receipts. He also told me that the t-shirt company—which turned out to be bogus—was minority-owned and D.C. incorporated, knowing both would please me. The bottom line is, there was no company. Michael was just stealing money from the campaign, in addition to ripping off my credit card.

I knew it would be embarrassing if it came out publicly that one of my most trusted campaign employees was stealing money from me and from my campaign. But by far my greater thought was that crime should not pay. I really believe that no bad deed should go unpunished (and this time I purposely mangled the idiom). It was obvious that this guy was a thief, and he probably stole from the Council and others. I knew that if I did not do something, he would continue to steal, hurting more people along the way. So I went down to the U.S. Attorney's office and filed charges. To hell with any embarrassment that might come to me as a result! None of this took away from the hurt I felt. I had trusted him, and thought we were friends. He even had said he loved me like his family.

Now back to the Amex card. In all the years I had that card and every other one, I had always paid the entire amount each month in full. Now these fraudulent charges, which I refused to pay, added up to thousands of dollars. And in spite of my calls, they kept charging me, and the interest just went up and up. That's when I got an attorney friend involved. He wrote several letters to Amex on my behalf reiterating that these were not my charges and that the company was culpable because they had allowed the charges without my permission. They never responded and the charges never disappeared.

Amex then ruined my credit rating, which had been perfect before. Needless to say, I cancelled the card. I should have sued them. I was being denied credit all over the place. In fact, I was setting up a new charge account at a store in New York while buying my daughter a coat, and it was refused. Then Amex had collection companies go after me through calls and letters. I told them to stop harassing me, and that Amex was the culprit—not me. Years later, the harassment finally stopped and I was able to restore my good credit rating. To this day, I won't get an Amex card, despite their multiple solicitations. FU Amex!

Back to Michael: I had to go before a D.C. grand jury and testify. I presented my case with all the back-up documents. I explained that this was a man I knew and trusted and therefore I found this hard to do. But I felt it was important for me to get justice and for him to get a wake-up call, which might turn his life around. And that's exactly what happened.

The jury did indict him. The prosecutor was ready to go to trial and so was I. But instead, Michael pled guilty and took a deal. I was glad to have won the case while avoiding a more public display. Although I would not have minded embarrassing him through a trial, I would have minded hurting his family—even though I did not know them—in such a visible way.

Michael served time for a couple of years. Another stipulation was that he had to pay back each dime, which he did. That wasn't the main point for me, but I did think that making him pay would help ensure that it would not happen to anyone else. And it didn't.

After he was released from prison, he moved to Florida and went into the restaurant business. And he wrote me a letter. He told me how sorry he was, that he still loved me very much, and understood what I did. He said, "You had always been my friend and I'm ashamed of what I did to you." He even sent me a gift—a cute pot holder. I wrote him back a nice thank you note. I learned that Michael died several years later.

Johnny Runs with the In Crowd

My brother Johnny worshiped the police and fire departments in every town we lived in or visited, and especially D.C.'s. So we always tried to take him to a fire station when he was here. As I started to get more political inroads, I tried to make sure Johnny had fun opportunities to meet impressive people, especially in the fields that so enthralled him. It was easy for people to be kind to Johnny as his disability was obvious; and because he was so adorable, most would gladly take some time for him.

When Johnny came for Thanksgiving in 1994 after the election, I took him to visit with D.C. Police Chief Fred Thomas at police headquarters. I had a special relationship with Fred through the Metropolitan Police Boys and Girls Clubs, and he and his wife Gigi became dear friends. (Sadly, we lost Gigi many years ago.)

Johnny and I were sitting in Fred's office visiting with him (and he couldn't have been nicer to my brother) when suddenly gun shots were fired in the building. The Chief and other officers immediately ran toward the squad room where the shots went off. Johnny and I were then locked in Chief Thomas's office and we stayed locked in there for hours. I even called my kids to explain the situation: "We're locked in a room and there are shots being fired outside." "What?!" my kids exclaimed as they went into a panic, which made me seem calm in comparison. But Johnny and I ended up fine. Very sadly, Metropolitan Police Detective Henry Daly died, along with two FBI agents, Michael J. Miller and Martha Martinez, and another seriously injured. Police headquarters is now named after Henry J. Daly.

Not long after, Johnny and I had an only positive experience. I was able to get us into a relatively small ceremony on the White House lawn, where President Bill Clinton was honoring a sports team. We sat in the first row on the South Lawn. Right after the program, President Clinton looked at Johnny and walked right over to him. He gave him a big bear hug. We got a great photograph of the three of us, which was the icing on the cake.

Another big shot in law enforcement who was a friend for many years was Richard Pennington. I also met him through my work with the Metropolitan Police Boys and Girls Clubs. He had risen to become Assistant Chief of Police in D.C., and then he went on to become Police Chief in New Orleans. He mentioned, "If you ever come to New Orleans, give me a call." So one time when I went there with Johnny, I did give him that call. I made it out of ear-shot of Johnny so he wouldn't be disappointed if I couldn't reach Richard and work something out. Richard did come on the phone immediately and was enthusiastic about getting together.

He did have an event that evening, but said he'd try to meet up later. I told him we'd be at dinner at a certain seafood place in the French Quarter. Not long after Johnny and I sat down and ordered, here comes Richard, all 6'4" of him in his full uniform—the New Orleans Chief of Police—and a complete surprise to Johnny. I thought he'd have a heart attack he was so excited. Afterwards, the three of us walked around the streets of New Orleans. Richard went on to become Police Chief of Atlanta. But he's most known to me as Johnny's hero on that fun evening. (Sadly, I just read today, May 9, 2017, that dear Richard had died at age 70.)

Making memorable moments for Johnny was one of the highlights of my own life. So many people are blasé, bored, and just basically unappreciative. But Johnny was totally the opposite of that. Whatever you did for him came back to you a million times over because of his enthusiasm and sheer joy. I still miss his sparkle and his voice saying things like "Yippee!" He was so alive with so little, while so many with so much are so the opposite.

Back to My Kids

Steph applied to public interest-oriented law schools, and was so pleased to be accepted by one of the best, City University of New York (CUNY) Law School. She had a great experience at CUNY where she made many friends and was President of the Jewish Law Students Association.

Doug started out working in New York as a Production Assistant on the *Charlie Rose Show* on PBS. I was so impressed by that, but Doug told me, "Don't be, Mom. I'm getting coffee for his guests"—but they included people like Ken Burns and Maya Angelou, who recited a poem for him, which he was really touched by. He went on to CNN as an Assignment Editor, which he was quite good at and enjoyed. Soon, though, Doug wanted to spread his wings and take off for London to work as a freelance journalist. But first he had to get a work Visa. He came to D.C. and went to the United Kingdom Visas and Immigration Office with only a letter from one possible source of part-time employment. They told him that wasn't going to be adequate. Several hours later, he walked out with a Visa. That was my son Doug.

Doug was able to travel a lot from London as a foreign correspondent, doing on-air work for such entities as NPR, and MSNBC from Rwanda. He also wrote pieces for the Christian Science Monitor on his travel in Iran, and for the *Sunday London Times* on Cuba, etc. In fact, he was able to piece together a salary from this freelance work, including hosting an early Internet talk show, which earned him more money in his 20s than I ever earned. In addition, Doug was a singer-songwriter-musician, and in London, he had his own band and I got to see him perform to an audience of several hundred, which was certainly fun for a stage-type mom.

Hilary, who had been living in New York since she was 17, began working for *U.S.News & World Report* after she graduated cum laude from NYU. She worked there for six years at various jobs and ended up being an Assistant Manager of Marketing. She then went on to *USA TODAY* for four years, where she was a Marketing Supervisor and then promoted to Marketing Manager. While working full-time, she was also active with different comedic writing side projects, including a very popular newsletter for a time—and even, as mentioned, did a bit of acting.

For five and a half years after college, Hilary lived with a young man named Mark in the Gramercy Park/Murray Hill area. Hilary met Mark at a family wedding, and I do mean family. Keeping with

Levitt tradition, Mark was actually a cousin, but in this case, a very distant one—at least more distant than I ever dated.

I got busy when my kids moved to new apartments, as they would call me in to help arrange things and hang up their pictures. I was quite good at that, and loved having opportunities to offer these skills. If they hadn't asked, I would have barged in anyway.

Although Johnny was my older brother and not my kid, I still thought of him that way. I looked so forward to going away during the holidays and spending time with Johnny and long-term dear friends. At Christmas time, I would go to Johnny's musical program at Marbridge in Austin, where he sang in the chorus, and then drive us to San Antonio. There we would spend several days with Aunt Doe, who you may remember as being like another mother to me since I was eight, and her daughter, my "sister," Linda. On the way back, we'd stop and visit with June (my friend from high school) and Lamar Hankins in San Marcos. We would also sometimes visit my ex-fiancé and other "brother" Ivan and his precious wife Bunny in Dallas. Johnny was their family too.

CHAPTER 28

Not Just the Car Passed Inspection

Back in 1988, I became responsible for two cars—my husband's old Mercedes and my red Chrysler LeBaron convertible. D.C. required cars to be inspected every year in those days, so twice a year I drove down to the inspection station on Half St., S.W.

In June of 1988, I had announced I would not be seeking reelection to the Council. Soon thereafter, I was at the inspection station when a man who worked there came up to me and said, "Councilmember Schwartz, I'm really sorry about your husband. I've watched you throughout your career starting with the School Board and you did such a good job for the city. I want to thank you for your service. We will miss you on the Council." He said it in a really sweet, caring way, and I was touched by his kind words.

From that time on, twice a year, this same man would come over and find something small but significant to say: "How are you and the children?" "Are you still with the Metropolitan Police Boys and Girls Clubs? I went to one in my neighborhood as a kid." Just small conversations. This went on for years. Soon I noticed his nametag said George so I'd call him that. But he never called me Carol, even though I said to, just Councilmember Schwartz.

In the spring of 1994, I was at the inspection station and for the first time in around 10 visits George did not come up to me. I asked someone, "Where is George?" And he responded, "He took a day off." I remember thinking, "Pooh." Months later, as I was driving to the station, he came into my mind for the first time since I was last there and I thought, "I hope he's around today."

Sure enough he was, and came walking over right away. As he approached, I thought, "What an attractive man." I had never really noticed before in all those years and could not believe I hadn't. Why? I guess I have always just been able to separate my personal and public lives, and in most situations, do not look at men as men, just people. But here I was now looking at this nice and handsome man in a whole different light. Maybe it was my being single for six years and relationships not working out. I don't know. But regardless, I actually sort of flirted for the first time in my life.

I said to him, "George, do you have a family?" (I knew nothing about him other than his first name, he worked at the inspection station, lived in Ward 8, and he had gone to the Metropolitan Police Boys and Girls Clubs as a child.) He mentioned he had two grown children, some grandchildren, and had been legally separated for nearly 20 years. Then I got bolder: "Do you have a girlfriend?" He answered, "Yes, I have been dating someone for a while but we're having problems. How about you?" "I had been going with a guy for several years, but we're not together now." I handed him my card (something I rarely ever did even when asked) and said, "Why don't you give me a call. We could go out for coffee." (Turns out, George didn't even drink coffee.)

In the early part of 1995 (several months after losing the Mayoral election) and after not having heard from George and not really ever thinking about him, I again had to go to the inspection station. Then I thought, "Oh dear. How embarrassing! George never called. What do I say?" George came right over and before I could say a word, he said, "I'm sorry I haven't called. I still have your card. But that lady I told you I was going out with, we continued on for a while and only just recently broke up." I was not sad to hear the news.

I then asked him if he knew anyone who would be interested in an old car. We had bought the kids a car many years ago, which was worn out and besides, the kids had moved away and could drive their dad's Mercedes when they were home. George said he had a good friend who dealt in used cars, so I said, "Well, use that card I gave you to call me about the car at least."

He did. He came over to the house on Springland Lane, as I still hadn't moved yet. We sat in the kitchen and we visited for a little bit before he took the Chevrolet, which his friend did sell for me for not much but at least I was rid of it. I moved to my new apartment in March and soon, George called for a real date.

He came to take me out to dinner. When I greeted him in the lobby, he had on a gigantic gold choker necklace with all three of his initials sparkling in diamonds. He also had on a huge gold watch and lots of big gold bracelets and rings—but at least no earrings. Everyone knows I like jewelry—but not on men. I thought, "Oh Lordy. Please spare me." I'd only seen this man in a uniform and now before me stood a combination of a slightly toned-down Mr. T and a much more macho version of Liberace. He still looked quite attractive, at least the parts of him that could be seen through the glare. (I may be exaggerating just a teense—but not really.)

We walked down to La Tomate, a nice Italian restaurant on Connecticut Ave. I did enjoy George's company. He had a great smile and a wonderful deep voice. And I had seen what a sweet person he was over those years. He expounded on why he had not called earlier without me even asking. He said, "As we know, in break-ups, you can go back and forth for a while before it's really over. I did not want to call until I was sure we were totally broken up for good."

After, I suggested we get a pint of ice cream and share it on a public bench. He was game and we sat grabbing spoonfuls of Ben and Jerry's. Just a hug goodnight as he said goodbye at the door of my building. He did say, "I really want to take you out again." As I thought he was adorable, I replied "I'd love to go out with you as well." But he probably didn't expect what I told him next in my straightforward way: "To be honest with you, George, I can't stand any jewelry other than a watch and a ring on a man and your gold jewelry is so extreme, I can barely look at it." Not surprisingly, he took great umbrage. So that was it. I didn't hear from him.

Afterwards I kind of regretted what I had said and thought maybe I should have bitten my tongue. But I really hated all that glitz. (And I know that does sound hypocritical coming from big-necklace me—but aren't we all hypocrites about something?) Sooner or later, though, I knew it was bound to come out of my mouth as it bothered me that much. So overall, I was glad I said something early on even though I was a little sad at missing out on what appeared to be a good guy. I could tell from our few casual meetings at the inspection station, our one former talk at my house and our recent dinner, that George liked to run the show. He was a leader, both in life and relationships (which I like). I doubted that I would ever hear from him again.

Maybe a month later he called. The minute he picked me up, he said, "I think you'll be happy to see that I don't have the neck-lace on. But I'm not going to give up wearing my bracelets and my rings as I do every day" (and combined, those were at least 15 in number). I agreed this was a good compromise. Over the next 10 years, I would learn that compromising at all was not his specialty, and I had actually scored a great victory with the necklace.

George is six and half years younger than I am. When we met at the inspection station in 1988, I was 44 and he was 38. When we started dating, I was pushing 51 and he was 44. Yet he was al-ready a grandfather by then. His daughter had two children and his son had five children, as I recall, with a few moms. George had always been very close to his own mother, who had died years earlier. We sometimes went to visit her grave at Mount Olivet Cemetery in Northeast D.C. She had been an elevator operator at a downtown building for decades. His father, who had been in the service, was a butcher who later became a taxi driver. He lived in Ward 7 and by then could not drive a cab as he was legally blind. I became very friendly with his dad, George Sr., and two of his sisters, Arlene and Joan, as well as Joan's husband, Henry. But unfortunately, Joan passed many years ago.

George had gone to Mackin Catholic High School in the late '60s and was a basketball superstar. He was about 5'11" but was a real jock. He was High School All-American, regional best of everything, and his team's highest scorer when his high school was known, according to *The Washington Post*, as "a basketball powerhouse."[142] If those far outside shots, which were his specialty, counted for three points then as they do today, no one would have come close to his average. George was awarded a full basketball scholarship to Arizona State University, and many have attested, was on his way to the NBA.

After his high school girlfriend back home had a daughter when he was 18 and a son when he was 19, he came back to Washington, married her, and went to work for the D.C. government. He knew then that the NBA would never happen, but he did play pro ball for a couple of summers in Europe and Canada.

When we started dating, he also had a part-time job from 4 to 7 p.m., working with kids in an afternoon program, which I thought was great. He really wooed me those first few months in early to mid-1995, giving me flowers and attention.

Then one weekend we planned to go to Rehoboth late one Friday afternoon. I was all packed and ready to go. He never came to pick me up. He never even called. When I called, he didn't answer his phone. Saturday came and went, nothing. Same with Sunday. I couldn't believe it. Finally, he called Monday or Tuesday, apologizing profusely. He said that Friday afternoon, he went home from work to pack and just fell asleep. (He did have some degree of narcolepsy and this wound up happening a lot.) But why no call Friday or Saturday or Sunday? He said he felt so badly he didn't know what to say.

I was crazy about him at that point. But this was just too much. I wrote a note: "I cannot be involved with someone who will blow me off for a weekend and not even call—someone who would just leave me sitting there with no idea of what was going on ..."

After a few weeks, he called to apologize again. He swore he would never leave me hanging like that in the future. However, he continued to come late for dates, usually having fallen asleep, or so he said, and sometimes he would not show up at all. He was so undependable. When he did show up on time, I'd be so relieved. What kind of relationship is that—when you're relieved that the person actually shows up?

George liked to be on his own: play basketball some and occasionally work on cars on the weekends. He was just a loner and non-attentive. I think he suffered from depression and often just took to his bed. (Unfortunately, with only a few exceptions, these have been the type of men I attract, but more on that later.) I also think he was spoiled as a child being the youngest of eight and by former women in his life. I guess his prior girlfriends (and there had been a few) just put up with his unreliability and doing as he pleased because he was so cute, so sweet, smelled divine, and was such a good dancer. I joined right in for all the same reasons.

George was really a nice person, though. My kids met him early on in our relationship, and they just loved him. So did my friends. I always ultimately based people's character on how they treated my brother. He was wonderful with Johnny. And Johnny adored him. George was clearly one of his favorite people in the world. When George was good, there was no one better. But too often he was nowhere to be found.

Now and then it would get to me and I would call it quits. I probably broke up with him more than we were together. Every time I did, he would become the most attentive person—writing notes, calling, showing up with flowers and candy, usually making sure they were on public display, often coming to my office with all of the above and always saying, "I love you."

During George's non-attentive times, I wondered if he had other relationships. But then I would think, "Who knows ... or even cares! Let them put up with this."

I ended up putting up with this not-so-good relationship off and on for about ten years. Why? He was very cute and so nice when he wanted to be. And I was a real workaholic when I was working. And in January of 1997, less than two years after we started dating, I was back on the Council. With that 60-hour workweek schedule, his not being around was less noticeable to me. And in fact, it was helpful not to have someone clingy—and George certainly was not that—except when we broke up. The relationship also kept other people at bay. I still got some come-ons back in those days and it was so convenient to say I was involved. And it made me look like a "normal" person that I had somebody, although I really didn't most of the time.

I give credit to George for one surprising thing: he helped me discover that my legs were not so bad looking. I always thought my legs were not very nice-looking, so I spent most of my first 55 years hiding my legs beneath long skirts and dresses, stopping right above my fairly decent ankles.

One Christmas, George, Johnny and I were in Midland, Texas. While there we went to Swartz's (the way my mother used to pronounce my name), a ladies' store I certainly could not afford when growing up. Now that I could, I still hated to spend that much money on clothes. But Swartz's was having a big sale and I needed suits for the Council. George said, "These are really pretty," as he pointed to two blended silk suits that were on a half-price rack. "But they're too short. They cut off at the knee and I don't like my legs," I said. "Why? You've got shapely legs like a baseball bat," he said. I wasn't sure how that could be a good thing, but I tried the suits on anyway and they looked pretty nice, so I bought them. (You can view them, one red and the other blue [the suits, not the legs], in the very unflattering portraits of me standing with the rest of Council which are on display at the Wilson Building.) After that, I started wearing shorter clothes, which now in my old age, have gotten even shorter. Once the neck and face went, I had to draw attention elsewhere.

I am grateful to George for another thing: my now signature perfume. I used to wear anything and everything—whatever anyone gave me. Our first Christmas together, George gave me a White Diamonds gift box. It was Elizabeth Taylor's brand. I immediately loved it—and not just because it was Elizabeth's, and George picked it out. Okay, maybe a little at first. But I really started liking it, especially when I got compliments all the time. Thanks, George—and Elizabeth.

Also on the positive side, George and I had fun times, especially playing cards. He was really a good player of various card games and we did it for hours on end. George was smart, though undereducated. He had an amazing memory about the things he cared about: sports, cars, and he knew every word of every song from decades ago. I love to dance and George was a great dancer.

Even though I was in a much better financial situation than George, he paid for many of our dinners out. I did pay to take him for a long weekend to Las Vegas for his 50th birthday in 2000. But he was in such a depressed mood—I guess about turning 50, or maybe just his normal mood—that he refused to dance even when we were out where others were dancing. I guess it was then—after over five years together and halfway across the country—that I finally started realizing that this was not the right person. But it took me another half a decade to really say, the end.

Back in 1996, right after I won the at-large Council seat, "The Reliable Source" column in *The Washington Post* called after a picture of George and I dancing together at the victory party appeared in their paper. A few days later they wrote a short article about us: "Some people go through D.C. auto inspection and find only frustration and rejection. D.C. Councilmember-elect Carol Schwartz found inspector George ... and, ultimately, romance" with a photo of us dancing. The picture included a caption which said the two of us had our differences: "She's a Republican and he's a Democrat." It was cute. The column also remarked that George was separated. (I had been honest to the columnist who asked, "Has he ever been married?" I said, "Yes." They said, "Widowed or divorced?" I stated, "Legally separated for 20 years."[143])

Because of being Catholic, George had been reluctant to divorce, even though he and his wife had been apart for two decades when we started dating. George always told me that he and his "former" wife had consistently told each other that they would get divorced easily if one or the other wanted to. In 1998, as I was getting set to run for Mayor again, and remembering that article from a couple of years earlier, I said "George, I don't want to get married." (I didn't want to get married to him or anyone.) I continued, "But it is very hard for me as a public figure to be with what looks like to the outside world, a married man. Would you finally get that divorce you've talked about?" He said, "I'll think about it." He didn't do anything then. And I never asked again.

Four years later, in 2002, when I was running for Mayor yet again and we were in the midst of one of our breakups (and now I'm serious and he knows it), he called and said, "I've got something to tell you. I think you'll be happy. I'm divorced." He had told his wife he was ready. And it was simple. They just went to court and provided two signatures. I said upon hearing the news, "Well, that's nice." He was so upset with me that I wasn't excited about the divorce. From my point of view, why should I get excited in 2002 when he didn't get the divorce when I asked him to in 1998 for my Mayoral campaign nor in 2000 for my Council reelection? He did it only during one of our last breakups when I just didn't care anymore!

We continued to break up sporadically and he would come back to me, sending flowers and cards, saying he loved me. He always said he loved me. Although he consumed a great deal of my life, toward the end, about nine years into the relationship, I began to say to George: "I am a very forgiving person, in fact, too forgiving, especially with those I love. But I want to tell you something. I know from my history that I reach a point when I say, that's it. I realize I don't have much credibility with you after taking you back so many times over these many years. But I do reach that point and I feel it's getting close." Soon thereafter, I did reach that point and I *did* break it off for good. He couldn't believe it when I finally did it. But did it I did. This time, it was really over.

After our final breakup, I saw George about every six months or so. We'd have dinner or lunch. But it was only as friends. Then about eight years ago, my daughter Hilary was doing a comedy show on Capitol Hill. I invited a lot of my friends, including George who promised to come. I said, "Are you sure you are going to come? I'm reserving a spot for you and there's limited seating." Sure enough there was one empty seat. He didn't show. That was it—not even a friendship—and I told him so. When you don't show up for me, it's one thing. But not showing up for my kid ... I haven't seen him since.

And there was another big resentment by then as well. When we finally broke up for good in 2004, he never let anyone know. I still don't think he's telling anyone. In fact, I just talked to his sister recently and she was shocked that we were no longer together, and we had broken up 13 years ago. For all that time, he's acted like we're still together. I know for a fact that when people ask, "How's Carol?" he says, "Great." "Give her my best." "I will." His deception—or just being private or whatever—has deprived me of a few opportunities. Here's an example:

At a friend's wedding about 10 years ago, a nice-looking and classy man came over and said he thought I was an outstanding public servant, and we talked for a moment. I didn't find many men appealing in those days, but I thought he was enormously so and distinguished looking. And I could tell he was smart as well.

Then another man who was the husband of a friend came over when I was talking to this gentleman and asked, "How's George?" I said that we'd been broken up for years. "Really?" was his response. "I just saw George and he said you're great." I remarked that George tends to do that. But I did notice that when I said that George and I had been broken up for years, that attractive man just looked taken aback. "You're not with that George guy?" he said. "When I lost my wife a few years ago and started dating, I wanted to ask you out. But this friend (pointing to the other guy) told me that you had a longtime boyfriend. And just about a year ago, I started dating that lady there, and we're engaged." I looked over and saw his fiancé, a very age-appropriate, pretty and classy woman. I thought good for them, but an ongoing bad for me.

Unfortunately, I've had other similar experiences like the one at the wedding regarding George over these many years. And I have become resentful that a basically nonexistent relationship I was in for a decade may still be keeping people at bay another decade later. And this time, I have *not* been a willing participant.

When I was really into George at the very beginning, my daughter Stephanie said to me, "I really like George. He's so handsome and sweet. But is he smart enough for you?" I said, "Stephanie, I've had smart." After George and I broke up for good, someone said to me, "But he's such a good dancer." I said, "I've had good dancer." Now how about smart, good dancer, attentive, not depressed—and a good guy? Among those who are available, probably doesn't exist!

Pride in All of Who We Are

When I was with George, I was conscious of being an interracial couple. Most people were accepting, but at times I noticed the negative looks we would get. Though it was way past the time for it to happen, at the beginning I did ponder what it would have been like if George and I had a child.

Once at a wedding of friends who happened to be a mixed-race man and a black woman, we were sitting at the table with several mixed-race young people. I asked them what they racially considered themselves to be. Every single one, in spite of their white parents being at the nearby table, said "Black." I said, "Not even mixed race?" "No." Then I, being me, followed up with, "But don't you think that denies the existence of your white parent?" I knew that if George and I had that biracial child, and that child only said "Black," I would resent—and be terribly hurt by—what I would consider to be the erasing of me because I happen to be white.

Years later, I was grateful when the census finally had the option of "mixed race" on their form. But I must admit I regretted that President Barack Obama still chose only black on the questionnaire, which of course he had a right to do. And I understand the history where a person was considered black if they had one drop of black blood. But why are we now, in this day and time, willingly embracing those separatist vestiges? And what about

President Obama's mother and grandparents who he talks about so often? Why should they be erased because they are white? I actually felt badly for them.

I also do understand where those of mixed race who say "I'm black" are coming from. They want to show pride in their minority status, and they should. I have certainly felt similar pride as a Jewish person. And of course everyone has—and should have—the choice to do what they want to do. But I do hope they will consider acknowledging the full parts of themselves, not only to show respect and love for their entire family, but also to show respect and love for their full selves—whatever that may be.

I would want my grandchildren and great-grandchildren to feel that way. If they were all products of intermarriage, I would certainly want them to say, if this be the case, "I am African American, Caucasian, Asian, Jewish and Christian." Why deny parts of it? Why not keep the entire heritage alive? Why not embrace all of who we are, especially when it could also help transcend human barriers? Why not, "I am Black and I am White"?

Why Not Share a Dancer?

As I mentioned a little bit ago, George and I had lots of fun on the dance floor. Soon I found at weddings and other events, some of my friends, married and not, would knock me over to dance with him. At first I didn't mind—except for the ones who insisted upon grinding against him.

My sharing of a dance partner was not new. I was always empathetic at parties seeing a woman sitting alone. I'd even ask my husband David if he wouldn't mind dancing with her. Yet when I became a widow, I noticed that no one sent their husbands or boyfriends my way to do the same. I always thought that if people were lucky enough to be with a man who danced, why not share?

In 2014 when I was at the Red Cross Ball in West Palm Beach, a man named John Caliste I didn't know was sitting next to me at the table. We started talking and he even asked me to dance a couple of times. I could tell he was younger, but still in the range, had such a great sense of humor, was so smart, attractive, attentive—and a good dancer. I said to myself, "He's perfect." Then I said to myself, "He's too perfect. I bet he's gay"—and he is. John has become a good friend and a frequent dance partner. We each get our own ticket, and then go together to events like the 2015 Red Cross Ball in Florida, as well as the Opera Ball at the Kennedy Center last year and its Gala this year. We also dine out occasionally.

Now back to the point I was trying to make: As John was asking me to dance several times at that Ball in 2014, and I was having such a good time with him, I started thinking about another single woman at our table. I began to feel badly for her, so with John's permission I ran over and asked her to join us. The three of us danced individually together and before I knew it, she grabbed John's hand and started jitterbugging across the floor, leaving me standing alone. No good dance—I mean deed—goes unpunished. But I still think we should share a dancer—good or not so good.

A Sad Spring

A terribly sad episode occurred in 1995. Steve Sellows, an intellectually challenged and well-known D.C. resident was beaten to death on a street in his neighborhood. Steve was a volunteer with many groups, some political like my 1994 Mayoral campaign. I was proud to be on the Council when we made sure that a street was named in his honor, Steve Sellows Way, in Northeast D.C.

In 1995, my father's older brother, Uncle Albert, who had lived in New York since his teens, was dying of prostate cancer in a Connecticut nursing home near his only child. It was a year after my dad died and I had always been close to Uncle Albert. So I called my cousin Andrew, Albert's son, and said I'd love to come and see my uncle. Andrew said no, he doesn't need any company. But I was determined to go, even without his permission. I took the train to Danbury, Connecticut, and walked a couple of miles from the train station to the nursing home. I spent several hours with Uncle Albert, saying goodbye, and then walked back to catch a train home, feeling very sad—but glad that I had made the trip.

A Reunion of Some College Friends

Around then, several friends, a few of whom were sorority sisters at the University of Texas, had a reunion in Snowmass, Colorado over the weekend of July 4th. These gals were all originally from San Antonio and grew up as friends. And they were all married. Even though I didn't qualify for either of those two categories, they invited me along. They had their husbands there on our first reunion and it was really a great time.

Since then we've had many reunions, but they made the decision to leave the husbands at home. We've gone to San Antonio, one couple's place on South Padre Island, Texas, and my place in Rehoboth Beach. We've done a cruise, and met in Florida and just a couple of months ago were in Las Vegas for Patty and Larry Fallek's 50th anniversary celebration. These friends—Patty, Susan Becker, Carolyn Colvin, and Sandy Schwartz—have been special in my life and our times together have meant a lot.

Some Nice Honors

In October of 1995 I received an honor from my high school, the place where I became driven to impress. I was one of a select few inducted into the Midland High School Hall of Fame. The program listed me as Carol Levitt Schwartz, Class of '61, political activist, social-political commentator, former teacher, now in Washington, D.C. I went to Midland for the ceremony and walked onto the Midland High School football field (just 20 miles from Odessa High, about which *Friday Night Lights* was written) with my fellow inductees, two former professional football players. Especially given the pain of my childhood there, both at home and out of it, it was a special honor—and one I will never forget.

Also in 1995, the International Republican Institute (IRI) asked me to become an instructor at a seminar series it held for Turkish Mayors, entitled "Civic Action and Democratic Reform" in that country. We flew to Istanbul in the afternoon and then drove to a magnificent resort on the edge of the Black Sea. The first night we were having a welcome dinner with dignitaries from all over Turkey. My luggage was the only luggage that did not arrive. And it was a Sunday night and the resort stores were closed. What to do? What I did do is make the best of a not-so-good situation. I always carried an extra pair of underwear in a shoulder bag along with my toothbrush and toothpaste, my makeup and jewelry. I took a bath and put on my raincoat, which I had traveled with. In those days, when I had a waist, I wore belts so I belted my raincoat, put on my makeup and jewelry and off I went. Everyone said, "Oh, you got your suitcase." I had not, but I was glad I passed.

It was an interesting seminar. I don't think these Turkish Mayors in 1995 expected to find a Jewish female former Councilmember as their instructor. They were a little aloof at first, but it all worked out fine. I would give them specific experiences I had as both a member of the School Board and the Council, and warned them of certain pitfalls. Most of them went out of their way to tell me how helpful I had been to them as they were new to these positions in their emerging democracy. A fellow instructor was Stuart Holiday, now the President and CEO for many years of the Meridian International Center.

In 1996, I was asked to be part of the official U.S. delegation to Croatia to observe their election. It was a wonderful experience to witness again, individuals voting for the first time. One of the other U.S. delegates was Kip O'Neill, son of Tip—a nice guy just like his dad.

Then in 1996, I received the honor of carrying the Olympic torch as a "Washington Community Hero." That same exact torch which I held, and which went through many more hands before and after me, eventually lit the cauldron to start the Olympic games in Atlanta. And the person who did the last lap and who lit it was none other than Muhammad Ali, who was already suffering from Parkinson's disease then, 20 years before he recently passed away. It was great to see it again last year as that lighting was replayed at the beginning of the 2016 Summer Olympics.

Carrying the torch was quite an exciting experience until I had to put on the uniform—white shorts and top (not my most flattering outfit)—and then had to run uphill—when I could barely walk it—in front of a huge crowd. The worst part is that Tay and Roger's son, Phil, captured it all on video, so I got to actually see what I was afraid I looked like. I did enjoy, though, that the video was looped to the theme from *Chariots of Fire*. By the way, if I had ever had enough money in my Mayoral campaigns to license a song, I often thought that should be it. Either that or the *Rocky* theme. I guess, in retrospect, the best choice would have been "The Impossible Dream" from one of my favorite musicals, *Man of La Mancha*.

And here came another nice opportunity: Barbara Davis Blum and I became friends back in the 1980s through mutual friends. She had served in the Carter Administration and then became CEO of the Women's National Bank, which was the first federally chartered bank owned and managed by women. It later changed its name to Abigail Adams National Bank. I was asked to become a member of its Board of Directors in the 1990s. It was an honor, and I enjoyed doing it for several years.

In the late '90s, a known business person with national connections asked me out to lunch, saying that he was interested in getting me on some corporate boards as many wanted to increase their representation of women. As soon as we sat down at the Hay-Adams restaurant, he, a married man, asked me if I was dating anyone. I told him all about George, who I was with at the time. Then the meeting ended quickly with no board discussion. It became quite obvious that this man *was* looking to increase the representation of women—but only in his personal life.

More Losses

All the while, personal losses continued. The mid-'90s was still a time before the advent of protease inhibitors to combat HIV and AIDS, so unfortunately, I saw more friends pass away. Dear friend Charles Epps died in October of 1995; then Hank Carde, another good friend; as well as sweet David Watkins—all of whom I visited in the hospital. I was so sad about the losses and so fearful of losing even more beloved people. And I did.

Among them was Tom Mader, a wonderful friend since the early 1980s. Tom, Executive Director of the Friends of the Kennedy Center, came up with the idea of the annual Kennedy Center Open House with day-long activities open to all—and for free—to connect with the surrounding communities. Tom was a very handsome and interesting man.

Tom was gay but unfortunately closeted for much of his life, probably due his Catholic upbringing. I would see him around town with attractive guys. But whenever I got together with him, which was often, he'd talk about the girls he was dating. This went on for years. Then, in the late '90s, nearly two decades into our friendship, we met one night for dinner and that changed. He sat down and started talking about a gal he was seeing. By this point, I'd had it. I got up, took my coat, looked at him, and said, "Tom, I am tired of this. I know you are gay. Everyone knows it. And it would be helpful to your gay friends to just come clean. Instead we still have to go through this charade. I'm not doing it anymore." I went to the door and he came running after me. We sat back down, and we had an even closer relationship from that time on.

Terribly, we lost Tom to AIDS in 2004. Several of us gathered with him in bed before he left to be near his family in hospice care: Phyllis Freedman, who was his chief caretaker, Jay Fisette, Bob Rosen, and myself. I still miss Tom. His photo is on my refrigerator. I have all the beautiful notes he sent. The paintings he left me are still proudly displayed. And I stayed in touch with his mother in Wisconsin while she well enough to do so.

(I really wanted Tom be comfortable enough with himself to admit who he really was. And I also cared because when one keeps herself or himself closeted, it does harm to the cause. I have even begged friends to come out, saying, "If you would just do that, it would make it so much easier for others here and everywhere—and in the future.)

Enter the Financial Control Board

I kept a close eye on the workings of the D.C. government during the eight years after I left the Council on January 2, 1989.

The overspending of Mayor Sharon Pratt Kelly from 1990-94, coupled with the outrageous budgets of Barry's first three terms from 1978 to 1990, finally caught up with the city. Now with Marion Barry back in office as Mayor in 1995, D.C. faced a $700 million deficit. Barry asked Congress for a bail-out, even though he didn't balance the request with reductions in the humungous city staff and spending. Instead, Congress—now controlled by Republicans—instituted a five-member Financial Control Board in 1995, giving it responsibility for fiscal oversight of the city, which by the way, had been requested by Democratic Councilmember Kevin Chavous in a *Post* op-ed piece.[144] With the inception of the Board, the Mayor's office was basically rendered impotent as was the D.C. Council; and a CFO was installed—Anthony Williams.

One of the many actions of the Financial Control Board was the firing of the Superintendent of Schools, Franklin Smith, at the end of '96, and putting in his place retired Army Lieutenant General Julius Becton, a Virginia resident with no real education experience. The Control Board also replaced our elected Board of Education's authority with a five-member hand-picked Board of Trustees, who also had no real educational experience. I'm sure all had good intentions, but under this new non-educational/management-type regime, the test scores did not go up either.

CHAPTER 29

Another Council Run

An at-large Council race was set for November of 1996. The current occupant of the non-majority at-large seat was still Independent Bill Lightfoot. He had announced he would not be seeking reelection at the end of his second term, and went back to being a registered Democrat as soon as he left office.

Just as he was prepared to run against me in 1988, I was prepared to run against him in 1996. By circumstances in both cases, we never had to go head to head. I said to the *Washington Blade* on May 24, 1996 in response to a question about rumors of my running: "Yes, I'm thinking about it ... The thought of playing a role in helping the city at this particular time is appealing. But I'm not there yet. I'll have to make a decision in about a month." In June, I entered the race.

Although there were many disturbing changes in the District, or maybe because of them, I felt a call to serve the city again. Those changes ran the gamut from the Financial Control Board's takeover of D.C. to the closing of the decades-old Higgers drug store on Connecticut Ave. in May of 1996, which to me it was indicative of the struggles of the few independently owned businesses we had and our lack of effort to keep them—and attract more. I knew we could do better.

But the main reason I wanted to run is to help bring financial responsibility to the Council body (as I did when I voted against the bloated budgets in the 1980s) which I thought would help wrestle control from the Financial Control Board—and give D.C. back at least the limited Home Rule we had before.

In that at-large Council campaign, I spoke of wanting to expand jobs—and businesses, upgrade city services while reducing waste, lowering taxes, and tackling our ongoing problems, such as alcohol and drug addiction and the racial and economic divide.

I also wanted the Council to take on a more serious role in oversight as well as ferret out problems rather than being surprised when they became headlines in the newspaper. (I used that line a lot.) I won my old seat back by a large margin—getting 96% in the primary (well, I only had a few write-ins as opponents) and garnering nearly 74,000 votes in the general election.

Back on the Council

The first day of my new Council term in January of 1997, Chair David Clarke made a surprising speech in a closed gathering of the

Council. He spoke of doing a bad thing to me back in 1987 during my first term by reducing the number of committees when it came time for me to chair one. He actually said, "I did a terrible thing to Carol. I denied her a committee and I have felt awful about it ever since. Although we do not give newly elected members a committee, this time, I want to make it up to her."

That year the only other newly-elected Councilmember was Sandy Allen, a Democrat, who beat Barry's handpicked Ward 8 successor, Eydie Whittington. Dave said to Sandy—with all of us present—that he hoped she didn't mind if he, in order to make up for the past injustice, gave me a newly created committee and not her, a Democrat. Sandy said she didn't mind at all. Although the Committee Dave Clarke added for me, Local, Regional and Federal Affairs, was not a major one and had fewer committee staff, I felt grateful to have it—and felt redeemed by his kind words.

After the meeting, I went up to Sandy to say thank you directly. She said, "Carol, I don't know if you remember me, but I briefly worked at the Council when you were here in the '80s. You were always so nice to the staff. You were one of our favorites. I'm glad you're back now, and was happy to do this for you." We became dear friends then and remain so to this day.

Not long after I came back, we had to move to One Judiciary Square as the Wilson Building was scheduled for renovation. The plans for the Council Chamber continued the awful configuration of decades, where the Council sat at the head of a very long room with narrow rows of chairs going way back. This was a problem because: 1) it was a narrow area and the dais had to be in a rectangular shape, only a few of the Councilmembers could look out directly at the audience, or be seen directly. Over half of the members had only their profiles in view and some at the farthest corners weren't viewed at all, and 2) the audience's chairs went so far back, some observers could barely see or hear anything.

When I saw that the new plans kept that same impossible configuration, I said, "Wait just a minute. Here's an opportunity to finally rectify an ongoing problem." Instead, I suggested that we change it from a vertical arrangement to a horizontal one so that when you entered the room, all Councilmembers would be equally visible at the center and far closer to the entire audience. The suggestion was enthusiastically embraced and the plan was changed. The benefits are there for all today. (I thought about putting in an illustration for comparison, but figured at this point, you got more of the picture than you ever wanted.)

The Council was more than a full-time job, though defined as part-time. I found that I spent 40-60 hours a week on Council business. Most others made it a full-time job as well. Some members, though, had additional paid outside employment, sometimes making as much as $250,000 a year for it.

Another Run-In with Congress

Marion Barry, who was Mayor at this time, and I had a few surprising views in common. We were both concerned about the perpetual dependency that welfare created for the able-bodied and able-minded and were happy when President Clinton passed a work requirement called Workfare, originally proposed by President Reagan. Marion and I were also united on the bill I introduced to invoke the death penalty for the killing of police officers in the line of duty (and not in self-defense or after provocation). The bill also required that juveniles convicted of first or second-degree murder of a police officer had to be confined until age 30. Marion, as Mayor, obviously couldn't vote but he spoke publicly and fervently in favor of the bill. The only other supporter on the Council was Harold Brazil and therefore when the measure was voted on, it was defeated 11 to 2.

Right after that, Senator Kay Bailey Hutchison from Texas offered legislation which forced the District to enact a law similar to my own, in fact written practically verbatim. I obviously wanted my legislation to pass or I wouldn't have introduced it. It was something I had strong feelings about then and nearly 20 years later, still do. However, I also have strong feelings about the District being able to decide on its own what laws we want to enact and which ones we do not—without interference from Congress.

So I went up to Senator Hutchison's office. After a cordial few moments, I said to her, "I need you not to bring your bill forward. It's just an imposition on the District of Columbia. The citizens have spoken through an overwhelmingly majority Council vote."

And then Senator Hutchinson said, "The United States Constitution gives Congress the authority to oversee the District of Columbia. The Constitution gives us the power." I said: "Kay, you're absolutely right. You have the power. But let me tell you, this Constitution you are quoting and which I have great affection for, had it been so perfect the way it was written in 1787, you as a woman would *not* be sitting here in the United States Senate. You not only would *not* be sitting here, you wouldn't even be able to *vote* for the people who are sitting here. So the Constitution—an admirable, wonderful document—obviously had to be changed over the years to rectify the injustice of having only white male landowners be the *only* ones who could vote or hold office. Another injustice that needs to be rectified is the fact that the District of Columbia, a jurisdiction made up of over 500,000 people [at that time], larger than a couple of states, is treated so unequally by not only having taxation without representation but also having to live under the whims of Congress. That needs to be changed, too. So the fact that you *can* do this as a member of Congress does not mean that you *should* do it." (And I said that all in practically one breath.) Our meeting ended. And in spite of all my articulateness that day, she did not withdraw the bill.

Not long after, a hearing was held by the Senate Committee that received Senator Hutchison's bill. I went up to the Hill and testified *against* what virtually was my own bill. I said basically the same thing to the Committee members that I had said to Kay herself, sans the woman part as none of these Senators were women. I also said to them that it was not easy to testify against something I cared so much about and had supported. But I have always cared and supported *more* the right of the District of Columbia to be a true democracy and make its own decisions.

The Committee never brought the legislation forward. I do not know if that was a result of my testimony or Senator Hutchison not pushing the issue after our meeting, or none of the above. Regardless, I was grateful for the results. And I am also grateful that Kay obviously has gotten over my lecture on the Constitution—and my not following up on her offer to help during the 1994 Mayoral race—since over the years when I have seen her, such as on planes heading to or from Texas, we have had warm conversations. And I did see her in October of 2015 at our 50th college reunion at the University of Texas, where she introduced me to the President of UT with generous praise and even exhibited pride in my career. I feel the same way about her esteemed service.

Today, I still wish that D.C. would enact similar legislation to the one I, with support from Marion, pushed in 1997. I do understand that people have legitimate concerns about severe punishment such as the death penalty, much of it fear about an innocent person being found guilty. Marion and I felt then that due to the various appeal processes that it probably would not happen. Today, with those processes still in place, combined with all the DNA and other forensic advances, those chances are certainly lessened. We as a society put a lot of expectations on individuals who put themselves in harm's way for us for not huge salaries. And we should expect a lot—including equal and respectful treatment. And if that doesn't happen—and it's proven—they should be held accountable and dismissed or worse. But what are we doing to protect the vast majority of good people who protect us? And how are we going to keep people in this dangerous profession if the pressure we put on them is not met with a commiserate amount of interest in their well-being?

Legislative Initiatives Defined

In my 16 years on the Council, I probably introduced, co-introduced or co-sponsored thousands of pieces of legislation, including resolutions. Resolutions basically honor individuals or events, or state opinions on various subjects, in the "Whereas ... Therefore, be it resolved ..." format. Obviously, I will not talk about resolutions much as well as the vast majority of legislation I was involved with. But I will highlight some in this book, only ones I introduced or co-introduced, and those which were most important to me. I will not deal with the legislation I just co-sponsored (merely added my name to) unless it was truly noteworthy. In this section I will talk about some legislation, while others that were particularly significant to my career and/or received a lot of publicity at the time, will be discussed in greater detail later and chronologically. Bet you can't wait!

Most of the legislation that I introduced or co-introduced over the years was my own initiative. I literally thought many of them up late at night—always tackling a problem in my mind until I came up with some solution.

(I'm a night owl I think by choice. I may have the proclivity to be an insomniac, but I don't give myself the chance to be one as I stay up very late—actually very early in the morning—to avoid any chance of sleeplessness. I used to do my best thinking then. But as I'm getting older, I still stay up very late, but find now I do my best thinking earlier in the day, and that day is now starting earlier as well. So here I am, both a night owl *and* an early bird. If you don't believe me, just look at the circles under my eyes.)

A lot of legislation at the Council comes by way of special interest groups, and I have sometimes introduced those initiatives, but not too often, though I have signed on to some as a co-sponsor. Also legislation can come from the Mayor's office; and if you chair the relevant subject-matter committee, you may agree to introduce it on the Mayor's behalf. Still, most of my introduced legislation really was my own, including a few compromise pieces of legislation where I tried to reasonably and responsibly modify some that were too extreme upon introduction.

As soon as I got on the Council, I started trying to tackle major issues within our government that I cared about and knew needed improvement, such as tax reform, bringing business and jobs back to D.C., and helping resolve the parking issues of residents and the few shoppers we had at that time. Other initiatives presented themselves during my time on the Council, like DUI protections and employee safeguards for reporting wrongdoing—issues I cared strongly about as well.

I viewed my job as a balancing act. In dealing with most matters, if one group walked out of my office high-fiving each other and the other was devastated, I felt I must have done something wrong. There should be give and take—a compromise—to reach the right solution, knowing more often than not, both sides have legitimate points (unless they're pushing discrimination or other types of similar injustices for which, in my mind, there are no legitimate points). By using my common sense, empathy and sense of fairness, people and interests were better served—and extremes were prevented.

Whistleblower Protection Law

In 1998, police officers came to my Council office stating they had suffered retaliation because they blew the whistle on supervisors who had required them to falsify timesheets. I brought the issue to the Council and pushed for an investigation. Jack Evans, who chaired the Committee on the Judiciary (which had the police under it), and Kathy Patterson, who chaired the Committee on Government Operations (which included government procedural issues) welcomed an investigation and proceeded to schedule a joint hearing. This episode with the police, as well as other instances in the past I was aware of, pushed me to begin amending our somewhat nebulous whistleblower protections to create the strongest whistleblower protections law in the country.

After months of research and input from experts, on April 1, 1997, I introduced the "District of Columbia Whistleblower Reinforcement Act." It stipulated that workers would be protected if they unearthed waste, fraud and abuse in government, and required those at a supervisory level to do so. I also made sure that any employee who was already on probation or in the process of dismissal—and not in retaliation for whistleblowing—could *not* cloak him or herself in the law to avoid separation. The bill unanimously passed the Council in 1998 after going through the Committee on Government Operations. Several years later, the federal government used our law as the blueprint for its own. It remains one of my proudest accomplishments.

Early Legislative Initiatives

Here is my first example of a late-night brainstorm: In February of 1997, a little over a month after I got sworn in, I proposed free parking on Saturdays and weeknights to encourage shopping in the city. At that time, we had a dearth of businesses and restaurants, and the few we had were basically empty on nights and weekends—quite different from today. Everyone including our own residents ran to the suburbs for their shopping and eating needs, especially to the malls where free parking was readily available. My proposed free parking at those designated times passed the Public Works Committee in January of 1998, and then the Council in April of that year. And it did help bring some business.

On rare occasions, though, I was on the opposite side of the business community. Although I am pro-business as I like the jobs, services, taxes and vitality they provide, residents and their well-being are my main concern. Therefore, early in 1998, I introduced the bill that lowered the threshold for drunk driving from 1.0 to .08 for blood alcohol level. The Metropolitan Washington Council of Governments (COG), on which I served as a representative of the District, had studied the drunk driving issue and had passed a resolution calling on all jurisdictions in the metropolitan area to make the change. The state of Maryland had defeated it in its legislature, and the Commonwealth of Virginia had refused to deal with it at all, as had the District. It was not a favorite piece of legislation of restaurant and bar owners, and they lobbied strongly against it. However, I brought it forward and made sure it got passed by the Council before the end of the year, putting D.C. at the forefront of positive regional change in battling drunk driving. Maryland and Virginia eventually followed.

Another area of keen interest has always been protecting the rights of victims of crime. Thus, in December of 1997, I co-introduced with Councilmember Harold Brazil a comprehensive victims' rights bill that gave victims access to all information as well as counseling and medical services.

A piece of legislation I thought up at night centered around the following: We were finding agencies were not enforcing fees and fines, such as health code violations by restaurants or garbage violations by them as well as by property owners. Often this was due to lack of staff. This non-enforcement affected our quality of life, including less control of rats, and we were also losing out on needed revenue. In 1998, I introduced the "Fee Collection Incentive Act" to encourage the enforcement of our laws by declaring that a certain percentage of money collected would go back to agencies to boost their collection ability by hiring more staff. This was a built-in incentive to protect our health and well-being.

Making it Easier for Residents to Park

Residential parking has been an issue many have struggled with in our densely populated city. People would have to drive around for long periods of time trying to find parking near their home, particularly in crowded neighborhoods. This also could become a safety issue if residents needed to walk long distances at night. After another late-night brainstorm, I introduced legislation that allowed for parking closer to the corners and at certain non-emergency loading-type areas during the non-busy hours from 10 p.m. to 7 a.m. This opened up many parking opportunities nearer to residents' homes then and thank goodness, still does today.

Another issue I tackled was handicapped parking which D.C. allowed to be totally free and endless on any street, whether metered or not. My staff did a survey of downtown meters, especially near federal office buildings and found that about 75% of those spaces was taken up by Maryland and Virginia cars with handicapped placards—absurdly exceeding the percentages of those who are disabled. And those cars were staying in the same spot all day. I then went about trying to stop this abuse while being sensitive to those who legitimately need accommodation. The solution: Meters would now give double the time for money inserted for those in need of that extra time. Meanwhile, illegitimate placard holders were no longer given a free and unlimited ride, and spaces were opened up for the legitimately disabled as well as residents and shoppers from anywhere.

Persistence Pays Off ... Sometimes

Sometimes you and your colleagues come up with some good ideas that unfortunately go nowhere. Any bill introduced goes to the relevant committee and it could just sit there through an entire Council period of two years, and then die. When elections are held in November and the Council is reorganized in January, if you are still interested in pursuing your bill that died in committee the year before, you can reintroduce it, where it could face the same fate, get passed as is, or be changed.

Harold Brazil and I introduced a bill entitled the "D.C. Telephone Fraud Act of 1998," which was designed to protect consumers. The bill required specific telephone solicitors to obtain a Certificate of Registration from the Department of Consumer and Regulatory Affairs, which would establish regulations for them. The bill permitted the prosecution of people engaged in telemarketing fraud and misrepresentation. Civil and criminal penalties for violators were imposed, and a fund was established to compensate the victims of such fraud.

The bill sat in committee until it died. The next year we reintroduced it verbatim and this time, added on some co-sponsors. Still nada. Then in 2000, the "Seniors Protection Amendment Act" was co-introduced by many, including Harold and myself, and it became law in 2000. Here's what it did: established standards and requirements for telephone solicitors; permitted the prosecution of persons engaged in telemarketing fraud and misrepresentation, and established civil and criminal penalties for violators. Sound familiar? It replaced the original victims' fund with counseling and testifying opportunities. Just a tweak, a different name—and the chair of the committee getting credit—did it.

The above showed you just have to be patient, adaptable and persistent to get things accomplished. Other times, even with all the patience, adaptability and persistence in the world, you still may come up empty-handed. Regardless, it never stopped me from trying and trying—again and again.

A strong example of trying again and again was my legislation requiring school uniforms/standard attire (such as white shirts and black pants or skirts of certain length) in our public schools. I must have introduced it three or four times, one time with Councilmember Kevin Chavous. I thought uniforms were important as an economic equalizer, preventing a situation where some students can afford to wear designer clothes while others cannot. Standard attire can ease students' feelings of competition—and the pressure that puts on parents. Uniforms are certainly part of the appeal of private schools—religious and others—where the vast majority require them. With school uniforms, fashion is no longer a distraction and the emphasis can be on study. I know it's pie in the sky to wish for a day when girls' skirts and leggings are not totally revealing all their parts and guys' jeans are not held up by their knees. Uniforms could also take care of that.

Unfortunately, the legislation never went anywhere, though many charter schools now have a uniform policy, and public school rules do now allow for individual schools to have it if a majority of parents say yes. But just imagine parents of pubescent kids or teenagers in today's world saying yes when their children, like most, don't want it. It's even hard for principals to make this decision as kids can transfer to other schools. Therefore, I did hope then—and still hope now—that uniforms/standard attire will become the policy of our school system for all the above reasons.

Another Death of a Good Council Chair

On March 27, 1997, Chair of the Council, David Clarke, died of brain cancer. I was sad and had been since he told us all that he was struggling with the disease. I found Dave to be intriguing as he was not the stereotypical outgoing politician. He was actually socially shy and seemed to hate most of the public appearances he was required to make, but he always did show up—and usually on his bicycle. And it was obvious to all sectors of the city that he loved D.C. and its residents, as he did his lovely wife Carole and bright son Jeffrey. Dave was a fine public servant who served us very well. In the March 29, 1997 *Washington Post*, Colbert King wrote, "He taught us all—black and white—that it is possible to live beyond our largely self-imposed strictures of race."[145]

(An aside: I went to the Internet to make sure I was spelling Carole's and Jeffrey's names correctly. I learned that Carole's maiden name was Leavitt, and that she was a special education teacher. I had no idea that we shared both names—in pronunciation—as well as initial professions. The last I heard Carole was in the Peace Corps out of the U.S., but I hope she'll learn about these similarities and find them as curious as I do if she remembers me.)

Help from the Feds, but at a High Price

Around the time Dave Clarke was very ill, the Clinton Administration sent over a plan to take back some of the federal responsibilities D.C. had. The "Federal Plan," later renamed the "D.C. Revitalization Act," emanated from the D.C. Financial Control Board's analysis of the structural imbalance between D.C. and the federal government. That analysis showed that D.C. was carrying costs usually covered by either states or the feds. These included federal court costs, Medicaid, and the pension liability for formerly considered federal employees (prior to Home Rule in 1974), such as teachers and police officers.

In order to shed more light on the District's unfair burden—usually assumed by states—let's zoom in on Medicaid. As Appleseed's 2008 comprehensive report on the D.C. Revitalization Act explains: "States generally assume the nonfederal share of Medicaid expenditures. New York City was the only city outside of D.C. that paid a portion of Medicaid costs, and that level was 25%. By contrast, the District was forced to pay 50% of its Medicaid costs—the largest burden borne by any city in the nation."[146]

At the same time, I want to point out that the District has an unbearable tax disadvantage in that we can neither enact a commuter tax nor tax income at the source (where it is earned), which every other city in the country can do. Why can't we? Because Congress won't let us. Not the Constitution, but Congress itself.

Thank goodness Representative Tom Davis, Republican Congressman from Northern Virginia, who chaired the House D.C. Subcommittee, and Eleanor Holmes Norton, the Democratic non-voting member of the House for the District, took up the cause of this structural imbalance laid out by the Control Board. They put together a plan which would address the federal courts, the problematic Medicaid issue, and the original federal pension system. That plan then was sent on to the White House.

One of the things I'm the proudest of in all of my political career occurred around that plan when it came over from the White House to the D.C. Council. And it all took place totally behind the scenes. Even though it was my first year back on the Council when the plan came to us in 1997, I jumped in with full force. Here was the problem with the plan: For the favor of taking back a few financial obligations that should not have been ours in the first place, the plan also proposed taking our federal payment away. That payment was the only money we received for the untaxed land (41%) used by the federal government and for all the city services, such as police and fire protection, road repair, etc., which the D.C. government provides to it. The annual payment was $660 million (which it had been for years in spite of inflation). This amount was a small portion of the value of the goods received and had nothing to do with the original "structural imbalance" issue.

I was furious at even the suggestion that we give up the federal payment which we deserved more of—and certainly not *none* of. I attended every single closed-door meeting between the D.C.

government and the Clinton Administration's representatives. I was going to make sure that we as a city did not get screwed as we normally did and unfortunately, still do. Because of my interest, attendance, and maybe because I chaired the Committee on Local, Regional and Federal Affairs, I did much of the negotiating while the plan was at the Council. Only a few Councilmembers even came to the meetings, much less spoke up. Those exceptions were Charlene Drew Jarvis and Linda Cropp, who were very engaged.

We fought hard for the federal payment. The Clinton Administration people kept saying that the only way we're going to get this—the federal courts, Medicaid, and the pension system—through Congress was for the feds to have some money to pay for them. I came back with, "The federal government pays for the federal courts in every jurisdiction in the country and those jurisdictions aren't paying the federal government for doing that. Why should we? Same is true of Medicaid!" They kept shooting back with, "But it won't pass Congress. That Republican Congress will insist on taking the federal payment back." I said, "Then let *them* do it. Why would you, representing a Democratic President not be fighting on the side of this Democratic city? And why would the Clinton Administration even think about taking the blame? You must know how inequitably we are treated. Why would you add to that?" Still no movement from them.

As the meetings proceeded over weeks and weeks, I decided that since we could not make them let us keep the federal payment, I would just negotiate for them to take on more of our unfair burden, such as the federal felons. We had been forced to be responsible for federal felons, such as John Hinckley, who shot four people including President Reagan and James Brady—people who were not D.C. government-related but were in federal positions. Why should D.C. taxpayers have to pay for these prisoners—especially since we would no longer even have a federal payment to help us with the burden of such unfair and outrageous expenses?

Fortunately, the Clinton Administration finally did see the merits of most of these arguments and took the federal felons off our hands. I was proud to be part of getting the best deal possible for D.C. within that rigid framework we were forced to deal with.

Years later, I ran into Ed, Clinton's top negotiator on this issue, who said, "Carol, you're a tough advocate I would want on my side anytime. By the time it was all over, you got out of us things we never thought we'd end up doing."

P.S.: When the D.C. Revitalization Act was enacted on August 5, 1997, we initially were pleased to see a one-time federal payment of $140 million included—still far less than the $660 million we got before, but at least something. My first thought was, "Since they did it this year, they'll probably do it the next and succeeding years as well." Well it turned out, it was just an add-on to fund a federal public transportation project—Barney Circle, a sort of freeway on Capitol Hill, which the feds wanted. A couple of years later, as Chair of the Committee on Public Works and the Environment, I was instrumental in killing that project and directing the money to the 11th Street Bridge instead, which we needed and wanted, and is being used and enjoyed by many today.[147]

In Case You Haven't Had Enough of My Kids ...

Steph graduated from law school in 1998 and went to work for New York Legal Aid in Manhattan. She did great work there for seven years, spending most of her time either in the court room or in jails, trying to ensure fairness in the justice process. Around this time, she lived with a guy named Andrew. After several years together, he took her to Israel and proposed at the Western Wall in Jerusalem. The wedding was planned for May 2002 at the Mayflower Hotel. But Steph decided after four and a half years to call it off. I was sad but supportive. Thank goodness she and Andrew are still friends. In fact, he called me recently when he was in D.C. to ask me out to brunch.

Steph, Andrew and her friends rented a place near Woodstock, New York for part of the summer for a few years. There, we had a mother-daughter weekend with a couple of Steph's friends. This included Belinda and her mother Deborah, and Gwen and her mother Arlene. Hilary, who in addition to her marketing job was tutoring public school students in the city, came up with a mother-daughter version of *The Newlywed Game*. It tested how well we knew one another with Hil being the moderator. When Stephanie and I won game after game, Steph was shocked as she thought she was often "neglected." But when I was able to answer questions like, "What did Steph as a child want to be when she grew up" with "prison guard," she realized that I was paying more attention than she thought. Another interesting one of Hil's questions was, "Would we rather our child have a sex change operation or join a cult?" All the daughters thought we'd rather they join a cult and all we mothers answered the opposite. We did a similar reunion at my place in Rehoboth a couple of years later. Such fun!

While in Europe, Doug earned a master's degree from the London School of Economics in International Relations. Afterwards, he did a Fulbright in Madrid, where his apartment was right on the Plaza Mayor and where Hilary and I had a wonderful week's visit. I also enjoyed an occasional visit with Doug at his home in the Notting Hill section of London, just a few blocks from the famous flea market on Portobello Road. I've always been able to depend on Doug for great locations! (Now it's Santa Monica, California.)

Whitman-Walker Clinic

My volunteer work took a lot of time, energy and money, but I needed to do it. It was just part of my reasons to get up in the morning. On the Whitman-Walker Clinic Board of Directors and others on which I served—as well as in my Council role—I took membership seriously and exercised strong oversight. In spite of being a boat rocker, I was elected for many terms by the Clinic's membership—and appointed once by the Board—serving for a total of 17 years. My tough questions often empowered other less aggressive members to speak up more which, albeit not usually welcomed, is often helpful to the organization and its leadership.

I want to give a shout-out here to Jim Graham, who was a founder and for years the Executive Director of the Whitman-Walker Clinic. When I left the Council in 1989, Jim immediately asked me to put my name forward for election to this Board. I was grateful for his initiative—particularly since he was such a partisan—in getting me involved with an organization that had such value to the community, especially during our devastating AIDS crisis in the '80s and '90s. Some special friends I made during my years there were Yvette Lindsey, Jay Haddock, Chuck Hicks, Victor Shargai, Bob Alfandre, Dr. John Robinson and Joe Perta.

(Sadly, Jim Graham passed away on June 11, 2017. I wrote the above a year ago. But I also want to show appreciation that at my 2008 Council election night "defeat party" and at a later announcement gathering, Jim was a comforting presence, who sure seemed intent on my return—a loving gesture from a memorable person.)

The schedule of the monthly meetings of the Clinic's Board was quite challenging. The Board held its meetings on the first Monday of each month, starting at 6 p.m. And the Council held its big monthly legislative session on the first Tuesday of each month with a breakfast meeting starting at 8 a.m. But in my 17 years on the Board and nine of them on the Council, I don't think I ever missed one of the Clinic's Board meetings. Often I'd be at the

Board meeting on 14th St., N.W. until midnight and then a few hours later would be at the Wilson Building for a minimum of 12 hours. But that was fine as all my jobs—both the unpaid ones and the paid Council one—were important to me. And I loved doing them. I also learned about issues while volunteering for non-profits, which informed my Council agenda.

Whitman-Walker sometimes had financial challenges, which forced us to reduce expenses and staff. That frequently happened because the Clinic would be owed thousands, even hundreds of thousands of dollars, by the D.C. government. Often non-profit charitable organizations do provide services via the competitive bid process and subsequent contracts with the D.C. government, and then sometimes would either not get paid at all or have to wait for years to get paid in full. The same thing often happened to small businesses who receive competitively bid contracts.

Witnessing the incidents mentioned above, as well as having other valuable groups inform me of similar problems, led me to introduce one of my first bills when I came back on the Council in the mid-'90s. The legislation stated that if the city did not pay what was owed to vendors under contract—with no dispute—within a certain timeframe, interest would be added on to the outstanding bill. It was unanimously passed by the Council. I just knew that if the government had to end up paying more with the passage of time, it would discourage it from expecting these thin-margined charitable organizations and small businesses from having to *carry* the D.C. government. The bill became law. But the problem continued. Why? Because the non-profits and businesses were so afraid that if they charged the interest due, the D.C. government would punish them by not giving them a contract in the future.

After I became aware of that new issue, I called together a group of non-profits. I told them that if they banded together and stayed united on charging the now-required interest, then the D.C. government would have no choice but to pay the interest without threat to any of them. Sadly, I doubt if they held firm. It is beyond me why the powers-that-be don't just pay on time, penalties or no penalties, in order not to put at risk those vulnerable groups it owes, needs—and supposedly values.

And it's so frustrating to literally lie awake some nights figuring out a way to rectify a problem, come up with a solution, have my staff write up the bill, introduce it, get it passed—usually unanimously—see it become law, and then the bad beat I tried to rectify just goes on. That was one of the reasons I wanted to be Mayor.

Open House

One of the volunteer boards I served on was Safe Haven Outreach Ministries starting in 1998. It operated a shelter and rehabilitation center near 8th and M Sts., S.E. at that time. The year before I went on the Board, I had the honor of receiving their Trusted Public Servant Award. As with many of those well-intentioned non-profits, funds were needed, so in 2000, I had a fundraiser at my apartment for the group. The day of, I got home from work early to get things set up and of course the staff from the center came early as well. And they unexpectedly brought about 20 of their clients—ex-offenders with some drug problems.

I must admit I had a moment of "Oh dear." With these type of affairs or a social party at my place, I have always said to all in attendance, "Just feel free to go around and look, but no closets or drawers." This time I thought to myself, "I'm not going to change my routine" and took a deep breath. So I said exactly that to the attendees, even before the fundraiser started.

And my instinct was so right. There was not one thing disturbed or missing. And each of the clients told me how much they appreciated getting to just look around on their own. Life is so interesting. My experience with these ex-offenders with substance issues was perfect. Other times, not so. I have found several people going through my drawers and sometimes something missing. But not with this group. Once again, don't be so quick to judge.

Some Nice Recognitions

I did my volunteer work because I needed to do it. It was probably as much about me as the people I tried to help. I certainly never expected any awards for it or my Council work, yet I did occasionally receive some. In 1998, I was inducted into the Women's Hall of Fame which is part of the D.C. Commission on Women. I also received the First Annual Humanitarian Award from the legendary Sholl's Colonial Cafeteria in 2000, as well as the Excellence in Leadership Award from the National Log Cabin Republicans in 2000, which was presented at a lovely and well-attended dinner in Philadelphia at its National Conference.

I received in 2001, Hillel's Excellence in Leadership Award at GW University. Also in 2001, at its annual meeting, the Metropolitan Washington Council of Governments (COG) bestowed its most prestigious award on me—the Elizabeth and David Scull Metropolitan Public Service Award. All were deeply appreciated.

CHAPTER 30

Mayor Not Quite For Life

The takeover by the Financial Control Board rendered Mayor Marion Barry almost powerless. But still in early May of 1998, the early polls showed Barry running ahead of the Democratic pack, even though at the same time, most voters did not want the Mayor to run again.[148] Then on May 21, 1998, the decision was made: Marion Barry announced he would not seek reelection for Mayor—a move I applauded because I knew how hard it was for him not to even try to be Mayor again. Even in that powerless time, Marion did succeed in helping to get the Verizon Center built and paid for by Abe Pollin. He also did all the work to plan and develop a new and needed convention center, which opened under the next Mayor's tenure. Kudos to Marion for those.

Competitors for the 1998 Mayoral race started lining up before Marion Barry decided not to run. Councilmember Kevin Chavous from Ward 7, Councilmember Jack Evans from Ward 2, and at-large Councilmember Harold Brazil entered the Democratic primary, followed by a few lesser-known candidates.

At that point, *The Washington Post* immediately started pushing Anthony Williams, the CFO of the Control Board, with one praising article after another, including one big picture after another, all on the top of the front page of its newspaper. And then came the "Let's Draft Tony Williams for Mayor" movement—seemingly orchestrated from start to finish.

A Control Board Out of Control

The Financial Control Board and its CFO Anthony Williams had rendered not only Marion Barry inconsequential, but also the elected Council as well as the Board of Education until they basically did away with the latter. This Control Board, made up of five members appointed by the President and confirmed by the Senate, began serving in early June of 1995. The Board and its CFO were given much credit for getting the District's finances in order. But upon closer look, it seemed like they could have used their own Control Board. As you read a portion of the following article, remember that this was a *temporary* group, which had been in existence for a year and half at this point. Also keep in mind that the Control Board/CFO, while renting a high-priced downtown space in 1996, had been charged with undoing the District of Columbia's financial problems, which included overspending on salaries and non-competitive, overpriced contracts.

In the long piece by Jonetta Rose Barras entitled "Bureaucratic Oversight," which was published in *Washington City Paper* on December 13, 1996, Barras wrote:

"... when Control Board members finish sniping at District bureaucrats for their spendthrift ways, they return to their plush offices and plot the expansion of their own bureaucracy ... the independent CFO has been leading a similarly privileged life amid the budgetary ruin of the District."

Barras goes on to describe the Control Board's offices: "The carpet is freshly laid. The glass-fronted conference room, complete with mahogany table and maroon leather chairs, would fit seamlessly in a top-five law firm. Down the hall, in a more expansive and finely furnished room, sits Williams, who calmly explains why he splurged on his office renovation: ... 'The [$93,000] allocated for this is by no means lavish. ... Yea, you can look at the time this is happening, but the District had not devoted resources or made a commitment to financial management. This is part of building that infrastructure.' ..." *[My take: Yes, every temporary office needs a $93,000 "infrastructure renovation."]*

Jonetta Barras goes on: "The city's appointed helmsmen ... the Board and its kin, the untouchables in CFO Anthony Williams's office, have awarded high salaries, awarded noncompetitive contracts, and duplicated existing municipal functions—just the sort of bureaucratic sprawl that made their appointment a must for the city in the first place. ... With carte blanche from his District-bashing overseers, Williams is free to hire aides at will, pay hefty salaries, pass out inflated titles, and create new offices."

Jonetta continues: "Williams, who has bashed everyone from the Mayor on down for budgetary lapses ... proposes to increase—not decrease—his fiscal 1997 budget by $3 million ... While the District eliminated almost 7,500 jobs ... The CFO's ranks, however, are moving in the opposite direction. Williams proposes to hire an additional 24 people for his office." Barras then said: "... city regulations prevent Williams from hiring aides at salaries exceeding the $81,200 cap ... Williams circumvented the law and added seven administrators at $100,000 each excluding benefits ... the Control Board has offered lavish raises ... Clearly, the large salaries cast the Control Board as an active participant in the same spendthrift culture it was established to eradicate ... its freewheeling spending is camouflaged by its use of consultants and contractors."

She goes on: "The Control Board rarely issues requests for proposals—a staple of clean and efficient government—when a contract is up for grabs. According to the Control Board's Executive Director [John Hill], 'We've done a number of contracts because of [the] speed necessary to get a contract done.'

... Of course, public officials always use speed and expeditiousness as a justification for doing business in noncompetitive ways."

In the article, Councilmember Kevin Chavous aptly summed it up: "Power corrupts absolutely ... If you have an appointed body that doesn't have to answer to the people, then you have unfettered discretion to run amuck' ... It is so easy to replace old cronies with new cronies.'"[149]

Introducing Anthony Williams

Anthony Williams is smart. Because he had been an accountant, comptroller and a CFO, he was often called a "bean counter." His credentials are impressive. He had received a B.A. from Yale and a J.D. from Harvard. He also has a compelling story as an adopted child in California who was so reserved that his cognitive abilities were questioned when he was young. He sure proved them wrong. That widely circulated story, and his intelligence and vitae primed him to be a star in the eyes of D.C.'s influencers.

In his career, Williams had worked in Connecticut, Boston and St. Louis. He came to the Washington area in 1993 to become the Department of Agriculture's Comptroller in S.W. D.C. During his tenure there, he did not choose to live in the District of Columbia, but instead, he and his wife Diane rented a home in Virginia.

When the Control Board took over D.C.'s financial matters in the mid-'90s, Jeffrey Thompson, accounting company executive and future multimillion-dollar holder of D.C. contracts of all kinds, recommended that the Financial Control Board hire Anthony Williams to be city's Chief Financial Officer. (This is the same Jeffrey Thompson who later agreed in 2014 to a plea bargain for allegedly funding a Mayoral shadow campaign.)[150]

After Williams was appointed by the Control Board to that high-paying CFO position in 1995, he was required by law to move into the city within six months of taking the job. However, it took him seven months to cross the bridge. And according to the talk of that time, he did not hire his own movers or do it himself.

When I got elected to the Council again in 1996, Williams was CFO and he invited me to lunch at the Control Board headquarters at 14th and M Sts., N.W. Once in his office, the first thing I noticed was the new wood paneling. I could only imagine how much it must have cost to panel that temporary office for that temporary Board. As a fiscal conservative, especially with tax dollars, this observation and cost analysis were not unusual for me. (And I had all of these thoughts way before I read Jonetta's piece above.)

We had lunch on a big mahogany dining table with elegant linens in this large, beautifully appointed office, with a sitting area, and were served a lovely meal by a waiter. I couldn't help thinking how hypocritical it was that the Control Board and CFO were put in place to get a handle on the city's finances, ridding it of waste, and here was all this opulent spending on such important and lasting things as wood paneling and waiter-served lunches. After that, I used to say to all who'd listen, "Please save us from our saviors!"

The Anthony Williams Push—and Me Pushing Back

There was a much-publicized "Draft Tony for Mayor" movement, which I always knew was basically feigned and not community-driven as described by the *Post*, except for Mr. and Mrs. Paul Savage of Ward 7 and Marie Drissel of Ward 2, who were just about the only ones ever quoted. I believe, as do others, that Tony had mostly orchestrated that movement from day one from the CFO's office. For instance, I later learned that my elegant lunch with Williams was not an unusual event. Many of the elected Advisory Neighborhood Commissioners—and there are about 450 of them—had been invited at one time or another to sit around that same table for lunch. The "draft" worked. Williams resigned as CFO and soon after announced his run for Mayor.

Personally, I was disturbed that this person who wanted to be Mayor here did not even register to vote in this region, much less D.C., until June 18, 1996—after several years in Virginia and nearly a year into his CFO position. It appears he continued to vote absentee in Connecticut while living in Boston, St. Louis and Virginia. He finally voted in D.C. in 1996, but sat out the '97 special election. When confronted with this in 1998, he said, "I didn't vote. I regret that. But 95% of District citizens didn't vote as well." I guess that makes it okay. [151] Silly me always believing that political leaders should lead—or at the very least, vote.

Regardless, Williams's educational pedigree did have much appeal to many. Also the fact that most people did not know him had its own appeal. People love an outsider, someone they don't know. With them, you can fill in the blanks, and make them more perfect than the people you do know. People we're acquainted with have faults. We think strangers don't. It's like seeing an attractive person across a crowded room. One thinks, "She won't just shop 'til she drops with my money" or "I bet he doesn't snore so loudly"; but they may end up being even worse. It's awfully easy to put our hopes into people we do not know—both personally and politically. And the media does this too. This dynamic was at work in this election, when other well-known and competent Councilmembers had to battle Williams as underdogs.

Anthony Williams had some advantages, but he clearly had little connection to the city. I know there are instances where well-known people move into a new community and run for high office, like Robert Kennedy and Hillary Clinton running for Senate in New York after a short time there. But can you show me a place, especially a big city, where someone has only lived for two years (didn't grow up in the town and then returned, but just arrived—and only because the job required it) and then runs for its top executive and administrative elected office and to become the face of the place? Could I have actually moved out to Maryland (and only because I had to), with not having been involved in community activities like voting, and then after two years, have gotten the *Post*'s never-ending endorsement for Governor before I even announced my candidacy? I doubt it—even if I was a male.

But thank goodness for journalists like Jonetta Barras (who lived in D.C.) and others at the *City Paper* then who saw Williams as not just a shiny new object who never did any wrong—as was shown in that article. And where was the *Post* when all that similar stuff they criticized in the D.C. government was going on at the Control Board and in the CFO's office? Probably sitting around that mahogany table in Williams's office or its own office one block away, plotting the "draft Tony" movement, likely financed by none other than Jeffrey Thompson, who was, I'm sure, raking in non-competitively bid accounting contracts from the Control Board and CFO, while opening up bank accounts in anticipation of the multitude of healthcare contracts soon to come once Williams got to be Mayor and joined with the Control Board to close down D.C. General—in spite of the unanimous protestations of the elected Council—and then licking his lips as he started to plan those 125 shadow campaigns around the country he would finance in the future with D.C. taxpayers' money. (This, my cynical take, may be deserving of an award for the longest non-sentence in a publication ever—and I wrote it in one breath.)

Taking on Tony

Despite the big push for Williams by the *Post* and the Savage/Drissel families, I decided to enter the field myself. I had just come off the best showing ever as a minority party candidate in the prior Mayoral general election in 1994. I also found it hard to believe that D.C. voters would go for 1) an outsider who was an extension of the Control Board, designed by Congress to weaken our independence, 2) a person who had not chosen to live in the city until he had to, 3) a man who would likely put business interests above people's needs, and 4) an individual who had shown little interest in voting for any office in D.C., except for maybe voting for himself for its top position as Mayor. But being the ongoing realist I am, I knew I had, once again, a big mountain to climb with so little chance for success—in fact, it would take a miracle.

I know I was critical earlier about the spending of both the CFO and the Control Board, and it was deserved. At the same time, though, Anthony Williams was given a lot of credit for putting the city into financial order and much of that credit is deserved as well. And I also give credit to the members of the Control Board, who served without compensation. All of them helped enhance our reputation, which was in need of enhancing.

Personally, I found Tony engaging with his quick and dry sense of humor, which I always appreciated. I also enjoyed his and his wife Diane's company and became, over the years, very close to his mother, Virginia Williams. I have invited all three to parties at my home and they have come on occasion. I actually like Tony.

So whatever I say about Tony is my professional evaluation. I recognize that I have envied what I have considered his free ride. I would love to have gotten one myself, but was never fortunate enough. However, the facts are the facts; the professional experience was the professional experience.

And here's a professional experience which is also a fact: In 1997, Tony callously fired 165 city workers in agencies including the public schools, the police department, the Department of Human Services, and the University of the District of Columbia, without notice and without appeal. Most of those fired were minority women. I would certainly fire people who failed to improve after giving them limited probationary notice and necessary training, but to just fire people out of the blue with no notice seemed unconscionable to me. And it does not appear that they were fired for wrongdoing as they were given their accumulated benefits, etc. But fired they were. While this was happening, Williams gave an additional severance payment of $55,000 to the outgoing Director of the lottery agency—and went ahead with the agreement after it was discovered that the same Director had misused government credit cards to pay thousands of dollars in rent for a luxury apartment in downtown D.C.[152] I felt that showed his priorities—and was indicative of things to come.

Now I'm In

On June 17, 1998, I announced I would again run for Mayor and delivered a statement at Freedom Plaza in front of the Wilson Building. My two daughters were there, but my son Doug was living in London at that time so couldn't be with us. Many friends and supporters came. My new colleague David Catania was also there. He was a Republican who had been elected in the 1997 special election for an at-large seat. We were friendly at the time, or so I thought. My daughter Stephanie's then fiancé Andrew was present as well that day and told the girls that he didn't like "that guy" (David) because after the speech, he had overheard him say, "Let's wind up the old girl one more time." I myself only heard about it much later, and was glad not to have heard it that day. And by the way, "the old girl" was a mere 54 at the time.

My friend Cornelius Baker was the Chair of my election committee and once again, Richard Smith, a Democrat and friend, was my Treasurer—two African American men. I found an office at an empty space on 7th St. and New York Ave., N.W. After I used it for a couple of campaigns, it became a popular space for other candidates over the years, like Jack Evans and Anthony Williams.

For the first time, I hired a media consultant: Tom Ochs, who had approached me and who was a partner with Bob Squier in a Democratic political consulting firm, which had never taken on a Republican candidate before. Tom described me as a personal candidate, not a company one. As a 20-year resident of D.C. he said he had voted for me a couple of times and was tired of sitting on the sidelines, as he told the *Post* on June 14, 1998.[153]

Even with Tom and many volunteers, it soon became clear we were facing a juggernaut. I won the Republican primary uncontested. Anthony Williams won the Democratic primary with 50% of the vote, followed by Councilmembers Kevin Chavous at 35%, Jack Evans, 10%, and Harold Brazil at 4%. I had hoped that Tony's primary numbers would be lower, but there they were—50% in a primary made up of nearly 80% of the overall voters. And the boost he got from contributions, especially business interests, and from the free media time he consistently received, especially from the *Post*, made surmounting him in the general election a fading possibility. At one point he had raised $1 million to my $188,000. The fact is that money often decides our political fate.

Although Williams was seen as a clean slate and someone not connected with the financial problems of the past, I certainly fell into that latter category too. I was never viewed as part of the past financial irresponsibility, especially because on the Council I was the lone voice voting against those ballooning budgets in the mid-to-late '80s. And then I was gone from 1989 until 1997. So no one could blame me for those years either. And even in my recent time back on the Council, I had put in tax-cutting legislation to keep our tax base as well as fought against waste in government spending. I had a history of fiscal responsibility, not giving away our land to developers, and although pro-business, not letting anyone take undue advantage. I even rejected the idea of giving a signing bonus to lure a city manager, proposed by Tony and the Control Board, saying "We are not the NBA." I would often add, "We are Washington, D.C. and people want to be here."

Williams was also for cutting taxes and creating a business-friendly environment. He spoke of things I talked about as a Republican. In fact, he was probably to the political right of me, and certainly less focused on social services for our needy. It's no wonder even the conservative *Washington Times* was behind his candidacy. And although the *Post* credited me with being the better politician with my "hey buddy" style, they were obviously taken with him. In its endorsement of Tony, the *Post* concluded: "Her strengths as a council member are considerable, as are her campaign skills and ability to connect with voters on a personal level. But this is a different city from when Mrs. Schwartz was fighting the good fight alone against Mayor Barry. The city needs not just a politician but a resourceful effective manager. She is the better politician of the two; he is the proven manager."[154]

(Even Tony admits he never had the personal touch. In an October 29, 2015 interview with the *Post Magazine*, which looked back at his tenure, Tony, with his appealing self-deprecation, said: "What? I'm not warm and fuzzy when people recognize me? ... I had a rap for being standoffish and aloof. Now I'm standoffish and aloof but I'm not running for anything."[155])

During this time in 1998, the District population was changing. Many black middle class families continued to move to the suburbs, and although whites at that time were a clear minority, the white population diminished less than the African American population in those years. And it was not surprising that the District was attracted to someone new as Mayor as much of the city's population was new as well. The Tax Revision Commission found in

1995 that 60% of people filing taxes in D.C. lived in the city for less than five years. The city was changing.[156]

As opposed to the first Barry race in 1986, where black versus white was a dominant feature, the picture was less clear now with even more African American voters supporting me for Mayor than in the past. Lots of black residents resented Williams as an outsider and a tool of the federally appointed Control Board, which had usurped our little bit of Home Rule. And many seemed to admire my toiling in these fields for so many years. In fact, my slogan that year which I put on the posters was: "Bring It Home."

I also got support from other seemingly unlikely backers, including the Sierra Club. This was a coup as a Republican. They said they supported me for my advocacy of recycling and public transportation. And they appreciated that I had spoken out, voted against, and helped stop the development of Children's Island (an environmental preserve), which was about to be made into a theme park and would have given a developer a 99-year lease for that treasured land—while we were under the Control Board.

A Positive Voice

This time I received favorable attention from *The Afro-American* newspaper, which on August 22, 1998 wrote, "To Anthony Williams—the *Post* is trying to make you feel so secure that you might forget that the winner in the Sept. primary will have to face Rep. Carol Schwartz in the general election—that friendly, hard-working lady who almost beat Marion Barry in the last election. Don't listen to them."[157]

Other black journalists such as Adrienne Washington of *The Washington Times* spoke of Williams's free-ride candidacy and unpopularity with some people who saw him as a Congressionally appointed outsider. On October 10th, Washington wrote, "Every D.C. worker is saying for the first time, 'I'm voting Republican.'" Another of her articles in *The Times* on October 16, 1998 stated: "D.C. Mayoral Race Is Really About Home." In it, a 42-year-old African American resident who planned to vote Republican for the first time said he would not vote for "no carpetbagging, bow tie-wearing black man ... [who] fired a lot of people."[158]

Surprisingly and finally, *The Washington Post* even mentioned Williams's firings as CFO in an October 24, 1998 article, though only a few days before the election and not on the front page.

Distrust of Williams inspired some of my support. In the September 8th *Washington Times* article, "Beware of Bowtie Bandit's

Bandwagon," a senior citizen was quoted as saying, "I still don't know who Anthony Williams is." Another said, "What's really offensive is carpetbaggers who believe that hometown, homegrown folks who can't be forced to go along with their underhanded takeover plans ought to be shut out or shut up." [159]

There were other articles, and some were supportive. In the *InTowner* in June of 1998, a 43-year-old gay African American government employee said, "What's wrong with Carol Schwartz? [She] understands the city's problems. She is concerned and sincere about city issues. She's not on a power ego trip like those others. I think Carol Schwartz would make a great Mayor." [160]

A decent number of former Barry supporters came to my side. One of them was Effi Barry, former wife of Marion and a lovely woman I liked a lot. I was so surprised when she called to say she wanted to help, and she did. Also of great help was Lawrence Guyot, a former civil rights leader and labor organizer. In the June 18th *Washington Post*, Guyot drew a direct link between Barry's and my populist style, and spoke about how after working for Barry for 20 years, he was now crossing the line for me. "I went to jail for the right to be a Democrat," Guyot said. "But when I look at Carol Schwartz she is the closest thing I see to Marion Barry." [161]

In the *Post* on September 17th, Guyot said about Williams: "This man is a federal candidate. If we elect him, we would be using the ballot, for the first time in my American history, as a method to validate occupation ... thank God we have an opportunity to stop this." [162] And in the October 16th *Times*, Guyot said, "Schwartz is the Democratic candidate in this race and the other candidate is the personification of Republicanism at its worse." [163]

Campaigning always energized me and others noted so. In a *Washington Post* profile that described my "ever-present laugh," Bernard Demczuk said, "I view it as feeding her fuel tank. ... This is not labor for her .. She gets energy from being on the street, having people touch her and touching people. Tenacious? Yeah. Principled? Yes. But, really, this is love for her."

That same *Post* piece captured a moment when I saw my posters illegally tacked to trees and got on the phone to rectify it. I was involved in every detail. "She's that way at home, too, where every knickknack must be in place," the articled noted. "'I'm a control freak. .... I was so unable to control every aspect of my life, my father, my husband, my brother, bless his soul. This is something I can control.'" [164] I could control some aspects of my life and campaigns—but unfortunately with both, not the outcome.

Trying to Bring It Home

As I said, my campaign slogan for my posters was "Bring It Home." This campaign was about home—and who had allegiance to Home Rule and truly serving our home city. A proposal I offered during the campaign spoke to making commitments to those who are committed to the city. I offered teachers signing bonuses of $5,000 if they agreed to stay with our public school system for at least five years. I tried to encourage voters to feel the same about engagement and loyalty. As I told the *Current* on September 16th, "I know we always look at the new. I want you to look at this woman who has always been there for you."[165]

I was excited to receive the support of the Missionary Baptist Ministers of D.C., a large group of prominent African American pastors. They said, "[She is the] best candidate, loves the city, paid her dues ... [She's] sensitive to the faith community. We trust her integrity which is above reproach. She earned the right to be the next Mayor of the District of Columbia."

That was quite a tribute to this white Jewish girl from Midland, Texas. In accepting their endorsement, knowing how they had selected their own leadership, I said, "I appreciate that you picked your leadership from the inside and now you are doing the same with me. You didn't go with some outsider, some stranger. You went with someone in the family and I'm grateful." The group seemed to love that and applauded appreciatively.

In this election I felt I was running against *The Washington Post* more than I was running against Williams. The paper was certainly more engaged in this than he was, as he rarely campaigned and skipped many debates. But I guess when the *Post* is touting you every two minutes, you don't have to be so engaged. But I sure had to be. I even told *The Washington Times* in a sit-down with editors (which Williams skipped) that "I have never seen anybody get a free ride [from the press]" the way Williams had.[166]

Marion Barry resisted endorsing Williams throughout the primary, but soon enough I guess he felt he had to. Then he worked hard for the guy. I know that party allegiance is strong, but part of me couldn't believe it. When Marion tried to say hello to me on the campaign trail, I spoke to him pointedly: "Don't even try to talk to me. You picked a stranger over a friend." (Of course I ran against my friend Marion twice, so who was I to talk?)

Marion said I must understand that he could not possibly endorse a Republican, to which I stated, "You mean it's better to pick an outsider who tried to take away your powers?"[167] Not just tried, but actually did.

Thank goodness there were lighter, less bitter moments. After receiving a standing ovation at a church, a woman said to me, "TV doesn't do you justice, girl. You look so fat on TV."[168] Imagine how far down you are to think of that as a "lighter moment."

And speaking of churches, my first introduction to Virginia Williams, Tony's mother, was at a church as people were arriving for the service. My friend and then supporter Johnnie Rice was walking ahead of me and tried to hand her a piece of my literature, not knowing who she was. Virginia responded, "Get that shit away from me!" Hard to believe, but we really did become good friends. As I mentioned, Virginia attended a lot of parties at my house. And I have many beautiful handwritten notes from her. Both Tony and one of Virginia's best friends, Judith Terra, still tell me when I see them, "Virginia loved you so much." And I loved her too.

Speaking again of churches, this reminds me of a less light moment that took place during the primary. It was at a huge public candidates forum at a very big church in Ward 8, sponsored by the Washington Interfaith Network, a powerful coalition of activist churches who got contracts from the city for community efforts like housing, and I guess wanted more. They were interested in hearing our views about their projects.

It was one of the rudest settings I ever found myself in. They demanded to know from each of us, "Will you commit to this [one of their projects]? Yes or no?" Then, "Will you back [another one of their projects]? Yes or no?" When I tried to say, "I maybe could say yes, I would consider it, but I would need to know the price and who the recipients would be ..." they immediately interrupted and said, "The answer must only be YES or NO." That's impossible to do unless you're going to just give lip service. I have always honestly spoken my mind, and pandering was never my forte. In fact, when put in those kinds of situations, I become even more stubborn. What right did they have to speak to anyone, much less D.C. elected officials, in that rude and intimidating manner?

But I was obviously totally alone in those thoughts. Every single one of the other Mayoral candidates before the primary all said yes to all the questions. I thought it was irresponsible to promise millions of dollars to fund projects that haven't been properly researched, without knowing the cost—and all with the need to ignore our procurement laws. But I said in front of those hundreds and hundreds of people—maybe even a thousand—as well as their powerful leadership, NO. And I felt really good about it. I especially felt good when, as I was leaving, I saw the multitude of cars in the parking lot with mostly Maryland and Virginia tags. (By the way, I subsequently told the leadership: "You can be strong and even tough without being rude.")

On October 31, 1998, I received one of the most special honors of my career: a full-throated endorsement from *The Afro-American* newspaper, which has had such an esteemed history. In the publication's own words: "*The Afro-American* newspapers were founded in 1892 by John H. Murphy Sr., a former slave and Civil War veteran. We are independent in all things and therefore holding to no political party. Our job, as we see it, is to endorse the candidates who we think can do the most for our people."

The endorsement was a full-page piece written by the publisher herself, Frances Murphy, who is the granddaughter of the papers' founder, and it first covered a great deal of my background and achievements at length. Please indulge me as I repeat a few of the other words here:

"Ms. Schwartz, a Republican, is facing strong opposition from Democratic candidate Anthony Williams, mainly because he has more money to spend and there are more Democrats registered in D.C. than Republicans ...

As she [Ms. Schwartz] says, 'I do not just talk the talk. I walk the walk.' We like Ms. Schwartz for many other reasons. Yes, she is an astute politician and well-liked by all residents who make up D.C.'s various races, creeds and colors. She understands our need to be treated fairly—equal schools, clean neighborhoods, good police protection for all. She looks you straight in the face, gives you a warm handshake and does not shy away from answering questions. Yes, she is a bundle of energy that moves fast, places a kiss here and there, but she also thinks on her feet and does not hesitate to follow through to solve problems. ... Her plan for education is well thought out. ... Ms. Schwartz can point with pride to her many accomplishments during her long service to D.C. D.C. needs her political know-how now. Vote for Carol Schwartz for Mayor and help her bring democracy back to D.C. We can trust her to bring it home."[169]

I still have a blown-up version of that endorsement in my home as it meant that much to me. Thank you, Frances.

In the end, I received 30% of the vote, which was still not that bad when you consider the political/demographic/money/media (with the exception of a few) climate. And I knew that there were good things to do on the Council. I also recognized that my strong oversight role would be needed now as much as ever.

First Woman President
(of the Metropolitan Police Boys and Girls Clubs
in their then 61-year history)

Police Chief and friend Fred Thomas
(left of me) at swearing in

Friends Alda Douglas Proctor
(left) and Marilyn Johnson

Friends Barbara Chinn, Tom Mader, Pat
Hawkins, Richard Smith at swearing in

AIDS Walk with Whitman-Walker
(Jim Graham, Eleanor Holmes Norton
and Tipper Gore)

Working hard to observe
the Croatian elections

Carrying the Olympic torch
(sorry the motorcycle
covered most of my outfit)

Lucile, my dear friend and
neighbor in Rehoboth

With Hil and Steph in Rehoboth

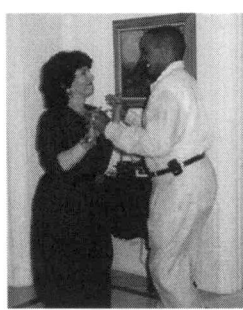

George and I dancing
in the hallway

George and me

Greeted with
balloons and flowers

Friend Richard Smith,
Campaign Treasurer, sadly
passed away in 2001.

Judy Smith, close friend and Campaign
Treasurer, with her and Richard's family

Volunteers working hard at
campaign headquarters

Pride Parade during the
1996 Council campaign

1997 Council Swearing In

Johnny and me

With Marion and Johnny

With my kids in front of Wilson Building

Meeting Bill Clinton at the White House
with the D.C. Council

Pictured: The District of Columbia's Historic Seat of Local Government
The John A. Wilson Building (1904 – 1997; September 2001 and Beyond)
Councilmember Carol Schwartz, At-Large
1350 Pennsylvania Avenue, N.W., Suite 105
Washington, D.C. 20004

**Hey, It's Good To Be
Back Home Again!**

Best wishes to you and
yours for the Holidays,
and for the New Year ahead!

~ Carol

My holiday card the first year after my return
to the D.C. Council and the Wilson Building

With Johnny in Greenville, Mississippi
at our parents' graves

In Greenville with my
"twin" Beth Stovall

Dear friend Alice Banks
(Harry Singleton on right)
at a Republican function

Texas college friends reunion
In Snowmass, Colorado

In one of my
subtle jackets

In Rehoboth
with staff
and significant
others

Picture taken at
family gathering
in San Antonio

As President of the Metropolitan Police Boys and Girls Clubs, I had tough assignments such as hosting unattractive celebrities like football player Charles Mann (also a friend) and singer Michael Bolton.

Reception at *The Washington Post*
(Ben Bradley, Donald GrahamKatharine Graham)

I was honored to be the recipient of the first Sholl's Colonial Cafeteria Award for Community Service.

Me and Eartha Kitt
(Isn't she beautiful?)

Johnny and me with Bill Clinton
at an event on the White House lawn

CHAPTER 31

Grow Where You Are Planted

After losing the 1998 Mayoral race, I was almost resigned to the fact that I would never get the top job of my dreams—notice "almost." A friend bought me a pillow that said, "Grow where you are planted." It sits in my bedroom area and became my motto for my remaining time on the Council. I did grow where I was planted in the late '90s and 2000s—and not just in weight. In fact, I had a particularly productive time then on the Council.

Legislation and Other Initiatives: Fighting to Reignite Business

I was passionate about incentivizing business in a city in need of it. Thus, I pushed for tax-free holidays when shopping is necessary, such as during back-to-school and the winter holidays. In 2000, I introduced the back-to-school holiday event that took place over 10 days in August, and then in 2001, added the tax-free period during the holidays, which went for 10 days from the Friday after Thanksgiving through the Sunday of the next week. They both unanimously passed the Council and successfully went into effect. Each stated that any item of clothing or accessories (belts, scarves, jewelry, ties, socks, etc.) which cost $100 or less per item would be free of tax. I added school supplies to the list for the back-to-school event.

In addition to encouraging people to shop in the District (including our own residents), a strong motivation of mine was to give a break to those who need it most and at a time when they had to spend some money whether they could afford to or not. A sales tax is a regressive tax. Rich and poor pay the same rate, and therefore, it most adversely affects the poor. These holidays helped alleviate that extra burden, at least for a brief time.

The first day of each tax-free holiday, I organized a press conference at a different store (including both department stores downtown and individually owned shops in various parts of the city like H St., N.E.) to make sure people knew about these tax-free windows. I then tax-free shopped myself, which did tend to receive good coverage in the news. And it was fun, me doing one of my favorite activities—tax-free or not—and for a good cause. Colleagues often joined me as well, and I remember two particularly enthusiastic ones were Ward 8 Councilmember Sandy Allen and Ward 4 Councilmember and now Mayor, Muriel Bowser.

And we got good results—from November 23 to December 2, 2001, the former Hecht's downtown reported sales up 40% from the previous year over the same time period. Urban Outfitters in Georgetown reported being up 13% with the manager stating that people were "psyched about it."[170]

Unfortunately, none of us have that opportunity today in the District of Columbia as the Council got rid of the popular tax-free shopping holidays not long after I left the Council in 2009. Now only Maryland and Virginia have them, although they started theirs after ours—and now sadly, our residents head there.

Legislation and Other Initiatives: Fighting for Driving Safety

As mentioned, in early 1998, I successfully pushed to lower the drunk driving threshold from 1.0 to .08 for blood alcohol level, making us the first in the region to do so. After I took over the Committee on Public Works and the Environment in January of 1999, I continued taking on the issue with a sense of urgency, mainly because of the high number of pedestrian deaths in our city. I made sure the District had stricter penalties for drunk driving, which included the revocation of drivers' licenses; and even when the license was reinstated, a breathalyzer device could be installed on the steering wheel, which would not unlock if the test failed—real cutting-edge stuff in those days.

I have also tried to be reasonable in the few areas where we went overboard. For instance, we passed the open container law, which meant a person could not drink alcohol on the street or sidewalk. Afterwards, when the enforcement started including people drinking on their own front porches, I made sure that the law was amended in 1998 to allow for that.

And then in mid-2005, a 45-year-old lawyer was arrested in D.C. after she was tested at .03 for alcohol level. This arrest got wide news coverage and made me aware that too much leeway was being given to arresting officers. I became the principal author of legislation to clarify our DUI law. Though we should have zero tolerance for alcohol-impaired driving, we should have reasonable standards that allow for a woman to have a glass of wine at dinner. We also should not harm our hospitality businesses needlessly. We clarified that below .05 was tolerable, and made the level from .05 to .079 a judgment zone which would require other factors like a sobriety field test to determine a DUI.[171] Still tough, but now fair.

Back in 1999, I helped make sure that our teen driving laws were strong, given the high number of teenage deaths and injuries. Along with Kathy Patterson, I instituted graduated driver licensing requirements, such as limiting the number of unrelated passengers to two in the car when a 17-year-old was driving. My daughter called me a "kill joy," but I said we were just trying to keep kids from being killed on a "joy" ride.

Then at the end of 2003, the Committee on Public Works and the Environment, which I chaired, brought forward the "Distracted Driver Safety Act," which called for the use of hands-free devices for phone use while driving as well as prohibiting other forms of possible distraction. We were an early mover in passing this law, following forerunners New York and New Jersey. This was important especially in a city which has such a dense population and so many pedestrians and bicyclists. Motorists who did receive a first-time infraction could have the fine suspended if they provided proof of acquisition of a hands-fee device. I made sure the law was rolled out with much lead-time before implementation, and we had ongoing contact with the media, the cell phone companies, as well as groups like AAA to help us get the word out.

Legislation and Other Initiatives: Fighting to Protect Our Property

Another thing that used to keep me awake at night was trying to figure out ways to stop the giveaway of our valuable property to developers. When we were deadsville—able to roll a bowling ball at night through a downtown street, hitting no one—I could understand the need for giving developers a good deal, but still even then felt it should only be in exchange for at least some public benefit. I consider public benefit to be: 1) affordable housing, 2) grocery stores, restaurants and other shopping in underserved areas, and 3) mixed development downtown that would give us housing (i.e. condos and rentals) to enliven deadsville.

I often took my concerns directly to the Mayor. On November 22, 1999, I wrote Mayor Williams a letter, which stated: "I oppose the unsolicited proposal by the Oliver C. Carr Company to acquire the city-owned building that houses the Department of Employment Services at 6th St. and Pennsylvania Ave., N.W. ... As you know, this site is considered the last great development site on Pennsylvania Avenue and has an estimated value of $40 to $60 million. ... I do not believe it is in the best interest to allow the Carr Company to acquire this valuable development site through bypassing the competitive bidding process ... if the District intends to sell it, I ask that a formal request for proposal be issued to allow for a competitive selection process. ... Moreover, we may want to keep the building so D.C. can have a presence on both ends of Pennsylvania Ave. ..." That deal was abandoned. (A few years later, Mayor Williams sold the site to the Newseum in an unsolicited offer, but at least this time we got benefits: $50 million for it, $25 million in affordable housing money, and a tourist attraction.)

As soon as charter schools were mandated by Congress, they started coming after our surplus property. An alarm went off in my head that people who were starting charter schools could come in, get our property and then go out of business by failure or maybe even design, gaining possession of our property in the process. I was not going to allow that. With my one general counsel-type staff member, I wrote legislation that would give long-term leases but no permanent possession, and would ensure that the long-term lease stays only with that charter school—not allowing the lessee to sublet our property in the future. This enabled the property to remain what it was leased out to be—a school.

I introduced the bill at a Council legislative session on September 16, 2003 and immediately, the charter schools came down to the Wilson Building in droves. They said that this legislation would keep them from getting loans from the banks for renovations and for operations. My intent was certainly not to be a roadblock for charter schools, even though I had initially opposed them. Besides, I knew the charter school people would just run to Congress, which had established them, and that the legislation would be overturned. Therefore, I withdrew the bill on October 31st with a self-imposed commitment that stated, "I plan to bring this legislation back after working with the various stakeholders to identify and address their concerns while, at the same time, ensuring District assets."

Because of my limited personal legal staff of one person—although we found some time to talk to the banks and the charter school people—we didn't have all the time needed to put together the accommodating legislation. And I could not use my Public Works and the Environment Committee's legal person to work on an educational issue as she were already flooded with our Committee work. Therefore, after several months, Kathy Patterson, who chaired the Committee on Education, and who was very aware of the charter school needs but also shared my worry about the property issues, asked if she could reintroduce improved legislation similar to my own initial one, and stated that she had more legal help via her Committee staff. Of course I said "of course" and we went on to ensure our property was protected.

I also tried to safeguard historic properties, which enhance our community. On September 5, 2002, I wrote a letter to Mayor Williams about the demolition that he allowed of a dilapidated historic property at 901 R St., N.W. It said: "... [there is an Act] which mandates that if the Mayor determines that a historic structure ... is an extreme and immediate threat to the safety and the welfare of the general public and the owner does not make repairs within a reasonable period of time, the Mayor may enter the property and make repairs ... to prevent demolition by neglect." And the letter explained that the Council had even established a fund for paying the costs. It said: "The Council passed this law because it understands and appreciates the value of these structures to the city. Sadly, lack of enforcement by the Executive, however, renders the Council's efforts ineffective and meaningless."

Not only did I try to encourage historic preservation of our properties, I also fought against the proliferation of huge signage around town which would negatively impact the ambience and beauty of our city and overshadow its magnificent historic sites and surroundings. I spoke strongly against the signs but when I could not prevail, I was at least able to force limitations on them.

I have been gone from the Council for over eight years now, and am saddened and maddened by the number of those huge, imposing and obnoxious signs which continue to proliferate. At least recently, the city has been taking steps to rid us of some signs which they say were constructed illegally or are a danger to the public. But I believe we must remain ever-vigilant—especially with those neon ones—or we'll wake up one day and be Las Vegas. Heaven forbid!

There are other issues related to surplus property which I tackled and which will be discussed later. So, for those of you who enjoy this stuff, stay tuned. For the rest, beware!

Legislation and Other Initiatives:
Fighting for Responsible Contracts

Procurement contracts was another one of those lie-awake-at-night concerns of mine. Tony Williams and later Adrian Fenty did more and more contracting out of city services. Contracts involve too much taxpayer money and are used to provide too many basic government services. If they don't get necessary scrutiny, they are ripe for abuse. Now let's talk about it:

- **To Be Approved or Not To Be**

For many years now, the Council has approved contracts that are worth $1 million or more. That additional level of approval was started decades ago because of crony contracts, many of them not competitively bid, and a procurement system or lack thereof that was suspect at best. So it was put in place to solve a problem and to ensure a more transparent process. And for the most part, it has worked well and has not impeded the operations of government and in fact, has stopped some of the previous shenanigans related to contracting.

In the last several years, mainly due to media coverage and editorials, there has been pressure to take the Council out of the contract approval process because of the fear of the influence campaign contributions by businesses can have. I know that can be an issue. But it is still harder to buy off a 13-member body, as the Council is, than just a Mayor and his or her pertinent administrative staff, which was the risk when contracts fell under Executive control only.

Regarding the legitimate issue of potential conflict with campaign contributors and elected officials, there is definitely a need for change, and not just at the local level. But keep in mind, there are reporting requirements and limits on campaign contributions now as well as on gifts.

In regards to the Council approval process of contracts, I do believe there is a need for involvement by the Council, and that its oversight is an important safeguard. But maybe some tweaking is in order. Currently, a holdup of a contract requires the will of three Councilmembers. Maybe it should require more in order to guard against frivolous or worse motives. There should also be a requirement that the Executive send those contracts for ongoing services (not emergencies) over within a certain timeframe to allow for a time-limited review by the Council. That way neither the Executive nor the Legislature can hold up needed services.

Government being run by private contracts is an ever-growing area which I don't like. But if it's going to be done, it should be transparent—and most of the time it is not. Having Council oversight and approval of contracts, which involve gigantic amounts of taxpayer dollars, is essential. It puts these contracts out in the public eye and that's important too. More open discussion about such large expenditures is certainly better than none—which is what happens without that oversight. I do believe that our elected officials, who we can un-elect or recall, are the people to do it.

We've seen too many sweetheart deals to leave it in the hands of one branch of government, whose head also receives even more of that questionable money via campaign as well as inaugural contributions from the business community. Where there is abuse by anyone, elected or appointed, it should be called out. But why would anyone think we'd be better off just having those decisions made by that one elected person and/or his or her appointees—usually behind closed doors—rather than by the 13 duly elected Councilmembers—in an open forum?

(In reading through the book again to do the final edit—where I often added instead of deleting, sorry—I read again about an impoundment lot lease/sale debacle, which I was able to squash, as well a ridiculous warehouse lease, which I was able to change [both of which you'll read about soon—just wanted to wet your appetite]. But it made me realize that instead of taking contract approval away from the Council, maybe we should add leases, which are multiple, and so totally behind the scenes that they never see any light of day. Maybe they should.)

- *Putting Approval to Work*

As mentioned, contracts worth $1 million or more are subject to approval by the Council. When I was a Councilmember and taking the contract approval process very seriously, it became very interesting to see the multitude of $999,999 contracts that soon surfaced behind the scenes to avoid going through the legislative body. I had a good time finding those contracts and pointing them out at our Council meetings. I then began to insist upon seeing every contract above $900,000 and asking tough questions about each, as well as requesting an audit of such contracts. At that point, all the $999,999 trickery ceased.

Another trick then used by the Executive was separating a big contract into mini-contracts to avoid Council oversight. So I amended the procurement law to make sure that oversight would be required for any smaller contracts going to a single vendor for similar work and which added up to a million dollars or more. Between my big mouth and my rewriting laws, it became harder for the Administration to devise ways to deceive me than it was to just put forward contracts legitimately.

I knew contracts were important to keep the wheels of government moving, so I never held them up needlessly. But I did make the Executive aware that I was not going to put up with its sleight of hand of sending contracts over for approval at the last minute as emergency legislation to avoid scrutiny—and then try to blame the Council. Finally, they stopped these evasive acts and cooperated better—for the most part.

I also wanted to get the best deals possible for taxpayers while still fighting to make sure approval procedures were followed. In May of 2003, as we were going through financial cut-backs and implementing a hiring freeze, I strongly urged that the government push for savings in contracts as well. I wanted all agency heads to ask each contractor to cut no less than 5% from their billings, and especially for contracts worth more than $150,000 per year. My suggestion was taken. In December of 2003, I wrote the Mayor a letter congratulating him on getting a 5% reduction in the contract for the red light/traffic photo enforcement system.

However, unfortunately, in the same letter I had to take him to task for executing the contract before it was approved by the Council. The contract had actually expired in mid-November and the contract wasn't even sent to the Council for approval until December 2nd. As red light enforcement didn't stop in the interim, the new contract clearly was executed prior to official approval. Similarly, the recycling contract came to us just days before it was set to expire, thus that contract also went through without proper approval. As I said in my letter to Mayor Williams on December 10, 2006: "I would hate to think what kind of legal battles we as a city could be in for should the Council disapprove a contract that your Administration had already executed."

In my many years on the Council and as a private citizen reading about deals, I've seen our city too often give away the store. As a Councilmember, I actually became so fed up with the city and its taxpayers being taken advantage of that I started personally renegotiating contracts. For instance, in 2008, there was a deal where D.C. was renting a police warehouse which required the city to be stuck with an 18-month lease, and then we would have to pay for a rate hike if the property was not vacated by May 1, 2009. We needed that property and could not turn around on a dime to find an alternative. I jumped in and met with the landlord, and the lease went from an 18-month requirement to a month to month lease with no rate hike. *Washington City Paper* said the renegotiated deal saved the city hundreds of thousands of dollars. This is just one example of several contracts I renegotiated, another being a bus shelter contract which saved us millions. And I kept improving on the procurement law in order to stop shenanigans. In 2008, *Washington City Paper* named me "Best Friend of the D.C. Taxpayer" for these types of efforts.

Legislation and Other Initiatives: Fighting for Tax Reduction

Residents of the District have paid a high tax burden over the years, especially in the area of income taxes. I worked hard to lower that burden. It was actually self-destructive to have such high taxes because we were forcing the middle class out of the city. And many of our wealthier residents would just establish residency at their vacation homes, so we would lose those income taxes entirely. I constantly repeated this same refrain: "In our zealous effort to gouge that extra nickel out of our residents, we are ending up with zero nickels. How stupid is that?"

Our tax burden only added to the unfairness in a city that already lived with the injustice of no voting representation in Congress. Many residents said, "Enough. I'm out of here." The population decline at the time proved they were true to their word. D.C. residents also had to live with subsidizing suburbanites as Congress would not allow us to have a commuter tax or tax income at the source, as every other city in the country has—and does. Even our so-called Democratic friends in Congress blocked these revenue streams for D.C., especially when it meant protecting their commuting constituents and in some cases, themselves.

There was not much I could do about the unfairness of the federal action or inaction, but I could do something about our own self-imposed tax burden. In my prior term on the Council in the mid-to-late 1980s, I did have some successes in coupling our estate and inheritance taxes with the federal level as well as reducing the top marginal income tax rate from 11% to 9.5%, with a then not very fiscally conservative Council. One of the pleasures of being back in elected office in the mid-to-late '90s was working with a far more fiscally responsible body. Many had learned the hard way (i.e. through the Control Board) that overspending and overtaxing was not the way to go. I was glad back then in the '80s to help move us in the needed opposite direction—and *now* in the '90s to work with likeminded colleagues to continue to keep us going in that right direction.

On March 2, 1999, I introduced the "Tax Reduction Amendment Act," co-sponsored by Councilmember Jack Evans (I had asked him to co-sponsor as he chaired the relevant committee), which included income tax reductions for individuals in three income brackets: less than $10,000, $10,000 to $20,000 and more than $20,000. On April 15, 1999, Jack, Chair of the Committee on Finance and Revenue, introduced the "Tax Parity Act," co-introduced by me and others, that appropriated the income categories as defined in my original bill six weeks earlier, along with other various tax reductions. I was proud to see us working together to make our taxes more comparable to the surrounding jurisdictions.

Unfortunately, in February of 2002, there was an effort made by Mayor Williams to freeze the rollbacks we initiated with the Tax Parity Act three years earlier, because national revenue projections came in at a lower level. I then wrote a letter to my colleagues saying that this rollback would only perpetuate "existing negative perceptions of our government. ... One of the great frustrations about this government ... is that we are so often seen as unreliable. We giveth, then we taketh away. ... if revenue projections are healthy enough, I am inclined to support going forward with this year's installment of the tax reduction, or at the very least, putting in a trigger for a refund if projections and/or revenues improve by summer." The latter is what we did—and the rollback occurred.

In 2002, some members of the Council, along with the Mayor, passed legislation that put a new tax on residents' non-D.C. municipal bonds. I was not one of them; in fact, I voted no. D.C., unlike other states, has very few municipal bonds of its own. People often purchase these types of bonds because they are tax-free and they are owned by many across the economic spectrum. Here again, this kind of tax can be self-defeating in that residents can move elsewhere in order to have a larger variety of these tax-free municipal bonds to purchase. Not only did I vote no then, but I also co-introduced legislation later that would repeal the bond tax, which did happen. However, it kept coming back. And in April of 2004, during the budget process, I identified $5 million in the Committee on Public Works and the Environment (which I chaired) and divided it between offsetting the proposed tax on out-of-state municipal bonds and the proposed healthcare provider tax, as well as increasing affordable housing funding. (This additional money was usually the result of hiring more parking enforcement officers who brought in more revenue.)

In 2005, many of us supported the legislation called the "Pension or Other Retirement Income Exclusion from Income Tax Amendment Act" (how's that for a title?) as we thought it was a useful way to help ease the financial burden of seniors, many of whom were living on fixed income. I felt in D.C., if it moved, we taxed it—actually, it didn't even have to move. This bill did not pass then and is still being introduced without success.

Other such efforts continued which were successful, including my joining with colleagues in introducing tax relief to those who renovated properties in neighborhoods we hoped to revitalize. We also gave some tax credit to first-time homebuyers in revitalization zones and then everywhere, as well as capped property tax increases that can occur in any one year.

Legislation and Other Initiatives: Fighting for Victims

I've always been a fighter for the vulnerable. One of the reasons I wanted to be in elected office was the enhanced ability to carry on that fight. In 2001, I introduced an amendment to the Human Rights Act to include the prohibition of harassment including sexual harassment

I also took on another problem involving alcohol and abusive behavior that too often happens on campuses (and we have many) by introducing the "Hazing and Binge Drinking Prevention Act of 2002." It made it unlawful to haze, or otherwise cause bodily injury to any person at any school, college and university in the District of Columbia.

Around 2005, I introduced bills with Councilmember Kwame Brown related to domestic violence in an effort to protect people subjected to such suffering. That year, I also introduced with other Councilmembers the "Emergency Care for Sexual Assault Victims Act" to provide emergency after-the-fact contraception to victims of sexual assault who request it after the hospital informs them of that option, as required by this law. It was enacted early in 2009.

Another significant moment of which I am very proud was led by Councilmember Vincent Orange. He approached me about co-introducing legislation that would commemorate D.C. Emancipation Day. He felt that it should be a bipartisan effort, especially since Abraham Lincoln was a Republican. We were the two co-introducers, and were joined by our other colleagues as co-sponsors. D.C. Emancipation Day highlights April 16, 1862 when President Abraham Lincoln signed the "Compensated Emancipation Act," freeing more than 3,000 slaves in D.C. That Act preceded the emancipation of slaves throughout the United States in 1863. D.C. Emancipation Day later became a holiday—an effort also led by Vince Orange. Seven years later, I received the D.C.

Emancipation Day 2015 Recognition Award, which they called the Eagle Award, for this effort.

Me and Chris Rock

I'm giving you a break here from "legislation and other initiatives" to tell you a story. My children always came home in those days for Thanksgiving. One time in the late '90s over the weekend, it was a cold wintry evening, and the kids and I decided to walk to the video store then on Columbia Road. We got a couple of movies and one of the kids suggested a Chris Rock stand-up performance they heard was good. As we were watching the latter, Chris started talking about Marion Barry. To paraphrase, he said something like, "Can you believe those people in D.C. reelected that guy who was on crack cocaine? How bad was the person who lost to him? They must have been on heroin." We had no idea that was coming, but we sure laughed hard when it came.

As crazy and coincidental as this may sound, here's the rest of the story: Maybe four months later, I was sitting in my Council office on the first floor of the Wilson Building on Pennsylvania Ave. when I heard a lot of commotion outside the window. I asked a member of my staff what was going on and he said, "They're filming a Chris Rock movie where he's going to be running for President." I immediately went outside and walked up to him (but not in the middle of filming) and said, "I'm that person who lost to Marion Barry—the person who is on heroin." He seemed to enjoy the encounter and we took a picture together. Now that you've had a little break, back to ...

Legislation and Other Initiatives: Fighting for Education

I was always concerned with attracting and retaining good teachers. Thus, I co-introduced a housing fund for teachers who specialized in math and science in exchange for a five-year commitment to D.C. Public Schools in order to attract educators in those understaffed fields. (There was a clause stating that if the commitment was not met, they would have to pay back the money.) We on the Council later pushed for housing assistance programs to attract new police officers, firefighters, and at that point, all types of teachers to the District.

The D.C. Public Schools had stopped providing vocational education programs many years before. I believe the basis was the old tracking system where many minorities were put into those programs whether they wanted to be or not. And once on that track, it was practically impossible to get off. However, in 2005, Kwame Brown, Vincent Orange and I decided that the time had come to offer students the option to pursue vocational careers (many of which pay good salaries), and we successfully asked others to join us. We unanimously called for the establishment of a commission to analyze the feasibility of reinstituting vocational programs into the D.C. Public Schools, and *not* with the "tracking" aspect, which then did lead to those types of needed options.

I also continued introducing and pushing for the school uniform policy, and let me tell you why ... (Just kidding.)

Legislation and Other Initiatives: Fighting for Special Education

Having a lifelong passion for special education as the younger sibling of a brother with special needs, and as a teacher of special education, I have had great and ongoing concerns about the lack of such programs in our public schools. As mentioned, when I moved to Washington in January of 1966 seeking a special education job with the D.C. Public Schools, I was told that there were no special education programs. That was amazing as my brother Johnny had gone to one in the public schools in Oak Ridge, Tennessee in the late 1940s. Sadly, the basic lack of special education programs in D.C. in the '60s went on for another half a century.

Even in the 2000s, most of our children with special needs were not being offered many programs and certainly not close to home. A court order of thirty years earlier stated that if a child does not receive adequate special education in the D.C. Public Schools, the D.C. government needed to pay for an adequate program elsewhere. Thus, students with special needs were going to mostly private schools mostly out of state, far away from their families—and D.C. taxpayers were paying a fortune for that practice. This had another result: As our school system population started declining, our special education population grew as families flocked to D.C. for free access to the best and most expensive private special education programs in the country.

The whole practice became a vicious cycle. Because we had no programs, our growing special education population went to very expensive alternative schools. And then because our educational financial resources were being directed to those high-priced schools as well as to high-cost transportation to get those children to and from them, we never had the money to start good special education programs within our own schools. Of course, some students with really challenging needs may require private placement and that should be provided. But the vast majority are better served near their families and in settings where they can get special attention while being mainstreamed into programs with non-special education students when possible.

So in 2007, I pushed for a reform amendment to require a detailed plan for special education services and an analysis of educating students in private settings, and then I recruited eight co-introducers and co-sponsors. The bill received only a public hearing and no Council action, but I do believe it helped serve as an impetus to start turning things around. And the situation did get somewhat better, starting under the leadership of former Mayor Vincent Gray and former School Chancellor Kaya Henderson. There is still much work to be done, but at least finally we are heading where we need to go.

Legislation and Other Initiatives: Fighting the CFO

Once we got the government back from the Financial Control Board on September 30, 2001 (after D.C. had four consecutive balanced budgets—and I was proud to have participated in that balancing), no legislation could be passed without a fiscal impact statement. [172] So in order for the legislation to go into effect, there would have to be money built into the budget for it. The CFO would always tell us that every position hired would cause a fiscal impact of blank amount of money, which would include salaries and benefits. So it was always a huge fiscal impact to add positions. By the way, I agree wholeheartedly with this reasoned approach to sound fiscal management.

However, there are positions that actually bring in far more revenue for the city than they cost in salaries, including benefits. Therefore, I took on the CFO about this issue. When I chaired the Committee on Public Works and the Environment, I fought him by saying that certain positions are revenue producers, not reducers—so all new positions should not be treated equally. For instance, for every new parking meter person, a significant amount of money could be added to the city coffers. Not only did their own positions get covered by the money they produced, but a lot of extra money came in on top of that.

Our CFO Nat Gandhi balked at the idea at first—"A new employee is just money out the door." But I threw back at him that he had used my same rationale when he hired new people in his tax office. "Nat, when I asked you last year about hiring new people for your office, you said those people would bring in more money. So do ticket writers." I fervently and consistently made that point—and eventually won. Because of that, we now recognize positive impacts as well—and not just in the CFO's office.

I soon added lots of new parking meter people, much to the chagrin of drivers who get tickets, including those from the suburbs. Finally needed turnover of parking spaces occurred, which helped residents and shoppers—while revenues grew. I know there is resentment about tickets from everyone, residents and suburbanites alike. But we have a choice here. We all know that tickets are not caused by parking meter personnel but by those of us not abiding by the signs—and of course those signs should be easily readable and comprehensible. And if there is a question of whether the ticket was deserved or not, there is an available and understandable appeal process. We *do* have a choice. (And P.S. I get and pay for tickets here, and occasionally in the suburbs too.)

I also worked very hard to keep parking meter fees and tickets reasonable, and fought back on the efforts of Mayors Williams and Fenty to raise them while I was there—killing them one time and halving them others. I must say that I am disturbed by the new very expensive fees. It appears to be an effort to benefit only the parking garage magnates—and certainly not us or our businesses.

Legislation and Other Initiatives: Saying No for Good Reasons

I took negative positions on some issues that on the surface seemed worthy, but just on the surface. For instance, Potomac, Maryland heiress Betty Brown Casey wanted to gift the city a Mayoral mansion—actually not gift, but lease for free. But it appears she needed the city's help in getting four adjacent acres of neglected and overrun National Park Service land added to her property. So not as charitable as it sounded. On top of that, the mansion was to be located on two-lane Foxhall Road—not easy to access. If that weren't enough, the city would have to pay for most of the ongoing maintenance, security, entertainment costs, etc. In doing some research, I found that only a couple of larger cities had Mayoral mansions, and those that did found them problematic. Governors of states do have official homes, but most of those governors did not have a residence in the town where they must work—the state capital—so there was a practical need for them.

At first, most members thought it was a great idea. But when I raised all my legitimate concerns about location and maintenance costs, as well as shared the research I did, some lost enthusiasm. The idea never came to fruition. I was awfully glad. Today, that property has large, beautiful, and expensive homes, and produces a lot of tax revenue for the city—instead of draining it.

In November of 1999, I voted against a bill entitled the "George Washington University [GW] Revenue Bond Approval Resolution." I did so in order to express my displeasure at GW buying up income taxable properties—way out of its campus plan—then making that property part of the University, and therefore, tax-exempt. I had expressed this concern on the record before as well as directly to the then President of the University, Stephen Trachtenberg. I said, "GW is becoming an octopus with its tentacles usurping Foggy Bottom." Steve responded, "We are the second biggest employer in Washington, behind the federal government." I said, "That's great. But that still does not give you the right to take our real estate not on your campus and make it tax-exempt." Then he said, "Alright. We'll just move to Virginia." I said, "Fine. I'm sure all your students who pay your ridiculously high tuition—maybe the highest in the country—will enjoy being out in Virginia instead of a few blocks from the White House. Goodbye," as I did my best fingers-to-palm wave to him. In spite of that, Steve usually gave $100 to my Council campaigns and we are friendly when we see one another.

P.S. I read recently that GW sold the old Howard Johnson hotel across the street from the Watergate complex—which it had bought nearly 20 years ago to use as a dormitory—to a developer who plans to put 250 apartments there. I wonder how much non-taxable profit the "octopus" likely made from that. But at least I'm glad to see it become apartments so maybe many employed people will live there and then pay taxes of various kinds.

In the 2000s, a developer was building a large resort/center in Maryland. I was at an exhibition hall and saw the model of his project, and at the bottom was a gigantic sign that said "Washington, D.C." I went over to the developer and said, "It is not in Washington, D.C. and it is very misleading to say Washington, D.C." We had just opened a Convention Center that was *actually* in Washington, D.C. And this facility would be in direct competition, especially if people bought into the Washington, D.C. claim.

Later, Mayor Williams, Jack Evans and I were walking around and the developer stopped us, and said, "I want to have a direct water taxi service to D.C." Both guys said, "Fine!" I knew not to say "fine." I knew he would bring his guests over after they had eaten and pick them up before their next meal, and they would have little time for shopping in the real Washington, D.C. And guess what? I was right because that's exactly what his buses are doing now. I said at the time, "No, I don't think so. But if we decide to let you, it will cost you plenty." I sure wasn't going to make it easy for him to steal our hotel guests, especially under such deceit.

Back around 1997, the Council conducted a hearing on Mayor Anthony Williams's nomination of the Reverend Willie Wilson to be a member of the Board of Trustees of the University of the District of Columbia. As you may recall, just a few years earlier, there had been an incident in Southeast D.C. involving a customer and a Korean grocery store merchant. According to the owner, the customer was trying to create chaos and he asked the person to leave. And according to the customer, he or she was told to leave for no reason. I don't know what was true or not. All I know is that many of the media reported that Rev. Willie Wilson staged a boycott. He and others stayed outside the store for days protesting and put a barricade around it. That's okay. However, as also mentioned, Rev. Wilson was quoted throughout the media as saying about the store owner that residents should "cut off his head and roll it down the street." That is *not* okay. He certainly never retracted it, and in fact, seemed pleased with his own words.[173]

At the hearing for his nomination to the Board of our only taxpayer-supported University, I let my feelings be known. I said, "Someone who would speak like that, of cutting off somebody's head and rolling it down the street, is not the kind of role model our youth and others in our University need as a leader." I announced I would be voting no. I received calls and letters calling me a racist for not supporting Rev. Wilson. At the January 4, 2000 Council meeting, where the vote was to take place on his nomination to the University of the District of Columbia Board of Directors, I made a statement to counter those charges, which I am excerpting liberally from here:

> "I have not lasted in public office in this town, on and off for over 25 years, without being fairly politically savvy. And I know that it would probably have been politically smart if I just slipped out to the restroom or just stayed home feigning the flu, and missed this vote. Or I could have just shut up and voted yes. But I would be remiss, only for the sake of political expediency, not to vote my conscience.
>
> In response to the concerns I raised to Rev. Wilson directly at the Education Committee hearing on December 20th, he used phrases such as, 'Sometimes things need to be said.' 'I can live with

myself.' 'I do not intend to bring anybody down.' 'My responsibility is to speak.' 'I could never be so dishonest so as to not speak.' These are my same feelings today.

Maybe if I had just arrived in D.C. a couple of years ago or had no memory, this nomination would be okay with me. But I have lived here for 34 years and I do have a memory. I remember Rev. Wilson denouncing school desegregation during a memorial service at Howard University. In my view, and in Justice Thurgood Marshall's view, desegregation was right. In my view, the divisive rhetoric was not. I remember the weeks-long demonstrations aimed at a business owner who did wrong. In my view, the boycott was right. The divisive rhetoric was not. I remember Rev. Wilson's words aimed at the former head of the Control Board.* In my view, the Home Rule cause was right. The divisive—and insulting—rhetoric was not.

I have long said—and sincerely mean—that my only intolerance is of intolerance itself. I will cast my vote today against what I see as intolerance and divisiveness—certainly things that are not needed at our sole public institution of higher learning.

Rev. Wilson and I have always had a cordial relationship, despite the fact that he has not been a political supporter of mine. And by the way, if I only supported my supporters down here at the Council, then I would rarely cast a yes vote on Mayoral nominees. But that is not the case. I have voted favorably on literally hundreds of nominees, the vast majority of whom were also racial minorities. Check the record! I have never taken it personally that Rev. Wilson has never supported me and I have never called him a racist because of it. Now that I am not supporting him, I hope that he too will not take it personally and that we will maintain our cordial relationship.

I have been on this earth nearly 56 years and I defy anyone to find anywhere or any place where I uttered a racist word or acted in a racist fashion. It has never happened, nor will it ever. In fact, my life has been about uniting—not dividing—people.

To Rev. Wilson's supporters, I say, be mad at me for not supporting this nomination—that is fair. But to brand me a racist because I do not support him is *not* fair—nor does it deal with reality. It should be pointed out that today there are two other African Americans nominated to the UDC Board—Professor Charles Ogletree and Mr. Reginald Gilliam—and they will get my vote. But Rev. Wilson will not."

*Reverend Wilson had called the well-known and respected African American Chair of the Control Board, Andrew Brimmer, an "Uncle Tom."

His nomination passed with everyone's support, except for me and Kathy Patterson who voted no.

CHAPTER 32

Never-Ending Challenges

But back in January of 1999, I began chairing the Council's Committee on Public Works and the Environment. After chairing the Committee on Local, Regional and Federal Affairs, which I was grateful to Dave Clarke for giving me upon my return, I was excited to have such substantive areas under my watch. I immediately found my stride and loved doing the real oversight that this jurisdiction definitely needed. It was a big challenge, but one that was most welcome by me and my staff.

We worked really hard. I held more than 100 hearings in just a span of a year and a half. Practically every time I turned on Channel 13, the television station that featured Council meetings and hearings, I saw my aging face while questioning a witness. People on the street would tell me, "I watch you all the time on Channel 13." I would say back to them jokingly, "Get a life."

I was consistently firm with government witnesses at my hearings, making points with the aim of being constructive and causing improvement while being fair. I would often hear from viewers who remarked, "You always ask the question I was thinking."

One of my major pushes was to get rid of all the gas-guzzling SUVs that the Williams Administration workers as well as the Mayor himself were all riding around in and which had become the standard D.C. government vehicle. Gigantic, expensive, gas-guzzling and environmentally hazardous—what were they thinking? Not only was this step important to encourage use of vehicles which are better for the environment, but SUVs were big contributors to the enormous wear and tear on our roads and the huge expense of fixing them—not to mention the huge initial cost of buying or renting them. I put in legislation on December 4, 2001 that would ban the use of these vehicles except in cases of emergency, and made sure the bill became law.

The speech I wrote when I introduced the legislation was among my all-time favorites. It included: "It's not like the Mayor and D.C. workers have to navigate over hundreds of miles through mountainous terrain here in Washington, D.C.!" Thank goodness the legislation passed the Council unanimously and soon after went into effect. Meanwhile, most of the damage was done—the vehicles were already bought, ordered or rented. (And as recently as 2011, a Council report showed that the law was not being adequately followed.[174])

One of my other first environmental efforts revolved around recycling. During the Barry and Control Board days, the city's few efforts at recycling had been abandoned. I worked hard to successfully restart them, and the Williams Administration proved to be a good and willing partner.

The Battle for Self-Determination

We had our usual challenges with Congress, which tried to force socially conservative riders onto our budgets, such as trying to ban our medical marijuana and needle exchange initiatives—that we as a Council had passed and I had voted for. After that happened, Anthony Williams, a Democrat, as well as a few Democratic Councilmembers attended a fundraiser for Republican Ernest Istook, Chair of the House Appropriations Subcommittee which was responsible for those riders. The Councilmembers who boycotted the fundraiser in protest of Congressional intervention: Carol Schwartz and David Catania—the then Republicans.[175] Now, isn't that notable?

In 2000, I co-sponsored a contraceptive insurance bill introduced by Charlene Drew Jarvis to provide, among other things, coverage for contraception for women. But Congress would not go forward with it without a conscience clause, which was so broad that everybody could be exempt, and it held up the bill for years. Because men's contraception like vasectomies were covered, I could not understand the uproar—or I guess I could. The legislation was passed by the Council but was pocket vetoed by Williams, meaning the Mayor delayed signing and then it expired. Maybe he didn't want to deal with it in Congress.

In October of 2000, when I found out that the funds given to D.C. to help victims of crime were in jeopardy of being taken away by Congress and would revert to the U.S. Treasury because Mayor Williams had not submitted an expenditure plan, I called and asked Tony to put together such a plan immediately. I then I wrote to members of Congress after he submitted the plan to ask that they reconsider, saying, "The District of Columbia has no shortage of victims who could benefit from the availability of these funds ... and I will try to help ensure that it is spent, and spent well." We did get to keep the funds.

When Congress held up our ability to spend our own local dollars on our needle exchange program, we at the Whitman-Walker Clinic, concerned about the spread of HIV/AIDS through dirty needles, started an outside charity to fund the program. I made sure I was the first donor with a check of several hundred dollars.

Then in December of 2001, I wrote letters to Congress asking that they allow us to spend our own money for programs we felt were important—domestic partnership and needle exchange. On December 19, 2001, I received a letter from Chuck Hagel, a Republican Senator from Nebraska, who said, "I voted in favor of the [appropriations] bill ... [which] includes provisions that *allow* the District to use local funds to implement a needle-exchange program and lifts the federal ban on the implementation of the D.C. Domestic Partnership Act. While I do not support these provisions, I believe that the District of Columbia should have the flexibility to use local, *not federal*, money for programs as they see fit." Boy, how I wished there were more Senators, especially Republican ones, like him. (As an update: Our Domestic Partnership law was implemented in 2002. And the ability to use local funds for needle exchange program was finally granted in 2007—after many years and maybe many lost lives.)

But the battle was not over. On February 8, 2008, I felt compelled to write President George W. Bush about our needle exchange program as we had heard that he might ban it again. Here's what I wrote:

"Your record of compassion and commitment in the global fight against HIV/AIDS is an admirable one, and I commend you for it. However, I must take exception with your Administration's attempt to intervene in our local fight against the disease.

Fourteen percent of District of Columbia residents who are HIV-positive became infected as a result of contaminated needles. As you know, this year Congress agreed to permit the District of Columbia government to spend its own local funds on programs that seek to slow the transmission of HIV by making clean needles available to intravenous drug users. ... I find it unconscionable, therefore, that our efforts to strengthen a proven method of HIV prevention might be again impeded as a result of an action by our federal government.

No other state or local government in the country is restricted from providing local funds for needle exchange programs; in fact, there are 210 needle exchange programs in 36 states. I urge you to treat the District like any other jurisdiction by allowing us to allocate our own local funds as we see fit, especially when it can be a matter of life or death."

Thank goodness, we were able to keep the program, which has made a real difference in the fight against the spread of the disease.

The Battle Continues for Voting Rights

My passion for getting D.C. the voting rights it deserves and pays for through our federal income tax has been the bane of my existence for the nearly 52 years I have lived here. I have tried to tackle it from every angle, including being present at rallies for the cause, whether they be in the U.S. Capitol building years ago or symbolically putting teabags in the Potomac River at the edge of Georgetown years later. Not wanting to leave any stone unturned, I wrote letters to jurisdictions all over the country, including thanking members of Congress in our corner.

Earlier, in 2000, I took my plea for D.C. voting rights to the Republican Convention in Philadelphia. I helped write and pay for buttons that read, "Let D.C. Vote. It's Only Fair," as well as flyers that put our plight into its proper unjust perspective. Here are the points made in the leaflet:

- The U.S. is the only democratic nation that denies citizens of its capital city the right to representation in its national legislature.

- D.C.'s own local budget is paid for by its own local taxpayers in spite of the fact that 41% of its land is used by the federal government and cannot be taxed; and services provided to the federal government are not reimbursed. (*And by the way, the inadequate federal payment we once received to at least help compensate for the land and services is no longer provided by the federal government.*)

- Residents of the District of Columbia assume every responsibility and burden of American citizenship. For example, D.C. suffered more lives lost in Vietnam than 10 states.

- The District of Columbia residents pay nearly $2 billion in federal income taxes—the second highest per capita tax burden in the nation. (Today, it is over $4 billion.)

- Yet, District of Columbia residents are denied voting representation in the U.S. Congress.

And the second side of the handout highlighted the words of prominent Republicans who spoke out for D.C. voting rights:

- "The Republican Party supported D.C. voting representation because it was just, and in justice we could do nothing else." (Senator Robert Dole [R-KS] in 1978, speaking about the 1976 Republican Platform)

- "It should offend the democratic sense of this nation that the citizens of its Capital ... have no voice in Congress." (President Richard Nixon in a message to Congress, April 28, 1969)

- "We simply cannot continue to deny American citizens their right to equal representation in the national government ... this basic

right is a bedrock of our Republic that cannot be overturned."
(Senator Howard Baker [R-TN] in 1978 as Minority Leader)

Note that the above quotes were made by Republicans in 1969 and 1978, when the District of Columbia was made up of well over 70% Democrats and 70% African Americans.

There were other examples of Republican quotes and some more recently than the year 2000 that I have included below, which could not fit on the small handout—but can fit in this one-thousand-page book. (Okay, a little exaggeration here). I have included a few more recent ones and some may even surprise you:

- "They should also be entitled to representation from Congress." (Senator Prescott Bush [R-CT], George W. Bush's grandfather, in 1961 when pushing for D.C.'s right to vote for President and Vice President)

- "It has long ago been established by court decrees, as well as by American political tradition, that the right to vote in federal elections is a right that flows directly from the Constitution to each citizen of the United States. This right is one belonging to national citizenship and it arises out of the very nature and existence of the nation itself." (Senator Barry Goldwater [R-AZ] during a Senate debate, 1978)

- "The residents of the District of Columbia deserve the right to representation if for no other reason than simple fairness." (Senator Strom Thurmond [R-SC] during a Senate debate, 1978)

- "The need for an amendment [providing representation for the District] at this late date in our history is too self-evident for further elaboration; continued denial of voting representation from the District of Columbia can no longer be justified." (Chief Supreme Court Justice William H. Rehnquist as Assistant Attorney General under Nixon, 1970)

- "'No taxation without representation' is a fundamental principle of our democratic society ... there is nowhere in the world that a U.S. citizen can move to, still owing federal income tax, and lose their rights to voting representation in the U.S. Congress; nowhere, that is, except to our Nation's Capital, Washington, D.C." (Congressman Dana Rohrabacher [R-CA] before the Committee on Government Reform in 2004)

- "This transcends partisanship. We need to start giving the vote to people who haven't had the vote in the District of Columbia, and that's the right thing to do, not the partisan thing to do." (Congressman Chris Cannon [R-UT] in 2005)

- "It's hard to make a straight-faced argument that the capital of the free world shouldn't have a vote in Congress." (Congressman Tom Davis [R-VA] in 2003)[176]

At the 2000 Republican Convention in Philadelphia, I felt strongly that our Party, which is so proud of democracy and liberty, should resurrect support of the cause and even include it in its Party platform. Obviously, even with that well-written and distributed brochure and the button with "Let D.C. Vote—It's Only Fair," we were not successful. But I'm glad we tried. Republican resistance to District voting rights, despite prominent Republicans supporting it in the past, showed me how far Republicans were drifting away from their core values and has been one of the major reasons for my growing frustration with the Party.

But the Democrats sure don't deserve a pass here either. No Democratic President in decades has ever made it part of his agenda, in spite of receiving around 90% of D.C. residents' votes in the General Election. The only time Bill Clinton mentioned it was on the stage of the University of the District of Columbia several months before he left office, but at least he did use our Taxation Without Representation license plate.

Barack Obama, who in 2008, got 92.5% of D.C.'s vote in the General Election, rarely said a word about the need to alleviate the injustice of our lack of voting rights anytime or any place, even though people have begged him to do so. And in 2011, President Obama used D.C.'s self-determination as a bargaining chip to reach a deal with then Speaker of the House John Boehner to avoid a government shutdown. He gave away the city's right to fund abortions for low-income women using its own money, saying, reportedly, "John, I'll give you D.C. abortion."[177] This sparked widespread disappointment among D.C. rights proponents. I like him, but this hurt. And I wish he had been more sensitive to our legitimate concerns and more of an advocate on our behalf—and not just on this abortion issue, but on the many others, especially full voting rights and autonomies.

In addition, over the years, when the Democrats have held both Houses of Congress and the Presidency, we have not been anywhere close to their front-burner. A valued exception was Senator Joseph Lieberman, who put legislation forward every session, but unfortunately he is no longer in Congress. Where are the national Democratic leaders on this critical cause? Obviously too busy, along with their Republican counterparts, bringing democracy to every corner of the earth except to the federal taxpaying citizens of their own Nation's Capital. Shame on all of them.

Two More Midlanders in Town

I got to know George W. and Laura Bush a bit after he became President. Actually, we first met many years earlier when his father was Vice President and my husband and I had been invited to a brunch at the Vice President's home at the old Naval Observatory on Massachusetts Ave. On the rare occasions I saw him, he would mention my parents as they had volunteered in his first Congressional campaign, whose jurisdiction would have included Midland if he had won. "The Levitts, who owned the General Clothing Store. God rest their souls," he would say. His words about my folks always touched me.

Many people ask me if I knew the Bushes when I was growing up in Texas. The answer is no—for several reasons: 1) We lived on opposite sides of town. 2) They were a few years younger so we would not have crossed in school. And, 3) George went away to boarding school when he was 13 and then his folks moved to Houston soon thereafter.

Even before the Bushes came to D.C. as President and First Lady, in my ongoing efforts to fight for a bigger tent in the Republican Party, I wrote a letter to then Texas Governor George W. Bush, asking him to choose a pro-choice female running mate like Olympia Snow. Despite our Midland, Texas commonality, he obviously did not listen to me.

When they first moved here, I tried to get them engaged in our city. An example: As Chair of the Metropolitan Washington Council of Governments (COG) in 2001, I invited them to kick off Summer Quest, a successful reading program in local public libraries across the region.

On March 28, 2003, I wrote to the President to get their help on a very important issue:

"I have an idea that may be of interest to you and to the First Lady. We have a tremendous need in our city to restore a National Historic Site dedicated to one of our greatest Americans, Frederick Douglass. The house and grounds, located in Southeast Washington, have landed on the National Park Service's list of the country's "Ten Most Endangered National Parks." We have a marvelous opportunity to help preserve a significant part of the legacy of this great African American patriot, statesman—and Republican ... and hope you will become involved with this issue."

I sent a copy of the same letter to Karen Hughes, then at the Republican National Committee, as well as to federal government entities like the National Park Service, etc. Then on June 23, 2003,

I received a letter from the U.S. Department of the Interior signed by the Regional Director of the National Capital Region. In it, he said that the Speaker of the House of Representatives, a Republican, had recently announced at a press conference that Congress would make available provisions of $1 million to aid in the restoration of the site. I was so happy.

When the President did other helpful things, such as recommending the transfer of federal land to D.C., I wrote a letter to express my appreciation, as well as a letter on August 24th to recognize his wanting to transfer 17 federal parcels to the District of Columbia: "... the District's ability to raise revenue and provide services for its residents and visitors is significantly dependent upon its ability to collect tax on properties within its borders. Development of these parcels will go a long way toward that end."

Even though he did a couple of these helpful things, I always wished he had been a better friend to the District and our plight of no voting rights in Congress. In fact, he was never anywhere to be found. But at least his grandfather, Senator Prescott Bush (R-CT), had certainly been a good friend to the District by rounding up the Senate votes to pass the 23rd Amendment, which granted D.C. Electoral College votes—and his support of representation.[178]

Colleagues, Friends and Fundraising

Back in May of 1999, the government of Taiwan, at its expense, invited members of the Council to visit the country. Linda Cropp, then Chair of the Council, picked eight of us to go. We flew to Taipei and met with many leaders there, where we learned a lot about their government and culture. We were supposed to see other parts of the country but because of storms, couldn't, yet very much liked Taipei, its people and its museums. The rest of the group was going on to Hong Kong at their own expense, and I had decided not to join them on that leg having already been there on a personal trip a few years earlier. Kevin Chavous, Jack Evans, Sandy Allen, David Catania and others, though, begged me to go, saying it just wouldn't be as fun without me. Being a person who loves flattery, that's all I needed to hear and off I went to Hong Kong—again. Councilmembers really got along in those days. It was close to being a family.

Meanwhile, at home, I held fundraisers at my apartment for different causes such as the Women's Campaign Fund, a national bipartisan group which supports women candidates. Senator Susan Collins attended one of the events as well as then Senator and former Vice President Joe Biden. His well-known gift of gab was on full display that evening. Many guests were fascinated as Biden held court for over two hours in one of the side rooms. I am particularly fond of both of these fine public servants.

I loved having parties in my big and gracious apartment. I think it made me feel less guilty about having all that space just to myself. Around that time, one of my best friends, Cornelius Baker, celebrated his 40th birthday and we used the occasion to do a fundraiser for the Whitman-Walker Clinic, which we were both very involved with. Many other events followed, including a fundraiser/birthday party in January of 2001 for my then friend and colleague on the Council, David Catania.

I used to always love to do a spring open house for several reasons: 1) to celebrate warmer weather coming, 2) to enjoy seeing friends, 3) to reciprocate for all the invitations I received, and 4) to get it all done in one fell swoop—to save money and time. I especially always enjoyed doing them because of Dan Ezell, who would come to help and who has become a good friend. Among my favorite guests, in addition to some mentioned elsewhere, are Kitty Kelley, Gloria Minott, Esther Coopersmith, Melanne and Phil Verveer, Kojo Nnamdi, and Joy and Carl Stern.

Staff as Family

I treated my Council staff as a family. We worked hard, but we also had a lot of fun. I was demanding in that I wanted to do a really good job and could be impatient in the process. I raised my voice some, but tended to laugh louder. I also read every single word of every single report, and edited them all, leaving me sleepless many a night. I'm sure it drove my staff, who had to make the corrections, crazy, but I couldn't curb my enthusiasm for what I perceived as perfection, especially when you're dealing with public documents that represent our government at work.

I tried to make sure we had some good times away from the office, including taking the whole staff to my getaway place in Rehoboth every other summer for the weekend where we had mattresses on the floor and people sleeping on the couch. We always began with my treating for the buffet at Rusty Rudder. And then in the days afterwards, I got the benefit of the good cooks and grillers in my office. Such fond memories.

But I know that sometimes I treated them too much like family. I have a lot of loyalty, often even when not deserved. That was me—high expectations most of the time and yet, too forgiving some of the time. I did find it hard to let people go, but occasionally I had to. Although we had a full docket at work, I did also try to be considerate of my staff with evenings and weekends. Thus, I usually went to Council-related events during those times alone, even though it would have been much easier on me to have one of them there, as most other members did. Regardless, I was blessed to have had a large number of good and loyal staff members. And I remain proud of having had among the most diverse staffs of any Council office all my years there, proud of the work we did together—and the ongoing friendships that were developed.

Family as Family

And I always had some fun with my family. On December 31, 1999, to celebrate the millennium, my family and I got close seats to the amazing concert at the foot of the Lincoln Memorial. We took in the new year with the President and celebrities and it was quite a memorable event.

Then in 2000, my girls Stephanie and Hilary, my brother Johnny, and I (my son Doug was still in London), along with my two Aunt Bettys, Uncle Seymour and Uncle Joe, and my first cousins (Seymour and his wife Martine, Becky, Bev and her husband Ross, and their children David, Selena, Arielle and Jonah Luc) on my mother's side of the family, took off on a sentimental journey. They started in Brownsville, Tennessee, where my beloved Grandma Carrie was originally from. My immediate family and I could not join them there because of my work schedule, but we hooked up in Memphis a day later.

Then we went on to Greenville, Mississippi, where my grandparents lived, my mom and her two brothers were raised, and where Johnny and I were born. First, we stopped by my grandparents' old house at 613 S. Washington St., where the new owner graciously let us in and which was filled with such warm memories. But it was so bittersweet. All the family who had lived there had now passed away. The glorious trees in town had been diminished due to a bad ice storm. The once vital downtown, where my family had a grocery store, had died like most small downtowns around the country. And the lovely view of the Mississippi River from the levy was now obstructed by a casino. It was still a wonderful and meaningful visit. And the beautiful Hebrew Union Congregation downtown still stood tall, proud, unchanged—and open, despite its dwindling membership.

We visited the Main Street Cemetery, where a portion is set aside for Jewish families and kept up by the temple, and where my grandparents as well as my mom and dad had been laid to rest. I continue to contribute some financial support to the synagogue in Greenville because of its importance to my family (my folks were also married there), its historic significance, and because I worry about its future and the cemetery's without such support. From Greenville, we stayed a couple of days in Baton Rouge, where my mom and uncles had gone to college and which remains home to some of the family. There we joined with other cousins Jean and her husband Will, and Joe and his wife Tricia, and Becky's son, Prentiss. Afterwards, Johnny, the girls and I went on to spend two days in New Orleans—one of my all-time favorites.

I was also close with several of my paternal cousins, in fact, all the offspring of Uncle Earl and Uncle Albert. Uncle Albert's you know about—Andrew. Uncle Earl had two children, Bruce and Brook, who I am very fond of as well as Bruce's wife, Emily, their children Scott and Alex, and Brook's husband, Philip.

As Doug had been in Great Britain since 1996—nearly five years—it enabled him to get a dual residency there. One of the things I enjoyed most during that time was to go visit him in London, sometimes with the girls, sometimes alone. During summer recess from the Council, I had two special and memorable short trips with Doug in Europe. One was to a family friend's wedding in Florence, Italy, which is one of my top cities in the world, and another to Prague, Czechoslovakia which I loved. I never take pictures when I'm traveling as I want to spend time taking in the sights instead of mainly looking through a lens. But I took rolls and rolls of pictures in Prague as I was so enthralled with the architecture and the various colors of the buildings.

In November of 2000, when I won reelection to the Council, Stephanie and Hilary were in D.C. But they were much more keyed into the Presidential election. In fact, Election Day, when I thought they were out campaigning for me, they were actually on the Key Bridge (which connects Georgetown to Virginia), holding up Gore/Lieberman signs. They both went to bed, too nervous as the contest became too close to call. So close that a month later Gore made his concession speech. By then they were back in New York, and I called to comfort them. They were inconsolable. Steph was sobbing. I told her in the future she cannot get so emotionally involved in politics, which was quite ironic coming from me.

At my swearing-in ceremony on January 2, 2001 at the Walter Washington Convention Center, I chose to only have my brother Johnny with me and had him hold the Bible as I took the oath. He stood by smiling as I gave my speech in front of a large crowd, who were there for all seven Councilmembers being sworn in that day. As I turned to walk off the stage expecting Johnny to follow me, how surprised I was to hear his voice on the microphone, giving his own speech. I did let him go on for a couple of minutes— "I'm so glad to be here today ... D.C.'s a great place ..."—and then I walked up, took his hand, and he waved to everybody as we walked off to a far bigger applause than I got after my speech.

Nation as Family

On September 11, 2001, Doug had just arrived in town several days earlier from his nearly five years in London and was planning to drive later that day to Nashville where he was relocating to pursue a career as a singer-songwriter instead of doing it occasionally. He had rented a U-Haul truck that he had just loaded up with some of my furniture the night before and had it parked right on the side street next to my Connecticut Ave. apartment building.

Usually the television is always on in my home—most of the time just for company—but that morning it was not. Doug and I sat in my corner office, chatting. My daughter Hilary called from her Chelsea apartment in NYC and told us to turn on the TV. Doug and I immediately started crying as we saw both towers on fire. We were horrified and felt so badly for those poor people and their families. And we were scared for our own family there. We knew Hilary was okay but had not heard from Stephanie who worked downtown.

Then came the plane right into the Pentagon just across the river from D.C. And we learned that another plane had gone down in Pennsylvania. It had been heading to Washington to hit the Capitol building or the White House. I will always be grateful for those brave souls on that plane who kept the terrorists from coming to D.C. May they rest in peace.

Stephanie worked at Legal Aid in Manhattan, about 15 short blocks north of the World Trade Center, so she heard the crashes in her office. On TV, when the towers fell, it looked like the entirety of lower Manhattan was being engulfed, and my daughter Hilary was hysterical thinking Steph was in harm's way. Stephanie wound up seeing the towers fall as she rode her bicycle northward toward her home on the Lower East Side. She called up, screaming and crying. She was safe, but she had seen far too much. We were so grateful, but like everyone else, felt so devastated for the families who lost their loved ones. The only good thing that came out of that horrific day is that the nation united in the shared trauma and sorrow—and we became like a family.

Later in the day, Doug went down to check on the U-Haul and found it had been broken into, but nothing was missing. It turned out that since we live in downtown D.C., just a few blocks north of Dupont Circle and only about a mile or so from the White House, security officials had viewed that truck as a security risk and had gone through it.

For weeks after that terrible day, I was teary constantly. Within a few days, I came up with an idea to have our school students collect pennies to help build a memorial to D.C. lives who were lost in New York as well as at the Pentagon. I called the Superintendent of Schools, Paul L. Vance, asked him to join me in heading up this effort, and he enthusiastically said yes. We both felt better ourselves for this, especially knowing that it gave D.C. school students an outlet for their own pain.

Initially the Williams Administration asked for just $100 to $150 million in security aid of the $40 billion available from the federal government to assist localities in improving emergency preparedness following the attacks of September 11th. I spoke out at a Council hearing that as the Nation's Capital we should be asking for a billion dollars, not 10% of that.

I also wrote a letter on October 5, 2001 to the Mayor in which I appealed to him to ask for that billion dollars to ensure that we, the seat of the federal government and long considered a prime target for terrorism, would be adequately protected. In the end, the District did ask for $735 million as well as millions of dollars' worth of grants. I was relieved we were finally requesting and getting the money we needed and deserved.

Then, on June 12th of 2006, I wrote a letter to the Under Secretary for Preparedness of the Department of Homeland Security, with a copy to the Secretary of that Department, about my dismay at their decision to cut federal counterterrorism funding to the national capital region by nearly *one-half*, and said:

> "It does, in fact, run counter to the recommendations of the National Commission on Terrorist Attacks, which stated that 'homeland security funding should be based strictly on an assessment of risks and vulnerabilities ... Washington, D.C. and New York City are certainly at the top of any such list.' ... The

Commission's two chairs, Thomas Kean and Lee Hamilton ... jointly wrote that, 'It is scandalous that we still allocate scarce homeland security dollars on the basis of pork-barrel spending.'"

Council of Governments

In addition to being busy on the D.C. Council, I was also very engaged with the Metropolitan Washington Council of Governments (COG), a regional organization that brings together leaders from local governments in the D.C. metro area. When I was a member of the COG Board in the mid-to-late 1980s, it consisted of 17 jurisdictions and then more recently, 23 jurisdictions, such as Montgomery and Prince Georges County, Maryland; Fairfax and Alexandria, Virginia; the town of Rockville, Maryland, to name five. I went back on the COG Board when I returned to the Council in 1997. I was Chair of its Transportation Planning Board (TPB) 1998-99 where I helped institute an advisory group.

I was selected COG's Board Chair for the year 2001 and started serving in January. So on September 11, 2001, Executive Director Michael Rogers and I were in charge of leading the coordinated regional response to those tragic events that day as well as preparing the region for any God-forbid future events. We immediately established the Committee on Homeland Security and Emergency Preparedness. I became Chair of that Committee for the remainder of the year as well as the following one. The group (which included appointees from the relevant federal agencies and organizations such as the American Red Cross and the Board of Trade along with other regional representatives) started meeting on a regular (at first weekly, then bi-weekly, and for the next year, monthly) basis. It was quite a challenging schedule and agenda. But I remain proud of the coordinated systems we put in place at that time, which stand today.

And that enormous undertaking wasn't the only thing on our plate. Affordable housing is at a troubling level in D.C. today, although efforts are being made to address it. But even back in 2001—16 years ago—I recognized the growing problem in this area. Then, it was not just the lack of affordable housing specifically here in D.C. that was the issue, but the fact that the District was carrying practically the whole load of public housing for the entire region. As it was standard for a Chair of COG to pick a primary focus during her or his year as the leader, I decided back in January of 2001 to make regional affordable housing my focus.

Obviously, September 11th affected some of the time we could spend on the matter of affordable housing, but we still put together a well-received and comprehensive report outlining principles and goals, entitled *Finding a Way Home: Building Communities with Affordable Housing*. This report included a regional map which visually displayed with black dots where public housing could be found. As expected, D.C. proper was practically one big dot. Prince Georges County had some, while only a few random dots could be spotted elsewhere in Maryland and Virginia. In addition, we put into motion concrete plans by 1) securing private funding to award rental security deposit assistance to families in need, 2) partnering with Freddie Mac to target predatory lending practices affecting home owners, and 3) endorsing the establishment of the Washington Area Housing Trust Fund, working with Kerry Donley, then Mayor of Alexandria, Virginia. We went on to raise money for the Trust Fund from the regional jurisdictions who were members of COG and from Congress where we succeeded in securing $500,000 one year and then $1 million. Mayor Donley and I co-chaired the Washington Area Housing Trust Fund from 2002 to 2007.

It was good to have a perch from which to advocate for the sharing of public housing across the region instead of one or two jurisdictions having to carry the whole burden. I used that perch to advance the cause of recognizing that affordable housing for lower and middle-income residents was an issue we should all embrace, regardless of jurisdiction. It was a worthy effort.

On COG, I met many wonderful and impressive people and became friends with a lot of them, including Nancy and Jim Estepp, Bruce Williams and Geoffrey Burkhart, Bob and Roberta Dorsey, Cathy and Gerry Connelly, and became better friends with Jay Fisette, who I knew from the Whitman-Walker Clinic, and his partner Bob Rosen. It was actually fun to get to know regional leaders who I had seen on television over the years. We at COG decided to capitalize on these new relationships by not only working on mutual areas of interest, but also by socializing some. I was helpful in starting an annual dinner, usually around holiday time, in the various jurisdictions. We held the first one at my apartment.

In May of 2001, several of us on the COG Board, along with a couple of others who had particular expertise in the area of transportation, were picked by the Marshall Foundation to take a trip it financed to Copenhagen, Denmark; Berlin, Germany; and Lyon, France to see various exemplary transportation solutions. Among the six selected participants were Rushern Baker (former Maryland Delegate and now Prince Georges County Executive), Kate Hanley (former Chair of Fairfax County, and then Secretary of Virginia), and Ulysses Currie (Maryland State Senator). It was an interesting and enjoyable group and trip—except for when my wallet was pilfered brilliantly in Lyon by several young females (who the police described as gypsies). What happened was one blocked the door for a second, which appeared to just be rude, while others held up my shoulder bag, unzipped it, grabbed my wallet and rezipped my purse. They were long gone before I discovered it missing when I went to buy something. Well, at least I had my passport locked up back at the hotel.

A Tree Grows in Washington—Actually Many

Since 1973, our beautiful city of trees had lost 64% of its canopy. The District was losing 5,000 trees a year.[179] This loss also was having a public health consequence as trees remove pollutants in the air, reduce heat, control water run-off during storms, etc. Something had to be done.

Therefore, I was very pleased that in December of 2001, Councilmember Phil Mendelson brought forward the "Urban Forest Preservation Act," which was a collaboration with environmental groups. I was very much with them in that we had to do something to save and replenish our greenery. However, the legislation was too extreme. Phil and I, who were the only ones attending the hearings on the bill, encouraged witnesses to help clarify the language as it was too confusing and broad. The legislation as written also required such a large administrative staff that there would barely be enough remaining dollars for the trees themselves.

We re-wrote the bill. I brought it out of the committee after it passed there, and then shepherded it through passage by the full Council. We ended up with the strongest tree law in the nation. And it was one that could realistically be implemented without breaking either our bank or those of private citizens. It did show we were serious about not only preserving the trees that we had left, but planting many new ones. I felt good about the legislation and having partnered with Phil collegially to broker workable compromises to keep D.C. beautiful and green.

We made tree planting and preservation a priority. We planted thousands of trees, using capital dollars, and trimmed thousands more. We also got a $60 million boost from the Casey Foundation. Thank you, Betty Casey. You helped make a huge difference.

More specifically, a permit would be needed for anyone (private property owners or developers) seeking to cut down a tree with a circumference of 55 inches or more, and a fee would be charged. They could avoid those fees, though, if they planted new trees. I also pushed through legislation which required posting a notice seven days in advance on any city tree slated for removal unless it was dead or of potential danger.

We received kudos on the tree law from tough critics like Jim Dougherty of the D.C. Chapter of the Sierra Club, who called the bill "a great compromise."[180] It was especially important to have acted as we did then, rather than knowing that if we did *not*, the next generation would say, "Why didn't they do something about our diminishing canopy?" Well, we did—and I'm mighty proud.

And I kept on doing. In later hearings, I learned there were problems in maintaining the trees that we were finally able to plant. I asked, "Are the saplings we're planting being watered?" The answer: "No." "Why not?" I asked. "We don't have watering trucks." "Well, let's get watering trucks," I declared—and couldn't believe I had to declare it. And I made sure that money was put in the budget for watering trucks and drivers.

Sometimes in government it comes down to being as ridiculously simple as that. How could we possibly get through this insurmountable hurdle? Maybe by doing the obvious. Before you plant any more saplings that will just die in their infancy because of lack of watering after you spent the money to buy them and paid the workers to plant them, not to mention all the expense you put out to remove the saplings after they die, why don't you just get watering trucks and people to drive them? Lordy! Why should I be the one to recognize that as a problem, and then rectify it? Isn't that the job of the tree planter, or someone in the Mayor's office, or one of their many well-paid "consultants"? No wonder I wanted to be Mayor! That kind of frustration was one of the reasons I ran and ran and ran. ...

Quitting Smoking

I started smoking when I was one-month shy of 18 years old. My parents smoked all my childhood—Mom, cigarettes incessantly and my father, cigars. Our small house reeked of it. The worst was our car, where the windows were always up and I felt nauseous because of all the smoke. The only grandparent who smoked was Grandpa John, who also smoked cigars like his son.

But his wife, my Grandma Bonnie, hated smoke, so she only allowed him to smoke in the apartment every day in February, which was his birthday month. Family and friends sent boxes of cigars to him then. Afterwards, Grandma would air out the apartment, and dread the next February 1ˢᵗ. When he got to be about 80, he quit, and then he started lecturing my father to do the same. No progress was made until he told him that if he stopped, he'd give him $100. Now, my dad was middle-aged and not poor at that time—but he did quit so he could collect that $100.

Most of my friends in Midland started smoking cigarettes at 11 or 12. I took no part in that. I was going to be different. But then I went off to college and while studying for my first finals there in December of 1961, my two roommates and I began smoking together. And with everything I ever did, I did it with great gusto. Every day, all day, never less than a pack a day—but never more than a pack and a half. I must admit I smoked first thing in the morning and every night before I went to sleep, and I enjoyed every single cigarette. About 35 years in, I began to be annoyed at myself about it. I would think, "You've worked so hard not to be enslaved at this point in your life by anybody or anything. And here you are enslaved by this three-inch stick of tobacco. You've escaped drinking and any type of drug, but you are totally addicted to those damn cigarettes. They rule your life. You don't even want to go to a movie because they interfere with your smoking time. You need to take control." (I actually said those exact things over and over again in my mind.)

Several years later, in 1999, my son Doug said, "Mom, we lost one parent to suicide already. I wish you would stop smoking." That was an additional wake-up call. I knew I needed to do it for myself, for my children, for a sense of control. I had heard about Zyban and bought it. I decided to follow the program exactly as instructed. The program said to start taking the pill 8 to 14 days before you wanted to quit. I picked the 11ᵗʰ day. It said to go out of town and do something different from your normal life. I decided to go to Baytown, Texas with Johnny in September of 1999 to visit Ivan's mother, who I remained close to. I would never have smoked in her home under any circumstances anyway. The program said to have someone air out your house, closets and your car while you were gone. I did that too. My determination, the Zyban pill, which took a little of the edge off, and the change of scenery worked. I stopped smoking for several weeks; and even when I first got back to D.C. and my normal routine, I was okay.

Then I thought, "I'm fine. I can now just mooch those couple of cigarettes a day I really miss—the ones after mealtime." And off I went—and was soon back to smoking my normal pack or so a day.

In the late spring of 2001, I really became disgusted with myself again and decided to repeat the program. I made reservations to visit my Aunt Betty and Uncle Seymour in Denver (another home I would never smoke in) in order to be there for her 80th birthday on July 11th. I started the Zyban program on June 30th and quit smoking on my travel day of July 10, 2001. I have not had a puff since. I've learned that Zyban is a form of Wellbutrin, which is cheaper than Zyban and now there is a generic form of Wellbutrin that is cheaper still. (I mention that for those of you who may want to quit yourself.)

I also added to the program my own regiments to deal with some of the most difficult habitual issues: the act of deep breathing, the oral fixation, doing something with your hands, and keeping busy after meals. The regiments included:

1) For several months before stopping, I smoked less. When I would get an urge to smoke, I would start doing deep breathing, which helped get me through that moment. And I would wait through several urges (which by the way, only last a minute) before I would smoke. 2) I also started smoking lighter cigarettes, which I didn't like as much. 3) I continued the deep breathing after stopping smoking every time I got an urge, and they were often in the beginning. 4) I cut plastic straws the exact size of a cigarette and would keep them in my car and purse. I used them especially when driving or talking on the phone, as I did not think you could do either without smoking. So there I would be, talking on the phone, breathing through a straw. It actually helped. 5) I started sucking on cough drops, and was glad when they came out with a sugar-free variety, and prefer the defense drops now, especially the citrus flavors. 6) My daughter Hilary, who only smoked briefly in college, started putting toothpicks in a card case in her purse when she quit. Whenever she felt the need to smoke, she would reach into her purse and get out her card case, take out the toothpick, and put it in her mouth—just staying busy while the urges came. (All of these six things helped so I'm passing them along in hopes that others might at least try to quit.)

The first year or so, as I would pass people smoking on the street, I wanted to rip the cigarette out of their hands—not to throw it away in disgust, but to smoke it myself. Then after a couple of years, it got better. But still a girlfriend, who had quit decades earlier, and I would talk occasionally about how when we were older in the nursing home and we were told we were going to die soon, we would take up smoking again. Now, 16 years in, I would not take up smoking under any circumstances and am awfully proud of myself for having given it up. I do remain more sympathetic than disgusted when I see people smoking on the street, and often walk up and in a nice way try to tell them to think about quitting. Then I say, "If you ever decide to do so, please call me and I'll help you through it," giving my phone number if they haven't turned their backs on me yet.

Quitting smoking ain't easy, but it sure is worth it not to have your home, car, clothes and breath reek, not to have your furniture and clothes have tiny little burn marks, not to constantly cough (which I always said was post-nasal drip and which, by the way, miraculously disappeared after I stopped smoking), actually have your friends want to be around you, and be able to watch your teeth and gums decay only from old age and not helped along by smoking. Oh, and not unimportant: it could lengthen your life.

CHAPTER 33

Name Shame

In early November of 2001, I was sitting in my bed on a Sunday watching D.C.'s NFL football team play, one of my favorite pastimes in my favorite place. I can't remember if the team won or lost that game, but I do know that I vowed that afternoon that I would never say their proper (or in my opinion, improper) name again. It had bothered me for years, but for some reason that day, my eyes became wide open. Unfortunately, here, I have to spell out the name to explain the issue as I am writing this book, but I am not saying it aloud even as I write it.

That evening, I decided that refusing to use the name personally was not enough. I needed to do something much more dramatic. I just had a hunch that this was a racist name. I could not imagine a team called "blackskins" or "yellowskins" or "whiteskins" being thought of as acceptable. Why was this acceptable?

I started writing a resolution that I intended to get voted on by the Council at its Tuesday legislative session. I had decided to do it as an emergency piece of legislation, which means you can bypass certain time-allotted procedures. I sure felt racism was an emergency, so it should qualify. I knew the resolution would have to be distributed by the close of business on Monday, so there I was on Sunday night in that same bed, writing the "Whereas's." I had gone at first to a recent dictionary, which described it as a "disparaging slang term meant to insult," exactly the same definition as the n-word for Black people, the k-word for Jewish people, the w-word for Italian people, and the s-word for Latin people. Exactly the same except it disparaged American Indian people.

I stayed up very late working on it, and then got up early so I could get it to my staff to research some of the factual information. I had the "Therefore be it resolved" section down pat, though, which called on the owner of the team, Dan Snyder, to change the racist name. I hardly slept as I was excited about finally trying to right an ongoing wrong.

After including the research done that Monday morning on the deplorable origins of the word, the resolution was circulated to my colleagues by 5 p.m. and read as follows:

"RESOLVED, BY THE COUNCIL OF THE DISTRICT OF COLUMBIA. That this resolution may be cited as the 'Sense of the Council in Support of the Washington National Football League Name Change Emergency Approval Resolution of 2001.'

Sec. 2. The Council finds that:

(1) The term 'Redskins' was derived during a time in our nation when a bounty was offered on Native Americans, and those killed by the bounty hunters were scalped as proof of slaughter so that bounty could be collected.

(2) Bounty hunters began referring to the scalps of the dead Native Americans as 'redskins,' much like pelts from beaver were referred to as 'beaverskins' and the pelts from deer were referred as "deerskins."

(3) The term 'Redskins' is viewed by many sensitive and progressive-minded individuals as a demeaning, dehumanizing racist insult that embodies a history of degradation and slaughter.

(4) The team name 'Redskins' is offensive and hurtful to many Native Americans who are citizens of this nation and to all people who reject racial stereotypes and bigotry as socially and morally unacceptable.

(5) The Council and the citizens of Washington, D.C. are proud of the National Football League franchise and desire a team name that instills pride as well.

(6) While changing the name of the city's National Football League team may not be a simple task, it is the right thing to do.

Sec. 3. It is the sense of the Council that the Washington Redskins' owners change the team's name prior to the 2002-2003 football season."

I introduced the emergency and the sense of the Council resolution (as printed above) on Monday, November 5, 2001. The next day, during the legislation session there was a discussion, all favorable toward the intent and content with the exception of Harold Brazil (D-at-large). Harold stated, "I don't know why we care. The team is incorporated and practices in Virginia, and it plays in Maryland." I responded, "If they were called the Vienna, Virginia Redskins or the Raljohn [Landover], Maryland[181] Redskins, then maybe I wouldn't care so much. But they are called the WASHINGTON Redskins." The resolution passed 12 to 1.

Then in December of 2001, a month later, as Chair of the Metropolitan Washington Council of Governments (COG), I took the issue to the group. Normally COG resolutions dealt with important yet very non-controversial issues such as, "We desire clean air in the region" and, "All of us want better regional transportation." Now here I come with, "Change the name of our beloved, honored, legendary, favorite team." How sacrilegious can one get? I knew this would take some lobbying. In all my years on the COG Board, I had never been called by a colleague about a matter, nor had I called. Well, I changed that, at least this one time. I worked the phone and lobbied each COG member individually.

Many were on board right away. Several were concerned politically because of ties to the team or because they represented areas that included team activities. I understood but suggested that maybe they weren't going to be feeling well the day of the vote.

That day arrived, January 9, 2002, and a similar resolution was passed by COG, and this time 11 to 2 in favor with five abstentions. As I said at the time, "... we are simply stating our concern about the ongoing use of the term ... and requesting that it be replaced with a term that does not offend, and does not hurt Native Americans and all people who reject racial stereotypes, racial slurs and bigotry." COG's action was certainly considered newsworthy. We were on the front page of *The Washington Post* with a picture of the body with a vast majority of us holding our hands up proudly to vote in favor.[182]

On March 3, 2002, I wrote an editorial in *The Washington Post*, which put the name into historical context and gave further rationale for the pressing need to change the name of our team:

'Name Shame'

"I don't believe that George Preston Marshall meant to dishonor American Indians when he changed the name of the Boston Braves to the Redskins in 1933—four years before the team moved to Washington. I don't believe Dan Snyder means to dishonor Native Americans by keeping that name and that fans—myself included—mean to be racists when singing 'Hail to the Redskins.' But the time has come to have another team name. Times and sensitivities change.

In 1993, 'redskins' in standard dictionaries was defined as 'American Indian.' However, recent editions of the American Heritage, the Merriam-Webster and the Princeton University dictionaries define 'redskin' as offensive or a disparaging term for a Native American.

The team says 'Redskins' was derived from the American Indians' practice of painting themselves with red clay before battle. Maybe. But another origin of the term comes from the days when bounty hunters received money for killing American Indians and, as proof, presented bloody scalps called 'redskins.'

You can love the team and its traditions as I do and still support a name change. Traditions are important but not when they are hurtful. And when teams' names change, the world does not stop spinning.

Bullets owner Abe Pollin heard the plea of those who cried out for a name change because of gun violence, and through a community-wide competition, a new name was born. The Wizards now have Michael Jordan and a decent record. Times and sensitivities can change.

The Redskins seem to have no problem with change. Name the area, and it has seen changes: the owner, coaches, management, quarterbacks, uniforms, stadium, and rising prices for tickets, parking and concessions. The only sign of stability is the racist name. This issue is not about every Native American-type name or emblem. That debate will continue. It's about having the dehumanizing name 'Redskins' associated with our proud region. California will not allow one of its citizens to have a vanity plate reading '!REDSKN' because it said 'Redskin' was racist, and the courts upheld that decision. Yet in this region, the name is held up as a banner for the world to see.

In 1992, the *Post* endorsed a movement to change the team's name. WTOP radio refused to say 'Redskin' on air for two years. But Jack Kent Cooke arrogantly proclaimed, 'I will never change the name,' and he didn't. And the movement faded.

That may happen again despite strong votes by the region's elected officials requesting a name change. But as the *Post* stated in that 1992 editorial, 'To say that the use of the term "redskin" is well-intentioned or that it is not meant to be objectionable, sidesteps the real issue. This is not a term fashioned by American Indians. The nickname was assigned to them, just as the pejorative designation 'darkies' was once imposed on African American slaves. That was wrong then; and this is wrong now ... We can do better.'

The times—and our sensitivities—require that we do."[183]

One discussion I had with an African American colleague and friend kind of tells the tale. Her husband was associated with the team and she said firmly to me one day, "I don't know why you're making such a big deal about the team name. And besides, the American Indian profile on the helmet is quite dignified-looking." I responded, "Okay, then why don't we change the name of the team to the Washington n-word and put your proud profile up everywhere. How do you feel? Or we could change it to the Washington k-word and put my proud profile up. Is that okay?" She paused reflectively and said, "I never thought about it that way."

The resolutions requesting a name change could not force the organization to do anything. Only the owner of the team can change the name. But the then and still present owner Dan Snyder continues to stick to his stubborn refusal to right this wrong. But it was an important statement we made at that time back in 2001, and it's sad that 16 years later we're still where we were with a disparaging and hurtful name.

Because of being a vocal and visible promoter of the name change, I did become the target of vicious verbal attacks, including death threats. Even more death threats came my way when I received some national attention.

After the passages of the resolutions, I was invited onto some Fox News programs seen nationally, and was interviewed on two separate shows by Bill O'Reilly and Sean Hannity. I knew what I was walking into when I said yes to the shows, but I thought it was important to have a public discussion about it, even among those not prone to agree. Hannity started the interview wondering how a Republican from Midland, Texas could care about such a cause. They both really just used the opportunity to berate me about my "political correctness." Maybe political correctness can sometimes go too far, but too many use the term to write off hurtful issues that don't affect them personally. If the team was called the "Washington Whities," or the "Washington Crackers" with either Hannity's or O'Reilly's proud profile on display, I'm sure people at Fox News, including those two, would not then just scoff it off.

I have not taken offense with terms like "Warriors," "Braves," "Chiefs," (other than Cleveland's logo), and maybe I should, but our team's name is blatantly egregious. I was proud to have taken a very unpopular and public stance on this very important issue and well ahead of today's outrage.

We should have been outraged for far longer. A U.S. District Court Judge in Alexandria, Gerald Bruce Lee, "questioned why the team ever chose the name, pointing out in a ruling in 2015 that Webster's Collegiate Dictionary defined the word as 'often contemptuous' in 1898, 'seventy years prior to the registration of the first Redskins Mark.'"[184] And according *The Washington Post* on June 30, 2017, "One of the earliest points of contention came [in] ... 1972, when ... Native American leaders met with then-Redskins President Edward Bennett Williams to change the name." He did not, but "the team scrapped 'Scalp 'em' from its fight song."[185]

Now some recent history on the court battles: In 2015, a Judge Lee ordered the cancellation of the team trademarks. The team, backed financially by the NFL, kept appealing. Then recently the Supreme Court weighed in on another trademark case that had implications to this. In that case, the Court unanimously backed the First Amendment right to free speech, saying it overrode even the use of disparaging names. Even though it ruled constitutionally as it did, I do not believe that the Supreme Court gave its stamp of approval to racially disparaging names. Now in the general matter of our football team's name, our collective conscience should say morality should prevail—First Amendment or no First Amendment. Just because you can doesn't mean you should.

There have been a couple of polls in the last 13 years that show that most American Indians don't care. Who were the American Indians? What kind of questions did they ask? How did they ask them? I have no idea. Of course we know there will be some who don't care. Or maybe they're just glad to get any recognition, disparaging or not. But some really do care. Regardless, decent people who want to be helpful in ridding our country of disparaging terms will continue to care. And here are some examples:

Just a year or so ago, Sidwell Friends School, led by the students—and after the polls—expanded its dress code to not allow themselves to wear clothing with the team name or logo. And on June 22, 2016, *The Washington Post* editorial board responded by publishing a piece entitled, "Mr. Snyder's Losing Battle with the Next Generation." [186] I have been proud of the *Post* editorial board which has written many compelling editorials over the years calling on the team owner to get rid of the name. And *Post* columnist Courtland Malloy, a champion of the cause for decades, rightly continues beating the drum for the change. Kudos to all of them.

On the other hand, in 2013, Dan Snyder told *USA Today* he would never change the name. "It's that simple. NEVER—you can use caps," he said. I've always wondered why Snyder wouldn't do the right thing and just change the damn name. Is it financial? If he thinks it is, maybe he needs to think again. If he changed the name, the old team name memorabilia would become very valuable. And fans would have to purchase a new jacket, new scarf, new t-shirt, new sweatshirt, new cap, new blanket, new mug, etc. I just can't understand why that wouldn't work out well for him.

So whether it's about doing the right thing, "political correctness" (also known as sensitivity), or just to build good will, it needs to be done. And I am sure that any name change pain that may occur will be gotten over eventually, and will certainly not last as long as the pain this name has caused—and the bad example our region, especially D.C., has set with this shameful name.

Distrust of the 'Trust'

Not long into Williams's tenure, there came before the Council in the Administration's Fiscal Year 2000 budget a proposal to set aside $54.3 million of taxpayer money to be given to a public-private partnership, which was called the D.C. Children and Youth Investment Trust Corporation ("Trust"). It was sold to us as a partnership whereby the D.C. government would give public dollars and the Board of the Trust would raise private dollars. Maybe if it envisioned that the government would match whatever private dollars were raised, that might have been one thing. But here we were expected to just hand over tens of millions of dollars and have faith that the Trust might do its part—which it didn't. Meanwhile, the Board could hire their friends and spend our money however they wanted. Again, our taxpayers' dollars at work!

I had a hissy fit and went on to publicly say such things as: "Why are we giving our money to an outside group to decide how to spend it on our children and youth with no guarantee of transparency or a competitive bidding process? Why are we spending money to set up whole new outside administrative mechanisms when we already have that mechanism within our government to give money through a competitive and transparent process to worthy youth-oriented programs? Isn't this a waste of money—money that could be spent directly on kids? And most importantly, this thing just seems so ripe for misuse and abuse!"

But it became apparent that it was a done deal. Originally, Williams was going to appoint the entire Board for the outside group. He finally compromised, because of my raising these questions, with his making four appointments including the Chair, and with the Council making three. Originally, it was envisioned that all the Board members would be business people, who were also supposed to raise money for the Trust. Not sure that ever happened.

As the Trust was getting off the ground with its $54.3 million of our local money, we learned that $12 million in federal funds too was being rerouted to the Trust. As Sewell Chan of *The Washington Post* reported, while "the city is failing to keep up with the national decline in welfare caseloads," that money "intended to make District welfare recipients self-sufficient" would be given instead to the Trust.[187] So now the Trust would have as much as $66.3 million to spend instead of the mere $54.3 million the D.C. government had given it to begin with.

At the time and for many years afterwards, Tony Williams would say to me, "I don't know why you're always picking on my children and youth investment trust." But I always felt this whole thing was irresponsible, open to abuse and somewhat scary. As I publicly said at the time and said to him repeatedly, "This baby is ripe for thievery. Why would we give decisions about our children as well as our money to outsiders?" And boy was I right. Soon enough, that Trust became known for giving money to friends and relatives of its directors and staff, which was easy to do without a transparent procurement process that we at least attempt to have in spending other taxpayer dollars.

Ten years later, the activities of the Trust really blew up in their faces. And now, it is bankrupt. *The Washington Post* editorial page on May 14, 2016 *at last* wondered why it was allowed to survive for so long in its piece called "The Failure of the D.C. Trust": "Only now, finally, are plans being made to shut down the operation—and D.C. taxpayers find themselves paying the price."[188]

And in his column in *The Washington Post* on April 20, 2016, Colbert King wrote:

"The current state of affairs with the failing nonprofit D.C. Children and Youth Investment Trust Corporation, known as the D.C. Trust, is a crying shame. No, make that a public outrage. This week, according to *Post* reporter Aaron C. Davis, the D.C. Trust's board voted to dissolve the 17-year-old organization 'to cover debts from exorbitant spending on and by staff, including the misuse of the organization's credit cards.' ...

People who have been footing the bill for the D.C. Trust for years—namely, D.C. taxpayers—need to know what led to the shutdown. ...

According to the Office of the CFO, from fiscal 2007 through fiscal 2012, the District provided the D.C. Trust with approximately $124 million ... the auditor couldn't tell when, how or where District funds were used by the D.C. Trust, let alone whether the money effectively served the needs of the city's children and youth. ...

Not that the D.C. Trust didn't already have a head-shaking history. The D.C. Trust was used by former D.C. Councilmember Harry Thomas Jr. to embezzle more than $350,000 intended for youth baseball programs. In 2013, Capitol Hill rapped the D.C. Trust for lacking controls to administer a $20-million-a-year federally funded school voucher program. ...

On behalf of D.C. taxpayers, who will be held accountable? Yes, that word so disliked by public functionaries, accountable."[189]

Not exactly and I'm sure better written, but close to what I had been saying starting when it began 17 years earlier. Now, I really would *love* to have that conversation with Tony Williams about my picking on him with my distrust of *his* Trust. I'll bring along all of the info we know on the outright thievery from the Trust by many. And while I'm at it, I'll "pick on" Adrian Fenty who was Mayor from January of 2007 to January of 2011, when the Trust was also provided with over a hundred million of misspent and fraudulently spent D.C. dollars. In actual fact, it was the taxpayers of D.C., along with its children and youth, who were the ones who got picked on—actually far worse—by the Trust itself.

A Divided City

Williams also took some actions many considered divisive in 1999, early in his tenure as Mayor. For instance, he, working with the federally appointed Financial Control Board, shut down D.C. General (Washington's public hospital) in spite of the unanimous disapproval of the duly elected Council—and with nothing to take its place. Soon after closing D.C. General, Williams proposed getting rid of the elected Board of Education.

These contentious stances were being brought forth while the population in the District was changing and the economic divide was becoming more pronounced. In the 1990s, the black population shrunk by more than 4% while the white population increased 10%. In the early 2000s, African Americans still made up the majority of the population, but it had fallen to 60% and would fall more over the subsequent decade. As mentioned, the District had become a city of newcomers—one in four residents moved to the city in the five years before the 2000 Census was taken.[190] Real estate prices were climbing, forcing many middle class and poor residents out of the city. And the income gap that was plaguing the country was particularly wide in the District. We were sadly on our way to becoming more of a divided—and less economically diverse—city.

With this backdrop, Williams made it known that he wanted the ability as Mayor to appoint a five-member Board of Education—replacing the elected nine-member body we had. The media loved it but the public, not so much—especially those of us who rued the fact we had so few elected officials as it was.

We all knew we needed to see major improvements in our school system, which despite some strides made in the late '70s/early '80s, continued to fail too many of our students. However, there had been no data to show that a non-elected School Board actually improved the education of children. I felt it was no small thing to get rid of a big part of the limited Home Rule and the first elected body granted to us by Congress in 1968 (six years before it allowed the Council and Mayor to be elected positions).

In February of 2000, months after the initial request, Mayor Williams finally agreed to abandon his proposal for a five-member School Board, all appointed by him, in favor of a compromise which Adrian Fenty and I had fought hard for when we didn't have the votes to keep the fully elected Board. I did reluctantly vote for that compromise Williams put forth as I had helped fashion it—a hybrid body of nine members, made up of five elected including an elected President, and four appointed by the Mayor and approved by the Council. Our back was against the wall and the compromise was certainly better than an all-appointed Board.

I was proud to have at least saved five elected positions, and especially the Chair, and to have gotten Council approval of the Mayor's appointees. I also made sure there was a sunset provision so that we would go back to an all-elected Board in four years. (Of course if the hybrid board was working well, the Council could always extend this sunset provision, or do away with it entirely.)

The hybrid school board proposal, though, required voter approval as it was an amendment to the District's Home Rule Charter. A referendum was placed on a ballot and a special election was set for June 27, 2000.

The day before the citywide vote, I announced to *The Washington Post* that I would be listening to my conscience and my real non-compromised feeling about the hybrid school board issue—and would be voting no.[191] It was not just my disdain at the idea of getting rid of some of our few elected positions. I was also disgusted by the targeted mailings that took place before the election. Knowing that the strongest support for Mayoral appointees was in the white areas of the city, even though the public schools remained about 95% black, supporters of the proposal sent out multiple mailings to households in *only* the predominantly white Wards—by design. And already reluctant me became nauseated by such tactics and therefore, voted no.

The measure passed 51% to 49%. The vote was divided racially—voters in white-dominant Wards 1, 2, 3 and 6 favored it while the black-dominant Wards 4, 5, 7 and 8 rejected it.

Many African American voters appeared to share my concerns about further reducing the ability of the city to choose its leaders. And many felt this would reduce black political clout. My friend Dwight Cropp, who was then Professor of Public Administration at George Washington University, explained that many young white voters who are new to the city knew little about the struggle for Home Rule in the District of Columbia. David Bositis, a Senior Researcher at the Joint Center for Political and Economic Studies echoed that in *The Washington Post*: "Taking away the vote from the black population of Washington is a very sensitive issue."[192]

The hybrid School Board election also exposed an concerning ethical lapse when the Williams Administration was called out for using government workers, equipment and an elementary school building to campaign on behalf of the proposal. The Board of Elections and Ethics determined that Williams's position gave him an "unfair advantage" over the opponents.[193] But in spite of those "unfair" shenanigans, the vote was amazingly close.

In 2000, we rolled out the license plates with the important slogan, "Taxation Without Representation." How ironic that in the very same year, we dissipated our own representation.

Speaking of Dissipating Our Self-Determination

Even before Tony brought forward his desire to appoint a five-member Board, I got a call one evening at dusk in my office from Jim Kimsey, who had donated to one or two of my campaigns even though I did not know him well. He said, "I am demanding that you vote for the Mayoral takeover of the schools, which Williams will soon propose." I certainly was turned off by that tone, but I did express to him my fervent desire to see more elected officials in D.C., not less. He then became even more aggressive, which then caused me to finally say that I was not going to tolerate his tone any longer, and that given his residency in Virginia, which had plenty of elected officials, I did not feel he had a right to tell me and others in D.C. what to do. He hung up, thank goodness.

I never took well to these business types, whether they supported me or not, when they started directing me—and us—what to do. I had the same problem with Terry Golden, who at least lives in D.C., when he served starting in the late '90s as Chair of the Federal City Council (a regional group of movers and shakers) and would come to testify at the Council. It was never, "We think this is an idea worth pursuing" or "We have a suggestion." It was always done in a dictatorial, somewhat threatening manner: "We feel strongly that you *must* do this." I don't know about you, but that kind of attitude, especially from mostly outsiders, gets on my last nerve. In fact, I said to Terry on the record after he expressed one of the group's many edicts—and not the first time, "Terry, if you and the Federal City Council want to run the city, why don't you just run for Mayor?" On second thought, maybe they had.

Driving Toward a Better DMV

While chairing the Committee on Public Works and the Environment, we made much needed improvements to one of the most unpopular agencies—the Department of Motor Vehicles. There were many complaints from residents about long lines, numerous closed windows, and not being treated well by employees when they finally did get to the window. Something had to be done. I conducted hearings and a few things became clear.

The way it was working was that when DMV employees took a day off, there were no fill-ins, and therefore their co-workers had to cover for them—thus the closed windows. So these remaining employees were overworked through no fault of their own (they actually showed up for work that day, keeping the line from being even longer), *and* were making the lowest salaries of anyone in the D.C. government. So by the time a customer came up to the counter, he or she had been waiting so long that they were on edge and inevitably took it out on the employee, who wasn't so affable either due to their own circumstances. Not a good scenario.

At hearings, I often spoke directly to residents who were watching us on cable TV. I asked those viewers to confront what we're really expecting from DMV employees—that they cover for those absent because we don't have enough staff while making the lowest wage, *and* on top of that, have stomachs of iron and the patience of Job. "Who could stand being put in that situation? I know I couldn't."

I pointed these things out so that people would act more humanely to those who work in our government under that type of pressure. And to help the workers out with their pressures of meeting our service needs, I found money to hire more people at DMV and to raise their salaries.

Also in fairness, I strongly suggested that DMV supervisors take rude employees who don't like people out from behind the windows and give them something else to do. Maybe they'd like filing or data entry better. If not, free them up to look for employment elsewhere which they might like more.

Another major problem I highlighted was that we did not notify people of all deadlines, like when their car registration was expiring. That registration deadline was on a sticker on our windshields, but how often does anyone look at that? The first notice residents got that their registration expired was when they got a $100 ticket on their windshield. It was just a "gotcha" moment.

So I made sure we began to send out expiration notifications in all categories—drivers licenses, registrations and inspections. And remember, those days these things were required more often. I'm pleased with the changes I helped make. The complaints were lessened and we found that DMV went from being probably the most hated aspect of our government to one less hated.

These days, residents' contact with DMV is minimized because such things as car inspections are required less often, so now the agency is probably even more less hated. Of course government can appear to be more efficient if it doesn't do as much. I too like not having to go to DMV as often. But when I sometimes see low-maintained and not so safe-looking D.C. cars on the street in our densely populated city with lots of pedestrians, I wonder if fewer inspections is a good—or safe—thing. I'm just not sure we should put government's efficiency and our convenience above safety.

Other Life Lectures

In my ongoing efforts of trying to make things better, I often try to extend that to the personal sphere as well. Whether it be me, a family member or friend who is leaving an unbearable job or relationship, I believe instead of just totally cutting and running, we have an obligation to try to make it better for the next person. It can be done by either having a rational and constructive conversation as you leave, or maybe even a nicely worded note later on. A little time and effort is involved, but maybe it *can* be better for the next you or me.

Now that I'm talking about extra time and effort, I'll make it a twofer. I put a lot of those into every relationship I have. I try to call on birthdays, send congratulations and sympathy cards—just check in with the people I care about. And when they're sick, I visit or certainly call. I try to be there when they are aware of it. And in each and every case, with very few exceptions, when people pass away, I have avoided the guilt that many people feel about not keeping in touch or having not been there. And then, the not-there people are running to the funeral as a way to make amends. Of course it's nice to go to the funeral, to pay respects to the family and to honor the person. But I think it's so much more important to show that respect, honor and attention when they are alive.

On second thought, make it a threefer. Whenever I have a big decision to make when I'm actually totally in charge of the decision and no one else is involved, I don't write the pros and cons down on a piece of paper, which is an okay strategy too. Instead, I project myself into the future, imagining the decision has been made one way, and ask, "How do you feel?" Then I do the same thing with the alternative decision. "How do you feel?"

Many decisions I have made throughout my life are arrived at exactly this way, whether they be personal or professional. If I feel regret while imagining having made a certain decision, I know I should go the other way. To me, barring life or death situations, regret is the worst. Try this projection technique sometime. It certainly has helped me make difficult decisions.

Okay, I can't stop. Make it a fourfer ...

Therapy: to Have or Not to Have?

I truly believe that if my husband had gone into therapy on a regular basis during anytime of his 48-year life, he would still be with us today, of course save for an accident or illness. (When I refer to therapy, I also mean to include any medications which might result from that therapy.) Even when I begged him during our 21-and-a-half-year marriage to go get therapy, he refused other than briefly during a couple of crisis times. Instead, he self-medicated since he was 16 years old with Jack Daniels bourbon. Thus, we lost him violently and tragically in 1988.

I believe that my own father, who made my life and others miserable most of his life, could have been helped by therapy. Because of both situations, David and Dad, and the grief my teenage children went through after their father's death, I made sure they got the help they needed.

To be honest, though I am a strong proponent of therapy, I have not sought it for myself because I have found that I have been able to get through a lot of my whole life by being my own therapist—and by being my own best friend. But I do not think I suffer from clinical depression, but the kind more situational. My "glass-half-full" mentality—as well as yelling sometimes—has served me well up to this point.

However, I have seen therapy and medications change many lives for the better, and I would encourage those who need it to do it. It is a different era today, praise the Lord. So different, in fact, that I feel out of it by not doing it.

Watching family and friends survive and thrive with therapy is a beautiful thing. But I am very concerned about the high cost, especially given the frequency of need. Most therapists charge $200 to $250 an hour at a minimum which can easily amount to

$1,000 a month in after-tax money for just once a week. For someone who needs it and is not wealthy, that can be overwhelming.

I know therapists are professionals who went to school to get there, and I know they would argue that other professionals like lawyers or other doctors may charge as much or more. But who needs a lawyer on a once or twice-a-week basis or a doctor or dentist on a once or twice-a-week basis? Not many people. And on top of that, unlike most doctors and lawyers, many therapists work out of their homes instead of paying rent at an office and then even deduct that space on their taxes. So I wish that therapists would consider the necessity of their service to the well-being of their patients, and would not add to their burden by having them worry constantly about how to pay such high prices on a longer term basis. Just something for therapists to think about ...

Taking It to the Streets

Back to the Council: In the late 1990s/early 2000s, our streets were in a state of chaos. This was the beginning of the era of much-expanded Internet and cable television, and more and more cables had to be laid underground. As fiber optic and utility companies were digging up the streets, it was all being done in a completely uncoordinated fashion. As soon as one street was dug up and repaired, here came another company who would submit its $24 for a permit to dig up that same street again.[194]

I worked with Dan Tangherlini, Director of the D.C. Department of Transportation, to get the situation under control. A moratorium was put on road cuts to create a coordinated plan, which we came up with pretty quickly. No company could get a new permit if it was currently exceeding a 45-day limit on another road cut. Also, an all-out call went to pertinent companies when a cut was open to come in and lay their cables, as a street permanently restored could not be dug up again for a certain period. We needed those companies to know we were serious so I pushed through legislation for substantial fines for blocking traffic, working without a permit, and other violations.

After all that effort, having a new plan, and establishing fines, Mayor Williams, in his usual appeasement to businesses, just pushed the coordination plan aside during a few-months period in 2000, and we had over 500 permittees just doing as they pleased. The bulldozer sound just went on, and the traffic remained at a standstill. It was so frustrating to be promised coordination by people in the Administration only to end up with promises as empty as the potholes they were creating.[195]

Fortunately, it all finally shaped up. My persistent nagging on the issue may have helped. More orchestrated cuts started to happen. And increased inspections and fines also helped to get the undue street repair and traffic situation under control.

And then there was the Lockheed Martin giveaway: While earning $35 million to process and collect D.C. parking tickets, Lockheed Martin was given a pay raise by the Executive by way of a temporary extension of the contract (circumventing Council approval) with additional money paid *supposedly* for program enhancements. Five months into the extended contract, I learned through questioning at one of my Committee hearings that the "enhancements" were non-existent. In a letter to Mayor Williams, I wrote: "What is especially unsettling to me is the fact that we spend our taxpayers' hard-earned money needlessly. Why we would give this company more money without the additional services is beyond me."

Trying to Save Lives

I have seen many people whose lives were cut short by not getting an organ donation and others whose lives have been saved because of them. Thus, in 2001, picking up on a discussion with a dear friend and health professional Marilyn Johnson, I introduced legislation to give paid leave to government employees if they served as an organ or bone marrow donor. This was to encourage more people to give of themselves, knowing that they would not lose pay while they were losing an organ or a partial one.

Then in 2006, I co-introduced with Linda Cropp a piece of legislation to establish incentives for a private employer to provide paid leave for this purpose as well. Both bills were passed into law.

Human Rights Campaign Award

On October 13, 2002, I got the incredible honor of receiving the National Capital Area Leadership Award from the Human Rights Campaign (a leading national LGBTQ rights organization) at its annual gala dinner for my work on behalf of its constituents. My award was one of three presented that night, with the other two being national honorees—Director Steven Spielberg, who was presented with the National Equality Award, and radio talk show host Cristina Saralegui, who received the Civil Rights Award. It was such a memorable and hard-to-believe evening. It was tele-vised as well as captured on the front page of the Style section of the *Post*. There it was big and bold—a picture of Steven Spielberg and keynote speaker, Congressman Dick Gephardt, standing on either side of me. We were laughing and talking, making it look like I was the center of attention—almost as if they knew me. That photo remains a prized possession. My daughters, who joined me that evening, seemed more impressed with me than at any other time of our lives—at least for a few minutes.

Thank goodness for *The Washington Post* photo. We as a family are so bad about taking pictures and rarely ever even bring a cam-era along—and this event was before cell phones with cameras. This time, though, we did bring a camera, but the only photo we took had my two daughters in the foreground, with a blurry me on stage with the other equally blurry honorees. Strangely enough, my daughters had handed the camera to Spielberg's friend and cinematographer to take that photo. I think that's less of a statement about his skill than our cheap, crappy camera.

Some Name-Dropping (and There'll Be More)

I have been lucky that my official roles (both elected and vol-unteer) have afforded me opportunities to meet well-known people. I have met Bishop Desmond Tutu, the Dalai Lama, Pope John Paul II, and Queen Elizabeth, to name a few. In the mid-2000s, a friend and former journalist Charles Krause brought to my attention World Refugee Day and the fact that Angelina Jolie was going to be in D.C. for the occasion. I did a Council resolution to honor Jolie's work on behalf of world refugees. On the day I presented it to her, I was able to spend some time with Angelina at both the luncheon and then on our own in the anteroom before the presentation. She is drop-dead gorgeous and I was impressed with her grace and quiet softness.

A particularly memorable encounter occurred back around 1980. One evening a client of my husband invited us to a large gathering at a hotel where the honoree was Clare Boothe Luce, the first American woman Ambassador abroad, a Congresswoman, as well as a writer who authored the famous, groundbreaking play from the 1930s, *The Women*. She also had been the wife of Henry Luce, the publisher of *Time Magazine*. Clare was around 80 then, and quite an interesting and attractive person. In my usual want-ing to meet everyone way, I went up to her afterwards and mentioned to her that I was an admirer. Next thing I know, she invited David and me to the Watergate to have a drink with her and some of her friends, where we spent an incredible two hours with a group of about eight people, listening to Clare Boothe Luce regale us with fascinating stories from her life.

I have purchased tickets to the Kennedy Center Honors since it began nearly 38 years ago—way up in the nosebleed section. It's an event full of celebrities and I have used my utter lack of shyness to introduce myself to anyone and everyone before and after the taping. I have even had some short conversations with Joanne Woodward and Paul Newman, Sidney Poitier, Ginger Rogers, Aretha Franklin, Gene Hackman, Smokey Robinson, Harry Belafonte, Jack Lemmon, Stevie Wonder, Clint Eastwood, Chita Rivera, Loretta Lynn, Robert Redford, Paul McCartney, Carol Burnett, Herbie Hancock, Dustin Hoffman, Rita Moreno, Morgan Freeman, James Taylor, Meryl Streep, and if that's not enough, there were many, many more. It is my favorite D.C. evening out.

Letitia Baldrige

Twenty years after meeting Clare Boothe Luce, I became very good friends with another neat person, Letitia Baldrige, who was the Social Secretary to Clare when she was Ambassador to Italy as well as White House Social Secretary to Jacqueline Kennedy when she was First Lady. Letitia was the author of many books, mostly related to manners. Starting when I ran for the Council in the mid-'80s, I received a $100 check from a Letitia Baldrige with a lovely handwritten note wishing me well, and then received the same in every subsequent campaign. Surprisingly, I never made the association to *the* Letitia Baldrige until many years later.

In the early 2000s, I received an invitation to one of her book signings at the Ritz Carlton. I ran by on my way home from work, planning to just stop in, buy a book, get it signed and leave. When I handed Letitia the book, she looked up and said, "Carol Schwartz, I've been a fan of yours for years. I bet you have no idea how special you are." And that's basically what she put in the book. The organizer who witnessed this came over and asked me to sit with Letitia on the dais. Of course I responded favorably and did—and was glad to have done so. We had a lot of time to visit during dinner, and her talk afterwards about the Jacqueline Kennedy book was enthralling. I became even more of a fan of hers.

Afterwards, as I was leaving, she was standing there with her cane waiting for a cab. I asked if I could give her a ride and it turned out to be just a few blocks away. As I dropped her off, she mentioned she'd like to have lunch sometime and I said of course. She called the office the next day to schedule. After that, we became very close and talked at least once a month, had lunch, dinner, or a visit every few months even at her assisted living home during her last years until she died on October 29, 2012.

At one of those lunches, she mentioned something about turning 80 soon. I simply asked, "Well, what are you doing?" thinking maybe I'd take her out to lunch around that time, and she responded, "Nothing." I then said, "We're doing something." So on February 9, 2006, I gave her an 80th birthday celebration—a luncheon with some friends and family at my home, which was featured in *Washington Life* magazine.

Letitia was the most engaging conversationalist I have ever met. Her father had been a Congressman, and she had grown up in society, and was as classy as they come. But she was so caring and down to earth too; and as much as she liked to talk, she was a wonderful listener and booster of spirit and ego. Letitia, even at the assisted living residence, continued to work practically up to her last breath. She needed to—both financially and psychologically. And her work ethic was even more remarkable considering her severe osteoarthritic challenges of many years and the acute pain associated with them. No one ever made me feel better about myself than Letitia. (Three other neat people have come close, but I'll talk about them later.) I will miss Letitia as long as my memory allows me to do so.

One Letitia story told by her at one of my dinner parties: She was in an ambassador's home sitting at a huge long table surrounded by many guests with about a dozen pieces of silverware at each place setting. When the first course came, everyone just sat there, looking at her, the manners expert. She picked up one of the utensils and everyone followed suit. The same went on for the whole meal. When the ice cream-type dessert arrived in its bowl, the last utensil remaining was a fish fork. She said she just picked it up and dug right in with a smile on her face. I'm sure Letitia told it better.

Human Rights
Campaign Award
Night (Dick Gephardt,
Steven Spielberg,
Cristina Saralegui,
Melissa Etheridge,
HRC Executive Director
Elizabeth Birch)

Steven Spielberg with
my lovely daughters

Visiting a school

The Dalai Lama
(GW President Steve
Trachtenberg leaning in)

Visiting a library with
Alma Powell

At the DMV inspection station

Dancing at a senior fitness event
at Freedom Plaza

Dear friend Letitia Baldrige

Union gala

Chris Rock and one of the
world's worst pictures of me

Speaking of Midlanders ...

At Midland
College for the
Hilda Simmons Levitt
Poetry Contest with
English Chair
Larry Griffin
and College
President
Dr. David Daniel

To Carol,
With Best Wishes.

CHAPTER 34

2002 Election

In 2002, I had no intentions of running again against the incumbent Mayor, but circumstances took a turn. Democrats running for Mayor had to get 2,000 valid signatures from registered Democratic voters to secure a place on the ballot. D.C. Watch journalist Dorothy Brizill discovered that more than 80% of the signatures on Mayor Williams's petitions were fraudulent. Many pages included signatures in the same handwriting and had names such as "Mickey Mouse" and "Kelsey Grammer." Mayor Williams had hired Scott Bishop and company to gather the signatures, but it turned out that Scott and his daughter spent most of their time making up names around the kitchen table rather than bothering to go out into the elements. As a result, Mayor Williams's name was not going to appear on the ballot in the Democratic primary. He would have to undertake a write-in effort.[196]

Many residents were outraged about the transgression. A criminal investigation began and the campaign was fined $277,700. But a business-friendly incumbent Mayor in D.C. finds that to be mere pocket change.[197]

Even though the people he hired committed the fraud, the candidate's campaign was of course ultimately responsible. How sad that the only person paying enough attention to uncover this blatant fraud was an activist citizen and journalist. But kudos to Dorothy—and D.C. Watch! (And by the way, there were other transgressions I mention in the announcement statement below.)

As the fraudulent signature debacle unfolded, people began to ask me to run, but I said no. When primary day arrived on September 10th, Williams did secure the Democratic nomination—and he even won the Republican nomination—all by write-ins. (That should have been a warning to me.) I, not a candidate, received the second most write-in votes in the Republican primary. When Williams shockingly chose to accept the Democratic nomination, the Republican Party was free to present a nominee.

Since I was the runner-up by write-in votes, leaders of the Republican Party came to my house and begged me to run. As everyone knows, I've wanted to be Mayor for a long time—and have never required being asked much less begged. But this time I really was a reluctant candidate, and they did have to twist my arm. And some of my colleagues were even whispering to me, "Run, Carol, run."

But in full disclosure: I do think I finally welcomed the opportunity to get my concerns about his Administration on the table, many of which I've outlined in this book. So the petition debacle gave me that chance and very importantly, this campaign would only last about six weeks. Therefore, I ultimately said yes.

My entry was so late in the race and the decision was made so quickly that during my announcement on September 26, 2002, at the corner of Martin Luther King Ave. and Good Hope Rd., S.E. in Anacostia, we brought out old t-shirts and cut the dates off of old campaign posters. My statement was less in tatters:

"Deciding to run this time has been difficult—terribly difficult.

Last time, when I lost to someone people barely knew, I became reconciled—albeit sadly—to the fact that this job of Mayor that I wanted so badly and had worked toward for 30 years was not meant to be mine. When people asked me to run a year ago, six months ago or even six weeks ago, I never wavered. 'No' was the answer—the constant, consistent answer.

But recently just saying 'no' started filling me with a sense of regret—regret for me personally, regret for the sake of our city, regret for the sake of democracy.

I have always believed that political competition improves the quality of government for all. The people deserve a choice.

This will be an uphill battle.

My opponent offers a record which shows some progress. Washington is, in some respects, a better city today than it was four years ago. But this is still a deeply troubled and divided city. Tony Williams's stewardship has been marred by ethical lapses, questionable judgment, and a cold lack of compassion for our poorest and most helpless citizens.

If you don't believe me, ask the members of the D.C. Board of Election and Ethics about my opponent's outrageous and illegal efforts to get his name on the ballot, or about the consultant fees he took from companies doing business with the city while he was running for Mayor the last time, or about the three times he has been fined, more than any public official in our history.

Ask the voters in Ward 7 and 8 about the last four years under the Williams Administration. Ask them if their lives have improved, if their schools have improved, and ask them if they have better hospitals and healthcare than they did four years ago.

I say to you today, we can—and we must—do better!

The tangible difference between Anthony Williams and myself is my vision for the city, my commitment to this city, my passion for all the people of this city and the quality of leadership I have demonstrated over the course of my long public career. I have a true, demonstrated history of fighting for the rights of all our people—fighting for good government, for honesty, for compassion and for competence in the public life of this city long before it became fashionable to do so—and long before our present Mayor was forced to leave Arlington, Virginia in 1996 to take up residency in D.C. as a job requirement.

And we must take a closer look at those in our city who Tony Williams has ignored. Even during the recent time of economic boom and prosperity, the poor in our city have gotten poorer. And I believe it is the obligation of all of us to focus our intelligence, our goodwill, and our resources on those parts of this city where there is the greatest need—and where good government, coupled with strong, competent, compassionate and engaged leadership can make a difference.

Keeping our home values up is a worthy goal. In fact, the Council's tax-reduction policies helped get those values up. But there must be more. There must be affordable housing for those who hung in there with us during the tough times and are now being priced out.

A bloated and very expensive bureaucracy is back. Big time.

And of great concern are the appalling ethical lapses that have occurred under Mayor Williams—lapses that, in my opinion, have been too easily forgiven.

I can assure you that accountability (fiscal and otherwise) and high ethical standards—coupled with competence, compassion and creativity—will be the hallmarks of my Administration.

Last week at the Jewish High Holiday services, we read these words, which moved me and helped bring me here today:

"Birth is a beginning
And death is a destination
And life is a journey
From childhood to maturity and youth to age
From innocence to awareness and ignorance to knowing
From weakness to strength or strength to weakness
And often, back again
From fear to faith
From defeat to defeat to defeat
Until, looking backward or ahead
We see that victory lies
Not in some high place along the way
But in having made the journey stage by stage
A sacred pilgrimage"

The "defeat to defeat ..." part was right on target. But I felt it was worth the journey—an effort to bring competition to the race.

In September, *The Washington Post* described a divide in which Williams's most solid support came from the increasing number of upper-income white voters flocking into the city, while his biggest detractors were the least affluent African American voters.

This was also a time when incomes for whites rose while those for blacks dropped. Many residents were likely not happy to see a 92% increase in government managers making $100,000+ during Tony's tenure. I often said that Williams made Marion Barry look like a piker when it came to a bloated bureaucracy.[198]

Mayor Williams had an overwhelming financial advantage with much coming from business interests. By mid-October he had raised $1.3 million (or so said the campaign reports) to my $100,000. And the Mayor was reaping benefits from businessman Jeffrey Thompson and his network of donors (or maybe supposed donors). Of course, Jeffrey Thompson had spent the last four years reaping contracts from the Mayor, so he sure had the money.

In fact, a decade after this race, in 2012, *The Washington Times* reported that Jeffrey Thompson's financial benefits from the city had its roots in the Williams Administration, a link I have mentioned. During his tenure, Thompson's accounting firm won hundreds of millions of dollars in contracts. And after Williams got rid of D.C. General (the public hospital serving mainly low-income residents), Thompson started a private company, D.C. Chartered Health Plan, which then won city contracts worth at least $800 million with much of the services supposedly going to poorer residents. For instance, his company secured a no-bid contract to open a 24/7/365 clinic for those low-income residents. However, the around-the-clock promise was never fulfilled.[199]

In hindsight, the nexus between the closing of D.C. General and the gigantic contracts accountant Jeffrey Thompson immediately started receiving in the healthcare field, where he had no experience, should have been something that even a blind person could see. But it was, and has been, basically ignored by *The Washington Post*. Remember, Jeffrey Thompson was there from the beginning as he was the person who recommended Williams in the first place to become CFO to the Financial Control Board back in 1995. And interestingly—but not surprisingly—soon thereafter, Thompson went from being a little known accountant to having a mega-accounting firm with guess what—financial contracts from the Financial Control Board and the CFO. And here we are, a few years later, giving that same accountant hundreds of millions of dollars of healthcare contracts (which were not even his expertise)—and in some cases, non-competitively bid. Everybody would wish for such a sweet gig!

I have always found it very fascinating that the media took great glee in—and gave wide coverage to—the ethical scandals in the Marion Barry Administrations during the '80s and '90s, and well they should. As someone who ran against Barry, I must admit that I did so as well. The *Post* then rediscovered their glee right as Mayor Gray was heading into office in 2010, which is fine. The difference is I had the same negative and "glad they were caught" feelings about other administrations that were found doing wrong. (And oftentimes I was the one doing the finding.) But when it came to the Williams and Fenty Administrations, both promoted and endorsed by the *Post*, the media did not report misconduct or minimalized it—over and over again (with a few rare exceptions).

For instance, in the 2006 Mayoral election, when *The Washington Post* finally ran that Adrian Fenty had been admonished by the D.C. Bar years earlier for mishandling an elderly client's finances, it was run in a small, short column on B2 in the middle and right beside the fold. It would have taken a sleuth *and* a microscope to find it. But I bet if that story was about Fenty's opponent, it would have gotten a far more visible placement, like A1 above the fold.

There sure seemed to be different standards for some. In my world, wrongdoing is wrongdoing, regardless of who is doing it. I am an equal opportunity pouncer, and made no apologies about it then—nor do I now. I just wish the media would do the same.

Back to the 2002 Mayoral Election

(Note: It was really hard to concentrate on the campaign at times due to a horrible thing happening in D.C. while the election was going on. From October 2nd to October 24th of 2002, a sniper with a young accomplice was terrorizing the whole region. He was finally captured, but killed 10 people and critically injured three more during that awful time. Still I had to force myself to concentrate on campaign issues, even as that nightmare unfolded.)

The shady dealings I saw in the Williams Administration disturbed me and I couldn't ignore them. At a campaign forum that fall on Capitol Hill during that Mayoral race, I brought up another suspect deal Williams was calling for, which would pay developer Doug Jamal $12.5 million for a property in Prince Georges County that he had recently bought for $1.5 million, even though he had made no improvements to the property. *City Paper*'s "Loose Lips" column downplayed the accusation, calling my assertion "hitting a double" and not a political home-run. But soon an investigation which I started of that deal turned into a major story—and resulted in an indictment. No one was downplaying it then.

In addition to calling out sweetheart deals, I noted that as the economy grew, the Administration still ignored many of those who needed attention. Statehood-Green Mayoral candidate Steve Donkin pinpointed the dynamic: "This is a kind of curious election. What's going to happen is that most of the city's conservative Republicans will end up voting for the Mayor, and most of the liberal Democrats will end up voting for Mrs. Schwartz."[200]

The Washington Post acknowledged that I had "been a consistent advocate of lowering the city's tax rates while pushing in many cases for better social services, including treatment for drug addicts ..." and that I also have a "progressive streak when it comes to social issues such as abortion and gay rights," which I appreciated. My platform included getting police officers out of their cars to walk or bike the streets. And I promised to personally stop by group homes and shelters to make sure agencies are treating people in their care well. "I've seen too many things that have made me cry. ... This is not going to happen on my watch," I said in the *Post* regarding incidents that have occurred at our facilities.[201]

I also gave voice to concerns all of us on the Council had that Williams did not give us any credit for improved services. It is something that outraged me. As the *Post* reported from a debate, I told Williams, "You do I, I, I. [In fact,] the supercans were solely brought by me. The trash trucks were solely brought by me. I will say, I shared with you the trees.'"[202] Although I take credit for a lot myself, I also always give credit to others as well.

I did feel positive about my theme of "Taking Care of Business and People" and felt very energetic. One photo on the cover of the *Post* had Tony Williams and me at a campaign forum. I was shown in mid-statement, my finger pointed, while Tony rested his head on his hand with his eyes closed. It made for quite a visual.[203]

I did get a lot of attention from *The Washington City Paper*'s "Loose Lips" column, but its articles focused on my fashion and jewelry choices, as well as my use of the endearment "honey."[204] One column even made light of my "hair spray" and I wrote back to explain that "I don't use hairspray—my hair sticks up on its own." Although I knew that sardonic was the tone of the column, I felt this was indicative of the sexism I often had to unfairly fight despite my strong and deep record—and this time, it was written by a woman. The *InTowner* newspaper even took issue with one of those articles, calling me a "person of supreme substance and critical understanding of matters of public policy ... and high ethical standards."[205] I must say that "Loose Lips" did wind up giving me its endorsement with the headline, "Vote Honey!"[206]

Many of my former Democratic supporters rallied again, including Effi Barry, Roscoe Dellums, Lawrence Guyot and former School Board colleagues Barbara Lett Simmons, Calvin Lockridge, and Conrad Smith, which was always very encouraging. I also got a great deal of encouragement from people on the street who said, "Thank God you're running."

The Current Newspapers endorsed me saying, "Mrs. Schwartz is far better suited to move the District forward ... Mrs. Schwartz would be a superior manager."[207] So did the InTowner, saying, "... she is a person of high ethical standards without the slightest inclination to even allow for actions by herself or her subordinates that might give even an appearance of conflict of interest. What a refreshing thought for D.C.!"[208] (I do want to thank Davis Kennedy and Chris Kain of the Current Newspapers and P.L. Wolff of the InTowner for their various endorsements over the years.)

In the 2002 race, even The Washington Post said that, unlike Williams, I was not dogged by scandal: "Without question, Mrs. Schwartz brings the kind of energy and commitment to public office. ... She has been a candidate in nine campaigns and—in contrast to Williams—has never been fined by the Board of Elections and Ethics." And the editors even said, "... residents inclined to give Mrs. Schwartz their vote will find themselves on solid ground as well: She is a fine public servant, a tireless voice of common sense and compassion, and an elected leader who has always put the city's best interests first."[209] But they endorsed Williams, though noting that my late entry enlivened the Mayoral race. That should be my slogan: "Enlivening Mayoral Races Since 1986." I did, though, truly appreciate the kind words then and now.

In the end, I wound up with my fourth defeat. This time against Williams, I secured 35% of the vote—five percent more than the first time and five times more than the percentage of registered Republicans. I spent only $200,000 to his over $2.6 million (including primary spending, yet excluding the many outside groups' expenditures on his behalf), and only campaigned for less than six weeks. In fact, Williams spent about $33.00 per vote (including the write-in effort) while I spent a mere $4.40 per vote.[210]

And what was most interesting about the results is that my *highest* percentages came from Wards 7 and 8. This was a complete reversal from my races against Barry. I felt good about that—and I sure needed something to feel good about.

Post-Campaign Depression

Despite the decent results in such a short time and spending so little money, I must admit that right after that campaign, I felt depressed. Even though I was ambivalent about running, once I was in the midst of the campaign, I got my hopes up, unrealistically or not. I guess it's part of the psychology of a campaign. You can't really be in it without some hope of winning, even if the odds are long. That hope keeps you going. And you need to keep your spirits up, especially for those who are supporting you. Plus, during this campaign, I was getting so much positive feedback—so many people coming up to say, "You've got my vote," or giving a thumbs-up when they drove by. It's natural then to get swayed into thinking you have a real chance. And then you don't. It's quite a comedown—especially when it's the fourth time.

I tried to pick myself up by reminding myself that more than one out of three voted for me. Although a clear minority, that's still 50,000 people—bigger than the town I grew up in.

However, that positive thinking quickly dissipates. And you are left with the combination of the initial hope, then the comedown, the exhaustion from nearly 24-hour days, *plus* knowing what was really going on in the Williams Administration—and now seeing it would just continue—and feeling like you were the only one who cared. That made me terribly sad.

It was a real letdown emotionally—and a lot of that emotion was about being really upset with my colleagues. I knew from working alongside them how frustrated they were with Mayor Williams. They resented his unilateral style and outright disrespect of the Council.[211] They didn't like working with him any more than I did. But out of Democratic Party loyalty and/or siding with the one most likely to win, or whatever reason, just about all of them supported the Mayor's reelection, or at least did publicly.

With hardly a minute to rest, the only one-day delayed Council legislative session was scheduled to take place on the Wednesday after the Tuesday loss. That morning, my disappointment, frustration and exhaustion reached a boiling point. I went in early to air out my feelings to the Council Chair, my friend Linda Cropp. I cried and even talked about quitting, even though I don't think I would have. I was just tired and sad. I then went back to my office to get ready for the meeting. The next thing I remember is seeing Kevin Chavous, Kathy Patterson, David Catania and Sandy Allen coming into my office, hugging me and saying such things as, "We need you. Don't quit." It was a real lovefest and one I desperately needed at that very moment.

I honestly don't think I ever would have quit despite my chagrin and hurt feelings. I found my Council work too worthwhile, did feel that I was actually needed, and it was too big a part of my life for me to ever leave by choice. And besides, I would never have burdened the city with the cost of a special election.

A Dirty Deal

In mid-July of 2002 –during the election and months before I thought about entering the race—as the Council was going into its summer recess, Williams tried to push through *emergency* approval of a contract with Douglas Development. The contract covered that land exchange I talked about in the campaign, which was highly suspect from the start.

Alarm bells went off in my mind at that July meeting, which was the Council's last one before our summer recess. What was the state of emergency? I had to speak up immediately. If I did not question the emergency then and there, the exchange would have taken place and it would never have been publicly vetted—which I'm sure was the point of the "emergency." So I challenged the emergency nature of the action as well as the underlying exchange to such a degree that it was taken off the July emergency agenda.

Then a few months later, in September, as the Council was coming back into session, Mayor Williams sent down the bill with the contract which contained the same exchange, and it came to my Committee on Publics Works and the Environment. My office had already started doing research over the summer on this supposed "emergency" deal as we were sure we had not seen the end of it. So we were loaded for bear.

This *was* a sweetheart deal second to none. Here the Mayor was giving away a much more valuable property between 4th and 5th Sts. on Massachusetts Ave., N.W. for $350,000—a property that Doug Jemal urgently needed as he was constructing a building around it. And in the same deal, the Mayor was purchasing an out-of-the-way property for an impoundment lot in Prince Georges County from Jemal for $12.5 million—36 times more than what the city was getting for its downtown property. And Jemal had bought that totally inconvenient property for just $1.5 million four years earlier and had made no improvements to it—but still was getting a quick $11 million profit in a not good real estate market. Some great deal—for Doug Jemal.

I found this to be indeed an emergency—*for the city*. And I was intent on rescuing us from it. I jumped in and asked the Williams Administration: 1) Why in the heck did you try to sneak the approval of this lousy deal buried in an emergency agenda through the Council in July? 2) Why are we asking so little for our valuable property? 3) Why are we paying so much for Jemal's property, which is so hard to access that D.C. residents and others would have to take a bus through Prince Georges County—as the impoundment lot was not near a Metro stop—to get their towed cars back? 4) Why are we giving Jemal a profit of $11 million with no improvements in just four short years in a down market? A combination of those questions and their lack of viable responses made me even more suspicious. My reliable instinct said, "This stinks to high heaven." I decided to hold a hearing right away.

I went to Councilmember Jim Graham, who had the Office of Property Management under his Committee (since the matter involved both public works and property). I said to him, "We need to schedule a joint hearing immediately on this issue," which we did for October 21, 2002 to meet the hearing notice requirement. That same day, before the hearing, I asked the D.C. Auditor to do an independent audit of the Mayor's proposal. In the letter requesting the audit, I wrote, "I found this deal to be replete with troubling facts, which make me question the ethics of it."

On October 21st, as I was walking in the door of the Council chambers to begin the hearing, Jim Graham walked toward me in the hall and said, "I got Mayor Williams to agree to take back the proposal so we don't need to hold the hearing now." I said, "Oh yes we do. Congratulations on getting him to withdraw it, but I can assure you they'll find another way to get it done. Besides, this deal does not pass the smell test, and it would be irresponsible to just let it go." He argued with me to do just that. I went on to say that I was afraid that this might be just one example of giveaways to developers and that we need to out it publicly so it will stop.

After more back and forth, I said, "Now I'm going inside to start the hearing. If you choose not to take part, that's your business." I walked in to gavel the meeting to order and within a few minutes, Jim joined me. And once we got into it, he really got into it too, and made quite a name for himself due to what we unearthed. He became dogged as well once I insisted that we get the party started—and I was proud of him.

The hearings went on to reveal deep corruption in the Office of Property Management during that time. Regarding the impoundment lot deal, we soon learned that the then Office of Property Management's Deputy Director Michael Lorusso gave the appraiser wildly inaccurate information and thus, the impoundment lot at 4800 Addison Rd. in Prince Georges County was valued at way above its true market rate. As Yolanda Woodley reported in *The Washington Post*: "In a letter to Lorusso, appraiser Cushman & Wakefield said the estimated value was based on information provided by Michael Lorusso. The letter also cited 'extraordinary assumptions' that contributed to the increased value, including being told that the city's three-year lease, which costs $1 million a year, had been extended for nine years. City officials say there is no such extended lease ... The appraisal states that the 'rental rate is significantly above what 'typical' landlords and tenants would agree to in the normal course of business.'"[212]

How interesting that an employee of the D.C. government would be adding value to Jemal's property. Yes, the District's DMV had started recently renting the property from Jemal for $1 million a year, which I complained about at the time but I was told it was only temporary. At any rate, the $1 million was an inflated rental price, according to Cushman & Wakefield. And now they were using and even extending that inflated rental price to jack up the purchase price, when we obviously wouldn't be renting anymore as we would own the property. That is, unless Jemal and his emissaries in the Williams Administration expected us to do both, pay for the property and rent it. I wouldn't be surprised!

Regardless, this was certainly a fraudulent appraisal which had been done under the direction of a top-level executive in the D.C. government. And that doesn't even include the giveaway of our valuable historic property on Massachusetts Ave., N.W. in the heart of D.C. Wow. I still feel grateful to have found that deal in the packed emergency agenda in July before we recessed, to have taken it off that agenda, to have insisted on holding a hearing and made sure we had it, and to have outed this abomination. Otherwise, D.C. residents and others would have paid top dollar for the worst-located impoundment lot in the country—if not the world.

Once the D.C. Auditor Deborah Nichols started researching this deal at my request, much was uncovered. According to an article by Yolanda Woodlee that spring: "D.C. auditors called in the

FBI and found that several leases to Douglas Development were over-valued and that many deals were designed to circumvent Council approval."[213] This Administration was basically writing blank checks to a very rich developer. I began calling the Office of Property Management, the Office of Property Mismanagement.

We also discovered that Deputy Director Lorusso, who fashioned this "deal," received gifts from Jemal including cash on two separate occasions, a Rolex watch, and trips. After all that—bogus information to the appraiser which jacked up the price we'd have to pay for Jemal's property, gifts from Jemal, *and* pleading guilty to bribery charges—Michael Lorusso was able to *step down* from his position as Deputy Director of the Office of Property Management. He was not only *not* fired as he should have been, but instead he was allowed to step down and *then* received *severance pay* and a *nice parting letter* from the Williams Administration for his service. I was appalled then and explicitly expressed that to Mayor Williams. (Then, according a September 17, 2017 *Washington Post Magazine* article on Jemal by Jonathan O'Connell, "Lorusso later pleaded guilty in federal court to agreeing to have the city buy a property Jemal owned in Prince George's for three times its appraised value and issuing millions of dollars in other payments to Douglas Development."[214]) I remain appalled at the mere thought of it—and am so proud I got that "party" started.

An indictment was also handed down on Jemal for bribery.[215] He was acquitted by a jury on those charges but found guilty at the time on a separate charge of defrauding a mortgage company. Most importantly, the effort exposed deals that were ripping off the taxpayers and let Mayor Williams and his Administration, as well as the people doing business with the city, know that the members of the Council were watching and doing their due diligence. And this, by the way, would never have been noticed if the Council was not involved in the contract approval process.

Around that time, Mayor Williams made another attempt to take over the schools and appoint all the School Board members himself. Councilmembers Sandy Allen, Adrian Fenty, and I again fought for more elected members, not the fewer we had agreed to earlier—therefore, a stalemate. I always thought "there was enough on the Mayor's plate to keep him busy, and it would be good to see areas already under Williams's direct purview—like the Office of Property Management—get its act together before he tried to take on additional important responsibilities like all of education," and I said those exact words at the time.

First Person Singular

Between all the hard work, I received a nice honor toward the end of November 2003. *The Washington Post Magazine* selected me as one of the first to be featured in their "First Person Singular" column (now called "Just Asking"). They wanted me to talk about two subjects, my brother Johnny and being a Republican. I emphasized Johnny, and they chose their preferred subject, my being a Republican in a Democratic city:

"I didn't start out to be a Republican politician. I was an individual who happened to be a Republican who was very interested in the city. ... it became an issue ... Every other word was 'Carol Schwartz: Republican, Republican.' In this town that was like waving a red flag at a bull. Democrats here aren't just Democrats. They are staunch Democrats. But I don't mind being different. I don't mind causing discussion. ... I hear it all the time: 'You're the first Republican I've ever voted for in my whole live.' And then I say something cute like, 'God hasn't punished you yet.' I think the [Democrats who vote for me] have forgiven me. Or looked the other way. They've watched me for a lot of years. I think they think they're getting more good than bad, so they kind of close their eyes, hold their nose and vote for me. Obviously they've not either forgiven me or gotten over it enough to elect me Mayor. I would love to lead the city. I must admit, when you put as much time and attention and caring into the city and always come up short, it's painful to lose."[216]

Speaking of Republican, I was asked to be on the Advisory Council of the Republican Women's Federal Forum in 1997 and served on it until 2013. It is a group of Republican women made up of the spouses of Senators, House members, and Supreme Court Justices, as well as a select group of female elected officials like myself. We met about eight to ten times a year for lunch at the Capitol Hill Club and had speakers for each gathering, which the Advisory Council helped obtain. Several of the members started mentioning that they had heard I had a beautiful apartment, so I took the bait and invited the Advisory Council to my home. I really enjoyed being part of the Federal Forum and have missed so many of the people there since I chose to leave at the end of 2013 when I was no longer a Republican.

A Set-Up

My sweet daughter Stephanie has always been bothered when I'm alone socially. She often makes suggestions of available people we know, but I resist. In the winter of 2003, when George and I were on the outs for about the tenth—and last—time, Stephanie decided to fix me up with an attractive lawyer in private practice she had seen in court over the years. She approached him one day and asked if he was married or involved. He told her no and she said, "Well, I'd like to fix you up with my mom." I'm not sure if that was the follow-up he wanted, but he said, "Okay"—and called. Sounds like he was as desperate as I was.

As I was going up to New York anyway in several weeks, we made a date. He came and picked me up at Hil's apartment, where I was staying, and Steph made sure she was there as well. Then off we went for a lovely dinner downtown, to a movie, and then on to Brooklyn for cheesecake at Junior's—a first for me, but not the last. We had a great time and Ron even called to thank Stephanie for the fix-up. We stayed in touch. He came to D.C. for the opening of our new D.C. Convention Center. All my colleagues and friends there were impressed, and the females said, "Really cute!"

Then one day, I went by his NYC office to meet him as we were going to an art show featuring his friend's work. Upon my arrival, he went to the Internet to show me articles about himself, which was fun at first. But literally two hours later, by then having missed the art show, and now being deluged with his reading out-loud letters clients had written to him, I knew he was not right for me. For one thing, how could I ever have time to read him my letters from constituents if he never stopped reading his? Just kidding, I think. I still went up to his place afterwards, which was a lovely house in Harlem and we had a nice evening at a great jazz club. Anyway, I did appreciate Steph's good intentions and the love she showed.

The Road Not Taken

By 2003, the dispute over Klingle Road had been going on for 12 years. Klingle Road, one of the few roadways that crossed Rock Creek Park and connected the eastern and western parts of the city, had been temporarily closed due to a storm run-off. Many of us wanted it reopened—including Councilmember Adrian Fenty whose Ward was adjacent, and Chair Linda Cropp—as it was a vital, albeit small, conduit. But the Sierra Club pressured Councilmembers to keep it closed as a road and instead, asked us to spend over a $1 million to turn it into a bike and walking path—despite having many of both in Rock Creek Park already.

Even though I had always been at the forefront of pushing environmental issues, I parted ways on this one. Rock Creek Park is over 2,000 acres of recreational parkland. What was so wrong with taking just a few of those acres to fix a small, already existent roadway, which had for decades allowed for people on opposite sides of the park to easily intermingle?

With all that environmental lobbying, in 2003, Mayor Williams sent the Council legislation that would permanently close the road to vehicular traffic and turn it into additional parkland. It was defeated by a vote of 8 to 5. Linda Cropp and I, both proponents for years, decided to use this opportunity to actually get Klingle Road reopened. We knew that any legislation we might put forward to reopen the road would probably be vetoed by the Mayor—requiring nine votes to override. So smart women that we are, we decided to attach verbiage and funds to reopen Klingle Road to the Budget Support Act instead, making it very difficult for Williams to veto his own budget to kill off rebuilding Klingle Road.

Linda and I went about getting the approval of the Park Service to start the process, which first called for a federal environmental study—that ended up taking far too long. Then in 2008, Mayor Fenty, with my encouragement, tried to move the reopening along by putting money in the budget with help from Councilmembers Muriel Bowser, Jim Graham and myself. Unfortunately, our efforts were all for naught.[217] Klingle Road still remains closed. And the Sierra Club never endorsed me again. And then I stopped giving it my annual check of $100. How's that for one-upmanship?

P.S. On September 11, 2017, Mark Segraves of NBC4 reported that just 100 days after Klingle Road was opened solely as a biking and hiking trail with gravel on the sides—all costing $6 million—it is falling into disrepair. (The road had lasted for nearly 100 years before being ruined in a flood in 1991.)[218] So the Sierra Club finally got its way and we now have gravel being strewn around beautiful Rock Creek Park instead of a repaired, functioning road. It appears that the road itself did not want to be just another trail in the Park!

Casablanca: The Movie Was Better

One of my dearest friends in the whole world is A. Cornelius Baker, who I call Corn. He came to volunteer in my first Council campaign in 1984, a couple of years after he graduated college, and we've been wedded at the hip ever since. Some of my best times involve Corn and his buddies, who have also become mine.

In August of 2003, Corn and I went to Casablanca, Morocco, which we both could not wait to see due to our romantic images from the movie. We sure could have waited to see it as it is about as romantic as Siberia. We had a great time anyway. The next day we were joined by Sam Paschal and his then partner. Off we went through Morocco by car, first to Marrakesh and then on to Fez and Tangiers. Those sound so exotic—and they are. I liked the interesting architecture, mainly the mosques; and Tangiers with its magnificent seaside views was quite extraordinary.

I had been especially looking forward to their souks (outdoor bazaars), but that turned out to be annoying because every step you took, you were surrounded by people trying to sell you something. And no matter how hard you tried, you could not escape. The only way to avoid it was to hire a guide, who then would take you only to his cousins' expensive shops. Regardless, my favorite nightgown for the last 14 years is one I bought at the souk for $3—with no cousins involved. In fact, I have it on this very moment. I sure wish I had bought more. But I'm not going back to that souk.

I did love the food and the great company of those guys. In fact, we had such a good time together that we went on another adventure two years later to Buenos Aires, Argentina, and by then, Corn had met his lifetime partner, Greg Nevins, who added, along with Ernest Hopkins, to the fun. Boy, do I love my gay guy friends and am so glad they ask me to tag along on occasion.

In fact, in the spring of 2016, Corn, who was working at the State Department on global AIDS issues, asked me to join him as he was going to a Vatican conference on AIDS in Rome. Before he got the offer out of his mouth, I said yes, found a cheap flight (through my wonderful travel agent, George Spina at Pillsbury & Co.), and off we went. We were supposed to fly from D.C. to New York and then directly on to Rome. Because of the New York flight cancellation, we ended up in Detroit, totally the opposite direction from our destination. We eventually got to Rome the next evening instead of the next morning as originally planned. Only Corn and I together could make this beginning a dream trip. But the rest really was. We went to many sites that first night in Rome and had a yummy meal at the Piazza Navona. Saturday, we took the wrong bus to the train because of me, but got to see a lot along the way. We spent the afternoon and night in Florence. And after several museums, on Sunday afternoon I headed for Venice for a repeat visit after decades, and Corn went back to Rome to work. I joined up with him again for a few days of the valuable conference and then headed home after a wonderful unplanned-for week.

CHAPTER 35

Always Needing to Be Alert at Work

I remained concerned over the dramatic rise in middle managers making over $100,000 in the Williams Administration. In fact, in 2003, I called for an audit of city salaries making $90,000 or above a year as they were using a scheme of paying $99,999 to avoid the $100,000 threshold that would require Council scrutiny (similar to what was done with contracts).

At the same time, I was worried about the trend of contracting out services in vital areas. For instance, the Department of Mental Health was laying off employees and cutting services while spending millions on outside consultants. How mentally healthy is that?

Then here comes the scandal concerning the overuse and misuse of government-issued credit cards. Overriding Mayor Williams's veto, we on the Council froze the credit cards right away until new and more limited procedures could be put in place. As I said in *The Washington Times* on July 30, 2003, "Current spending rates will allow [the Williams Administration] to spend $65 million by the end of the fiscal year"—while credit card expenditures in fiscal year 2000 totaled less than $1 million—a $64 million hike.[219] One of the good things about the outing of these kinds of abuses is that it hopefully discourages them from happening again—or at least for a little while.

And then a few months later, we learned that the former President of the Washington Teachers Union, Barbara Bullock, pled guilty to stealing more than $2.5 million from District teachers. On November 13, 2003, I wrote a letter to Dr. Vance, Superintendent of D.C. Public Schools (DCPS), which spoke of the recent scandal and then went on to say:

> "At least part of that money [$2.5 million] was obtained when DCPS, at the request of the union, deducted a lump sum of $144 from each member's check for union dues. Of course, it was later discovered that no such dues were authorized by the union membership. This appears to make DCPS complicit at worst or complacent at the very best. I would like to know what procedures were in place at the time, or have been put in place, to ensure that requests from the union for payroll deductions have actually been approved by the membership."

And then I took on Suzanne Peck, the head of OCTO (the Office of Chief Technology Officer). Suzanne was a wealthy woman who lived in Virginia and made sure she took each Councilmember out to lunch on occasion and contributed to their campaigns.

I had no problem with her at first, other than the fact she lived in Virginia, and also not knowing how she avoided the requirement of moving into the city within 180 days. Then a whistleblower in her office made me aware that Suzanne had hired a friend who lived in North Carolina as a consultant for OCTO, who was oftentimes going back and forth to his home there at D.C. taxpayers' expense, while his consultant salary was hundreds of thousands.

At a hearing on OCTO, I brought up the consultant issue, and she went ballistic (which emphasized where there's smoke, there's fire). After the hearing, Suzanne walked up into my face in the hallway and said, "I am a very wealthy woman and I don't need this job or to take this crap." I said, "Suzanne, I am very wealthy woman and I don't need this job, or to take your crap of ripping-off-our-taxpayers—of which you are not one." She actually smiled.

Government by Contract

Another absurd contracting-out problem surfaced in a media report in February of 2003 about the District's parking meter contract. I wrote Mayor Williams on February 6th asking him to please investigate—and never heard back. So on March 4th, I had a hearing on the matter and then wrote the D.C. Auditor asking her to perform an audit on the contract. On March 14th, I wrote the Mayor a follow-up letter on the findings:

> "... the contractor not only collects coins from our meters, but also counts and reports that revenue to the District, and there does not appear to be a method in place to independently confirm that meter revenue reports submitted to the city by the contractor actually reflect the revenue collected. Is it really in our best interest to trust any contractor who gets a percentage of our revenue to be the only accountant minding our store's receipts?"

The Administration also wanted to contract out basic public works services like trash collection. But I said, "Not on my watch." These contracting-out plans would get rid of the trash trucks, workers, everything, and put it all in private hands with the theory that it was cheaper. I said both publicly and privately at that time as often as I could, "Of course a contractor will tell you that they can do it cheaper, even with their profit margin built in. Of course they're going to give you an initial low bid. You grab it and then you start buying out our workers (who then go to work for the contractor) and start getting rid of our equipment and our facilities that house that equipment. And then guess what happens? The contractor starts raising the price of the contract. And we are now held hostage—with no workers in the government who can pick up the trash, no equipment, no place to house it even if we had it. Smart way for a government to do business," I said facetiously. Thank goodness, the issue went away, at least then.

Contracting out is not the panacea that some may think, especially for citizens. In March of 2015, a *Post* article stated that the private operators of Northern Virginia's toll lanes reached a settlement in a class action law suit filed a year earlier. The suit said the operators "routinely failed to notify drivers in a timely manner that they had missed tolls and were accumulating fees and fines—in some cases amounting to thousands of dollars." Why is government giving private profit-making companies, and in this case, an Australian company, authority over public roads? These are exactly the shenanigans we should expect to happen. Why should citizens have to locate one another after such mistreatment and enter a class action suit to rectify those shenanigans? And why didn't the government itself go after the contractor *it* put in place, which harmed its citizens who were just driving on their own roads?[220] And now they're dramatically raising the fees and tolls.[221]

And look what's happening at the Justice Department, which on August 18, 2016, announced its "plans to end the use of private prisons after officials concluded that the facilities are less safe and less effective at providing correctional services than those run by government." Deputy Attorney General Sally Yates also stated:

"[Private prisons] simply do not provide the same level of correctional services, programs, and resources; they do not save substantially on costs; and as noted in a recent report by the Department's Office of Inspector General, they do not maintain the same level of safety and security."[222]

When Will We Ever Learn?

Even here at home: In August 2016, the District's 911 emergency line went down for 100 minutes from 11:35 p.m. until 1:15 a.m. on a Saturday night. And the reason: "... a contractor trying to shut off an alarm accidentally hit a master turnoff switch." Lo and behold, the contractor was working for a private company hired by the D.C. Department of General Services.[223] I will never understand why we don't hire our own people, who we can train, oversee, and evaluate to do such vital work for our residents.

And on November 1, 2016, six people were killed with 11 injured in Baltimore by a school bus hitting vehicles. The bus was operated by a firm that has a contract with the Baltimore City

Schools. Maryland MVA discovered that the school bus driver hired by the private firm was not authorized to drive a commercial motor vehicle at the time.[224] Again, contracting out is no panacea.

And if padding friends' pockets is a problem with a government-run program, what's the padding like with the private firm that the government hires? We will certainly never know. At least we have a shot at knowing when the government runs the show through Council oversight, an independent Inspector General, protected whistleblowers, and ongoing governmental audits.

And now we have the President wanting companies to have our valuable public facilities. Today, May 24, 2017, I read on the front page of *The Washington Post* an article entitled "Privatizing Assets to Modernize the Rest" with the subheading, "Plan would try to entice state, local governments to sell public facilities." It states that "The Trump administration, determined to overhaul and modernize the nation's infrastructure, is drafting plans to privatize some public assets such as airports, bridges, highway rest stops and other facilities ..." His budget "called for spending $200 billion ... to 'incentivize'" entities' "spending on infrastructure."[225]

Why not just spend the money to fix the infrastructure directly rather than having cities and states sell their assets or lease them for 99 years to private companies, who will supposedly help with infrastructure? Now Trump is trying to put the aqueduct—D.C. and Virginia's water—into private hands. Imagine our high bills and how much we'll have to pay to get it back when he's gone.[226]

Okay, folks, the bottom line is private companies will own or control our assets. When these companies have control through purchase or nearly hundred-year leases, they can either re-sell or re-lease at huge profits or they can set exorbitant fees for planes that land or cars on the roads, with no real accountability as has been the case in Virginia. This whole Trump scenario is perfect *for* the profits of private companies (present ones and those that will rush in to grab a piece of that lucrative pie)—but *not* for us. Now Maryland Governor Hogan is proposing a public-private partnership for roads, saying "... the plan would not cost taxpayers any money."[227] Sure. If it sounds too good to be true, it *is*. Beware.

Always Feeling the Need to Be on Top of Everything

No wonder I didn't have the time to raise money or start campaigns early—or have a relationship. I was too busy being on top of all kinds of issues—some of which came into my office and others I thought of myself—and then feeling the need to do something about each and every one. To give you who are still with me a break between "contracting out" and "lead in the water," here are a few examples:

'On-Top-of-Everything' Letters

October 31, 2003
Mr. Jay Leno,
The Tonight Show

Dear Mr. Leno:

I am writing to thank you for a joke you made in your opening monologue on your October 6th show. While I cannot recall your exact words, you were discussing a coach berating his players in the locker room for their use of racist terms. The punch line was that, at the end of his lecture, the coach says to his team, "Now let's go out there and beat those Redskins."

While I appreciated the humor, I especially appreciated the issue it addressed. "Redskins" is, plain and simple, a racist term, and I am grateful for your bringing that to the attention (albeit in a lighthearted way) of your many viewers."

April 10, 2003
Ms. Paula Shugart, President,
Miss Universe Organization

Dear Ms. Shugart:

I purposely set aside time to watch the recent Miss USA Pageant, in large part because I am so proud of Ms. Shauntay. Hinton, Miss USA 2002, who previously reigned as Miss District of Columbia. Imagine my dismay when no mention whatsoever was made of the District of Columbia by anyone when discussing Ms. Hinton!

In addition, the brief biographical film spoke only of Ms. Hinton being from Starkville, Mississippi, implying that she had won Miss USA after being Miss Mississippi. I found it more disheartening that viewers did not know Ms. Hinton won Miss USA in 2002 as the representative from Washington, D.C. as they were never informed of this fact.

... I would still appreciate an explanation as to why the District of Columbia was not mentioned in reference to Ms. Hinton during the 2003 Miss USA Pageant. I look forward to your response.

I cc'd this letter to the Chair and CEO of NBC as well as to casino owner and pageant promotor, Donald Trump. I do not recall getting a response from any of the above. And by the way, in case it's not clear yet, Ms. Shauntay Hinton represented the *District of Columbia* the year she served as Miss USA.

September 18, 2002
Mr. Bill Hanbury, President and CEO,
Washington, D.C. Convention and Tourism Corporation

Dear Mr. Hanbury:

It has been brought to my attention that on the Washington, D.C. Convention and Tourism Corporation's official website, the Confederate flag and items that include depictions of this flag, such as boxer shorts, baseball caps, throw rugs and sportswear, are offered for sale. ...

The Convention and Tourism Corporation's website should make all people feel welcome, reflecting the values of our community as we attempt to draw visitors to the District. I do not think it is an appropriate venue for the sale of the Confederate flag and items with its depiction.

(Note the date: 2002.)

January 11, 2005
Robert L. Nardelli
Chair, President & CEO,
Home Depot

Dear Mr. Nardelli:

As a District of Columbia citizen and an at-large member of the Council of the District of Columbia, I am pleased to have Home Depot as a corporate citizen of the District. However, I was disturbed by a letter I received from another resident, Mr. Chris Colwell, alleging that he received abysmal customer service at the Rhode Island Avenue Home Depot here in the District. As a result, he indicated that he would now take his business to the Lowe's in Maryland.

As you can see, the loss of this customer and others like him would be detrimental to both Home Depot and the District of Columbia. I would greatly appreciate it if you would investigate this matter and respond accordingly.

March 28, 2001
Ms. Loren Berkheimer, Washington, D.C.

Dear Ms. Berkheimer:

I received your March 16th communication requesting that I vote against New York Gov. George Pataki's plan to increase sentences for those convicted of marijuana-related offenses. As I am not a member of the New York State Legislature, I am afraid that I cannot honor your request, but thank you for sharing your views with me.

I told you I answered all my letters, and even initiated my own.

Lead in the Water

In early 2004, *The Washington Post* broke the news that the lead levels in D.C. water exceeded the EPA limit. This was truly alarming and was made much worse by the fact that D.C.'s Water and Sewer Authority (then called WASA, now DC Water) delayed informing the public of the hazard; and when WASA finally did inform the public, it buried the information in mailings and left out crucial details.[228]

When I learned about it, I pounced. I immediately scheduled an emergency hearing and went on to conduct 11 more. I also put forward a proposal that we establish a joint Mayor/Council Task Force on WASA and the lead problem, which the Mayor and I would co-chair, made up of all the pertinent players (local and federal) in an effort to rectify this health crisis right away. Mayor Williams agreed and the Task Force started meeting on a weekly basis in the Wilson Building where City Administrator Robert Bobb and I alternately chaired the meetings.

At the first hearing on the issue, I laid into WASA officials for endangering the public and hiding the water test findings: "The facts are alarming, and the fact that [the information] was hidden from us is also alarming. WASA ... I say shame on you ..."[229]

They had the audacity to come back with the assertion that WASA had a policy of complete openness and honesty. I didn't hold back: "Where do you live? Do you come from outer space? ... If nothing else, I hope this hearing provided a wake-up call that your concern has to be elevated."[230]

The EPA also bore responsibility in failing to monitor as well as having approved purposely misleading and vague communication to customers about dangerous levels. I said about the EPA: "They too were negligent for nearly two years ... now for them to come back and talk about fining WASA up to $32,000 a day for violations that they signed off on is hypocritical at best ... And by the way, any fines paid by WASA will come from the ratepayers which are you and me."[231] And shouldn't WASA, at this point, be spending any money it has to *rectify* this situation instead of paying it in fines to a co-culprit?

This crisis was a top-of-the-hour local news story. It got some national coverage and the state of our water was even mentioned on an episode of *The West Wing*. I ended up handling much of the response—whether by default or design. Between the regular group meetings, the hearings, the well-attended weekly news conferences the Mayor and I were holding, I must have spent at least 20 hours a week on this issue alone for months.

This was one of those areas where I would lay awake nights trying to think of ideas to help. Contaminated lead levels are seriously hazardous, especially for kids under 6, pregnant and nursing women, cancer patients, and people living with HIV/AIDS. In those circumstances, water needed to be boiled. I was constantly urging WASA both at hearings and meetings to do this or that, such as offering free water filters to homes with service lines that could be tainted, and getting information out to the most vulnerable populations—which they did.

Through the Committee's hearings, we learned that back in 2003, a water quality manager had even sounded the alarm to her bosses about the lead levels and the need to take action. She was subsequently fired. In the *Post*'s investigation, this same former quality manager provided documents that showed that the heightened lead levels were caused by chemicals added to the water, which had been suggested by the federal government in order to avoid the expense of replacing pipes.[232]

Councilmember Adrian Fenty kept calling for the firing of the head of WASA. Mayor Williams rejected the idea. I agreed. Not that I wanted to give a stamp of approval to the WASA chief, but I did not think it would be productive to fire the head person in the middle of a crisis when we desperately needed to have someone who knew what was going on and how to rectify it. And I felt that reading resumes right then was not the best use of our time.

WASA ended up distributing over 30,000 free water filters, greatly expanded testing, offered free blood tests to residents, and put in place a new treatment method. It also hired an adviser on public health, which is something I wish they had done before, but at least I was glad to see it happen then.

I kept trying to think of solutions and protections for the future. In April, I introduced legislation to protect people in condos and apartments, including public housing. It called for the owner of those buildings to conduct a lead-level test on the tap water upon the request of a resident. I also made sure the drinking fountains in the schools were tested.

Even after the crisis passed, I felt we should compile all the knowledge we had gained and all the steps we took in confronting this health hazard in order to prevent similar chaos from arising down the road. Therefore, I got the D.C. Council to agree to have the Committee put together a published report, albeit an enormous amount of extra work, but I felt it was important. The D.C. Council Report, which was an investigation into the whole crisis with recommendations for the future, was released on December 21, 2004. (Kudos to my staff.) The report faulted WASA, the Army Corps of Engineers, and the EPA for the contamination. And thank goodness, by the end of that year, water was lead tested and determined to be at lower, acceptable levels.

After the crisis, I worked with WASA on an ambitious plan to replace more than 23,000 lead pipes across the city by 2010. These were potentially dangerous pipes which had been underground for over 100 years. The agency would fund the pipe changes up to the private property line, and then would work with banks on low-interest loans and other tactics to help residents with the cost for replacing the pipes on their property. Mayor Williams called for holding off until we saw the results of new chemicals in the water and best practices from other cities. But as I told the *Post*, public officials "would like to pass these problems on to another generation so that they don't have to spend the money or have the disruption, but I'm worried about the next generations, too."

This is a national problem as well. Just look at Flint, Michigan, where thousands of children have been exposed to water with extremely high levels of lead. And now more jurisdictions around the country are facing the same issue. A recent *Washington Post* headline read, "In some cities, 1 in 7 children have dangerous blood-lead levels."[233] Even with this national emergency, too little is being done, as "Under federal law, the vast majority of schools don't have to test the water ..."[234] Meanwhile, the dangers are clear: A March 29, 2017 *Post* piece was headlined, "Lead Exposure Alters Trajectory of Children's Lives Decades Later, Study Finds" and subheaded, "Kids with higher levels found to have lower IQs, socioeconomic struggles."

Meanwhile, here at home, some alarms have gone off. In June of 2016, it was reported that excessive lead contamination was found in six water fountains in four libraries. Thankfully, the same day, the D.C. government said in a *Washington Post* article that "they will lower the maximum acceptable level of lead in public drinking water, making the District standards far stricter than those set by the EPA."

But maybe we need to do more, particularly with pipes connecting to homes. Very troubling was a 2010 Center for Disease Control Report on D.C.'s lead problems, which was covered in the

Post. The report indicated: "... water supplied to almost 15,000 homes might still contain dangerous levels of lead despite the partial replacement of lead pipes at the homes from 2004 to 2008. ... Children living in houses, in which the city-owned section of lead pipe has been replaced, have blood lead levels indistinguishable from those of children living in houses with intact pipes."[235] It seems like half-measures are not working. I worry that if we don't fully replace the old pipes in our old city and stay on top of this issue, we could face a crisis much worse than the one in 2004.

Pats on the Back

Thank goodness during this time in the early and mid-2000s, some nice things happened. In 2004, I received one of the most prestigious awards in the city: the Whitney M. Young Community Service Award from the Greater Washington Urban League at their beautiful and well-attended annual event. My daughters were there with me to help celebrate this unique honor.

Before that, in 2002, I was given the Certificate of Appreciation for Exemplary Work on Racial Justice Issues from the Indigenous Peoples' Fourth Annual Conference. That year I was also presented with the Housing Leadership Award from COG. And I enjoyed having the opportunity in 2002 to be the keynote speaker for HUD's National Women's History Month event, where they presented me with a nice plaque.

Speaking of pats on the back, how about more for the extraordinary women in American history? Around 2006, I became aware of a movement which started in 2003 to build a National Women's History Museum on the Mall. I gave several contributions to the effort and attended some fundraisers as well. At one, I met and had a picture taken with Meryl Streep (sure wish I could find it), who is a huge supporter of the effort. What a nice, talented role model she is. I do hope that we will see such a museum in my lifetime so that girls and young women can be inspired by our nation's female trailblazers in countless categories.

Ongoing Hazards

Toward the end of 2004, I experienced a situation that only happened a couple of times in my career—voting against a bill I co-introduced. Councilmember Kathy Patterson brought forward legislation, which the Sierra Club pushed, to ban railway companies from carrying hazardous material through the District, and she asked me to co-introduce it, which I did. I recognize that people can say, "Well, if it's not in your backyard, it's going to be in someone else's." But in this case, I can say two things: First of all, I was elected to take care of D.C.'s backyard, not someone else's. Secondly and legitimately, D.C. is the Nation's Capital and the seat of government, and has special vulnerability because of that.[236]

The legislation came before my Committee because it was transportation-related and I held a hearing on it where CSX, the railway company, testified and stated at the time that it was company policy, understood by the federal government, not to talk about which trains/cars had any such materials on them and which routes they would be on, for obvious reasons. There were also legal issues with our ability to impose such a ban that were related to interstate commerce. I then started meeting behind the scenes with the executives of CSX to work out an agreement to accomplish in the back room what would have been very difficult, if not impossible, to do by legislation. We ended up getting assurances that the company would indeed voluntarily bypass the District, although not advertise the fact. I understood and was pleased to have accomplished as much as I did, especially after I learned about the legal issues involved if we did it legislatively.

Meanwhile, the Sierra Club was pushing for the out and out ban legislation to pass. I reassured my colleagues more vaguely in public because of the previous reasons, and more specifically behind the scenes, and emphasized the legal concerns. Most were comfortable with the understood agreement, but Kathy, the co-introducer, and a few others wanted the legislation voted on regardless. Of course, I knew if there was a vote, all the Council would vote for it, looking like they were trying to protect the citizens and maybe to appease the Sierra Club. I knew that a vote would only succeed in jeopardizing the agreement—and thus would be less helpful in protecting our citizens rather than more.

There again, I refused to be intimidated to do something that not only pandered but blew apart a real solution. The bill wound up passing 12 to 1 (as I predicted) with me, the other original co-introducer, voting no. Soon thereafter, CSX, with the federal government as an amicus curiae (friend of the court), went to court and that legislation which had become "law" in D.C. was determined to be unlawful in that it violated the Interstate Commerce Act, and therefore was overturned. Just another example of a lot of political show—a lot of "sound and fury, signifying nothing"— when we had a real but quiet solution in the bag. So infuriating.

CHAPTER 36

My Beloved Brother

I still saw Johnny every three or four months, even during my busiest work periods. Most years I went to Austin to see him in the Christmas program at Marbridge where he was in the choir, and then usually we went on to visit my "sister" from childhood, Linda, and her family in San Antonio. Johnny often came to Midland with me for Mom's poetry contest in April. And he would come at least once a year to Washington to visit. I so enjoyed Johnny's company as he gave me unconditional love. I used to joke to him: "Johnny, you're not just the President of my fan club, you're its only member." And he would laugh every time and say, "That's not true."

Back in 1992, I threw a wonderful surprise 50th birthday party for him at the Marriott on the River Walk in San Antonio. Dad knew, but thank goodness, as requested, didn't tell. Johnny walked in, thinking he was just going to dinner—and a small ballroom was filled with lots of friends and family from all across the country.

In 2002, I threw a really fun 60th birthday weekend for him in Washington with most of our family and many of our friends from here and out of town. The weekend consisted of a dinner in my apartment on Friday night, a buffet lunch on Saturday there as well, a party with 60 people and a DJ at the Washington Hilton one block away on Saturday night, ending with brunch on Sunday at the Cosmos Club five blocks away with the out of towners.

Steph did name tags for the Friday night gathering, which I thought were so clever that I still keep them on my refrigerator. Here are a couple of examples: For Uncle Joe, "Hi, my name is Joe. Ask me about skinning a fish." For Aunt Betty Jane, "I'm Betty. I survived Carol's house tour." For herself, "I'm Stephanie—the main reason Carol isn't a grandmother."

At the big party on Saturday night, Johnny, who loved all things political, was thrilled with the big surprises that awaited him after dinner. One was Council Chair Linda Cropp reading him a resolution from the Council honoring his 60th birthday. Another was a proclamation from Mayor Williams. The finale was a letter from President George W. Bush, wishing him well on his big day. Steph, Hil and Doug sang Johnny a song they wrote and he, sitting next to George, was grinning from ear to ear. We all spent the rest of the evening dancing to music played by DJ Lady Smooth. Johnny really loved to dance—and was good at it.

We set up a podium as we did for his 50th birthday in San Antonio where he had made a long and memorable speech. But I did notice the speech at his 60th was shorter and less energetic. Still, it was a joyful occasion and he seemed very happy. With his disability, Johnny wasn't expected to reach 60. But I wanted him to live forever.

Nearly two years later, approaching his 62nd birthday in June, I really didn't like the way he looked. With a family who loved to eat, Johnny had been a bit chubby most of his life. Then he became diabetic in his later years, took pills, and needed to stay away from sugar, although he always cheated. Still, he got thinner, which I guess was good for the most part. But then he started looking too skinny. He also had experienced stomach issues most of his life, including a hiatal hernia. But now, I worried about something more serious. So I had him come up to D.C. and I took him to have a full MRI done. Doug was in town and sat with him during it, which sure helped Johnny. I was so grateful to see the results which showed no sign of cancer. What a relief—or so I thought.

I had a trip to Austin planned for August of 2004 and I had doctor appointments set up for him while I was there as he was still having some stomach problems although he kept up his routine. But a week before the trip, I got a call from Marbridge saying Johnny was quite ill and had been rushed to the hospital. Thank goodness Linda from San Antonio and Sandy Schwartz, a friend of Johnny's from the temple in Austin, who I had met several times, went to the hospital as soon as I called them so they could be with Johnny until I could get there. Linda even confessed to my daughters over the phone that it looked very bad.

Stephanie, Hilary and I flew down that day. Johnny was hooked up on machines, basically unconscious. It was so painful for the three of us to see him like that. I just kept rubbing his feet and patting his arm. The doctor said the breathing machine was the only thing keeping him alive. And we then had to make the most tortuous of decisions to let him go. I broke down. The last and most beloved member of my birth family was gone.

Of all the deaths of loved ones I had experienced, this was the saddest for me. Johnny was the sweetest person in my life then and had defined me in so many ways. Still does. I protected and fought for Johnny all my life, and I felt incomplete being without him. Still do. Even though I miss him so much to this day, I get great comfort saying, "Hi Johnny" every time I pass his picture on the table next to my closet. Johnny was truly the love of my life.

In memory of Johnny, we had a lovely ceremony with all the people at Marbridge near Austin. Steph and Hil were really so helpful in the planning of it and the calling of family and friends. Doug, who flew in late the night Johnny died, led all the residents in a rendition of "Lean on Me." And he played a recording he had recently made of Johnny talking about his plans for the fire and police departments. My ex-boyfriend from high school and his wife, as well as Ivan and Bunny, my ex-fiancé from college and his wife—all of whom loved Johnny—came in from out of town. In fact, Ivan, after arriving from Dallas, drove down to San Antonio in the middle of the night to pick Doug up at the airport and then they drove back to Austin. Other friends came in from Midland and elsewhere. My colleagues from the Council were wonderful, calling and sending flowers. Such a sad time, but I did feel surrounded by love.

And that continued in Greenville, my mom's hometown and where Johnny and I were born. There we were joined by my loving aunts, uncles and cousins from Baton Rouge and Denver as well as sweet local friends like Hazel Edwards. Johnny was laid to rest next to my grandparents and our mom and dad. There was my family in a small patch of grass in the Jewish section of the Greenville, Mississippi Main Street Cemetery—gone.

Keeping Their Spirits Alive

They may have been gone, but I was going to make sure they were not forgotten. Back in 1994, soon after my dad passed, I started a student activity fund at Marbridge for those who could not afford many of the outings that Johnny and some of the other residents could. I named the fund in Dad's honor as he had made some similar contributions over the years. After Johnny died in 2004, I renamed it in honor of him as well. It is now the Stanley and John Levitt Student Activity Fund, and I still fund it today.

I continued funding the Hilda Simmons Levitt Poetry Contest at Midland College, which Dad started to honor her talent. I sponsor it every year, and go down every other year for the ceremony. Through friends in Odessa, Texas, Marion Luper and Nelson Allison (who I met through Lettie England), I became friendly with Jenna Welch, Laura Bush's lovely and spunky mother. Sometimes I would pick her up in Midland to take her to dinner at the guys' house 20 miles away, with Lettie there too. The four of them (until Nelson passed away) and then three, often attended the poetry awards presentation at Midland College, adding to the festivities. It is a fitting way to keep dear Mom's memory alive.

Taking My Campaign Colors on the Road

I purchased a used car in September of 2005. I needed to get rid of an 18-year-old red Chrysler LeBaron convertible, which I had paid for at least 14 times over because it was a lemon from year one. But since David had bought it for me about five months before he died, it was hard to let go of in spite of all the problems it caused—both at the time of purchase and thereafter. I definitely wanted a convertible to take its place, and I figured it would be another red one since I had owned several.

Then, in Rehoboth I saw this bright yellow 2002 Pontiac Trans Am/Firebird collectible convertible with a black top and interior, and complete with two black firebirds painted on the front hood. I thought, "This is even too over-the-top for me." But I drove it with its Corvette engine and its six-gear stick-shift plus reverse—and fell in love, but still felt self-conscious about driving it in public as it was just so "out there." I decided I would sleep on it.

I drove back to D.C. and got my daughters to look it up on the Internet to get their thoughts. Both said it looked like fun and that I should get it. They also learned its value was above the asking price, so I called the guy in Rehoboth and said, "I think I want it but can you do a little better on the price?" His response was, "Carol, I had just gotten the car as a trade-in when you came by and had no idea what its real value was. Since you were here yesterday, I went on the Internet and saw I was undercharging you, but I will keep with my offer. Now I also have three other people on a waiting list for it. So Carol, as we're friends, I would suggest if you want it that you get your ass back here to pick it up real quick." I loved his style. Steph and I both took off from work that afternoon to get my ass there.

The first day I parked the car in front of the Wilson Building, and did not mention it to anybody. Within a few hours, I got two calls from the media asking about my new "wheels": the *Post* and *Washington City Paper*. I said to one, "If anyone had any doubt that I was in the midst of my mid-life crisis, now they need not." And to the other, "That car makes *me* look subtle." *City Paper*'s "Loose Lips" wrote in its column, it's "so wonderfully out of place among the imports and SUVs in front of the Wilson Building."[237]

It's always amusing to see other people's reactions when I get out of the car—not some young muscular guy as expected, but a graying lady, at that time 60 years old and now 73! When my son was in town later and met the car, he asked, "Didn't it come with a muffler?" and walked away fast. Barbara Blum was the first friend to ride in it a couple of days after I bought it, and she fell in love immediately too. I guess it's a middle-aged-plus woman thing.

I still own it and it became quite the talk of my subsequent campaigns, particularly because it shares my campaign colors of 40 years—yellow and black—although I didn't set out to get a car to match my posters. I've only had it for two campaigns—both losers—but I don't blame the car. I still enjoy it as much as the day I got it. And even though it started out as the solution to my mid-life crisis, it's ending up as the energizer of my old age.

2004 Election

I didn't have strong opposition for the Republican primary in September of 2004, and got nearly 83% of the vote. I won reelection once again for my at-large seat on the Council in November of 2004, getting nearly 94,000 votes—my largest number for the Council, and it set a record for the non-majority seat. (That record just got broken in 2016, with now over 100,000 more residents in D.C. than there were in 2004.)

I was grateful that so many people felt I was doing a good job and wanted me returned. It was also particularly rewarding to get so many votes as a Republican during the highly contested Presidential election between Bush and John Kerry, when party loyalty and tensions are at a high. As far as elections go, this was a relatively non-stressful one—and that was nice for a change.

Street Fighting Woman

In December of 2004, while still chairing the Department of Public Works and the Environment, I pushed legislation to raise registration fees for gas-guzzling cars (like my own, although I use public transportation a lot), lower them for more environmentally friendly cars, and cut them in half for hybrid cars.[238] It continued my reward good behavior, punish bad behavior philosophy. This step was important to encourage the use of vehicles which are better for the environment, and to get more money for the use of vehicles like SUVs that were causing enormous wear and tear on our roads and to offset the costs associated with repairing them.

Speaking of wear and tear, since potholed, damaged roads have long been a scourge on the District, I was determined as Committee Chair to help rectify that situation. Whenever I had an oversight hearing with Dan Tangherlini, Director of the Department of Transportation (DDOT), we spent a lot of time arguing about this issue. He said there were hardly any potholes, and I said, "The streets are a mess." So one day I said, "Let's resolve this now, Dan. You and I are going driving and we'll take a firsthand look together at the state of our streets." Then I adjourned the meeting and took Dan out in my Trans Am convertible. We bounced over a good number of potholes, proving me right, that is, until the car broke down on us and we had to be towed away.

Dan and I did come together to work on getting permanent financing for street repair in the mid-2000s. We established a perpetual source of income for fixing potholes and ongoing street and sidewalk improvements called the Rights of Way Fund. For many years it worked beautifully, and we saw the difference all over town. Unfortunately, after I left the Council and Dan left D.C. government, it disappeared. And we have certainly seen the bad results of that poor decision that the Council and Mayor made those many years ago in the abysmal state of many of our roads. A *Washington Post* story on July 20, 2015 reported that the cost of fixing aging roads and infrastructure in the Washington area exceeds available funding by $58 billion.[239] Dan and I worked so hard to take care of this never-ending problem on an ongoing basis, at least on D.C.'s end, and how disappointing that it was all in vain.

Dan Tangherlini and I had our share of disagreements—and then coming together to solve problems. Yet I always liked him and thought he was a good public servant. I guess he felt the same because when he moved to another position in 2006, he wrote me a letter for which I'm grateful, that said among other things:

"From the first days of my tenure, your vigorous oversight set a tone and expectation for our agency that resulted in a much better DDOT. Knowing that you would be asking me about an issue or problem was all that was needed for my staff to find the answer or solve the problem. In this way and others, your demanding excellence has been greatly appreciated."[240]

During my time on the Council, I received the James B. Hunter Leadership Award in 2002 from the Washington Area Bicycle Association, which I was very pleased about. I think they appreciated my efforts on road repair and the special attention I gave to their concerns. I'm not sure they always appreciated, though, my lec-turing that cyclists also must follow the road rules like everyone else. I would say at hearings that too often we see bicyclists whizz-ing between cars and ignoring street lights and stop signs.

I even had a hit and run with one, and I wasn't the one hitting and running. I was sitting at a light, minding my own business, and the next thing I know I got hit by a bicyclist—a huge bang! I im-mediately rolled down my window, not out of anger at first, but out of concern that the person might be hurt. But before I could say, "Are you alright?" he jumped on his bicycle and raced off. And there I was left with a huge dent in my car, which cost me $800 to repair. It should be incumbent on everyone who is on the road, whether they be drivers, cyclists, or pedestrians, to act responsi-bly and follow the law—like not leaving the scene of an accident.

Trying for Dedicated Funding for Metro

Just as I worked with Dan to establish a perpetual fund for street repair, I also felt strongly that there should be a dedicated source of revenue for the Washington Metropolitan Area Transit Authority (WMATA), though I had never served on its Board. (Now I realize maybe I should have forced my way in.) This idea of dedicated funding had been discussed for many years at COG and had been recommended for the region by COG and others on the Blue Ribbon Panel on Metro Funding, which wrote a report. As Chair of the Committee on Public Works and the Environment, I held a hearing on that report on May 5, 2005. That same day, I wrote to Mayor Williams to seek his help in getting started at the Executive level a serious and urgent regional discussion with Gov-ernor Mark Warner of Virginia and Governor Bob Ehrlich of Maryland on the need for such dedicated funding. In it, I wrote:

> "As you likely know, Metro is the second most heavily used rapid transit system in the country, and it is the only public system without a dedicated source of funding to pay for its operations and maintenance requirements. Establishing a dedicated funding mechanism may be a bit more complex here than elsewhere in the country because a number of jurisdictions are involved, but I am more and more convinced that it is something that is needed. ...
>
> I certainly agree that the federal government needs to be a partner in any plan for dedicated funding if for no other reason than nearly 50 percent of Metro's ridership is made up of federal workers. Because our neighboring jurisdictions in Maryland and Virginia must have buy-in at the state level, I hope that you will

agree with me on the need to discuss this with your counterparts in our neighboring states."

Similar discussions continued through the years. In fact, I remember our voting on the Council to raise our sales tax some to get that perpetual dedicated fund going on the condition that Maryland and Virginia did the same. But a regional and federal buy-in never occurred. Today, we are suffering the awful consequences.

A Streetcar No One Desires—Except for the Profiteers

Instead of benefiting that Metro system, which serves hundreds of thousands of people, hundreds of millions of dollars is being spent on another project serving practically no one.

I have watched the H St., N.E. streetcar issue as a citizen for the past nearly nine years. It has annoyed me the whole time. First H St. was torn up to lay down wide, bumpy tracks (which cars and pedestrians have to maneuver around), while parking and sidewalk space was taken away. We had worked hard years ago and at great expense to put cables underground only to find them uglying up H St. and some of Benning Rd., N.E. And now they're not only talking about, but have plans to extend this eyesore through K St., N.W. and on to Georgetown. How did this all happen?

In the early 2000s, under Mayor Williams, with enthusiastic support from Dan Tangherlini, then head of transportation, streetcars started being pushed. They were looking at Portland as the streetcar model. But unlike D.C., it did *not* have a good subway system so needed an another form of transportation. I got invited to go there by the Administration, as did other Councilmembers. I declined as I was more interested in dedicated funding for Metro.

But in the past seven or so years, D.C. has spent well over $200 million, including a $48.8 million car barn.[241] And this is for a line that has yet to extend to the now planned seven miles.

In the year and half the small stretch has been open, the city has tried to attract ridership. It's done ads; the cost to ride is free. However, when it is in service and not in repair, it seems that the free cost is too high. I guess soon we will have to pay riders to get on. (And meanwhile, people are having to wait 45 minutes between trains at night for a Metro train they actually use.) So now streetcars, which have so few riders, are an enormous money-drainer and not well-liked—*must* be expanded, according to the plans. How can being a money drain and not well-liked, plus having little to no ridership and ugly wires, equal expansion? Who could possibly be thinking: "What does beautiful D.C. need? Oh, I know, more congestion on K St., N.W., and hideous hanging wires. And we should spend at least a billion dollars more for it." Only the profiteers could be thinking that.

I believe the non-riders on H St. have the right idea. Please let's learn from them—and get off this "train," and put our time, energy and money into the Metro trains—and buses—that really matter.

My Gifted Son

Doug has always been ambitious, energetic, and participated in every activity in school. He always pushed himself to succeed. Even after his father's passing as he just turned 16, he seemed to go through high school and college fairly smoothly considering. Yet in grappling with his dad's tragic death in adulthood, he has often expressed his feelings through profound songs and writings.

After a couple of years in Nashville, Doug moved to Los Angeles, where he got engaged and then unengaged. (That made three in the family.) Soon he was not only pursuing writing songs, but also other types of writing connected to his political and social interests. He started a project called *Greyhound Diaries*, in which he describes trips he's taken around the country on buses, talking to people of varied backgrounds to illustrate the struggles of those who habitually ride the bus. He's recorded these journeys not only in words and songs, but in photographs he's taken as well.

About 15 years ago, Doug called and said he wanted to change his name for professional reasons. He explained that when he saw his name on CDs or a marquis, "Doug" was overpowered by "Schwartz" (which I know is true from my own experience as it is very long and bold—eight letters and all those consonants). I braced myself. "Oh no." I was sure he would pick the polar opposite of Schwartz, something really not Jewish. It hit a nerve—as so many family members hid or denied their Jewishness—and I thought here we go again. He'll pick a name like Doug Jones.

Then he told me the surname he chose: "Levitt," his middle name and my family name. (We had named him "Douglas Levitt Schwartz" to keep my maiden name going.) He also said he was using "Schwartz" as his middle name. I was so relieved and said, "You're not changing your name. You're just reversing the order." He would now go by Doug Levitt. Not only was I relieved, but more than that, I was touched.

It's only a little awkward when I introduce him: "Meet my son, Doug Levitt." Since most people don't know my maiden name, they think he is the product of another marriage of which there has been none. But, Johnny, Hilda and Stanley Levitt would be very proud, as is Carol Levitt Schwartz.

Hilary Spreads Her Wings

My daughter Hilary worked in marketing for two big media outlets for 10 years, making good money with good benefits. She wasn't really happy in this career. I offered her the opportunity to go to graduate school like I had done for both Steph and Doug. But she said she would just be wasting my money as she wasn't sure what she wanted to study. This offer and refusal went on for years and finally I suggested, even insisted, that she do a sabbatical on me for one to two years to figure out what she wanted to do.

Hilary has particularly enjoyed comedy writing, and has innate abilities in that area. While she was at *U.S. News* she wrote a really funny newsletter poking loving fun at the show *Melrose Place* and other popular soap opera-type shows at the time, and even took some acting classes in the evenings.

During her hiatus from work, Hilary took some writing work-shops and started hitting open mics. And now, she's been doing stand-up comedy for 16 years. She makes some income from it. She also worked as a substitute teacher for a time, then full-time for a production company and a technology company that focused on education. Hilary even had a stint taking tourists out on a seven-seat bicycle around Times Square, until it was made illegal. (Maybe I shouldn't have insisted she take that hiatus.)

She's traveled doing stand-up, including in Rehoboth and Dewey Beach, and often does shows in the New York region and occasionally the D.C. area at venues including the Birchmere.

Hilary has had several relationships, but she has shied away from marriage and children. She explains it this way verbatim: "I feel unworthy while also feeling that no one is worthy of me."

Gaby

Throughout my career, I have been honored to be featured in various local news outlets as well as some national ones. But the media outlet I was most thrilled to be in during the spring of 2005 was the newsletter from the Washington Animal Rescue League (WARL).[242] My daughter Stephanie had moved back to D.C. right before the holidays of 2004 for what I had hoped would be for good, but turned out to be for only a year and a half. It was wonderful not only to have my daughter home, but we took the opportunity to co-adopt a dog, our precious Gaby.

Steph and Hil, who was in town, fell in love with her at first sight—an adorable spaniel/chow/lab? mix, all black. I would soon joke that we had gotten a dog to match our wardrobe. The girls had called me at work and said that they had narrowed the choices down to two and needed me to come out to help make the final selection. I did go—and Gaby stole my heart with her warm dark brown eyes. She had been slated to be euthanized at a herding facility in Georgia when she was brought to WARL through another relief group. It was clear Gaby had had a tough time of it.

At the Rescue League, they called her Godiva, but given my figure—and hers—the jokes would be too easy, as they had been with Candy years before. I asked Steph if it would be alright if I picked a new name, and she said fine as long as it was a Hebrew one. So I started working from the "G" and came up with Gabrielle, with the adorable nickname, Gaby. When I told Steph, she immediately looked it up, and sure enough it was Hebrew from Gabriel, meaning "God is my strength."

The weekend we brought Gaby home, she was in heaven and so were we. That Sunday night as Steph and I were having dinner (Hil had gone back to New York earlier) at the kitchen table with Gaby nearby on the floor, I was sitting there thinking, "Thank you, God, for bringing Stephanie home and for Gaby. Life is perfect."

At that moment, Gaby started flailing her arms in the air in a convulsive state. It was frightening—and Steph and I both began to yell, "Do something, do something!" I immediately ran, got a blanket, wrapped it around Gaby, and put her in crying Stephanie's lap. I called a vet. We then threw on our coats over our nightgowns and carried her to the car while I cried, "Why can't anything ever be normal?" We drove to an animal hospital where they kept her overnight. It turned out that she had epilepsy, which had been undiscovered. We picked her up and took her to WARL to be checked out there too and they told us we could return her, but we said, "No way!" Gaby had several more episodes over the years, but they subsided years ago (knock on wood).

My brother Johnny, who had died August 18, 2004, had the sweetest brown eyes. But when you looked at him, he would always turn his eyes away. We got Gaby at the end of December of 2004, only four months after Johnny passed away. One day, Gaby was sitting on my bed, looking at me with her sweet brown eyes and I kept looking back at her. She would catch my eye like Johnny and then would look away. At that moment, I who had never believed in this kind of thing, felt that Johnny had returned in a new form but still a beautiful creature with special needs and precious kind eyes. It made me love Gaby even more, if that was possible.

Now back to the newsletter: The Rescue League asked us if it could highlight our adoption in its newsletter and of course we said yes. As you may recall, all of my pets have always been rescue animals of sorts and with great pride, I can also say that my 12 grandpets have all been rescues too. The article was headlined: "Councilmember Carol Schwartz and daughter Stephanie Schwartz adopt homeless special-needs pooch." It went on: "'We have a happy, loving family, and we wanted to share that love with an animal in need,' said Stephanie. [She continued:] 'That Gabrielle has epilepsy makes us want to do even more to make her life a good one.'" I added, "'Visiting the League reinforced my conviction that adopting homeless animals—who desperately need our help and love ... is our responsibility.'" Not too long after adopting Gaby, my chief of staff John Abbott also adopted a dog from WARL, and my friend Aleida then got a rescue dog as well.

Gaby had an especially hard time trusting men (WARL said it was obviously due to past abuse). During Thanksgiving of 2005, my family was all here together. Doug took Gaby out and stopped by the nearby 7-11. Once Doug tied her to a poll to run into the store, she escaped the leash (which maybe I hadn't put on properly), sped across Columbia Road, and headed back to the apartment building. When Doug approached, she ran down Connecticut Ave. at the height of rush hour. She could so easily have been hit by a car. Poor Doug had to make the phone call: "Gaby's missing." We all ran out of the house. I, crying, got in the car to drive to look for her. Hilary and Stephanie ran on foot calling her name. At California and 18th Sts., blocks away, a girl looking out of a window yelled to Hilary, "Are you looking for a dog? She went that way." Hilary ran up the block and Gaby appeared out of a yard. Hil carried her to 18th St. as I was driving by. When I saw her, I cried again, this time with relief. I had been so scared—what a blessing it was that she was safe—and that she was in our lives!

(I went on the Board of WARL in 2011. We merged with the Washington Humane Society in 2016. Now we are called the Humane Rescue Alliance—caring for animals throughout the region.)

CHAPTER 37

National Pastime vs. National Capital

When my husband David and I were first married, we went to see the Washington Senators' baseball games. It was one of our favorite things to do. Sometimes after work, we'd go over to RFK Stadium, eat hot dogs, and watch baseball. What relaxing fun! But unfortunately, in 1971, the Senators were stolen away and became the Texas Rangers. I hated to see them leave, and I always wanted to see a team back in D.C.

For years both as a private citizen and Councilmember, I'd write a letter to Major League Baseball (MLB) every three to four years that said, "We're the Nation's Capital without the national pastime. Bring us a team." I found one I wrote on February 5, 2002 to Commissioner Bud Selig, which ended: "I look forward to working with the stakeholders in the effort to secure a Major League team for our city, and hope that you will see the logic [which I outlined] in returning Major League Baseball to Washington."

On September 29, 2004, two years after my last letter and 33 years after the Washington Senators left, Tony Williams announced that he had worked out a deal to bring the Montreal Expos to Washington. I was thrilled at the prospect and became one of seven Councilmembers (out of 13) who went to hear the big announcement at the Carnegie Library. The six other Councilmembers present seemed to have already signed on. Tony called us up to speak. I said I was so pleased that the Mayor had brought us a Major League Baseball deal. He interrupted and said, "I guess that means you're going to vote yes." (The deal still needed to be voted on by the Council, and it needed seven votes to pass.) I said, "Mr. Mayor, you know me. I'm going to have to look at details of the deal first." I went on to say, "But I really love baseball and have been trying to get it back since it left. And I've gotta tell you folks, it's nice to have a choice. So, Tony, thank you for giving us that choice."[243]

Soon thereafter when I looked at the ballpark financing bill, I found that we, as a city, had to *pay* for everything and the owners *got* everything. And I mean everything. The deal required D.C. taxpayers to pay for the land, the new stadium, and all the infrastructure while the owners even got the profits from the naming rights. Although wanting baseball, I knew I could not sign on to the deal as negotiated—I mean *not* negotiated.

A little background: When the Expos were sold, instead of allowing one owner to buy the team, Major League Baseball (made up of all the team owners) bought the team itself. All the owners knew the value because there were cities across the country, like Washington, that wanted a team. So they banded together, bought the Expos, and planned to then resell it at a great profit and split the winnings. Smart on their part. But I wanted us to be if not equally—at least somewhat—smart.

The Major League owners were in an advantageous position, knew it, and used it. And because Tony Williams wanted to get a baseball team to Washington so badly, he said fine to anything. The owners wrote the contract they wanted, and he signed it—which was certainly his prerogative. But now, I, as a Councilmem-ber, had the prerogative to get us a better deal before I signed on. Even though I wish he had been a better negotiator for us—as we are not Podunk, we are the Nation's Capital and baseball wanted to be in D.C. as well—I still was grateful he brought us a deal.

As I started to do research with my staff, we found the arrange-ment of the city paying for everything was not standard. In many jurisdictions, the owners of the team had to pay for the stadium and then the city threw in the infrastructure. In fact, a new sta-dium is being built without taxpayer dollars in Inglewood, California to accommodate a football team returning to Los Ange-les, with city expenditures only being used to cover infrastructure and transportation, although the developers did get tax breaks.[244]

This is exactly the kind of arrangement made by Marion Barry with Abe Pollin, then owner of D.C.'s basketball team, for its arena. When Pollin wanted to bring the team to D.C., he said to the city, "I'd like you to build me a facility." And Marion, who was Mayor then, said (and good for him) that he'd certainly provide the infrastructure and some tax benefits, but Abe would have to build the structure himself. Now Marion may have had to say that because of the Financial Control Board being in place, but regard-less, that's exactly what happened. Abe Pollin built the then MCI Center, now the Verizon Center; and as a result, he helped us build a living downtown.

(As an aside: Long after Abe Pollin moved the then named Bul-lets from Baltimore to Landover, Maryland in the 1970s, I ran into him one day walking on Capitol Hill. When he said, "Oh hi, Carol," I said back at him, "I don't even want to talk to you. If you were going to move your team from Baltimore, why didn't you move it into Washington? We needed the team." Then, when I ran into Abe again after he had moved his team into the city in 1997, he said, "Are you happy with me now?" I was, and gave him a hug.

Abe was a good man and a great philanthropist, and is missed since he passed away in 2009.)

Because of that MCI/Verizon Center history and the experience of other cities, I found this current deal with D.C. paying all to be unpalatable, as did some of my colleagues. But because we were fighting against: 1) powerful Major League Baseball, 2) an obviously too overly enthusiastic Mayor, 3) an equally enthusiastic Chair of the Council's Finance Committee, 4) many in the city and its suburbs, and 5) the media—all deprived of baseball for years in D.C.—and with 6) an already signed "non-negotiated" deal, we, the opponents, were taking on quite a challenge.

When the Council had its initial hearings, a huge crowd showed up, by far most wanting baseball. The support appeared overwhelmingly in favor. However, polls later showed that a majority of D.C. residents were not so enthusiastic as they learned about the dollars D.C. would have to expend, with many wishing that our funds would go elsewhere to other priorities. Needless to say, all the suburbanites were in favor. Why not? They weren't directly paying for anything, and the traffic in their neighborhoods would not be affected. They came to our hearings about the seemingly done deal. Voicing their support was fine. But booing those of us who dared to ask any questions was not.

The contract details were becoming more concerning by the day. First, our CFO Natwar Gandhi, in October of 2004, upped the cost estimate of the stadium from the initial $440 million to $530 million. Then D.C. Auditor Deborah Nichols upped it to $584 million. And these numbers did not even include infrastructure, expanded Metro costs, the environmental cleanup of the site, etc.

The baseball deal was up for a first vote on November 30, 2004, and it already appeared to have the majority it needed—seven votes—to pass. Lee Smith, my Legislative Assistant, and I were in my office late the night before. We were frustrated at the thought of the deal and the cost involved. We felt we needed more details to back up my fight so decided to go through the whole contract line by line before the meeting the next morning. We then came across the most alarming stipulation. It said that if the city did not deliver the baseball stadium on time, we, the city taxpayers, would have to pay an uncapped liability to the owners. There was no ceiling. It could be trillions of dollars.

Get this: The team would be entitled to recover "compensatory damages from the District, including without limitation, lost profits from private suites, club or other premium seats, concessions, parking, naming rights and other advertising, and other costs" if we were late in delivering the stadium we were paying for. All of these dollars potentially going to already very wealthy out-of-town people at D.C. taxpayers' expense was just too hard to stomach. And the "potentially" part appeared too real to me as we had union contractors building the stadium, so if they decided to strike, we would have little control over the timeline, not to mention unpredictable things like weather conditions. It was an unacceptable scenario, and I found the thought of it repugnant.

Lee and I discovered this detail at about 3:00 in the morning. I said, "Oh my God. We've got to stop this." The vote was to take place a few hours later, so I had to go about it thoughtfully. I could speak up about it on the dais, but I just knew that was not the way. I said to myself, "I doubt there's a chance with the other six apparent yes votes, but we may have a shot with our Chair Linda Cropp, the apparent seventh vote, as she is certainly fiscally responsible."

I decided not to say anything to Linda too long before the meeting. I thought if I did, she might call the Mayor to raise this concern, and he would try to "promise" his way out of the uncapped liability with no real binding agreement.

Councilmembers began to take their seats on the dais around 9:30 a.m. before the meeting started at 10:00 a.m. I strategically walked up to Linda at 10 minutes to 10, and kind of moved away the person who was by her side so I could sit next to her. I said, "Linda, you need to see this." And I showed her the clause on the uncapped liability. She said, "Oh dear." I said, "Uncapped, it could be 100 trillion dollars. How could we possibly vote for this? We just found it a few hours ago in the middle of the night."

Linda's vote was an abstention, and she upped her own conditions on the contract, adding the need to go after private financing to offset the public investment. That first vote still approved the deal with six in favor (Sandy Allen, Sharon Ambrose, Harold Brazil, Kevin Chavous, Jack Evans and Vince Orange), four opposed (David Catania, Adrian Fenty, Jim Graham and me), and three abstaining (Linda Cropp, Phil Mendelson and Kathy Patterson). Although it passed, a second vote was required. And since there was a majority still not in favor (either voting "no" or abstaining), the deal was not assured at this point.

Because of the imbalance of the contract, not surprisingly, I voted "no" during that first vote on November 30, 2004. As much I loved baseball and wished for its return, I loved D.C. taxpayers more and was determined to do better by them in spite of the odds. Mayor Williams became so concerned that his bet that the Council would just fall in line was falling apart that he even made an unprecedented move of cancelling a trip to be in the Council chambers during the debate that day, which lasted for hours.

After the vote, the Council, ably led by Linda, worked to amend the deal to get some concessions for the city. There was a meeting of all the big players of Major League Baseball, including Baseball Commissioner Bud Selig and President Bob DuPuy, and the Council in a small conference room in the Wilson Building. Many of us attended. But the most vocal opponents of baseball, Councilmembers Fenty and Catania, did not bother with real negotiating. Catania dropped by for a minute and Fenty came in, texted for a while, and left. You could always find them, though, in front of the media, and David at some hearings ranting at Nat Gandhi, our CFO, who he was mad at for not killing the deal outright. I, on the other hand, saved the bulk of my ranting for the parties on the other side of the table.

At that important meeting with the leadership of Major League Baseball, I sat at the table and when it was my turn, I looked at that group of powerful men and said, "You all should have come in and talked to us a long time ago—especially because we were so evenly divided—and not just ignored us elected officials, which was very disrespectful. I could maybe see your doing that to us if the vote was 12 to 1 or even 10 to 3. But still, our legitimate concerns should have been heard. That being said, now let's talk about where we who have not voted in favor are coming from. Most importantly, this uncapped liability has got to go. You can try to shut us up or pay us off. You can try to do whatever you need to do to get the votes you need. But if you don't do anything about the uncapped liability, I guarantee I will make your lives miserable by talking to the taxpayers and the media in a big-time campaign. I did some on the dais the other day, but it will get worse."

They tried to intimidate me by saying, "You know, there are lots of other cities that want us." So I called their bluff: "Then go to Phoenix. Go to Las Vegas. I know you want to be in the Nation's Capital just as much as we want you to be here. Let's be fair to the citizens of this city who are fronting the bill for all this. You didn't need to sock it to us. And this contract really did sock it to us. And that's just not right. All of you are very rich and you are going to be made even richer by this deal. You don't need to screw us in the process. So let's sit down and talk." And we did. And things got a little better—at least then.

Major League Baseball came back with a $19 million capped liability if the stadium was not built on time, which many of us found, albeit a cap, still too high. Linda Cropp also put in the agreement that building the stadium would be contingent on securing private funding for half the cost.

Even with the deal adjusted with Council amendments which I supported, I was a no vote on the second reading of the overall deal on December 14, 2004, still due to such a large liability as well as the escalating costs. But this modified deal did pass the Council, 7 to 6, with Cropp, Allen, Ambrose, Brazil, Chavous, Evans and Orange voting yes; Catania, Fenty, Graham, Mendelson, Patterson and me voting no. However, I did vote for the Ballpark Financing Resolution that day to keep the ball rolling while the troubling aspects of the deal were being worked on.

The Mayor, though, was furious at Cropp for making changes to his deal. And Linda had a great response: "I keep hearing that we had a deal with baseball. Well, I have had a 30-year-plus deal with the citizens of this city. That deal trumps any other considerations with Major League Baseball."[245]

That's when Major League Baseball started to really play hard ball. They then rejected the Council's changes. MLB President Bob DuPuy called the legislation "totally unacceptable" that "does not reflect the agreement we signed and relied upon." MLB halted all business and promotional activities for the newly named Washington Nationals and stopped selling season tickets.

Although some editorial writers, including Colbert King and Sally Jenkins in the *Post*, expressed support for our standing up against being taken by the rich baseball owners, there was much backlash, some vicious. In Colbert King's December 18, 2004 column, he excerpted an email to Chair Cropp from a baseball supporter that included hateful racist language, which I also found to be deplorable. In Colbert's column, he put the blame for the deal on the Mayor: "Who but the politically tone deaf Williams would have gone out and negotiated a stadium financing deal that 69% of D.C. residents would reject?" And he pointed out that the Council's push-back reflected the community's sentiment. Colby even quoted longtime newscaster Jim Vance, who when learning of Major League Baseball's rejection of our deal, said, "Great. Let them go screw some other city."[246]

Mayor Williams did not speak to Cropp for several days as tensions grew. Then a week later, on December 21, 2004, a new vote was cast on a reconsidered financing bill after marathon negotiation sessions. There were some concessions, including keeping the stadium at a $535 million budget. We would continue to pursue some private financing, but the Council conceded that the building of the stadium would not be contingent on that. The Council passed the deal, 7 to 6 (with Graham, Catania, Fenty, Patterson, Mendelson and me voting no). I was still a no vote, due to my continuing worry that stadium costs would exceed that $535 million budget (with the city being solely responsible for cost overruns), the continuing large liability, as well as MLB not doing enough for our residents, like some community benefits. Even with this 7 to 6 vote, the battle was not totally over as a stadium lease agreement still needed to be negotiated.

In the meantime, though, the Nationals did play their opening season starting in the spring of 2005 at RFK Stadium. In July, the Nationals had their first gay baseball night sponsored by Team D.C., an umbrella organization of local LGBT sports teams. I was happy to attend Nationals' Night Out and was surprised that the only other elected area representative I saw at that event was Montgomery County Councilmember Howard Denis. I found it interesting that the only two regional elected officials supporting that evening with their presence were both Republicans. It appeared that *The Washington Blade* felt the same as our picture was in its next edition.[247]

In early November of 2005, three technical amendments were added to the original financing bill to correct inaccuracies. Some of us on the Council wanted to reopen that whole deal and to look at building a stadium adjacent to RFK, which could save up to $200 million, but at this stage, it was not really feasible given the vote a year earlier. I did vote to approve those amendments wanting the process at this point to go forward.[248]

In late November of 2005, a majority of us on the Council demanded a vote on the stadium lease agreement, which needed to be completed for bonds to be issued to begin stadium construction. Baseball officials and D.C. Mayoral representatives had been negotiating behind the scenes and were trying to keep the Council out of the process. But we insisted on the vote as we were worried that costs were exceeding the approved $535 million by as much as $100 million more, which the city would be responsible for at that time. For example, the $535 million did not even include the $54 million needed to pay for the financing fees on the bonds—a newly discovered expense. Not only were costs rising but transparency on actual costs was lacking—actually non-existent.

Another reason we demanded a vote on the stadium lease agreement was that in the beginning of 2005, 10 months prior, three new Councilmembers had been sworn in, and deserved to weigh in. These three new members had all successfully campaigned against the baseball deal and all defeated people who were in favor. Kwame Brown defeated Harold Brazil for an at-large position, Vincent Gray won against Kevin Chavous in Ward 7, and Mr. Comeback, Marion Barry, defeated his and my friend, Sandy Allen, for the seat in Ward 8.

And there were more unresolved issues. We were still waiting on the agreed-upon $20 million to be paid by Major League Baseball toward stadium costs. And MLB had refused to give a $24 million letter of credit for rent payment insurance in case of a terrorist attack or players' strike, which also had been agreed upon. In addition, the Council learned that the Administration had taken away $55 million from the stadium budget (I guess to make the numbers look better) which were to go to Metro upgrades and infrastructure, promising to get the money from the federal government and private funding instead. This was a go-to promise on various occasions which never seemed to materialize. But this one really scared me because large crowds could cause injuries or death if the Metro station was not expanded. "We can't just depend on the feds or find a buddy to call from heaven. That's irresponsible," I was quoted as saying on this issue in The Washington Post.[249] And all this was in addition to the escalating costs.

On December 19, 2005, I laid out my thoughts on the city bearing cost overruns in a public statement:

"As a Sunday Washington Post article pointed out, of the last nine publicly funded stadium deals, six had cost overruns ranging from $30 million to $115 million. However, only one of those deals required the public to foot the entire bill for the cost overruns. I do not want the District to be the second. ... We must get this right. If we do not, we jeopardize our hard-earned financial stability and could lose our limited Home Rule. It happened before and, unfortunately, it could happen again. I, for one, will not be complicit in bringing back a federally imposed control board. If a no vote from me means baseball walks—and I hope it won't but it might—I know I will be among those who will be blamed. But I would rather be blamed now for being responsible than be blamed later for being irresponsible."[250]

Eventually, the Council was successful, aided by Linda Cropp, in getting a vote on the lease agreement for the stadium, which took place on February 6, 2006. We on the Council rejected the lease agreement, 8 to 5. Voting in favor were Cropp, Evans, Ambrose, Orange and Patterson. Voting to reject were me, Fenty, Graham, Catania, Mendelson, Barry, Gray and Brown. We eight no votes knew full well we were putting the future of the sport in the city on the brink, but we refused to be on the hook for potentially endless cost overruns. And we knew voting no was our only negotiating tool. The lack of a cap on burgeoning costs plagued us the most, but we also wanted a lower liability cap, and more public benefits as well.

The tense negotiations went into high gear after we voted the lease down. *The Washington Post* described the scene: "'I'm very, very disappointed,' Williams said. 'I beg and implore the Council to reconsider the deal, even tonight.'" City Administrator Robert Bobb was running back and forth among Councilmembers to get a deal that would work. "He huddled with Carol Schwartz (R-At Large), who had also voted no."[251]

There were three or four who could not be swayed. However, four of us could be, and knew this was our shot at getting the best deal possible. It was important we hold this team of Councilmembers Barry, Brown, Gray and myself together for leverage. The Administration was trying to "buy" Barry and Gray off separately with promises such as not closing schools or doing a recreation center in their Ward, and they only needed two of the four of us to have a win. I said, "We have to be strong. We can't let them pick us off. Here is our chance to get some things the city needs."[252] The guys could not have agreed more, and we did hold together.

We took another vote close to 1:00 a.m. on February 7, 2006 once an absolute cost cap of $611 million was put in place with airtight language, which said that the owners would pay any cost over that $611 million. We set in stone a much better liability cap, which MLB officials were furious about, but then agreed to. That part stated that if the stadium did not open on time, now the city would be liable for just $5.3 million (the cost of a year's rent at RFK) instead of the $19 million they had agreed to earlier. And we were able to negotiate some other sweeteners. We got a kids' baseball academy across the river, paid for by MLB, as a citywide benefit. Vince was instrumental in this and made sure it was in Ward 7. We also wanted more free tickets for our inner-city youth for the games—and we got them as well.

I finally thought we were at the point where I could vote enthusiastically for baseball—and in good conscience. We did the best we could for the city and taxpayers while negotiating against a monopoly. The stadium lease contract passed 10 to 3—with the four of us (Barry, Brown, Gray and me) as well as Mendelson now in the yes column, but only after we made important changes for the city. *The Washington Post* described the outcome: "It was a remarkable ending to what had been a fairly grim day of arm-twisting, name-calling and frantic messaging about the murky fate of a stadium lease agreement with Major League Baseball."[253] We five originally no votes that day made a big difference. And I am so proud of each and every one of us. And I'm glad, in the end, we were able to vote yes.

On March 7, 2006, the Council approved the construction contract by a vote of 9 to 4 with me voting in favor. (Phil Mendelson joined the other three in voting no.) Right afterwards, Major League Baseball signed off on it as well. It was done. Baseball was truly back in the Nation's Capital. Construction broke ground on May 4, 2006 and the Nationals continued to play in RFK until the new stadium was opened.

(Interestingly and disgustingly, Mayor Williams received tickets to the games from the owners right away and was told to make sure that he shared the tickets with the Council. But Tony refused to give any tickets to the Council—not even to those members who had supported the baseball deal with no changes from day one. Unfortunately, this kind of disrespect from him was legendary and made it hard to have a decent working relationship.)

The Lerner family, developers who live in the area and have been behind projects like White Flint and Tyson's Corner, became the new owners. The city paid a lot, and the growth of the Anacostia waterfront area that we hoped the stadium would spark stalled for years due to the economy, but is now finally happening big time. We have done well with baseball. We get a small percentage of the tickets sales and some of the concession taxes. And most would agree that the team, the Washington Nationals, has been good for D.C.—and we for them.

In fact, in the last two years, the Nationals have been the National League East champions. This year, I hope the Nationals go all the way to become the *national* champions.

Those stadium negotiations remain one of my proudest moments in office. I know I was helpful, along with others, in modifying the original deal and leading us to something better.

I've always liked the behind-the-scenes nuts and bolts. When it comes to making sure the city is protected, I become like a mother hen, for better or worse. In fact, Gregory McCarthy, who is Vice President of the Nationals, told me for a while afterwards that every time he saw Bud Selig (who just got elected to the Baseball Hall of Fame), Bud never failed to ask, "How's that Carol Schwartz?"

That March 7th evening of the final vote and after all was said and done to bring baseball back to D.C., I held a celebratory cocktail party at my apartment. The Mayor, the Lerner family, the CFO, the Councilmembers, the City Administrator, and many others who were part of the process were in attendance. I felt it was a great way to bring us all together civilly, especially after all of the tension that had previously gone on. It worked, and was a fun, relaxing, and truly celebratory evening for everyone.

CHAPTER 38

A New Council Session Begins

I was sworn in again for my at-large seat on January 2, 2005. In my statement, I called for us to focus on voting rights and affordable housing. How sad that here we are, over 12 years later, with no real progress on the voting rights issue, even though our last two Mayors have made it a priority. And affordable housing is better due to the efforts of this Mayor and the last as well, but still has a way to go, especially in the face of our increased gentrification.

I decided to do something a little different with Johnny gone for this 2005 swearing in. Normally he or my children came. But this time, I wanted to have all of my staff (or at least as many as I could get) from my years in elected office stand with me on the stage as I was sworn in. I had become close to most of them during their time with me and I wanted them to get recognition for their service as well. Dozens showed up and stood with me. It certainly was different. It was also a great reunion and lots of fun. The audience seemed to appreciate it too.

The incoming Councilmembers were sworn in that day: Kwame Brown, Vince Gray and Marion Barry, who was entering his third time on the Council (1975, 1993 and now 2005). Although I was very sad to see my dear friend Sandy Allen go, who was also a key ally on a lot of the issues I cared about, I knew that my old friend and rival Marion would be an ally on some, as well.

Speaking of issues, I continued to try to press the federal government on just causes, and here's one: After Bush's second inauguration, a few weeks after ours, I wrote the President urging the Administration to reimburse the District for the full cost of his inauguration, instead of his requiring the District to dip into our Homeland Security funds—to the tune of $11 million—to pay for it. I tried to appeal to fairness as well as federal precedent by writing, "The alternative could result in the District being unable to fully respond in the event of a terrorist attack, or else raiding local funds, hurting residents who depend on receiving the most basic housing, health, education and other services from the city." (I hope and think the letter was successful but I'm not really sure.)

Light and Fun Coverage

At the start of the new session, in January of 2005, *The Washington Post* profiled the Councilmembers, and asked us fun questions. One was: "What is something people don't know about you?" My answer: "I play a mean game of ping pong." Another

question: "Which celebrity would play you in a movie?" I so
wanted to say Heidi Klum. Picturing myself being played by a tall,
thin, gorgeous blonde with a German accent struck me as hilari-
ous. But then I thought people would not know who Heidi Klum
is (as *Project Runway* was brand new), or worse, they may think I
was being serious and thus, must be nuts. I also thought of Jackée
from *227* (a TV show set in D.C.), who my friend Patrice said I
walk like. But I was afraid people would think I was trying to pass
for black. So instead I went with Kirstie Alley from *Cheers*.[254]

Also around this time, *Washingtonian Magazine* did a feature in
which they asked several local celebrities to send in a prom photo
and caption. Of course, my parents would never even think about
taking a prom picture. So I asked the publication if I could send a
freshman-year college photo of me and my boyfriend Ivan at a
dance instead. They said sure. In the photo, my long hair was done
up in the best early-1960s beehive I could manage—it nearly hit
the ceiling. It made me at five feet three and a half inches look like
I was six feet tall. In the caption, I said, "I thought I looked good
in the photo, but now I realize my hair should have been higher."

Welcome Back, Marion Barry

We took the official Council portrait in March of 2005. Spirits
were up. Marion was running late (what else is new?) but when he
arrived, he said, "I want to be next to Carol" and did. I retorted, "I
want to be 19 and thin for this!"[255] There was good camaraderie
then, and Marion always brought a burst of energy.

Before I bought that understated Pontiac Trans Am I told you
about before, I had gotten a year earlier another old used car,
which I still have and love, when it works. (Actually I love it even
when it doesn't.) Marion saw the car, a 1994 Jaguar, and said, "Oh,
I forgot how much I love those old Jaguars." Not long after, parked
close to mine in front of the Wilson Building was a near replica.

An aside (if you're not interested in cars, skip this part): I have
two cars because they are old and in the shop most of the time—
one very classy and the other, not so much—and because my kids
can have a car when they visit from New York and California. And
I had never driven anything but an American-made car and was
proud of it. But in 2004, when I was helping my daughters look for
a car as their 1988 car had died, I came upon the rear end of an old
Jaguar and my heart started pounding. I thought at the time, "Oh,
if only a man would affect me in such a way these days." Anyway,
I asked what year it was—"1994"—and now figured the mileage

was really high—"only 37,000"—and then just knew it would be really expensive—it was "$12,500." I said, "I'll give you $11,000" and drove it away, giving my kids my dad's 1992 Buick. (So now all of us had cars that barely ran—but at least it was better than their 1988 car that didn't run at all.)

Now let's leave cars and go back to Marion. One of my favorite times with him—which was probably not his—was the following: On a trip around 2006, as part of Mayor Tony Williams's delegation to South Africa, Marion happened to be staying in the room next door to mine. The first night in Johannesburg, there was quite a bit of noise emanating from Marion's room very late so it was obvious that some of the group had gathered there. I decided to go over and join in. (Now I know what you're thinking—and I did lead you astray to keep your interest.)

The real activity amidst the laughter and talking was a card game called bid whist. Marion was playing with Stan Jackson, a high-level government official, as his partner against Diane Williams (Tony's wife) and Vince Orange (a fellow Councilmember). I had never seen the game, but I enjoyed watching the four of them play. It was also fun listening to their trash talk back and forth and getting to know the younger staff members there.

The next night we gathered again. But this time, Diane said that she would have to leave right away as Tony had said, "Tonight's my night." The three guys were really upset as none of the young people played. I then said, "I've never played bid whist, but I do play bridge and this is sort of similar; and I got a gist of it watching last night, so I'm willing to be your fourth." Marion and Stan, who had played together for years and were quite good at it, were very pleased to continue. Vince Orange, on the other hand, though pleased to go on, was quite nervous about having a new partner—especially one who had never played the game before.

As we started to play, Vince would make sure he had the highest bid so he got to play the hand instead of me. I caught on pretty quickly and then began to overbid my partner so I could play the hand. And we beat the hell out of the well-known champions, Marion and Stan. Boy, were those three guys shocked—and after that, I got new-found respect in a whole new category. And they saw I was a pretty good trash talker myself. (And by the way, I never played cards again with them as I decided it would be better to quit while I was ahead.)

The next day, we landed in Capetown and were supposed to go directly from the airport to a concert by Jay Z, where we were to to watch from backstage. Unfortunately, my card partner's luggage did not arrive and being loyal colleagues, we waited with him and missed the concert. (I'd never do that again.) When we got to the hotel, the Mayor and Diane and the other Councilmembers went up to the VIP lounge for food and drink. I stayed in the lobby with the staff as we were planning to go out and see the town—as none of us had been there before.

While getting organized in the lobby, in walks Jay Z who I immediately approached in spite of a security guy, even taller and bigger than he is. We shook hands (and his were the softest I ever touched) and I told him we were sorry to miss his concert—as if he knew about us. Two seconds later, here comes Beyonce—absolutely breathtakingly magnificent looking. I was thrilled beyond belief thinking, "What could possibly be better than this, being here in Capetown, South Africa with A-listers, and the luck to be in the lobby at this moment?" As I turned to walk out the door to the waiting van, in front of me walking in was a statuesque woman in stunning garb with an entourage following her. It was none other than Winnie Mandela. Of course I backed up and politely nodded to her. That made it even better. And the VIP people missed it all. I'm glad I stuck with the staff.

Target of the Times

Councilmembers had always had the right to park on the street when on official business, whether they had been appointed by the President of the United States pre-Home Rule or starting in 1974, elected by the citizenry. This parking ability by elected officials is true in every jurisdiction I know of. However, in 2002, Mayor Williams's Director of the Department of Public Works, Leslie Hoteling, reacting to a question that had been raised about Councilmembers' parking, decided we could no longer do so.

Councilmembers, for the most part, drive their own cars and pay for their own gas, even when on official business. We did have the opportunity to use government vehicles, which come with gas, but in my 16 years on the Council, I never once used a government vehicle. I think most other Councilmembers didn't take advantage of that opportunity very much either.

And besides, the 535 members of Congress in the Senate and House have parking privileges in D.C., as do many executives in the Mayor's administration. But after being unable to move the Director from her adamant stance against following the practice of decades (who was probably being directed by the Mayor), and as Chair of the relevant committee, I took it on and sponsored an amendment to enable our 13 Councilmembers to have the ability to park while on official duties. This was restricted to available curb space, and we could not park in loading zones, during rush hour on restricted streets, and near firehouses or fire hydrants.

During the vote on that amendment, 10 were in favor with Phil Mendelson, Kathy Patterson and Sharon Ambrose voting no.[256] Interestingly, soon thereafter, I was driving to an event happening during rush hour at 14th and K Sts., N.W. and there on 14th St., blocking traffic during rush hour—a no-no even under the Council's more flexible rules he voted against—was then at-large member Phil Mendelson's car. As soon as I legally parked mine, I went in and told him, "I just called the police about your car"—but smiled after he gave a worried look. And not long after that, at an event in Georgetown, I passed as Kathy was getting into her car, parked at the corner and jutting out into P St. with her Councilmember tags clearly displayed. I just said, "Hi, Kathy." I wanted to say, "Nice space," but from the look on her face I didn't have to.

Then in 2006, *The Washington Times* went on a rampage with article after article and even editorials lambasting me for pushing for the Council's "unwarranted parking indulgences." I always knew the culprit was Wes Pruden, Editor-in-Chief at *The Times*, who lived in the Kalorama/Adams Morgan area near me and who obviously did not have a garage space. It was a real obsession on his part, and I am *not* exaggerating when I say that there had to be at least 20 mentions of my name and this issue that spanned several years. (In fact, Phil Mendelson recalled it to me recently.)

I tried to let it go, but after about the 10th incident, I started writing letters to the editor, using reasonable arguments to put the matter into perspective: the D.C. Council gave themselves parking flexibility that the 535 members of Congress gave themselves more than 50 years ago; Councilmembers are not using government-paid vehicles but are driving ourselves in our own vehicles, while buying our own gas; we often have multiple engagements to attend each day and evening on official business, many of them at the same time, so it can be impossible to keep that schedule without some accommodation—and every other jurisdiction allows their elected Councilmembers this type of flexibility.[257]

But it was for naught. His onslaughts continued—until his time at the *Times* was over, which was right before I left the Council.

Taken to Task, Times and Again

I had more than my share of issues with *The Washington Times*. This was ironic since I was probably the only person in local political life in D.C. who had had her own home-delivered-paid-for-by-me-personally subscription to the *Times* since it started in 1982. But anytime I did something they deemed wrong, they were quick to attack; anything they thought right, they either didn't bother to find out about it or chose to ignore it. Yes, we elected officials are not perfect. But the media needs to be more taken to task for their own agendas, blind spots, and for the occasions when they are flat-out wrong. Here is what I wrote the *Times* editorial board on November 3, 2005:

> "The commendation of the Council's swift action to correct the confusion concerning the District's DUI laws in *The Washington Times*'s October 22nd editorial was appreciated. However, I continue to be baffled how every time I do something you do not like, my name is in the paper ... But when I step in to take the lead to address issues such as the DUI matter—something on which I acted promptly to clear up and minimize further embarrassment and damage ... [my name is nowhere to be found] ... A little credit every now and then from the *Times* when it is deserved would be appreciated.
>
> Then, a little over a week later, I read the lead editorial ... in the Sunday, October 30th *Times*, in which you discussed the plan put forth by Education Committee Chair Kathy Patterson to raise business taxes and postpone the Council's approved rollback of residents' income taxes in order to spend $1 billion on school facility construction and improvements.
>
> The editorial states that '... Carol Schwartz ... and other veterans should be telling Ms. Patterson hands off.'"[258]

Imagine, calling me out on that issue above, which I'm not even responsible for. But in this case, I had already taken care of the damn thing two weeks earlier by calling it out and helping to get Kathy to table the issue. The newspaper was obviously too busy writing their editorial to check the news. And by the way, we did find the money for schools as well.

Finally, a Department of the Environment

In 2005, I pushed through legislation to approve a separate Department of the Environment. My goal was to provide a coordinated voice on environmental issues and to ensure that the Department received cabinet-level status. Before then, environmental issues had been spread throughout the government—some with public works, some in the health department—but receiving not much attention from anywhere. This new Department worked with all levels of government on relevant issues, and the environment got the status and attention it deserved. I was very proud to have finally brought it about, along with a longtime employee of mine, Adam Maier, who was my then Committee Clerk.

For other work I did while chairing the Committee on Public Works and the Environment, I received some awards: the Legislative Award in 2005 from the Cable Telecommunications Association of Maryland, Delaware and the District of Columbia, and WASA's Board of Directors Leadership Award in 2006.

A Small Effort to Help

In early September of 2005, some evacuees from Hurricane Katrina were brought from New Orleans to D.C. We greeted the arrivals who were being housed at the D.C. Armory. I and others immediately got to work trying to do what we could for their recovery. The huge clothing drive I had not only envisioned but had begun to organize, including getting a space for free, turned out not to be feasible. Instead, I ended up going to Hecht's department store and they came through with a truckload of donated items, which my staff and I were pleased to deliver to the individuals and families at the Armory. There but for the grace of God go I.

Taxi Tension

Improving our cab service is an issue I knew needed tackling. In 1985, I proposed changes to the "Taxicab Establishment Act" because of the total control given to the Mayor and the general lack of public confidence in the system—and often for good reason. The bill allowed for five of the public Commission members to be appointed by the Council Committee with oversight—instead of all the Commissioners appointed by the Mayor—and for the Council to approve the Chair and the removal of any member.

Then in 1986, I joined with Councilmember Betty Ann Kane on a bill that established criminal penalties for driving without a valid license with fines up to $500. It also called for mandatory revocations of permits for cab owners who let their cabs be driven by illegal drivers. The legislation went nowhere. I then brought forward the same bill the next year and this time, Betty Ann joined me. Still nothing. But at least this time we got a shout-out from a *Washington Post* editorial on April 17, 1987, entitled, "Bad Cabs:

Does the Council Care?" which said, "Maybe this year, given evidence of mounting outrage among honest cab drivers as well as the general public—enough Councilmembers will sense the desperate need for tough action and will insist upon enacting Mrs. Schwartz's proposal ... Schwartz notes that this is the same bill that Democrat Kane originally proposed; the only thing different this time is that the situation on the streets has clearly worsened."[259]

There was also lots of justified anger at cab drivers for refusing certain customers going certain places. When I came back on the Council in 1997 and then two years later, chaired the Committee on Public Works and the Environment, it was a fight that I took on with full force. I had great empathy for those who were passed by. I received many calls and letters from them, and I witnessed the problem firsthand starting back in the '80s. I had a staff member, my Legal Counsel, who lived in Southeast and wore a suit every day. But he could never get a cab on Pennsylvania Ave. outside the Wilson Building. I would have to go out to hail the cab and then bring him forward. How sad is that? And many of the drivers who passed him by were the same color as he was.

In 2004, following my recommendation, the Chair of the Taxicab Commission included funds for diversity training in the 2005 budget. We also instituted a fine of $250 for refusing a passenger, which doubled for a second offense, and ultimately revocation of the taxi license. I had concerns about cab driver safety too. So I established and put in money to start a revolving low-interest-loan fund so drivers could afford to get protective windows and an emergency alert device on the roof of their cab.

By the way, I was pleased to see Mayor Gray finally tackle the appearance and uniformity of our taxicabs. He appointed Ron Linton in 2011 as Chair of the Taxicab Commission, and changes were made. Today, thanks to them, we look good as a city with those orangey red and gray cabs which all take credit cards and give printed receipts. I think even the cab drivers are glad as they can at least be somewhat competitive with the outside unregulated groups. And recently, the Bowser Administration and its Department of For-Hire Vehicles have said that more competitive improvements are coming, including new apps and digital meters.

Speaking of Taxicabs ...

... you should use some, or else all of you Uber riders out there are one day going to wake up, after having put all the standard taxicabs out of business, and there will be nothing but Uber-type transportation. You will then be constantly in a state of surge pricing, and you will have no one to blame but yourself. I know that standard taxis are not perfect, and having competition like Uber and Lyft has been helpful in improving them, such as taking credit cards, nicer looking vehicles, and being able to use an app.

Remember that taxicabs are regulated while the others don't have the same requirements. The taxis have to pay a fee to drive on the streets while the others don't. The taxi drivers have to take a course to know where they are going instead of having someone untrained dangerously looking at or listening to directions. The taxicab companies are also required to have a certain number of their vehicles be accessible for the disabled, and D.C. law requires that taxicab drivers have background checks, including fingerprinting. Cab drivers also pay taxes on their income. (Now I know these alternative transportation companies are reporting income now due to new requirements, but it had to be forced on them.)

Regarding the fingerprinting issue, an article in *The Washington Post* on December 24, 2016 reported on Uber threatening to leave Maryland due to its new rules and referred to a California lawsuit that alleged "Uber mislead the public with claims that it had 'the best in the industry' background checks." The upshot was that "Uber agreed to pay $25 million in fines and [to] stop referring to its background checks as superior ..."[260]

And for those who think that Uber and Lyft are better when it comes to discrimination, think again. As reported in *The Washington Post* on December 28, 2016, Senator Al Franken, on November 2nd, "voiced concern after an independent study found black riders in two cities faced longer wait times and higher ride cancellation rates." In addition, "... Franken took aim at Uber for altering its privacy settings to track riders' movement for several minutes after their ride concludes."[261] I could go on and on as the damning articles keep coming. Instead, I advise you to take a few minutes away from "calling" an Uber to read those articles.

Regulations *are* important—and this non-level playing field is unfair. Most of you would agree, I'm sure, if you just stop to think about it. And make no mistake, when it's just the alternatives left, history has shown they often merge or there is collusion on pricing. So I would suggest that you split up your use between the old and the new. Or otherwise, the cab companies and taxicab drivers will be totally pushed out of business, and then your prices will go up—way up—and your service, with no real regulation and little competition, will go down—way down.

My 60th Birthday Party

My dear friend Tay threw me
a wonderful birthday lunch.

Ann, Ardith, Corn, Hilary and David
watch me visiting with a gorilla.

William and Alda Douglas Proctor
at the evening party I had
at the Cosmos Club

Herb Miller, Tom Kaufman and David
Myerson, who did the eulogies at David's
memorial, at a happier occasion

Colleagues Charlene Drew Jarvis,
John Ray and Jack Evans

Hilary, Elsie, Bunny and Ivan

Friend Linda Cropp reading a Council
resolution honoring Johnny's 60th

With kids at campaign office

Volunteers for the 2002 campaign

A true honor to receive the
Whitney M. Young
Community Service
Award from the Greater
Washington
Urban League, led by
Maudine Cooper
(who later became a friend)

2002 Mayoral concession

Johnny and I dancing
on New Year's Eve
at friends' country club

Precious Gaby,
a rescue, who we
adopted at the
end of 2004

My beloved brother
Johnny loved every
joyous moment.

CHAPTER 39

Open for Business

I took on another fight to keep D.C. open for our hospitality business, though it was an uphill battle, my specialty. Now please go with me to the early to mid-2000s. Even I today would be on a different page. But back then, we were just getting more bars and restaurants to finally open in the city and gaining some vitality. It was nothing like today; it was a very different time. And in this case, at least Anthony Williams and I were right in step together.

An all-out smoking ban in workplaces was on the table, including for restaurants and bars, which was being pushed nationally by the deep-pocketed Robert Wood Johnson Foundation in New Jersey. In September of 2003, Kathy Patterson and Adrian Fenty introduced that smoke-free workplace legislation and only Phil Mendelson co-sponsored. The rest of us, 10 in number, shared a similar concern about hurting our one thriving industry, hospitality. I had quit smoking for years at this point and did not like even being around it, so it was certainly not a personal preference.

The legislation was assigned to my Committee on Public Works and the Environment, and I eventually held a public hearing. I was expecting the testimony to be slanted toward the advocates of the bill, but instead most spoke fervently against the ban, including many restaurant and bar workers. The same proved to be true in the subsequent hearing on the issue. This was surprising to me, because I always joked that most people in D.C. are against the death penalty—except for cigarette smokers. I actually said that exact same thing at one of the hearings.

To me, an all-out ban was extreme and hurtful to our city, but I also shared the concern about the health and ambience issues of the proponents. Therefore, I introduced legislation in December of 2003 to incentivize new and existing establishments to go totally smoke-free by giving them tax credits for doing so and to ensure that they remained smoke-free, there would be periodic inspections and subsequent penalties for violations. There were seven co-sponsors of my bill—Linda Cropp, Sandy Allen, Harold Brazil, David Catania, Kevin Chavous, Jack Evans and Vincent Orange—and it signaled that a compromise on this issue in the future might be in order if the eight of us stayed together.

Then on March 10, 2005, a year and a half later, basically the same legislation for an all-out smoking ban reappeared, co-introduced by the former three as well as Vince Gray and Kwame Brown. It was again assigned to my Committee which I'm sure was done in hopes I would bury it, which pleased the eight-member majority on the Council for the same reason as before—to avoid hurting our hospitality business.

A Falling Out

Back in 1997, David Catania, who I hardly knew, called and asked me to support him for the Council in the December 2nd special election. But I declined because my policy had always been not to support anyone against a Council colleague. A special election was needed as Linda Cropp had become Chair in her own earlier special election following the untimely death of David Clarke. And because she was an at-large member when she ran for Chair and won, a vacancy on the Council was created. Under election rules, the Party (in this case Democratic) could appoint someone to fill the vacancy until a special election could be held within 90 days. The Party appointed Arrington Dixon from Ward 8, who had formally been Chair and a Ward 4 Councilmember.

Arrington ran for the permanent seat as did several other Democrats. In special elections, there is no primary, and therefore people from minority parties can run as well. David did run as a Republican; and with the Democrats split and a 7% voter turnout, he won. He came on the Council mad at me because he said he had done some work in my '94 Mayoral campaign and I had not helped him in return. He kind of lashed into me about that, and I told him that my policy had always been not to support anyone against an existing colleague because we were such a small body and we needed to be able to work together after an election.

Within a fairly short period of time, though, David and I did become friends. In fact, we were pals and hung out occasionally as well as talked on the phone. With David, I had finally met my match in the talking department, and I enjoyed his sense of humor, although often a little harsh for me in a Don Rickles way. He was also smart, which I appreciated. David was my kids' age and he did make me feel like a substitute mother. (He had unfortunately lost his own several years earlier.) I later learned that he did the same with other older females on the Council, including Linda Cropp, Sandy Allen, Sharon Ambrose and Kathy Patterson. In the early 2000s, I held a birthday party/fundraiser for him in my apartment. Later, he said that he named a cat after me—Morty Schwartz.[262]

Also back in 2000, even though I had never contributed to a candidate in a Presidential election before, due to David's arm twisting, our being friends, and my wanting to be helpful to David, I agreed to contribute $2,000 to George W. Bush. David was a big bundler for that campaign and raised over $50,000 for Bush that year, at least enough to get him and his partner invited to the Bush's ranch in Crawford, Texas. And I never even got a thank you note from either of the guys—David or George.

One night in 2004, David generously shared the results of a poll he was aware of—which I still have— funded by the D.C. Chamber of Commerce. It had included the names of every elected official in D.C., and polled only likely Democratic voters. It revealed that I had tied Marion for the highest name recognition at 90% and that I led the field with a 75% favorability rating. (Adrian Fenty was second with 65%, and David had a rating of over 50% as well.) David said to me, "If you can't get elected Mayor here as a Republican with those kind of numbers, no one can." I knew then that he was looking for a way out. And George Bush certainly accommodated him a few months later.

In May of 2004, David spoke out strongly against Bush's stance favoring an amendment banning same-sex marriage and said he would not be voting for the President. In response, the D.C. GOP stripped David of his Delegate spot at the Convention. I did agree with David's position against the ban. But I resigned as a Delegate mainly in sympathy and support of David, and said so at the time in a letter to Betsy Werronen, Chair of the D.C. Republican Committee, on May 27, 2004:

> "We have had numerous discussions of late regarding my Council colleague, David Catania, and his response to the President's call for an amendment to the Constitution that would prohibit same-sex marriage. As you know, this proposed amendment has caused significant discomfort with many in our local Party, including myself who find it odious and unnecessary. The President's position on this may have placated a certain segment of the National Party, but he has alienated others. For David, as a loyal Republican who raised tens of thousands of dollars for the President for both his first election and for his reelection effort, the amendment issue has been particularly troublesome and his reaction to it has been both emotional and understandable.

> I have expressed to you my strong feeling that David, as a duly elected official and as a leader in our local Party, should be treated with some deference. I have also said that his quarrel with the President should not affect his stature within the D.C. GOP, nor should it diminish his role at the 2004 Republican National

Convention. You obviously disagreed, and have now decided not to certify him as a Delegate.

David has been an enormous asset to us, providing able and energetic leadership. I am proud to have him both as a colleague and as a friend.

Because of my personal and professional relationship with David, and because I feel that he was not treated with the respect he deserves, I hereby resign as a Delegate to the 2004 Convention and decline your appointment to the Rules Committee."

I received several letters commending my action of dropping out of being a Delegate in support of David, which was nice. And then I received this one from a registered Republican in D.C.: "Now, if you would just quit the Republican Party, you would make an honest woman of yourself (e.g., Republicans don't join the looney left and whine about the name of the Redskins football team.)" I wrote back: "I take seriously the notion of a "Big Tent," and continue to believe that the Republican Party should be open to people with a range of views. Apparently, you disagree." (See, I told you I answered all my correspondence.)

Then in September of 2004, four months later, David changed his registration to Independent.

Regarding David, I must admit that by 2005 (and having nothing to do with his registration), I started to pull away a bit. We sat next to each other on the dais and he would chat a lot. Some of that included talking about personal matters pertaining to others. One instance in particular really disturbed me. A fellow colleague had told me confidentially about a marital separation, which I had never mentioned to anyone. Soon thereafter, David, who was quite friendly with the person, started telling me intimate details about the separation. That certainly was a wake-up call to me. If he was talking in such detail about other people, maybe he was doing that about me as well. And he was always asking about my social life—who I was dating and what I was doing. (And in those days, I actually had something to talk about.) So I started to become more closed in my responses and not as available socially as I had been.

We did not have many professional conflicts, though. I did have some issues with the way he talked to witnesses from the dais, which sometimes verged on abusive. I would counsel him that there were ways to be strong and tough without humiliating people. Otherwise, we were usually on the same page as both of us were fiscally conservative and more liberal socially.

When the smoking ban legislation first came up in 2003, David and I were in full agreement. Then when it was reintroduced in 2005, there again, David and I saw eye to eye. Both of us were concerned about the bill's effects on restaurants and bars, which really were an economic engine in a city in need of one at that time. He constantly expressed his wish for me to "keep it buried"—as did many other members—in my Committee.

(Again, you must realize as you read this whole long smoking ban discussion that we are talking about 13 years ago when the movement for smoking bans started. And many of us then were civil libertarians, especially when it came to a legal activity, the need for economic vitality, and choice. Today, I, as a non-smoker for 16 years, am very glad to be surrounded by smoke-free environments. But I still feel that the position I took then was best for the reasons stated.)

In May of 2005, David and my relationship hit a crossroads. It was over earmarks. As mentioned often, I've always been a watchdog of taxpayer dollars. One of the things I've fought against was sole-source contracts. We on the Council legitimately took on the Williams Administration time and again for bypassing procurement rules to give non-competitive (sole-source) contracts/deals.

And make no mistake, earmarks are sole-source contracts. Earmarks are line-items in the budget that give taxpayers' money to favored people, companies or groups without a competitive process. I understand wanting to give money to accomplish worthy things. Then we should put out a Request for Proposal (RFP) and get competitive bids to accomplish those worthy things, and not just give away the money with no process. It appears to me too much like, "Hey Buddy, come and get it."

And some feel the same. For instance, Colbert King later wrote in his 2008 column, "What D.C.'s Elves Do with Your Taxes": "Earmarks help [politicians] stay in office ... they can help favored groups without worrying about merit or the competitive process. These acts of generosity often get repaid through votes and campaign contributions."[263]

On May 9, 2005, during our Fiscal Year 2006 budget deliberations, there was going to be an administrative, closed-door meeting of the Council where we would discuss the various committees' budget submissions before voting on them. As usual, I was up most of the night, and this time not in the office but at home. I was reading committee budget reports, including their mark-ups, which did not come to us until about 5:00 p.m. as I was leaving the office. While reading through each that night, I noticed no-bid grants (earmarks) in David's Committee on Health budget—nearly $14 million worth of them—given out mostly in increments of $200,000 to $500,000.[264]

I remember thinking at the time, "How interesting—and hypocritical!" Just that day, I had watched David light into Robert Bobb, the City Administrator, at a public hearing because Robert had given out a sole-source contract of about $250,000. It was for an activity related to the new baseball stadium and was given to someone Robert knew from Oakland, who had been instrumental in getting the stadium opened there. David went on and on with his attack—and no one was better at that. In this case it was a twofer, hitting at baseball while simultaneously expressing his horror at even the thought of sole-source contracts.

The next day, at the May 9th Council administrative meeting, I asked to be called on right after the Chair opened the meeting. I said, "I read every report last night and early this morning. I was very disturbed to see, sort of buried in one committee's report, $13 to $14 million worth of earmarks." We were behind closed doors. I didn't mention David's name, nor the committee, nor did I look at him. I went on to say, "We constantly and legitimately give Mayor Williams hell about his sole-source contracts. Earmarks are just that—sole-source contracts."

The minute I mentioned the nearly $14 million earmarks, David stared at me with what could only be described as blood-curdling hatred. Then he just went off. As reported in *The Washington Post* on May 26th, David "blew up at Schwartz. Then he turned dramatically to Councilmember Kathy Patterson (D-Ward 3), a leading proponent of the smoking ban [he had been against] ... Catania told Patterson: Get that ban bill ready and send it to his committee! He'd move it out."

It was obvious that Mr. "Keep It Buried" did that just to get even with me because I had the audacity to question his close to $14 million worth of earmarks. The same *Post* article expressed surprise at his changing his mind on the smoking ban because the year before, David had even urged the D.C. Elections Board to reject a ballot measure for the ban. In spite of his private expressions to me and his public ones to the Elections Board, in the *Post* article, when asked about his change of heart, he claimed, "'Frankly, I had been deferring to Councilwoman Schwartz.'... But 'as soon as I felt that respect for a chairman's prerogatives was not being reciprocated, I felt I didn't need to be restrained anymore.'"[265] How nice to have such power over him! And what about David's going to the Election Board to get them to reject a ballot measure for the ban? I hadn't even gone that far myself.

Despite David's petulant outburst, at the meeting I continued to discuss the important matter at hand—the near $14 million worth of earmarks in 2005 money, so over $17 million today. I noted that a few individual earmarks had been done over the years for revitalization purposes, but never anything like this and never just by one committee. I spoke against this wholesale giveaway, hoping we wouldn't allow it in this fashion. Instead I urged that the needs emphasized by the Health Committee report be pushed up to the Executive with money attached so that they could be fulfilled by the competitive procurement process. Chair Cropp concurred with my concerns. It was then decided that an amendment be put into the budget legislation asserting that the earmarks would be only for one year and would have to go through D.C.'s procurement process, which did have an exception for sole-source but only under certain conditions.

As soon as I got back to my office, I received countless calls and emails from all of the organizations who were the beneficiaries of David's multi-million-dollar largesse. He obviously had done a mass email, telling them I was trying to take away their money. I told the many who contacted me that I was trying to make sure that we abided by the law and not to take it personally.

And as a result of my exercising fiscal prudence which was not unusual for me, not only did David give me a look that could kill, blow up big time at me, change his mind on the smoking ban, and sic his pals on me, he also did not speak to me for a few years. Literally, did not speak to me. I would pass him in the hall and he would not say a word. It was crazy. (But I understand that this is not unusual for him in that he has done it to others before and since.) At least I didn't have to hear intimate details about people's personal lives any more.

He continued, though, to talk about me in his own inimitable snarky way—sometimes even doing caricatured drawings of me. During administrative meetings, he would say to others such things as what I heard him say to Sharon Ambrose (it was always loud enough for me to hear): "Look at Carol's hair," and proceeded to say something negative about it. And I always thought it was my best feature. Oh well ...

Back to the Ban

After David's blow-up in the closed-door meeting on May 9th, where he turned to Kathy Patterson and said, "Now you've got your smoke-free bill," it was immediately re-written as a health bill and referred to David's Committee on Health. It was all over but the shouting. I worried, though, as it was not the right time for such overreach.

By 2005, only Montgomery County, Maryland in our entire metropolitan region had banned smoking in restaurants and bars. I could just envision patrons wishing to smoke, or wanting to hang out with friends who did, simply crossing the line into other places in Maryland or anywhere in Northern Virginia, and thus giving their expendable dollars to those jurisdictions. And my vision was based on reality.

The Washington Post reported on November 14, 2003 that bar and restaurant patrons were leaving Montgomery County in droves to patronize establishments—many of them in the District—where they could smoke. According to the *Post* article, smaller to medium-sized Montgomery County restaurants and bars (other than large family-style chains) had lost an average of 30% of their business on weekdays and 50% of their business on weekends after implementation of the smoking ban. So the fear was real. *The Washington Blade* echoed that feeling with its headline: "Gay Clubs Fear Devastating Impact of D.C.'s Smoking Ban."[266] We had worked so hard to gain a booming hospitality industry—why would we now undermine it? I didn't know why we could not delay until more surrounding areas went smoke-free—or at least do a compromise.

I never just said no. I went to work immediately on a total compromise bill, which I wrote with staff in a couple of days, there again lying awake at night, trying to come up with compromises that made sense—and were not self-destructive. I introduced that bill on May 17, 2005, the same day the "Worker Occupational Safety and Health Amendment Act of 2005" was introduced.

In a *Washington Post* op-ed piece on May 29, 2005, I laid out my proposal, which follows:

'Compromise on Smoking'

"I was a smoker for 40 years, but I have not had a puff in nearly four years. Now that I have quit, I don't like being around people when they are smoking. But I also don't like the government taking away my legal choices.

Four smoking-related bills are before the D.C. Council. Three would ban smoking in bars, restaurants and nightclubs. The fourth, my bill, encourages—but does not mandate—more restaurants and bars to go smoke-free.

'The Smoke-Free Restaurant, Tavern and Nightclub Incentive Amendment Act of 2005' provides restaurants and bars that go smoke-free with a two-year tax credit equal to 25 percent of annual sales. Businesses that take advantage of the tax credit would have to remain smoke-free permanently or pay back the credit they receive.

In addition, my legislation requires the installation of high-performance ventilation systems (with specific standards) in any restaurant, bar or nightclub that permits smoking. It quadruples the annual business license fees for establishments that allow smoking.

Penalties for businesses that fail to enforce their smoke-free designations would be set at $200 for a first violation, $500 for a second offense, and $1,000 for subsequent violations. Violators also could have their business licenses revoked. Individuals who light up in establishments that prohibit smoking would be subject to a fine of $100; the current minimum fine is $10. My legislation directs that, after costs, funds collected through increased license fees and penalties be used for anti-smoking and health education programs.

Our city finally has come alive. We have a vibrant nightlife and plenty of diverse venues from which to choose. According to Smokefree D.C., the District already has 287 smoke-free restaurants and bars, but if a blanket smoking ban is implemented, some businesses won't survive, jobs will be lost, and the government will lose tax revenue.

The Restaurant Association of Maryland, citing figures from the Maryland comptroller, says that since Montgomery County imposed a smoking ban a little more than a year ago, the number of liquor-licensed businesses dropped from 507 to 402. In a city in which hospitality is the number one industry, that statistic is worrisome, especially when competition for restaurant and bar business is just a five-minute Metro ride from the District.

Further, in jurisdictions in which smoking bans have been enacted, cigarette smokers simply step outside, thereby creating more noise and litter in the neighborhoods.

Of course, I care about the health of workers. I also care about their being able to keep their jobs or to choose where they work.

People who do not want to patronize establishments that allow smoking already have a choice not to do so. And one day, as fewer and fewer people smoke, smoke-free establishments will be the norm. My legislation will hasten that day. Meanwhile, government should not be denying people the right to choose."[267]

Afterwards I added the following provisions (not verbatim) to my compromise legislation:

- Any employee who wished not to work in smoking areas could choose not to and would not be penalized.

- Any restaurant that wished to retain a smoking environment had to have 75% of their dining space designated smoke-free.

- Any bar that wished to retain smoking had to have 50% of its area devoted to smoke-free.

- Any smoking areas had to be in the back of the establishment, totally separate from the main area, and no one had to go through it to get in and out of the place, or to go to the restroom.

Getting on the Ban-Wagon

On a Sunday night, June 19, 2005 to be exact, I was out walking our dog Gaby and ruminating about this whole smoking ban issue. It had become like a train that everyone was now jumping on that I knew could not be stopped and would lead to damaging our one bustling industry. What to do? What to do? And all of a sudden I came up with an idea that, albeit ludicrous, would at least maybe draw attention to the business-hurting path we were on. I ran home—I hope Gaby had finished her business—and immediately started writing well into early morning hours, and finished my part. On Monday, I had my staff start doing the health research related to the issue, which I planned to insert. Both had to be ready for the legislative session on Tuesday, June 21st.

During the hearing and ongoing debate about the total ban bill, one of my colleagues, Jim Graham who had been a private naysayer to the ban, now was on board and in public kept repeating that smoking kills, over and over again in just one speech, and would always say, "1st, 2nd and foremost." Others were constantly quoting health statistics related to smoking. So I took it to the next logical conclusion. I put out a press release at the end of the next day, which stated that I would be making a major introduction of a bill related to the current smoke-free bill, the "Worker Occupational Safety and Health Amendment Act of 2005." I stated I would be doing so at the Council's Committee of the Whole, prior to our legislative session the next morning, which was June 21st. Interestingly, since the smoke-free debate had become such a public one, there were many cameras and microphones there. I also had never been a Councilmember who held many press conferences or put out alerts, so this was unusual for me.

When it came time for introductions of new legislation, here is what I read:

"All my life I've been around people who drink, and I don't—and never have. My personal preference is to be around people who do not drink. I am tired of going to a bar or a restaurant and having these noisy and often sloppy—or worse—drinkers disturb my night out.

I never thought I could ban drinking just because I didn't like it, but now I know I can. The impending smoking ban has empowered me. My personal preference *can* prevail. And I know many people who don't drink now, even if they did in the past. Why should they and I have to be bothered by non-sober individuals, with their often offensive behavior and smelly breath?

Obviously, I can't say this bill is about my personal preference as that would seem selfish. So today I am introducing the "Worker Occupational Safety and Health Amendment Act of 2005, Part II."

We all know that bartenders and wait staff are constantly harassed by drinking customers. Bouncers are even beaten up by drunks. I care about these workers and their safety. I know they have to support their families and they have to work in these establishments. I want to help them, and the only way to do this is to *ban all* alcohol in *all* bars, restaurants and nightclubs. The workers I'm protecting may not say they want this—in fact, they may say the opposite, as they did *en masse* about banning smoking at the hearings in December of 2003 and on June 14, 2005—but I know what is best for them.

And not only is drinking a worker safety issue, but it is also a health issue—1st, 2nd and foremost. It is a *public* health issue. Drinkers don't just hurt themselves, they can—and do—hurt others.

Let's be honest. People are dying. Pure and simple, drinking kills. People drink in bars and restaurants, then get in their cars and drive off with an increased likelihood of maiming or killing their fellow citizens or of going home and abusing their spouses or children.

Indeed, according to Mothers Against Drunk Driving, about three in every ten Americans will be involved in an alcohol-related crash at some time in their lives. Further, in 2002, the most recent year for which complete statistics are available, 17,419 people died in alcohol-related traffic crashes—an average of one every 30 minutes. These deaths constituted 41% of the total traffic fatalities. Additionally, more than half a million people were injured in crashes where police reported that alcohol was present—an average of one person approximately every minute. This certainly impacts on our healthcare costs as well.

The need to be sober and drive safely is worth more than the license to drink.

And drinkers don't just hurt others with their vehicles—but also with their fists, or their guns or knives. According to the Bureau of Justice Statistics, about 40% of all crimes are committed under the influence of alcohol. The National Council on Alcoholism and Drug Dependence, Inc., finds that, on average each year, about 183,000 rapes and sexual assaults involve alcohol use by the offender, as do just over 197,000 robberies, about 661,000 aggravated assaults, and nearly 1.7 million simple assaults, and certainly some of them on hospitality industry workers.

Alcohol is also likely to be a factor in incidents of domestic violence. In a 1998 study, two-thirds of victims who were attacked by someone they knew reported that alcohol had been involved.

Now, I know I should have waited until the Robert Wood Johnson Foundation decided to make banning alcohol part of its national agenda and, through its emissaries, given me my marching orders—but sometimes I like to lead rather than follow.

I know some will say that drinking is legal, and that people should not have this choice taken away. But this is a health issue, 1st, 2nd and foremost, so there should be no choice. It is also a life and death issue.

Nearly 110,000 people die every year from alcohol-related causes, according to the National Institute on Drug Abuse and the National Institute on Alcohol Abuse, and alcohol-related mortality ranks third among causes of death in the United States. Alcoholism is associated with 25% of all general hospital admissions, often for liver disease, which affects more than two million Americans. And up to 40% of heavy drinkers develop cirrhosis, which is a leading cause of death among young and middle-aged adults in the United States.

So drinking does kill—in many ways, in many forms.

Now, I'm aware that some will say that not serving alcohol of any kind in our bars, restaurants and nightclubs will drive away business to the suburbs. That's ridiculous. We're D.C. We're the Nation's Capital. Our residents won't go anywhere else. And, of course, suburbanites and tourists—especially international visitors, who certainly don't care about wine with dinner—will continue to come to our non-drinking bars, restaurants and nightclubs.

The fact that we had double the rate of restaurant and bar sales tax growth of Montgomery County after it enacted its smoking ban does not mean our growth will slow in similar fashion. Maybe there will be a momentary "dip" in our economy, but soon we'll have triple-digit increases in our hospitality industry. After all, we're D.C.

If it doesn't work out, and our revenues suffer, we can always raise taxes and fees to make up for any difference. Or find other economic engines like growing corn or wheat in our wide open spaces.

Obviously, I expect a majority of my colleagues on the Council—and, of course, the Mayor—to sign on to my new legislation because it's a worker safety issue and it would be "heartless" of them not to. And let's not forget that it's really a health issue—1st, 2nd and foremost.

I know the big liquor lobby, 'using their industry's blood money,' will try to kill off this legislation. But I know where to go for competing money—so New Jersey and the front door of the Robert Wood Johnson Foundation—here I come. I do hope they are not mad at me for not waiting for any marching orders. I'm sure all the health organizations will sign up to fund the lobbying campaign as they have the anti-smoking effort. And the unions will rally for worker safety, even if it means losing a lot of those same workers' jobs. And the gay and lesbian activist groups—who, I learned from the smoking ban, actually want government in their business—will be out there in full force. I guess the ACLU here—unlike in other jurisdictions—will just continue to sit it out.

Now, I'm not banning alcohol. People are still free to drink at home—for now. I'm just legislating that liquor cannot be served in bars, restaurants and nightclubs because I don't want it to be served. I will allow tea, soda and milk—for now. And if the drinkers insist on drinking alcohol—and they will—they can just step outside on sidewalks with their flasks and drink. And, of course, the disturbance they will cause in the neighborhood will be minimal or non-existent.

By the way, I did hear that there are many restaurants—perhaps over 100—that are alcohol–free already, but finding them may entail a call or a click. I'm awfully busy. And besides, why should I have to spend the time and effort?

I even thought about maybe not totally banning alcohol but trying a compromise piece of legislation that would encourage more alcohol-free environments—sort of a carrot-and-stick approach. Establishments that convert to alcohol-free would get financial incentives since they might think they'd lose money if they don't. Silly of them to think that, but they do. And then a stick—among others—would be to pay more to the government to get a license to serve alcohol—a discouragement. And then I thought about having that extra money go to anti-drinking and other health education programs. But why bother with that approach, which would probably accomplish my desire to see more alcohol-free establishments when I can just ban it outright. So much easier and so much quicker.

Yes, I come to you today a changed woman. It had just never occurred to me that I could simply choose to ban a legal choice for consenting adults in a private place where the public does not have to go, and where workers do not have to work, and then get six other people to agree—and then just do it. Thank goodness, the smoking ban lobby taught me a lot. Thus, the "Worker Occupational Safety and Health Amendment Act of 2005, Part II" was born.

I'm also now looking at some other legal choices to ban—like driving or sex—for they, too, can be dangerous to your health and the health of others.

I look forward to your co-sponsorship."

There was much laughter in the chambers and much coverage—even in the national news. Of course I withdrew the bill later that day as I didn't want the world to think we weren't allowing drinking either. I was still pleased I made an important point.

In the end, only Marion Barry and I voted for my smoke-free compromise legislation, which I offered as a substitute when the total ban was voted on at first reading (December 2005) and then at second reading (January 2006). The total ban passed, and interestingly, it included verbatim some of the language of my compromise bill, such as funds going to health education programs. Still, there were many in the community who shared an unease with this government overreach. Writer Christopher Hitchens, who testified at an open hearing, said, "I mean, really, you're treating us like children."[268]

Strangely enough, the ban bill that did pass had an enormous loophole whereby any business that showed economic hardship could be exempt from the non-smoking law, and there was no real definition of what constituted "economic hardship." Councilmember Adrian Fenty described it as a loophole so big, "you could drive a tobacco truck through it." Also strangely, during the final vote, Jim Graham—who was constantly saying "smoking kills"—made sure hookah bars (which are nothing but smoke) were exempted from the ban by adding an amendment to do so. I said at the time, "But Mr. Graham, you said smoking kills. Why are you trying to kill off the hookah bar workers?"

Mayor Anthony Williams himself was in favor only of incentives for going smoke-free and against a government mandate, just like me. In fact, after the smoking ban passed the Council and went up to his office for signature, he refused to sign it, a symbolic display of his disapproval. I was proud of him.

Mixed Smoke Signals

Some may find it ironic that I later did not support marijuana recreational legalization (except for medicinal use which I voted *for*) considering my viewpoints on smoking choice and my absurd take on banning alcohol. But cigarettes and alcohol were already legal substances. I find it more ironic that those who spoke so forcefully for the total smoking ban jumped on the marijuana bandwagon so quickly and strongly—maybe they didn't realize that smoking marijuana is actually smoking. Some leaders even pushed for legal smoking at designated clubs opened solely for that purpose and in public outdoor spaces—even though some studies say that marijuana secondhand smoke is more carcinogenic than cigarette smoke. I guess we should all just realize that smoking is bad. Unless, of course, it's smoking a substance that is mind-altering—and considered hipper. What hypocrisy! This kind of thinking does not make sense to my non-altered mind.

Just today, October 18, 2016, legislation was debated at the D.C. Council that would raise the age for buying cigarettes from 18 to 21. It would also institute a fine for anyone under 21 smoking in public: $50 for publicly smoking cigarettes and $25 for publicly smoking marijuana. That's my town![269]

CHAPTER 40

Steph Heads Back North

I don't know why Stephanie didn't want to stay in Washington. Okay, most of her best friends and sister were in New York. But she had a good job waiting tables at Logan Tavern (after deciding she needed a break from lawyering). When I went there to eat, it was fun to watch her sauntering up to the table. And I mean sauntering. It's a good thing she has such a good personality or she would have been gone after the first day.

Steph did try to get a job working as a lawyer representing D.C.'s abused and neglected children. She got waived into the bar here in preparation. (I went to the bar swearing in and the judge happened to be the woman who bought my house. She made mention of me, a Councilmember, being there and introduced Steph and me. Then she asked the inductees to raise their hands. At that very moment my phone went off and I ran out the door, not being able to see all of what I came to witness. I learned an embarrassing lesson the hard way. Steph forgave me—not sure the judge did.)

Steph submitted papers to the court way in advance, to be among the applicants for the jobs available. The list of eligible people was supposed to be out in March. Summer came. Still no list.

When fall rolled around and the list—affecting so many people—was still not out, six months after it was due to be, she applied for *one* job with the Administration for Children's Services in New York and as un-luck would have it for me, she got it. I truly believe that if the D.C. Court (run by the feds) had kept their timeline, she would still be here, and I remain mad at their delay. But fate stepped in. And the worst part was that Gaby moved too. Steph and Hil were going to be living together in New York so it made more sense for the two of them to take care of Gaby than me alone with my 60-hour-a-week job. I have stayed quite involved and have negotiated very liberal visiting rights (in fact she's sitting next to me right now).

Go and Stop

In July of 2005, there was an effort being pushed by the owner of a hotel in Georgetown to do away with the Whitehurst Freeway in order to enhance the view from his hotel rooms as well as the value of his property. Of course everyone in proximity of the freeway knew it was there when they bought—other than the ones who did so prior to 1949 when the freeway opened. The Williams Administration kept doing expensive studies on the matter.

Now, I do happen to be against building freeways through neighborhoods. I stopped one around Capitol Hill (Barney Circle Freeway), as well as decades earlier as a citizen, fought a northern extension of 395 past New York Ave., which would have uprooted a historic African-American cemetery. But this freeway had been there well over half a century and the impact on the surrounding residential neighborhoods should it close would have been intolerable. So I firmly pointed out often and loudly the traffic chaos that would ensue on M St. and residential roads nearby as people from D.C. and the region went to and from downtown during rush hours. And I questioned why we kept doing expensive studies of something that would benefit so few. The studies finally stopped.

In mid-2006, I filed a bill to take on the speed-trap cameras throughout D.C. I was quoted in *The Washington Times*: "'As I drive around the city, [they] seem out of sync with the nature of the road,' said Schwartz. 'The one that drives me crazy is New York Ave. It's a divided highway, not a pedestrian in sight ... it's a blatant "gotcha" and what gets us legitimate criticism.'"[270] After that, it went away. I also called for re-evaluating speed limits to ensure that they make sense. Some seemed too high and others too low. Of course cameras can have value, especially where schools and pedestrians are present. I've always felt that our over-using them as revenue streams can be counter-productive as you can also lose existing revenue when people decide to stay home.

Tied to the Whipping Post

Around this same time, I ran afoul of *The Washington Post* regarding legislation to ban Councilmembers from discussing Council business outside of an open meeting. The *Post* had banded together with other media outlets to write a bill that ensured that no discussion of any kind could take place among elected officials who work together. The original bill called for a $1,000 fine to be levied if three committee members were discussing business outside an open meeting. There would also be criminal penalties. It was indeed extreme. I didn't feel we should worry about every conversation we might have in the hallway with colleagues without possibly incurring a $1,000 fine. And what if we seemed to violate it twice? I shudder at the consequences. Probably the guillotine—in an open forum.

I do believe in transparent government. But there are some benefits to having occasional discussions outside an open meeting in order to reach compromises, and where Councilmembers don't feel the need to censor themselves or play to the public—as well as to develop some camaraderie. Now that I'm thinking about it, I wonder how the co-introducers got together to co-introduce the open meeting bill that would not allow them to get together. Since there were more than three of them, I certainly hope they had a meeting that we and the media were all invited to, with proper notice, but I don't recall getting that notice—as if there was one.

I worried that such an overreaching bill would, in fact, impede the work of government. Regardless, the proponents were pushing the bill as written and would not even discuss—openly or not— any compromise. Therefore, when that bill was on the docket for a vote in a committee on which I served, and had the needed votes to pass it, I purposely denied the meeting a quorum by not going, and getting others to not go as well.

The Washington Post went ballistic in an editorial. The newspaper called the move "disgusting and cowardly." Those were very strong words. Therefore, I wrote the following op-ed piece in response, which the *Post* ran on July 10, 2006.

'Improving but Not Crippling Our Government'

"Yes, I helped deny a quorum to mark up the D.C. Open Government Meetings Act [editorial, July 1], and I make no apologies for doing so. The ability to deny a quorum is a legal tool—akin to Congress's filibuster—available to Council members as they go about their job of serving District residents. In this case, my purpose was to protect them from irresponsible legislation. (And it worked, somewhat: After twice being denied a quorum, the Committee Chair finally presented a substitute bill that at least reduced from $1,000 to $100 the fine for three committee members discussing business outside an open meeting and eliminated the *criminal penalties*.)

Nonetheless, my using a perfectly legal tool to try to bring about a better law was labeled "disgusting and cowardly" by this newspaper—quite strong words. Considering that the *Post* has a vested interest in getting this bill passed, its statement didn't surprise me. After all, *Post* representatives helped write the bill. And of course a newspaper wants unfettered access to all government meetings. The *Post*'s support for this bill is both self-serving and a conflict of interest. I find its intimidating tone and bullying tactics to merit the same strong words it used on me: "disgusting and cowardly."

With this legislation, no consideration was given to the fact that the ability to hold some meetings out of the public eye can work to benefit the public. Take the rent control issue, for example. In an effort to reach a compromise that would ensure that we protect our residents without forcing landlords to stop providing rental housing, closed meetings were held to see if the parties could reach a compromise.

If we had been required to make those meetings open to the public and abide by the stringent notice requirements, the parties would not have been able to negotiate effectively without feeling that they had to censor themselves. We wouldn't have the rent control bill we now have, one that has the support of both renters and landlords.

The overreaching 'open government' legislation is before us today only because of electioneering and press-pandering. It is not needed; we already have a law stating that no official action can be taken unless it happens at an open public meeting. Just turn on Channel 13 and you can watch these open meetings ad nauseam.

Of course, in this election year, we are going to go there whether we need to or not. But it's important that we do so in a constructive manner that does not hamstring our ability to do our work, and do it as amicably as possible.

The D.C. Council, unlike other legislatures, is under constant scrutiny from Congress. It could be undone if it aired too much of its dirty linen in public. Anyone who watches our numerous open meetings and endless public hearings knows we are capable of doing some yelling. But not being able to freely and candidly discuss issues among ourselves on occasion will inhibit our ability to get things done on behalf of those we represent. I don't want to pass my colleagues in the hallway and be able to discuss little more than the weather without worrying that we are breaking the law. For us to be unable to talk—not vote, not act, but talk—is insane.

One suggestion for improving our open-meetings law should be implemented. A 1999 study by the public advocacy group DC Appleseed made 33 recommendations to strengthen Council operations. Only one dealt with the District's open meetings law. It suggested that for closed breakfast meetings the Council provide minutes of any discussion of items on the agenda of the public meeting to follow. At the Council's next legislative meeting, I will have an amendment that would make this change, as well as others, to expand our law without crippling our government."

The Post took my original title for the editorial, "Improving but Not Crippling Our Government," and created its own self-serving one—"Open Government Is Overrated."[271] Usually the paper tells you what the title change is. This time, they did not. Speaking again of "disgusting and cowardly." It was a cheap and mean-spirited shot that had the newspaper's agenda all over it. I had legitimate concerns. They were obviously legitimate as the bill was altered to reflect them. But the *Post* title for my piece misled the public purposely and created a shorthand way to harm me and to undercut my valid argument. And it really did get used to harm me later. That title—written by the *Post*—would soon be weaponized by political nemeses to help do me in. And it succeeded.

In the end, my denying a quorum opened the door to moderating the bill in significant ways, such as reducing the ridiculously large fine and *eliminating jail time*. The final law became more feasible without draconian measures—and I was very glad to have accomplished that even though I became the *Post*'s whipping post.

Openness in government is very important, but it must not hinder the equally important workings of that government. *The Washington Post,* on November 15, 2016, reported on a discussion among the Council and Mayor on lessening the size of their 2017 inaugural viewing stand—the type of conversation that would best take place outside of an open meeting as it could negatively impact D.C.'s relationships with the President and with Congress, which we have to depend on.

And, on July 2, 2016, I watched an interesting discussion on C-SPAN with politicians and journalists entitled "Political Polarization," which was filmed not long before it aired. It talked about the gridlock between Congress and the President as well as partisanship among members of Congress, and emphasized how in the past, there was more civility and camaraderie because members tended to socialize together, making compromise easier. Very stringent open government laws have the unintended and opposite effect of contributing to isolation rather than working together and compromising, which should be the goal.

The subject of political polarization was also addressed in an August 2016 article in *The Atlantic* by Jonathan Rauch entitled, "How American Politics Went Insane." In it he writes, "Today, federal law, congressional rules, and public expectations have placed almost all formal deliberations and many informal ones in full public view. One result is greater transparency, which is good. But another result is that finding space for delicate negotiations and candid deliberations can be difficult." He cited some examples where things got done in government because they negotiated freely, such as: "In 2013, Congress succeeded in approving a modest bipartisan budget deal in large measure because the House and Senate Budget Committee Chairs were empowered to 'figure it out themselves very, very privately,'" as a Democratic aide put it.

All votes should be made in public and the discussion on the day or days of the vote should be in public. But not being allowed to meet behind the scenes, in some instances, can weaken government, not help it. Of course the media wants total access, but they also decry that nothing gets done because elected officials are not compromising. Can't they see how their own demands stand in the way of what they're asking for?

One need only look at the well-known relationships between Tip O'Neill and Ronald Reagan as well as Ted Kennedy and Orrin Hatch to see that it's possible to have friendships and get things done. Under the original open government bill brought by the media, if either of those two went out for the evening with another colleague or two who happened to serve on the same committee, they could each get a $1,000 fine and criminal penalties. Please!

And how do you think the Voting Rights Act and the Civil Rights Act—done only in an open forum in the 1960s—could have gotten passed by Lyndon Johnson? Another please! You can't have it both ways. At least what I did by denying that quorum made sure those guys back then would only have gotten a $100 fine—but thankfully no criminal penalties—for their camaraderie and ability to make progress happen on our country's behalf.

Helping Women Around the World

There are non-profit organizations like Vital Voices that empower women leaders and entrepreneurs around the world. In the mid-2000s, that group asked me to become involved by hosting delegations of women from various countries in my office to talk about how I first entered elected office, about D.C., and about issues facing women, especially in political life. Then in 2006, they asked me to be part of a training session in Istanbul, Turkey with the first elected women in the Parliament of Afghanistan. Interestingly, the Constitution of Afghanistan requires a certain percentage of women to be elected. I was one of the trainers there and I focused on teaching them how to write and pass legislation as well as giving them some pointers on serving their electorate.

In 2007, the group held a huge conference in Kiev, Ukraine where there were hundreds of women from all over Eurasia. I had an opportunity to do some training there as well. I found it thrilling to see women of all ages, many of whom had never worked outside their homes, now engaged in the political process in these emerging democracies around the world. And I was so pleased to be a part of their experience and growth.

(Since I had never been to that part of the world, I decided to go to Moscow on my own for a weekend. It was an expensive country, but interesting. I especially loved the Armory which is filled with all my favorite material stuff: old paintings, furniture, jewelry and silver. I hear the Hermitage in St. Petersburg has even more of those things and I do hope to go there one day, but not until Vladimir Putin becomes a better citizen of the world.)

Over decades, I've used opportunities to encourage women to run for office here in the U.S., and to help them acquire the skills to do so as well as fulfill the job itself. I have done this through local groups, national organizations, and casual conversations.

But I remain very frustrated at how little progress we've made even today, with women only making up 19% of the 435 members of the House and 21% of the Senate. Yet in 1943, when there were only nine women in the House and none in the Senate, Representative Clare Boothe Luce was being highly touted as a Vice Presidential candidate. And here we are 74 years later, with neither a woman Vice President or President, and only three having been on the major tickets. We are being eclipsed by the rest of the world, where there were in the 1960s, Indira Gandhi leading India and Golda Meir, the head of Israel. And today, women are the heads of government in Germany, the United Kingdom, Taiwan, Norway, Switzerland, Nepal, Bangladesh, Croatia, Namibia, Chile, Liberia, Lithuania, Serbia, etc. In this regard, a usual leader of the world, the USA, is NOT. It's not only frustrating, it's sad.

A Groundbreaking Groundbreaking

On November 13, 2006, I was invited to attend the groundbreaking for the Martin Luther King Jr. Memorial overlooking the Tidal Basin abutting the National Mall. I had made a contribution to the Memorial, but I'm not sure if that's the reason I was invited. Regardless, I was thrilled to be there, especially since my son Doug was in town. As we walked in, the person next to us was Oprah Winfrey, who we exchanged a few words with.

A little later, I got the pleasure of introducing Doug to two individuals who actually were people I considered friends: Dorothy Height, President of the National Council of Negro Women, and Congressman John Lewis, both of whom could not have said nicer things about me to my son even if I had paid them. Doug was certainly excited to meet them as they had been heroes of his as well.

But by far the most impressive thing that day with its delightful informality, was the actual groundbreaking for the Memorial to honor a great American who deserved it.

(Dorothy, an extraordinary woman, died April 20, 2010 at age 98. She is my number two neat woman, who always made me feel special—even though she was the special one—and who is still very much alive in my heart. I was thrilled that recently the United States Postal did a stamp in her honor.)

Bad Ideas Gone Wild

The *Post* and I did agree when it came to a very misguided move relating to schools. The Council originally voted 12 to 1 to place on the ballot a measure, introduced on April 4, 2006 by Kathy Patterson and eight other Councilmembers, to amend the Home Rule Charter to include the right to "free high-quality public schools." You would guess correctly that I was the lone dissenter. It's a phrase that sounds positive enough on the surface, kind of like "motherhood and apple pie." But I saw the inserting of that language in our Home Rule Charter as an invitation to law suits. *The Washington Post* in an editorial agreed: "When Councilmember Schwartz offered an amendment that would have prevented parents from using the measure as a basis for suing the school system, the rest of the Council voted her down. As a result, the legislation practically invites families to file lawsuits."[272]

The city already was paying private school tuitions for over 2,000 special needs students because past legal language allowed parents to sue when the schools did not reach a certain standard. As a result, in 2006, according to the *Post*, those students, 4% of the student body, consumed 15% of the school system's budget.

The school system had just gotten out of that court order from the 1970s. We did not need to open up those same risks again and this time, to *all* of our students in *all* of our schools. I noted when I voted against the measure that the District at the time had 2,143 lawyers per 100,000 residents—that's well over 12,000 attorneys in D.C. alone. And I added, "Isn't that something? I can see the lawsuits now and so will you."[273]

In the end, every member of the Council voted to table the bill so it was not included on the ballot due to the lawsuit fears that I had raised. That really was a big win for me, having turned all my colleagues around, but even more—a big win for our taxpayers.

Speaking of bad ideas gone wild: All the while, I fought against the practice of earmarks because I knew once it got started, it would be "Katy bar the door." I refused to allow one earmark into any of my committee budgets. Even when a committee member or colleague would ask to include one, such as Mary Cheh did one year for an environmental group in her Ward, I said, "You'll have to find another avenue as I refuse to have my Committee report have any outside earmarks in it."

I did try to find money for other inside government agencies and their needs within our Committee budget. For instance, in 2001, I ensured that the Interim Disability Assistance Act (IDA) was fully funded in FY 2002—in spite of the Mayor not funding it—by redirecting $742,500 to IDA, as well as directing $500,000 the next year to the libraries to keep them from having to cut their hours. I also sent some funds to the University of the District of Columbia for specific programs such as adult literacy several different times over the years.

A Really Big Win

As Anthony Williams's second term drew to a close, a proposal was pushed by the Mayor and his emissaries behind the scenes to build a new central library at a cost of $275 million (and we all know initial costs go up) on the site of the old Convention Center. Some outgoing Councilmembers promoted it as a kind of monument to the Mayor's legacy. I thought the stadium might qualify.

As nice as that idea sounded, I couldn't rationalize spending $275 million dollars of city money on a non-revenue generating project—in fact, just the opposite as libraries eat up revenues. In this case, it was even worse to do it on such high-priced real estate. And we already had a central library just a few blocks away. Turns out there was a second plan (speaking of behind the scenes) to sell that property, the Martin Luther King Library, which had not even been discussed. Here was a twofer and I was "fer" neither.

If the MLK Library was out as a library for whatever reason, I even suggested using the historic Carnegie Library. Although historic and not very large, I had already talked to historical preservationists about possibilities for expanding this beautiful, underutilized District-owned facility. And the Carnegie was just across the street from the Walter E. Washington Convention Center as well as the new proposed library location.

Because we have neighborhood libraries all over the city, I felt that any new library so centrally located would basically be used by tourists, suburbanites and let's be honest, the homeless. Besides, the Internet was already here big-time, so many were starting to question large libraries anyway. And to top it all off, the price tag for this library was outrageous: $275 million. (I'm aware that I have repeated this amount three times, but I was so appalled by it, I can't help myself.)

Meanwhile, a large state-of-the-art library had just been built in Rockville, Maryland for $26 million—less than one-tenth our amount. I pointed out the $250 million difference in cost in meetings over and over again. I also kept emphasizing that this was one of our most valuable pieces of land and we had just spent a fortune on building a new convention center, which at least has some opportunity to pay for itself. So why would we put catty-corner to it a revenue drain instead of a revenue-producing convention center hotel or revenue-producing condos and/or revenue-producing high-end stores?

The proponents kept mentioning, "But Seattle did a big central library downtown and people now come downtown." I responded, "Well, we already have a central library downtown which we can refurbish. And besides, we are not Seattle, whose draws downtown up to that point had been a fish market and a big needle. We have lots of attractions, like the White House, the Capitol, the Washington Monument, the Lincoln Memorial, the Vietnam Memorial, and all the Smithsonian museums to name a few. And I really don't feel like spending $275 million (now make it four times) on this prime real estate, which will then cost us at least tens of millions of dollars a year in services and upkeep."

Actually the deal was sealed from the get-go. They had their seven votes, and because of the "legacy" argument, others were leaning toward voting in favor as well. But that did not stop me. I kept working to persuade colleagues to vote no and had six who said they would. At the Committee on Education, Libraries and Recreation meeting on November 21, 2006 when the legislation to establish the new library was moved—legislation unless it's an emergency, goes to the relevant committee first—I then moved to table it and spoke very strongly against the library and certainly on that valuable site. The vote to table passed, three to two, and therefore the issue should have been over.[274]

But then Mayor Williams pushed to bring it up at the Council's last legislative session of the year on December 19th, right before he was leaving office, as an emergency. Some emergency! I still worried as they were really trying hard to get the extra two yes votes they needed for an emergency above the seven they already had. The day of that session, I was really nervous. But by the time of the vote, which was late in the evening, Councilmember Sharon Ambrose, a sure yes vote, had left as she was quite ill. Knowing they didn't have even seven votes now, much less the nine needed, they withdrew the emergency bill. I was so relieved.

During the debates, I had offered another suggestion on several occasions: Let's spend that money to refurbish our neighborhood libraries, which are actually used by our residents. To the disappointment of some but to the benefit of our community libraries, that's where funds went. Many have been beautifully refurbished and enjoyed now by so many of our residents, including our children, as well as by others.

In addition, I continued beating the drum for the site of the old Convention Center to be maximized to its greatest potential in terms of use and revenue. I wrote Mayor Williams advocating for mixed-use development on the site. And soon after the next Mayor, Adrian Fenty, took office, I wrote him a similar letter with ideas on how to utilize that valuable piece of property:

> "Wonderful mixed-use development projects have been thriving for years now in the very nearby suburbs of Arlington, Virginia and Bethesda and Silver Spring, Maryland. Each of these projects feature retail, dining, office, and housing components, and could, I am confident, be replicated here successfully—perhaps even more successfully. Just look at our revitalized Chinatown/Gallery Place/Verizon Center area which features the same sort of mix that I am suggesting for the old Convention Center site. Why wouldn't we want to coax folks to explore a wider array of stores and restaurants a mere two blocks to the north?

Flash forward. Today on the old Convention Center site sits City Center with its luxury living quarters and high-end stores and restaurants, all of which I envisioned, and which are a huge revenue generator for the city. (And there's still a little room for more.) Every time I pass by it, I smile. In fact, I had dinner there with friends not long ago.

A New Mayoral Election

In 2006, a new Mayor would be elected as Anthony Williams chose not to run. Tony and I had our differences over his eight years in office, but I did like him personally. I found him engaging and very much appreciated his sense of humor as well as his compelling personal story. I believe he did help enhance our city's reputation. I backed his desire to see the city grow by 100,000 residents in the next decade, which echoed Alice Rivlin's vision. (Alice was the former Chair of the Financial Control Board and is now a Senior Fellow at the Brookings Institution.)

The Democratic primary's main contenders were Council Chair Linda Cropp and Councilmember Adrian Fenty. Adrian had been a Ward 4 Councilmember since 2001 while Linda had served on the body since 1991 and prior to that, served on the Board of

Education and had been its President. She also had leadership experience as Council Chair, as well as the endorsement of Mayor Williams. In many ways, Linda was a natural successor. However, some, especially *The Washington Post*, had become infatuated with Adrian Fenty, as did many in the media. He was a young, handsome native Washingtonian of mixed race, who was also a marathon runner—and who gave out his cell number to everyone in the media and was available to them night and day.

Adrian was just 35 when he ran for Mayor, about 23 years younger than Linda. He did a major door-to-door campaign, and the paper loved to describe him racing up the steps to the doors of voters with accompanying flattering pictures. Meanwhile, the newspaper in their profiles of Linda, who is a very pretty woman, picked one unflattering photo, taken at her announcement, where her mouth was open and her face distorted, and ran it over and over again. The only other photo I remember highlighted her back as she was walking.

These articles and pictures seemed intent on emphasizing her age and were in stark contrast to how Adrian was treated. Of course there was a difference in age and Linda was not a marathon runner, but she was still only 58 years old! I guess that would obviate most men in elected office too if they were held to that same standard. The clear bias in content and images was sickening. It so smacked of ageism and sexism.

I kept saying to myself, "Stay out of this, Carol. It's not your fight." But in a way, maybe it was. I started cutting out *all* the clippings of the *Post*'s coverage of Linda and Adrian and put them in a folder. I then called Donald Graham, the Publisher and Chair of the Board of the *Post*, and made an appointment, which was a very rare thing for me to do. I sat at a table with Don and showed him each of the articles and photos. I then said, "I know you all may have a favorite in the race. But Linda Cropp is a good, respectable public servant and what you are doing to her is unfair journalism."

Don looked at everything in the folder, nodded to me in what I perceived as agreement, walked out of his office and into the Metro Editor's across the way. In a few minutes, he came back and walked me over there, requesting I show the Editor the material and discuss the matter. Thank goodness that awful picture subsequently disappeared and the coverage became a little more fair. I never told Linda until many years later, or anyone else until now.

I did not publicly endorse through most of the race. I tried to be consistent about not endorsing any of my colleagues against another. But the day before the primary, I finally came out for Linda. I did a walking tour with her, Mayor Williams and others in high-traffic areas in Northwest like P between 14th and 15th Sts. and released a statement that evening which encompassed my feelings: "Are we electing a Mayor or are we selecting a track and field star? Okay, maybe Linda won't lead in the 50-yard dash, but we are fortunate to have such a seasoned and experienced person. We could have Linda's leadership and keep Adrian's energy on the Council." I also got on the phone and started calling people. Hardly much and certainly too late, but at least I felt better to have done a little publicly.

Adrian won the primary, 57% to 31%, guaranteeing his win in the general election where he had two lesser-known opponents and got 89% of the vote. And sadly, we lost Linda from public service. As the 2007 session began, there were only two women on the Council—and not even one African American woman. It was quite an unwelcome contrast to when I began in 1985 with Councilmembers Hilda Mason, Charlene Drew Jarvis, Nadine Winter and Wilhelmina Rolark (and seven women in total). Thankfully, the special election months later would bring two more: Muriel Bowser to fill Fenty's Ward 4 seat and Yvette Alexander to fill the Ward 7 seat vacated by Vince Gray, who had been elected Chair.

15 Seconds of Fame

Adrian Fenty was sworn in as Mayor on January 2, 2007. That night he had a gala inauguration ball at the D.C. Convention Center. After Adrian spoke with his lovely wife Michelle, who I like a lot, by his side, the music started. Marion began dancing by himself on stage. In order to not make it look as awkward as it was, I started dancing with him and then later, others joined in as well.

The next day, I learned that there was a video of us dancing on YouTube. It actually made it to YouTube's number two watched video that day. I think it had more to do with Marion than my dance moves (although impressive). See for yourself by searching "Marion Barry dancing" on YouTube (second video down). Or at least it was there a few months ago.

CHAPTER 41

School Takeover

Soon after Mayor Adrian Fenty took office, he moved to take Mayoral ownership of the D.C. Public Schools with a Chancellor reporting to him. The elected School Board would be reduced to a State Board with no real power and little function other than teacher certification requirements. It was a surprising turn of events as Adrian had been vociferously against the Mayoral take-overs proposed by Anthony Williams. But now Fenty looked to New York City and the Chancellor set-up, orchestrated by then Mayor Michael Bloomberg and Chancellor Joel Klein.

In fact, Adrian insisted that we take a one-day trip to New York to meet with Bloomberg and Klein to get a briefing on their system. After visiting a few schools and a meeting at one of them, we went to Gracie Mansion for lunch, and I enjoyed visiting with Bloomberg. It was also nice to talk that day with Klein about the time he had spent in D.C.

Fenty received strong backing from the editorial page of *The Washington Post*. The *Post* really pushed the takeover, implying that it was the only way to reform education, which should have been no surprise as it further explained their multiple endorsements of Fenty in the Mayoral election. I also wondered if there was a little conflict of interest at work here too as the Washington Post Company also owned the education company Kaplan, which provided consultants in addition to products focused on educational reform efforts.

I did know that schools needed to be reformed, and in fact had worked on it for decades. I also realized that dramatic steps had to be taken. However, I was against the Mayoral takeover as it was unproven (even New York did not have statistics yet)—and extreme. And I felt that the Mayor with all the other areas of government that needed improvement had enough challenges already. Mostly, though, I was against it because in a city with so little voting opportunity for its residents, I thought it was wrong to take away nearly half of our democratically elected people who actually do policy.

I was not just a naysayer, but offered an alternative to a full takeover and outlined those ideas in the following op-ed published on January 27, 2007 in the *Post*:

'Better School Reform'

"I appreciate Mayor Adrian Fenty's willingness to take a central role in improving public education in the District of Columbia and certainly share his desire to make our schools not just better but great. When Mayor Anthony Williams proposed taking control of the schools two years ago, I also believed he meant well.

Interestingly, Adrian Fenty, then a member of the D.C. Council, opposed that takeover, as did I. He has changed his mind. I have not.

I am concerned that we would be dismantling the Board of Education just as we elected a dynamic President and added elected members and Mayoral appointees—all of whom are impressive and have promised strong oversight. We have a Superintendent—found through a joint effort and national search two years ago—who has laid a foundation for needed improvements. The D.C. Council has also put in place $200 million a year to modernize school facilities. We have assembled the components necessary to hasten reform.

Added to this mix is our new Mayor, who obviously wants to be more involved in education. I am sure he would use his office to support the Superintendent and School Board and to coordinate the relevant city agencies. Why would we not give the assembled team a chance, at least for a limited time, to prove its mettle?

I don't want education to become just another of the myriad things for which the Mayor is responsible. Running the schools is a full-time job, and the Mayor already has a daunting task ahead of him with the many agencies that need fixing.

I fear that the plan for a Mayoral takeover may push us to the brink—which threatens citywide consequences, not just schools.

We all want our students to achieve more. I fully agree with the Mayor and my Council colleagues that the status quo cannot remain. We must put our schools on the road to success. Toward that end, I will ask the Mayor and the Council to consider five recommendations that, taken together, should get us where we all want to go:

- First, the Board of Education should be given three years to achieve measurable improvements that indicate the system is turning around. If these people, working with the Council and the Mayor, cannot get the job done in three years, a complete takeover can and probably should occur. By then, hopefully, other agencies will have been fixed.

- Second, the Mayor and the Council should have line-item authority over school spending. The Superintendent, with approval from the Board of Education, would submit his budget to the Mayor for his changes. He would then submit it to the Council, which would decide on the schools' budget, as it does for all other agencies.

- Third, the Mayor should be given control of some underperforming schools—one high school and all its feeder schools—and be evaluated on their progress after three years. This is similar to the frequently cited Los Angeles model, where Mayoral control is being tried at selected schools. We could compare the progress at Mayor Fenty's schools with similarly low-performing schools under the control of the Superintendent and the Board. Data on the effectiveness of Mayoral control are scarce, but this would provide firm, relevant facts upon which to base a decision.

- Fourth, the Superintendent should have ex officio cabinet-level status so that he may become a partner with other cabinet members, who can provide greater assistance in meeting the social, health and other needs of our students in a timely manner.

- Fifth, the Council should outlaw social promotions. We do not help our students by advancing them before they're ready. In fact, we handicap them—in many cases for life.

- This plan would allow the Mayor to demonstrate the benefits of his plan without wholesale experimentation with our school system and its students."

Under the plan I proposed, the Mayor and the Council would have line-item budgetary control for the first time, and thus greater accountability. And, importantly, our limited democracy would not be kicked to the curb in the process.

The Mayoral takeover did pass the Council, with only Phil Mendelson and me voting against it. To this day, I stand by that vote and would do the same exact thing. It was a vote, however, that got me on the bad side of the *Post* editorial board, or maybe it just added to its list. The editorial board has brought that vote up consistently since then.

Michelle Rhee was selected as Chancellor by Klein, Bloomberg and the *Post* ... I mean, Fenty. Rhee was given the largest salary of any school head in the whole D.C metropolitan area—$275,000 with a $41,250 signing bonus, etc.—at age 37 and without even a master's degree, and not one day's experience as a Superintendent/Chancellor or even a Deputy. [275] I had concerns about a lot, but relating to the "etc." part above, I wrote a letter to Mayor Fenty on June 6, 2007, which said:

"[I] received a copy of the contract that you extended to Ms. Michelle Rhee today. What exactly is 'the most favorable pension available to any DCPS official' as promised in clause number 12 of the contract? Please provide me a detailed description of what this contractual obligation entails? I look forward to receiving this information before the vote on Tuesday, July 10, 2007."

I never heard back.

Rhee's experience consisted of three years of teaching in Baltimore for Teach for America, and then setting up a company that recruited teachers for cities such as New York. And for being this middleperson, others said she got paid around $150,000 a year. Straight from there, Rhee, now as Chancellor, was given unprecedented control of the entire D.C. Public School system with very little, if any, oversight (which turned out, in the long run, to be *none*—except some by the Council).

Michelle is smart, attractive and articulate. She quickly made a national name for herself through vast coverage in the media with her plan to clean up the system. *Time Magazine* featured Rhee holding a broom on its cover. And it was just the beginning of her reign as a media celebrity extraordinaire.

Even though I did not vote for the takeover, and certainly had concerns about her lack of credentials, I tried to be a team player and did vote for Rhee's appointment as I wanted to be helpful. As she started making abrupt decisions and taking actions with no warning or due process, I tried to tell her, behind the scenes, that these things could be done—and also quickly—but more sensitively and fairly. Unfortunately to no avail.

An abrupt decision put into motion was firing 96 people in the central administrative office.[276] In this case, she needed action by the Council to do so as it involved the budget to pay them for severance and benefits owed. It was all done under the guise of, "We do not need this number of people in the central office. Instead, we need science and art teachers in the classroom." Okay, who wouldn't buy into that? So of course we voted yes—only to find out shortly thereafter that the mostly older African American women in the central administrative office had been replaced by a *greater number* of young people at higher salaries in that same central office. Soon 100 central office employees were making more than $100,000 a year. And sadly, the kids in the schools never got their science and art teachers.[277] They had just been pawns in that whole process. And where was the *Post* coverage when this fraudulent bait and switch was going on?

It was so hard to stomach, watching these inhumane and deceptive kinds of things, and then seeing the media be unaware it was going on—or just refuse to cover it. Personnel who weren't under a cloud were being pushed out without even a quick evaluation. It was just so unfair. Then even higher-paid people were brought in to be exactly what we didn't need more of—central administrators. It was so misleading—and such a wrong tone. The broom was out of control—sweeping out the old because they were old, while sweeping in the new because they were not old.

Many veteran instructors were replaced with young teachers from Teach for America. I like the Teach for America program and always felt that its emphasis on inner-city and rural schools is very important. I also have found their recruits to be smart, well-meaning and sincere. But studies have shown that they often stay in those types of schools for only a couple of years, add it to their resumes, and move on. I did not think then—and I do not think now—that this is the way to anchor a stable and dependable school system. A cadre of good veteran teachers, who are there for the love of teaching, with a smattering of new energizing Teach for America types coming and going, is the better answer.

There were so many areas in which things could have been done better. Rhee and many of her administrators appeared to be so arrogant. They did not have to answer to anybody about anything. Whether it be school closings, principal and teacher firings, overblown salaries, they were all-powerful and all-knowing. Although the Council did get some brief briefings, any concerns raised were usually ignored, ridiculed, or written off as anti-reform, and even anti-children. In my view, there could have been more respect and collaboration—while still getting the job done.

When I first wrote this section, I had said, "As the years have gone by, her results have proved to be mixed." But now that I've reviewed articles, I find her tenure to be more troubling than just "mixed." Most alarming were indications of widespread cheating on standardized tests from 2007 to 2010. *USA Today* broke this story in a 2011 investigative piece which found that D.C.'s soaring test scores coincided with an enormous amount of erased and changed answers. *USA Today* zeroed in on Noyes Education Campus to shed light on these findings:

"In 2006, only 10% of Noyes' students scored 'proficient' or 'advanced' in math in the standardized tests required by the federal No Child Left Behind law. Two years later, 58% achieved that level. The school showed similar gains in reading." [278]

Amidst this "achievement" *USA Today* found, "The consistent pattern was that wrong answers were changed to right ones."

The problem was not at a single school, but citywide: "Noyes is one of 103 public schools that have had erasure rates that surpassed D.C. averages .... That's more than half of D.C. schools."

D.C. Public Schools' testing company, CTB-McGraw-Hill, verified the issue, flagging 46 D.C. public schools for "high rates of wrong answers changed to right ones."[279]

Coincidence? Seems unlikely. As a 2011 *New York Times* piece stated, "At some schools, they found the odds that so many answers have been changed from wrong to right randomly were 1 in 100 billion."[280]

Michelle Rhee touted the soaring test scores. Teachers and principals were rewarded with lucrative bonuses for those supposed improvements. On the other hand, using those tests, "She let go of dozens of principals and fired at least 600 teachers."

DCPS was held up as a "national symbol of what high expectations and effective teaching could accomplish." But as *USA Today*'s investigation showed, some cheating on tests can help.

In 2008, D.C.'s State Superintendent of Education pushed for an investigation into the high erasure rates, but she was "met with resistance from Rhee's staff,"[281] and soon thereafter left the school system. (No wonder I wanted to keep a strong, elected Board of Education in place to oversee the Chancellor's office.) Rhee then hired her own consultant who miraculously said that everything was A-okay, except for a single school.

And according to a *New York Times* story, when veteran education correspondent John Merrow followed Rhee for a segment for *PBS NewsHour*, Rhee "asked if his crew wanted to watch her fire a principal." The camera captured the firing while "the principal seemed dazed." Merrow said, "I've been reporting 25 years and never seen anything like it."[282] How cruel can one be.

Michelle Rhee did bring us her deputy, Kaya Henderson, who was Chancellor for nearly five years after Rhee. Kaya continued reform, but in a more inclusive and humane way. She, though, left the system in September of 2016.

Thank You, Washington Post

I have certainly done my fair share of pointing out what I considered to be the bias of the *Post*, not only editorially, which *is* its job, but also in its reporting, which is not. However, I do want to say how I have appreciated over the years when I was in public office, the *Post*'s willingness to publish my pieces, even those that disagreed vehemently with their positions, like my school reform one. I have also appreciated the couple of times I have needed to talk to one of the really higher-ups, both early on and even at the end, that I have had the opportunity to do so. Thank you, *Post*.

A Committee with No End

In January of 2007, I took over the Committee on Government Operations, which had legislative oversight of the Executive Office of the Mayor and the City Administrator's Office, the Board of Elections and Ethics, and the many Mayoral Commissions, to name just a few of the over 30 areas covered. But I really wanted to also oversee workforce development, as I had special interest in creating jobs for our residents and the training that goes with it, and Vince Gray, as Chair, was helpful in allowing me to do that. It was a lot on my plate as well as my small staff's since additional positions did not come with it. But I was thrilled to have the opportunity to impact on so many important facets of government.

One of the most fun times during those couple of years was deciding to host a potluck dinner at my apartment, inviting all the diverse Commissions which included African Affairs, Latino Affairs, Asian and Pacific Islander Affairs, LGBT Affairs, Women, and the Commission on Human Rights, and others, along with the Mayor's Offices of such, and having it come to fruition. There were at least 150 people present with probably 300 different yummy dishes, many of which represented the various cultures. I loved every minute of it, especially the connections that were made. Some still talk about it, and obviously I'm one.

Challenges with Another Mayor

Before Adrian Fenty got elected Mayor, he was known as a Councilmember who concentrated on constituent services during his six years on the Council. I recollect that he pushed for the ban of single-container beer sales (which I opposed because I thought it discriminated against those who couldn't afford a six-pack) and voted no on the baseball stadium and the school takeover. He did introduce a school capital improvement bill, which got the ball rolling on our needed modernization of schools.

I had an innate fondness for Fenty when he arrived on the Council as he and my son Doug had gone to Wilson High School together for a time before Adrian transferred to Mackin Catholic High School. But it was hard to get too close to him as he tended to be standoffish with his colleagues on the Council. Never nasty or mean, just somewhat aloof.

But some of Fenty's actions after he became Mayor had troubling aspects to them. For one, Fenty was very outspoken about former Mayor Williams's disrespect for the Council, which was evident through Williams's too regular failure to consult with us on important city decisions and even his withholding baseball tickets that he received from the Nationals, which were intended to be transferred to the Council. Since Tony's actions bothered Adrian then, why would he replicate them? But he did.

For instance, Fenty did not notify us of his plan to fire 1,000 city workers in a deal he made with Congress. And then he, a naysayer to the baseball stadium throughout the process, even used those same Council-intended Nationals tickets to exert his power. In April of 2008, when Fenty sent over the baseball tickets, four Councilmembers, including me, were excluded from the distribution list—Fenty's list, not the Nationals. Vincent Gray, Chair of the Council, went to bat for us (cute pun, eh?—especially when you learn he was a baseball player himself). He returned all the tickets and said, "No exclusions." Finally, tickets for all were delivered an hour before the game. What a petty and childish act of disrespect, which many of us felt was indicative of the overall tone of his Administration.[283]

Tickets aside, the moment of disrespect from the Administration that got to me the most was this one I'm about to relate: Chair Gray was a strong ally of Fenty's during the school takeover fight. A lifelong Washingtonian and public servant, both in the D.C. government and in the non-profit community, Vince was a fervent Home Rule advocate. Thus, I'm sure it was hard for him to support the school reform package, which made the elected School Board basically advisory for a few "state" functions. But Vince did support it. He was a key figure in this effort as he was not only Council Chair but Chair of the Committee of the Whole, where education then resided.

Then after working so hard to give Fenty exactly what he wanted, this is how he was rewarded: When the Mayor selected Rhee as his Chancellor, he brought her into town over a weekend and introduced her to the Federal City Council (a group of business people, many of whom reside in the suburbs) and *The Washington Post* editorial board (many of whom reside in the suburbs). Vince Gray, Chair of the elected D.C. Council and chief ally in getting the all-powerful Chancellor here, was totally ignored that entire weekend and all day on Monday. It wasn't until 11 p.m. on Monday night at the John A. Wilson Building that this chief ally, Chair Gray, got to meet Michelle Rhee—just 10 overnight hours before Fenty introduced her to the Council at its breakfast meeting—and just 12 hours before the introductory Fenty-Rhee press conference. Such dismissive treatment of a courageous ally was hard for me to watch.

Also troubling: The Williams Administration got into some hot water at the end of its tenure for giving 30 senior workers inappropriate cash bonuses. The Council subsequently outlawed such severance payouts in October of 2009. Then, two months later, as Fenty was leaving office, though, he ignored the law and handed out more than $500,000 worth of bonuses himself.[284]

Under Fenty, managerial salaries also ballooned. I said to *The Washington Post* back in September of 2007, "I am not opposed to our employees being fairly compensated. However, I believe some of these packages which are being paid for by taxpayers are exorbitant and quite possibly ridiculous." The Mayor wanted maximum salary caps to be set $100,000 *higher* than the previous cap. I fought it. In the end, a compromise was reached that did allow for six agency heads to be compensated at a rate that did not require Council approval.[285]

Mayor Fenty also tried to get his nominee for D.C. Attorney General, Peter J. Nickles, who happened to be his godfather and who lived in Virginia, waived from the residency requirement. Even *The Washington Post* editorial board wrote an unusual editorial which said that we should waive in Peter Nickles.[286] At that point, as Chair of the Committee on Workforce Development and Government Operations, the matter came to me. I had only allowed one waiver before and that was because the person's wife was physically disabled and they had retrofitted their home in Virginia to accommodate her. In this case, I could find no good reason other than Mr. Nickles preferred Virginia. So why should our D.C. Attorney General—such an important position—not live and pay taxes on his salary here? Thus, I refused to do the waiver, despite all the pressure—and Mr. Nickles bought an apartment in the city. I was glad to have him as a resident as I personally liked him.

(An aside: Leslie Hoteling, who was Director of Public Works under Mayor Williams—and a Virginia resident—had tried to get me to give her a waiver from the requirement that she move into the city years before. I said, "Absolutely not." So she did come in and bought a house at 14th and W Sts., N.W., just a block from the Reeves Center where she worked. Years later, as she was retiring to a rural area in Virginia, she thanked me for refusing her waiver request as she made a fortune on that D.C. house.)

Also troublesome were contracts being awarded to developers who happened to be Fenty's fraternity brothers. The Council ended up appointing a Special Counsel to investigate the awarding of $86 million to his fraternity brothers for a deal that skirted Council approval and where those "brothers" appeared to be just high-paid pass-throughs.[287]

There seemed to me to be too many areas of concern. In particular, I did not want to hand over government property to developers in apparent sweetheart deals, especially when we might need that property in the future. And I sure did not want to see us in the position of then having to buy back our needed assets from those same developers at the exorbitant price they would have set. I could see this happening even more vividly, given the many schools closings under the new Chancellor. Like I said in *The Washington Times* on December 5, 2007, "We need to get a mindset that shows we value ourselves. This land is ours. It belongs to our family first and foremost if we have need for it."[288]

To this end, I proposed legislation that would require the Council to decide whether a property was still needed or not for public use *before* it could be sold or leased. Absurdly, the process of both saying "we don't need" and "here's the sale" had been contained in the same legislation before. I made sure it was separated. Today, as our city grows and we may need more schools and recreation and senior centers, we must be even more mindful of preserving our property for our own use above all else.

But here again, when we should have been deciding what to do with our property, Mayor Fenty proposed a Southwest Waterfront Development Corporation—another basically private entity to deal with our land. At this point, you can probably imagine my response—and you're right. I made 11 amendments to the legislation when it came forward from the Finance Committee, and made sure that the D.C. government was very intimately involved in all aspects of this Corporation. I bet you never heard of this group. You know why? My 11 amendments made it so unappealing to the Mayor and his friends to be bothered with it—though Fenty's then wife, Michelle, was hired to do some legal work for the Corporation.

Then there were the usual issues with expiring contracts coming to the Council for approval at the very last minute. One of these expiring contracts compromised health insurance coverage for District employees. Shortly after the Christmas holidays, my office received calls from D.C. workers about the cancellation of their health benefit plan. I wrote the Mayor, saying that, "Employees had made their healthcare decisions in a timely fashion only to move into the new year with complete uncertainty about their insurance—something that can be completely traumatic."

I soon learned that none of the health benefit contracts had been submitted to the Council until the day before winter recess and long after the open enrollment period had closed. I wrote: "I am troubled by the manner in which this was handled. Why are contracts worth hundreds of millions of dollars collectively submitted to the Council for approval at the last possible minute? This is an unsound and cruel practice from not just a fiscal perspective, but from a physical and mental well-being perspective."

Another issue that was preventable: In early 2008, D.C. held the Presidential primary which included Barack Obama and thus, turnout was high.[289] The election operations were overwhelmed. I couldn't understand how they could not have predicted the crowd during such a historic vote in this majority black city. When questioned at my hearing, a representative countered: "[Boxes] could only hold so much." I said, "Well, then, let's get a bigger box!" This exchange was actually quoted verbatim in the paper.[290]

Getting Older and Colder

When I was working, I would always try to find at least a couple of long weekends, if not a whole week, during the cold winter months for a warmer break in West Palm Beach, where I own that same one-bedroom apartment.

Through friends, I was introduced to Lois Frankel, the Mayor of West Palm Beach and now the Congresswoman for that area. They put us together at a luncheon in 2008 and we clicked right away—a real Democratic Mayor and me, a then Republican wannabe. Lois actually said she knew of me through her time spent in D.C., including law school many years earlier. Lois is a really bright, hardworking elected official, who had also been the Minority Leader of the Florida State Senate before being elected Mayor where she revitalized downtown West Palm Beach which had been dormant for decades before. Her rare free time is often spent painting. Lois is quite talented in that regard and has her large vibrant pictures displayed in her home and office.

One Christmas eve in West Palm Beach, after we finished having dinner at her son's wine bar/restaurant, The Blind Monk, we decided to head to a movie theater at City Place. All the movies we had verbalized interest in had already started so we just stood there. I really wanted to suggest Tyler Perry's *A Medea Christmas*, which was due to start soon but was hesitant to mention it. As we were walking away from the theater, I finally said, "You wouldn't be interested in seeing *A Medea Christmas*?" and she said, "Gosh yes! I really wanted to suggest it myself." So there we were Christmas eve, yukking it up with Tyler Perry and an equally appreciative full crowd of his fans. This past Christmas day it was *La La Land* with her mom.

I have a lot of good friends who have been growing older like me and spend much of the winter in Florida, and we hang out, along with new friends I've made there. Some of these are: Mary Ann Lundgren, Carol and Shelly Schuman, Judy and Stuart Treby (sadly, Judy passed away two years ago), Judy and Ahmed Esfandiary, Mildred and Howard Amer, David and Rebecca Burka, Shirley and Arnold Schreiber (we lost Arnold several years ago), Karen and Bob Croce, Joan and Arnold Weiss, Francine and Pierre Lapter, and Alex Armstrong and Jerry McCoy, who have a place in Sarasota where I've spent wonderful times with them. I also spend enjoyable times with Florida friends like Eileen and Frank Brennan, Katherine Waldren (who was just elected to the Port of Palm Beach Commission), Christopher Bates, Inge and Phil Bowdre (he unfortunately died a few years ago), Marsha and Kevin Hennessey, neighbors Joan McCrosky, Miriam and Ariel Pagan, Pat Sokolosky, and Bridget Cunningham and Bob Billings. I also appreciate Ted Lefman who checks on my apartment when I'm not there. They and Florida have been a great break for me.

(You may be thinking here that *you* need a break from my mentioning friends. However, please realize I would have felt awful not doing it as they are a very big—and nice—part of my life.)

An Emergency with No Response

For years, I had been pushing for the separation of Emergency Medical Services (EMS) and the Fire Department, which in D.C. have somewhat inexplicably been part of the same department with each receiving dual training. This configuration has put our firefighters in the position of having to do health treatment too. This system has never made sense to me as a good firefighter may *not* make a good EMS professional and vice versa. Imagine having a heart attack and a fire truck shows up. (Actually you don't have to imagine; that's what has been happening here for years.) This has obviously caused many bad situations on top of reported issues of poor training and low morale, especially for EMS workers.

I pushed for a split of the two important functions (of course, continuing strong coordination) with legislation in 1999, 2001,

2004, 2005, and again in 2007. The 2004 introduction was with Kevin Chavous and we got six co-sponsors. But despite the five introductions and having eight Councilmembers sign on, it never happened; and to this day, the agencies still operate under one umbrella. The only difference is that now some of that ambulance service is being contracted out—hardly my idea of a remedy!

Employing Our Residents

D.C. has a First Source program, which requires contractors in government financing and development to employ a certain percentage of District residents. We were finding that enforcement of the program was lax. And often, when companies were non-compliant, they would simply incorporate under another name to get out from under fines and other enforcement measures.

So in 2007, I along with Councilmembers Marion Barry, Kwame Brown, and Harry Thomas Jr. introduced the Office of First Source Compliance Act of 2007. It would have established an office within the Department of Employment Services to ensure compliance with such agreements. It also required each bidder for a contract to provide documentation of past and present compliance prior to a new bid. Finally, it would have ferreted out those who file under another name, and set up a two-fines, then a third-strike-you're-out system.

That bill stalled, but in 2011, the first source compliance program was given stronger teeth. A hotel in my neighborhood was recently made to stop work due to non-compliance with First Source. I am glad to see this enforcement so that our own residents are given the most opportunities possible for employment. But below is a resident who should not have had an employment opportunity:

Largest Theft in D.C. History (That We Know of)

In 2007, another scandal broke in the D.C. government, which involved the largest known theft by an employee in its history. Harriette Walters, a manager in the tax office in charge of property tax refunds, embezzled $48.1 million from the city spanning over two decades by funneling a large part of that money to shell companies. She wound up being sentenced to a 17-and-a-half-year federal prison term. Ten others, including Walters' friends and relatives, were sent to prison as well. Fifteen tax office staff members were fired or forced to resign. And the D.C. Chief Financial

Officer Natwar Gandhi came under fire for allegedly not heeding a warning from D.C. Auditor Deborah Nichols, appointed by the Council, about potential problems.

Years earlier, Gandhi put in place a system whereby he signed off on tax refunds *only* of $250,000 or higher, but seemed to consider lower amounts as "micro-managing," as was stated in a November 16, 2007 *Post* article by Nikita Stewart.[291] The lack of oversight with apparently no one minding the store was astounding, and is well-documented in a later *Post* article by Del Quentin Wilber as he reported on the sentencing of Walters:

> "Walters has admitted that she exploited lax oversight in the tax office to issue more than 230 fraudulent property tax refund checks to friends and co-conspirators starting in 1989. Between 2000 and 2007, her most prolific period, she issued 152 fraudulent refund checks worth $42 million.
>
> Walters gambled heavily and made 45 trips to Las Vegas and Atlantic City. She had expensive tastes. She charged more than $2.3 million during shopping sprees at such high-end stores as Nordstrom and Neiman Marcus ... she had a personal shopper.
>
> When agents raided her Northwest Washington home, they discovered a trove of luxury watches, designer purses, and expensive furniture.
>
> Known as "Mother Harriette," Walters often gave cash and checks to friends and co-workers. She distributed $1.2 million in checks and an undetermined amount of cash to her colleagues from 2001 to 2007, according to authorities.
>
> The scheme unraveled in 2007 when the bank manager [at Bank of America who deposited $18 million in fraudulent checks] lost his job. An employee at SunTrust Bank grew suspicious when Jayrece Turnbull, Walters's niece, tried to deposit a $410,000 refund check. The bank employee alerted the FBI."[292]

How could this have gone on unnoticed so long and so ostentatiously? How could Chief Financial Officer Nat Gandhi, who served as the head of that office from 2000 to 2007 when the most egregious actions took place, have been totally unaware, especially since he had been warned by the D.C. Auditor? And Dr. Gandhi was a product of the Financial Control Board, having served as the Deputy to then Chief Financial Officer Tony Williams, and then as CFO himself, during the Control Board period of the 1990s. Once again, I say, save us from our saviors. The real lesson here is that strong oversight is important at every level of government. Gandhi survived the scandal, but needless to say, his reputation was damaged.

COG'S 50th Anniversary

The 50th Anniversary of the Metropolitan Washington Council of Governments (COG) was marked in the year 2007. At the beginning of that year, COG asked me to be the Chair of its 50th Anniversary celebration, which was quite a unique honor. We put together a forum about the future of the region, a commemorative book, and a real big party in November to culminate the festivities. All of this was done with strong committees and the able leadership of our Executive Director, David J. Robertson, who served with COG for decades and was one of the finest, nicest and smartest public servants I ever met.

Interestingly enough, I helped raise over $350,000 from outside groups to fund our anniversary celebration, and even made the calls directly myself—something I've never been able to do for my own campaigns! We had the Futures Forum luncheon at George Washington University with Jim Vance of NBC4 as our moderator, four panelists, and Leonard Downie Jr., Executive Editor of *The Washington Post*, as our keynote speaker. (Sadly, Jim passed away several months ago.)

We scheduled the night of November 15, 2007 for the 50th Anniversary Gala with months of advance notice going out to our membership. The D.C. tax office scandal broke on Wednesday, November 7th. Instead of scheduling an emergency hearing on this news-breaking story anytime during that week after, Chair Gray scheduled the hearing for the 15th, knowing full well, especially because he was Chair of the COG Board then, that the COG Anniversary was starting at 6 p.m. that same evening. Why not delay one more day and start the hearing on the 16th, if not days before?

I could hardly believe it and called, wrote, did everything I could to try to have him use another day, but to no avail. I stayed at the hearing until 5:00, but then as the Chair and host of the celebration, I had to leave to go to the Gala. There were about 500 regional leaders gathered at the Mellon Auditorium. We had a lovely reception first and then started dinner about 7:30, along with the program, which I was MC-ing. Specials guests included Virginia Governor Tim Kaine (now a Senator and former Democratic Vice Presidential candidate), Congressman James Moran, and former Maryland Governor Parris Glendening, among hundreds of others, mainly notables.

It was a wonderful event, marred only by looking out at the crowded audience and seeing several totally empty tables, including a few in the front, reserved for D.C. officials, who had all RSVP'd yes weeks before. Governor Tim Kaine managed to fly in from Richmond in the rain for the celebration. But my own D.C. Council Chair could not manage to either schedule appropriately or adjourn the hearing that he had waited eight days to have. That hearing finally did end at 9 p.m. so my D.C. colleagues came over at about 9:15 before the 10 p.m. ending. It was just so disrespectful to an organization that deserved better, especially from its Chair. Was I annoyed? You betcha. And obviously still am.

COG is special and I loved being involved with it for decades. I said that night: "This is a marvelous organization that has made a difference in so many ways during the past 50 years. We are a family of more than 250 public officials, and many business and civic leaders, representing almost five million people in the National Capital Region. This family shares common values and doesn't let boundaries and barriers prevent us from doing what is best for the region we love and the communities we serve." (It now has 60 years of outstanding regional cooperation, and the population of the region is now over six million.)

CHAPTER 42

Sick and Safe Leave

On a spring day in 2007, a Sick and Safe Leave bill was brought forward and all 10 of my colleagues' names were included, either as co-introducers or co-sponsors, everyone except me. (Note that two seats were vacant awaiting a special election.) When the paper the next day listed the 10 members who had signed on when it was presented and cited me as the only one who did not, I did add my name as a co-sponsor that day as I favored the idea despite some strong concerns.

I had perused the legislation quickly on the dais and I liked its purpose of giving sick leave to workers who were not otherwise provided it, and the fact that it included employees who were victims of domestic violence, and thus the "safe" in the title. The leave would be earned through hours worked—starting after 60 days of employment—so it would apply to part-time workers as well. However, when I saw that this original bill stated than any employer with six or more employees would be required to provide up to 10 days of sick and safe leave per year, and even those with fewer than six employees would have to provide five days, I felt it was too extreme in days given and would put too many of our struggling businesses out of business, especially smaller ones. That is why I did not sign on the first day.

The legislation had been promoted by 26 organizations including unions and public interest groups like the D.C. Employment Justice Center and the Fiscal Policy Institute. It came to me as my Committee was now Workforce Development and Government Operations. Since it dealt with the private sector (as government workers already got sick leave), it could have easily gone to the Economic Development Committee or the Health Committee or another. I never really delved into it, but I presumed all those well-meaning Councilmembers who supported it were glad to see it sent it to me, the initial lone non-signer-on-er, to have it just die in my Committee—or so they thought.

The activists started demonstrating outside my office door practically immediately. Despite the fact that I had a lot of the government with over 30 boards, commissions and agencies under my purview, and had more than my share of work to do, their constant demonstrations either outside the Wilson Building or in front of my office certainly kept their legislation on my radar screen. But after years of serving, I was used to those kinds of things so that's *not* the reason I decided to act.

The crux of the legislation really played into one of my whole philosophies of life and that is basically subsidizing the working poor, with the emphasis on working. I have always had an intolerance for able-minded and able-bodied people who just live—or are allowed to live—off the public dole. I think it's not only bad for taxpayers, but also bad for them. But with this issue of sick leave for workers, you are talking about individuals who are not just sitting at home, but who go to work, really wanting to better their lives and those of their families. And it is not their fault that the only jobs that they can find are part-time and have no benefits. So I knew I wanted to do something.

Behind the scenes, I started to look into the issue and found out that there were major national drug store companies in which 51% of their workers were part-time. And why? Obviously to deny those workers any benefits. And these were not small businesses—quite the contrary! I became even more anxious to do something about it. But I knew that these 26 organizations were politically strong individually and certainly collectively, and that it would be hard to move them from their original extreme legislation, or so you would think with 10 introducers/co-sponsors.

Meanwhile, I want to add that none of those ten movers of the bill ever asked me to go forward and/or work on it. *Not one.* But on my own, I became passionate on the subject.

It seemed so inhumane not to have any sick leave. Every time I entered a drug store and saw the person behind the counter, usually an African American woman, including many older ones, I thought about how, if she had woken up that morning with a bad cold, her decision was either to stay home and lose her pay or go into work sick. What a lousy decision to have to make—and so unfair. And how is it in society's best interest—or even the business's best interest—to force someone to make such an awful choice? So the worker, trying to avoid losing the needed pay, comes in, coughing and sneezing all over the money taken in and change being given back, spreading germs everywhere. This is in no one's best interest. Most importantly, it is inhumane to put any working human in that position.

So about six weeks after the introduction, I called an evening meeting of the 26 organizations that had authored and brought the bill to the Council. Representatives from about 20 of those organizations showed up at a conference room I had booked in the

Wilson Building. My staff and I were the only other people in attendance. This meeting will be ever-present in my mind as one of the most satisfying moments in my long career.

I said to those very progressive people that I believed in the cause, had not signed on that first day as I thought it was extreme and that it would put businesses, especially smaller ones, at risk. I then said to them my two conditions before I'd work on the bill.

One was, "I will dissipate the bill. I will water it down. I will make it a shadow of its former self. But I will deliver you sick leave legislation that will make us the first 'state' in the nation to do so and only the second jurisdiction after San Francisco."

My other condition was that after working with them and the business, university and hospital communities et al, whatever compromise bill I put forward and got the Committee to vote on "would NOT be changed when it left my Committee and went before the full body." I went on to emphasize the point by saying that I do not intend to take on this very controversial and cutting-edge issue, which might put my political career on the line, and then just be the conduit for their piling back on the same extreme measures after I had worked so hard on a good compromise bill.

I then looked each of the 20 or so representatives in the eye and asked each of them if they would swear that they would agree to both of those conditions. Every single one of them did. And then I asked that they contact the six organizations which did not have a representative present and get back to me with their willingness to do the same. They did get back to me, and each of the others agreed to my conditions as well.

I had never made that strong of a demand in my then many decades of being in a position of making public policy. And here I was asking it of 26 single-minded and staunch activists. It took a lot of gall, but I really needed their assurance to act and they knew it. I so wanted to help, but I was not going to put all the blood, sweat and tears into this sort of (at the time) earth-shattering position to be left with the original "killer of business" bill.

Interestingly enough, I trusted them and their assurances, even though my common sense and experience told me I was naïve to do so. But I did trust them, and each and every one of them, individually and organizationally, hung in with me throughout this enormously tough effort. And I, even knowing as we moved along, that my career would probably end here, hung in with them as well. And I've never regretted it.

I started immediately after that evening to organize meetings with the Board of Trade, the Chamber of Commerce, the Consortium of Universities, the Hospital Association, and many other vested parties. And I did start "dissipating the bill" with the intent of putting in place realistic legislation that would deliver sick leave to workers which was as palatable as possible to business—and certainly more palatable than the original bill. These negotiations went on for several months and I did try to take private sector legitimate concerns into account. Of course, all of these business interests preferred for the bill to just die. But since 10 Councilmembers had initially signed on and I, the 11th, was now taking the lead in advancing it, their only choice appeared to be to get the best bill possible. I would also get together either by phone or in person with advocates for the legislation to let them know the details of what was going on.

Finally, right before Christmas and the Council recess, I did get the Committee to pass the bill unanimously. We changed the original bill that was based on San Francisco's, which gave five to 10 days. In our bill, we reduced the number of maximum days from 10 to seven and reduced them further based upon the size of the business. So large businesses (51 or more employees) would give seven days; medium-sized (31 to 50) would have six; small (11 to 30) would give five; and micro (10 or less employees) would give three days instead of the original 10 days for six or more workers and five days for one to five workers. We also made sure that employees could earn sick time only after a 90-day probationary period instead of the original 60 days. We then added a requirement that only employees who spent 50% of their work time in D.C. would qualify. We excluded independent contractors, students in work-study programs, and critical healthcare workers. And we added domestic partnerships under the definition of family. We worked very hard to strike the right balance.

Barbara Lang, President of the D.C. Chamber of Commerce, immediately the day of the vote issued a press release that they had scored a good victory in that the bill was far better than the one originally introduced, and that they had worked well with the Committee Chair (me) to address their concerns.

Yet over the holidays, the garage owners, some of the wealthiest people in the private sector, started having a hissy fit and began riling up everyone in the business community to protest the bill. Of course, I became aware of all this and scheduled a meeting in January with the business community on their turf. And all the big business owners, developers, restauranteurs and garage titans came out in droves.

My staff and I arrived prepared with very understandable charts in hand, which compared the original bill to the "dissipated" version passed by the Committee a few weeks earlier. After distributing the charts, I started a PowerPoint presentation, allowing time for questions and the airing of additional concerns. But the group was so angry and impatient that it was hard to continue the presentation. They just wanted the bill killed. They were not interested in hearing any of the details of how far the bill had come in addressing their issues.

At first I tried to remain respectful, patient and listen, but their belligerence got to me. They were literally yelling at me and I must admit, although far outnumbered, I raised my voice some as well. What I had hoped would be an informative and "look how far we've come with your legitimate concerns being addressed" session became a "die, bitch!" session. Many were actually threatening me about my reelection, which was coming up soon. I, who had been such a friend of the business community with decreased taxes, tax-free holidays and free parking, and had taken on the smoke-free issue on their behalf, was now their worst enemy. But more significantly, I knew the fight for the bill was going to be harder than ever.

At the first reading of the legislation (and there are always two readings except in emergencies), which took place on February 5, 2008, the very organized and well-financed business community did two effective things:

One, they paid people to arrive as soon as the building opened, to sit in the chairs in the Council Chamber to hold them for the private sector people who would arrive right before the meeting began. Each of them had on a t-shirt handed out by the business community that I believe read, "Don't Kill Business!" That left the advocates for the bill—with or without t-shirts—with few or no seats in the chamber. Most were then forced to sit in a far-off room with the proceedings piped in—making it look like most people were against the bill.

And two, the business people had lobbied the Council hard to table the bill, ostensibly to buy more time for "compromise," claiming that the Chair of the Committee had made no such efforts after all those months of my doing exactly that. Everyone knew that this tabling maneuver was really a "kill-the-bill" tactic. And we all knew it would never have made it off the table should it wind up there—except for possibly many years later. But I knew also that if we beat the effort to table the bill that a vast majority, if not all, would be forced to vote to pass it as it was important to other of their constituents; and after all, they all had already signed on to it even when it was far more extreme.

The business community had six votes to table the bill—Chair Vince Gray, Councilmembers Jack Evans, Kwame Brown, David Catania, Muriel Bowser and Yvette Alexander. (Muriel and Yvette had been voted in by that point in a special election.) I had seven votes to oppose tabling—me, Marion Barry, Phil Mendelson, Jim Graham, Mary Cheh, Tommy Wells and Harry Thomas Jr. I had reconfirmed those anti-tabling votes at the end of the day on Monday, walking around to each of their offices. I also revisited the pro-tabling votes to ask them to reconsider.

One of those tabling votes, Muriel Bowser, said she would consider switching if I made an additional amendment that would require fewer days for some of the smaller businesses in her Ward. I told her that I had already compromised the bill to such an extent that I really did not want, at this last minute, to go back to the 26 organizations to ask for more. And besides, I did have my seven votes—all of whom had just reassured me late that day.

That Tuesday morning, March 4, 2008, I arrived on the dais early for the legislative session that was supposed to begin at 10 a.m., and where the first reading on the bill was to occur. As I sat there, waiting for the meeting to start, I began to get a premonition that the bill might be in trouble. That premonition became even more pronounced as two of my votes, Marion Barry and Harry Thomas Jr., were not on the dais at 10:15 a.m. I reached Marion on his cell phone and said literally, "Get your ass in here now," which he did soon thereafter.

When Harry finally arrived, I just knew that he had switched. I'm not sure how I knew. It may have been his expression. Regardless, I just knew. I motioned to Ed Lazare of the Fiscal Policy Institute, who was one of the leaders of the Sick and Safe Leave advocates, to meet me in the back. There, I told him I was worried, and that I needed to find a new vote (maybe just a backup but I had to have a new vote), and that the only way I could get it was with an additional amendment. He said, "Carol, we trust you. Do what you have to do."

I went over to Muriel and quietly said to her, "Now would you switch if I amended the bill by raising the employee threshold? "

She said, "Yes." I then knew we had it in the bag. I just knew my instinct about Harry was right and that now we'd still be okay.

When we got to the portion of the meeting on this issue, I moved the bill and discussed it, using some of the arguments that I mentioned earlier, such as workers having no choice because these businesses made sure their jobs were only part-time to avoid any leave, and how *inhumane* it was for these businesses, regardless of size, to deny *any* sick leave.

Right after I spoke, the motion to table the bill was made. (Tabling always takes precedence over the previous motion and is not debatable.) As the Secretary of the Council called out the names to vote for tabling, there were five "ayes," and sure enough, when they got to Harry Thomas Jr., he voted yes to tabling with a big smirky smile on his face, knowing that a seventh "aye" (and the winning one) would follow. His smile and vote prompted smug looks on the yes-to-tabling votes' faces, as well as those of the business community seated in the chamber, all basically saying, "Victory is ours!"

Not so fast. Muriel and I just glanced at each other. Coincidentally, she was either the last to vote or second to last. When it came her turn, Muriel voted no. Her totally unexpected no to tabling, which I had just secured unbeknownst to anyone but the three of us (her, Ed and me), certainly took those smug looks off their faces. The victory instead belonged to the people who really deserved it—the workers.

Now the Council was forced to vote on the bill itself. This first-reading amended version, which I had changed, adjusted the business categories from four to three, keeping the maximum number of sick and safe days at seven instead of the original 10. Businesses with 100 or more employees would provide up to seven days. Businesses with 25 to 99 employees would provide up to five days. And businesses with 24 or less employees would give up to three.

Sick and Safe Leave easily passed, 11 to 2. Only Jack Evans and David Catania stuck with the business people and voted no. That was especially interesting in that they had both signed on to the original bill, which was far more repugnant to the business community than the one before them that day. On second reading the next month with the inclusion of wait staff and bartenders in the excluded category, all 13 Councilmembers did unanimously vote for Sick and Safe Leave. And I always knew that would be the case once hiding behind tabling the bill was off the table.

It was one of the hardest, most nerve-wracking, frustrating, deceptive, time-consuming and character-revealing (and not always in a good way) experiences of my life. But I am grateful for having had the fortitude to see it through to the end. I am also grateful to the advocates who truly compromised, recognizing it was the smartest strategy to make the bill become reality, and to my colleagues—Marion Barry, Muriel Bowser, Mary Cheh, Jim Graham, Phil Mendelson and Tommy Wells—who stayed the course.

And as I suspected, my career figuratively did end here (more on that later). But I remain proud of that law and would fight that same fight all over again to get the same result. I also encourage other jurisdictions to take on this same just cause. And now, nearly 10 years later, it should be a far less arduous path, especially with other jurisdictions having bought in, including: Milwaukee, Connecticut, Seattle and other cities in Washington, California, Massachusetts, New York City, Philadelphia, Pittsburgh, Vermont, Minneapolis, Chicago, Montgomery County in Maryland, Jersey City and other cities in New Jersey. Regardless, it's worth the effort. I was pleased when President Obama on September 7, 2015 unveiled an executive order requiring federal contractors to offer employees up to seven days of paid sick leave. It has become obvious that our legislation has been used as a prototype by the feds and these other jurisdictions as the number of days is the same.[293]

I described the sick leave issue as a win at the beginning of this section. It truly was a win that really mattered, especially for hardworking people and their families—a win that makes me smile.

On with the Show

Some of the most fun events I have participate in are benefits for the TheatreLab, which is a non-profit theater education center. One of their great programs is called "Life Stories," where individuals in prisons, seniors in assisted living homes, wounded veterans, and at-risk youth tell their stories through creative self-expression. They are probably best known for their work with homeless women at N Street Village, which resulted in a performance at the Kennedy Center and a documentary. They also give acting scholarships to students who cannot afford the classes.

At past annual fundraising events, TheatreLab invited elected officials and local news people to act out scenes from Shakespeare. Not professional actors, clearly, and with no rehearsal, we just read our lines with scripts in our hands with our pajamas on.

The first time I did it, we were at St. Columba's Episcopal Church late at night. That year I was paired with WAMU radio show host Kojo Nnamdi in *The Taming of the Shrew*. I'm sure you can guess who played the shrew. Kojo had actually been an actor so he was quite good and that made me look even worse. (By the way, Kojo has been a good friend since the mid-1970s when he had a television show at Howard University and interviewed me fairly often back when I was a leader on the Board of Education.)

Years later, I was paired with NBC4 TV reporter Tom Sherwood at the TheaterLab's own auditorium—with Tom on the stage and me up in the balcony—to perform the famous balcony scene from Romeo and Juliet. One problem—other than the fact that I cannot act and was playing at 68 years of age, a 15-year-old—is that there was no lighting whatsoever up on the balcony. Even reading glasses couldn't help. Tom was fine on the well-lit stage, but I was rendered speechless—a rare event.

Tom read his lines and then the audience waited with baited breath for mine. Silence. But then I thought, the show has to go on. These people have paid good money to hear us do Shakespeare. It was time to improvise. I just began making up the lines. "Romeo, oh Romeo? Where are you?! Art you there? Romeo, I can't find you! There's no light! I love you, Romeo!" Just making up gibberish. Soon Tom and I could not stop laughing, nor could the audience. "Romeo, are you there?! Romeo, answer me!!!" I sure learned that night that I needed to stick to my day job.

This actually happened many years ago and I look back on it with some humor, but mostly embarrassment. Others have fonder memories. They still bring it up to me and Tom, saying, "Now that was a fun night." In 2013, TheaterLab presented me with its Organizational Stewardship Award—obviously not for acting.

Equality

I was honored to be named the Best Straight Ally, by both *Washington Blade* readers and editors three times (2003, 2004, 2006), and to be named Local Hero-Female by the *Blade* in 2008.

I have always been a strong supporter for domestic partnership rights and worked hard, along with others on the Council, to help make them the most expansive in the country. Then in 2004, gay marriage was made legal in Massachusetts. As D.C. talked about doing the same, some supportive individuals and groups appeared to be cautious. They were worried, for good reason, about Congress, which constantly interfered in our business. That concern centered on the fear that Congress might roll back not only any new law but our hard-won domestic partnership rights. Having spoken up against Congress in fight after fight (voting rights, gay and lesbian adoptions, needle exchange, our medicinal marijuana law) and losing three out of four, I shared those concerns.[294]

I stated so at a Human Rights Campaign rally. Some then vehemently questioned my commitment. So to clarify my position, I wrote a commentary for *The Washington Blade* that ran on May 30, 2008. This beginning excerpt spells it out: "I am not opposed to same-sex marriage but progress requires strategy. ... Do I oppose same-sex marriage? No. Do I have any personal, moral or religious issues with same-sex marriage? Absolutely not. But was I willing yesterday—or am I willing today—to risk sacrificing our hard-fought domestic partnership laws, which took 10 long years for Congress to allow us to implement? Again, the answer is no. Will tomorrow be better? Yes, I believe it will, and I certainly intend to help that day along."[295]

If I had been on the Council in 2009, I would have voted yes to recognizing marriages from other states. And in 2010, I would have voted yes for same-sex marriage in D.C., which did pass into law that year. I have been thrilled to see such marriages passed into law in so many states, including New York in 2011, and hailed the Supreme Court decision in 2015 that makes it legal everywhere now.

I was very happy my own daughter Stephanie married her female partner, Jackie, of four years, in October of 2012 in New York. Jackie is an extremely smart, lovely woman who I am very fond of as well as her family. Unfortunately, they separated two years ago and are in the process now of a non-contested divorce. I was sad but supportive.

Steph had been bisexual over the years, including, as mentioned, being engaged to a man in the late '90s. But every time she was with a woman and I "outed" her telling my friends she was a lesbian (as many think saying "bisexual" is a cop out), five minutes later Steph would be with a man and I'd have to "un-out" her. Even with a man, Stephanie felt so strongly about the right of members of the LGBT community to marry that she really did not want to marry herself until her lesbian and gay friends were able to. It is wonderful now that there is true equality in this area. It is finally as it should be—including the right to divorce.

Punishing Good Behavior

Each year in May, elected officials and other D.C. government personnel above a certain grade level and/or having certain responsibilities must file a financial disclosure form with the Office of Campaign Finance. In the 2008 filing, it listed any holdings you have, including stocks worth $5,000 or more in companies that may do business with the District of Columbia government, any outside employment you have, as well as any gift that was given to you costing $100 or more from anyone or any entity doing business with the D.C. government. (Now, nine years later, any stocks worth $1000 or more must be listed regardless of whether the company does business or not with the District; and gifts of $100 or more must be reported regardless of the giver.) Relating to my stocks in that 2008 filing, I and my financial adviser tried to find out what companies did business with the District of Columbia, and that list was impossible to obtain as they said it fluctuates constantly. Therefore, I just listed all my stocks worth $5,000 or more, whether relevant or not. I had no outside employment, so there was nothing to report there.

I also always kept track, along with my Administrative Assistant, of any tickets or gifts or meals that might be worth $100 or more and reported them. In one case, a restaurant owner (who was a friend of my uncle for 40 years and who owned one of my favorite eateries where I took my children to dinner for major family occasions and always paid), told the waiter that he was covering the bill for my birthday. I said, "Thank you very much, but you must tell me how much the bill would have been so I can report it." He gave me the amount (about $250). I paid a cash tip to the waiter and then reported the gift in full, as I had no idea if the restaurant did business with the D.C. government or not (it does not by the way). As always, I erred on the side of caution.

Each year, organizations such as the D.C. Chamber of Commerce would give each Councilmember two tickets to their major annual events, as well as tickets to the Mayor, and those tickets at that time were being sold to others for $400 each. In this case I knew that the D.C. Chamber of Commerce had some hospitality-type contracts with the D.C. government, so I felt required to report those tickets with the total value of $800. There were tickets from other organizations, and since I did not know whether they did business with the city or not, I reported those tickets as well.

In May of 2008, I filed my 2007 financial report with the Office of Campaign Finance as required by law. Then an article appeared entitled "Carol Schwartz's Bounty," in big, bold print, citing all the "freebies" I had reported. Well, lo and behold, I guess I was the only one who did so, even though I was certainly not the only Councilmember at many of the functions I attended. The amazing part is that the article was able to cite those gifts *only* because I actually reported them—unlike others.

I certainly know, as should the media, that both the Mayor and Councilmembers are likely to get treated to free dinners and events by business people who really do business with the D.C. government, unlike the restauranteur I had reported. Freebies are regularly offered. Even these days (and I've been gone from office for over eight years), when I pay a cab driver, he sometimes says, "I'd like to treat you to this ride." My response is now and before: "Thank you, but you have to earn a living." If I had taken the offer and the ride was $100 or more, I would have reported it.

Unfortunately, instead of applauding my taking the gift section of the financial filing seriously—and questioning why other Councilmembers had not reported so fully—I became the bad guy. So much for honesty is the best policy!

A Close Call

Clearly, I have always prided myself in being honorable and ethical. But there was one time where I got tested to the nines. After we re-drew the boundaries for the Wards, needed after the census count, I received in the mail a Ward 2 sticker, though I live in Ward 1. But Ward 2 is just across the street.

Connecticut Ave. was the dividing line and I actually made sure that my side of Connecticut Ave. stayed in Ward 1 as that's where I had moved to years earlier because of its diversity—and I'm sure others had as well. But here in my hand was a Ward 2 sticker, and it was hard to send it back. Ward 2 is downtown, Georgetown, Dupont Circle, Logan Circle, the Verizon Center—all the places I drive to and can't park in. Oh dear ... But honorable, ethical me sent it back and requested my Ward 1 sticker. And I've regretted it ever since—but I know I would do same again. Darn ...

Senator Kay Bailey Hutchison at an event in my home

The High-Heel Race

In 2007, with comedian
Dick Gregory, who passed away
in August of 2017

Marion and Nelson, a couple of 65
years, at their home in Texas with
Jenna Welch (Laura Bush's mother)

With Marion Barry and Jack
Evans as part of Mayoral
delegation to South Africa

Doug's and Hilary's headshots

Dorothy Height at the Martin Luther
King Memorial groundbreaking

Friends did a potluck 65th
birthday party at my apartment.

Dear Uncle Seymour and Aunt Betty
visit me in Florida.

Jay Leno, who happened to be
performing at Midland College
the night of Mom's poetry contest

2007 Holiday Card, taken with guests
at the annual
Office on Aging Holiday Party

Parading and campaigning

Meeting with delegation
of African legislators

Me and Corn

CHAPTER 43

The Fight of My Life

I was up for reelection for my Council seat that November and it turned into one of the most difficult experiences of my life. A striking incident and harbinger of what was to come happened at the Gay Pride Parade on June 14, 2008. I had very recently announced that I would be running again for the at-large seat on the D.C. Council, and my daughters, who were in town, had gone out to hang up posters along the parade route. They called me very upset as they discovered along that same route, brand new posters in my signature yellow and black campaign colors, which read, "Ask Carol Schwartz why she is against marriage equality." And this was weeks after my piece in the *Blade*, which explained I was not. The signs were misleading and even worse, illegal. Public political messages are required by law to cite the organization that paid for them. These signs had no such verbiage.

That afternoon, as I along with other elected officials lined up our cars, I noticed David Catania behind me with a huge vindictive grin on his face as he looked at me. I knew why.

Kevin Naff, editor and owner of *The Washington Blade*, without my ever saying a word, cited David as responsible, as if it were common knowledge. Kevin called the signs "cowardly." Fortunately, most along the parade route did not take the bait. I heard a few barbs, but the majority of watchers were people who knew my history. Their comments were positive, including a few memorable ones such as, "F... 'em, Carol!"

I saw a car carrying a young man with a sign: Patrick Mara. I did not know him or what he was running for. I soon learned.

To be honest, I was a little ambivalent about running initially for several reasons. I was seriously overworked. I know I did it to myself by taking on a Committee (Government Operations) that had a lot under its purview already and then being able to add, with Vince Gray's approval, far more which was of particular interest to me, like Workforce Development—all without additional staff. And speaking of staff, maybe because of this additional work stress or just differences in personalities, my gang, who had always been like family, now too often were squabbling like one.

The other reason I was a little ambivalent was that most of the camaraderie on the Council among its members was disappearing. The Council had always been a lot of work, especially if you did it full-time and took it as seriously as I did. But it could have its moments of fun, particularly if there was congeniality among its members and staff as well as the Mayor. The Wilson Building in the '80s and most of the '90s met that standard. You'd walk down the hall and people would stop and visit, or at least say hi. That had changed—not only less camaraderie, but less civility as well.

But then I realized the Council was not only what I knew, but it was also what I was good at. And more than anything, I valued making a big difference in many people's lives. Legislating and active oversight afforded me that opportunity on a wholesale basis.

As usual, I did not get out there in the campaign as soon as I needed to. That was always the case with me, not because I was arrogant about getting reelected (though I did know I had fairly good name recognition and I heard my positives were high), but because 1) I hated to be distracted from my Council work, and 2) I hated to raise money. Thus, I would put off setting up an office and hiring campaign staff for as long as I possibly could.

The Plot Begins

In the meantime, David Catania was clearly determined to get me off the Council—and he used Sick and Safe Leave as his vehicle. He teamed up with those most upset about it. These comrades included parking magnates like husband and wife, Bud and Cherrie Doggett, construction company owners like John McMahon and his son Brett of Miller & Long, and corporate millionaires like William Dean of M.C. Dean (the company he inherited from his grandfather and which employed David), as well as Barbara Lang, President of the D.C. Chamber of Commerce. It is clear that they and David all came together to plot my undoing. The group backed a Republican opponent rumored to have been picked by Catania— Patrick Mara, then a former lobbyist and part-time bartender.

I was not wrong about the orchestrators. Even *The Washington Post* in 2013 (five years later) reported who was behind this and why: "He [Mara] challenged former Councilmember Carol Schwartz in the GOP primary. Earlier that year, Schwartz had pushed through a bill requiring paid sick leave for most workers in the city, prompting Mara to run against her with the support of business groups and Councilmember David A. Catania ...."[296] (I not only didn't write that article, I wasn't even interviewed for it.)

David tried to keep his backing of Patrick Mara quiet until it was reported in the *Washington City Paper* that Catania made his staff devote hours to the Mara campaign from the get-go and they were also very visible at Mara's primary election night party.

This group supporting my opponent used a Political Action Committee called "Citizens for Empowerment"[297] and other PACs to send out a multitude of highly negative and misleading communications about me during a two-month period before the Republican primary in September. This included 17 push polls, which are calls to voters and often push "fake news," and 13 mailings full of much of the same.

On August 22, 2008, Mike DeBonis in the *Washington City Paper* verified the use of these PACs for these negative mailings. DeBonis wrote that Citizens for Empowerment was "largely funded by Miller & Long Construction and electrical contractor M.C. Dean" (that's in spite of not even being corporate citizens in the District as they are headquartered in Maryland and Virginia respectively). Here are fuller quotes from DeBonis's article: [298]

"Patrick Mara is doing a great job of challenging At-Large Councilmember Carol Schwartz in September's Republican primary. The first-timer, for starters, has nearly matched Schwartz's $100,000-plus campaign war chest.

And Mara won't have to spend a dime of it on negative campaigning—the PACs have it covered.

For one, there's the Citizens for Empowerment political action committee, the anti-union outfit funded largely by Miller & Long construction and electrical contractor M.C. Dean. Not only did the PAC donate to Mara's campaign, but mail has started showing up in Republican mailboxes bearing the 'Paid for by Citizens for Empowerment PAC' label.

One such mailer obtained by LL [Loose Lips] shows a gentleman holding an empty pocket out of his pants alongside a smaller picture of Schwartz, under the headline 'tax-and-spender: raising our taxes, wasting taxpayer dollars and supporting labor unions.'

Then there's the Nation's Capital Committee for Good Government, which has yet to spend a significant dime on the race, aside from funding a Web site that declares the group's 'initial goal is to help elect Patrick Mara At-Large Councilmember.'* ...

Mara says he's aware of the mailer and the Web site, but declined to comment on the propriety thereof. 'I can't control what others are doing,' he says. 'I'm trying to focus on the campaign.'"

Note: The National Capital Committee for Good Government gave $2,000 directly to the Mara campaign on July 3, 2008 ($1,000 more than legally allowed). Actually, it looks like there were $16,000 worth of over-the-limit contributions in the 2008 Patrick Mara for Council report.

The main PAC used to support Mara and target me, Citizens for Empowerment, was started in December of 2005, according to the D.C. Office of Campaign Finance Report. It collected a total of $331,950 until its last donation on November 6, 2008, right at the time the 2008 Council election ended. M.C. Dean and the Dean family contributed a total of $140,000, while Miller & Long/the McMahon family contributed $135,000. The other large contribution was $50,000 from Sigal Construction.[299]

In digging further, I discovered that Citizens for Empowerment appears to be the Political Action Committee arm of a nonprofit called the D.C. for Economic Empowerment Coalition (DEEC), whose address as listed on the "Non-Profits: Find the Company" website is M.C. Dean's address in Dulles, VA, with the contact being William Dean.[300]

It is apparent that the Citizens for Empowerment PAC, which was started at the end of 2005, was used to fight the agreement for an all-union-built baseball stadium, but by the end of 2007, as I was moving the sick leave legislation forward, it was then used to punish me as well.

A 2008 report by the Local Laborers International Union corroborates the efforts of the D.C. Economic Empowerment Coalition against the stadium and its connection to M.C. Dean:

> "The D.C. Economic Empowerment Coalition or DEEC, has spent significant sums on mailings and advertisements maligning the stadium project. ... the DEEC's sister organization and Political Action Committee, Citizens for Empowerment, is heavily funded by M.C. Dean, a Virginia electrical contractor, and Miller & Long, a Maryland contractor ... Even the DEEC web site [was] held in the name M.C. Dean."[301]

While the Citizens for Empowerment PAC/M.C. Dean connection was going on from 2005 to 2011 (overlapping the time the PAC was actively supporting Mara), David Catania was General Counsel of a subsidiary of M.C. Dean called Open Band. This corporation held contracts with the D.C. government, maybe making his employment—and even his votes and speeches against the baseball stadium—at risk of a possible conflict of interest. He earned $125,000 in this part-time job with Open Band. Then, in 2011, while still on the Council, Catania took a senior executive position at M.C. Dean directly, with a raise in salary to $240,000 per year for the part-time job.[302] On November 11, 2011, *The Washington City Paper* quoted William Dean, who described David's new role as a "jack of all trades, frankly."[303]

In a *Washington Post* article in 2014, when responding to whether his affiliation with a company with D.C. contracts was a conflict of interest, he said, "At the company, there was a firewall."[304] However, as an elected Councilmember, he actively worked to replace a fellow Councilmember with a candidate who he pushed as better serving the business interests of entities like his employer, a non-union contractor with D.C. government contracts.[305] And it certainly looks like it was done with the significant financial backing of that same employer. Sure doesn't sound like much of a "firewall" in my estimation.

I know many will say I am bringing up this situation out of bitterness and because I have an ax to grind. And I do. I did resent how these deep-pocketed interests went after me with David apparently leading the way. But I have been out of elected office for nearly nine years—and these issues go way beyond me. The public complains for good reason about the revolving door between government and lobbyists/business interests. In this case, where the employer of a Councilmember was heavily supporting a candidate with its PAC while that Councilmember was very involved with that candidate's campaign, there is not even a door. It is everyone huddled together in a room—near Dulles Airport in Virginia.

There was another PAC which I suspect was involved in supporting Mara as it was started in 2008 and was funded by many of the same operatives who directly supported his campaign, according to finance report filings. These were obviously people who did not want to give any amount of sick leave. This was BUD'S PAC and it raised $82,300 from 2008 to 2009. Its main contributors were the parking magnate Cherrie Doggett and John McMahon of Miller & Long at $35,000 apiece. Other contributors included Irwin Edlavitch of Atlantic Parking, Marc Slavin of MarcParc, George Vradenburg, Barbara Lang, Julyan & Julyan, the Altman Corporation, the D.C. Chamber of Commerce, THE Jeffrey Thompson, and the ubiquitous M.C. Dean. Many of these same people and entities also supported the D.C. Chamber of Commerce PAC and the Washington Board of Trade PAC, who were giving to newcomer Patrick Mara as well during that time.

(Speaking of William Dean of M.C. Dean, there was an article in *The Washington Post* on November 26, 2016 about his lavish affairs. It seems that his most recent Halloween party included "treats" like cocaine, topless women [which the reporter implied was like many of his fetes], and allegedly much worse.[306] So glad to be on the outs with that crowd!)

Executing the Plot

The anti-sick leave group knew they would have a hard time ousting me in the general election, as I had gotten 94,000 votes in the 2004 general election just four years earlier—the largest non-Democratic Council vote until 2016 after the population grew significantly. My count included broad support among Independents and Democrats all over the city, and even in the 2002 Mayoral race, I got a significant number of African American votes, including in Wards 7 and 8. Therefore, they decided to go after me in the Republican primary (our primaries are closed) as they realized that only a couple of thousand people usually vote in it at most, thus making it easier to put together enough votes to defeat me.

Another of their first orders of business, other than raising money, was to change their own registrations to Republican, as exemplified by Barbara Lang herself and David's staff. David was then an Independent, but used his Republican bona fides. They ran out to all the Young Republican Clubs at all the local universities (except for Howard and UDC) to register hundreds of college Republicans. Their message was, "Your choice is a 64-year-old liberal who brought sick leave to workers or a conservative young Republican who would have voted no." Interestingly, in the general election, at forums around town Mara said he would have voted yes to sick leave—obviously playing both sides.

Then here came the negative and distorted 13 mailings and 17 push polls in a two-months span—worse than any I had ever gotten in all my time as a voter in D.C. They were outrageous. The mailings were huge and expensive, and the push polls went like this: "Hi, aren't you glad baseball returned to the Nation's Capital? Did you know that Carol Schwartz tried to deny you baseball?" I wanted to yell: "In reality, I helped bring baseball to D.C., and actually, it was the orchestrator of this push poll who tried to deny baseball to the region."

A Councilmember targeting another in this way was unprecedented. I even went to Council Chair Vince Gray and begged him to intervene, saying, "We just don't do this on our body. You need to talk to him." Vince just said, "You two work it out." About four years later, after David turned on then Mayor Gray as he was planning to run for Mayor himself, I ran into Vince and he said to me, "I now know what you were talking about with David." I replied, "Well, you two just work it out."

I had wonderful volunteers as usual on the campaign, and a truly terrific staff member named Kristan who worked day and night. I not only wanted to win for myself and to not have the challenger's nasty campaign prevail, but I also did not want to disappoint my workers. And I was concerned that since sick leave appeared to be the reason for all this animosity and challenge, my defeat might hurt that important cause.

Amidst all the negativity, here came a mostly positive piece by Marc Fisher in *The Washington Post* on September 4th—five days before the primary—which I'm going to quote from liberally:

'D.C. Benefits From Schwartz's Fight Against Corruption'

"After three decades on the D.C. Council and school board, after the death of her husband, after losing four campaigns for mayor, Carol Schwartz says she is 'sort of used to having things work out not so well. I've led kind of a chaotic life.'

But the District's only Republican elected official is an eternal optimist, as sunshiny as her bright yellow convertible and as big a booster as this city has ever had.

It's fashionable in this year when the political mantra insists on urgent but undefined 'change' to conclude that elected officials who have been around for a long time must be cleared out to make way for a new generation. ...

It's certainly true that Schwartz is no comfortable fit in the GOP of Sarah Palin. Schwartz is a champion of gay rights, a self-professed liberal on most social issues and architect of the District's new law requiring businesses to grant a few days of annual sick leave to workers—a move that has the city's business establishment coughing up big money to get rid of her.

But going back to the Marion Barry era, Schwartz, now in her fourth term as an at-large council member, has been a rare fiscal conservative in a government that views taxpayers as a bottomless source of cash for every fly-by-night contractor ...

When her deep adenoidal voice rings out in a council hearing room, it's often the public's only chance to discover how the millions vanish and how little the people get in return. Not a real Republican? Well, maybe, but it is Schwartz who has spent the past year and a half preventing movement on Barry's bill that would give ex-offenders special protection under the city's human rights law. 'I don't think if you are a jewelry store, you should have to hire a jewel thief and if you don't hire them, they could sue you and the city has to pay for the lawyer,' Schwartz says. 'I mean, please.' And she's frozen for nearly two years a bill that would force such large retailers as Macy's or Target to pay the city's $11.75 [in 2008] an hour 'living' wage.' She says: 'It would chase away exactly the kind of retailers we're working so hard to bring into our city, so I bottled it up. And *I'm* anti-business?' ...

Only ... registered Republicans get to decide whether Schwartz stays or goes ... but the entire city benefits from Schwartz's non-ideological insistence that the city cannot afford the corruption and incompetence that has held it back for so long.

'She's beyond meticulous about knowing where every dollar is spent,' says Lawrence Guyot, a longtime Democratic activist who says he works to defeat all others save Schwartz and ... 'She is where the Republican Party should be, watching the spending without opposing helping people.' ...

After all those years in office, Schwartz is not exactly an outsider rebelling against the system. But she does still frequently poke the powers that be. I don't know whether Schwartz was right to stand up as one of only two council members opposing Mayor Adrian Fenty's takeover of the school system—the jury will be out on Chancellor Michelle Rhee's efforts for a good deal longer—but I do know that without Schwartz, hardly anyone would be keeping tabs on where the torrent of new school money is really going. ...

This newspaper's editorial board advised voters yesterday against returning Schwartz to office, calling her 'unrelentingly negative,' a term I'd think any legislator charged with overseeing a sprawling, profligate bureaucracy would wear proudly. ...

When I ask Schwartz whether she's confident of victory, she answers uncharacteristically monosyllabically: 'No.' Schwartz tears up at the prospect of losing because of her role in winning sick leave for the women who work the cash registers at chain stores. 'It's just a humane way of treating people who are trying to better their lives by working,' she says. 'Isn't that a Republican principle? If I go down on that one, I will really be proud.'"[307]

Unfortunately, though, my Republican voters were used to my breezing through the primary and thought it would be the same this time, or maybe they were just reeling from the onslaught of vicious mailings and calls to their home, so most did not bother to vote in spite of the fact the D.C. Republican Committee had gone out on a limb to support me in the primary. The *Post* did manage to vote—and it came out for Patrick Mara (as shown above).

Election night we gathered at campaign headquarters, which was on the second floor above the 7-11 at 12th and U Sts., N.W. I was hoping against hope. Then Mike Neibauer (*Washington Business Journal*) quietly informed me that their exit polls showed I would lose. I got 751 fewer votes than my opponent, while just 4,035 voters out of 30,000 registered Republicans participated in the extraordinary voter-light Republican primary.[308]

I was calm and collected then, and told my daughters who were quite devastated. I kept it together that evening as many supporters and colleagues came by, but I felt like I had been kicked in the gut. I hated to see such a vicious campaign win—given my feelings about never rewarding bad behavior—even if I hadn't been the target. But I must admit a part of me was just glad to have a break from the bombardment of those nasty, misleading slings and arrows that had been coming my way non-stop.

Losing My Sister

An even sadder thing than losing the election was losing the woman, Linda Garmon, who had been like my sister since we were both eight years old.

In 2008, Linda was diagnosed with stage IV lung cancer. I went down to visit her in the summer. My son Doug was traveling on his *Greyhound Diaries* project, and happened to be in Corpus Christi. He took a bus to San Antonio to be with "Aunt" Linda as well. Sitting at her bedside, she taught Doug the song written by her brother Buddy, "Truck Driver's Road." Thank goodness, he wrote the words down and still sings it—a song I have loved since I was about 15 years old. On August 8, 2008, Linda Gayle passed away. The deaths of both Aunt Doe and Linda remain very hard to think or talk about. And Johnny is in that same category.

A New Friend in the Midst

After the primary that Tuesday in September of 2008, my girls left late that Wednesday afternoon, and all I wanted to do was just head to Rehoboth to start my wound-licking. But I had read that Roberta McCain, the then 96-year-old mother of Senator John McCain, who was then running as the Republican nominee for President, was going to be speaking at the Capitol Hill Club on Thursday at noon. As I had seen her on TV and liked her spunk and views about a woman's right to choose, I wanted to hear her in person. So I decided to make my escape to Rehoboth after. Thursday morning I packed up my car and drove up to Capitol Hill. When I entered the large room, I was one of the first people there, and I put my purse on my seat, which was near the front.

I then turned and saw Mrs. McCain walking in the doorway, probably 30 feet away. Her vivid blue eyes seemed to be fixed on mine. I had never met her so I was sure that she was not looking at me, so I turned to check behind, but there was no one there. She then started walking toward me. Other people were approaching her and she seemed to be batting them away. She came right up to my face, a little taller than I am, and said, "Carol, I am so sorry you lost the election. I watch you all the time on television on that Council channel, and you are the best Councilmember I have ever seen. You do your homework. You always ask the questions I'm thinking should be asked. I am heartsick you lost that election."

I was so touched I wanted to cry, but waited until she turned to sit down at the assigned table next to mine, at which point my eyes welled up with tears. It was the most consoling, helpful thing at that moment of my life. It was kind of like God had sent me an angel at a time when I sure needed it.

Mrs. McCain spoke, and what a good speaker she was. I went over to tell her that afterwards and to thank her for her kind words. And she said, "I'm your neighbor. I live in the building next door to you." It was so interesting that she knew that, but I didn't. She proceeded to say, "I would love for you to come over sometime so I could get to know you better." She gave me her telephone number and asked me to call soon. I did several weeks later, and she has become one of my dearest friends and one of the most important people in my life—one of those four neat people mentioned earlier who always make me feel good about myself.

And what an inspiration she is at now at 105 and a half years old. She had a stroke when she was 97, while traveling alone to Lisbon, so now is in a wheelchair and has some vision issues. But her mind is amazing, her beauty extraordinary, with such humor and kindness. A few recent examples of that mind: I came home from a trip on a Monday and called her to say I was back. And she said, "I thought you weren't coming back until Tuesday." (And she was right!) She knows my schedule better than I do. Last Wednesday, I took over Gaby (remember our dog, who she loves and who hadn't visited for a while). Roberta put her hand down to pet her and immediately said, "You cut her hair." We should all have her memory at any age, as well as her beauty and her heart.

Escaping and Returning

Then thirty-six hours after the primary loss and meeting Roberta, I drove to Rehoboth. I got a good night's sleep, and the next day my good friends Marc and Stephen came in to their nearby home and we hung out. At dinner that Saturday night, after we had gone to a movie, I decided to run a write-in campaign. It really had nothing to do with any conversation with them. It just came into my mind, and I knew I would do it. I went home and wrote my speech, went back to D.C. on Sunday, and announced on Monday, September 15, 2008.

I realized the Council was my life. I felt rudderless even at the thought of being without it. And I knew I would be lost without being able to impact people's lives in a big way. I had stated the night of the primary to a reporter, which ended up on the news, "What a loss. This was not just my job. It was my life." Too true.

I was also smart enough to know that write-in campaigns are very difficult, but knew that if I did not at least try, I would regret it. So here I was, interestingly enough, 24 years after I initially won my Council seat against Jerry Moore, who had staged a write-in campaign after losing to me in the primary, staging one of my own to save my career.

The announcement took place at the campaign headquarters at 12th and U, and even though it was a last-minute call-out, it was well attended by friends and supporters who were thrilled I had not given up the ship yet. I jumped off with this:

> "I'm here today to say, as Mark Twain once said, that the reports of my death are greatly exaggerated."

In my statement, I spoke about how the tone of my opponent's campaign also was an impetus to continue:

> "... to be honest with you, the idea of going forward with a write-in campaign and actually running against a candidate who is now being supported by many on the D.C. Republican Committee, which bravely and unanimously endorsed me in the primary, is a difficult thing to do. Working opposite those who did so much, so recently, for me is something I do not take lightly. But I also do not take lightly my primary opponent's extremely nasty, dishonest and unfair efforts to undermine my record—a record of which I am justifiably proud. Make no mistake, his tactics played a role in this decision to fight on—a risk he willingly took."

I also felt strongly—and stated so—about not letting "so few primary voters decide the final outcome of this election."

The D.C. Republican Committee, which, as I said, had backed me through the primary, now had to go with Mara. I did kind of understand, but I still felt touchy about it. I had hung in with the Party forever, even when it kept me from ever really having a chance to be Mayor, and here they were abandoning me for a candidate who participated in the dirtiest/nastiest campaign in Home Rule history. At least I tried to be understanding, until the Party put out word that in the general election, where you could vote for two at-large candidates (i.e., write my name in as well as vote for another), to just vote for one candidate—Patrick Mara.

Here I was again, still working hard at the Council and running around to every single event in the city for the next seven weeks. As usual, I walked the 17th St. High Heel Race in October, where men and transgender people dress in drag and race down 17th St. on heels higher than I've ever worn, even in my youth. I came across a tall person in costume dressed as "Carol Schwartz," carrying a giant pencil and my poster with the words, "Write in Carol Schwartz." I'd love to take credit for the idea, but I can't!

Also running in the general election was Michael A. Brown, son of Ron Brown (former head of the Democratic National Committee and Clinton's first-term Secretary of Commerce, who unfortunately died in a plane crash in 1996). Michael Brown was a Democrat turned Independent in order to run for the minority-designated at-large seat. His running as a self-described "Independent-Democrat," along with his father's notoriety, would give him a good shot in the general election. And Michael had just recently run for office twice—as Mayor against Adrian Fenty and as the Ward 4 representative against Muriel Bowser (both as a Democrat)—so his own name was quite familiar at that point.

Then the Board of Elections did ballot placement for the general. Since I was a write-in, I was not on the ballot. As luck or non-luck had it, Michael Brown got #1 on the ballot, a huge advantage.

Democratic colleagues Yvette Alexander, Vince Gray, Marion Barry and Harry Thomas Jr. endorsed Michael Brown as we got closer to the general election. Once that "don't support your colleague" spirit starts, it continues, which makes working together on a daily basis harder. And some of the unions, including AFSCME and SEIU local 722 I worked so hard with on sick leave, also endorsed Michael Brown. All this was hurtful.

I do appreciate P.L. Wolff of the *InTowner*, who "strongly" urged voters to write in my name and said: "It is her willingness to focus on much of the arcane stuff that is the grist for the bureaucratic mill that if left unchecked will translate into even more fiscal waste [and] that is one of the very important reasons why we need to return at-large Councilmember Schwartz to continue her good government crusading on behalf of us taxpayers."[309]

Adrian Fenty sent his consultant Tom Lindenfeld to help me. It got some media play and then I was left to go into my own pocket, as a loan, to pay for him and the workers he brought—which I did in full and which is still my own campaign debt. We had a slew of workers, both volunteer and paid, to cover the polls.

We worked hard to educate people about the need to write in my name, and to warn them that they would not find it on the ballot.

There was a lot of excitement in the air on election day, November 4, 2008—and it had nothing to do with me. Barack Obama was on the verge of being elected President, an exciting time for our city. In the end, I received way over 35,000 write-in votes. It would have been much more had we demanded a recount. As the votes were being counted on election night, on top of my validated 35,000, it was obvious to my vote-counting observers that many people had attempted to write in my name, and those were not being counted. Even a Board rep said that it could be as high as 50,000 votes including absentee ballots. But since Michael Brown, #1 on the ballot, had gotten at least 70,000 votes—an insurmountable number for me to overcome—I did not demand a recount. Plus, I did not want to add to the cost of the election and continue to look like a sore loser which, by the way, I was. My counted write-ins did beat Patrick Mara, whose name was actually on the ballot, which gave me at least some satisfaction.

Notably, Mara has run two other times since as the Republican nominee for an at-large seat on the Council—and lost both times. See, it wasn't so easy to get elected as a Republican in this town. I did it time and time again, and even when I ran for Mayor as a Republican, the least I got was 30% of the vote. Yet when it was all over, the D.C. Republican Committee never did anything to say thanks for those many years of service. Oh well ... I did it for all the right reasons—and not for a free ticket to a Lincoln-Douglass Dinner and a plaque, although that would have been nice.

David Catania continued vacillating between taking credit and denying credit for my defeat. When he was asked in 2008 before the election by Mike DeBonis, then "Loose Lips" columnist for the *City Paper*, if he was trying to get rid of me so that he could take over my beautiful corner office in the Wilson Building, he responded, "No. And I have no intentions of moving in there." But guess what? He did, and even kept most of my furniture. Then a couple of years later, David actually took credit for orchestrating my defeat in an article about him in the *Post*. Soon thereafter, I guess he learned that bragging about the power play which got me off the Council wasn't such a crowd-pleaser because he seemed to stop doing it— at least publicly. And then later, he would outright deny it. But who cares? I give him credit anyway.

In December of 2008, we packed up my office. I had donated some of my papers to George Washington University when I left the Council initially in 1989. Some additions were made in 2009, but my staff and I were so hurried and depressed that I'm sure a lot ended up in recycling. I do wish I had it all, especially now that I'm writing this. But I'm sure you're glad that I don't. Just imagine this book double in size!

As our last Council meeting in December of 2008—my last meeting ever—ended at 11:15 p.m., with an empty chamber other than a couple of my staff members who remained, I was presented with the Outstanding Public Service Award from the Council.

At the opposite end of the spectrum, earlier that month, at a more reasonable hour with a full house at their annual luncheon meeting, the Metropolitan Washington Council of Governments (COG) surprisingly presented me with the one and only, they said, "Three Decades of Leadership Award," to a very long standing ovation. At that event, I was so touched that I cried.

Soon thereafter, I walked out of the John A. Wilson Building, which I had walked into 24 years earlier for my first term on the Council when it was called the District Building, sad, tired and uncertain of the future I was facing early that January of 2009.

And no wonder I was tired. After I left the Council, the multiple jurisdictions within the Workforce Development and Government Operations Committee I chaired—with no additional staff—got split up into four separate committees, covered by four separate Councilmembers and their staffs. Between all that and the two campaigns, I was exhausted.

The Election Aftermath

I must admit that I was very sad after leaving office that January. My job had become such an important part of my life, the real reason I wanted to get up in the morning. Now here I was just turning 65 on January 20th with still lots of energy, wishing only to be back at the Wilson Building and instead arriving at the Social Security office. That was quite an eye-opener.

Because my retirement was going to be based on my highest salary, which was $90,000, it made a real difference. The Council had raised its salary several years earlier from $90,000 to $125,000 a year, but there was a rule that you had to go through an election cycle before receiving it. If I had made it past that election in 2008, my retirement and years of service would be based on the $125,000 figure rather than the $90,000, which now gives you an idea of the difference—and that mattered to me because I had worked most of the years between the age of eight and 65.

So that election not only devastated me emotionally, but it also hugely impacted me financially. And the fact that Patrick Mara at 33 or Michael A. Brown at 43 might walk in at that new salary made it worse—which you will learn later was still not enough money for a part-time job for Michael.

At the end of 2008, *The Washington Post* did a year-end summary in a special section, and at the beginning of it, there was a large picture of me hanging up my own torn-down poster. I looked so forlorn. It was a true depiction of how I felt. But I'd had other depressing times and made it through. I would do so again.

(And I did. In fact, in doing the research for this whole chapter of enormous money raising and enormous time spent plotting, I find it almost complimentary in retrospect that they thought I was so important and powerful that they needed to expend all that time, effort and money to get rid of me. Wow! Not only to get rid of me, but to wind up electing Michael A. Brown.)

Inauguration of Barack Obama

January 20, 2009 was the inauguration of our first African American President and my 65th birthday, in order of importance. I took great pride in the occasion, especially as my son Doug had been a surrogate for Obama early on in the campaign. I so much wanted to see the parade and asked Vince Gray if I could sit in the Council/Mayor viewing box. He immediately said, "Of course."

I arrived early, as we were told to do (even those of us who did not have tickets for the swearing-in itself at the Capitol). As I walked up to the back of the Wilson Building to go in and wait for the parade, Peter Nickels, D.C.'s Attorney General, saw me and called out, "Come up to the swearing in with me. I have an extra ticket." I rode up with Peter and was thrilled to be there. I loved seeing the parade, especially when our beautiful new first couple walked by, and was so moved by the history that was being made.

Reflections on Defeat

In the 2008 at-large Council race, particularly in the primary, I was up against a lot, including the coordination of many forces. And why did all those deep-pocketed, very wealthy individuals and business interests get rid of me? Because I supported a small amount of paid sick leave for their workers, a humane act which they really should have been doing anyway.

In my social and charitable activities, I often run into some of these parking guys and gals as well as other business types who fought so hard to deny their employees (who they made sure were only part-time in the first place) a modicum of sick leave. How charitable is that? Yet, they sure found the money, in fact, hundreds of thousands of dollars—not for sick leave—but to do me in.

Meanwhile, making them cover that small amount of sick leave for these past seven or eight years has clearly not left them bankrupt, as I see them making sure their names are plastered all over buildings, halls and organizations, which costs beaucoup dollars, as well as shopping big time at expensive antique shows all over.

At temple over the Rosh Hashanah holidays in the beginning of October, I read in the prayer book, "Be the same within and without," and I thought of them and their hypocrisy. "Within" their companies, not a penny for sick leave for their own workers, but "without," they will give six and half million dollars as long as their name is seen everywhere in a big and bold fashion.

Rabbi Lustig, at that same service, used a quote from Martin Luther King, which I also grabbed onto: "The time is always right to do what is right." What I did with sick leave was right. And there are *some* business owners who have given sick leave to part-time workers on their own, which is right. And good for them. But the fact I was punished by these very rich, selfish and self-serving individuals who did *not* give it on their own—certainly *not right*— is actually quite thought-provoking.

Do these bosses fail to realize that treating their employees humanely is not only important to their workers and families, but also for the betterment of their own businesses? Those workers have helped enable them to have the kind of money they have— and they should be valued. I hope that next time they will do what is right on their own; and then people like me in public positions won't have to force them to.

I remain proud of what I did, including compromising the bill to take in legitimate concerns I had myself as well as those raised by various business groups, much of which I solicited. And I have taken my punishment like a man, albeit a bitter one—but still not as bitter as the mostly men who came after me. Much more importantly, I would do it all again in the exact same way as I believe the greater good it served was worth even my defeat.

CHAPTER 44

Cruising

For my 65th birthday that year, which came three weeks after I left the Council, I took the kids on a cruise to Hawaii—a place I always wanted to go. I was really looking forward to it. I shouldn't have. How could anyone dislike the beautiful islands of Maui and O'ahu? Somehow we managed it.

I was still reeling from the loss and being bludgeoned by the opposing campaign. So I thought it would be good to get away for a relaxing time with my family, who are usually good company, to celebrate my big birthday. But my kids, especially Steph and Doug, seemed like they were avoiding time together—going to bed right after dinner and awakening at 5 a.m., when they could grab hours of solitude. Hil was her usual less-than-enthusiastic self, but next to the others, she was a dream.

Unlike the Caribbean cruise over the holidays twenty years earlier, when we had a great time together and went to all the shows no matter how corny, I had to beg them to participate. And they still didn't. I should have known the first day that things were not going to work out so well when we boarded and found the buffet wrapped in cellophane because of some bacterial outbreak. Little did I know then that that would turn out to be the highlight!

The best times we had were playing ping pong on the ship. We could have saved thousands of dollars by just going to an arcade. To this day, I don't like the sound of a ukulele. Oh, and I cracked a tooth on board to boot. Losing the election was a day at the beach compared to that cruise. And the election cost less.

No personal offense is intended to truly beautiful Hawaii and its nice people—just to my children.

A Surprising Phone Call

On February 20, 2009, around 1:30 p.m., when I was in West Palm Beach getting a respite from the cold in D.C and still getting over that Hawaii trip, I got a phone call. It was Marion Barry. "Hi Carol. What's up?" "I'm in Florida. What's up with you?" If I had turned off those judge shows and turned on CNN that day, I would have known what was up with him—that he was getting that kidney transplant operation that he had needed for a while. He then told me that he was just about to go into surgery. I said, "When?" "In a few minutes," he answered. We chatted a bit, until I heard a voice say, "Mayor Barry, it's time to go." I wished him Godspeed.

I knew we were friends and fond of each other, but I never would have expected to be the last person he called before a life-threatening surgery. I thought he was just joshing with me. But several hours later, I got a call from a friend in D.C., who said, "Did you know that Marion had his kidney transplant at 2:00 today and he's doing okay?"

A few weeks later, when I was back in D.C., I realized it was Marion's birthday (March 6th). I gave him a call and asked him what plans he had. He said he wasn't doing anything. "Well, do you want some company? We could bring in dinner." He said, "Sure." I was on 14th St. when I called and a chocolate store was right there. I bought some for him and drove over to his house where we just sat and visited. Then his friend Kim, who had given him her kidney, came over. When I said I was just going to go out and get us dinner and asked if she'd like to join in, she said, "Let me go get it." I gave her money to pick up food from the Player's Lounge, which was one of his favorites—and mine too.

I then asked him, "Marion, was I the last person you called before your surgery?" "Yes," he said. "Why?" He answered, "Carol, I always liked you. I just kept thinking about you and I needed to talk to you." I was so touched. It was really one of the more flattering—and unexpected—things that ever happened to me.

My Guard Is Up

After leaving the Council, I went out several times with two different men I had met during the latter part of my Council work—both attractive, smart and nice. But I instinctively knew that they might not be there for the right reasons, and soon they proved me right. One owned a company which did business with the city—and maybe wanted more. He asked me to be on his board. The other did diversity training and wanted to do business with entities in the area, and asked me for some help there. I did neither. Instead, I stopped going out with either. But they do both keep in touch occasionally. (In fact, one just called last week.)

When you become a "somebody," you really have to be alert about separating the wheat from the chaff—in these cases, not too alert because they were obvious quite soon after asking for the first date. Times like this, I wish for the south side of Midland where no one could ever accuse me of having money, social position, notoriety or connections.

Now I am so on alert that I'm hardly interested, and the same goes for most men these days. But I did have a good run for many years with many different and interesting men entering my life in one way or another. You could line them all up and you would not visually see the similarities. They were white, black, Jewish, Protestant, Catholic, Muslim, rich and not, tall, short—definitely a wide variety. But several commonalitics with rare exceptions were wonderful speaking voices, nice looking, strong personalities, usually a sense of humor—and some degree of depression.

Also being a strong professional woman can make coupling more difficult. Some of my friends have said, especially years ago, that they had men who told them they would like to take me out, but they were too intimidated by me and what I did. Since I only like strong men, they would not have worked out anyway.

But I guess even today if the right person came my way, I might let my guard down. It would need to be someone nice, loyal, independent and fun. Now, considering my own love of my independence, I would add geographically undesirable. As poet Kahlil Gibran said: "Let there be spaces in your togetherness." I do believe that can make things more interesting.

Many of My Best Friends Are Gay

Thank goodness for my friends. I continue to be blessed with a lot of them, and many of them, gay males. My friend Jeffrey, who is gay, asks, "Do you ever hang out with anyone who is not gay?" I reply, "I do sometimes, but only if I have to"—joke. They are a big part of my life, whether it be my phone time, travel time, or just thinking good thoughts time. I used to often state that "Some of my best friends are gay." Now I say, "Most of them are." That is true—and I'm glad.

Doug and Jen's Wedding

In March of 2009, my son Doug married Jennifer Steen, a beautiful woman (if a tall, thin, gorgeous, blue-eyed blonde can be considered beautiful). Jen was from Minneapolis, and had been educated at Duke University and then Harvard Law School (obviously smart too). They had both lived in New York and then moved back together to California, where they married at Inn of the Seventh Ray in Topanga Canyon. Jen took Doug's name, which surprised me as she had been a very successful lawyer in a large Wall Street firm for many years with her name. But I was so touched when that lovely woman became Jen Levitt carrying on my family name, which would not have been otherwise. Even though I know it had nothing to do with me, I was very happy. (I know Johnny, Hilda and Stanley Levitt are very happy too.)

It was such a joy to see this wonderful couple who were obviously so in love, exchange their vows. Although Jen's mother Ellen and I had gotten acquainted during long conversations on the phone, it was also wonderful to meet all our new family in person: Ellen and Lee Hoffman, Cheryl and David Steen, and Jen's brother Bobby, who has since married Ellyn Sawyer Steen, and they recently had daughter Rose.

Since Jen was a product of a Norwegian Christian father and a Jewish mother with not much Jewish upbringing, I had no idea if their wedding would have any Jewish elements. Therefore, I was pleasantly surprised that Jen and Doug got married under a chuppah (a canopy in a Jewish wedding ceremony), and that Doug stomped a glass that belonged to his dad (another Jewish tradition that speaks to luck). And before the ceremony, they signed a Ketubah (an ancient Jewish wedding contract). They were married by a friend of Doug's, who did a great job and had us all in stitches throughout by repeating over and over again: "By the authority vested in me by the State of California through the Internet for a day, I hereby ..."

(A sort of cute and funny related story about Jewishness: A few years ago, the girls and I went to Santa Monica to visit the Levitts one Thanksgiving, which happened to coincide that year with Hanukkah. Thinking that Jen and Doug probably would not have a menorah, I brought one from D.C. The girls thought the same, so they brought one from New York. As we walked in with our menorahs, a lovely one Jen had gotten was standing on the table. It was a menorah plethora.)

At the wedding, Doug sang a song he wrote to Jen followed by a fun evening of dancing. My dear aunts (both Bettys) and Uncle Seymour were there, which made everything even more special. It was the happiest day of my life. I even used those exact words when Steph, Hil and I got back to the hotel room we were sharing in Santa Monica: "This is the happiest day of my life!" Right then, Steph told me she had dented the rental car earlier in the day. I guess they thought my happiness created the perfect cushion to break the news. So now my "happiest day" is permanently linked with haggling over damage (albeit minor) with Alamo Rent a Car.

Fleeing the Nest

Now with my new-forced freedom, I decided to make the best of it. When I first got off the Council, since I always did a lot of non-profit volunteer work, many offers to be on boards came my way. I loved each one of those prominent organizations, but knew I would take the work far too seriously to get any real time off; and if I didn't take it seriously enough, then I would feel guilty. So even though I remained on my old boards, I did not add any new ones then as I wanted to travel more while I still could. And about that time, here came a good traveling companion.

Similar to my meeting Roberta McCain and becoming dear friends after the loss of the primary, I became good friends with another interesting woman not long after losing my Council seat. I had met Vicki Bagley several years earlier when she approached me at an antique show in Palm Beach, and said she had admired me from afar for many years. Of course, I knew who she was from her successful life of running a real estate company and as publisher of several known magazines, as well as a renowned social hostess—and I certainly admired her as well. After that, we shared several meals over the years, but never spent much time together. Then, not long after I was no longer working, I saw Vicki on the street and we said, "Now that we're both retired, let's become real friends." And we did. And off we went a-traveling.

Vicki had a place in Chautauqua, New York and we went there. She came with me to Rehoboth Beach. Vicki is very intelligent, curious and a good conversationalist. We also had a mutual interest in museums and shopping. We went to a Renaissance Weekend (my first time) in Charleston, SC. And then we started planning bigger adventures. We spent three and a half weeks in Asia, starting with four days in Singapore, then boarding a 16-day cruise where we hit Thailand; South and North Vietnam; South Korea; Hong Kong; Shanghai; Nagasaki, Japan, ending in mainland China where we spent four days in Beijing. Fifteen months later, we spent a whole month traveling through much of India. Then in the spring of 2013, we spent a month living in an efficiency apartment off the Rue Saint-Honoré in Paris.

Vicki was used to all the finest things. She stayed at the best hotels and always traveled first class. But I remain grateful that she "dumbed down" for me, and would stay at hotels with very few stars if any. I would tell her to at least go ahead and fly first class.

She'd say, "No, I'll sit back in coach with you." She was a good sport and we had such fun.

I used to joke that once I wasn't working 60 to 80-hour weeks, if someone said, "Do you want to go to ...," I wouldn't even wait to hear the rest of the sentence—I would just say "Yes." And that was somewhat true. An example: In July of 2010, I got several offers from a few different dear friends. Cornelius Baker and Carl Schmid were going separately to the International AIDS Conference in Vienna, Austria, where I had never been. Then Marc Albert and Stephen Tschida asked me to go with them to Gestalt, Switzerland, also where I had never been. So I coupled the two trips and did both, plus a couple of other places I had never seen, Zurich and Budapest, on my own. There are other examples of such adventures, but since this is not a travelogue, I'll quit here.

But let me talk a bit about Marc and Stephen. I had met Marc back in the early '90s when we were both members of the Board of Whitman-Walker Clinic. Since Marc served one term and our meetings were full of Clinic work, we never really got to know each other well. Then, in the late '90s, we started running into each other in Rehoboth Beach, where they own a house a couple of blocks away from mine. Their walking route to the beach and shopping was by my house. Soon Marc started knocking on the door, and as usual, I was in my granny gown. After a while, I had to tell him to look at my blinds. "If they are closed, do not knock." But he kept knocking and I'm so glad he did because we have become such good friends—kind of like family. In fact, his now spouse Stephen told Marc's mother that if Marc were straight, he would be married to me. Of course, that makes me feel good, but I know it's not true. When we're together, if he notices a woman, which is quite rare, she is young, thin and lovely—not an overweight old broad like me.

Fleeing the Nest to My Other Nests

In these last few years, I also have finally been able to spend more time in both West Palm Beach, where I still own the one-bedroom condo we had bought for my mother-in-law nearly 40 years ago, as well as my cute Cape Cod house in downtown Rehoboth Beach. Since the place in Florida had not cost much and was in a modest development, it has been easy to handle financially. I kept it because I knew I would get older and colder. Glad I did, as I did. It has given me great pleasure as has the place in Rehoboth.

Some more of my dearest friends came from my time in Rehoboth, including Linda and Irv Pine. After David passed, I spent a
lot of time with them there and in Florida where they went in the
winter until Irv passed years ago. Linda then moved back to her
home state of Pennsylvania, but we stay in touch. Another dear
friend is Eddie Bullock who I met when he owned an antiques
store, and then he worked at Back Porch, which is my favorite restaurant in Rehoboth. Others I like are Semra's, Nicola's and Claws.
Eddie fell in love with Paul Barr and they moved to Pennsylvania
and married, but we still get together. Other close friends are the
Ryan family—Elizabeth, Sheila and John—who used to own the
store, Faraway Places; and Denise and Roger Willey, who live in
Milton and who have always been so helpful to me.

I often say about the house in Rehoboth that, "It was the best
thing I ever did for myself, except for my three children." Occasionally I humorously add, especially in front of my kids, "It's the
best thing I ever did for myself—period." I have a plaque on the
wall in my bedroom there which says, "It's never too late to have
a happy childhood." Rehoboth exemplifies that to me.

My other favorite places to go are New York City, where I have
good reason with two daughters nesting there for many years (but
I have loved it since I was 10 years old) and Los Angeles with
Doug, Jen et al there.

Another favorite place is Santa Fe, New Mexico, with its endless number of American Indian jewelry shops and relatively new
dear friends there. I stay at the same place every year—the Residence Inn with its family-like staff. I started going to Santa Fe
about 15 years ago with my good buddy Barbara Blum, who was a
member of the Board of the Institute of American Indian Art
(IAIA) for many years. Its annual meeting takes place during Indian Market week in August and I would go for about four or five
days with Barbara every other year. Now, I go from 10 to 14 days
every year and stay on my own, and hang out with her and other
friends, including: the remarkable American Indian leader La-
Donna Harris, who I met through Barbara as well as former
Washingtonian Craig Lemm, and Susan and Ernest Holmes.

I have become good friends with Marcia, owner of Shalako,
which has the largest amount of old pawn American Indian jewelry I have ever seen (and I've seen a lot). Marcia has hung out
with me here in D.C. as well. Another good friend I have made
there is Ali MacGraw.

And it is THE Ali MacGraw. About eight or nine years ago, I was at an antique show in Santa Fe. I went up to a booth, and behind that booth stood Ali. I could hardly believe my eyes. Who's not been a fan of hers? I immediately started gushing. She was so nice and modest, and started asking me lots of questions about myself. We had a great conversation for five minutes or so, and that was it. The next day, I was standing in front of IAIA, waiting for Barbara, talking to several people I knew, when someone came up from behind me, pecked me quickly on the lips, said "Hi Carol," and sped off. The people I was talking to said, "Oh wow! That was Ali MacGraw. I didn't know you were friends with her." I replied, "I didn't either."

Over the next couple of years, I would run into Ali and we would always exchange information, but neither would call. Finally, we said, "Enough is enough" and we made plans to go out to dinner. Since then, we have a beautiful friendship, which includes phone conversations during the year and several get-togethers when I'm in Santa Fe. I often tell her that I enjoy dropping her name more than any other. Recently she's been touring in the stage show, *Love Letters*, reunited with Ryan O'Neal, who I enjoyed meeting a couple of times when I saw the production in Los Angeles in October of 2015 and several months later in June in Baltimore. They tour occasionally around the country and it is great! See it if you can. Ali is now designing clothes with some indigenous women in South America, and did a fashion show in Charleston in February of 2017 and several other places since.

In August of 2015, I was in Santa Fe with my kids—as I had decided to do a year-and-a-half-later celebration of my 70th birthday. I took them to dinner at Geronimo, a nice restaurant on Canyon Road. Unbeknownst to them, Ali and I had arranged for her to show up and surprise them at dessert time as she was working earlier. They had heard me talk about her over the years, but probably thought our friendship was just a figment of my imagination. But there she was and she actually raved on about me and our friendship. Boy, did I go up in my kids' estimations. Ali is neat friend #4 (along with Letitia Baldrige, Dorothy Height, and Roberta McCain)—and they're all #1 in my book. And boy, does Ali make me feel good about myself—she's always such a booster— just like those three other extraordinary women.

Backyard Buddies

But I can't go another minute without talking about two of my bestest friends, Tay Hahn and Elsie Smith. They're really like my sisters. These are the people I talk to least several times a week as we check in on each other.

Tay, in our nearly 50 years as friends, has always been my confidante. There is nothing I would not tell her. I trust her more than anyone. She is also smart and very knowledgeable about so much; thus, I often go to her for information. And Tay is often my reality check as she is deadly honest. I love and need that—and her.

Elsie is so fun and full of life. We became friends nearly 40 years ago when her then husband and I served together on the Board of Education. They divorced several years later, but both stayed my friends. Elsie and I hang out—movies, lunches, shopping, trips to Chicago to visit her daughter and Rehoboth, sometimes to hang out with my gang. We often talk at night when we're both watching our cerebral choices on TV—*Dancing with the Stars*, *The Voice*, or *So You Think You Can Dance*. I always know who she's rooting for—the black person. (And if there are several African Americans, then it's the darkest one.) I often joke with her that I'm only white person she ever rooted for—and I'm glad she does. What a joy she is in my life!

Other friends I talk to often are Cornelius Baker, Marc Albert and his mom Molly, Linda Cropp, Jeffrey Slavin, Judy Smith, Carol Schuman, Sandy Allen, Judy Irwin and Carl Schmid who I've mentioned earlier. Then there's Roscoe Dellums, a dear friend with whom I email back and forth. And really close friends who have remained so from teenage years are Ann Wylie and Carol Pensky, both of whom are in town, and college friends Ivan and Bunny, Patty and Larry Fallek, and Sally and Stan Bernstein, who are in Texas, Texas and California respectively. And another good friend I pal around with—along with her husband Alfredo— is Gloria Piedra, who I met 40 years ago when she became like family. She has been my hairdresser for 35 years and is at Gloria's Hair Salon in Georgetown. A wonderful friend has been Tom Kaufman, who was David's law associate/ partner and friend for many years, who has been so helpful to me with legal issues over the years—and to whom I am very grateful. Other dear friends are D.C.ites Alex Armstrong and Jerry McCoy, and Maria and Bob Burka. And Ardith and David Myerson in NY are still like family after 50 years.

One of my favorite activities is a once-every-several-months bridge game with three dear friends of many years: Ann, Cornelius and Marc. We're so busy talking that our game is not improving, but who cares!

But my best friend is the whole world is h Lumbi Trochez. Aleida has worked for me for 30 years (starting a year before David died) and in the beginning, five days a week and now two days. She has been there for my darkest hours and happiest of times. I could not lead the life I've led without her. She not only helps me with the house, she helps me with bills, filing, the animals, and the scrapbooks. And she comes the closest to being my therapist of anyone. We really confide in one another and we're always there for each other. I really think and often say, thank God for Aleida.

Actually, I've often thought over the years that Aleida and my daughter Hilary were two of the nicest people I've ever known—really too nice. They were always allowing people to run all over them—whether it was their friends or their family. Because of two separate incidents, I made it my business to try to empower these two sweethearts. They took the lessons well, and now I have both of them in my face most of the time. The other lesson here is: Be careful what you wish for. By the way, I am still glad.

Speaking of friends, I have always tried to be a good one. Even though I talk a lot, I can also be a good listener. And I keep confidences, even when not asked. I just know instinctively what should be shared and what should not. Even when I find out things about people who I am not particularly fond of, I do not choose to advance the news. I am not so pure that I do not enjoy gossip. I do. But it stops with me.

I'm not a real astrology person. I don't look up people's characteristics and only once in a while read my and my kids' horoscopes, giving very little validity to it. But let's talk about it anyhow. I'm an Aquarian, but actually on the first day so I just missed being a Capricorn. (I always claim to have the best characteristics of each and dismiss the worst in both.) I've become conscious, though, of the fact that so many of the most important people in my life have been Aquarians. Three out of four grandparents were and the fourth only missed by 13 days. Many of my friends are and most of them are interesting and enjoyable, like two of my "neatest" people: Letitia Baldrige and Roberta McCain—and two loves. But in a couple of cases, they have also been relationships that are among the most complicated and painful.

Avoiding Boredom and Depression: Mindless TV

So many older people I know become depressed. And no wonder. Every time I would visit most of them, they would have either CNN or Fox News blaring in their room with their eyes totally affixed to the screen all day long, watching constant repeats of the most depressing and/or aggravating news imaginable: terrorists attacks, floods, political chicanery, mass domestic shootings, and then the non-stop commentary of the talking heads about the above. Life is depressing and aggravating enough, especially as you get older, without sitting yourself in front of a television, of your own free will, to get further down and annoyed—even if it's for free. Why add to the bleakness with entertainment choices?

So I decided that was not going to be me—and it isn't. You will see me sitting in front of the TV watching those few favorites I mentioned earlier along with: *Judge Judy*, who I appreciate as an equal opportunity teller-offer; and *Family Feud* with Steve Harvey, who I love to watch because he makes me giggle; and *Jeopardy*, which I could do well in, at least in some categories, if they would just give me 24 hours to answer; and thanks to Tay, HGTV where I watch people either buy a house or remodel one (and I get to guess which they choose) on *Love It or List It*; and where I get to travel around the world with *House Hunters International* (and get to guess which place they choose too); and when I get tired of choosing, I go back home to my Texas roots and accents with *Fixer Upper* (whose only problem is we all wish we had a handsome, fun, and agreeable partner like Chip and perfect kids like theirs); and thanks to Stephanie, The Food Network, where I get to see chefs compete in a three-course meal during *Chopped*, (and I get to guess who wins—usually not the woman but they're getting better lately); or I get to guess at the pick for the next *Food Network Star*. Nothing really too depressing or aggravating here.

I actually cannot just sit and watch TV so I play solitaire while it's on—not on a computer but with a deck of cards as I really enjoy shuffling, and it keeps my fingers nimble.

I also like *The Closer* with Kyra Sedgwick playing a nifty Southern police chief as well as Kerry Washington in *Scandal* until the show starting making everyone evil and violent. I like *Nashville* and was sad when it left ABC because I don't have CMT on my cable in D.C. as it only comes inexplicably linked with the sports package. I have always loved the *Law and Order* franchise—all of them. I think they are brilliantly done, but I refuse to watch those late at night as they can cause sleeplessness. Reruns of *The Golden Girls* and the movie *Miss Congeniality* also remain favorites. (You may be sneering now, but I bet you've watched them too. If not, you should.)

Even though I like a good drama in the theater, I do tend to want to escape, especially when I'm spending my money, to a lighter and livelier world, like romantic comedies and tap-dancing-type musicals. There are some more somber movies and shows among my favorites, such as *The Shawshank Redemption*, *Les Misérables*, and *Driving Miss Daisy*. But I find them not just sad, but redemptive, hopeful, and affirming of humanity.

My all-time favorite films are *To Kill a Mockingbird*, about goodness, and *Gone with the Wind* about pluck and survival. (Speaking of, I used to have a crush on Leslie Howard's Ashley, the sensitive man when I was very young; but later, so preferred the macho Rhett Butler as played by Clark Gable.) Another favorite is *Last Picture Show*, set and filmed in a small town in Texas.

Now I may still get depressed or aggravated or have insomnia on occasion, but at least my leisure activities are not contributing—and in fact, are helping to take them away.

Show Time

Over the years, many people, including family, have told me they thought I should have a talk show. Some have told me that I'm curious and ask good questions. And some have said they like my voice. They've mentioned a TV talk show, but I actually think at my age, I would look better on the radio. I've decided that the problem with either is I'd rather be both the host *and* the guest. Just jump from chair to chair: "Carol, what do you think about ..." Jump over: "Well, I have lots of things to say ..." I'm sure the offers will just start rolling in.

In the meantime, I spend a lot of time and even some of my resources on our local theaters, which are extraordinary. We are so fortunate to have the number of quality performing arts centers as we do in D.C. and the surrounding areas. Some of my most wonderful memories, especially during these not-working-full-time years have been the enriching experiences at the Kennedy Center, Studio Theater, Arena Stage, GALA Hispanic Theatre, Shakespeare Theater, etc. If you haven't done so yet, treat yourself. You'll be glad you did. I also love movies and my movie pals are Marc, the team of Corn, Sam, Ernest and Bob, as well as Elsie, and Judy Smith. Or I often go on my own at the last minute. I walk to

West End on 22nd or Atlantic Plumbing on 9th, bus or drive to Avalon and Georgetown, or Metro to E St. To be honest, I like going by myself the most because I can be totally absorbed only in the movie—and I don't have to share the popcorn.

Losing Aunt Betty Jane

My beloved Aunt Betty who lived in Denver had been a breath of fresh air my whole life—so sweet, caring and attentive. She had breast cancer many years earlier, and then near her 90th birthday, it returned with a vengeance. My other Aunt Betty and I flew into Denver to celebrate her July 11th big birthday. As always, she was beautiful, this time with a pretty wig, and we have pictures that captured her and that special occasion.

A week or so later, I was at friends Pauline Schneider and Diane Camper's summer party in Betterton, MD and Gwen Ifill was there, who I knew casually. Gwen was Aunt Betty's favorite newscaster in the world, and she watched her every night on PBS. So since Aunt Betty was so ill, I asked Gwen if she would mind saying hi to her. She graciously said yes. When Aunt Betty got on the phone, I said, "I have someone here who would like to talk to you" and handed the phone to Gwen. At that moment, Aunt Betty was in seventh heaven. Thank you, Gwen.

(Unfortunately, though, on November 14, 2016, Gwen Ifill, who I really liked and admired and had just visited with at a play at Arena Stage, died. It appears she had cancer, which was diagnosed a year earlier, but about which she kept quiet. Gwen, who was so brilliant, so strong, so vital in contributing to the world around her, is sadly now gone. But what a send-off she had at Metropolitan A.M.E. Church with a huge crowd including Michelle Obama. I was so glad to be there with my daughter Hilary for the fitting tribute to her.)

By the end of September of 2011, Aunt Betty was in the hospital growing weaker each day. I went to visit. It was so hard to see that vibrant, so full-of-life woman so dissipated. It was also hard to leave her, but her children were coming in later that day. As I was leaving her room in the intensive care unit to go to the airport after many days there, I turned around to wave and Aunt Betty, so weak and in so much pain, sort of smiled and winked at me. It was like she was trying to say to her devoted niece that everything was okay and to not be so sad—she was ready to go. Aunt Betty died two days later on October 1st. That precious wink—and that precious person—is forever ingrained in my mind and my heart.

After Having Lost Many Loved Ones ...

I had always been a person who sort of feared death and did not want to get older and face it. But as the years have gone on and I have seen so many people dear to me, both friends and family, pass on, I fear it far less.

Other than the tragic sudden deaths like in a car accident, I have found that most people are ready or even at peace at the thought. The pain of either physical or mental illness have ravaged their lives to such an extent that they actually look forward to leaving. I've certainly also found that to be the case in people who are way up there in age when their various senses and capacities have left them—and any quality of their life is gone. Those experiences have given me comfort.

And speaking of comfort, for a long time after Mom and David died, I dreamed about them often and they were usually recurring dreams. With Mom, it was her standing on top of her gravesite in a white choir-type robe singing happily. Since my mom never sang nor was she religious or happy, it certainly was an unusual dream. But she seemed so filled with joy in those images that it gave me then—and continues to give me—great comfort.

This is the recurring dream about David: He was showing me around a beautiful farm-like environment with lots of hills and greenery. And he seemed so content. That's the vision of him that still comes to mind, and it also gives me much comfort.

I find it interesting now that I'm writing this that although I have dreams about other people in my life then and now, they are the only two who appear in the same dream again and again—and each in such peaceful visions. I sure hope that's true as both seemed not to get much of that in their lifetime when I knew them.

CHAPTER 45

Grandma

After so many losses, how wonderful it was to finally get a gift I had longed for, for decades—and in this case, gifts. In early 2012, Doug came into town to perform at the Millennium Stage at the Kennedy Center. He sang his original songs with a band, and spoke in between about his *Greyhound Diaries* project, a journey he has taken across the country for 11 years spanning over one hundred and twenty thousand miles.

Jen also came on this trip. After the performance, when I went up to say hi to everyone, one of the band members said, "Is this the future grandma?" or something similar. That's how I found out that I was finally, at age 68 and a half, going to be a grandmother for the first time. Doug and Jen had not told me yet, but had planned to do so that night when we had dinner after the show. Later, I just sat in my car and cried because I was so happy.

Soon, we received other surprising and fabulous news: twins—a girl and a boy. Truly special gifts. Sylvie Emeline and Walker David, known as Wally, with the last name Levitt, arrived on September 3, 2012, and they were so welcomed—and they are so adorable and very much loved by all who know them.

By the way, when aunts Stephanie and Hilary were about five and four years old, Steph would sometimes say, without prompting, "When I grow up, I'm going to have four children—two girls and two boys." Then I would turn to Hilary, who was usually nearby and ask, "Honey, how many children do you want?" Her response: "I don't think I want any." And that never changed.

Steph, though, did try when she was in her early to mid-40s to have her first child, which included lots of hormones, seven artificial inseminations and four in vitros. She actually got pregnant twice—once with twins about the same time as Jen, which she sadly lost, and then later, another one. After Jen and Doug's children arrived, she abandoned the effort. She said to me that a big part of the reason she was trying so hard was to make me a grandma. Bless her. Sylvie and Wally took the pressure off of all of us—and have been such a blessing to the whole family.

I often tell young women that if they are delaying having a family, that's fine. But if they think they might want a child in the future, they should freeze their eggs. I have seen too many wait too long. Why not at least give yourself the option?

Vince Gray: A Victory and a Cloud

Meanwhile, on the D.C. political front, the Mayor was up for reelection in 2010. The Chair of the Council Vincent Gray was Mayor Adrian Fenty's main challenger in the Democratic primary. The result: Vince Gray won 54% to 44% with Wards 4, 5, 7 and 8 (majority African American) supporting Gray and Wards 1, 2, 3 and 6 (majority white), and *The Washington Post* backing Fenty. I had concerns, as were stated earlier, about Adrian's actions when he was Mayor. But I do appreciate his doggedness in the schools issue and his helping to accomplish the modernization of schools, libraries and recreation centers after the Council, including him, spawned the idea and allotted the money. I ran into him not long ago in New York and we had such a great visit.

Soon after Vince was sworn in as Mayor, a scandal erupted. In March of 2011, a minor candidate in the 2010 Mayoral race, Sulaimon Brown, said the Gray campaign paid him—and promised him a job—to stay in the race and continue bad-mouthing incumbent Mayor Adrian Fenty. The *Post* gave the accusation wide coverage.

Then in the latter part of 2011, an investigation led by U.S. Attorney Ronald Machen ensued, regarding an alleged shadow campaign operated during Gray's Mayoral effort, funded by a local businessman we've heard much about, Jeffrey Thompson.

We would soon discover illicit activity by several Councilmembers, including on the part of my successor.

More Clouds Gather: Crises on the Council

The years 2009 to 2014 were scandal-ridden for the D.C. Council. It started with earmarks, which I had sounded the alarm on a few years earlier, when David Catania put nearly $14 million worth of earmarks in the Health Committee budget. And as I feared, once it got started, everyone wanted a piece of that pie.

When I was on the Council, I continued to rant against earmarks, and not just at a private meeting, but publicly at Council sessions, including during the Fiscal Year 2008 Budget process in 2007. One day, Marion Barry said, "I agree with Councilmember Schwartz about these earmarks." As it turned out, two members of the Finance Committee miraculously—and almost instantly—found $8 million in earmark money to shut Marion up. It was those dollars that got Marion in trouble because that money was quickly funneled into questionable non-profits. This provoked an investigation and rebuke of Marion in 2010, and resulted in his losing his committee for a year.[310] I must admit I got some vindication for my "I told you so" warnings many years earlier.

Now let's look at Councilmembers' Constituent Service Funds. Each Councilmember has one. The amount that could be raised from private donors each year when I was there was $40,000 for constituent needs, such as funeral costs and electric bills. But sometimes the Fund went to sports tickets or for self-promoting causes. Then when I chaired the Committee on Workforce Development and Government Operations, several of my colleagues came to me to lobby to raise the amount from $40,000 to $80,000.

I declined, thinking that $40,000 annually was already adequate, especially given their reported uses. The approaching members went on to say that they would just get together and figure out a way to go around me. I countered, "Fine, I will then introduce a bill to *lower* the amount that you can raise each year, and we'll have a nice public discussion about the Constituent Service Funds." Not surprisingly, the issue was dropped. Lo and behold, soon after I left the Council in January of 2009, Councilmembers doubled the annual amount they could raise for their Constituent Services Funds to that $80,000.

Then in 2012 and 2013, three Councilmembers had to leave office amidst federal charges. In January of 2012, Ward 5 Councilmember Harry Thomas Jr. resigned his seat and pled guilty to federal embezzlement charges.[311] He had used earmarks from the D.C. Children and Youth Investment Trust Corporation (the public-private partnership Anthony Williams had started) to do so. Remember, I fought vehemently against its establishment, ruffling Williams's feathers. I had worried that this public/private Trust (certainly more publicly funded than privately if at all) would just open the door to malfeasance, and stated so at the time.

And sadly, I was proven absolutely correct, as Mr. Thomas schemed to set up fraudulent youth charities to embezzle money from that Trust, and then received kickbacks. He pled guilty to stealing more than $350,000 of public funds, which he used to buy non-youth-supporting things like a luxury Audi, a Victory motorcycle, and numerous getaways to golf resorts for himself. He was sentenced to a "getaway" of three years in prison.[312]

Then in February of 2011, recently elected Council Chair Kwame Brown came under fire when he ordered a "fully loaded" SUV on the bank account of the D.C. government, with features like a DVD entertainment system, power moon-roof, and polished aluminum wheels. But then disaster occurred. The first vehicle arrived with a gray interior instead of the desired black one "like the Mayor's." No trade-in was allowed by the company, so of course with that earth-shattering deficiency of gray instead of black, another SUV had to be ordered—again on the D.C. government. And this was 14 years after my legislation in 1999 which forbade non-emergency use of SUVs for financial and environmental reasons, regardless of interior color. In June of 2012, Kwame Brown was charged on a separate count of bank fraud—and resigned office.[313]

In 2013, my successor on the Council, Michael A. Brown, was charged with taking bribes (in the form of $55,000 in cash stuffed in a duffel bag) from someone he thought was a businessman seeking favorable contracts. Instead, it was a federal agent. Michael had already been defeated for reelection to his seat after controversies such as non-payment of over $50,000 in income taxes[314] and large amounts of unreported expenditures and contributions.

During the 2008 race (the one where Michael succeeded me), it was alleged that he took an illegal contribution of $125,000 from a businessman and D.C. contractor. Guess who? Correct: Jeffrey Thompson.[315] Michael Brown's illegal activities went from very large to smaller infractions, such as his driver's license often being suspended for unpaid violations. In May of 2014, Michael Brown was sentenced to 36 months in prison for the bribery charges.[316]

At this point, I wonder if those who sought to get rid of me could be really happy with the results of the at-large Council election in 2008, when I lost and Michael A. Brown, who even intended to expand sick leave once there, won. With or without my write-in effort, unknown Republican Patrick Mara was *not* going to win the race against known Democrat-turned-Independent Michael A. Brown as I could have—and politically savvy David Catania and Barbara Lang probably knew that just as well as I did.

Regardless, I certainly was unhappy as a regular taxpaying citizen watching from the sidelines in 2013 as the antics of some Councilmembers, including Michael A. Brown, wreaked havoc on our city's reputation.

And remember the Constituent Service Funds? As the city was beginning to go through these various ethical crises, the members responded to calls from the media and residents and decided to do an ethics reform bill. In the legislation that passed at the end of 2011, one of the few modifications made was to lower the annual limit of the fund—back down to the $40,000, where it was before I left three years earlier.

In later ethics reform legislation, an independent Board of Ethics and Government Accountability—separated out from the Board of Elections and Ethics, which then became the Board of Elections—was created to police and sanction all D.C. employees, including elected officials, who violate the public trust. I thought that was real progress.

A Warm Applause

As a result of Harry Thomas Jr. resigning and pleading guilty to federal embezzlement charges, a special election to fill his Ward 5 seat was held in mid-May of 2012. Kenyan McDuffie won and was immediately sworn in. Even though I did not know Kenyan, I decided to go to my first Council event since leaving over three years earlier. I sat toward the back. There were several other former Councilmembers there who got introduced to some applause.

When Kwame Brown, who was Chair then, introduced me last, there was a standing ovation that went on for at least a minute. I thought at first I was imagining this, but Channel 13, the Council channel, had captured and repeated it, which I then taped. It was a touching outpouring of affection from the packed chamber, mainly made up of Kenyan's family and friends from Ward 5. It was such affirmation of my 24 years of service. It was impromptu, but heartfelt—and meant a lot to me.

Hit the Road, Jack

A favorite thing to do when I'm in Florida in February is to go to the Miami Beach Antiques Show. It has about 5,000 vendors (not really but seems so), and I love looking at all that stuff. In 2012, I had done it all, but decided to stop by the antique flea market on Lincoln Rd., a few blocks away. As I was browsing, a very attractive man started following me. He was tall, well-built with a shaved head and although casually dressed, had a sophistication and seemed just a little younger than I. He finally approached and asked me to go to one of the nearby places to have a coffee. I've never been an easy pick-up so initially said, "No, thank you."

As soon as he turned to leave, I thought how stupid. Why couldn't I just have coffee? So we did. I learned his name was Jack, he lived in England, but had been born and raised in Amsterdam. His accent was far more British though. He had been married but no longer, had a part-time job as a firefighter, but his main business was dealing in silver antiques—the reason for his being in

Miami Beach then. The only things I said about myself were my first name, that I was the mother of three adults, lived in Washington, D.C., and that I had years before been in elected office there. Then we parted with Jack asking for my full name and number which I did not give.

Afterwards, I thought how stupid again. What could be more perfect than an attractive firefighter with an English accent who likes antiques and is so geographically desirable across the ocean? Oh well ... A few days later I called home to get messages off my machine in D.C. and there was one from Jack. (He had obviously done some research.) When I returned to D.C. in March, Jack started calling and emailing often. That went on for months. He was spending a lot of time in France where he was building a house on a piece of property he owned. Now he had all the above and a house in the south of France. I was not smitten, but interested and looked forward to his communications. After about eight or so months, I began getting a nagging feeling that he was married and confronted him by phone when he called one day. He admitted he was, but of course said they were in the process of ... whatever.

He knew that was it for me, but he did continue to call and email occasionally. The next February at the antique show, I did agree to meet him for coffee one morning—but only that. He started in on his political views for the first time which were just so far right and annoying. And even though he was still attractive and well-built, I was not at all attracted to him. (Another example of our always making the stranger into glitter and gold.) In fact, his being married was now my favorite thing about him.

It Was 'Just [His] Imagination'

In April of 2013, I was in New York and decided to go to the opening of *Motown: The Musical* since I so love the Motown sound. When I got to the theater, lo and behold, there stood Berry Gordy (and that is the correct spelling). I went over to congratulate him on the opening of his musical. He grabbed me and gave me a big hug and kiss, like he knew me. He said, "So glad you're here. It's been so long. Let's get together after the show. There's going to be lots of fun things to do." Then, straight-talking, truth-telling me stupidly said, "I think you have me confused with someone else. I'm Carol Schwartz from Washington, D.C. and I don't think we've met before." He then said, "Excuse me. I thought you were someone else." I should have just played along and kept my mouth shut. Another time when honesty was not the best policy.

Then in December of 2014, I was at the Kennedy Center Honors with my daughter Stephanie when Usher, standing near me, said, "You're gorgeous." That too was "Just [His] Imagination." (He must have also confused with someone else—but again, I was sure glad.)

Blessed with Four, Now All Gone

I was blessed to have four wonderful uncles, each of whom were also lots of fun. The two from my dad's side: Uncle Albert, who was my NYC pal, passed on March 29, 1995 at age 82; and Uncle Earl, who I visited with in both D.C. and Williamsburg, Virginia, where he lived for over 60 years. Uncle Earl was the second sweetest person in the Levitt family (after Johnny of course), so when he left us at age 87 on July 7, 2006, I was very sad.

Now to my mom's side: Uncle Joe, who was the baby of the Simmons family and who lived in Baton Rouge with Aunt Betty Jean, was 6'2", always had a twinkle in his eye, and was quite straightforward. My daughter Stephanie just reminded me that we had, at her request, invited ourselves for Passover about ten years ago, and when we arrived, Uncle Joe immediately asked, "When are you leaving?" He also kept calling our visit, "the invasion." As you can see, he was lots of fun—and honest. Unfortunately, we lost him July 9, 2008 at two months' shy of 86.

Uncle Seymour was a dear presence in my life starting when I was a camper in Colorado and continuing until we lost him at age 93 on October 6, 2013—two years to the month after we lost his wife of nearly 69 years, Betty Jane. Uncle Seymour had started having memory issues several years before Aunt Betty died, so after she passed and he was at a facility in Denver, his daughter Bev and her husband Ross moved him to Cleveland near them. I visited him in both places during those two years as I wanted to be there for him as he had always been for me. What a dear man.

These important-in-my life losses reminded me of what a small family we are. I never had a chance to be an aunt as David was an only child and I only had Johnny as a sibling. And my children have no first cousins. Thank goodness we have Sylvie and Wally.

Leaving the Party

I am no longer a Republican. In December of 2013, I changed my registration to Independent. I decided I was not going to start a new year being in a Party that had become practically impossible to identify with. I then took on the label that does truly represent my political philosophy, certainly today, and I guess has for a long time. I have always taken each issue as it comes and tried to do what made sense, including, as often as I could, voting for the person rather than the Party. Independent seemed to fit.

By 2013, the Republican Party was not the one I embraced over 60 years earlier. I had for decades been proud of the Party I joined. It had room at the table for lots of ideas, as exemplified by Abraham Lincoln, Theodore Roosevelt, Dwight D. Eisenhower, Nelson Rockefeller, Everett Dirksen, Howard Baker, Mark Hatfield, and John McCain—before and after his Presidential run—to name a few. It no longer did. So I had to finally say goodbye.

The current Party had become entirely too socially conservative—so much so that some of us who are moderate-leaning were not only made to feel unwelcome but have been targeted as not conservative enough. It probably started way back with the entrance of the Dixiecrats—Southern Democrats such as those I grew up with in Texas and Mississippi—who I didn't want to be part of then, but all of a sudden they became Republicans. Although I recognize that initially some were courted by the Republican Party, many others came on their own. And they certainly altered the Grand Old Party I signed onto—and in my mind, not for the better. And then here came the Tea Party, which was also not my cup of tea.

I must admit that I remained a Republican, even when the Party began to drift away from me, because I didn't want to shrink an already shrinking tent of moderate voices within it. I didn't want the far right to totally take over the Grand Ole Party of Lincoln without at least a fight. I supported and contributed to the Republican Main Street Partnership—founded by Amo Houghton, former moderate New York Republican House member—which tried to keep people of my ilk from leaving the fold and to attract more of us. I have also personally contributed to Senator Susan Collins (R-ME) who I respect for her independence.

In addition, I fought hard to stay for years because it was helpful to the city for me to be a Republican when I was in elected office. But then I wasn't in elected office anymore, so that motivation no longer existed. And even more importantly, I just became uncomfortable with the rhetoric of too many. I didn't belong anymore—and I didn't want to belong. I've often said in the last few years, "I didn't leave the Party. It left me." So in December of 2013,

I made the move to Independent. And I'm especially glad now that I got out way before the 2016 Presidential election!

I feel comfortable saying I am an Independent, but I miss being able to vote in a primary and being politically associated. Sometimes I think maybe we should start an Independent Party or the "Middle-of-the-Road" Party so like-minded people (and I do believe that's most of us—neither left nor right) can bond and expand. Maybe something to think about in the future.

Happily Turning 70

On Saturday, January 18, 2014, two days before my 70th birthday, I had a casual party at my apartment with my children, some close friends, and favorite activities. There were all my preferred foods, card playing in two rooms, and dancing in the foyer. Doug and Hilary both performed for the group—Doug singing and playing the guitar and Hilary doing some comedy. Then Stephanie (who is actually a good singer)—not to be outdone—started something like "ballet dancing" in the hallway while humming some music. (This routine has been reprised by her often over the last several years.) It was really a fun evening—and one of my best birthdays ever.

The Shadow Around Vince Envelopes Him

Woes continued for Mayor Gray. On July 9, 2012, prosecutors, led by U.S. Attorney Ron Machen, charged 2010 Gray campaign aide, Jeanne Clarke Harris, with helping to funnel $653,000 in illegal funds to Gray's campaign, which she admitted to. Again, the funder, sources at the time said, was none other than Jeffrey Thompson. [317]

(I think it's important to point out here that great efforts were made by the media, especially the *Post*, to imply that Jeffrey Thompson was an outgrowth of Vince Gray. But I would like to remind everyone that it was not Vince Gray—or even Marion Barry—who created this monster. It was Tony Williams and the Financial Control Board.)

Mayor Gray asserted that he had no knowledge of a shadow campaign. The day after the campaign aide was charged, the Mayor expressed disappointment about the campaign activities and when asked, indicated he had no intentions of stepping down.

Later that same day, Councilmembers Muriel Bowser, David Catania and Mary Cheh each called separately for Mayor Gray to resign.[318] Not surprisingly, the former two became candidates in the 2014 Mayoral election.

During his call for the Mayor to step down, Catania even called Vince Gray a "joke."[319] It's one thing to question the issues related to the campaign. But how belittling and disrespectful a thing to say about a recently elected Mayor, who had spent his professional life in public service as Executive Director of both the Association of Retarded Citizens and Covenant House, as a Director of the Department of Human Services in the early '90s, and as a Ward 7 Councilmember, who had led the Council as its Chair. Vince also had no formal charges against him relating to the matter at hand. And he was someone who David before prided himself in being pals with—until David decided he wanted to be Mayor.

After the campaign finance scandal broke, it appeared to be trial by media, whose constant coverage did a number on the Mayor's—and the city's—reputation. Even though there continued to be no indictment for Gray, the shadow of the shadow campaign made him vulnerable to strong competition for reelection. Muriel, who had been gearing up for her own run for Mayor with the Fenty machine backing her, announced her candidacy in March of 2013. Also back in December of 2012, David began telling people of his plans to run for Mayor and established an exploratory committee, with its side benefits, in December 2013, and then officially announced in March of 2014.

The Mayoral primary was set for April 2014, which was our earliest ever (and earlier than most) as it previously was held in September. The feds had required earlier primaries for all jurisdictions in the country to allow time for armed services members in far-away places to have their ballots counted in the primary and general elections. The Democratic candidates became Mayor Vincent Gray, Councilmembers Muriel Bowser, Jack Evans, Vincent Orange, and Tommy Wells, restauranteur Andy Shallal, and a few others. David Catania, an Independent, would face the Democratic nominee in the general election in November.

Interesting aside: I rarely watched Council meetings because I found that it made me a little sad about not being able to participate, but one morning in September of 2013, I did. And within minutes of turning it on, there was Muriel Bowser introducing the "Carol Schwartz Sales Tax Holiday Act of 2013," co-sponsored by Yvette Alexander, Anita Bonds, Mary Cheh, Jim Graham, Kenyon McDuffie and Tommy Wells. (As you may recall, the Council had done away with my Sales Tax Holidays four years earlier and not long after I left.) What an amazing coincidence that I was watching! Although I was pleased at even the thought of seeing it back again as it gives our residents a needed economic break and local businesses a boost, I sort of felt that it might just be political. I guess I was right because the legislation, even with seven introducers—a majority on the Council—never went anywhere.

Muriel, who supported me in my 2008 reelection effort and who I had supported for her Ward 4 seat, was running second behind Gray in the polls. One poll in February of 2014 for the Democratic Mayoral primary showed Vincent Gray at 28%, Muriel at 20% and Jack Evans and Tommy Wells were at 13% and 12%, followed by Andy Shallal at 6% and Vince Orange at 4%.[320]

Then three weeks before the April 1st primary, a bombshell erupted. Jeffrey Thompson, who was accused of orchestrating and financing the shadow campaign, claimed that the Mayor did know about it. This was in exchange for a plea deal where Thompson would *not* serve any prison time. Thompson's assistant had just gotten three months in a halfway house and six months of home confinement for having carried the money back and forth.[321] Now we have the culprit with the money saying the Mayor knew, and then getting *zero* days in jail, instead of possibly 10 to 20 years. Who wouldn't say what he was saying?[322]

Now I don't know if the Mayor knew or not. But regardless, I certainly would not take the word of Jeffery Thompson just "spilling the beans" under those circumstances. However, here was the U.S. Attorney having a press conference. How often does a U.S. Attorney anywhere have a press conference, period, especially for a case that did not involve murder or mayhem? But three weeks before the primary election, we got one. The timing was too unfair to stomach and too coincidental not to envision a conspiracy. Notably, in December 2015, nearly five years after the allegations surfaced, the new U.S. Attorney announced that he had dropped the investigation against Gray citing lack of sufficient evidence.[323]

That press conference, though, on March 10, 2014 frightened District voters into thinking an indictment was forthcoming. Many thought, "We'll elect a Mayor who won't be able to serve." So the number two person, Muriel Bowser, with *The Washington Post* endorsement, became the candidate coalesced around. Muriel went from being 8 points behind Gray in the polls to besting him by ten points, 43% to 33%, in the primary on April 1, 2014. It would now be Muriel versus David in the general election.

Alex and Aleida Lumbi Trochez

V.V. and Poochie

Two lights of my life and great
losses, Linda and Aunt Doe

Uncle Seymour's 90th birthday
in Denver with Aunt Betty and
beautiful to-be daughter-in-law Jen

Santa Fe, New Mexico

Dear friends Barbara Blum
and LaDonna Harris

Good friend Ali MacGraw, and jewelry designer and friend Federico

Me and
Roberta
McCain
on
Sept. 29,
2017

My 65th birthday cruise
(We look happy, but we weren't.)

Guess who's 105 and a half
(and it's not the person on the left).

Steven Tschida and Marc Albert,
friends, on their wedding day

With friends Sandy Allen, Carl Schmid
and Alejandro Barrera (my 68th
birthday dinner at Logan Tavern)S

Doug and Jen at their wedding

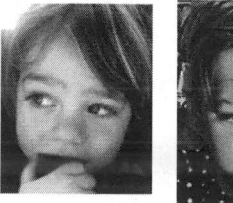

Wally and Sylvie, my adorable and brilliant grandchildren!

CHAPTER 46

Could It Possibly Finally Be My Time?

I, sitting on the sidelines at that point for over five years, after having lost my seat on the Council, had thought any opening for me to be Mayor had passed by long ago in spite of people continuing to say, "Wish you were our Mayor ... I voted for you for Mayor." Now, everywhere I went, many people yelled "*Please* run for Mayor" from their cars, couples would mouth it to me across restaurants. Friends said, "This could be the race you could win."

Not only having that encouragement, but looking at the scenario, I started to agree for these reasons: 1) Muriel, a Ward representative, was not yet well-known citywide. She was a native Washingtonian who had great potential. (In fact, I had told her when she was new on the Council that I saw her as our Mayor one day.) But Muriel was thought of as too aligned with Fenty. And many believed that she was not ready and had not substantially distinguished herself on the Council. 2) David had shown leadership ability over his years as an at-large member, but that was often overshadowed by his widely acknowledged difficult temperament. And there were some questionable issues with him consistently having that part-time job with M.C. Dean, a firm that had contracts with the D.C. government.

I started to agree that maybe, "This could be the race I could win." And my mind started racing with all the concerns I had about the city, which involved corruption, gentrification, giveaways to developers and infrastructure decline. Maybe now would be my chance to be in a position to finally do something about them as Mayor. But I was still vacillating.

Probably the deciding factor had to do with writing this book. I started it in November of 2013. The first thing my daughter Hilary and I did was go through my over 100 scrapbooks which I had begun assembling in the mid-1960s. The scrapbooks were many and huge because 1) I put several packets of extra pages into each scrapbook before I even got started, and 2) I not only kept my programs from entertainment activities and articles from my political career, but I also kept cards and letters from friends and family, and articles about them as well. Going through those scrapbooks took many, many months.

And then when I started writing the book about my life in the early spring of 2014, a few months after turning 70 (which I did in January), I realized that I didn't just want to review my life and write about it, I wanted to continue to live it.

And I thought, what if this is the time? How could I pass it by? I've always lived my life avoiding regret at all costs, and it wasn't going to change now. As I've often said, I never wanted to be the old woman in the rocking chair on the nursing home porch, going back and forth, thinking, "I could have, I should have, why didn't I?" Now I can rock back and forth, thinking, "Why did I?" And that's still better than the other.

I told very few about my thoughts of running other than my kids. Even most of my closest friends did not know. I did that because I knew I might change my mind, and also because if I did decide to run that I wanted to keep the "surprise" element in place—and some of my friends aren't the best secret keepers. I especially wanted to do the "surprise" in that I knew my fundraising ability was nil to none mainly because of my hesitancy to do it. Thus, I had to take advantage of the free publicity that a totally unexpected announcement might make in the media.

I went back and forth on the decision until the end of May. I thought Doug seemed okay with the idea. Hilary was into it. In truth, Hilary may have been most interested in leaving her day job, and helping my campaign was a great exit strategy. My daughter Stephanie was not enthusiastic for various reasons, including her fear about my reaction to another loss. That was not an issue for me. I had lost before, and had become quite accustomed to it.

The Decision Made

I decided to announce on June 9th, which is usually around the time I had entered a Mayoral race in the past. We had a lot to do. First, what about office space and phones? Then I decided, why spend money on office space when I have a well-located and big apartment on Connecticut Ave. near buses and Metro. Phone? I already had two lines. I also had a large number of office supplies from past campaigns that were easily retrievable. Since I knew I would not spend time and effort raising money, these choices made the campaign more doable. (Later, I did rent a small vacant space in the basement of my apartment building for a few months to house posters and campaign materials.)

I was aware that since I had been out of political life for five and a half years, I would have to reintroduce myself to many as well as introduce myself to the newcomers. I then went about writing an announcement statement, which did both as well as articulate my motivations for running. It read as follows, in my typical non-succinct style:

"Hi, I'm Carol Schwartz, former D.C. Councilmember At-Large. In the five and a half years since I have been out of elected office, my name has not been in the paper that much nor should it be; but whenever it is, I am often referred to as the "perennial mayoral candidate." Well, it's been 12 years since I ran for Mayor. That was in 2002; it's now 2014. That's a long time. But since I'm still referred to in that vein, I might as well be what I'm called. So today I am announcing my candidacy for Mayor of the District of Columbia.

My kids have been upset when they have read this "perennial" label in the media, thinking after my more than 40 years of good service to our city that I deserve a better label. I sure agree.

But the dictionary defines perennial as constant, lasting, unfailing, unchanging, abiding, enduring. Well, I'm guilty of all the above—and proud of it. They are actually some of the qualities we should look for in a Mayor. And I am glad those in the media who use it think that I possess them.

This time, though, I have undergone a change, and obviously it's not a facelift. I am now a registered Independent and have been since late last year. I am finally registered to exemplify what I really am—a true Independent. When I switched last year, I had not decided to run for office. But now that I am running, I am glad that I did so earlier, because I can say to the Democrats who have supported me even when I was a Republican, and those who have wanted to support me, that at least now I am meeting you halfway.

I am not nor have I ever been simply a label. What I really am is a person who has lived in D.C. for nearly 50 years, a person who chose D.C. I did not follow a relationship, a family, a job, or a college to get here. In fact, 48 and a half years ago I left all of those things back in Texas to move to Washington. I chose D.C. because I fell in love with it on a short August visit in 1965. I loved its beauty, its history, its diversity, its people. And that feeling has not changed.

My love for D.C. is a good part of why I'm running, as well as my great sense of responsibility about its welfare. During this five-year break from political life—and many of you may remember, that break was not of my choosing—I have watched closely from the sidelines and have been concerned about what is happening in our city's present and what its future will look like. While I have been extremely happy to see our town develop and thrive—the groundwork which I helped lay during my years in elected office, along with many others then and since—I have become more and more troubled as many of our longtime fellow residents are being left behind or pushed out. Our glorious diversity is being threatened.

I have also been very upset as I've watched, in this case, thank goodness from the sidelines, as some of our elected officials did us and our city's reputation in. Any corruption is too much—and D.C. has gone beyond the pale. And it concerns me that my former body, the D.C. Council, created the circumstances that opened the door for some of these unethical shenanigans to take place, circumstances I tried to stop when I was on the Council. For example, a few officials did severe wrongdoing using earmarks and their Constituent Service Funds. Earmarks are sole-source contracts that Councilmembers gave out to favored groups.

As my former colleagues well know, I tried to stop earmarks when I was on the Council, but unfortunately, was not successful. However, I was successful in stopping members of the Council from raising the amounts collected for their Constituent Service Funds, knowing that they were ripe for misuse. Regrettably, as soon as I left, the Council unanimously doubled the amount the Funds could raise each year, and earmarks got even bigger in number and amounts. Both abuses finally blew up in their faces, and then, and only then, did they regroup—somewhat.

Real leaders don't wait until they get into trouble to know certain things are risky and ill-advised. They know instinctively, using common sense if not experience. Sadly, most turn a blind eye and even participate in those antics, and only after the damaging headlines come out, do they speak out and act surprised, saying "How could that possibly have happened?" Maybe one answer is that they themselves helped open the floodgates.

So another major reason why I am running is because I think there is a void in the kind of leadership that speaks up long before the flood comes. I want a leader who has the wisdom to recognize chicanery before the "you-know-what" hits the fan and who has the courage to take it on and stop it before it hits. I have not seen that leader in this general election. I may not be alone in this feeling, given the low voter turnout in the primary and the general lack of enthusiasm now.

Today, our citizens are in need of someone who will fight for their interests, someone who will help earn back our reputation; someone who will be beholden to no one but them; someone who can be tough when it is needed but also is always fair; someone who will balance competing interests and still get the job done; someone who will protect our city's property for our own workers, students, and residents, and for future generations, instead of practically giving it away; someone who will value and care for our most vulnerable; and someone who will help D.C. continue to grow and thrive while using our best efforts to include everyone.

I believe I am that someone. I have a long history of making a positive difference in our city even when it meant going against the tide, whether it was running against Marion Barry twice when few had the courage to do so; voting against the reckless and irresponsible budgets in the 1980s which led to the Congressionally created Financial Control Board in the 1990s when I was six years gone from the Council; whether it was fighting against sole-source contracts of every kind and governmentally established funds that were independently managed—both were not only ripe for thievery but used for such; whether it was authoring a resolution, in spite of being a big fan, that called on Dan Snyder to change the hurtful name of our football team back in 2001, which I got passed right away by both the D.C. Council and the Council of Governments; standing up for students starting in the 1970s way before education reform was fashionable; or fighting to secure sick leave for workers that I believe they deserve (and for which I paid a very bitter price in my defeat for reelection—but of which I remain very proud).

This passion for making a difference led me to the Board of Education, from the mid-'70s to the early '80s, where I was elected Vice President three times, and where among other things, I brought back standardized tests; fired an inadequate superintendent to make way for two very successful ones; championed Banneker Academic High School; wrote columns and created bumper stickers to promote our public schools; instituted back-to-basic curriculum; advocated for a longer school day and year as well as stronger evaluations of teachers; and as a result of all this, we saw test scores rise.

It continued with my first term on the Council of the District of Columbia in the mid-to-late '80s, where I lowered the income tax from 11% to 9.5%; fought for seniors to remain in their homes by allowing them to defer rising property taxes until they decide to sell; and lowered D.C.'s inheritance tax (the highest in the country then) to match the federal level, to name a few.

It continued during my last three terms (1997-2009) on the Council where I created the Department of the Environment; made us second in the country to require hands-free devices while driving; shepherded the nation's strongest tree law through the Council; rebooted recycling efforts; co-introduced the measure to mark Emancipation Proclamation Day; banned government purchase of SUVs except for emergency use; upped the registration fees for gas-guzzlers and lowered them for hybrids; created two annual tax-free holidays for back-to-school and holiday purchases; prohibited the harassment of students based on sexual orientation; removed most parking meter fees on weekends and evenings; promoted the lowering of income tax from 9.5% to 8.5%; loosened parking rules for residents overnight; unearthed and stopped government "sweetheart deals"; personally renegotiated several city contracts to save tens of millions of dollars; exercised vigilant oversight which greatly improved city services; pushed for the separation of EMS and Fire services; stood up for medical marijuana; strengthened drunk driving laws (including lowering the threshold from 1.0 to .08 in 1998); voted for baseball after ensuring that the District got the best deal possible out of Major League Baseball; promoted organ donation; established a perpetual fund for street, bridge, sidewalk, and pothole repair (which was done away with after I left the Council—I presume to go to more earmarks—and look at the results); enacted the strongest Whistleblower Protection Law in the country (which was replicated by the federal government); and provided safeguards for victims of domestic violence, to name a few.

There is hardly any area in our city where I have not participated. I have been a volunteer for 45 years with valuable community groups starting in 1970 and continuing today: I counseled drug addicts at the Blackman's Development Center; served as Vice President of the Parents Pre-School Council, worked as a volunteer tutor at Malcolm X Elementary School in Anacostia; served on the Board of the Metropolitan Police Boys and Girls Clubs for 25 years, and was its President; devoted 17 years to the Board of the Whitman-Walker Clinic (1989 to 2006) and was its Vice President; have been on the Advisory Board of the Kennedy Center for 30 years and was the multi-year chair of its Education Committee; have been a 20-year member of the Board of the Hattie M. Strong Foundation, which gives out education grants and scholarships to future teachers; served as Regional Co-Chair of PFLAG's year-long 30th Anniversary Celebration; give fundraisers for causes like the Women's Campaign

Fund; and serve on the Board of the Washington Animal Rescue League, to name some. And my children went nowhere but the D.C. Public Schools—all three of them from pre-k or k through grade 12. So whether you pay me or not, or whether I am in elected office or not, I am always giving my all for our city.

The only way to know what kind of leader a person will be is by looking at who they have been—what they have done and how they have done it. We all know that people don't really change. So trust more in what you've seen in the past, not what you're promised for the future. Look at who has a long and deep record of getting results, while treating people with dignity and respect, and not just at election time. Look at a leader who is known, trusted, constant, unfailing, enduring; in other words, perennial. I hope that as you look, you will recognize me as that leader—and will vote for me as your Mayor.

And if you do, I'm excited about what we can accomplish together. We can prove that you can take care of business and take care of people. We can fix our streets and make them safe. We can protect our greenery and do drug treatment. We can do development and have affordable housing. We can educate our children and our adults, and do real job training for real jobs while celebrating our diversity— and keeping it. And we can work at finally getting the full voting rights we are owed as well as the budget and legislative autonomy we deserve. We can do all this as we optimistically look toward the future while embracing our rich and diverse history and those who made it. I hope we have the opportunity to start that strong and united future together on November 4th."

(Okay, so it's 2,093 words or 11,911 characters, which is equivalent to about 85 tweets. But as I told you before it's my life—not a tweet—and I wanted to list my unique and lengthy qualifications for that job—even if no one read it because it was too long.)

Out of the Gate

Hilary, who was helping me, is very smart and talented. As usual, I was my own Campaign Manager—and remember, I did win some elections. Hilary served as my Deputy Campaign Manager and worked 18-hour days. But of course we needed help to get everything done in a few short weeks. That's when I probably got one of my best ideas of the whole campaign: grab Phil Hahn, the son of my great friends Tay and Roger. Phil, who was not working at the time, is as equally smart and talented as Hil. I called him up and he was willing and enthusiastic about coming to help. Hilary joked that we really brought Phil in because we needed a website and he had a computer. Neither Hil or Phil had built a website before but they got right to it and we held our own in that arena. And they brought great senses of humor and fun to the effort.

We were able to compile a comprehensive list of press contacts with the help of some friends. In the early afternoon of June 9th, we clicked "send" and out the press release went. It was surreal—and even exhilarating—going from our own little world to the phone ringing off the hook within seconds of sending the email. Reporter Tom Sherwood emailed and said that "the Twittersphere was exploding" after the announcement. It was just the reaction I was hoping for when I decided to keep it under wraps.

But the enjoyment did not last long as right away David Catania fired accusations that I was "set up and bought off" by the Bowser campaign to take votes from him. His campaign manager even referred to me with a reference to the Mayoral candidate allegedly paid by Gray's campaign to stay in the race against Fenty. In my political career spanning four decades, which included two terms on the School Board and four terms on the Council, no one would have ever said I was not my own person. But the accusations, false and ridiculous as they were, were broadcast through traditional and social media. I ended up spending the first few weeks batting down those offensive and untruthful rumors.

The day after my announcement, I went on Bruce DePuyt's *NewsTalk* show and spent a large part of the interview answering questions about the last time I talked to Muriel (I said hi to her at a Memorial Day party) and being confronted with quotes about how we supported each other's elections for the Council, which I assume was supposed to be rock-solid proof of our "conspiracy."

Fortunately, I received a legitimizing nod from the *Post*, which ran an editorial saying voters should "welcome having choices."[324]

The first Friday after I announced, Kojo Nnamdi asked me to come on the *D.C. Politics Hour* where he and Tom Sherwood interviewed me. One of the first questions asked by Tom was about my thoughts on the legalization of recreational marijuana. I stated that I had supported and voted for medicinal marijuana years earlier; and I said that if I had been on the Council, I would have voted for the decriminalization of marijuana because of the disproportionate nature of who was being sent to jail and who was not. (By the way, I have also never been in favor of going through people's homes and arresting them only for their use.) I did say that I would be voting no on the initiative for legalization of recreational use which would be on the next ballot, because we already had too many addicted people we needed to take care of without giving our stamp of approval to more.

I knew at the time that answer would be hurtful to my candidacy, but I try never to deceive. My two major opponents both publicly bought into the initiative, which I'm sure served them well at the polls as it passed by 65% to 28%.

I still feel comfortable with my response back then. And now with the synthetic type of marijuana and with heroin usage on the rise, and deaths from it quadrupling from 2005 to 2015[325] and now outnumbering deaths from gun homicides,[326] as well as seeing special high schools opening now for kids as young as 14 who are addicted to drugs and alcohol, that feeling is stronger than ever. On January 27, 2017, *The Washington Post* reported that marijuana was responsible for the fatal crash by the Amtrak engineer south of Philadelphia in 2016.[327] An article called "Faces of the Epidemic" in a recent *People* talked about two brothers dying, saying "... the two liked to party ... with recreational drugs, first using marijuana and cocaine in high school, and later moving on to heroin." Another man named Steven also overdosed. His dad "watched his son ... spiral from occasional marijuana use into severe opioid addiction ..."[328] We need to beware. (Some may say, "I bet she drinks. Why can't I do marijuana?" Well, I neither drink or do any kind of mind or pain-altering drugs. So I am aware enough to beware.)

Putting It All Together as Best We Could (With Little Time and Less Money)

My dear friend of over 45 years, Bob Burka, willingly took on the role of Treasurer with my daughter Hilary's and former Treasurer Judy Smith's assistance. (My Treasurers for decades had been the Smith family, both Democrats, first Richard until he passed away and then Judy. We became wonderful friends 35 years ago when we met through our boys playing peewee football.) My close friend of also 35 years, Elsie Smith, a Democrat, was Chair of the campaign. A friend and supporter of nearly as many years, Milt Grant, volunteered to run yard signs around town and put up posters. Of course there were many other supporters, including Republicans—although I was no longer one—and quite a few new supporters of all persuasions. Another great aspect of the campaign was reconnecting with Ernie Pozzi, a former D.C. public school teacher, who was invaluable, hanging up posters through the night while getting signatures for the petitions all morning. Maudine Cooper, retired from heading the Urban League here, retired military man Ted Howard, a well-known Democrat Betty Smalls, Cheryl Wilkins, and Lawrence Parker, were four others who worked very hard. Our volunteers came from every Ward and represented the full spectrum of our city's diversity.

As soon as we announced on June 9th, along with answering phone calls and signing up volunteers, the first item of business was getting the petitions out in order to gather the signatures needed to get on the ballot. Acquiring all the required signatures was a major project in and of itself. In the past, when I had run as a Republican, considering the small number of registered Republican voters, I joked that I needed to get about three signatures. Now, as an Independent, I needed 3,000 of those babies.

And we intended to get far more than that to ensure that we had enough signed eligible names to pass any kind of scrutiny—in fact we wanted double. And unlike most other candidates, we did not hire anyone to gather them; we did it ourselves along with many volunteers. While collecting signatures out in the field, we had a volunteer operation back in the "office," certifying those names against the list of registered voters. I used the opportunity of gathering signatures personally, garnering 2,000 on my own, to engage directly with voters.

A few have said that I became an Independent before my final election for Mayor for political expediency. I switched for the reasons I explained, and if I had switched for expediency, I would have made that switch long ago to become a Democrat. Going from Republican (6% of the voters in D.C.) to Independent (17%)—a big 11% gain—although a little more palatable to the electorate, is not exactly expedient. And it's much harder to run a citywide election without a party behind you. Being on your own and needing 3,000 signatures is not easy.

Anyway, nearly 100 volunteers had asked to circulate petitions, and as we neared the deadline, 72 people turned in their sheets on fairly short notice. We pulled a near-all-nighter organizing and numbering the huge pile of pages. In the end, on August 6th, we turned in over 6,500 certified signatures to the Board of Elections—quite an accomplishment with only volunteers in just seven weeks. There were quite a few members of the media there that morning, and it was certainly one of the peak moments of the campaign. Maybe *the* peak. We should have quit there!

After we gathered the signatures, the office remained abuzz with volunteers stuffing envelopes, preparing packets and other tasks. Every donation got a timely thank you note as did our petition circulators. We also wrote and sent out numerous letters to past supporters as well as Advisory Neighborhood Commissioners, political lists, and whatever list we could get our hands on.

Dealing with Dirt

Not long after announcing, I started receiving phone calls from friends and strangers who told me they had gotten recorded calls from pollsters asking about the Mayoral race. One poll included approval questions on Muriel, David and Carol. And then came the obvious follow-up question, "Who will you vote for?" At that point, only two choices were provided: "For Muriel Bowser, press 1. For David Catania, press 2." The people who reported this to me stated they kept saying, "Carol Schwartz" and pushing 3. No luck. And at that point, they were hung up on. We learned from the media that that poll was paid for by D.C. First which turned out to be the PAC organized to support David Catania. Big shock! The PAC was chaired by Martin Janis of Atlantic Services Group (which is Irwin Edlavitch's company), and was largely funded by it and the other parking companies that funded PACs to defeat me because I got the sick leave bill passed.

There was another poll being received by Democratic voters that said I was a Republican, even though I was an Independent. It was obvious that these were push polls used to spread false information and cement the race as a choice between two rather than three candidates.

Then, soon after we sent a letter to D.C. Republican Committee members (who did not have a nominee and we knew David was courting them), *The Washington City Paper* reported about it. Not the letter that went to the ANCs, many political leaders, or former supporters—just this one. I had my suspicions—we had an alleged mole. I became suspect when this person started spending most of her volunteer time asking questions and wanting to see all of the campaign letters we had sent out. My suspicions were confirmed after we got copies of Catania's petitions in order to validate the signatures, and found the person's name among his petition circulators. No longer alleged, now just a mole. And even more ridiculous, I'm actually still friendly with this person.

Following this incident, Hilary and Ernie became so paranoid about double agents in our midst that they spent a morning driving around to supporters' homes (without my knowledge) to see if there were opponent signs on their lawns. They thought they were an ace pair of detectives, until they showed up at the homes and in every case saw my yard signs.

Hilary was just being protective of me. There were some good reasons. At times I was yelled at by supporters of David who had bought into the spoiler theory, not to mention the cruel words that were sometimes foisted on Twitter or in other comments online. As I had not run in six years, I had not been confronted before with the increased prevalence of social media. But unfortunately, this is a new day when any hateful person can say anything about anyone. And I'm aware that I have not been the only recipient of this kind of vitriol, especially when the writers can hide behind an anonymous profile online. But some of the messages were beyond the pale. There were a few that even wished for my death. Hilary got so upset when she read some of these posts that she started answering back. I would scream at her, "Ignore them. That will bother them even more." Sometimes I would just yell, "Stop Tweetering!" But thank goodness, there was much positivity and kind words along the way as well.

Press Coverage

This was a different kind of campaign for me, and there were new mountains to climb. This time, I had to battle for legitimacy as a candidate. There were articles citing, "the two leading candidates," naming Muriel and David. This was before any polls were done, or certainly legitimate polls.

I wrote notes, made calls, and finally got some meetings with the media to cite the unfairness of being overlooked and under-covered by them. Martin Baron, Executive Editor of *The Washington Post*, was responsive, gave me some time to plead my case, and could not have been nicer. (And that is the same Marty Baron who led the uncovering of the priest abuse scandal for *The Boston Globe*, which was the subject of the great Oscar-awarded Best Picture, *Spotlight*. I so admire him for that.) And due to Marty, I had another productive meeting with Mike Semel, the Metro Editor.

At one point, a journalist said that they were focusing on fund-raising to determine the leading candidates to devote the most space to. How about that for hypocrisy? Many in the media decry the influence of money in politics, but here they are using money as a measuring stick for who to cover, thus ensuring those with the most money would get the most coverage—and would most likely win. Isn't that undermining the campaign finance reform they usually promote?

Finally, the media did start including me more, probably just to make my calls stop. But be careful what you ask for.

I was soon featured in a profile in *The Washington Post*. It was a front-page piece by Marc Fisher. I heard positive feedback from a few on this article, saying it highlighted my warmth. But I didn't like it so much. First of all, the paper in its first edition featured my age prominently—three times on the cover page. Literally, and I repeat, three times on the cover page—sub-headline, fourth paragraph, and in the photo caption. Thank goodness, it was caught and the second edition only mentioned it *twice* on the front page. The title of either may just as well have been: "70-YEAR-OLD."

I have never seen them do that with a male politician, and there are lots of them that age—and older. Not surprisingly, "too old" started appearing in article comments online. This kind of ageism tends to get more directed toward women. Remember we used to hear much about Hillary Clinton in her late-60s being too old to be President, which only stopped when the older and male Bernie Sanders in his mid-70s entered the race—and same with the older and male Donald Trump being 70.

An interaction was highlighted in the Fisher article. A woman I met outside a grocery store told me about her daughter who had lupus and was very obese. I gave her some advice on that latter point. Since she had also said her daughter had a sweet tooth, I said, "So do I. But I now substitute cottage cheese mixed with blueberries and Splenda, and it helped me lose some weight. It really is a dessert-like treat." But the article made it look like I was recommending the dish as a cure for lupus, painting me as ridiculous and worse, callous. And there was absolutely no mention of my record as an elected public servant which spanned four decades. But that was a piece of cake in comparison to some of the other articles. Oh well ... At least they wrote about me.

As we tended to do in the campaign, we would take these annoying things and make a joke of them. This became a running one of those—my cottage cheese lupus cure. Phil even said if I lose the Mayor's race at least I would win the Nobel Prize for Medicine.

Kudos and Grateful Tears

In mid-August, I received a great boost from Colbert King, an esteemed regular Saturday columnist for *The Washington Post* for decades. I had been so frustrated trying to prove my worth to journalists who were often new and/or young and not aware of my serious record and history. Colby had called to ask for an interview, which we did for hours as I came with a written record of my legislative history starting with my School Board days. But I found it somewhat unnecessary as Colby's questions seemed to acknowledge his awareness of me and my work.

However, I know him to be straightforward and tough, so I waited for his column with great apprehension. Friday, August 15th, I received an email from him with the column attached. I cried when I read his piece, and many of his words stay ingrained in me even today:

> "Schwartz, undoubtedly, has the life experiences to work in the racially, socially and ideologically diverse stew that is our Nation's Capital.
>
> She's also encountered her share of bears in the woods—anti-Semitism during her Midland, Tex., childhood, the agony of a husband's sudden death, being a single mom having to make a living while guiding three children through the D.C. public schools and on to adulthood. Along the way, she's enjoyed both political victories and bitter betrayals.
>
> The words tough, courageous and compassionate fit Schwartz like a glove. She is one candidate who can claim to be 'unbought and unbossed.' Nobody pulls her strings. And after close to 30 years of casual observation, this much I can say: Right or wrong matters to Carol Schwartz. In this city, that's saying a lot."

I have strived throughout my career to live by the words he described. But those were his words, and I was more than grateful to have a man I looked up to a lot use them in describing me. His recognition was one of the highlights of not just the campaign, but of my entire career.

Focus on Education

A hot button issue was whether the next Mayor would retain Chancellor Kaya Henderson, who had been Michelle Rhee's Deputy and who Vince Gray appointed to the top post after he became Mayor. Backstage at the Bruce DePuyt's show on June 10th, a day after my announcement, a Ward 4 community activist asked whether I would keep Kaya Henderson on. I said "off the record" that I would. Although I had originally been against the Mayoral takeover, by this point the education system had already been through too much upheaval to make more changes. Besides, Kaya had a much less brusque style than Rhee when it came to parents and teachers. And our system was finally showing some improvement along with seeing the highest enrollment in years. Therefore, my desire to see her stay.

Muriel had refused to commit to retaining the Chancellor since she had announced her candidacy fourteen months earlier. Interestingly, that same night at an education meeting with some parents in Ward 4, she did commit that she would reappoint Henderson and made it public. I immediately realized that the community activist must have passed along my off-the-record comment that afternoon—or was it possibly just a weird coincidence? Regardless, since Muriel would likely be the winner as the Democratic nominee in this Democratic city, I was glad to see her commit to Kaya—and stability for a school system in need of it.

Meanwhile, David was taking another tact. He was portraying himself as the expert on education after being Chair of the Education Committee for a year and a half. But he is a convincing speaker and a quick study, and he won favor from many public school parents. Of course, using his position as Chair to give public money in a campaign period to new college funds and to give back the ability for special education parents—and the hordes of lawyers lined up—to sue the city probably helped.[329]

He also sweet-talked the Washington Teachers Union, and played them correctly by not only refusing to say publicly that he would keep Kaya Henderson as Chancellor, but saying he would *not* keep her in private. Yet, I knew from my experience on the Council with him that he was one of Michelle Rhee's biggest advocates and defenders from start to finish. Quite a turnaround!

(In fact, it was widely rumored that David had an arrangement with Adrian Fenty in which he would rubberstamp all his education wishes as long as David had total control over the Department of Health, where he put in some of his own staff and then proceeded to privatize most of its functions. According to Mike DeBonis: "From his committee perch, [Catania has] overseen wide-scale privatization of city health services—from drug and alcohol detoxification to care for the mentally ill.")[330]

Furthermore, one of the first things David did as Chair of the Education Committee was hire a private law firm to craft education legislation. He paid the law firm with contributions he had requested from those with school reform interests, including investors in charter schools—which are the nemeses of teachers' unions. When the Washington Teachers Union became aware that his walk did not jive with his talk, they backed away, and wound up not giving an endorsement to anyone, even though he may have thought he had it in the bag. (I wonder who gave them that information about the charter school contributors? ... It was fun to take on the king of dirt, and with just the truth.) I had been working hard to get their endorsement for myself and I got very close. But still, no endorsement was a win.

The Rag-Tag Team Produces

We were definitely the rag-tag team. We'd go to street fairs and there were the other campaigns with fancy tents. We would walk around with our posters which we had stapled onto stakes. It was good we were able to accomplish anything considering .. We did attempt to compete well where money wasn't the issue. We put together a full and attractive website ourselves. We did papers on issues like education, housing and economic development. We answered every single questionnaire in detail and there was a multitude of them; I was involved in each one, usually at 2 a.m. Afterwards, I went in to make the coffee so it could just be turned on in the morning for the volunteers. That coffee, a tuna fish sandwich, chips, and a few cookies were the only remuneration for the many good people from all over the city who came to help.

Our comprehensive plan on education, which we pulled an all-nighter for, received good coverage from the *Post* and from *Greater Greater Washington*, which called it "a detailed, thoughtful platform."[331] I talked about increasing the use of magnet schools to keep students as well as utilizing retired seniors as tutors with students who need extra and loving attention.

An important point I made is that we need to keep good teachers and principals where they are. We can do that by rewarding them with increased salaries instead of the present practice which usually incentivizes them to leave the classroom and the school setting to go into administrative positions to get that increase. Just because a person is good at working directly with kids does not make them a good administrator—and vice versa. Capable principals and teachers should be given a first shot at any administrative position, but an increased salary should not be the motive to make that move. Let's keep our best and brightest working directly with children by better compensating them for being there.

The education plan was an easy one as I had been public school educated from kindergarten through college, a special education teacher in two public schools, a volunteer in a cooperative public pre-school program, a public school parent of three for decades, a Board of Education member for two terms, a volunteer tutor in a public elementary school in Southeast D.C., a Presidential appointee and Vice Chair of the National Advisory Council on the

Education of Disadvantaged Children for seven years, a full-time consultant at the U.S. Department of Education to the Deputy Secretary, and a Secretary of Education appointee to the National Commission on Time and Learning, where I was Vice Chair and served for its three years. Certainly not as impressive as chairing a committee for 18 months, but at least a little experience.

My Bright Yellow Wheels

Before the campaign, my son Doug told me not use my yellow Trans Am convertible, which I had owned for nine years. Doug said that it was just not Mayoral. I know that. And I'm sure there may be a few who did not vote for me because of it, but I bet they would have come up with another reason anyway.

It's my car, though, and I love it, and if it had disappeared as Doug wanted, that may have been talked about as well. I also thought it might get me some attention I wouldn't get otherwise. And in fact, it did, actually getting even more coverage than I got. It was photographed. It was ridiculed. It was envied. Even some young people who criticized me on Twitter admitted my car was cool. Regardless, I just know that putting the top down and driving that stick-shift car all over town relaxed and thrilled me at times when I could use something like that. Still does.

Hot Button Issues

School boundaries became a hot-button issue during the election. The Gray Administration delivered plans to redraw school boundaries for the first time in 30 years. Change was necessary as some schools were overcrowded while others were underpopulated. But a problem in the plan was drawing a line along Rock Creek Park which I feared would affect the little diversity we had in our schools. I said in a press release that day on the boundary plan that I did not intend to turn back Brown vs. the Board of Education, so the blueprint would need some "tweaking" to avoid that. I had no idea when I wrote the word "tweaking" in that release that it would become the term everyone would start using.

There was talk of selling the Reeves Center, a government building at 14th and U Sts., to a developer for condos. I had a hissy fit. Why would we want to take a valuable government asset and have the beneficiary be one developer and its residents when it can be used for something which benefits all of us? And even if not for us today, it will still be there for future generations to have and to hold. All talk about the deal ceased. Hallelujah!

Campaign finance reform is always a hot button issue. In 2013, the Council passed much-needed reform in the wake of that most recent corruption crisis. Yet a significant loophole was conveniently kept open, and would only be closed after this 2014 election. By way of explanation: businesses, like individuals, are subject to a maximum contribution of $2,000 in a Mayor's race. However, a loophole allowed businesses to give that maximum contribution from each of their subsidiaries (LLCs) and therefore, bypass the $2,000 limit. The other candidates in this race just went about their merry way and took in a lot of money using that hole in the law. I brought up this issue often in debates. But the media never took the candidates to task for it; in fact, they barely said anything. It was obviously not their hot button issue.

I made the decision to close the loophole prematurely in my own campaign, even before the law went into effect in January of 2015, and called on Bowser and Catania to do the same. "Just because you can do it does not mean you should." But they kept raking in that LLC money. They were also using PACs, that often have no contribution limits, to send out mailings and robocalls from what they called "independent" organizations.

Taking Our Show on the Road

Our campaign did a fall "kick-off" event at Freedom Plaza. (I picked it because of its location across from our city hall, but not for its size, which is enormous.) My daughter Stephanie and her spouse, as well as my son Doug, came in for that. Because of storm warnings that morning, we were worried that we would be the only ones to show, especially since we scheduled it in the middle of the work day (our bad). And we were relieved when we ended up with about 60 very enthusiastic people. Longtime volunteer Lawrence Parker masterfully decorated the plaza with signs and balloons. I invited my favorite DJ, Lady Smooth, to play music. We all had a great time dancing and singing along to "Simply the Best" by Tina Turner. A Mike DeBonis piece on the event in the *Post* concentrated on the age bracket of the attendees, saying that "very few were under 50."[332] We know. Why else would we schedule it in the middle of a weekday? And besides, our attendees don't drive at night, even if they happen to be awake.

Seriously, age *was* a factor. It reared its ugly head earlier with the three "70s" in my kick-off profile. Although I had energy and ebullience, my opponents had youth—and in D.C., youth was in.

Will Sommer of *The Washington City Paper* asked what my campaign theme song would be. Since we were such a ragtag team, I chose off the top of my head, "Side by Side" with the lyrics, "Ain't got a barrel of money. Maybe we're ragged and funny. But we're traveling along, singing our song, side by side." Hilary and Phil made fun of my choice, which they felt did nothing to contemporize my image. I don't know what they were talking about, just because it's a tune from the 1920s. I had thought about making Tina's "Simply the Best" my campaign song, until we read the lyrics and found out it was all about obsessive physical love. I didn't think that quite fit what I was offering.

Actually I had wanted to use from the start, "Everything's Going to Be Alright" by Moms Mabley, who was a comedian and singer at her peak in the 1950s and 1960s. But we didn't have the time or money to make it happen, like too many other things.

CHAPTER 47

A 'Poll' or Whatever

On September 8th, Catania released the barest of information about an internal poll his campaign conducted which he stated showed him statistically in a dead heat with Bowser. In front of reporters that evening at a dark bar, he announced that he was three points behind Bowser and that I was many "multiples" of three behind him. (Maybe that was the poll my friends told me about in which you couldn't even vote for me if you wanted to.) The Catania campaign refused to give out any more details on this poll's results other than the vague he's three points behind. The most amazing part is that members of the press just ran with the results like it was legitimate, with the exception of Will Sommer from *The Washington City Paper*'s "Loose Lips" column.[333] I appreciated his reality check.

I knew that if the race continued to be perceived as being between Catania and Bowser, I would have even less of a chance. Not only that, but it was incredible that the poll showed the race was tied between Bowser and Catania when back in March, Catania stood 30 points behind Bowser in a hypothetical matchup.[334] Catania knew how shaky his poll was, and refused to give any backup information on it. Good for him for trying to manipulate the story, but bad for most in the media who played into it and for being so well-puppeted.

That September 8th when that internal poll got such wide coverage, I got depressed. I really felt like I had hit a wall. I was just so frustrated at the media, with whom I had to battle to be taken seriously, and yet who were so willing to let this BS PR-spin by Catania go unchallenged.

The only relief to my frustration that day was thinking, "Aha, I know how to fight this crap—just fight it with more crap." Hilary was just as depressed as I was, so we ran with it. We would just release our own "poll" even if no such poll had taken place. As we had learned from David's poll or whatever that was, it clearly didn't matter if there was legitimate backup or not. So we started typing away, laughing like teenagers the whole time.

Assistant Andre Strickland, a Democrat from Ward 8, enjoyed the process, but became worried about actually sending it to the press. But we brought him around by saying that we thought it was the best way to highlight the ridiculousness of the media's running with David's lack of data. Here is the release I sent out:

'Carol Schwartz Releases Internal Poll Results with AbsolutelyNo Backup Evidence'

"The Carol Schwartz for Mayor Campaign today announces results of a poll the campaign conducted. The poll was done by a credible polling firm (we can't say more than that, you just have to take our word for it). The poll was conducted among 1,001 registered voters, and the not surprising results: Our poll shows Carol with 75% of the vote, Muriel Bowser at 3%, Faith* at 1%, and David Catania at -3%, with 18% of the vote undecided. The margin of error is 99.9%. Notably among the 50+ age bracket, Carol Schwartz has 100% of the vote. Upon learning about these scientifically sound and encouraging numbers, Carol said, "And to think I had been worried about David Catania's recent poll (which in a way actually pleased me because most of his polls have not even included me as a choice). But then I realized why not conduct my own internal poll and release the results with no back-up evidence as well. Muriel, I look forward to seeing your internal poll results soon.""

*Faith was the Statehood-Green Party candidate.

Mike DeBonis of the *Post* tweeted the whole press release and said, "This is really pretty funny." And others let me know they found it amusing as well. Regardless, it was fun to do.

A Real Poll

The first legitimate media-taken poll was released by *The Washington Post* on September 17, 2014. It showed Bowser with 43%, Catania with 26%, and me with 16%. It was clear that Bowser had a formidable lead, but I wasn't unhappy with the results. In fact, I was pretty pleased that I did as well as 16% considering how long I'd been off the Council, how little money I had, and how recently I had entered the race. Some in the media echoed that by expressing surprise I was doing that "well" considering the same things. And the nice part was that the poll showed I was not acting as a "spoiler," pulling equally from Bowser and Catania. But I did know that if I didn't rise soon or slipped, it would really be over.

Then on October 1, 2014, a group called Economic Growth D.C. did a poll, which focused on frequent voters. While the *Post* poll surveyed a voter group which represented 48% African Americans and 43% white voters, the Economic Growth D.C. one polled 53% white voters, 42% black and 5% Latino. Their poll had

Bowser at 35%, me at 14%, and Catania at 27%. The group's executive director was quoted as saying, "What this says to me is the race is closer than a lot of people think it is," with Catania trailing Bowser by 8%.[335] It was curious to me that this independent organization's poll somewhat mirrored Catania's own internal poll.

On the brighter side, I received the endorsement of D.C.'s Tenant Advocacy Coalition (TENAC) members, led by Jim McGrath, and was grateful to have their support.

Debates Large and Small

The debates were another point of contention. At first there was talk that I would be excluded, but thank goodness, I wasn't. Then Bowser announced she would only be doing four debates and skipping all the rest, which caused some to be canceled. But there were still many that David and I did on our own.

The first of these was an arts-centered forum on Capitol Hill. It included me, David, Brian Moore (the Libertarian candidate), and Faith (Statehood-Green Party), who has run for Mayor more times than even I have and at age 90, made my then 70-year-old self seem young. She is a bugle-playing actress/artist/activist, who is very nice and always adds vibrancy to the proceedings. This forum had a high point as Faith yelled to the audience, "Vote for Carol!" I appreciated that as I have her, who I just had a visit with.

I was present at every debate and forum, except for one sponsored by the Georgetown Citizens Association, which had scheduled their debate on one of the most important Jewish High Holidays. I asked them to reschedule, but they refused to change the indelicate scheduling. That night I went to temple as I do each year on Rosh Hashanah and David had the forum all to himself. I did send several volunteers to pass out a letter with literature enclosed saying where I was.

I was very nervous at the first major debate with all three of us at American University as I had spent the last five and a half years only debating my children and a few friends. Speaking of, Doug was quite a help in this campaign, calling regularly to check in, flying in a couple of times, and helping to write some pieces. He gave good advice—some of it I took. But the biggest help was Hilary who was there working non-stop morning, noon and night, and with not that much remuneration. What a trooper.

That first debate did give me an opportunity to get wind of the scenarios that would follow. The three of us, Bowser, Catania and

I, were all standing in a small anteroom outside the stage area before the debate began. All of a sudden, Bowser left and David and I were then told to just go on stage and sit down. We got some applause as we waved to the audience while finding our seats. Just as we sat down, here comes Muriel, who stands in the center of the stage with both arms raised triumphantly, like "Now let the show begin." It was obviously orchestrated—and successful.

I had a few successes myself that night. I believe many in the audience appreciated my stating that I was appalled at the lack of fairness toward Mayor Gray, who had his reputation smeared four years earlier with still no indictment. I said, "If the U.S. Attorney has something to bring, he should bring it. If not, he should just shut up." I also scored by pointing out how my opponents were using the LLC loophole in raising campaign money, saying, "Even though you made sure it wouldn't apply to you in this election, you should have followed that law even before it took effect as I am doing. Leaders need to lead."

Our second major debate at NPR was hosted by Kojo Nnamdi, with questions being asked by Tom Sherwood of NBC4 and Patrick Madden of WAMU Radio. Fairly early in, Tom Sherwood asked David, "You used to talk about having caused Carol Schwartz's 2008 defeat for the Council. Did you play a part in it?" David answered that he had not. I then said that he had actually taken credit for it in a *Washington Post* article until he found it wasn't so popular. He denied that was the case, and immediately Muriel jumped in and said, "We just heard that Mr. Catania didn't organize the race against Carol, and everybody knows that that's not true ... he not only recruited the candidate, everybody who supported that candidate also supported him throughout all of his races. So it's obviously very clear."[336]

I did take opportunities during some of the debates to point out David's working for years for M.C. Dean, a D.C. government contractor, while he was a sitting Councilmember. For that part-time job, he made $240,000 annually until he left to run for Mayor in the beginning of 2013. Also a potential conflict was his support of the full 37-mile streetcar plan of which M.C. Dean would be a major beneficiary. During each debate, David used the line that he would wake up every morning and run toward the problems of the city. Yet he always neglected to mention that he often ran toward Dulles, Virginia for his work with that D.C. contractor. Muriel certainly mentioned this outside employment as well. His response each time was that this private sector experience would be very helpful to the city. And he emphasized that this work with M.C. Dean, including all of his international travels for it, had given him a rare commodity: a "special security clearance," which would be especially helpful to us. I'm still trying to figure out how.

Those bigger debates highlighted our smaller and cheaper organization. Bowser's and Catania's camps had hordes of people gathered outside the venues, many paid people as well as volunteers, and had posters blanketing the area. We had a few signs up with a handful of volunteers passing out literature. We finally did get our act together for the third one, an NBC televised debate at its studio. This time we blanketed the area with posters and people. But since it was in the middle of the day with a very limited audience, the only people who saw our impressive presence were the two other candidates and a couple of media people. The other camps had not even bothered to put up one sign. Oh well ...

As if things could get worse that day, they did. Only a couple of supporters from each campaign were allowed into the room where the debate took place. Of course, Hilary was supposed to be one of them. But unbeknownst to me, in her usual magnanimous manner, she offered her seat to a supporter we barely knew who happened to show up. (It wasn't really just magnanimous, as Hilary has told me, but it was because the debates made her nervous and she liked being able to pace in another room.) Anyway, the volunteer could not have been a worse choice. At the end of the debate, while the cameras were still rolling, she started screaming, "Why didn't you give more time to Carol Schwartz?" I thought Tom Sherwood, the moderator, would have a heart attack, and I was ready to join him. Instead, I just looked down at my notes and pretended I didn't know the person, which wasn't too far from the truth. The televised version ended with Tom murmuring behind him, "Shut up, shut up, shut up."

But even that debate had a peak moment. After David answered a question from Colby King about his employment with M.C. Dean with the usual how beneficial his $240,000 part-time salary from that contractor was to the city, I used that opportunity on television to present him with a thank you card I had brought, which read how grateful we the citizens in the District of Columbia were to him for his work at M.C. Dean, and especially appreciative of his "special security clearance."

Should I Stay or Should I Go?

Yet another poll was released by the *Washington City Paper* on October 24th, which showed me at 10%. Unfortunately, once it gets in the air that you can't win, it becomes self-fulfilling as people understandably want to make their vote count. In that poll, I was beating Catania at least in Wards 7 and 8 east of the River, which was a bit of a consolation when you try to find good news somewhere.[337] At that point, I even had thoughts of dropping out, but then decided I should stick it out. I didn't want to disappoint my volunteers who stood behind me as well as the people who wanted to vote for me, albeit then not that many. I also didn't know who would benefit from my leaving, so I didn't want to tip the balance. It turned out there wasn't enough votes to affect that balance, but fear of it is one of the reasons I stayed in. And I also felt good about raising important issues, such as ethical concerns, including campaign finance, as well as the driving out of long-term residents without sufficient affordable housing.

Whenever I got a little depressed about the election, and it was usually after a poll, I would head to Costco in Northeast D.C. I found it to be a place where "everybody knows your name"—and face. People were so warm and friendly, and made me feel like the most popular person in town, by saying things like: "I'm voting for you," "We miss you," "You are such a strong advocate," "Thank you for your service." (I really thought about trying to get a referendum passed pre-election that would only allow shoppers at the N.E. Costco to vote, but didn't have enough time or money for that effort either.) My time spent there was a real pick-me-up—and the free samples didn't hurt. But I do say as I'm leaving with my huge supply of stuff—and usually only me at home—"I won't live long enough to use all this."

A Sweetheart Deal?

There was something specific bothering me throughout the campaign. Although I did prefer Muriel to David, I worried about her large number of contributions from developers. I also had noticed that her main headquarters was a spacious corner building located in the newly popular Petworth neighborhood. My instinct told me that this might possibly be a sweetheart deal. So we did some research. I then issued a press release on October 28, 2014 which I am now excerpting below:

"I have tried to run a positive campaign. I have never done negative ads or mailings like the ones we have seen too often in this election. An exception has been in discussing David Catania's second job. But I had an important point to make. Now I have discovered another exception and another important point needs to be made.

Back in 2002, when I ran for Mayor, I paid a very high rent for a second-floor, low-ceilinged, small, dark space in the 4000 block of Georgia Ave., N.W. in Petworth: $6,600 for a two-month period. I verified this amount on my financial report on the Office of Campaign Finance website. For my 2008 Council race, before U St. was quite the booming corridor it is now, I rented a second-floor space at 12th and U Sts., and paid $5,500 a month after negotiating the landlord down from $6,000, for about 1,000 square feet.

Cut now to present when Petworth has become part of the economic renaissance in our city. It is where Muriel Bowser's campaign finance report of October 10, 2014 reveals that her campaign is paying $1,800 a month, an amount which appears to include utilities, for a very visible, very large storefront with two floors, three entrances, and many windows near a Metro stop and Starbucks. [And one block away from my former place.]

Curious about the low rent being reported, I had someone call to get a quote on what the space would rent for after November of 2014. An individual representing the owner of the property called back yesterday and gave a quote of $5,000 a month for one-third of the ground-floor space. It's incredible to even think that this same space went from $1,800 per month (apparently including utilities) to at least $15,000 per month in the one year or so since her campaign rented the space.

This morning, we only saw two retail rental spaces in the Petworth section of Georgia Ave. and inquired about them. One representative returned our call for 3901 Georgia Ave., N.W. The space is located in the lower level (going down a couple of steps upon entry) of a small, two-story, decrepit-looking building and offers "little sunlight." The rent is $2,700 a month, not including utilities.

Considering the amount of $15,000 quoted to us for the ground floor of the Bowser campaign space and discounting whether she has the second floor since we do not know, the best-case scenario is that for the 13 and half months she has occupied that space, her campaign has been the recipient of $202,500 worth of office space for which it seemingly only paid $24,300. The maximum contribution a corporation can make, under the campaign finance rules, is $2,000. It appears the corporate owner of this property has contributed $178,200 in free rent. And by the way, the company receiving the rent happens to be a government contracting firm located on K St., whose website lists the District of Columbia government as a customer.

Maybe there is an explanation for this apparently amazing deal, but it certainly is not found in the Bowser campaign's finance report. It is especially concerning that such a deal is taking place even before a new administration has been elected. I did struggle with bringing up this issue, but I do believe the public has a right to know. Right or wrong does matter. Or at least it should."

Nothing much came of the release other than some excited tweets from Catania supporters who called it "RentGate." Weren't they surprised when I, the supposed patsy of the Bowser campaign, exposed this information.

The Hatfields and McCoys

The other campaigns and/or their allies were very busy spending lots of money to raise the negativity factor through many mailings. The Catania campaign did a lot, including a mailing to specific Wards which linked Muriel to Marion Barry as well as a particularly offensive handout in which Bowser appeared to be puppeted. Unions sent out mailings in support of Bowser which included quotes from those who had experience with Catania and called him a "bully" and anti-union. This is one time I liked getting totally ignored.

There was another Catania mailing which featured a Bowser photo with the logo from the TV show *Scandal* with the heading "It's not just a TV show." But the piece only revealed that no one in his campaign watches the program because it basically equated Muriel with the show's hero, Olivia Pope. What could be more complimentary? (I do watch the show.) I could imagine recipients getting this postcard and thinking, "Ooh! Four years of *Scandal*! What could be better?" It may have gotten her more votes.

I did not go negative in my handout or mailing. I just went verbose. I know in today's world you're just supposed to send out a huge postcard with a couple of pictures—which include children—and the only verbiage being "Education is Good" and "Crime is Bad." I know the drill. But in my few mailings, I just have to tell you not only something, but everything I did and what I wanted to do to make D.C. better. I recognize it's too much. And I hope you recognize what is happening today is too little. Maybe there's a happy medium.

Stuck Between the Hatfields and McCoys

This is what I felt about the race: Voters were caught between two dueling entities for a couple of years, which I labeled election night to a reporter as the "Hatfields and McCoys." Those two candidates, David and Muriel, did not like each other and their supporters felt the same way. His voters showed disdain for her and her voters felt similarly. When I announced June 9th, I hoped to capitalize on the division between "not ready" and "mean," but without much time or money, it was impossible. (And I am responsible for those two failings. [Colby, take note!]) Each of their supporters feared the other so much that they could not take a chance that the other opponent would win. Any vote for me became not only wasted but could cause that dreaded result.

And now I must bring up another huge factor in that election, and it has to do with race. I do not believe it was directed at me—and it certainly does not take away from other factors that affected this election, like temperament. But I do believe that many African Americans in D.C. feel threatened by what is going on in our city. And I truly understand how they feel. It is real and it is hard. D.C. used to be a 70% black city and now it is 50%. Many black people are being pushed out of town; but let's be honest, many chose to leave. I think so many felt that if Muriel wasn't elected there would never be another African American Mayor. In fact, I nearly voted for Muriel instead of myself for the same reason.

I know I received many African Americans votes, and I am eternally grateful. But to those who liked me and even leaned toward me, but yet chose to go the other way, I get it. Now let's make sure that whatever color our leaders are, that we hold them accountable for maintaining and even growing the glorious diversity which is Washington, D.C.

The End

Bowser won the election on November 4th with 55% to Catania's 35%, and me with not much, only 7%—but still there were over 12,000 people who voted for me. Defying predictions, even with the demographic shifts in the city, it was not the closest general election in D.C. history. At least I still hold that title against Marion Barry in 1994, when I got 42% to his 56%.

(I have watched Muriel in her role as Mayor and I have appreciated her energy and conscientiousness in trying to tackle the various problems facing the city. She's made some mistakes along the way, but seemed to rectify them pretty quickly. I think she was more ready than we gave her credit for, and I am glad.)

I grabbed onto the only bragging rights I could find in that 2014 election. And here it is, after much research and calculations—and sorry, Jack! I spent the least amount of money per vote by far, $10.50. And I received three times as many votes as Jack Evans did during the primary, where his campaign committee alone spent $407 per vote, 40 times what I did. [338] So that's something. The only other something is the fact that I lost 15 pounds. Yet, it would have been much easier to go to a local gym or much cheaper to go the world's most expensive spa.

Some might have considered it an embarrassing loss, even in spite of the money versus votes I just talked about. I think my children maybe have thought that, and it has certainly crossed my mind on occasion too. But I am proud that I ran. I am proud I raised the issues I did. I am thankful for those supporters who hung with me this time as well as those who had in the past. Some I have mentioned, but now I want to give a shout-out especially to these friends: Alice Banks and Barrett Brick (both of whom we lost a couple of years ago), Crystal and Ron Evans, Reverend Nat and Diane Thomas, Laura and Bob Richards, Bob and Maria Burka, Elsie Smith, Judy Smith, Maudine Cooper, Jim McGrath, Ellie Roberts, Cornelius Baker, Joan Kloepfer, Renee and Wyatt Stewart, Ann and Bob Wieczorowski, Russ Binion, Dr. John Robinson, Jeanette Miller, Reginald Jackson, Ann and John Wylie, Sam Paschall, Rene and Bill Regardie, Carole Egloff, Bob Ray, Virgil Thompson, Betty Smalls (who both sadly and recently passed in their 70s), and to Mark Sibley, who hates to be recognized, but who was always helpful with the various financial issues.

Would I have run again under these same circumstances? Probably yes, even with the cost of wear and tear, money and ego deflation—and so little percentage. Other than the important issues that I brought up, there was another nice side effect. I did show a 70-year-old could go the distance both mentally and physically against two 40-some-odd-year-olds.

And personally, I also recognize that my regret had I not run would have totally overshadowed the embarrassment I felt after losing badly. There again, I refuse to be that old lady, sitting on the porch of the nursing home, rocking back and forth, saying "I could have. I should have. Why didn't I?"

CHAPTER 48

Reflections

Right after that election, I thought a lot about it as I had the Council loss. But this time it wasn't a depressed state that took over my thoughts, but more of an analytical one. So here is some of what I concluded:

I've always been a stubborn old bird of sorts, and more so as I get older. When I was very young, I never could really verbalize anything I was really thinking for fear of being hit or not being liked. But as I got older and grew in independence, the stubborn old bird in me would just take over, especially when I thought I was right. I know it cost me some popularity and I think I knew it would, but I really couldn't help myself. And ultimately I'm glad I couldn't. More good than bad came of it, not only personally but I do believe for the common good.

Some dramatic examples include keeping my Republican label when it ran totally against the tide, bringing back standardized tests to the D.C. schools, pushing Banneker Academic High School for inner-city public school scholars when it was considered "elitist," stepping on toes to stop government giveaways, battling smoke-free at its inception in D.C. when I really felt it would dramatically hurt our hospitality industry (although I'm glad everything is smoke-free for many years now), making sure workers in D.C. had some sick leave, championing the change in name of our football team, fighting the Mayoral takeover of schools and ensuring that an elected Board of Education of sorts was brought back, as well as standing up against the expanded recreational use of marijuana—each and every one cost me votes, endorsements, popularity and contributions.

I knew when it was happening that I should just stop because some of them were not even winnable causes. But I just couldn't stop. I always say that I'm a rebel with a cause. It's the truth. But I feel secure knowing that I've spoken up when others didn't and stood by my convictions. I feel satisfied that I used my voice, albeit not always applauded, to say the things I felt needed saying.

Another point: It's always bothered me that you can cast 100 votes and people can agree with 99 of them, yet you rarely hear from those people. But be against just one thing—cast that one vote out of the 100 that they don't agree with—and that's the one they remember. I ask you, how fair is that? Just something else I hope you will think about. This is not about me, but generally.

Usually I knew casting that "one vote" was making it harder for me. And it's such a dichotomy. Here I have wanted to be liked more than anything my whole life, and yet I'm willing to do the unpopular thing when it comes to my strong convictions, even if it risks not being liked. I guess sticking to those convictions is actually more important to me in the long run—than pandering to be liked. Regardless, I know I could not have done it differently. And this book has become another way to speak my beliefs. Thank you for listening.

My Winning and Un-Winning Slogans

Thinking back on my campaigns made me remember the slogans I've used. With them, I tried to capture initially what fresh air, later know-how, and always never-ending commitment I would bring to the city. And here are a few: Wake Up Washington, There for You, A Champion for Our City, A Strong and Needed Voice, Taking Care of Business ... and People, A Vote for Our City, For All of Us, An Oldie *and* a Goodie, For Our City's Sake.

Silver Linings

After the 2014 loss, there was something that made me feel somewhat relieved. And it reminded me of a thought I had after the 2008 Council loss as well: At least I did not have to be ever-present on television in the age of HDTV (High Definition Television). The circles under my eyes and wrinkles elsewhere looked bad enough on regular TV screens when I had been on the Council. And then here came HDTV. I'm not sure if I would have looked okay on it when I was 20 years old, much less 65 or 70. And I'm certainly not the face-lift type. A gal who won't even lose weight is not going under the knife. I also do not alter photographs to any real degree. I prefer for people to see me and say, "You look so much better in person" than, "What a good picture you take" or worse, "Oh my—you've sure aged." Speaking of overweight, I've learned that actually helps with age—my own form of Botox.

I know my children feel relieved that they don't have to campaign for me anymore, so there's a silver lining for them as well. There were lots of campaigns and they were always a big help to me, and I appreciate what they did during all those years.

In addition to missing out on HDTV, I was also very pleased that I got out before emails became an every-minute activity for everybody, not to mention Twitter, Facebook, blogs, Instagram,

Snapchat, "Snatchgram" (that's next), etc., etc., etc. And I who spent my entire career answering every single communication would have gone more stark raving mad than I am now.

And speaking of all those methods of communication, whatever happened to talking? I go out and I see people sitting at the multitude of wonderful restaurants we have in this city next to very young attractive people and yet no one is even looking at each other, much less talking. All they are doing is staring at either their computers or their phones. Why even go out, especially with other people? Does someone out there have an answer about that for me? Or maybe you're not even hearing my question because you're too busy on some electronic device. Maybe I should just Tweet the question to you, if I only knew how.

This new world seems to be more about instant gratification than anything else—which is not only anti-social, but can endanger yourself and others. So please put those devices down when you're crossing streets. I get so scared as I watch you. And I know of people who have died doing just that. Couldn't you at least make that a small break time, okay?

Goodbye Old Rival and Friend

On November 23, 2014, we all received the news that Marion Barry Jr. had passed away. He had struggled with health issues for so long, but he constantly rose back up like the phoenix, as he often did in his political life.

I was truly sad when he died. The event at the Convention Center honoring his life, which was organized by his wife Cora and son Christopher, was a moving and fitting tribute. Soon after his passing, I was honored to be asked by the *Washington City Paper* to share memories of him in a written piece. In "Marion Barry and Me," which ran on November 25, 2014,[339] I talked about how we met in the '70s, our similar backgrounds geographically and professionally, our common feelings on many issues and some not, my lecturing him about his behavior, and our friendship. Below are excerpts of other memories from the article:

"[Marion and I] had fun times together. During one official trip to South Africa as part of then Mayor Anthony Williams's delegation, Marion sat next to me on a bus. As usual, I chattered away: "Look at those beautiful purple trees." He said, "Can't you ever stop talking?" I replied, "Oh, I can." I absolutely shut up. He kept asking me to talk, but I wouldn't say a word. "Carol, talk to me." Then he took the bus's microphone and said,

"Everybody, please help. Make Carol talk to me. She never shuts up. But when she does, I miss her talking." Now I'll miss him telling me to stop talking.

Some other moments I'll remember: When my dear husband David died in 1988, only 14 months after I ran against Marion in 1986, he called right away and then came to my house. He didn't just come to pay respects, but he sat there for much of the day for a few days. I had met Marion's mother several times in D.C., and when I went to Memphis for a personal function in 2006, I took breakfast over and had a wonderful visit with his mom and sister.

Marion was an unforgettable character with his endless self-promotion and self-victimization. But all the while, he could get away with it because he was enormously charismatic—and endearing. Whenever I would go to fancy functions, people always wanted to talk to me about Marion Barry. Most wondered what D.C. residents saw in him. I would mention his charisma, and they would say, "That's ridiculous." Then I would say, "I bet if he walked in here now, you'd change your mind." They would scoff. Sure enough, sometimes he did walk in, and they would turn and say, "You're right." Marion Barry in his heyday was the best politician I ever met. (And by the way, the second was Bill Clinton, and the third, Ronald Reagan.) This does not discount his transgressions—nor should those discount the good he did for the city, especially during the early days of Home Rule and his needed voice in these last few years for those most in need.

I remain shaken and saddened as I, like others, thought Marion Barry was invincible. He personified D.C., and his passing is a great loss. I loved and appreciated Marion Barry Jr. and will miss him greatly."

His wife, Cora Masters Barry, invited me to Marion's private repast. I thought that probably all the Council had been invited, but when I got there, only Vincent Gray and I were present. It was nice to be included and it was so good to see so many of the D.C. political "old timers," of which I am one. When I was talking to one of Marion's really good friends—probably best friend—I said, "Did you know that I was the last person Marion called before his kidney transplant? That was so surprising to me." He said, "I'm not surprised. He always loved you."

And speaking of Marion and love, his greatest most lasting love was probably his son and only child, Christopher, who unfortunately died of a drug overdose in the early morning of August 14, 2016 at age 37. What a sweet young man. It's so tragic.

P.S. Christopher had asked to pass out literature for me in my last Mayoral election three years ago, making two Barrys—Christopher and Effie—volunteer helpers. I even think the third one, Marion, did so sometimes in his own fashion.

Fleeing the Cold but Not D.C.

Being born and growing up in more geographically Southern states (Mississippi, Tennessee, Oklahoma and Texas), I must admit I never got used to the cold. When I was working all those years, I really had no choice. Now I do. I usually go to Florida right after Christmas because I have always enjoyed the wonderful holiday parties regularly and sometimes given by friends Pauline Schneider, Carl Schmid and Alejandro Barrera, Ellen and Bob Bennett, Vivian and Marc Brodsky, Carlin Rankin, Judith Rogers, Marc Albert and Stephen Tschida, Pat and Phil Peters, Lars Etzkorn and Gregory Hoss, Linda Auwers and Jim Jones, Jay Haddock and Hector Torres, Sylvia Bergstom and Joe Rothstein, Bob Jerome and Bill Courville (which had always been the first until they recently moved to a smaller place), among a few others. I stay in Florida until early March, with usually a couple of trips up to D.C. in between. I always want to be in D.C. for our beautiful spring. (Since I usually celebrate my January birthday in Florida, I want to give a particular shout-out to three dear friends, Judy and Stuart Treby and Joan McCrosky, for making such a big deal of it.)

The one-bedroom in West Palm Beach, which we had bought for Ma in 1979, basically remains the same, other than painting and putting in new carpeting once 25 years ago, and adding some more up-to-date pictures and knick-knacks (well, on second thought, maybe not so up-to-date). I really have had a great time there over the years. I have friends who live in the development and elsewhere in Florida, all along the east coast from Miami Beach to Port St. Lucie, and Sarasota on the west coast. A memorable time there was spent with Beth Stovall, my "twin" (a friend who was born 30 minutes after me in Greenville where our mothers shared the hospital room), who came from California several years ago to celebrate our mutual 69th birthday. What a great gal she is. I really like her except she looks so much younger. Speaking of, my mom used to say in her 60s that she loved to go to Florida to visit her in-laws as it was the only place that made her feel young. Now in my 70s, I know exactly what she was talking about.

Since I spend some time in both my getaway places, West Palm Beach and Rehoboth, there's a rumor that sometimes rears its ugly head—usually at election times—that I am a resident of Florida, Delaware or both. Like I often say, D.C. is the only love affair I have not gotten over. I have always only been a resident of the District of Columbia and have paid my income taxes here since January of 1966, except those brief months in suburban Maryland when first married—51 years in all. You can check the tax records if you'd like. So to those who spread the rumor, and to those who hear it, please just know that it's wrong. D.C. is my proud home and primary residence. If I ever move, I'll let you know.

Thanks for the Hospitality

Speaking of those Christmas holiday parties reminds me of friends who have occupied me during other holidays and times which can be lonely as a single person, such as the Jewish Holidays. I've appreciated Dace Stone (who died 15 years ago), Diane and Allan Kullen, Dede and Marvin Lang, Barrett Brick (who died two years ago), Francine and Mel Levinson, Marion and Herb Cherner, and Judy and Stuart Treby, who often have included me for festive meals—and Esther Coopersmith's Thanksgiving dessert party. I also love Lynda Webster's annual tea at the Chevy Chase Club in September and Jeffrey Slavin's annual tea at the Woman's Club of Chevy Chase in October, each with their distinct lists of interesting and attractive women. Other friends who have come through with great invitations are Pauline and Diane at their getaway place in Maryland in July, Shari Barton's summer party until she passed away a couple of years ago, Susan and Stephen Porter, Tay and Roger Hahn on any Mother's Day I want to join in, and Ed and Bonnie Sands for July 4th in Ocean City. (Bonnie's father was Abe Rosenfield, co-owner with Bonnie and Ed of Calvert Woodley Liquor, and whose School Board seat I took after Abe resigned in 1974.) I also enjoy an occasional evening with several women in the building where I live: Linda Lee Johnson, Susan Conway, Michaela Keeling, Karen Croce and Sylvia Kurop.

Getting Lost in Good Company

On July 8, 2015, Congresswoman Lois Frankel (D-FL), a friend, invited me to join her at another Congresswoman's home on Capitol Hill for the evening. It was quite a special event with at least 30 people, mostly members of Congress, including the former Speaker of the House, gathered for a buffet dinner and to have an open, off-the-record discussion with a *Washington Post* columnist.

Other than some staff of the members, I appeared to be the only non-Congressperson and non-Democrat present. Lois has thrown me into smaller dinners with her colleagues, but this was far more monumental. I loved every minute, like when several of Lois's colleagues told me they appreciated my work on the Council.

As I was leaving this perfect evening, I asked Lois if I could give her a ride. And then she asked if we could take a colleague, Congresswoman Katherine Clark (D-MA), as well. I said, "Of course." It was sprinkling. We had two umbrellas and two of us were wearing heels. I led them to the car, which was not there. I said, "Maybe it's on the next block." So we walked there through the rain. No car. I did say around that point, feeling terribly embarrassed, that they should just go back to get another ride or get a cab. But they were too nice to leave me and in fact said, "It's so dark out here. We don't want you to be alone." This to the girl who drives all around town at night alone in her convertible—if she can find it.

We then started walking around in circles, in some cases together and often apart, yelling at each other down the block: "No yellow convertible yet!" "It's not here!" Finally, we joined forces again and said, "Let's go back to East Capitol Street to find a cab so we can drive around instead to look for the car." No cabs. At that point, I realized I had headed us north away from East Capitol St. instead of south. Then we easily found my car just a half a block away. How humiliating! Lois obviously got over it as we have hung out again since, but she said she'd drive—joke! They were sure good sports that night.

Just Saying ...

I love sayings, and have lots of them on pillows and plaques on the walls at home as well as had them in my former offices. Some relate to the kids. Many I just picked out, and some were given by friends, even on cards, but I like them so much that I have them displayed. I've even unconsciously made up some of my own sayings over the years, but just use them verbally because they're too long for a plague or bumper sticker.

<u>Sayings I Have Collected</u>

- "I don't have to attend every argument I'm invited to."
- "Sometimes a majority means that all the fools are on the same side."
- "Remember to breathe."
- "Eat right, exercise daily, die anyway."

- "Be nice to your kids—they choose your nursing home."

- "Live long enough to be a problem to your children."

- "Life is hard. It's harder if you're stupid." – John Wayne

- "Money isn't everything, but it sure keeps the kids in touch."

- "I smile because you are my son. I laugh because there's nothing you can do about it."(Pointed out by a friend, Ernie.)

- "Family: We may not have it all together, but together we have it all."

- "I see no good reason to act my age."

- "It's never too late to have a happy childhood." (My favorite.)

- "Lord willing and the creek don't rise." (A saying I have used since childhood, like "knock on wood" when I don't want to jinx something.)

- "Bread and butter." (What you say when you're walking with someone and something comes between you—there again, not wanting bad luck.)

- "Work like you don't need the money ... Love like you've never been hurt ... Dance like no one is watching."

- "If you don't like the road you're on, start paving another one." (From the movie, *Our Brand in Crisis*.)

- "There are two lasting bequeaths we can give our children: roots and wings."

- "Definition of antique: Grandma made it. Mama gave it away. I'm buying it back."

Sayings Friends Have Given Me

- "Lord, if you can't make me skinny, make my friends fat."

- "A woman is like a tea bag. You never know how strong she is until you put her in hot water."

- "Every wall is a door."

- "I won't stop eating chocolate. I'm not a quitter."

- "Grow where you are planted."

A Few of My Own

- "I have to work hard to maintain this weight. If I'm not careful, it starts dropping down on me. It's a full-time job to keep it up there." (This saying is one I usually use when I'm knocking over people to get to the front of the buffet line.)

- When anyone tells me I have great hair, my response is always, "Thank you, but when God gave me these thighs, I guess he decided to compensate."

- "Linner"—of course, that's a combination of lunch and dinner.

- When I go for thirds: "What does full have to do with it?"
- When shaking hands after October: "Sorry about my cold hands, but they won't thaw out 'til spring."
- "D.C. is the only love affair I have not gotten over."
- "Some people say they are minimalist. I'm a maximalist."
- When I do something stupid: "If I had a brain, I'd be smart."
- Going out with friends and ordering baby back ribs, some say, "You eat pork?" My response: "Are you kidding?—growing up in the South, I didn't know there was anything but pork."
- When showing people around my cluttered apartment, I say, "I know there's a thin line between good taste and overdone—and I crossed it years ago."
- "My house is dated—but so am I."
- "Don't put so much salt in. You can always add it, but you can't take it away."
- Speaking of salt, my dad was not big on sayings, but here's one he made up and used over and over again after he spilled either salt or pepper: "I'm not superstitious, but I'm going to make sure that nothing happens that will make me superstitious," as he tossed the salt or the pepper over his shoulder.
- When out shopping and a salesperson says, "That looks nice," I say: "Thank you, but no. At this stage, I only want 9s or 10s. I already have lots of 7s and 8s in my closet."
- Every time something about this new world aggravates me, I say, "I'm glad I'm old."
- If people say I'm nice, I often reply: "I'm not really a nice person. I just do nice things to not feel guilty."
- When people tell me I look good for my age, I say one of the following: 1) "Glad your eyesight is failing," or 2) "Being overweight is my own form of Botox." (Now I'm thinking of just adding more years to my age to get more compliments.)
- "It's easy to look good spending a lot of money; the best is looking good spending little."
- "I think anyone below 150 lbs is anorexic."
- "I'm a rebel *with* a cause."
- Whenever food or soda is brought to me quickly, I say, "What took you so long?"
- "It's not just the quantity of life; it's the quality too."
- When people ask, "Are you enjoying 'retirement'?" I answer, "At least I know now my work skills are better than my leisure skills."
- I take so many supplements that I often say, "I have been dead for years. I'm just a walking vitamin."

Staying Busy to Keep Away from Making Up Sayings

During my post-Council life, I have stayed busy. I very often visit older friends who are somewhat home-bound, such as Reverend Jerry Moore, Roberta McCain, and Vincent Reed (and his lovely, caring wife Frances), which is really a pleasure in all cases.

The same is true of 47-year friend Dwight Cropp, who had a massive stroke about five years ago. Linda, his dear wife of those many years, has been the caretaker of the century. When it didn't look like he would make it and certainly not have full mind capacity, Linda decided that was not going to be the case. She went to work. Now—and for several years—when I visit, and Linda and I are talking away and can't remember somebody's name from the past, Dwight, sitting in his wheelchair, pipes up and fills in the blank for us. Unfortunately, so many others I got great pleasure out of spending time with, like Alice Banks and Mary Pensky, are both sadly now gone.

And I have stayed busy with valuable organizations like the following: A couple of years ago, I got more involved with PFLAG (Parents and Friends of Lesbians and Gays), co-chairing its year-long 30th anniversary celebration, along with Montgomery County Executive Ike Leggett (and his wife Katherine) and then Arlington County Board Chair Jay Fisette—all of whom are friends. I had a fundraiser at my apartment to celebrate the 30th anniversary with the Co-Chairs and the nearly 100 people who were present.

My membership on the Kennedy Center Community Advisory Board continues after 32 years. Several months ago, our President Deborah Rutter talked to the group about 2016 being the 45th anniversary of the Kennedy Center as well as May 29, 2017, being the 100th birthday of John F. Kennedy for whom the Center is named. Deborah said that because of the Kennedy Center's renown as the national performing arts center, the fact that it is also the national monument for John F. Kennedy has been somewhat overshadowed, and that they're working on ways to rectify that. I then said, "I know we have a large bust of Kennedy in the long foyer, but you have to be inside to see it so maybe a way to highlight President Kennedy would be to build a statue of him in front of the Kennedy Center in the small garden-type plaza in between the two entrances." I do believe such a statue would help solidify its status as the true national memorial to a former President who vigorously promoted the arts. I hope they do one.

My work for over 20 years with the Hattie M. Strong Foundation continues too. Unfortunately, we lost our leader, Hank Strong, several years ago, but his son, Henry Strong, is ably leading us now along with his sister, Sigrid S. Reynolds. We no longer do the student loans, but instead now are giving scholarships to fourth-year college students and graduate students who are in the teaching field. Grants are the other component of the Foundation and they are focused on supplemental educational-type efforts for young people such as after-school, weekend and summer programs with emphasis on the disadvantaged population.

In 2014 and '15, Rabbi Bruce Lustig of Washington Hebrew Congregation (WHC) put together a "kitchen cabinet," which he asked me to be part of. I had been a member of the Board of Directors of the temple in the late '90s and had been given the amazing opportunity to speak before the whole congregation during their high holidays in 1987. I have belonged to WHC for 43 years now and am very proud of the work that the temple does in the community, including providing transitional support and housing to young homeless women and their children at Carrie Simon House since 1988 and its citywide Mitzvah Day activities in the spring. I am also proud of its universal advocacy through words and deeds for equal and civil rights here at home and abroad. On June 3, 2013, I was honored to be given the Avodah Award for community service by the temple.

Also in early 2014, I was appointed to the Home Rule 40th Anniversary Celebration and Commemoration Commission by Mayor Gray, and served along with former Council Chair Sterling Tucker, *Washington Informer* Publisher Denise Rolark, and George Washington University Assistant Vice President Bernard Demczuk. Our efforts culminated in a series of educational events related to Home Rule as well as a major citywide celebration at the John A. Wilson building on October 28, 2014. It was the last time I hung out with Marion Barry, and my daughter Stephanie made sure that she had a picture taken with him that night. Good thing, as he passed away less than a month later.

I have been on the Board of the Washington Animal Rescue League (WARL) for the past five years. I also did a fundraiser for WARL in 2013 in my home with a good crowd. The League, in the last several years, has done a wonderful program of taking dogs into the prisons where it has been shown that they are very therapeutic for the prisoners. I have also seen cats and dogs do wonders for seniors in nursing homes, such as the one Letitia

Baldrige was in. For decades, my brother Johnny and his special needs co-residents at Marbridge have had animals as loving pets. What a blessing they can be to every population.

The Humane Society and the Animal Rescue League merged in February of 2016. The combined name is the Humane Rescue Alliance, and I am on the joint Board. The Alliance takes in animals in need of a home from across the country. If you want a companion, there's no better one than a cat or dog. Think about adopting.

Speaking of ... My life and home have been filled with our beloved family rescues for most of the last couple of years. One reason has been that Hilary has spent a great deal of time in D.C. instead of New York because of helping me work on this book and the Mayoral campaign which intervened. The second reason would have had her here anyway because dear Gaby, who we had adopted in 2004 when she was about four, has been quite elderly in the past several years and could not get up and down the fourth-floor walkup in the girls' lower east side apartment building. And where Hilary and Gaby go, so do the cats V.V. and Poochie, thankfully, who Hilary adopted when they were about six. So I've had four additional female family members here for quite a while now. And I love their company even though ...

I am a real priss about my prissy apartment. Everything is always in its place—or at least used to be. Because of Gaby's older age and occasional incontinence, and Poochie's (until recently) stomach issues, it's not as prissy anymore. To protect my rugs from my wonderful grandpets, there is a maze of obstacle courses with chairs and pictures put sideways on the floor, blocking rooms. I am stepping over a small one constantly as I enter my bedroom. Obviously, my normal active entertaining mode has been halted for quite a while now.

And guess what? I couldn't care less. Miss Priss would rather have this precious time with these precious animals as long as I can because they have brought me more pleasure than all these possessions. So that too has kept me away from making up sayings.

In the fall of 2016, I was told I had been voted into the Washington DC Hall of Fame, headed by Dr. Janette Harris Hoston Harris, which was a wonderful and unique honor. Then on April 30, 2017, there was a beautiful awards presentation in a Capitol Hill hotel for the honorees, of which there was one in each category ranging from business to law to sports to politics. (Guess which one I was in? ... and it wasn't sports.) I was thrilled to be one of the few elected officials to be recognized in the category of politics in the Society's 17-year history. I had also been pleased in 2012 to be named one of the women who are making a difference in the region, a project by Karen McConnell-Jones. We were featured on the cover of *Prince George's Suite* magazine with a story entitled, "Great Women: How They Heal and Uplift."

New Doors Open

While engaged in my fifth Mayoral run, when I was busy 20 hours a day, it reinforced my need to be doing more things of value. Fortunately before I could decide what those "more" should be, along came some worthwhile and satisfying opportunities:

- *National Museum of the American Indian*

In May of 2015, Kevin Gover, the Director of the National Museum of the American Indian (NMAI) invited me to lunch and asked me to join its National Council. I gladly said yes. I had always had an appreciation of the American Indian culture and its people, and had started a collection of its jewelry about 20 years ago, especially the older type commonly called old pawn. As you may recall, I did a resolution in 2001 calling for a name change of D.C.'s football team. Although this was at the behest of only me, I later learned it was greatly appreciated by many American Indians.

The National Museum of the American Indian is part of the Smithsonian Institution and consists of three separate facilities: the Museum on the National Mall at 4th St. and Independence Ave., S.W. that opened in 2004 and offers exhibits, lectures, performances, and educational activities; the Cultural Resources Center in Suitland, Maryland, which is gigantic and houses collections and research artifacts; and the George Gustav Heye Center, the former Museum of the American Indian (that was founded in 1916, merged with the Smithsonian in 1990, and became part of the National Museum in 2006), which has a current location in New York City at 1 Bowling Green near Wall Street.

The NMAI is dedicated to advancing the understanding of Native American people and culture, supporting its traditions, and encouraging contemporary art. The Museum has two incredible new initiatives, which the Council is actively involved in. One is to ensure that school curricula have a much more balanced and accurate depiction of American history as it relates to American Indians. The second is to raise awareness about American Indian veterans, who in fact, constitute the highest percentage of any ethnic group to have served in the military up to a decade ago, starting with the American Revolution. That was a surprising discovery for me and probably for most. But it is true. Our goal is to build a memorial to honor American Indian veterans on the grounds of the National Museum of the American Indian in D.C. The legislation to do so was approved by Congress several years ago, but the Museum must raise the money to get it done, and the Tribes are being helpful in that regard. And we should be as well.

- ***The John Wayne Cancer Foundation***

In September of 2015, I was asked to join the new four-member National Advisory Board of the John Wayne Cancer Foundation. John Wayne beat lung cancer, and then 15 years later, in 1979, succumbed to stomach cancer. He expressed his wishes before he died that his money help others fight this terrible disease. His children started the Foundation in 1985 and it has supported cancer research, prevention and treatment ever since. The Foundation established the John Wayne Cancer Institute, chaired by Patrick Wayne, at Saint John's Health Center in Santa Monica, which does research and treatments, and has established a surgical oncology fellowship. The John Wayne Cancer Foundation, headed by Ethan Wayne, is also active in educational and preventive programs.

And then here came a third worthwhile and satisfying opportunity, and one that offered a chance to return to my natural habitat and work in an area that was right in my wheelhouse. You'll now have go to the next page to solve this mystery.

2014 Campaign

Turning in petitions

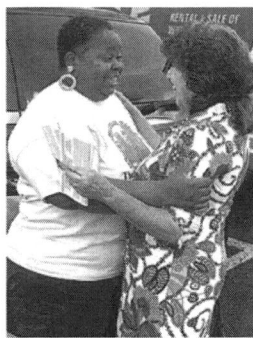

Not many votes,
but lots of love

Election Night: still smiling

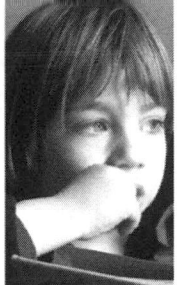

Sylvie and Wally's
5th birthday pictures

Sylvie and Wally with their pretty
mom Jen on their 5th birthday in NYC

CHAPTER 49

Brought Back In

In November of 2015, Mayor Bowser's Chief of Staff contacted me and said that Muriel wanted me to become a member of a major government board. I said I was so pleased to be thought of, but I was not interested in that board, and gave several reasons. I even told him that Vince Gray offered me that same position when he was Mayor and I had turned him down as well. When he said something like, "We'd like to make use of your talents," I did mention that I might be interested in the Board of Ethics and Government Accountability—a position Vince also asked me to take—if it were offered to me now. He said it might not be available, but he would get back to me. When he called the next morning with the offer, I said yes with great pleasure, appreciation and enthusiasm.

The Board of Ethics and Government Accountability is an independent Board whose members are appointed by the Mayor and approved by the Council for six-year terms, and who can only be dismissed for cause. Its functions include penalizing ethical lapses (by censure and/or financial retribution) of all D.C. employees from the lowest level to the highest elected official, as well as putting in place preventive measures such as ethical training to all divisions of the government.

I was ready for a weighty role that used my experience, judgment, and energy to serve the city. It's why I ran in 2014. After that race, though, I did not look for anything. I did not ask around. But here it came. And I was glad—and ready.

I always valued the role I played as a watchdog on the Council, and Muriel and Vince were colleagues who observed me doing it. But in both cases, I must admit I was surprised to be offered to play that role as an independent watchdog in their Administrations—knowing how dogged and tough I can be. I admire that they did. I'm not sure I would have even offered myself that job if I had ever had an Administration. But both Vince and Muriel did. The first time was not the time. The second time was.

When I look back over my life, and this book has required that of me, I realize that the most touching and satisfying moments of my fairly long life, aside from some personal ones, have been times when people who have observed my work, including colleagues, have shown appreciation of what I have tried to do and how I tried to do it.

In my statement during the required Council hearing prior to confirmation, I spoke about how I got here in my usual verbose fashion. I am sparing you most, but here are some pertinent parts:

"In my seven years out of government, in spite of my continued volunteer activities ... I have truly missed serving D.C. and its people in a broader way.... Now I'm ready, willing and able to take on a weighty role in our city government again.

Unfortunately, D.C. has suffered in the reputation department due to unethical behavior on the part of some government officials. I must say, though, that when people from other places point the finger at D.C., I do get angry, especially when it's used as a reason to continue to deny us our rightful voting rights in Congress—rightful in that we do pay federal income taxes. But let's be frank, unethical behavior is a problem everywhere. You don't even have to look far. Just look at our two surrounding states, where governors have been indicted, found guilty, and even sent to prison. Should we deny them their Congressional voting rights too? Of course not. But how about equal treatment for all? Regardless, D.C.'s obvious goal is to strive for the highest standards.

I always believed when I was in elected office that I not only had the ability to write rules on the Board of Education and laws on the Council, but I had the ability—and the obligation—to effectuate positive change by being a watchdog. And I am proud to have used that role to unearth wrongdoing and equally important, to give a needed wakeup call about practices that could lead to wrongdoing.

Those who hold trusted roles in government cannot just sit back and wait until trouble happens and the headlines start rolling in to know that certain things are risky, ill-advised or downright unethical. There must be the wisdom to stop troubling behavior before it blows up. Background checks and ethics training can help, but nothing can replace ongoing vigilance.

As most people who know me know, I am always sober and alert, and it's hard to get anything by on me. My former students and children sure learned that, though I do have a strong belief that you are innocent until proven guilty. It's also hard to get anything out of me that's confidential. I do take any responsibility seriously, and this one certainly is. Many who have witnessed my oversight—and my last committee had 32 agencies and commissions under its purview—have said, "You're tough but you're also fair." Those qualities—fairness, discretion, seriousness, vigilance, along with experience—are what I would bring to the Board of Ethics and Government Accountability. I hope the Council will give me that opportunity. Thank you."

The Council unanimously confirmed me and I started serving in January of 2016. It has been good to work for D.C. and its people directly again.

I have been on the Board of Ethics and Government Accountability for a year and nine months now, and have been pleased with the work my fellow Board members and I, along with our capable Board staff, have done. Mine is a four-and-a-half year appointment as I am filling the unexpired six-year term of a previous non-majority-party member. Originally the Board was three members in total, but it asked before I came to be expanded to five to cover its large responsibility. At first, I served with the original Chair and one original member. Now they have left, as has our Executive Director. So more recently, I have served with three newly appointed members. And I have enjoyed working with each and every one of them.

I have over two years left my term and wish to remain. The requirements for service are—and should be—that members of the Board do not participate in local political activities. Specifically, no member shall be a leader or hold any office in a District political organization or contribute to one; nor shall a member make speeches or publicly support or oppose a political candidate; nor use one's status as a member to attempt to influence any decision of the District government not within the Ethics Board's purview; and also a member cannot be a lobbyist or a felon. I believe this book does not run afoul of the above, nor do any of my present actions, or lack thereof. But in case it is decided that it does, I will either fight it or just resign. Getting this story of my life out is too important to me—and I am not choosing to delay it for another few years. If I need to leave, thank you Madam Mayor for the appointment, and to the present Board and any successors, I wish you well and continued vigilance.

The work the Board does is confidential until a decision is reached and a censure, fine, or both occur, unless a confidentiality agreement remains, which I certainly agree with and honor. But on July 6, 2017, the staff was briefing us in an open meeting about our October 2017 Ethics Day activities, and said that the planned featured speaker would be Michael A. Brown, my successor on the Council, who had just gotten out of jail a couple of months earlier for a huge ethical violation. I could not believe my ears and said, "I can just see the *Washington Post* cartoons now." It turned out that three *former* Board members, who preceded the four of us *present* ones, had negotiated a settlement with Brown to "conduct

12 live, in-person presentations" to "educate government employ-ees on the risks inherent in engaging in unethical conduct," as was stated in the August 20, 2017 *Washington Post* article entitled, "Former D.C. Official Who Took Bribes to Discuss Ethics."[340] The Board was able to deep-six this troublesome idea for that Ethics Day, and will continue to try to find a way through this challenge.

More on My Kids

Hilary is one of the most curious people I know. She is often reading about things she's interested in like the Middle East or lis-tening to some podcast about the history of English, economics, etc. She is also my go-to person for any technical issue, and even wrote up directions for setting up a DVR recording for me. Hilary loves animals, and has volunteered at a cat shelter for years. Seven years ago, she adopted two of the cats there—who they thought were sisters, and still volunteers sometimes. Poochie and V.V. were really beautiful, but quite overweight. I used to say just more examples of pudgy Schwartz girls, but now my two daughters are trim, so do not qualify anymore. But all the animals and I still do. (Sadly, precious Poochie passed away on August 19, 2017 at ap-proximately age 13, after suffering from many health issues.)

Recently, Hilary has joined the family passion of politics, mar-rying it with comedy, and was hired to write humorous blogs and videos for a political website during the 2016 national election. She has also been published in the books, *What Was I Thinking: 58 Bad Boyfriend Stories* and *Half Jewish: A Celebration*. She is such a talented comedy writer.

Hilary has spent much of the last several years helping me with various projects—the 2014 campaign and this book. Her time, ef-forts and smarts have been invaluable to me. And I have enjoyed her company as well, even when we're yelling at each other. I thank her lovingly for all of the above.

Stephanie had quite an interesting time upon her return to New York in the spring of 2006. To get to her job working as an attor-ney prosecuting child neglect and abuse cases for the city of New York, she traveled an hour each way from lower Manhattan to the Bronx by subway, and worked about 12-hour days. It was a hard, challenging, depressing, and frustrating job which she loved and was quite good at. Within no time they made her a supervisor, but she still continued her direct court appearances as well.

In 2015, Steph decided to use her many months of accumulated paid leave and to take a break from her stressful work. And that break was really good for her. Several months into it, she got some exciting job opportunities, including a judgeship for which she made it all the way through three interviews to become one of four who met directly with Mayor Bill de Blasio. That led to another appealing and unsolicited job, which she started in August of 2016. Steph is now a Referee at Manhattan Family Court. This role is similar to a magistrate judge. She has her own courtroom and chambers, and makes decisions on matters relating to visitation, custody and orders of protection. Steph is really happy in this new and important role and pleased that she will be able to continue her work protecting the people, including the children, of New York City. I am so proud of the work that she does.

Jen and Doug still enjoy their life in California. They both take full advantage of the beautiful weather there. They are always outside with their children on the weekends and in the early evening. Jen takes a frequent power walk and Doug is off on his bike as often as possible. Jen works very hard and is quite successful at her firm. Her mom Ellen and stepdad Lee moved 15 minutes away a couple of years ago and are very helpful with the children.

Doug has been off on a bus again, including registering voters for the 2016 Presidential election as well as continuing to record the riders' stories in words, songs and photographs. He is also a contributor to the *Huffington Post*. Still performing, he often gives his time and talent to those living in homeless shelters.

I have never seen better parents than Jen and Doug. The kids are involved in all kinds of activities: gymnastics, soccer, swimming, pony riding, tennis, basketball, baseball (which Doug coaches), not to mention the art classes they got in Gillybean, their pre-school. (And they are good at all of them according to this totally unbiased grandma.) They are such a loving family in addition to being good and smart people. And I am very proud of each and every one of them.

I often talk about not having regrets; and I want you to know that I have never regretted my marriage, albeit not so happy. My husband David was an extraordinary man. I adore my exceptional children and grandchildren, am appreciative of the important career I had—and the interesting life I have led. So no regrets in that regard either.

Family Matters

In August of 2016, my only remaining aunt turned 90 and it's hard to believe how much energy and sharpness of mind she has.

There was a wonderful three-day family reunion around that event. I went to Baton Rouge for five days and was so pleased that my children came in for the weekend. It was an orgy of eating in a state known for fabulous food. It now has none left as I ate it all.

On a more serious note, we were there the end of the week of the horrendous flood, where tens and tens of thousands of people were left homeless and carless. Many stayed at the same hotel we did, so we got to hear their tragic tales. The most astounding part was the attitudes that so many had. As I expressed empathy for what they had been through, I heard over and over again, "But I'm still here" or, "It's okay" or, "They were only things" or, "God will take care of me." I'm not sure those are the words that would have come out of my mouth had I suffered the same losses. But I so admired those expressions of hope.

Two weeks later, the weekend Hurricane Hermine was heading to Charleston, a cousin got married there. As we watched the storm approach, we were not even sure that Charleston would be there, much less the wedding. But thank goodness, all worked out. And 90-year-old Aunt Betty was there to celebrate with the couple as well. These events reminded me of how important family gatherings are, and even more, how important family is.

Speaking of Family ... Seriously

At this stage of my life, I feel good about most of it, other than the usual stuff that comes with aging like stiffness, neuroma in my feet, arthritis in my hands, and losing friends. I look back on my many largely surmounted challenges and accomplishments with great pride. I get satisfaction from my outside endeavors these days as well as fun times spent with my remaining friends.

I also have nice times with my family when I can. But there's something I want to talk about relating to family. I have hesitated to put in this part for reasons that will become obvious. But I decided to include it because I do not think I am the only parent who feels this way—especially those who are women and/or alone—and especially in today's world.

Therefore, I am going to make some general comments about "today's world" related to parent and child. In some cases, the shoe will directly fit my situation. In others, not.

I grew up in a time and place where you never called elders by their first name. If they were close, you used "Aunt" or "Uncle" in front of their proper name. Otherwise, you used Mr. or Mrs. or Miss (in that day). Now no matter how old you are or how close you are, it is "Bob" or "Jane." I find that to be somewhat disrespectful, especially when the person is a parent of sorts and who is much older than the person doing the calling.

I understand that someone who is close to their mother and calls her "Mom" does not want another mom or mother, but we should probably develop another term of some endearment for an in-law. I know if there's a grandma or a nana after children come that can be used sometimes. But what if there are no kids? And what do you do before and after the children are around? I called my mom, "Mom" or "Mommy." And I called my mother-in-law "Ma," which she seemed to love and appreciate. Maybe that's too close for some. How about "in-Ma" and "in-Pa"? I'm kind of joking, but not really. Or perhaps "Madre" and "Padre," or "Momsy" and "Popsy"? (Any of you want to make your own suggestions?) I'm just expressing a feeling many parents feel (but are afraid to say out loud). It's just another thing to think about.

I know that most of us as parents have tried to make sure that our children had more financially/materialistically than we did. But unfortunately, this pendulum has swung to the opposite end—resulting oftentimes in expectation and entitlement rather than appreciation. I have a plaque that I bought which says, "Money isn't everything, but it sure keeps the kids in touch." And sometimes even that doesn't.

I have often given money as gifts and have found that it just goes into a big pot. No one ever buys anything, and writes and says, "I just got a computer," "I got a new purse," "I went to a play" with the money you sent. Instead, when you give a check, you don't get the same acknowledgement as when you give a specific gift—which we all know is hard to do as people have different tastes. So I gave that up long ago. I did ask Jen, my daughter-in-law, this year in the card with the check to please buy something special with it. That day, she went out and made some purchases, and even sent me pictures of them. I was thrilled. Thank you, Jen.

My parents, as I have discussed, were not poster parents, nor did they give me unconditional love. But I did give them all their lives unconditional love because they were my parents. Even my impossible dad showed only respect for his impossible folks and in addition, called and wrote them often as well as his in-laws (all of which I appreciated). I did the same with them. That's what you were supposed to do. I took that Commandment—"Honor thy father and thy mother"—literally. Now, in writing this book, much of the sadness and bitterness of my childhood has surfaced. But they were never aware of it in their lifetimes. I tried to be there for them in spite of their lack of perfection—or anything even close to that.

The most recent generations, for the most part, do not give unconditional love or much respect to their parents. As this is the trend, it makes me worry about families now and in the future. If children see their parents' impatience with their own, what kind of example is that? And then, how can this be reversed? Maybe we do not need to go back to the days when kids could not express themselves at all to their parents, like me. But this opposite extreme we see today can be too hurtful and counterproductive to continue. I don't really know the answer. But at least I know that it should be thought about and discussed as well.

Other Thoughts That Should Matter

• *Back to the Lack of a Commuter Tax*

When I drive to Rehoboth Beach and have to go over the Bay Bridge, I pay $4 for that trip, while Maryland residents pay $2.50. Now, I could get an E-ZPass (and in fact, used to have one), and then would also pay that same $2.50. But that's where the similarity ends. For that $2.50 toll with an E-ZPass, I had to pay a $1.50 fee each month, while Maryland residents have no such monthly fee. So once again, I am penalized for driving on a Maryland bridge, whereas Marylanders are not. Yet those same Marylanders travel into D.C., many of them every day, and they do not pay a cent, equal or not. And we in the District have no opportunity to charge them a cent for the use of our roads, traffic lights, stop signs, police or fire personnel. Grossly unfair!

Commuters into D.C. have been unbelievably fortunate not to have a commuter tax or taxing income at the source as they would face in any other city in the country. They've gotten literally a free ride. The surrounding states they live in, though, do not hesitate to sock it to those of us who live here in D.C. Case in point above.

And they often take our government jobs, paid for by D.C. taxpayers. How lucky are they and how unlucky are we! And if the D.C. government dares to do a thing to stop such unfairness, like residency requirements for these jobs or something like a commuter tax, then their voting Congresspersons (and how lucky are they to have those as well)—Democrats *and* Republicans—jump in to slap us across the face.

And take our jobs suburbanites do. In a column by Colbert King on July 2, 2016 entitled "A City Run by Nonresidents," he states that, "Non-District residents dominated the D.C. government: 15,103 Marylanders, 3,579 Virginians and 429 residents of other jurisdictions vs. 15,191 D.C. residents, according to DHR [Department of Human Resources] data" and "... where salaries run from $98,697 to $139,288, non-D.C. residents hold 3,185 positions and D.C. residents 2,397." King sums it up beautifully and accurately: "Arguably, D.C. government is a pathway to the middle class—in Maryland, Virginia, and points beyond."[341]

Excepted and Executive Service positions controlled by the Mayor have a significant number of Maryland and Virginia residents—over 100—although they are required to move into the city within 180 days, if not waived. I think D.C. can do a better job itself here, but most of this is foisted upon us. Meanwhile, I still pay more than Marylanders to go across the Bay Bridge and no one cares. Those in federal roles responsible for keeping D.C. chained in their own self-interest should feel badly.

- ***Take Me off the List***

As I mentioned, I feel grateful for much of my life. But what I'm not grateful for is the marketing calls and all the solicitation mail. I send a contribution to a charity and then they spend every penny of it and more asking me for more. I often joke that if the marketing calls stopped, the phone would never ring and if I never gave a contribution, I would never get mail. Not true, but close.

Seniors tend to get targeted. They may end up losing their homes with all the reversible mortgage marketers. But probably the biggest cruelty which is being especially perpetrated on seniors is those fake IRS calls. They are endless, frightening and predatory. If IRS wants to get in touch with you, they do <u>NOT</u> do so by telephone. I have gotten some of these calls and have tried to contact IRS to give them the phone numbers which these messages are leaving me to call. Yet there is no way to get a human at IRS for a general comment or conversation. So I would strongly suggest that the IRS do a mass mailing, especially to seniors, as well as PSAs to forewarn about these bogus calls.

And IRS should also set up a hotline with actual people answering so we can report these calls and pass on the non-IRS numbers that are being left on our voicemails in hopes that they will be investigated. In a recent conversation, I heard that the number given is the last of a series of numbers used to make the call hard to trace.

It still would be helpful to give IRS those numbers and even more helpful if IRS would work with the FBI or somebody—even the Russians—to unravel this camouflage. And hopefully these creeps will have their operations shut down—and then be thrown in jail.

- *Answer the Friggin' Phone!*

Is it possible to find any resident/citizen/person of the United States of America who can answer the phone? When I call any commercial entity, I only get one of two things: a non-American or a robot. No wonder our unemployment figures are where they are. I know it may be cheaper to get someone in China or India or no one at all, but I as a consumer would rather pay a few cents more to people who could then go to work and pay taxes which would then make me feel better and might even lower my taxes. And that scenario might lower the company's taxes as well.

I am now going to pick and choose who I do business with where I have a choice. Maybe if we all joined together and do that, it would force the companies to hire our beautiful and diverse own—Americans. And I don't mean American robots; I mean real humans beings who can answer our calls *and* our questions.

Just the other day I called the phone company. The robot finally answered in a very pleasant-sounding female voice. And then she/it gave me a list of nine options, none of which addressed my problem. I then said, "Operator." The lovely-sounding robot then said, "Before I can transfer you to an operator, I need to find out what your problem is." And then she/it went on to repeat the nine non-relevant options. After three times, I started screaming at her/it. She/it said, "I need to know your problem." I wanted to scream, "My problem is you!" Instead I yelled for the tenth time, "Operator!" Finally, after a 24-minute, 22-second wait, I did get a human being who was helpful.

Why can't there just be more human beings? Maybe the multi-zillion-dollar-salaried executives of these companies could take a little less so they can hire a little more—humans, preferably Americans. Or else answer the friggin' phone themselves.

- *Unequal Height*

As I've watched basketball recently, it is obvious that mostly 6'5" and above players get hired these days with a few exceptions. They just have to put their hand up and drop the ball in the basket, not nearly as interesting to watch. Where is the place today for people like George who is 5'10" or 11"? During the Olympics, on the track field and in the swimming pool, who tends to win? It is usually the person with the longest legs and bodies with some spectacular exceptions.

So why don't we have categories in these sports—where there can be real competition for all—like boxing? In boxing, there are heavyweight, welterweight, featherweight categories, so similarly built people can fairly compete. They had the good sense to do that decades ago. Why shouldn't we do that now with basketball, track, etc. where size usually makes such a difference?

No one ever thought of Sugar Ray Leonard, a welterweight boxing champion, as less talented than heavyweight Joe Frazier. They both had equal prestige in the field. Why if you're not close to 7' tall, do you have little or no opportunity in much of today's sports world? I think we have a shot at making this inequity better.

- *Steering Money from Public Education to Money-Making Hands*

It started with Donald Trump's election. It continued with his handing the Department of Education to Betsy DeVos, who had very little experience with public education, and who now wants to hand all of public education to the educational money-makers under the guise of "education reform" and "school choice." By the way, I happen to be in favor of both education reform and school choice as my record can show. I always favored magnet schools and even got one started. Although I originally fought charter schools as Congress was shoving them down our throats (and my issue was more the latter than the former), I always supported the D.C. voucher program funded by Congress that enabled our low-income students to access private schools where qualified.

But what is going on now appears to be an effort to destroy public schools and pass the taxpayers' money into entirely private hands with no public oversight, which charter schools are known for having little of. They receive huge amounts of taxpayers' money with no accountability to those taxpayers. And some have done financial and educational harm. I know that may be true of public education as well, but elected officials and the people they appoint can do something about it. With charters, it's difficult.

Most of school options, like charter schools, are usually set up as non-profits, although a few may be for-profit. So you may ask, "How are these non-profits money-makers?" Well, investors in charter schools can take advantage of very generous tax benefits given to those who locate entities in economically struggling urban and rural areas. As a result, they can sometimes double their investment in seven years, according to an article by Alan Singer

entitled "Why Hedge Funds Love Charter Schools."[342] Additionally, some administrators of charter schools draw enormous
salaries.[343] So there are clear financial benefits.

Can't rich people care about education having nothing to do
with making money? How about going to a public school to tutor,
or send your employees there to help—or even your own children
to attend? Regardless, we need to make certain charters and other
options are held accountable—and are not just used by individuals
to make money through the "reform" movement.

In addition, charters are often allowed to choose their students,
a luxury traditional public schools do not have. Or they expel the
"problem ones," another luxury public schools are denied. And
then they brag about how their students perform better. Hardly
an equal playing field is at work here.

Although school choice could be beneficial to students who are
denied options—if they are truly given a slot and if the schools are
not allowed "student choices"—we still need to be wary as there's
lots of bait and switch that goes on, as described in the following:

A December 27, 2016 *Washington Post* front-page story entitled "Indiana's Voucher System Offers Hint of School Policy in the
Era of Trump," stated, "Indiana lawmakers originally promoted
the state's school voucher program was a way to make good on
America's promise of equal opportunity ... an escape from public
schools that failed to meet their needs. But five years after the program was established, more than half of the state's voucher
recipients have never attended Indiana public schools, meaning
that taxpayers are now covering private and religious school tuition for children whose parents had previously footed the bill."[344]
Wasn't the point to give *low-income* students those options, instead of helping existing private school parents pay for it?

On the federal level, a March 2017 *Washington Post* article said:
"The Trump administration is seeking to cut $9.2 billion—or 13
percent—from the education department's budget, a dramatic
downsizing that would reduce or eliminate grants for teacher-
training, after-school programs and aid to low-income and first-
generation college students." The title of the article is "Along with
13% cut, Trump Would Steer $1.4 Billion to School Choice."[345]

It's one thing to encourage options and choice, but to publicly
finance them at the expense of public education is another—and
that's what's happening here. And I feel that a real attempt to do
away with public education is underway.

We must make certain that the treasure that is public education—which throughout generations has taken every child regardless of whatever—is preserved. Because just like the privatization of government services I talked about earlier, once you go down that road and the schools, teachers, students and buses are gone, it's practically impossible to ever get them back—even if the alternative "school choices" are no better and no cheaper than what you had before. And once again, there will be *no* "choice."

- *Where Are the Future Jobs?*

Now we are heading toward driverless cars and I guess soon it will be driverless trucks on the highway. Of course we should trust robots and computers more than humans. I guess I am just more in interested in employing people—with or without families—than machines. Silly, outdated me.

Go into a grocery or drug store—there are more self-serve aisles than those leading to a human. Soon there will be no jobs at all, especially for those who are not Ivy League graduates. And now even they seem to be in trouble as reported by *The Washington Post* in an article which stated that " ... Goldman Sachs ... revealed that some of the investment bank's well-paid humans were being replaced by unpaid robots ... Over the past 17 years ... the number of stock traders ... has shrunk from 600 to two."[346]

I am so glad I am old because I'd rather do business with a live, even rude person than a lifeless, unfeeling machine. Have at this new world. As for me, I'm glad I don't have too many years left to watch the dissipation of more jobs of every kind—and humanity.

- *Don't Retire, Wait to Be Fired*

Now that I'm retired and can speak from experience, I tell all my older working friends not to stop working. I used to get so excited on Thursday night when I was working, just anticipating Friday and skipping from work toward two full days of no work and doing what I wanted. When everyday becomes a "weekend," it's not as fun. It's also harder to keep the brain alive when you're not using it constantly and you usually have far less to talk about when work is off the table.

I've certainly tried to fill my life with volunteer work, friends and family, travels, and even some part-time worthwhile and stimulating endeavors. But it's still different and not necessarily in a good way. My "retirement" was forced on me as I neared 65 in that I was "fired" from elected office. It hurt, but it also helped me in the long run by not having made the decision myself.

So I tell my friends to keep working if they like what they do until they get dismissed. Then when they are bored, lonely and put out to pasture, they do not have to blame themselves—just like I didn't have to.

- **Having Just Paid My Taxes**

I have always paid my taxes with something close to pride. I know government serves many purposes, including helping those in need—something I have tried also to do personally most of my life. Even when people tell me I should establish residency in a state with no income tax, I respond, "D.C. needs my taxes and yours as well." But then, as I learn that the richest people I know pay little to no taxes, including most likely our extremely wealthy present President most years, I am now really getting mad, and not only feel no pride, but feel suckered.

One daughter is a freelance writer and she pays her taxes every year. Another daughter works as a jurist in a family court, and she pays a lot in taxes. And so does their retired mother. Now I know that some very rich people say, "Well because of my deductions, I don't pay income taxes, but I do pay property taxes, sales taxes, etc." Well, I pay those taxes as well, *plus* income taxes.

I am now mad enough to have come up with a solution. And some of it stems from the whole taxation without representation discussions we had earlier. Since I don't live in a "state," even though I pay federal income taxes, I can't vote for members of Congress. So we have precedence here for denying people the right to vote.

Now I say that people who do not pay income taxes, thereby taking no responsibility for the workings of government, cannot vote for either members of Congress or the President, nor can they serve in any of those positions. How can you support America if you don't *support* America? So better yet, how about above a certain income level, if you don't pay any taxes, you can't do *any* voting—or maybe even saluting? How are those for good ideas?

'Your Time'

In the five times I ran for Mayor (1986, 1994, 1998, 2002, 2014), I always thought, "This is my time." And people were constantly saying, "Now is your time." It still happens. Just yesterday, leaving a library, the guard, as I walked out the door, said, "You must run for Mayor again. This is your time!" And I said to him, "Thank you, but I spent a lot of my time and a lot of my money thinking it was 'my time'—spanning four decades. But it's never my time. And it's okay." And he said, "Just try it again. This really is your time." I am not hallucinating and my daughter and others were witness to that. But I'm not falling for it anymore. I recognize now that in this case, there is no "my time." And it really is okay. I now have time to promote this book and watch things like *House Hunters International* (seeing the world while sitting at home).

A Visit to Grandma

Sylvie and Wally Levitt, as you may recall, joined the family September 3, 2012. (Remember my number 3 fixation!) I have gone out to visit them in Santa Monica, California every three to four months give or take since they arrived, usually on my own but sometimes with Hilary and occasionally Stephanie. Doug and Jen used to come to D.C. to join us all for Thanksgiving, but once the twins were born, two or more of us now head there instead.

Wally and Sylvie had never been to D.C. until Mother's Day of 2016. I think it was only their second trip by plane as two very active little ones are hard to do long trips with, and besides, it's difficult for Doug and Jen to get away from work. The girls and I were thrilled about their coming, and what a fabulous time we had. Hil and I met them at Dulles and then at Doug's request, we got the party started on Friday night at Ben's Chili Bowl, the original one on U St., N.W. We all joined up there, including Steph who drove in from New York, at the restaurant at 9 p.m., which could be considered late for three-year-olds to have dinner. But Sylvie and Wally could have cared less as they inhaled their burgers and cheese fries. Afterwards, they played and danced at the juke box until 11:15. What fun!

For those who have not seen my apartment, there's a knick-knack on every surface, including the floor, everywhere. I had decided to just grin and bear it. But first thing, Jen takes Sylvie's hand and I take Wally's, and we start our tour with Jen saying, "Now Grandma has lots of things and we have to be careful not to break them." And Wally said, "You mean I can't touch them?" I said, "Now, Wally, you know how upset you get if someone breaks your toys. And these are my toys." Later, Wally, at three and a half, said, "Grandma, what if I ask you first if I can touch something?" "Good idea," I replied. He only asked a couple of times. Once I said yes, once no. I would see him just walking around looking at everything like he was studying them. But he did not touch. I'm still amazed. (Older people should be as cautious as Wally.)

Sylvie was far less interested in the stuff. She liked to play games more, like pantomiming an animal and Steph, Hil and I would have to guess which one. One time Steph guessed, "Rabbit," and Sylvie said, "Good one (pause)—but no." A real diplomat is in the making.

The Saturday after they got in, I had a few people over to meet my grandchildren and to see Jen and Doug. The kids were so good, it's like we had given them tranquilizers (not guilty). I had told my friends how cute they are, but what grandmother hasn't? Several of them, many also grandparents, said afterwards, "They really are beautiful and adorable."

I always wanted to be a grandmother, and was getting to be sad—and even bitter—when it didn't happen until I was 68 and a half. But these two are filling my life with such joy that it makes up for all those years without them.

The Levitts have a tradition of holding hands before eating together as a family, at least on special occasions, with each saying what they are grateful for or care about. We did it at our first meal here at home. Our last meal during their visit was at Dupont Kitchen on 17th St., N.W. Wally said, "Let's hold hands," and we did. He then said, "I'll go first," and proceeded to say, "I love horses ... ah ... [while looking around the table] ... and our beautiful family." I, getting teary eyed, said, "I can't follow that. I think Wally said it all."

By the way, I just got back from New York where we spent Labor Day weekend with Sylvie and Wally and their parents, Jen and Doug. We were all celebrating their 5th birthday on September 3rd (remember, my favorite number—and now I have two more reasons). It was such a magnificent time together, for Steph and Hil too, as we watched the children discover New York City for the first time. They are both so sweet, curious about the world, and lots of fun. As I am an aging, their existence and the wonderful qualities they are already exhibiting give me great joy now—and also great comfort when thinking about the legacy of our family.

Running and Running ... and Now Looking Back

I feel good about the way I have conducted my life both personally and professionally. I have always tried to be a good person and act in a kind fashion toward others. Even when I get impatient or bark, I tend to get guilt-ridden right away. I can remember practically every nasty word I ever said and feel badly about it—and usually apologize soon afterwards. I do like people and I do give everyone the benefit of the doubt. You really have to work hard for me not to like you—either through actions toward me or toward others. Only a few have managed, really working hard at it.

I have prided myself in reconnecting when connections have been broken, not only between myself with someone, but between others where I can. I have always tried to keep in touch, especially at birthdays. Most of my friends who get sung to every year with my bad, croaky voice want to disconnect, but I won't let them. My friendships have been my lifeline.

When I first thought of writing this book, remember I wanted to call it, "An Interesting Life but Don't Ask Me to Live It Again." Sort of funny and accurate, but I didn't think it showed the gratitude I feel for my life, although not always an easy one. But it has been an interesting one. It's been a productive, maddening, scary, caring, sad, fun, frustrating, satisfying—truly a full—life.

For 50 years, one of my favorite of quotes is from *The Prophet* by Kahlil Gibran: "The deeper that sorrow carves into your being, the more joy you can contain." Unfortunately—and fortunately— I have found that to be true. You do appreciate good times far more when you've had bad ones. Here's a non-dramatic-scale example: Now just walking pretty normally after a year of the pain of an Achilles heel issue that caused me to limp, is a real delight.

Early on in the process of writing this book, I wrote one night on a small piece of paper these exact words: "Sorta started out a living nightmare and sorta became the impossible dream, with lots of sadness, fun, and attempts at good works in between." Now, finding and reading those words a few years in, I still feel the same. In retrospect, I appreciate the challenges of my childhood, which made me strong (but do not ask me to live them again). I appreciate the magnetic pull that brought me to Washington, D.C., my home of nearly 52 years. I appreciate my life, my career, my dear family and my many wonderful friends. I do feel truly blessed.

Speaking of my dear family, Johnny's 75th birthday would have been this week. Even though he's been gone for 13 years now, I still miss him every day. My daughter Steph wrote to me, "Sorry about Uncle Johnny. You were a really good sister." I sure tried to be. I think it was the thing I tried to be more than anything.

Many people want to go back in time and be younger. I do not, even though it would be nice to not have wrinkles and gray hair, and certainly nice to be more agile and not have the aches and pains that come with getting older—those of us who are lucky enough to be here and getting older. I guess I just appreciate still being around with a pretty sound mind and body. And I would not want to relive so many parts of my life that dealt with death and real problems, most of which I could not change or solve. I think I'll stay right where I am and just be grateful for these days of, for the most part, less trauma, except when recently my sweet grandcat Poochie was hospitalized again and then passed away.

I always wanted to accomplish things. I make lists practically every day, and most days I get much of my list done. I'm trying to be my own best friend now by patting myself on the back for what I've gotten done instead of my past tendency of just feeling badly about not completing everything. (I have also started taking my own advice I would give to people I love—and even strangers.)

I think we all recognize that some things are easier to get done like going to the post office and getting groceries. But there are often far bigger goals on that list, which are far harder. Such efforts can be tiring, aggravating, stressful, even infuriating, but some, with perseverance and not taking no for an answer, may pay off.

An example of a big pay-off: On October 18, 2016, I read in *The Washington Post* about President Obama's visit to a school where "he heaped praise." The article said: "President Obama first visited the District's Benjamin Banneker Academic High School five years ago, and he was so impressed with the students and staff that he decided to return ... to deliver what could be the last education-focused speech of his Presidency." It continued: "Banneker, a selective-admissions school in Northwest, has enough low-income students that its entire student body is offered free lunch, yet the school has a 100% graduation rate." Obama said to the students while he was there: "'You can't do any better than that. What all these numbers mean is that more schools across D.C. and across the country are starting to catch up with what you guys are doing here at this school.'"[347] (And in January of 2017, Anita Berger, Principal of Banneker, received DCPS's Principal of the Year.[348])

I got teary-eyed reading this article as I know that it would not have existed without my consistent push (along with Dr. Vincent

Reed) starting in 1980, 37 years ago, and not giving up in spite of the initial defeat, until it could open for students in 1981. How meaningful and satisfying it is to see the fruits of your labor—and I see them all around me. It's what I wanted my life to be about.

In my concession speech after the last disappointing election, I used a quote by the Reverend Martin Luther King that articulated my feelings perfectly then and still now: "We must accept finite disappointment—but never lose infinite hope."

We should all try to live by those wise words by encouraging each other to not lose hope and to not let fear and disappointment discourage us. Well-meaning people who have good will, tenacity, and the courage of their convictions *can* make a difference. And if we don't win all the time, it's okay. But at least we tried. At one point, I thought I wanted on my tombstone, "She tried," as I thought it was such a good trait. I have also wanted for decades to try and write the story of my life. I now have more than tried; the book is here—and I hope it is "good enough."

I must admit that even though it is written and ready to go, I am scared as I have been throughout my life. Will anyone read it? How much criticism will I and it get? All intimidating, scary thoughts. But once again, I'm jumping in, come what may—including the possibility of another defeat of sorts. Regardless .... defeat is still better than *not* trying.

My life has been full of losing and winning, disappointments and hope—and running and running and running ... And I didn't wait to be asked or get permission, I just jumped in, and I am glad. For those who helped along the way, thank you. And please know how much you are recognized—and appreciated.

I am comfortable with myself today, but more importantly, I take pride in having made the journey. "... From childhood to maturity and youth to age.... From weakness to strength or from strength to weakness. And often, back again. From fear to faith. From defeat to defeat to defeat. Until, looking backward or ahead, [I] see that victory lies not in some high place along the way, but in having made the journey stage by stage. A sacred pilgrimage."

And I am getting much closer to becoming that old lady I've often talked about, rocking back and forth on that nursing home porch. But now I am sure I will *not* be saying, "I could have, I should have, why didn't I?"

I did.

Picture taken September 21, 2017

Thank you for taking this journey.
Carol

ENDNOTES

[1] Nelson F. Rimensnyder, "A Champion of D.C. Voting Rights," *Washington Post*, 12/11/2005.

[2] Ibid.

[3] "Washington, D.C. – Historical Timeline of the Nation's Capital," DCVote.org, http://www.dcvote.org/fight-equality/washington-dc-historical-timeline-nations-capital (accessed 9/4/2017).

[4] S.E. Ruckman, "Nixon's Role of Self-Determination Focus of Talk," *Nativetimes.com*, 5/25/12, http://nativetimes.com/index.php/life/people/7232-nixons-role-in-self-determination-focus-of-talk (accessed 10/24/2016).

[5] Dugan Romano, "Carol Schwartz: A Crusader with Teeth," *Northwest Current*, 5/21-6/3/2011.

[6] Carol L. Schwartz, "Slighting the Minds of Our Children," *Washington Post*, 5/17/1977.

[7] Martha M. Hamilton, "Sizemore Problem Not Only a Legal One," *Washington Post*, 6/17/1975.

[8] Martha M. Hamilton, "Police Arrest 4 Supporters of Sizemore," *Washington Post*, 6/21/1975.

[9] "Sizemore to Fight Firing from D.C. Schools Post," *Jet Magazine*, 10/20/1975.

[10] R.C. Newell, "D.C. Schools Win Battle Against Head Lice," *Afro-American*, 11/29/1975.

[11] Caro L. Schwartz, "Slighting the Minds of Our Children," *Washington Post*, 5/17/1977.

[12] Loretta Lynn, *Still Woman Enough: A Memoir*, 2002.

[13] Dugan Romano, "Carol Schwartz: A Crusader with Teeth," *Northwest Current*, 5/21-6/3/1981.

[14] Carol Schwartz, "Carol Schwartz Reports," *Georgetowner*, 2/18-3/2/1976.

[15] Carol Schwartz, "Test Scores in D.C. Public Schools," *Northwest Current*, 10/5-18/1978.

[16] Michael Alison Chandler, "City-wide Analysis Shows that D.C. Preschool Quality Varies," *Washington Post*, 5/18/2015.

[17] Toni House and Calvin Goddard Zon, "Compromise Averts Strike of Teachers," *Washington Star*, Oct. 4, 1978.

[18] Carol Schwartz, "Carol Schwartz Reports," *Uptown Citizen*, 10/26/1978.

[19] Carol Schwartz, "Carol Schwartz Reports," *Georgetowner*, 9/22-10/4/1978.

[20] Kathy Sawyer and Joseph D. Whitaker, "Teachers Strike, but Schools Stay Open," *Washington Post*, 3/7/1979.

[21] *Washington Star*, 3/19/1979.

[22] Juan Williams, "D.C. Teachers' Dues Check-off to End," *Washington Post*, 2/23/1979.

[23] Laura Murray, "Teachers on Call as End of Strike Seen Nearing," *Washington Star*, 3/17/1979.

[24] Lawrence Feinberg and Milton Coleman, "Judge Tells Teachers to Go to Work," *Washington Post*, 3/25/1979.

[25] Laura Murray and Thomas Crosby, "Both Sides Cool to Barry's Efforts to End Strike," *Washington Star*, 3/11/1979.

[26] Laura Murray, "D.C. Teachers Back in Class as Court Determines Fines," *Washington Star*, 3/30/1979.

[27] Carol Schwartz, "Isn't It Wonderful?" *Northwest Current*, 4/12-25/1979.

[28] Andrew Giambrone, "Ten D.C. Public Schools Will Get Extended Academic Years," *Washington City Paper*, 2/3/2016.

[29] Elsa Walsh, "Shaffer-Corona Is Indicted on Theft Charge," *Washington Post*, 2/11/1987.

[30] Jody Beck, "Stalemate on D.C. School Board May Delay President's Election," *Washington Star*, 1/4/1980.

[31] Roger Glass, "Lockridge Elected," *Washington Afro-American*, 1/12/1980.

[32] *Washington Post*, 1980.

[33] "Ex-teacher Fills White House Post," *Lake Charles American Press*, 1/29/1981.

[34] Carol Schwartz, "Leaving a Cause I Love, Hassles I Hate," *Washington Star*, 4/30/1981.

[35] Gregory A. Smith and Alan Cooperman, "What Happens When Jews Intermarry," Pew Research Center, 11/12/2013, http://www.pewresearch.org/fact-tank/2013/11/12/what-happens-when-jews-intermarry/ (accessed 1/29/2016).

[36] Rachel Sadon, "D.C. Paid More in Federal Taxes than 22 States Last Year," *dcist*, 4/25/2016, http://dcist.com/2016/04/infuriating_tax_figure_time.php (accessed 7/6/2016).

[37] Committee on Homeland Security and Governmental Affairs, U.S. Senate, District of Columbia House Voting Rights Act of 2007.

[38] Justin Wm. Moyer, "D.C. Population Reaches Four-Decade High," *Washington Post*, 12/20/2016.

[39] "Annual Estimates of the Resident Population for the United States, Regions, States, and Puerto Rico: April 1, 2010 to July 1, 2016 (XLSX)," United States Census Bureau, (accessed 6/8/2017); Suburban Stats, suburbanstats.org/population (accessed 6/23/2017).

[40] Bennet Kelley, "10 Reasons You Should Care About D.C. Voting Rights," *Huffington Post*, 7/4/2015, http://www.huffingtonpost.com/bennet-kelley/ten-reasons-why-you-shoul_b_7728456.html (accessed July 6, 2016); "US Public Opinion about DC Voting Rights," DC Vote, 1/2005. http://www.dcvote.org/195/us-public-opinion-dc-voting-rights (accessed 7/1/2017).

[41] District of Columbia House Voting Rights Act of 2007 (110th Congress, S. 1257), GovTrack, 2007 (accessed 7/2/2016).

[42] Timothy Warren, "Senate Votes to Give D.C. Full House Vote," *Washington Times*, 2/26/2009.

[43] S. Amdt, 575: Text of the Amendment, United States Senate, Library of Congress, 2/25/2009.

[44] Fenit Nirappil, "Public Voice in Constitution Is Urged," *Washington Post*, 9/28/2016.

[45] Steve Birr, "Mayor Bowser Plans Big Fight with Congress over D.C. Statehood," *Daily Caller*, 4/16/2016, http://dailycaller.com/2016/04/16/mayor-bowser-plans-big-fight-with-congress-over-dc-statehood/ (accessed 10/2/2016).

[46] Martin Austermuhle, "In Push for Statehood, D.C. Leaders Unveil Constitution for State of 'New Columbia,'" WAMU, 5/6/2016.

[47] Andrew Giambrone, "District Line Daily: Constitution Restitution," *Washington City Paper*, 10/19/2016.

[48] Editorial, "The District Vote Is About More than Statehood," *Washington Post*, 10/21/2016.

[49] Petula Dvorak, "D.C. Residents Aren't Exactly Feeling 'New Columbia,'" *Washington Post*, 6/30/2016.

[50] Jerry Meandering, "Current Opinions," *Northwest Current*, 10/11-24/1984.

[51] Editorial, "Carol Schwartz for Council," Georgetowner, 11/8/1984; Gary Tischler, "Carol Schwartz: In the Running," *Georgetowner*, 8/24/1984.

[52] David Roffman, "Carol Schwartz for Council," *Georgetowner*, 10/26-11/8/1984.

[53] Mark Perry, "Endorsements," *Washington City Paper*, 11/2/1984.

[54] Gary Tischler, "Carol Schwartz Victorious," *Georgetowner*, 10/26-11/1984.

[55] Marcia Slacum Greene, "Bill Easing D.C. Rent Control Won Despite Early Odds," *Washington Post*, 4/18/1985.

[56] Ibid.

[57] Carol Schwartz, "D.C.'s Dead-end Budget," *Washington Post*, 3/31/1986.

[58] *Current Newspaper*, May 9, 1985.

[59] Carol Schwartz, "D.C.'s Dead-end Budget," *Washington Post*, 3/31/1986.

[60] Ibid.

[61] Carol Schwartz, "For the Record," *Washington Post*, 7/27/1990.

[62] Isaiah J. Poole, "Cable Contract Winner in City Seeks New Deal," *Washington Times*, 6/14/1985.

[63] Amy Stromberg and Linda Sarrio, "'Had Enough,' Councilwoman Says of Reports of UDC Extravagances," *Washington Times*, 6/26/1985.

[64] Editorial, "Should Young Violent Offenders Get a Second Chance?" *Washington Post*, 12/12/2016.

[65] Amy Brittain, Aaron D. Davis and Steven Rich, "How a Mercy Law Enables Criminals," *Washington Post*, 12/4/2016.

[66] Ken Cummins, "Barry's 'War' Over Hawkins," *Washington City Paper*, 6/7/1996.

[67] Tyra Wright, "Antioch Students Breathe Sigh of Relief Over Vote," *Washington Times*, 9/25/1986.
[68] Juan Williams, "A Black Mayor Betrays the Faith," *Washington Monthly*, 7-8/1986.
[69] Ibid.
[70] Ibid.
[71] Juan Williams, "A Black Mayor Betrays the Faith," *Washington Monthly*, 7-8/1986; Anne LaLena, "The Marion Barry File," *Washington City Paper*, 8/1/1986.
[72] Juan Williams, "A Black Mayor Betrays the Faith," *Washington Monthly*, 7-8/1986.
[73] Anne LaLena, "The Marion Barry File," *Washington City Paper*, 8/1/1986.
[74] Matthew Purdy, "Despite Scandals, D.C. Mayor is Expected to Be Reelected Easily," *Philadelphia Inquirer*, 11/3/1986.
[75] Peter Perl, "D.C. Finance Analyst Locked Out of Office," *Washington Post*, 2/9/1986.
[76] Juan Williams, "A Black Mayor Betrays the Faith," *Washington Monthly*, 7-8/1986.
[77] Eric Pianin and Joe Pichirallo, "Jose Guttierez's Telling Tale of Political Miscalculation," *Washington Post*, 3/31/1985.
[78] Juan Williams, "A Black Mayor Betrays the Faith," *Washington Monthly*, 7-8/1986.
[79] Tom Sherwood, "Barry Tours City Via Copter," *Washington Post*, 1/29/1987.
[80] Eugene Robinson, "Politicians' Reputations Can Be Buried by Snow Storms," *Washington Post*, 12/31/2010.
[81] Final and Complete Election Totals: Sept. 9, 1986 Primary, District of Columbia Board of Elections and Ethics, 9/19/1986.
[82] Arthur S. Brisbane, "Schwartz to Run for D.C. Mayor," *Washington Post*, 6/25/1986.
[83] Amy Stromberg and Elaine Rivera, "Schwartz to Run for Mayor; Says Race Not a Factor," *Washington Times*, 6/25/1986.
[84] Arthur S. Brisbane and Joe Pichirallo, "Schwartz Candidacy Livens Mayoral Race in District," *Washington Post*, 6/28/1986.
[85] Carrie Dowling, "Scaling Mountains with Mrs. Schwartz," *Washington Times*, 10/3/1986.
[86] Carrie Dowling, "As Child in Texas, Schwartz Learned to 'Beat the Odds,'" *Washington Times*, 8/17/1986.
[87] Tom Sherwood, "Carol Schwartz's Life: A Tale of Drive and Prejudice," *Washington Post*, 10/20/1986.
[88] Carrie Dowling, "As Child in Texas, Schwartz Learned to 'Beat the Odds,'" *Washington Times*, 8/17/1986.
[89] Christine Tierney, "Against All Odds II," *Washington Business Journal*, 9/8/1986.
[90] Lisa Hoffman, "D.C. Hopeful: If Midland Could See Her Now," *Dallas Times Herald*, 10/37/1986.
[91] Anne LaLena, "The Marion Barry File," *Washington City Paper*, 8/1/1986; Juan Williams, "A Black Mayor Betrays the Faith," *Washington Monthly*, 7-8/1986.
[92] Editorial, "Mayor's Race," *Washington Post*, 10/1986.
[93] Marc Fisher, "Farewell to Carol Schwartz—D.C.'s Last Republican?" *Washington Post*, 9/10/2008.
[94] Shannon Bradley, "The District Building," *Washington City Paper*, 1/16/1987.
[95] Editorial, "Mayor Barry: Beyond the Victory," *Washington Post*, 11/1986.
[96] Lisa M. Keene, *Washington Blade*, 6/17/1986.
[97] Vincent McGraw, "Schwartz, Beset by Tragedies, to Leave the Council," *Washington Times*, 6/3/1988.
[98] Ibid.
[99] Editorial, "Carol Schwartz: 'Time to Heal,'" *Washington Post*, 6/6/1988.
[100] Metropolitan Police Department, D.C., "A Study of Homicides in the District of Columbia," 10/2001, https://mpdc.dc.gov/sites/default/ files/dc /sites/mpdc/publication/attachments/homicidereport_0.pdf (accessed 9/1/2016).
[101] Sharon LaFraniere, "Lewis Says He Smoked Crack with Barry," *Washington Post*, 8/31/1989.
[102] Mike Folks, "Mistrial, Jurors Falter on 12 of 14 Counts," *Washington Times*, 8/11/1990.
[103] Alan Suderman, "Prison Advice for Harry Thomas from Other Elected Officials," *Washington City Paper*, 1/5/2012.
[104] Rebecca Watson, "A Memoir," *Midland College Literary Magazine*, 1994.

[105] Jonetta Rose Barras, *Washington Times*, 6/29/1994.
[106] Marcia Slacum Greene and R.H. Melton, "Lightfoot Drops Bid for Mayor," *Washington Post*, 9/16/1994.
[107] Cindy, "Here's a Vote for What Surname," *Washington Post*, 10/16/1994.
[108] Sam Fulwood III, "Barry Drew on Political Value of Racial Anger," *Los Angeles Times*, 9/15/1994.
[109] Adrianne Flynn, "Barry's Incredible Journey: The Masses Prove the Pundits Wrong," *Washington Times*, 9/18/1994.
[110] Marc Fisher and Eric Pianin, "The Riots and D.C.'s Underclass," *Washington Post*, 4/4/1988.
[111] Jonetta Rose Barras an and Clara Jeffery, "Poor Record," *Washington City Paper*, 11/5/1994.
[112] Ken Cummins, "This Year's Model," *Washington City Paper*, 11/4/1994.
[113] Howard Schneider and Nell Henderson, "District's Home Rule In Question," *Washington Post*, 11/13/1994.
[114] Ken Cummins, "Loose Lips: This Year's Model," *Washington City Paper*, 11/4/1994.
[115] Rene Sanchez, "Schwartz's Black Supporters Make a Political Leap of Faith," *Washington Post*, 10/16/1994.
[116] Adrianne Flynn, "Barry's Incredible Journey," *Washington Times*, 9/1/1994.
[117] Annette J. Samuels, "I Support Schwartz," *Washington Post*, 10/31/1994.
[118] "In Enemy Territory with Republican Carol Schwartz," *Roll Call*, 10/20/1994; Martin Well, "Schwartz Visits Enemy Territory," Washington Post, 10/1/1994.
[119] R.H. Melton, "Schwartz vs. Goliath," *Washington Post*, 10/17/1994.
[120] Rene Sanchez and Serge F. Kovaleski, "Barry-Schwartz Debate Awash in Invective," *Washington Post*, 11/5/1994.
[121] Yolanda Woodlee, "Foe Links Barry to Homicide Rate," *Washington Post*, 10/21/1994.
[122] Rene Sanchez, "Schwartz Calls for Accountability by Schools," *Washington Post*, 10/20/1994.
[123] Adrianne Flynn, "Schwartz Fires Away," *Washington Times*, 10/21/1994.
[124] Yolanda Woodlee, "Foe Links Barry to Homicide Rate," *Washington Post*, 10/21/1994.
[125] Yolanda Woodlee and Nell Henderson, "Barry: She's a Novice. Schwartz: He's Failed, D.C. Candidates Point Fingers Over Lunch," *Washington Post*, 10/27/1994.
[126] Nell Henderson, "Barry, Schwartz Depart from Usual Tactics to Engage in Partisan Politics," *Washington Post*, 10/24/1994.
[127] R.H. Melton, "Schwartz vs. Goliath," *Washington Post*, 10/17/1994.
[128] Amy Goldstein, "Schwartz Has Plan to Boost Healthcare," *Washington Post*, 10/17/1986.
[129] "A Republican with a Progressive AIDS Agenda," *Washington Blade*, 10/7/1986.
[130] "City's Renewal Requires Solutions to Crime Problem," *Northwest Current*, 10/19/1994.
[131] Cindy Loose, "Schwartz's Record Shaped by Willingness to Stand Alone," *Washington Post*, 11/5/1994.
[132] Rene Sanchez and Serge F. Kovaleski, "D.C. Mayor Slugfest, Barry-Schwartz Debate Washed in Invective," *Washington Post*, 11/5/1994.
[133] Rene Sanchez, "A Mayor's Race That's Too Hot to Cool Down," *Washington Post*, 11/3/1994.
[134] Ken Cummins, "Loose Lips," *Washington City Paper*, 11/4/1995.
[135] Editorial, "The Mayor's Race: Summing Up," *Washington Post*, 11/7/1994.
[136] Carol Schwartz, "For the Record: Letter to Marion Barry," *Washington Post*, 11/8/1994.
[137] Adrianne Flynn, "Barry Reclaims Office Over a Tough Schwartz," *Washington Times*, 11/9/1994.
[138] *Washington Blade*, 11/11/1994.
[139] Art Kramer, "Ward 3 Residents Planning Bid to Secede from District," *Washington Times*, 11/20/1994.
[140] Nell Henderson and Yolanda Woodlee, "Won Without Help of White Voters," *Washington Post*, 11/9/1994.
[141] Editorial, "Mr. Barry's Victory—and Challenge," *Washington Post*, 11/10/1994.

[142] Chelsea Jane, "Throwback Thursday-1964; Mackin High School Track Team Attacked by Youth Gang," *Washington Post*, 9/25/2014.

[143] Anne Gerhart and Annie Groer, "The Inspector Calls," *Washington Post*, The Reliable Source, Style Section, 11/2006.

[144] Vernon Loeb, "Kevin Chavous, on a Spinning Record," *Washington Post*, 8/26/1998.

[145] Colbert I. King, "He Stood for Something Large," *Washington Post*, 3/29/1997.

[146] "The D.C. Revitalization Act: History, Provisions and Promises," DC Appleseed Center and Our Nation's Capital, 2008.

[147] "The D.C. Revitalization Act: History, Provisions and Promises," Appendix One, Appleseed, 2008.

[148] Vernon Loeb and Yolanda Woodlee, "Mayor Says He Won't Seek Another Term," *Washington Post*, 5/21/1998.

[149] Jonetta Rose Barras, "Bureaucratic Oversight," *Washington City Paper*, 12/13/1996.

[150] Nikita Stewart, "'The Governor' of D.C.," *Washington Post*, 7/14/2013.

[151] Ken Cummins, "Halting the Williams Juggernaut," *Washington City Paper*, 7/3/1998.

[152] Yolanda Woodlee, "Williams Backed Payment to Lottery Chief," *Washington Post*, 9/5/1998.

[153] Ann Gerhardt and Annie Groer, "The Reliable Source," *Washington Post*, 6/24/1998.

[154] Editorial, "Tony Williams for Mayor," *Washington Post*, 10/25/1998.

[155] Joe Heim, "Just Asking, A Former Mayor Looks Back," *Washington Post Magazine*, 10/29/2015.

[156] Robert P. Strauss, "The District of Columbia's Individual Income Tax: A Research Report to the District of Columbia Tax Revision Commission," 1/6/1998.

[157] *Afro-American*, 8/22/1998.

[158] Paula Nickens, "D.C. Mayoral Race Is Really About 'Home,'" *Washington Times*, 10/16/1998.

[159] Lucy B. Murray, "Beware of Bowtie Bandit's Bandwagon," *Washington Times*, 9/8/1998.

[160] *InTowner*, June 1998.

[161] Michael Powell, "Schwartz Launches Third Bid for Mayor," *Washington Post*, 6/18/1998.

[162] Vanessa Williams, "Schwartz Hits Mayoral Trail with Zest," *Washington Post*, 9/17/1998.

[163] *Washington Times*, 10/16/1998.

[164] Saundra Torry, "Running Against the Grain," *Washington Post*, 10/19/1998.

[165] *Current*, Sept. 16, 1998.

[166] Ronald J. Hansen and Susan Ferrechio, "Schwartz Lashes Out," *Washington Times*, 10/30/1998.

[167] Vanessa Williams, "Schwartz Hits Mayoral Trail with Zest," *Washington Post*, 9/17/1998.

[168] Saundra Torry, "Running Against the Grain," *Washington Post*, 10/19/1998.

[169] Frances L. Murphy II, "Endorsements for D.C.," *Afro-American*, 10/31/1998.

[170] "Tax-free D.C. Sales Were Way Up," *Georgetowner*, 12/6/2001.

[171] Eric M. Weiss, "D.C. Council Votes to Ease No-tolerance DUI Law," *Washington Post*, 10/19/2005.

[172] Financial Control Board Website, Archived 10/9/2001.

[173] Richard Cohen, "Former D.C. Mayor Marion Barry Will Have to Cut His Ties to Racists, Anti-Semites," *Washington Post*, 9/16/1994.

[174] Mike DeBonis, "Probe Finds D.C. Fleet Agency Ignoring Laws for City's SUVs," *Washington Post*, 4/11/2011.

[175] Colbert I. King, "Rep. Istook's D.C. Pals," *Washington Post*, 10/16/1999.

[176] "Republicans and D.C. Voting Rights," DC Vote, www.dcvote.org/sites/default/files/documents/articles/republicanssayingwphotos.pdf (accessed 11/26/2016).

[177] Paul Schwartzman and Nikita Stewart, "D.C. Rights Proponents to Obama: What Gives?" *Washington Post*, 4/17/2011.

[178] Nelson F. Rimensnyder, "A Champion of D.C. Voting Rights," *Washington Post*,

12/11/2005.

[179] "District of Columbia Urban Tree Canopy Plan," D.C. Dep't of the Environment, 1/15/2013, https://ddoe.dc.gov/sites/default/ files /dc /sites/ ddoe / content/at-tachments/ Draft_Urban_Tree_Canopy_Plan_Final.pdf (accessed 6/10/2017).

[180] Craig Timberg, "D.C. Bill Would Assess Payment to Cut Trees," *Washington Post*, 12/4/2002.

[181] Former owner Jack Kent Cooke had named the town surrounding the stadium "Raljohn," after his sons, Ralph and John.

[182] Andrew DeMillo, "COG Deplores Redskins' Name," *Washington Post*, 1/10/2002.

[183] Carol Schwartz, Editorial, "Name Shame," *Washington Post*, 3/3/2002.

[184] Ian Shapira, "Federal Judge Orders Cancellation of Redskins' Trademark Registration," *Washington Post*, 7/8/2015.

[185] Ian Shapira and Ann E. Marimow, "Redskins Prevail in Long Fight Over Name," *Washington Post*, 6/30/2017.

[186] Editorial, "Mr. Snyder Is Losing the Battle with the Next Generation," *Washington Post*, 6/21/2016.

[187] Sewell Chan, "Welfare Funds to Go to Children," *Washington Post*, 8/10/2000.

[188] Editorial, "The Failure of D.C. Trust," *Washington Post*, 5/14/2016.

[189] Colbert I. King, "Answers Are Needed in D.C. Trust's Failure," *Washington Post*, 4/30/2016.

[190] D'Vera Cohn and Craig Timberg, "D.C. Racial, Economic Divide Sharper, Census Finds," *Washington Post*, 9/9/2002.

[191] Michael H. Cottman and Yolanda Woodlee, "Mayor Sees Racial Divide in Vote," *Washington Post*, 6/29/2000.

[192] Ibid.

[193] Ibid.

[194] Dan Tangherlini, "Smoother Streets" *Washington Post*, 8/20/2001.

[195] Lyndsey Layton, "Despite Promises, Road Work Still Chaotic," *Washington Post*, 8/13/2000.

[196] Brian DeBose, "Petitions More than 80% Invalid," *Washington Post*, 7/25/2002.

[197] Laura Bolt, "Today in D.C. History: Anthony Williams Forced to Run Write-in Campaign," *Washington City Paper*, July 15, 2001.

[198] D'Vera Cohn and Craig Timberg, "A Divided D.C. Poses Challenge for Next Mayor," *Washington Post*, 9/9/2002.

[199] Jim McElhatton, "Money to Thompson Goes Back to Williams' First Term," *Washington Times*, 5/8/2012.

[200] Elissa Silverman, "Prayer for the City," *Washington City Paper*, 10/25/2002.

[201] Craig Timberg, "D.C.'s Mayor's Race a Study in Contrasts," *Washington Post*, 11/1/2002.

[202] Ibid.

[203] Craig Timberg and Lori Montgomery, "Campaigns Suffer Since Attacks," *Washington Post*, 10/17/2002.

[204] Elissa Silverman, "Loose Lips: What the Hell," *Washington City Paper*, 10/4/2002.

[205] Editorial, "Who and What We Hope Prevails on November 5," *InTowner*, 10/2002.

[206] Elissa Silverman, "Vote Honey!" *Washington City Paper*, 11/1/2002.

[207] "The Mayoral Race," *Current Newspapers*, 10/9/2002.

[208] P.L. Wolff, "From the Publisher's Desk," *InTowner*, 10/2002.

[209] Editorial, "For D.C. Mayor," *Washington Post*, 10/29/2002.

[210] Carol Schwartz for Mayor Committee and Committee to Reelect Tony Williams Campaign Expenditures Reports, D.C. Office of Campaign Finance, 2002.

[211] David Vise, "Williams's Work Style Assailed," *Washington Post*, 7/1/1999.

[212] Yolanda Woodlee, "D.C. Officials Probe Attempt to Purchase Impound Lot," *Washington Post*, 2/13/2003.

[213] Yolanda Woodlee, "Ex-D.C. Property Official Promised $1.8 Million for Move to Jemal Building," *Washington Post*, 5/20/2003.

[214] Jonathan O'Connell, "The Fixer-Upper," *Washington Post Magazine*, 9/17/2017.

[215] Carol Leonnig and Yolanda Woodlee, "Top D.C. Developer Accused of Bribery," *Washington Post*, 9/28/2005.

[216] Tyler Currie, "First Person Singular: Carol Schwartz – D.C. Council Member," *Washington Post*, 11/23/2003.

[217] David Nakamura and Craig Timberg, "12-Year History of Klingle Road Dispute," *Washington Post*, 5/15/2003.

[218] Mark Segraves, "Multi-Million Northwest D.C. Trail in Disrepair," NBC4 Washington, 9/11/2017.

[219] "D.C. Council Overrides Mayor, Suspends Employee Credits Cards," *Washington Times*, 7/30/2002.

[220] Robert Thomson, "Deal Reached in Hot Lane Suit," *Washington Post*, 3/29/2016.

[221] Jeff Goldberg, "Express Lanes Near $30 in Fairfax County," *WJLA*, 5/9/2017.

[222] Matt Zapotosky and Chico Harlan, "U.S. to Phase Out Privately Operated Federal Prisons," *Washington Post*, 8/19/2016.

[223] Peter Hermann and Victoria St. Martin, "90-Minute Outage of 911 Line Was Caused by Accidental Flip of Master Switch," *Washington Post*, 8/30/2016.

[224] Lynh Bui, "Investigators Find No Defects in 2 Buses in Baltimore Crash," *Washington Post*, 11/5/2016.

[225] Michael Laris, "Privatizing Assets to Modernize the Rest," *Washington Post*, 5/24/2017.

[226] Robert McCartney, "Trump Wants to Sell Major Aqueduct," *Washington Post*, 6/7/2017.

[227] Robert McCartney, Faiz Siddiqui and Ovetta Wiggins, "Hogan Seeks to Widen 3 Congested Highways,"*Washington Post*, 9/22/17.

[228] David Nakamura and D'Vera Cohn, "D.C. to Create WASA Task Force," *Washington Post*, 2/5/2004.

[229] Ibid.

[230] Ibid.

[231] Ibid.

[232] "WASA Violated Federal Law in Not Properly Notifying Citizens," *Post.com*, 4/2/04, (accessed 1/10/2017).

[233] Brady Dennis, "In Some Cities, 1 in 7 Children Have Dangerous Blood-Lead Levels," *Washington Post*, 6/16/2016.

[234] Emma Brown, "A Legal Loophole Might Be Exposing Children to Lead in the Nation's Schools," *The Washington Post*, 3/18/2016.

[235] David Brown, "Study of D.C. Water Sharpens Understanding of Lead Threat," *Washington Post*, 12/11/2010.

[236] Spencer S. Hsu and Sari Horwitz, "Hazmat Rerouting Decision Delayed," *Washington Post*, 10/25/2004.

[237] James Jones, "Political Potpourri," *Washington City Paper*, 4/22/2005.

[238] Yolanda Woodlee, "City Raises Fees on Luxury SUVs," *Washington Post*, 12/8/2004.

[239] Antonio Olivo, "Funding to Fix Systems Falls Short," *Washington Post*, 7/20/2015.

[240] Dan Tangherlini Letter, 2/1/2006.

[241] Michael Laris, "How D.C. Spent $200 Million Dollars Over a Decade on a Streetcar You Still Can't Ride, *Washington Post*, 12/5/2015.

[242] "D.C. Councilmember to the Rescue at the Washington Animal Rescue League," *WARL Newsletter*, 2005.

[243] Elissa Silverman, "Diamond in the Rough," *Washington City Paper*, 10/8/2004.

[244] Robert Jablon, "Los Angeles-area City Celebrates Stadium Deal, Awaits NFL," *Associated Press*, 2/24/2015.

[245] David Nakamura and Thomas Heath, "Baseball Rejects Council's Changes in Financing Plan for D.C. Stadium," *Washington Post*, 12/16/2004.

[246] Colbert I. King, "Stepping Up to the Plate for the City," *Washington Post*, 12/18/2004.

[247] Lou Chibbaro Jr., "Gay Baseball Night Draws 1,100 to RFK." *Washington Blade*, 7/22/2005.

[248] David Nakamura, "New Hurdle for Stadium Lease Deal," *Washington Post*, 11/26/2005.

[249] David Nakamura and Thomas Heath, "D.C.'s Stadium Lease Talks Stumble," *Washington Post*, 11/28/2005.

[250] Carol Schwartz, "Current Thoughts on Baseball," Press Release, 12/19/2005.

[251] Lori Montgomery, "'No' Vote Was Only Start of Council Ride," *Washington Post*, 2/8/2006.

[252] Ibid.

[253] Ibid.

[254] "Public Lives, in Private," *Washington Post*, 1/6/2005.

[255] Yolanda Woodlee and Theola Labbe, "District Notebook," *Washington Post*, 3/17/2005.

[256] Avram Goldstein, "D.C. Council Votes to Give Itself a Break on Parking," *Washington Post*, 7/13/2002.

[257] Carol Schwartz, "Carol Schwartz on Parking," *Washington Times*, 1/22/2006.

[258] Carol Schwartz, "Letter to the Editor," *Washington Times*, 11/3/2006.

[259] Editorial, "Bad Cabs: Does the Council Care?" *Washington Post*, 4/17/1987.

[260] Faiz Siddiqui, "New Screening Option for Uber, Lyft," *Washington Post*, 12/24/2016.

[261] Steven Overly, "Uber, Lyft Respond to Senator's Bias Concerns," *Washington Post*, 12/28/2016.

[262] James Jones, "Loose Lips," *Washington City Paper*, 3/11/2005.

[263] Colbert I. King, "What D.C.'s Elves Do with Your Taxes," *Washington Post*, 5/17/2008.

[264] Eric M. Weiss, "Catania Reroutes Health Funding: No-Bid Contracts Raise Questions," *Washington Post*, 5/22/2015.

[265] Eric M. Weiss and Lori Montgomery, "Smoking Ban Finds an Unlikely Backer," *Washington Post*, 5/26/2005.

[266] "Gay Clubs Fear Devastating Impact of D.C.'s Smoking Ban," *Washington Blade*, 12/13/2005.

[267] Carol Schwartz, "A Compromise on Smoking," *Washington Post*, 5/29/2005.

[268] Eric M. Weiss, "Smoking Ban Gaining in D.C.," *Washington Post*, 6/15/2005.

[269] Perry Stein, "D.C. Bill Would Raise Age to Purchase Cigarettes to 21," *Washington Post*, 4/6/2015.

[270] Tarron Lively, "Schwartz Slams 'Out of Sync' D.C. Speed Limits," *Washington Times*, 6/15/2005.

[271] Carol Schwartz, "Improving but Not Crippling Our Government," [changed to "Open Government Is Overrated"], *Washington Post*, 7/10/2006.

[272] Editorial, "How Not to Fix D.C. Schools," *Washington Post*, 6/25/2006.

[273] Nikita Stewart, "Schools Measure in D.C. Off Ballot," *Washington Post*, 7/12/2006.

[274] Elizabeth Wiener, "Central Library Plan Stalls in Committee," *Georgetown Current*, 11/2/2006.

[275] Theola Labbe, "Rhee to Be Highest-Paid School Head in D.C. Area," *Washington Post*, 7/4/2007.

[276] Rachael Brown, "Rhee Fires 100 School Employees," *Washington Post*, 3/7/2008.

[277] Bill Turque, "Sizing up the DCPS Central Office," *Washington Post*, 2/14/2011.

[278] Jack Gillum and Marisol Bello, "When Standardized Test Scores Soared in D.C., Were the Gains Real?" *USA Today*, 3/20/2011.

[279] Ibid.

[280] Michael Winerip, "Eager For Spotlight, but Not If It Is on a Testing Scandal," *New York Times*, 8/21/2011.

[281] Jack Gillum and Marisol Bello, "When Standardized Test Scores Soared in D.C., Were the Gains Real?" *USA Today*, 3/20/2011.

[282] Michael Winerip, "Eager For Spotlight, but Not if It Is on a Testing Scandal," *New York Times*, 8/21/2011.

[283] Nikita Stewart, "Council Cries Foul Over Fenty's Distribution of Nationals Tickets," *Washington Post*, 4/11/2008.

[284] Gary Emerling, "Council to Probe Bonuses in D.C.," *Washington Times*, 10/2/2007; Nikita Stewart, "DC Gives More than $500,000 in Bonuses Despite Legal Limit," *Washington Post*, 12/15/2009.

[285] Nikita Stewart and Paul Schwartzman, "Fenty Salary Scale 'Scary,'" *Washington Post*, 3/7/2010.

[286] Editorial, "Residency Rules," *Washington Post*, 6/20/2007.

[287] Mike DeBonis, "The New Cronies: Adrian Fenty, Some Frat Buddies, and $86 Million in City Spending," *Washington City Paper*, 10/30/2009.

[288] "Council Eyes Delay in Sales of Property," *Washington Times*, 12/5/2007.

[289] "40% of Registered Voters Cast Ballots in the Presidential Primary—Historic Election," *Washington Post*, 2008.

[290] Nikita Stewart, "10,000 Special Ballots Being Counted," *Washington Post*,

2/16/2008.

[291] Nikita Stewart, "D.C. Hearing on Scandal Has Gandhi in Tight Spot," *Washington Post*, 11/16/2007.

[292] Del Quentin Wilber, "Tax Scam Leader Gets More than 17 Years," *Washington Post*, 7/1/2009.

[293] David Nakamura, "Obama Order Expands Sick Leave," *Washington Post*, 9/8/2015.

[294] "Stein Democratic Club Asked Leaders to Lay Low," *Washington Blade*, 3/26/2004.

[295] Carol Schwartz, "Still Fighting for a Better Tomorrow," *Washington Blade*, 5/30/2008.

[296] Tim Craig, "Patrick Mara Faces Critics in Council Bid," *Washington Post*, 4/3/2013.

[297] Mike DeBonis, "Catania Comes Out for Mara," *Washington City Paper*, 9/19/2008.

[298] Mike DeBonis, "Political Potpourri," *Washington City Paper*, 8/22/2016.

[299] Citizens for Empowerment PAC, Contributors Report, D.C. Office of Campaign Finance, 2008.

[300] Find the Company, District Economic Empowerment Coalition, http://nonprofits.findthecompany.com/l/596095/District-Economic-Empowerment-Coalition (accessed 10/7/2016).

[301] LiUNA Local 657 D.C. Works Building D.C., "Keep a Good Thing Going. The Washington Nationals Stadium Contract: A Model for the Future, 1/2008.

[302] Mike DeBonis, "David Catania Has a New $240,000-a-year Job," *Washington City Paper*, 11/2/2011.

[303] Ibid.

[304] Jonetta Rose Barras, "Catania and the Democratic Mountain," *Washington Post*, 9/11/2014.

[305] Mike DeBonis, "Friends Like These," *Washington City Paper*, 2/12/2010.

[306] Michael E. Miller, Ian Shapira and Peter Hermann, "Bill Dean Throws Wild Georgetown Parties. Now a Rape Is Alleged to Have Occurred at One," *Washington Post*, 11/26/2016.

[307] Marc Fisher, "D.C. Benefits from Schwartz's Fight Against Corruption," *Washington Post*, 9/4/2008.

[308] Election Results, D.C. Board of Elections Website, https://www.dcboee.org/election_info/election_results/election_result_new/results_final.asp?electionid=1&prev=0&result_type=3&party=-87 (accessed 5/1/2017).

[309] P.L. Wolff, "We Strongly Urge Voters to Reelect At-large City Councilmember Carol Schwartz by Write-in," *InTowner*, 10/2008.

[310] Aaron C. Davis and Mike DeBonis, "D.C. Council Censures Marion Barry for Taking Cash Payments from City Contractors," *Washington Post*, 9/17/2013.

[311] Del Quentin Wilber and Tim Craig, "Kwame R. Brown, D.C. Council Chairman, Resigns After Being Charged with Bank Fraud," *Washington Post*, 5/3/2012.

[312] Mike DeBonis and Tim Craig, "Harry Thomas, Former Council Member, Is Sentenced to Three Years in Prison," *Washington Post*, 5/3/2012; Del Quentin Wilber and Mike DeBonis, "Former D.C. Council Member Harry Thomas Jr. Pleads Guilty to Felonies," *Washington Post*, 1/6/2012.

[313] Mike DeBonis, "'Fully Loaded' Puts D.C. Council Chairman on the Spot,'" *Washington Post*, 6/20/2011.

[314] Tim Craig, "Missed Rent Payments Add to Michael Brown's Financial Woes," *Washington Post*, 4/19/2012.

[315] Ann E. Marimow and Mike DeBonis, "Former D.C. Council Member Michael A. Brown Gets More than 3 Years in Bribery Case," *Washington Post*, 5/29/2014.

[316] Andrea Noble, "Michael Brown Is the Latest D.C. Lawmaker to Plead Guilty to Federal Charges," *Washington Times*, 6/10/2013.

[317] Andrea Noble and Jeffrey Anderson "Vincent Gray's Scandals Promise to Tangle D.C. Mayoral Campaign," *Washington Times*, 12/2/2013.

[318] WTOP staff, "Catania, Cheh, Bowser Call for Mayor Gray to Resign," WTOP, 7/11/2012, http://wtop.com/news/2012/07/catania-cheh-bowser-call-for-mayor-gray-to-resign (accessed 10/23/2016).

[319] Alan Suderman, "David Catania: Vince Gray Is a 'Joke,' Should Resign," *Washington City Paper*, 7/11/12.

[320] Mike DeBonis and Scott Clement, "D.C. Mayor Vincent Gray is Top Democrat in Poll as Primary Looms," *Washington Post*, NBC4/WAMU/ *Washington Informer*/Marist Poll, 1/14/2014.

[321] Ann E. Marimow, "No Jail Time for Key Figure in Shadow Campaign for Former D.C. Mayor," *Washington Post*, 7/16/2016.

[322] Monroe H. Freeman and Abbe Smith, "Machen Tramples on the Mayor's Due Process," *Washington Post*, 3/21/2014.

[323] Patrick Madden and Martin Austermuhle, "D.C. Prosecutor Ends Lengthy Corruption Probe of Former Mayor Vince Gray," WAMU, 12/9/2015.

[324] Editorial, "Carol Schwartz's Entry Into the Mayoral Race Gives Voters More Choices," *Washington Post*, 6/11/2014.

[325] Lenny Bernstein, "Heroin Deaths Have Quadrupled in 10 Years," *Washington Post*, 7/8/2015.

[326] Christopher Ingraham, "Heroin Deaths Surpass Gun Homicides for the First Time, CDC Data Shows," *Washington Post*, 12/8/2016.

[327] Ashley Halsey III, "Amtrak Crash Report Cites Marijuana," *Washington Post*, 1/27/2017.

[328] Alexandra Rockey Fleming and Steve Helling, "Faces of an Epidemic," *People*, August 21, 2017.

[329] Emma Brown, "Catania Proposes Sweeping Special Education Legislation," *Washington Post*, 3/18/2004.

[330] Mike DeBonis, "District Might Be Back in Hospital Business," *Washington Post*, 7/9/2010.

[331] Natalie Wexler, "Carol Schwartz Bids to Become the Education Mayor," *Greater Great Washington*, 9/11/14, http://greatergreaterwashington.org/post/24166/carol-schwartz-bids-to-become-the-education-mayor/ (accessed 9/11/2014).

[332] Mike DeBonis, "Carol Schwartz Kicks Off Mayoral Run with Old-school Vibe," *Washington Post*, 9/9/2014.

[333] Will Sommer, "Catania Polling Memo Claims to Show Dramatically Tightened Mayor's Race," *Washington City Paper*, 9/10/2014.

[334] Mike DeBonis and Scott Clement, "In D.C. Mayor Poll, Bowser Surges Against Wounded Incumbent Vincent Gray," *Washington Post*, 3/25/2014.

[335] Will Sommer, "New Poll: Catania Closer to Bowser in Mayor's Race," *Washington City Paper*, 10/1/2014.

[336] D.C. Mayoral Forum, WAMU, 10/6/2014.

[337] Will Sommer, "Bowser Leads Catania by 17 Percent in Mayor's Race," *Washington City Paper*, 10/24/2014.

[338] Expenditure Reports for Muriel Bowser for Mayor, Catania for Mayor, Catania for Mayor Exploratory Committee, Carol Schwartz for Mayor Committee, D.C. Office of Campaign Finance, 2014.

[339] Carol Schwartz, "Marion Barry and Me," *Washington City Paper*, 11/25/2014.

[340] Peter Jamison, "Former D.C. Official Who Took Bribes to Discuss Ethics," *Washington Post*, 8/20/2017.

[341] Colbert I. King, "A City Run by Nonresidents," *Washington Post*, 7/2/2016.

[342] Alan Singer, "Why Hedge Funds Love Charter Schools," *Huffington Post*, 5/20/2014, http://www.huffingtonpost.com/alan-singer/why-hedge-funds-love-char_b_5357486.html (accessed 3/15/2017).

[343] Alan Singer, "Big Profits in Not-for-Profit Charter Schools," *Huffington Post*, 4/7/2014, http://www.huffingtonpost.com/alan-singer/charter-school-executive-profit_b_5093883.html (accessed 3/15/2017).

[344] Emma Brown and Mandy McLaren, "Indiana's Voucher System Offers Hint of School Policy in the Era of Trump," *Washington Post*, 12/27/2016.

[345] Emma Brown and Danielle Douglas-Gabriel, "Along with 13% Cut, Trump Would Steer $1.4 Billion to School Choice," *Washington Post*, 3/16/2017.

[346] Danielle Paquette, "Low-paid Jobs Safer from Robots," *Washington Post*, 5/16/2017..

[347] Alejandra Matos and Emma Brown, "Obama Touts Education Record at D.C.'s Banneker High School," *Washington Post*, 10/17/2016.

[348] Alejandra Matos, "Banneker's Anita Berger is Principal of the Year," *Washington Post*, 1/24/2017.